STUDIES IN GENERAL AND ENGLISH PHONETICS

Rhythm, intonation, exotic and familiar languages as well as computer-synthesized audio-communications, procedures in forensic linguistics, pronunciation lexicography, language change and sociological aspects of speech such as English regional accents and dialects in Britain and other parts of the world are topics covered in *Studies in General and English Phonetics*, a collection of thirty-eight articles which has been brought together as a tribute to Professor J. D. O'Connor, one of Britain's most greatly respected teachers and writers on phonetics. The foreword to the collection has been supplied by Lord Quirk, joining the many other world-famous names on the international list of forty-five contributors who include former students, colleagues and admirers of Professor O'Connor.

This volume on descriptive and experimental phonetics and phonology will not only be of interest to readers concerned with linguistics and phonetics but also to those concerned with the teaching of English as a foreign language and readers in many other fields. With its invaluable up-to-date bibliographical matter as well as the papers themselves, no university library will be complete without it.

Professor J. D. O'Connor

STUDIES IN GENERAL AND ENGLISH PHONETICS

Essays in Honour of Professor J. D. O'Connor

Edited by Jack Windsor Lewis

Routledge
Taylor & Francis Group

LONDON AND NEW YORK

5036

KH

First published 1995
by Routledge
2 Park Square, Milton Park, Abingdon, Oxfordshire OX14 4RN

Simultaneously published in the USA and Canada
by Routledge
711 Third Avenue, New York, NY 10017

First issued in paperback 2014

Routledge is an imprint of the Taylor and Francis Group, an informa business

British Library Cataloguing in Publication Data
A catalogue record for this book is available from the British Library

Library of Congress Cataloging in Publication Data
A catalogue record for this book has been requested

ISBN 13: 978-0-415-08068-2 (hbk)
ISBN 13: 978-1-138-86845-8 (pbk)

Typeset in Baskerville by Solidus (Bristol) Limited

8/13/19

CONTENTS

Foreword by Lord Quirk CBE FBA ix

About J. D. ('Doc') O'Connor x

The publications of J. D. O'Connor xii

About these studies xv

Part I General phonetics and phonological theory

1 On some neutralisations and archiphonemes in English allegro
speech 3
Tsutomu Akamatsu

2 The phonetics of neutralisation: the case of Australian coronals 10
Andrew Butcher

3 Some articulatory characteristics of the tap 39
Bruce Connell

4 Assimilations of alveolar stops and nasals in connected speech 49
W. J. Hardcastle

5 Field procedures in forensic speaker recognition 68
Herman J. Künzel

6 Voice types in automated telecommunications applications 85
John Laver

7 The effect of context on the transcription of vowel quality 96
Moray J. Nairn and James R. Hurford

8 Place of articulation features for clicks: anomalies for universals 121
A. Traill

9 Postura: clear and dark consonants etcetera 130
L. Van Buuren

CONTENTS

Part II Pitch, intonation and rhythm

10 Spelling aloud: a preliminary study of idiomatic intonation 145
    Patricia D. S. Ashby and Michael G. Ashby

11 Rises in English 155
    Alan Cruttenden

12 Documenting rhythmical change 174
    David Crystal

13 The social distribution of intonation patterns in Belfast 180
    E. Douglas-Cowie, R. Cowie and J. Rahilly

14 Principles of intonational typology 187
    Anthony Fox

15 Intonational stereotype: a re-analysis 211
    Jill House

16 Speech fundamental frequency over the telephone and
    face-to-face: some implications for forensic phonetics 230
    Allen Hirson, Peter French and David Howard

17 The effect of emphasis on declination in English intonation 241
    Francis Nolan

18 Nucleus placement in Spanish and English 255
    Héctor Ortiz-Lira

19 Rhythm and duration in Spanish 266
    G. E. Pointon

20 The boundaries of intonation units 270
    Paul Tench

21 Stylisation of the falling tone in Hungarian intonation 278
    László Varga

22 The teaching of English intonation 288
    Jack Windsor Lewis

Part III The phonetics of mother-tongue English

23 A 'tenny' rate 301
    John Baldwin

24 Pronunciation and the rich points of culture 310
    Nikolas Coupland

CONTENTS

25 Spelling pronunciation and related matters in New Zealand
    English   320
    Laurie Bauer

26 Quantifying English homophones and minimal pairs   326
    John Higgins

27 Consonant-associated resonance in three varieties of English   335
    John Kelly

28 Syllabification and rhythm in non-segmental phonology   360
    John Local

29 The vowels of Scottish English: formants and features   367
    J. Derrick McClure

30 A neglected feature of British East Midlands accents and its
    possible implications for the history of a vowel merger in
    English   379
    J. A. Maidment

31 Mixing and fudging in Midland and southern dialects of
    England: the *cup* and *foot* vowels   385
    Clive Upton

32 The low vowels of Vancouver English   395
    Henry J. Warkentyne and John H. Esling

33 New syllabic consonants in English   401
    J. C. Wells

Part IV The phonetics of non-mother-tongue English

34 Approaches to articulatory setting in foreign-language teaching   415
    Beverley Collins and Inger M. Mees

35 The English accent of the Shilluk speaker   425
    Y. M. L. Le Clézio

36 Segmental errors in the pronunciation of Danish speakers of
    English: some pedagogic strategies   432
    Inge Livbjerg and Inger M. Mees

37 Describing the pronunciation of loanwords from English   445
    J. Posthumus

38 What do EFL teachers need to know about pronunciation?   454
    David Taylor

    Index   464

FOREWORD

We returned to UCL from war service in October 1945, Doc and I, but whereas he had managed to finish his degree before enlisting, I had only just begun. So we first met on opposite sides of the lectern, he a young lecturer, wittily and effortlessly expounding English phonology, I an over-age undergraduate, admiringly and enviously listening – and trying to learn.

Despite the passing of nearly fifty years, the teacher–pupil gap has never closed, but to my pleasure and pride it soon narrowed to the point when I could call him friend as well as teacher, could refer to him as 'Doc' without feeling guilty of name-dropping, and in due course (we moved slowly in those days) could so address him without feeling presumptuous.

The department was led at that time by Daniel Jones (widely known – if not widely addressed – as D. J.), who seemed to me simultaneously shy and austere, not easy to know. In contrast, Doc was prominent among a group of colleagues who were delightfully at ease with each other and their students: A. C. Gimson, of course, Hélène Coustenoble (also known as Gim and Cou), Dennis Fry, Gordon Arnold, Olive Tooley, Julian Pring, Margué-rite Chapallaz, John Trim. And despite attacks by the grim reaper, it has been a special pleasure week by week to see several of those colleagues and friends foregather in the UCL common room – at a particular table, on a particular day: joined too, in consequence, by former students from the international community of those who have looked to Doc and his peers for advice, information, good company and sheer fun.

His peers? Well, no. It would be hard to find any colleague making claim to be his peer, for Doc is quite unique: *primus* no matter who else he is *inter,* even this splendid gathering of linguists intent, in the pages that follow, on honouring him.

Randolph Quirk

ABOUT J.D. ('DOC')
O'CONNOR

Professor Emeritus Joseph Desmond O'Connor of University College London is universally with happy informality known as 'Doc'. He was born on 10 December 1919 and grew up in the handsome spa and market town of Harrogate in what was then the West Riding of Yorkshire 200 miles north-west of London. His forebears had moved from Ireland first to Newcastle. His father was a postmaster in different parts of the country including Northallerton and Maidenhead. His mother came from Harrogate, where her father was at one time the mayor.

For his senior schooling, like a number of Harrogate boys, Doc travelled daily to the Jesuit foundation St Michael's College at Leeds. From there he proceeded to University College London in 1937. When the Second World War broke out he was in the final year of a BA Honours course in French. Despite the fact that his department, like the Department of Phonetics, had been evacuated to Aberystwyth he got a first. Before the end of 1940 he was off to the West Country to train with the Royal Armoured Corps. He served in the army throughout the war, like his friend A. C. Gimson rising to the rank of major. His talents had greatly impressed his teacher of French phonetics, the redoubtable Hélène Coustenoble, and in turn Professor Daniel Jones, the founder and head of the Department of Phonetics at UCL. In 1945 he returned to the department to join its teaching staff.

He has never been an avid globetrotter, though he did accompany Daniel Jones and other colleagues to take part in teaching courses on English in Denmark and in France. A notable stay was his several months in 1954 at the famous Haskins Laboratory in New York.

In 1964 he was persuaded to take over from Randolph Quirk the annual University of London Summer School of English, in its heyday the most remarkable course of its kind running in the country. While he was in charge, it regularly accommodated well over 200 participants and engaged as visiting lecturers many famous people from a wide variety of British walks of life. He conducted it with great good humour and modesty and was immensely popular with the students and no less so with his numerous teaching staff until he finally gave it up in 1973.

University College recognised his splendid contribution to his subject and his important part in the development of his distinguished department, through which have passed so many leading figures in the field of phonetics, by appointing him to a Chair of Phonetics in the session beginning in 1976. At his slightly early retirement from teaching in 1980 the title of Emeritus Professor was conferred upon him.

THE PUBLICATIONS OF
J. D. O'CONNOR

Doc's publications have been many and varied. He has written quite a number of reviews, some of books only available in French or Danish. He has written more books falling in that important and these days undervalued category of phonetic reader than anyone else has or is likely to. His masterpiece, the amazingly wide-ranging Penguin *Phonetics*, is of course very widely recognised as probably the best general introduction to the subject, rivalled only by Abercrombie's *Elements*. Happy the newcomer to the subject who is able to read both of them.

He is no less famous for the 1961/73 *Intonation of Colloquial English* on which he collaborated with his distinguished colleague Gordon F. Arnold. The highly effective and satisfyingly accurate recordings they made of a substantial amount of its text on more than one occasion have richly benefited many generations of students of the subject. His superb *Better English Pronunciation* was described in the *Times Educational Supplement* in March 1975 as a book 'which can quite safely be said to be the most effective one ever written to help the ordinary learner to improve his pronunciation'. Besides this he has written articles that have been acknowledged as classics of the literature of phonetics such as the 1953 *Word* article which earned a place among two dozen of the most seminal articles on the subject of *Phonetics in Linguistics* as selected by John Laver and the late Bill Jones in that 1973 volume of fundamental readings for postgraduates. The latest of his various fruitful collaborations was with his only daughter Clare Fletcher, who was also the other voice in the very lively recording that accompanied the 1973 Phonetic Drill Reader.

The following list is not complete – it takes no account of his broadcast scripts or teaching films – but it is hoped that it omits nothing of major importance.

1947   'The phonetic system of a dialect of Newcastle-upon-Tyne', in *Le Maître phonétique*.
1948   *New Phonetic Readings*, Berne: A. Francke AG.
1950   Review of K. L. Pike's *Phonemics* in *Le Maître phonétique*.

1951a   'Styles of English pronunciation', *English Language Teaching* 6.

1951b   Review of Trager and Smith *An Outline of English Structure* in *Le Maître phonétique*.

1952a   'RP and the reinforcing glottal stop', *English Studies* 33.

1952b   'Phonetic aspects of the spoken pun', *English Studies* 33.

1952c   'A transcription in Southern British English from *The Wind in the Willows* by Kenneth Grahame', *Le Maître phonétique*.

1953a   'Vowel, consonant and syllable – a phonological definition' (with J. L. M. Trim), *Word* 9, 2.

1953b   Review of Bullard and Lindsay *Speech at Work* in *Le Maître phonétique*.

1955a   *A Course of English Intonation*, Amsterdam: Meulenhoff.

1955b   'The intonation of tag questions in English', *English Studies* 36.

1956a   *English Intonation*, Stockholm: Radiotjänst.

1956b   Review of Abbé R. Charbonneau *La Palatalisation de t d en canadien-français* in *Le Maître phonétique*.

1957a   'The fall–rise tone in English', *Moderna Språk* (Sweden), 51, 1.

1957b   'Acoustic cues for the perception of initial /w, j, r, l/ in English' (with Gerstman, Liberman, Delattre and Cooper), *Word* 13.

1957c   'Recent Work in English Phonetics', *Phonetica* 1.

1957d   Review of D. Abercrombie *Problems and Principles* in *Le Maître phonétique*.

1957e   Review of P. Christophersen *An English Phonetics Course* in *Le Maître phonétique*.

1958a   'Synthesis of English vowels' (with G. F. Arnold, P. Denes, A. G. Gimson and J. L. M. Trim) *Language and Speech* 1, 114–25.

1958b   Review of J. R. Firth *Papers in Linguistics 1934–51* in *Le Maître phonétique*.

1960a   Review of P. Strevens *Aural Aids in Language Teaching* in *Le Maître phonétique*.

1960b   Review of Thomson and Lyons *Spoken English* in *Le Maître phonétique*.

1961a   *Intonation of Colloquial English* (with G. F. Arnold), London: Longman.

1961b   Review of J. Vachek *Dictionnaire de linguistique de l'école de Prague* in *Le Maître phonétique*.

1961c   Review of E. Sivertsen *Cockney Phonology* in *Le Maître phonétique*.

1962a   *BBC Course of English Pronunciation*, London: BBC Enterprises.

1962b   *BBC Course of English Intonation*, London: BBC Enterprises.

1963a   Review of A. Martinet *A Functional View of Language* in *Le Maître phonétique*.

1963b   Review of G. Faure *Recherches sur les caractères et le rôle des éléments musicaux dans la prononciation anglaise* in *Le Maître phonétique*.

1963c   Review of D. Pasquale *A Practical Handbook of English Pronunciation* in *Le Maître phonétique*.

1964   'The perceptibility of certain word boundaries' (with O. Tooley) in D. Abercrombie *et al.*, *In Honour of Daniel Jones*, London: Longman.

1965a   Review of J. Vachek *A Prague School Reader in Linguistics* in *Le Maître phonétique*.

1965b   'The perception of time intervals', *Progress Report 2*, Phonetics Laboratory, University College London.

1967a   *Better English Pronunciation*, Cambridge: Cambridge University Press.

1967b   Review of E. Henderson *Tiddim Chin* in *Le Maître phonétique*.

1968a   'The duration of the foot in relation to the number of component sound segments', *Progress Report*, Phonetics Laboratory, University College London.

1968b   Review of H. A. Koefoed *Fonemik* in *Le Maître phonétique*.

1968c   Review of B. S. Andrésen *Pre-glottalisation in English Standard Pronunciation* in *Le Maître phonétique*.

1968d   Review of P. Garde *L'Accent* in *Le Maître phonétique*.

1968e   'Daniel Jones 1881–1967', *English Studies* 49, 238–9.

1970   Review of D. Crystal *Prosodic Systems and Intonation in English* in *Le Maître phonétique*.

1971   *Advanced Phonetic Reader*, Cambridge: Cambridge University Press.

1973a   *Intonation of Colloquial English* (with G. F. Arnold), 2nd edn, London: Longman.

1973b   *Phonetic Drill Reader*, Cambridge: Cambridge University Press.

1973c   *Phonetics*, Harmondsworth: Penguin.

1973d   Review of D. Wilkins *Linguistics in Language Teaching* in *Le Maître phonétique*.

1980   *Better English Pronunciation*, 2nd edn, Cambridge: Cambridge University Press.

1989   *Sounds English* (with Clare Fletcher), London: Longman.

ABOUT THESE STUDIES

The contributions to this volume have been divided into four groups but the categories adopted inevitably overlap in various ways. In particular a number of items placed in part II Pitch, Intonation and Rhythm could equally well have gone into part IV The Phonetics of Non-Mother-tongue English.

PART I GENERAL PHONETICS AND PHONOLOGICAL THEORY

1 **Tsutomu** ('Steve') **Akamatsu**, who, like his wife Maryvonne, a fellow phonetician, has happy memories of sitting at Doc's feet at University College London, applies his 'functionalist' approach with logic and clarity to some well-known neutralisations in English phonology and draws our attention to, among other things, developments that have come about by 'loosening of articulation'.

2 **Andy Butcher**'s paper on some consonantal features in a variety of Australian languages reminds me irresistibly of the early reports of naturalists on the amazingly novel flora and fauna of the antipodes. Rich alike in its theoretical speculation and its solid body of field observations, it includes accounts of some types of human articulations little paralleled in the northern hemisphere where so much the majority of phonetic observers have functioned.

3 **Bruce Connell** starts from an examination by electropalatography of the tap articulations of a speaker of Ibibio, one of the Lower Cross languages of south-eastern Nigeria, and opens the discussion out into a searching reconsideration of the nature of tap articulations in general and of their relationships not merely with flaps but even with stops and approximants. He argues that solely distinguishing stops from taps by duration leaves out of account the at least equally important matter of linguo-palatal contact.

4 **Bill Hardcastle** deals with certain English assimilations in an immensely rewarding practical way using fairly recently developed techniques like electropalatography and laryngography to reveal to us the gross oversimplifications that merely auditory analyses have limited us to in the past.

5 **Hermann Künzel**, Germany's leading forensic phonetician, has produced an impressive survey of the controversial field of forensic speaker identification which is about as satisfying and authoritative a treatment of the topic as one could imagine at anything like a moderate length. Certainly, for anyone who feels inclined to dip a toe into this topic, there could be no better choice of the first thing to read.

6 **John Laver**, with characteristic lucidity and thoroughness, discusses the various possibilities and choices involved in the employment of computer-incorporated recorded vocal responses (whether of synthetic or of human speech) of machine to telephone caller for a wide range of possible situations. This important topic, which so recently belonged only in science fiction, is becoming a more urgent real-life problem day by day.

7 **Moray Nairn** and **Jim Hurford** used digital processing to excise steady-state portions of vowels from certain CVC contexts and provided the results suitably disguised along with the same vowels in their original consonantal surroundings to four professional phoneticians for transcription. Notable variability between the transcribers was found in the judgements of the vowel qualities. The results were seen to support the contention that formant transitions aid vowel identification and to throw doubt upon the complete aptness of the usual vowel chart 'as a map of the real human possibilities'.

8 **Tony Traill** examines data from assimilation and language change in the Khoisan languages of southern Africa (Bushman and Hottentot are the two best known) which provide an important new perspective on the natural classes of clicks for which the traditional purely articulation-based categorisations are shown to be unsatisfactory and best replaced by phonetic classifications based on their acoustic features.

9 Those who know **'Luke' Van Buuren** for the radical thinker he is will certainly not be disappointed with this paper in which in convincing and entertaining fashion he makes the case for the recognition of what he terms neatly the 'postura'. He is not afraid to point out where he thinks Daniel Jones was 'sloppy' and offers forthright condemnation of the unfortunate way the term 'labialisation' is traditionally misapplied.

PART II PITCH, INTONATION AND RHYTHM

10 **Patricia** and **Michael Ashby**'s stimulating experiment makes some fascinating points and raises still more. It reminds me of my frequently uncomfortable reactions to using an answerphone which gives a lot of useful information by a realistically synthesised voice which, however, gives all numbers on a rising tone but all zeros falling no matter what the context. The algorithm they produce should enable an important step forward in the design of chips to provide natural prosodies for synthetic speech.

11 **Alan Cruttenden** takes on one of the most widely discussed topics in current intonation studies and deals with certain rising intonations especially heard in more northerly British cities (in Ulster, Glasgow, Newcastle, Birmingham, etc.) and in regions around the rim of the Pacific Ocean (Australia, California, Canada). This account of the 'High Rise Tone' phenomenon is no doubt the fullest and most important treatment it has received to date.

12 **Dave Crystal** who, in association with Randolph Quirk and also in his independent work, has made some of the most notable ever contributions to the study of English rhythm, turns again to the topic with some characteristically lively comments on its possible future development. They are conveyed with a highly diverse and diverting variety of illustrative references and it is perhaps possible that his tongue edges just a little into his cheek at times.

13 The data that **Ellen Douglas-Cowie**, **Roddy Cowie** and **Joan Rahilly** have assembled have clearly justified their impression that it might be rewarding to compare the intonational habits of Belfast people by sex, generation and class affiliation. They rightly point out that sociophonetic investigations have unwarrantably been almost exclusively hitherto in the domain of segmental data and they convincingly point the way forward to a useful broadening of the field.

14 **Tony Fox**'s consideration of intonational typology started from fresh data, on a small number of general parameters, of eight prosodically disparate languages, viz. English, French, German, Cantonese, Mandarin, Japanese, Mende and Zulu. Among his many interesting conclusions is one that a category such as 'nuclear tone' is not tenable as a universal and in fact that a typology of intonation as such is not feasible since such inter-language differences can better be ascribed to the different overall prosodic structures of the languages rather than to the intonational features themselves.

15 **Jill House** throws herself energetically into the fray in one of the most extensively disputed areas of intonation theory, the analysis of tonal patterns considered to be related to the expression of stereotyped ideas. She brings to it insights that are the fruits of, among other things, work she

has done observing numbers of telephone conversations where enquiries of a repetitive kind are being answered. She displays a thoroughly independent outlook and offers some interesting conclusions.

16 **Allen Hirson, Peter French** and **David Howard**, two academic phoneticians and a former academic who is now Britain's leading specialist in forensic phonetics, investigated the pitch of the speaking voice as heard over a telephone line and in face-to-face communication from twenty-four youngish male subjects. Among their suggestions regarding the forensic relevance of their findings is one that, where fundamental frequency from a telephone caller is lower than that from a direct speech sample, it may be taken as strongly indicating that different speakers are likely to be involved.

17 **Francis Nolan** describes an experiment designed to contribute to the debate among tonologists as to whether declination, the progressive lowering of fundamental frequency that generally characterises intonation units, is an overall feature of whole units or derives essentially only from individual relationships with immediately preceding pitch accents. The experiment is closely modelled on a previous one by two American scholars but with an important modification in that emphases were introduced on particular items in the read-aloud lists that were their basis. His results were rewardingly positive.

18 **Héctor Ortiz-Lira** gives the results of tests carried out to provide experimental evidence of Spanish-speakers' departures from the norms of English sentence accentuation especially when English does not place the nucleus on the last lexical item in the word group. Thirty-five fairly randomly selected Chilean teachers were recorded reading dialogues. Interference from Spanish-language habits duly showed up in their restressing of given information and accenting of sentence-final adverbials etc.

19 **Graham Pointon** reports an investigation of Spanish rhythm based on six readings of the familiar IPA version of the Aesop fable *The North Wind and the Sun*. His measurements of the durations of the segments, of their syllables and of the inter-stress intervals confirmed him in his rejection of the traditional classification of Spanish as a syllable-timed language. He proposes instead to assign it to a new category, 'segment-timed', which he argues is also the most appropriate categorisation of infant speech.

20 **Paul Tench** addresses the topic of the intonation unit boundary. He carefully reviews the work of the chief writers to have most recently tackled this problematic field and in particular draws attention to the weaknesses of Halliday's handling of the problem, finally opting for an approach that profits especially from the work of Jassem and Pike.

21 **László Varga** gives an account of the parallels and dissimilarities

between the intonational treatment of stereotypical expressions in English and in his native Hungarian. In general he finds that the formal and functional properties of the Hungarian 'stylized fall' are remarkably though not precisely similar to those of the corresponding English phenomenon. Although he apparently accepts the Robert Ladd line in terminology, his discussion does something to undermine this questionable recent orthodoxy in the explanation of the semantic value of the pitch pattern in question.

22 This item, by the editor, deals with questions of the teaching of English intonation to those for whom the language is not their mother tongue. It argues that too many teachers are doubtful of the adequacy of their handling of the matter. It suggests that in spontaneous speech only tonicity presents real problems. For those who wish to read aloud literature as authentically as native speakers some traditional studies are recommended.

PART III THE PHONETICS OF MOTHER-TONGUE ENGLISH

23 **John Baldwin**, in discussing consonant capture, offers many interesting examples of the ways English-speakers may quite often be heard to depart from the traditional 'rules' by which the mainstream forms of English generally do not allow the final consonants of words to attach themselves to vowels beginning following words. He is able to draw for evidence on his files of observations as the country's longest active practitioner in the field of forensic phonetics.

24 **Nik Coupland** ventures into a very controversial area with his provocative comments in the hinterland between between phonetics and sociolinguistics. He sees all proper-name pronunciations as having rights and obligations attached to them. Among various comments regarding pronunciation and cultural identity, he points out how certain local anglicisations of Welsh words 'subvert Welsh ethnicity' at Cardiff where so many born and bred there like myself are less than enthusiastic to be labelled 'Welsh'.

25 **Laurie Bauer** offers us salutary help in avoiding too simplistic a view of the categorising of various versions of words as 'spelling pronunciations'. The conservative speaker may find his new data something of a chamber of horrors but he points out a direction in which we need not doubt that we all travel further every day. He adds some interesting speculations regarding what he thinks may be a tendency towards syllable timing and others about the social causes of the phenomenon.

26 **John Higgins** makes enterprising use of a database in the form of a very substantial English wordlist to establish remarkably complete accounts of

various types of English homophones. His findings illustrate, amongst other things, the fact that computers can now be used to take a good deal of the drudgery out of the compilation of useful practice materials for the teaching of English pronunciation.

27 **John Kelly**'s stimulating account of consonant 'resonance' contrasts that exist between the accents of three regions of England reminds one that there are more things differentiating people's accents than have yet been fully accounted for. It deals with complexes of articulatory elements which extend to different degrees over stretches of speech in various language varieties and points to new research opportunities in an area which, as he rightly insists, is not merely of phonetic but also of phonological interest.

28 **John Local**, from a basis of non-segmental Firthian phonology, Abercrombian word-rhythm analysis, etc., deals with matters of timing and rhythm in respect of word syllabification and ambisyllabicity. He illustrates his conclusions from his work on speech synthesis using his YorkTalk speech-generation system to impressive effect.

29 **Derrick McClure**, having examined the monophthongs of seven speakers from widely separated parts of Scotland, uses his spectrographic data to devise an economical distinctive-feature system for Scottish Standard English as a whole that is plainly strikingly different from what would be applicable to the other well-known varieties of Standard English.

30 **John Maidment** draws attention to a little noticed feature of a traditional-dialect mainly eastern and northern Midland value of the vowel in words such as *shirt* which has occurred in Lincolnshire, Nottinghamshire, Leicestershire, Cheshire, Staffordshire and his native Derbyshire in a form with a quality comparable to an ordinary version of *shot* or *short*.

31 **Clive Upton** begins with what happens to the *cup* and *foot* vowels at the transitional zones between dialect regions in northern and southern England where groups of words may show either a mixture of two different types of sound distribution or neither of two alternatives but an intermediate compromise sound. But he goes beyond that and, among various matters of note, he shows (with an illuminating map) that the ancient quality of the *cup* vowel has been found to have persisted in very southerly areas indeed.

32 **Henry Warkentyne** and **John Esling** draw attention to a vowel quality difference between Canadian English and General American that has been hitherto overlooked. They point out that, by contrast with the General American tendency to raise the 'ash' vowel /æ/, Western Canadian English seems to share the southern British tendency to lower it. Their data on 128 speakers of diverse age, class and sex taken from an auditory survey of Vancouver English made by Gregg *et al.* in 1985 clearly demonstrate that the

well-known /ai/ and /au/ differences are not the only ones of note between the Canadian and the General American accents of English.

33 **John Wells**, in his article 'Syllabification and allophony' in our sister volume *Studies in the Pronunciation of English* (ed. S. Ramsaran, London: Routledge, 1990: 85), confessed to being worried by 'the apparently wayward behaviour of /r/' in words like *memorise* in which it clearly begins the last syllable instead of belonging to the previous one as predicted by his theory of English syllabification set out in that article. His extension of that theory with the ingenious addition of a new rule of 'sonorant left capture' expounded in the present article means that he is now a happy man about such things.

PART IV THE PHONETICS OF NON-MOTHER-TONGUE ENGLISH

34 **Bev Collins** and **Inger Mees** are pioneers in the application of voice quality studies to language teaching, offering new techniques to the next generation of teachers. Their work makes new observations and raises many interesting questions. Just two are: 'How far can General American speakers be assumed to share a set of vocal-setting features?' and 'Are the specifically GA features that Danish users of English may acquire likely to increase their intelligibility and/or acceptability to non-GA interlocutors?'

35 **Yves Le Clézio**, in investigating Shilluk, a little-known and not populously spoken Nilotic language of southern Sudan, needed to record many of his specimen words with accompanying English glosses which have provided the materials for this snapshot of Shilluk-influenced English in which, among its various interesting features, we learn that confusion can occur between /p/ and /f/, between /t/ and /s/ and even between /k/ and /tʃ/.

36 **Inge Livbjerg** and **Inger Mees** demonstrate strikingly and with great practicality what pitfalls there are in the teaching of pronunciation if the teacher has not got an adequately precise and up-to-date knowledge of the phonetics of both the interfering language and the target model. It is very appropriate that some of their data derive from recordings of Doc O'Connor working with Inge on her English pronunciation a couple of decades ago.

37 **Jan Posthumus** addresses himself cogently to the widespread 'ignorance of the basic realities of loan-word pronunciation in native language settings', vigorously demolishing the fallacy that any departure from the precise phonetic values of the lending language is a regrettable fall from grace. He makes his case by reference to the behaviour of English loans in Dutch. The misapprehension taints the practice of the compilers of even

the best English dictionaries (*OED*, 2nd edn, 1989, p. xxxiii ominously refers to its 'phonetic representation of unassimilated foreign words'). Now that we are getting CD/ROM versions of dictionaries with audible pronunciations this is a truly timely topic to have raised.

38 David Taylor offers his optimistic recipe for 'a new lease of life for phonetics and phonology in the context of pronunciation teaching'. His proposal is that teachers should not focus on imparting a particular accent of English but should 'take the transcription itself as the target' because the transcriptions of Gimson, Wells, etc. represent 'something much wider' than is explicitly purported by their purveyors. It is interesting to consider how far he is recommending a new departure or the recognition of a fact of life.

Part I

GENERAL PHONETICS
AND PHONOLOGICAL
THEORY

1

On some neutralisations and archiphonemes in English allegro speech

Tsutomu Akamatsu
University of Leeds

Paul Passy (1906: 39) mentioned 'prononciation familière ralentie' in reference to pronunciation, in his opinion, best suited for teaching purposes. This style of pronunciation was later referred to as 'slow conversational style' (Jones 1945: 127) or that of 'natural, unstudied but reasonably careful and not rapid conversation' (Jones 1950: 9), and on it Jones based his formulation of the phoneme. The pronunciation of individual words as indicated in various pronouncing dictionaries, etc. is largely what one would expect in such a style.

When a language is spoken naturally, we find, more often than not, allegro speech. To observe and account for various phonetic phenomena, it seems important to distinguish between two levels of articulatory care characteristic of non-allegro speech and allegro speech, respectively.

Traditionally, the phonological system of a given language is presented in terms of non-allegro speech. This is perfectly legitimate, but there should also be some reference to the phonology of allegro speech. These two kinds of phonology are not mutually exclusive. What happens in non-allegro speech inevitably happens in allegro speech as well. One and the same speaker may exhibit features of both in free variation (see Martinet 1988: xiv).

As the rate of speech increases, co-ordination in executing the various articulations necessary in the production of a sound deteriorates simply because the speech organs find it increasingly difficult, in the progressively less time available, to maintain reasonably clear-cut implementation of them. A transition between an articulation and an adjacent one may be less than satisfactorily executed, giving rise to the phenomenon of assimilation whereby successive sounds become more or less homogeneous. Often a whole sound may be omitted.

These phonetic phenomena of elision, loosening of articulation and assimilation are among those which most characteristically and frequently

3

occur in allegro speech both within individual words and at word boundaries. According to Ramsaran in Gimson ([1962] 1989: 308–11), elisions occur most typically in allegro speech, while assimilations occur equally in either allegro speech or non-allegro speech. Both allegro and non-allegro speech can be formal or casual. Assimilations are more frequent in casual than in formal speech regardless of whether it is allegro or not. We shall be concerned here with assimilations in allegro speech. It is rare for a type of assimilation to occur in non-allegro but not in allegro speech. Assimilation can be unidirectional, i.e. progressive or regressive: for example, the occurrence of [p] (labiodental) as in *cupful* in allegro speech instead of [p] (bilabial) is due to regressive assimilation; the occurrence of [ŋ] (velar) as in *bacon* in allegro speech instead of [n] is due to progressive assimilation. Assimilation can be bidirectional: for example, the occurrence of [m̥] (voiceless) as in *campement* [kɑ̃m̥mɑ̃] instead of [p] in allegro speech in French results from the sustained lowered posture of the soft palate all the way from the first [ɑ̃] to the second [ɑ̃], with the result that what would be [p] in the non-allegro pronunciation of this French word is nasalised (Martinet 1969: 128–9).

Elision which results in the omission of one or more sounds in an individual word most frequently affects a close or central vowel in the immediate neighbourhood of continuants like [n], [m], [ŋ], [l] and [ɹ]. Witness, for example, the elision of such vowels in the first syllables in *police*, *correct*, *believe*, etc. (cf. Gimson 1962: 231–2). In English and German, for example, certain of the so-called weak forms are more characteristic of allegro speech than some other weak forms of the same words. Interaction of elision and assimilation in allegro speech is very frequent, elision being the starting-point in this case (cf. *haben* ['haːbən] > ['haːbm̩] > ['haːmm̩] > ['haːm̩] > [haːm] in German). One finds a useful account of this topic in German in Kohler (1977: 213–19). One example worth mentioning, so far as English is concerned, would be what is frequently given in dictionaries in the spelling *gonna* (i.e. *going to* used in reference to 'future') – variously pronounced as ['gɔnə], [gənə], etc. – which is associated with a complex interplay between elision and assimilation.

Loosening of an articulation can occur in non-allegro as well as allegro speech. Gimson (1962: 154) appears to associate loosening characteristically with allegro speech ('in rapid, familiar speech', as he puts it), when he refers to instances of incomplete closure of plosives (e.g. *baker* pronounced ['beɪxə]), though I have observed the same phenomenon even in *formal non-allegro* speech (e.g. *Buckingham* pronounced with [x] instead of [k]). Compare the phenomenon in German whereby *habe*, for example, is pronounced with [β] (fricative) instead of [b] (plosive) (Kohler 1977: 210).

Gimson (1960; 1962: 270–2, 274) draws our attention to 'the instability of English alveolar articulation', notably word-final alveolars. Though he makes no explicit reference to allegro speech in this connection, its involvement seems obvious. By 'instability of final alveolars' is meant the phenomenon whereby a word-final alveolar phoneme (/t/, /d/, /n/) is said to be regressively assimilated in respect of the place of articulation to some following word-initial non-alveolar phoneme (e.g. /p/, /b/, /m/, /k/, /g/): for example, the alveolarity of /t/ in *that* will be assimilated to the bilabiality of /p/ in *pen*, so that *that pen* will be pronounced [ðæp pen]. Gimson further mentions coalescent assimilation between word-final /s/ or /z/ and following word-initial /ʃ/ or /j/ (though I would postulate /i/ instead in these cases), e.g. *this shop, this year, those young men, is she.* I deliberately leave them out of account here since the type of assimilation involved is coalescent rather than regressive and the pattern of replacement is not quite the same as in the other cases. Below is Gimson's (1960: 8–9) presentation, somewhat modified.

1   /t/ > /p/ before /p, b, m/, e.g. *that pen, that boy, that man.*
2   /t/ > /k/ before /k, g/, e.g. *that cup, that girl.*
3   /d/ > /b/ before /p, b, m/, e.g. *good pen, good boy, good man.*
4   /d/ > /g/ before /k, g/, e.g. *good concert, good girl.*
5   /n/ > /m/ before /p, b, m/, e.g. *ten players, ten boys, ten men.*
6   /n/ > /ŋ/ before /k, g/, e.g. *ten cups, ten girls.*

Gimson understandably calls the result of the above type of phonetic modification through regressive assimilation 'a phonemic change'. He interprets [ðæp pen] as phonologically /ðæp pen/. The identification of such distinctive units, which are said to replace the 'original' alveolar phonemes, is traditionally made, as shown above, through simple recourse to the criterion of phonetic similarity.

An alternative phonological analysis is possible for those who operate with the concepts of 'commutation test', 'phonological opposition', 'neutralisation', 'archiphoneme', 'phoneme', 'relevant feature', etc., to whom I shall hereafter refer as functionalists. (For my own understanding of these concepts, see Akamatsu 1988, *passim*, or Akamatsu 1992, *passim*.) For functionalists these phonological changes are instances of neutralisation. To the best of my knowledge, no phonological analysis of such examples in terms of neutralisation in allegro speech has appeared in published form, hence my present attempt.

My first task is to characterise in terms of relevant features all the nine phonemes (/p/, /b/, /m/, /t/, /d/, /n/, /k/, /g/, /ŋ/) involved.

/p/	'voiceless	bilabial	non-nasal'
/b/	'voiced	bilabial	non-nasal'
/m/		'bilabial	nasal'
/t/	'voiceless	apical	non-nasal'
/d/	'voiced	apical	non-nasal'

/n/		'apical	nasal'
/k/	'voiceless	dorsal	non-nasal'
/g/	'voiced	dorsal	non-nasal'
/ŋ/		'dorsal	nasal'

The concept of 'relevant feature' (on which see e.g. Martinet 1965: 138–40) should not be confused with the concept of 'distinctive feature' employed in generative phonology: for instance, the relevant feature 'apical' implies that all the required articulations involve the tip (i.e. apex) of the tongue, whether these articulations are alveolar (cf. *tea*), dental (cf. *eighth*) or postalveolar (cf. *tree*). Note that a glottal plosive as a realisation of /p/, /t/ or /k/ in word-final position is precluded in the present discussion.

The word-final distinctive unit in each of the six cases mentioned further above which replaces an 'apical' phoneme is different from the distinctive unit identified (as a phoneme) by Gimson. Let me take just the first case (i.e. item 1 in the list). The opposition between /p/ ('voiceless bilabial non-nasal') and /t/ ('voiceless apical non-nasal') is valid in some contexts, say, word-initially (cf. *pan* /pæn/ vs *tan* /tæn/) but is neutralised before /p/, /b/ or /m/ (there is phonetically no distinction between e.g. *ripe* [... p] *pears* and *right* [... p] *pears*), as the opposition between the relevant features 'bilabial' and 'apical' is cancelled and the archiphoneme characterisable as 'voiceless non-dorsal non-nasal' which is the sum of the relevant features shared by /p/ and /t/ occurs. I indicate this archiphoneme as /p-t/ and do likewise, *mutatis mutandis*, for the other archiphonemes.

Below then are those distinctive units which Gimson identifies as the phonemes (/p/, /b/; /k/, /g/; /m/, /ŋ/) replacing the 'original' phonemes (/t/, /d/, /n/). I shall give, in each case, the phoneme which Gimson identifies, followed by the distinctive unit, the archiphoneme.

1 /p/ ... the archiphoneme /p-t/ 'voiceless non-dorsal non-nasal' associated with the neutralisation of the opposition between /p/ and /t/. It is realised by [p]. In the context where /p-t/ occurs (i.e. before /p/, /b/ or /m/: e.g. *ripe* /... p-t/ *pears* /p.../; *right* /... p-t/ *pears* /p.../; *right* /... p-t/ *mayors* /m.../), it is opposed to, among other distinctive units, /k/ 'voiceless dorsal non-nasal' (as in *thick* /... k/ *pen* /p.../; *sick* /... k/ *boy* /b.../; *sick* /... k/ *man* /m.../), /b-d/ 'voiced non-dorsal non-nasal' (as in *good* /... b-d/ *pen* /p.../; *good* /... b-d/ *boy* /b.../; *good* /... b-d/ *man* /m.../) and /m-n/ 'non-dorsal nasal' (as in *ten* /... m-n/ *players* /p.../; *ten* /... m-n/ *boys* /b.../; *ten* /... m/ *men* /m.../).

2 /k/ ... the archiphoneme /t-k/ 'voiceless non-bilabial non-nasal' associated with the neutralisation of the opposition between /t/ and /k/. It is realised by [k]. Where /t-k/ occurs (i.e. before /k/ or /g/: e.g. *that* /... t-k/ *cup* /k.../; *that* /... t-k/ *girl* /g.../), it is opposed to, among

other distinctive units, /p/ 'voiceless bilabial non-nasal' (as in *stirrup* /...p/ *cup* /k.../; *top* /...p/ *girl* /g.../), /d-g/ 'voiced non-bilabial non-nasal' (as in *good* /...d-g/ *concert* /k.../; *good* /...d-g/ *girl* /g.../), and /n-ŋ/ 'non-bilabial nasal' (as in *ten* /...n-ŋ/ *cups* /k.../; *ten* /...n-ŋ/ *girls* /g.../).

3 /b/ ... the archiphoneme /b-d/ 'voiced non-dorsal non-nasal' associated with the neutralisation of the opposition between /b/ and /d/. It is realised by [b]. Where /b-d/ occurs (i.e. before /p/, /b/ or /m/: e.g. *good* /...b-d/ *pen* /p.../; *good* /...b-d/ *boy* /b.../; *good* /...b-d/ *man* /m.../), it is opposed to, among other distinctive units, /g/ 'voiced dorsal non-nasal' (as in *big* /...g/ *pen* /p.../; *big* /...g/ *boy* /b.../; *big* /...g/ *man* /m.../), and /m-n/ 'non-dorsal nasal' (as in *ten* /...m-n/ *players* /p.../; *ten* /...m-n/ *boys* /b.../; *ten* /...m-n/ *men* /m.../).

4 /g/ ... the archiphoneme /d-g/ 'voiced non-bilabial non-nasal' associated with the neutralisation of the opposition between /d/ and /g/. It is realised by [g]. Where /d-g/ occurs (i.e. before /k/ or /g/; e.g. *good* /...d-g/ *concert* /k.../; *good* /...d-g/ *girl* /g.../), it is opposed to, among other distinctive units, /b/ 'voiced bilabial non-nasal' (as in *pub* /...b/ *concert* /k.../; *glib* /...b/ *girl* /g.../), /t-k/ 'voiceless non-bilabial non-nasal' (as in *that* /...t-k/ *cup* /k.../; *that* /...t-k/ *girl* /g.../), and /n-ŋ/ 'non-bilabial nasal' (as in *ten* /...n-ŋ/ *cups* /k.../; *ten* /...n-ŋ/ *girls* /g.../).

5 /m/ ... the archiphoneme /m-n/ 'non-dorsal nasal' associated with the neutralisation of the opposition between /m/ and /n/. It is realised by [m]. Where /m-n/ occurs (i.e. before /p/, /b/ or /m/: e.g. *ten* /...m-n/ *players* /p.../; *ten* /...m-n/ *boys* /b.../; *ten* /...m-n/ *men* /m.../), it is opposed to, among other distinctive units, /ŋ/ 'dorsal nasal' (as in *strong* /...ŋ/ *men* /m.../), /p-t/ 'voiceless non-dorsal non-nasal' (as in *that* /...p-t/ *pen* /p.../; *that* /...p-t/ *boy* /b.../; *that* /...p-t/ *man* /m.../), and /b-d/ 'voiced non-dorsal non-nasal' (as in *good* /...b-d/ *pen* /p.../; *good* /...b-d/ *boy* /b.../; *good* /...b-d/ *man* /m.../). The archiphoneme /m-n/ 'non-dorsal nasal' is the same archiphoneme as the one that occurs in allegro speech before /f/ or /v/ and is realised by [ɱ] (labiodental) as in *comfort* /...m-n f.../ and *anvil* /...m-n v.../.

6 /ŋ/ ... the archiphoneme /n-ŋ/ 'non-bilabial nasal' associated with the neutralisation of the opposition between /n/ and /ŋ/. It is realised by [ŋ]. Where /n-ŋ/ occurs (i.e. before /k/ or /g/; e.g. *ten* /...n-ŋ/ *cups* /k.../; *ten* /...n-ŋ/ *girls* /g.../), it is opposed to, among other distinctive units, /m/ 'bilabial nasal' (as in *slim* /...m/ *cups* /k.../; *slim* /...m/ *girls* /g.../), /t-k/ 'voiceless non-bilabial non-nasal' (as in *that* /...t-k/ *cup* /k.../; *that* /...t-k/ *girl* /g.../), and /d-g/ 'voiced non-bilabial non-nasal' (as in *good* /...d-g/ *concert* /k.../; *good* /...d-g/ *girls* /g.../).

7

Gimson (1962: 271) gives further examples involving regressive assimilation similar to the type we have looked at above. He mentions, for example, *Don't be late* /... mp b .../ (which functionalists may wish to re-analyse as /... m-n p-t b .../), *He won't come* /... ŋ k .../ (/... n-ŋ k .../), *He found both* /... m b .../ (/... m-n b .../), in which cases, according to functionalists, the resultant distinctive units are archiphonemes (not phonemes).

It will have been seen that, when analysed from the functionalist point of view, the phonological system of allegro speech in English will contain more distinctive units (to the extent that certain archiphonemes are to be added) than are identified in non-allegro speech. Some of these archiphonemes may well occur in non-allegro speech as well. It will have become clear that the functionalists' analyses above are crucially based on the concept of phonological opposition (that of neutralisation being consequent on it) and not on the concept of phonetic similarity.

The particular aspect of the type of regressive assimilation in allegro speech in English we have looked at above has implications at another level of the language. Gimson (1960: 8) gives the examples of *ran quickly* vs *rang quickly*, and *run for* vs *rum for*, and Gimson (1962: 271) adds a few more examples like *right pears* vs *ripe pears*, *like cream* vs *light cream* and *hot manure* vs *hop manure*, etc. In these cases, the members of each pair are shown to be phonetically identical (and consequently phonologically identical as well). Gimson (1960: 8; 1962: 271) says that neutralisation is involved. However, according to functionalists, one has here to do ultimately with 'syncretism' in that there is 'formal confusion without semantic confusion' for both speaker and listener. The formal distinction is obliterated because both *ran* and *rang* happen to have the same signifier /r æ n-ŋ/ [ræŋ] as a result of the neutralisation of the opposition between /n/ and /ŋ/, but the speaker has chosen one of the two words and the listener knows (without, however, being able to tell which) that the speaker *has* chosen one of them. Gimson does not mention syncretism in this connection. He is more interested in indicating how this sort of ambiguity may be resolved when he says (1962: 271): '[to the listener] the sense of an utterance [i.e. which word the speaker has chosen] may be determined by the context'.

The above is intended to be but a specimen treatment, from the functional point of view, of a limited number of allegro forms. No doubt it would be interesting to pursue a similar treatment in the same theoretical framework of many other allegro forms.

REFERENCES

Akamatsu, T. (1988) *The Theory of Neutralization and the Archiphoneme in Functional Phonology*, Amsterdam and Philadelphia: John Benjamins.
—— (1992) *Essentials of Functional Phonology*, Louvain-la-Neuve: Peeters.

Gimson, A. C. (1960) 'The instability of English alveolar articulations', *Le Maître phonétique* 113: 7–10.

—— (1962) *An Introduction to the Pronunciation of English*, 1st edn, London: Edward Arnold. Subsequent editions are 2nd edn (1970), 3rd edn (1980) and 4th edn (1989, revised by S. Ramsaran).

Jones, D. (1945) 'Some thoughts on the phoneme', *Transactions of the Philological Society* 1944, 119–35.

—— (1950) *The Phoneme: Its Nature and Use*, 1st edn, Cambridge: Heffer.

Kohler, K. J. (1977) *Einführung in die Phonetik des Deutschen*, Berlin: Erich Schmidt.

Martinet, A. (1965) *La Linguistique synchronique*, Paris: Presses Universitaires de France.

—— (1969) 'Réalisation identique de phonèmes différents', *La Linguistique* Vol. 5, No. 2: 127–9.

—— (1988) Foreword to T. Akamatsu, *The Theory of Neutralization and the Antiphoneme in Functional Phonology*, Amsterdam and Philadelphia: John Benjamins, pp. xiii–xv.

Passy, P. (1906) *Les Sons du français*, 6th edn (1st edn 1887), Association phonétique internationale, Paris: Librairie Firmin-Didot, Société des traités.

2

The phonetics of neutralisation: the case of Australian coronals

Andrew Butcher
The Flinders University, Adelaide

NEUTRALISATION: TRADITIONAL AND CONTEMPORARY VIEWS

In his classic introductory text, J. D. O'Connor (1973: 182) concludes a brief excursion on the topic of neutralisation with a typically laconic but accurate reference to the /p/–/b/ opposition in English. This opposition, he says, 'is neutralized after /s/ where only *what we agree to call* /p/ occurs' (my emphasis).

The concept of neutralisation has always been one of the corner stones of phonological theory: two or more closely related sounds which are in contrast in some positions in the structure of a language may be replaced in other positions by an *archiphoneme*, embodying the totality of distinctive features common to the two sounds. However, the phonetic realisation of archiphonemes has, until recently, remained a somewhat under-researched area. Phonologists have traditionally grouped such realisations into discrete categories, whilst not always agreeing as to how many there should be. Trubetzkoy (1939: 71–3) originally listed six types of 'archiphoneme representative'.[1] Both Martinet (1968: 3) and Lass (1984: 49–51), on the other hand, come up with a list of five categories, which do not exactly correspond with each other nor with those of Trubetzkoy. Nevertheless, most phonologists seem to agree that, in the case of bilateral oppositions at least, archiphonemes are realised in one of the following ways:

1   One member of the opposition is represented, to the complete exclusion of the others. Which sound actually occurs may be determined 'extrinsically', i.e. by the context. More usually, however, the occurrence is determined 'intrinsically', i.e. it is the so-called 'unmarked' member of the opposition which is represented. This type of neutralisation is exemplified by the 'devoicing' of syllable-final obstruents in languages such as German and Polish.

2   Neither member of the opposition is represented; 'ein Mittelding' (an 'in-between' sound) occurs which has features common to both. An

example of this type would be the realisation of stops after initial /s/ in English, where the most commonly occurring sounds are voiceless but unaspirated – hence we must 'agree to call them' /p, t, k/.

3 Representatives of both members of the opposition occur, *either* in free variation, as appears to be the case, for example, with the syllable-final voicing opposition in Danish, *or* in complementary distribution, as with the /e/–/ɛ/ distinction in most accents of French.

Such traditional categories are evidently based entirely on auditory impressions. Over recent years, however, a certain amount of interest has been shown in the instrumental investigation of the phonetics of neutralisation. This interest has focused almost exclusively on what are presumed to be examples of the first type of realisation, and specifically on the question of whether neutralisation is complete or only partial. Much of this research has concentrated on the study of final obstruent devoicing in languages such as German, Polish, Russian and Catalan (see e.g. Dinnsen and Charles-Luce 1984; Port and O'Dell 1985; Slowiaczek and Dinnsen 1985) and in many cases has claimed to show that underlying distinctions are preserved acoustically, although usually not perceptually. This has led Dinnsen (1985: 275) to conclude that 'the standard view of neutralization ... is, unfortunately, without empirical support', and to suggest that the concept is only viable if phonological theory admits a distinction between perception and production. Dinnsen does not explicitly consider cases of type 2 or 3, however, but only those where the archiphoneme representative has traditionally been described as identical with a realisation of one of the members of the neutralised opposition.

Meanwhile in a number of recent approaches to phonology – in particular lexical phonology – the concept of *underspecification* of segments has been utilised in dealing with (amongst other things) neutralisation and markedness (e.g. Kiparsky 1982; Clements 1985; Avery and Rice 1989). According to this concept, only unpredictable features and feature specifications appear in the underlying (lexical) representation. Predictable features and feature values are supplied by rules – either universal or language-specific. Thus Avery and Rice (1989), for example, suggest that the realisation of /t/ as [ʔ] in English occurs because /t/ is underlyingly unspecified for place of articulation. According to this analysis, /t/ only becomes [t] when the Coronal node of its hierarchical feature structure is 'filled in' by a phonetic implementation rule. Similarly Harvey (1991) argues that the characteristic phonological patterning of the glottal stop in languages of northern Australia can best be accounted for by regarding /ʔ/ as '*the* completely unspecified segment' in these languages.

Underspecification does not, in the view of most phonologists, appear to extend to surface representations: in most descriptions each phonetic realisation is fully specified. Keating (1988), however, has suggested that this may not be a necessary or even a useful assumption. She gives examples of the 'transparency' of phonetically underspecified consonants such as /h/ and /b/, as evidenced by the presence of vowel-to-vowel interactions across them. Keating does not explicitly address the question of neutralisation, but it would seem reasonable to suggest that the notion of phonetic underspecification could be applied to the description of at least one type of archiphoneme representative. Surface forms of type 1 would automatically receive the unmarked value for the feature(s) in question by a 'fill-in rule' – presumably [–voice] in the case of German syllable-final devoicing. Realisations of type 3 would receive feature values through context-sensitive rules which assign values either on the basis of structural position or through spreading from neighbouring segments. A 'position rule' could, for example, be said to determine the realisation of non-final /ɛ/ in French. Type 2 'Mittelding' realisations, however, would presumably remain underspecified even at the phonetic level, and would be 'transparent' with regard to the feature in question. The trajectory between segments on either side would be determined by phonetic rules governing the realisation of those segments, and the intervening underspecified segment would contribute nothing of its own to that trajectory. Under this interpretation, O'Connor's stops following initial /s/ in English would remain unspecified for [voice], and would allow a smooth transition from [–voice] for the preceding /s/ to [+voice] for the following vowel – an interpretation which would seem to fit the facts of glottal dynamics in English initial clusters.

Subsequently Boyce *et al.* (1991: 225) have questioned Keating's equation of phonetic *target* with phonetic *specification*, arguing that segments which are unspecified for a given feature may (or must?) nevertheless still have a phonetic target for that feature. On the basis of evidence from lip rounding in intervocalic /t/ and /k/ and from velum lowering in slow articulations of intervocalic /s/, they claim that 'independent targets for so-called "unspecified" segments exist, although temporal constraints may prevent them from being visible in the acoustic or articulatory signal'. According to this view, the English post-/s/ stops *would* be assigned a characteristic target value for glottal configuration at the phonetic level. Because this target would be intermediate between those required for the surrounding segments, it would only become apparent in the appropriate physiological signal when the articulation of the cluster was slow enough to reveal a 'steady state'.

Compared with the neutralisation of voicing contrasts, the neutralisation of place-of-articulation oppositions seems to be rather less common in the world's languages, perhaps because the latter are less often 'privative' – i.e. involving the presence or absence of a single feature. Reported cases appear to be almost exclusively instances of type 1 or type 3. There are, for example, cases of vowel-induced neutralisation, such as that cited by Hyman

(1975: 70f.) from the Cameroon language Fe?fe?-Bamileke, where the opposition between /c/ and /k/ is neutralised before /i/, and only a sound corresponding to the former occurs. In some languages place of articulation is neutralised in nasals occurring before oral stops and the former are said to acquire their place feature values from the latter. In Australian languages, place distinctions are frequently neutralised in word-initial and word-final positions, and the resulting archiphoneme realisations have traditionally been described as type 1, that is to say the resulting sound is regarded as equivalent to the realisation of one of the members of the non-neutralised opposition.

IMPRESSIONISTIC DESCRIPTIONS OF AUSTRALIAN CORONALS

Australian phonologies are well known for the richness of their CORONAL distinctions – about half of them have three distinct sets of CORONALS and a further one-third have four (see Busby 1980: 75–8: Hamilton 1989: 1–16). Furthermore, almost every language has a nasal phoneme corresponding to each oral stop and many also have a lateral at every CORONAL place of articulation.[2] The following chart shows a maximal Australian place-of-articulation inventory.

LABIAL	APICAL		LAMINAL		VELAR
	ALVEOLAR	POSTALVEOLAR	DENTAL	ALVEOPALATAL	
p	t	ʈ	t̪	c	k

The labels are those traditionally used by Australianists and are not necessarily an accurate reflection of the phonetics – although the phonetically more realistic term ALVEOPALATAL is used in preference to the more widely used PALATAL.[3] Linguists have traditionally grouped together the ALVEOLAR and POSTALVEOLAR sounds on the grounds of their similar phonological behaviour and a presumed common active articulator, the tip of the tongue. They are jointly referred to as APICALS, and can probably be traced back to a common proto-Australian order (see Dixon 1980: 155–6). For the same reason, DENTAL and ALVEOPALATAL sounds are grouped together phonologically as a natural class. They are usually referred to as LAMINALS, since they can be said to be articulated with the blade of the tongue.[4]

About a quarter of the languages in Busby's (1980) survey have a LAMINAL distinction but lack an APICAL distinction (most of these are found in the Cape York Peninsula). Just over 20 per cent have an APICAL contrast with no LAMINAL contrast (this type of system is found in many languages of Western Australia and the Northern Territory). A few languages (16 per cent of Busby's sample – mainly from eastern Queensland and eastern New South

Wales) have neither a LAMINAL nor an APICAL distinction. In the following sections, the term 'archiphoneme' is used in a very broad sense, to refer to non-contrastive APICAL and LAMINAL sounds, whether they occur in languages which lack the contrast altogether or whether they occur in positions of neutralisation in languages which do have the opposition in question.

There seems to be a general consensus that in 'double-APICAL' languages (i.e. where there is a contrast between ALVEOLAR and POSTALVEOLAR sounds) the former are articulated in a similar way to the equivalent sounds in English (see e.g. Dixon (1980: 135) – although which particular variety of English is seldom specified). This is explicitly stated to be the case in practical pronunciation guides for a number of widely scattered languages, from Adnyamathanha in the south (McEntee and McKenzie 1992: vi) to Gupapuyngu in the north (Lowe 1975: 4,15). At least two (unrelated) languages, however, are described as having somewhat more advanced ALVEOLAR articulations than are usual in English: both Gooniyandi (McGregor 1990: 51) and Kunwinjku (Carroll 1976: 11) are said to have ALVEOLAR sounds made just behind the top teeth.

Most Australianists appear to agree with Dixon (1980: 135) that the POSTALVEOLAR sounds are articulated with the tip of the tongue just behind the alveolar ridge. This is said to be the case, for example, in Western Arrernte (Strehlow 1942: 35), Murrinh-Patha (Street and Mollinjin 1981:196), Tiwi (Osborne 1974: 12), Yindjibarndi (Wordick 1982: 12), and many others. Some authors, however, make reference to a much more retracted point of constriction, often with contact being made by the underside of the tongue blade. Such sublaminal retroflex articulations are said to occur, for example in Adnyamathanha (McEntee and McKenzie 1992: vii), Djingulu (Chadwick 1975: 3), and Gupapuyngu (Lowe 1975: 5, 20).

There appears to be a good deal of variation also in the realisation of DENTAL sounds, both across languages which have this category and often also within them. The majority of 'double-LAMINAL' languages (i.e. those which contrast DENTAL and ALVEOPALATAL sounds) are described as having an articulation with the tongue tip protruding between the teeth or contacting the rims of the upper incisors. Once again the geographical spread of these languages is quite wide, including Wembawemba in the south-east (Hercus 1969: 17), the Arandic languages in the centre (e.g. Yallop 1977: 21) and Kayardild in the north (Evans 1985: 495). The key point emerging from descriptions of these languages is that the pronunciation of DENTAL sounds is normally with the tongue tip up, varying between lamino-interdental and lamino-dentialveolar, either from speaker to speaker or as a function of speech style and tempo. In a few double-LAMINAL languages, however, as Dixon points out, the tongue tip is said to be placed behind the lower front teeth in producing these sounds. This type of articulation is described for Gooniyandi (McGregor 1990: 51) and Yindji-barndi (Wordick 1982: 12) in the west, but also for Wangkumara in the centre (McDonald and Wurm 1979: 8) and for Yuwaalarraay in the east (Williams 1980: 6). There are just a few examples of variation between tip-up and tip-down articulations within the same language. This is said to be the case in Djapu (Morphy 1983: 17) and possibly Marrithiyel (Green 1989: 19).

In the vast majority of cases, ALVEOPALATAL sounds in double-LAMINAL languages are explicitly described as having tip-down articulations, either lamino-postalveolar or lamino-prepalatal. A typical description is that provided by Hercus (1969: 17) for Wembawemba, where 'the tip of the tongue touches the back of the lower teeth, while the blade of the tongue forms an occlusion with the upper teeth ridge and the palatal area immediately behind and above the teeth ridge'. The same kind of articulation is described for other unrelated languages such as Gupa-puyngu (Lowe 1975: 7, 17) in the north and Yindjibarndi (Wordick 1982: 12) in the west.

As we have seen, Australian phonologies are characterised not only by the richness of their systems of place contrasts, but also by the fact that these systems can be described in traditional terms as consisting entirely of bilateral and (at least in the case of the CORONALS) privative oppositions. It is, therefore, perhaps not surprising that neutralisation of these oppositions is very widespread. Even when one or both of the CORONAL contrasts is present in a language, its distribution is usually quite restricted. APICAL sounds do not occur very commonly in word-initial position in Australian languages (see Dixon 1980: 167) and in the majority of cases the distinction between ALVEOLAR and POSTALVEOLAR sounds is not maintained in that environment. Reports on the majority of languages state that it is a sound equivalent to the POSTALVEOLAR which occurs in this position. This is said to be the case, for instance, in Nyangumarta (O'Grady 1963: 5), Warlpiri (Jagst 1975: 22), and Kunwinjku (Evans n.d.: 18). In a few languages, however, it is the ALVEOLAR sound which appears to represent the APICAL archiphoneme. Such is said to be the case in Murrinh-Patha, for example, (Street and Mollinjin 1981: 196) and in Kitja (Taylor and Taylor 1971: 107). At least one writer (Wilkins 1989: 91) seems to imply that in Eastern Arrernte there is free variation between alveolar and postalveolar articulations, corresponding to a type 3 realisation of the archiphoneme.

Most double-LAMINAL languages do not maintain the opposition between DENTALS and ALVEOPALATALS in final position and many languages in any case have only a single LAMINAL category. The sound which is most commonly described as occurring in such cases is some kind of tip-down lamino-postalveolar articulation, which would appear to be indistinguishable from those of contrasting ALVEOPALATALS in most double-LAMINAL languages. Such is reported to be the case, for example, in Maung in the north (Capell and

Hinch 1970: 18), Yidiny (Dixon 1977: 32) and Dyirbal (Dixon 1983: 441) in the east and Ungarinjin in the west (Rumsey 1982: 3). Very few single-LAMINAL languages seem to have a tip-up *dental* type of articulation, but the atypical Western Torres Strait language appears to be one of these (Bani and Klokeid 1972: 178; Kennedy 1981: 113). Single-LAMINAL languages are, however, commonly reported as exhibiting allophonic variation between 'more dental' and 'more palatal' varieties of tip-down LAMINAL, with the realisation which is considered to be the predominant or 'major' allophone varying from language to language or even from dialect to dialect. Vowel environment is most usually cited as the determining factor in such variation, as, for example, in many dialects of the Western Desert Language (Douglas 1964: 10; Glass and Hackett 1970: 109–10; Goddard 1983: 23), whereby dental variants occur before /a/ and /u/ and alveopalatal variants occur before /i/. There is also dialectal variation, with the dental articulation being preferred in the west and the alveopalatal in the east. Similar variation is reported amongst the languages of north-east Queensland (Dixon 1983:441) and within the Kunwinjku-Mayali dialects of north-central Arnhem Land (Evans n.d.: 18).

Thus linguists appear to be in agreement that neutralisation of the Australian CORONAL contrasts, in those languages where it occurs, is complete. Moreover there is almost universal acceptance of the type 1 nature of the realisation of both of the CORONAL archiphonemes. The evidence of auditory impressionistic descriptions suggests that it is the more posteriorly articulated member of each opposition which most commonly represents the archiphoneme. This has led Laughren (1990a, b) to propose that it is the [–anterior] member of the opposition in each case which is 'unmarked'. Dixon (1980: 188), on the other hand, regards the ALVEOLAR as being the unmarked member of the APICAL opposition, whilst not denying the apparent frequency of the POSTALVEOLAR at positions of neutralisation, which he explains in terms of a preference for marked segments in initial position.

In the following section, I present some palatographic data with the aim of testing the above assumptions from an articulatory point of view. These data may also have some bearing on the question as to whether such neutralisations can appropriately be accounted for in terms of under-specification. If Australian CORONAL archiphonemes are phonologically unspecified for the feature [anterior], are they phonetically realised as the equivalent of the 'unmarked' member of the opposition (type 1)? Or are they realised as a phonetic 'Mittelding' (type 2) or do they have a realisation which is either freely variable or positionally determined (type 3)? Finally, if either of the latter types is found, are such segments phonetically 'transparent' as regards anteriority or do they nevertheless have a specific target value for the corresponding phonetic parameter?

PALATOGRAPHIC DATA ON AUSTRALIAN CORONALS

The articulatory data presented here were recorded in the course of a wide-ranging investigation of the phonetics of Australian languages (see Butcher forthcoming). There appear to have been only two previous instrumental articulatory studies, on individual languages (see Jernudd 1974; Proffit and McGlone 1975). For the purposes of the present study, direct palatography was carried out using much the same method as that described by Jernudd (1974: 84) and Ladefoged and Traill (1980: 37ff.). An almost black contrast medium was painted on to the top surface of the speaker's tongue. He or she then pronounced the word under investigation once only. A flash photograph of the speaker's palate was then taken, using a *Polaroid CU-5* close-up camera with a 3 inch lens and a 1:1 palatal reflector, which was inserted into the speaker's mouth. In the case of certain APICAL articulations, where no contact was found at the front of the mouth, the underside of the tongue was then coated with the contrast medium and the procedure was repeated. This usually resulted in a deposit of the medium behind the alveolar ridge, indicating that contact had been *sublaminal.* In such cases tracings from both photographs were subsequently combined to give a composite palatogram of the sound in question.[5] Linguagrams were made by coating the hard palate with the contrast medium and photographing the tongue frontally, using a 1:1 anterior extension against the speaker's chin. All the palatograms reproduced here are traced directly from such photographs and all the cross-sectional profiles are traced directly from alginate palatal impressions of the speaker. Palatograms and accompanying sagittal cross-sections are divided into zones according to the speaker's maxillary dentition, as shown in Figure 2.1. The zoning and labelling are almost identical to those proposed by Firth (1957: 151). This method of division has the advantage of being based on objective criteria and seems to tally well with traditional landmarks when transferred to the mid-sagittal profile (cf. e.g. Catford 1977: 143; Ladefoged and Maddieson 1986: 4). In particular, the border between the alveolar and postalveolar zones, as defined by the dentition, usually falls at the variously named 'edge', 'corner' or 'peak' of the alveolar ridge, in so far as one is discernible from the mid-sagittal profile. Also, the border between the hard palate and the velum at the midline (usually clearly visible on at least some of the photographs) almost always falls exactly on the line between the middle and back molars (7 and 8). Contact between tongue and palate on the sagittal cross-sections is marked according to the location of contact at the midline on the corresponding palatogram. The outline of the rest of the tongue (i.e. the part not in contact with the palate), however, is no more than a reasonable estimation of the shape of the tongue along the midline at the moment of maximum constriction, based on anatomical knowledge, phonetic experience and common sense.

ANDREW BUTCHER

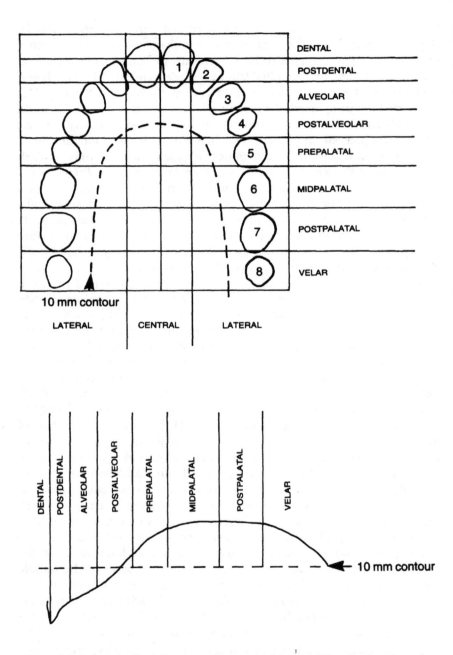

Figure 2.1 Anatomically defined tectal zones used in describing the location of tongue contact on palatograms

18

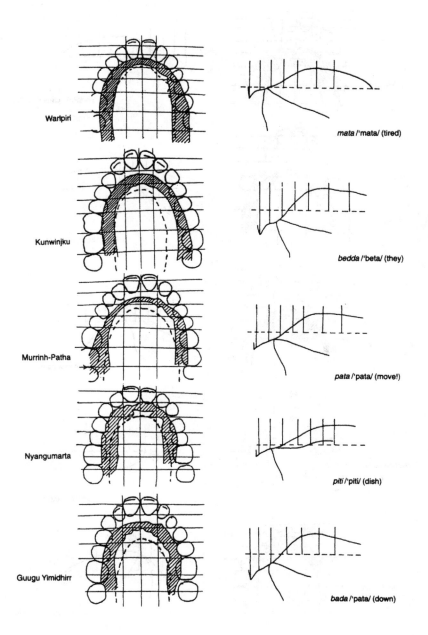

Figure 2.2 Palatograms and sagittal cross-sections of ALVEOLAR articulations in five double-APICAL languages

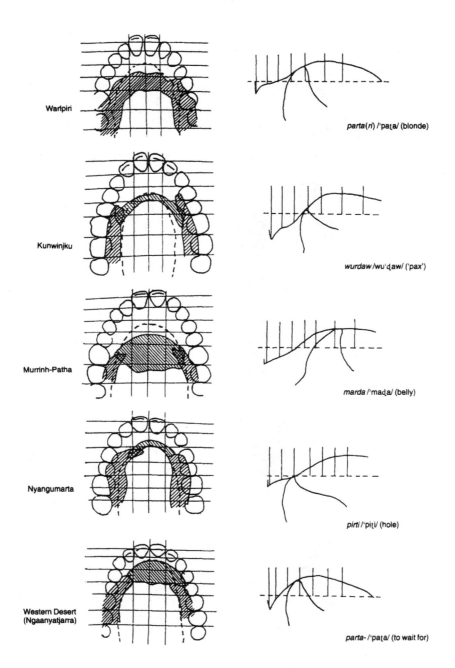

Figure 2.3 Palatograms and sagittal cross-sections of POSTALVEOLAR articulations in five double-APICAL languages

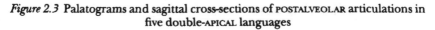

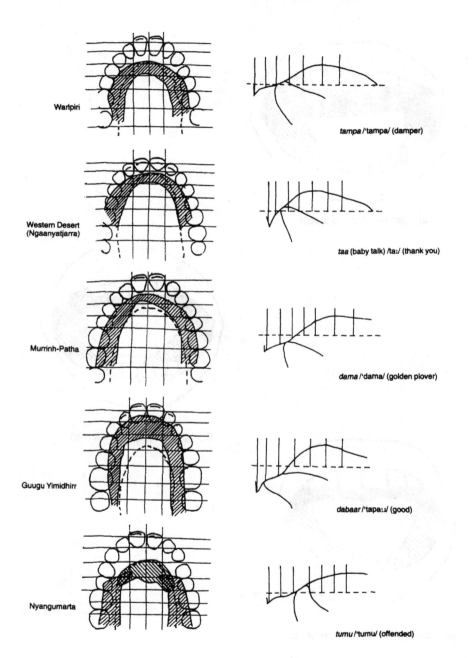

Figure 2.4 Palatograms and sagittal cross-sections of non-contrastive initial APICAL articulations in five double-APICAL languages

21

(a) *pata-* /ˈpata/ (to drop)

(b) *parta-* /paʈa/ (to wait for)

(c) *taa* (baby talk) /taː/ (thank you)

Figure 2.5 Linguagrams of intervocalic (contrastive) ALVEOLAR and POSTALVEOLAR articulations and an initial (non-contrastive) APICAL articulation by one speaker of the Western Desert Language (Ngaanyatjarra dialect)

In those languages, and in those contexts, where an APICAL contrast is made (i.e. between ALVEOLAR and POSTALVEOLAR sounds), static palatographic data from the present study show the ALVEOLAR sounds to be articulated in a quite similar fashion by almost all speakers. Figure 2.2 illustrates the way these sounds are produced in intervocalic position by speakers of five different double-APICAL languages. There is usually quite a narrow band of contact at the alveolar ridge, close behind the upper front teeth. This contact extends back along the midline of the palate to a depth of only 2–7 mm, sometimes intruding slightly into the postalveolar zone, and continues around the rim of the palate, usually broadening out to overlap the teeth at the sides. Both the narrowness of the contact and also the evidence from linguagrams indicate that the active articulator for all these speakers must be the tip of the tongue. Figure 2.5a shows a typical ALVEOLAR linguagram in which it can be seen that only the very tip and rim of the tongue have been in contact with the palate. Canonical APICAL ALVEOLARS thus appear to be truly both apical and alveolar in their phonetic realisation.

For the POSTALVEOLAR sounds static palatograms show contact in a broader band, typically in the range of 5–12 mm in depth, but occasionally up to 20 mm or more. Contact is usually centred at least as far back as the first pre-molars, and is thus in the postalveolar or prepalatal zone. Figure 2.3 illustrates these articulations. Contact patterns are much less uniform than in the case of the ALVEOLARS. Palatograms of successive repetitions of the same word in which the upper and lower surfaces of the tongue were each in turn coated with contrast medium clearly show that the active articulator is almost always the underside of the tongue blade (see Figure 2.5b). In fact, every speaker has a sublaminal articulation for every POSTALVEOLAR allophone almost all of the time. Whilst this generalisation is valid for the careful pronunciation of isolated words, it is quite possible that in spontaneous connected speech the tongue tip is more often used.

Contact bands vary in depth from 5 mm in the case of the Kunwinjku and Nyangumarta speakers to 21 mm in the case of the Murrinh-Patha speaker. Most of the sublaminal contact traces are smeared and plainly the result of movement of the articulators (a conclusion which is clearly confirmed by electropalatographic data from a subset of speakers – see Butcher forthcoming). The Nyangumarta speaker has contact only in the alveolar zone; the Kunwinjku and Ngaanyatjarra speakers have contact mainly in the postalveolar zone; the Warlpiri speaker has contact centred in the prepalatal zone; and the Murrinh-Patha speaker has contact extending at least as far back as the mid-palatal zone. It is not possible to determine precisely how much of this variation is language-specific and how much represents differences between speakers. However, what little data there is on within-language variation, in Kunwinjku (Jernudd 1974) and Warlpiri (Butcher forthcoming) indicate that differences between speakers of the same

ANDREW BUTCHER

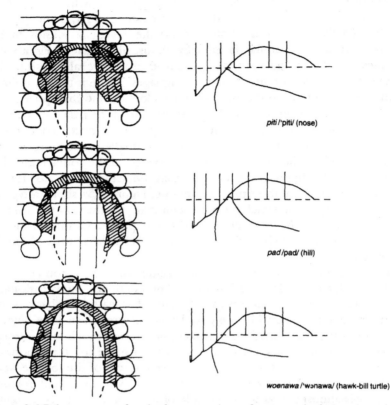

Figure 2.6 Palatograms and sagittal cross-sections of APICAL articulations in various environments in a single-APICAL language – the Western Torres Strait Language (Kalaw Kawaw Ya dialect)

piti /'piti/ (nose)

pad /pad/ (hill)

woenawa /'wɔnawa/ (hawk-bill turtle)

language may be of a similar order of magnitude to those revealed here.

None of the languages illustrated above has an opposition between ALVEOLAR and POSTALVEOLAR sounds in word-initial position. It appears that, despite the auditory impressionistic evidence from the literature, in all of these languages the neutralised APICAL category found in this position has a realisation of type 2 – a 'Mittelding' articulation somewhere between those of the two members of the (un-neutralised) opposition. As Figure 2.4 illustrates, this results in a contact band of comparable depth to that found for the POSTALVEOLARS (5–12 mm) but located somewhat further forward – often on the borderline between alveolar and postalveolar zones. There is indeed greater variation in these articulations, but they are only occasionally sublaminal – particularly in the case of the Murrinh-Patha and Nyangumarta speakers. Note the striking difference between the Nyangumarta and Guugu Yimidhirr palatograms. The Guugu Yimidhirr speaker

24

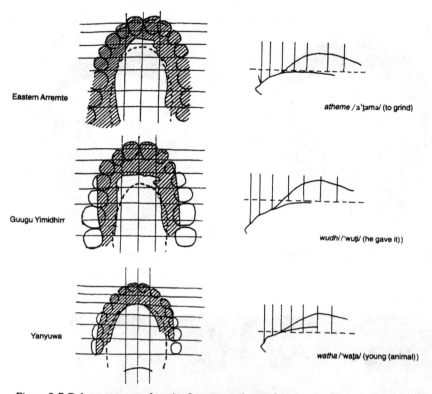

Eastern Arremte

atheme /aˈʈəma/ (to grind)

Guugu Yimidhirr

wudhi /ˈwuʈi/ (he gave it))

Yanyuwa

watha /ˈwaʈa/ (young (animal))

Figure 2.7 Palatograms and sagittal cross-sections of DENTAL articulations in three double-LAMINAL languages

appears to have a slightly laminal articulation for these sounds (it is nevertheless quite different from either the intervocalic laminal dental articulation or the initial neutralised laminal – see Figure 2.10). In general, however, initial APICALS maintain an apical articulation, as illustrated in Figure 2.5, which compares linguagrams of all three APICAL categories as articulated by a speaker of the Ngaanyatjarra dialect of the Western Desert Language.

Turning to the one single-APICAL language for which we have palatographic data, Figure 2.6 shows that the constriction for APICAL stops in the Kalaw Kawaw Ya (KKY) dialect of the Western Torres Strait language[6] is formed in the postalveolar zone and more often than not articulated with the underblade of the tongue. Variation, both free and allophonic, appears to be greater than in double-APICAL languages. Stops appear to be more likely to have sublaminal articulation than nasals, final consonants more than medial ones, and consonants in an /u/ environment more than consonants in an /i/ environment.

25

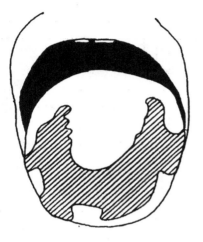

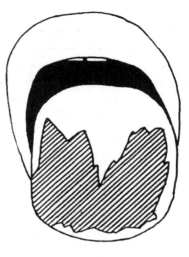

(a) *atheme* /aˈt̪əmə/ (to grind)

(c) *atyemeye* /aˈcəməjə/
     (mother's father)

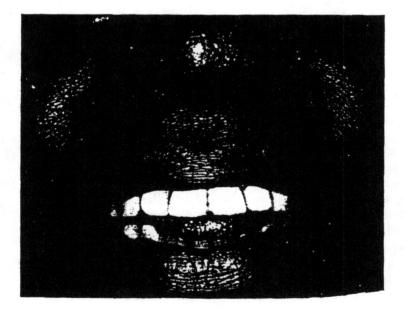

(b) *atheme* /aˈt̪əmə/ (to grind)

Figure 2.8 Linguagrams of contrastive DENTAL and ALVEOPALATAL articulations by
one speaker of Eastern Arrernte and frontal photograph of the former

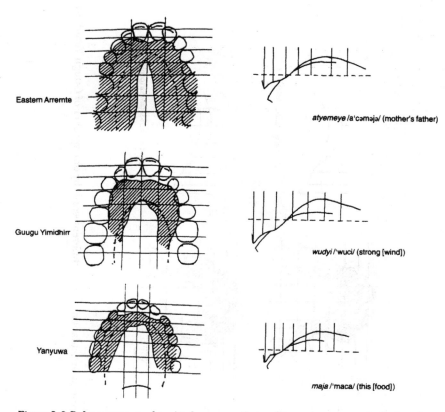

atyemeye /aˈcəməjə/ (mother's father)

wudyi /ˈwuci/ (strong [wind])

maja /ˈmaca/ (this [food])

Figure 2.9 Palatograms and sagittal cross-sections of ALVEOPALATAL articulations in three double-LAMINAL languages

Realisations of the DENTAL category in the three double-LAMINAL languages for which we have data all seem to involve lamino-dental articulations, with the tongue tip contacting the upper incisors or projecting slightly below them. Figure 2.7 shows static palatographic data from intervocalic tokens of these sounds in the languages concerned. In each case contact was registered on the very edge of the incisors and extends back between 13 and 20 mm to cover most, if not all, of the alveolar zone. The band of contact is thus about twice the depth of that found for APICAL ALVEOLARS, and is continued with a similar thickness around the sides of the palate, covering most of the teeth. Comparison of the palatograms with the sagittal cross-sections would suggest that, in order to achieve contact in just this area, without touching further back on the palate, the tongue must lie fairly flat in the mouth. The linguagram of an Arrernte DENTAL articulation illustrated in Figure 2.8a shows that contact on the tongue is made some 20 mm back along the midline – i.e. exactly on the area Australianists would

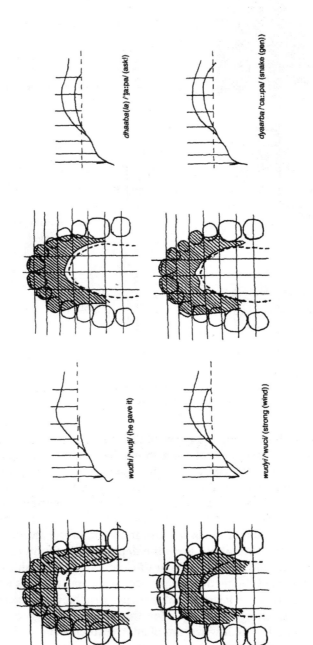

Figure 2.10 Palatograms and sagittal cross-sections of LAMINAL articulations in four different words by one speaker of Guugu Yimidhirr

dhaaba(la) /'ta:pa/ (ask)

dyaarba /'ca::pa/ (snake (gen))

wudhi /'wuʃi/ (he gave it)

wudyi /'wuci/ (strong (wind))

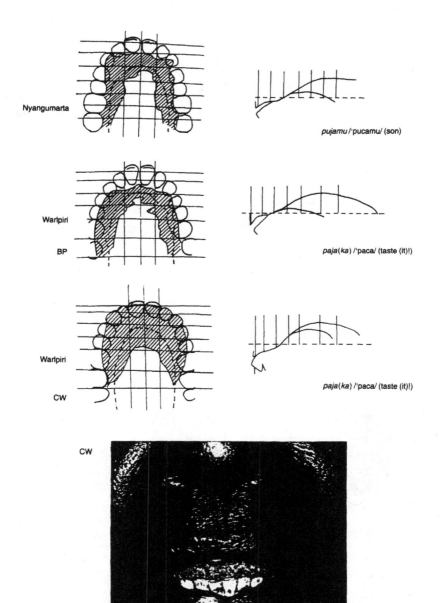

Figure 2.11 Palatograms and sagittal cross-sections of LAMINAL articulations traditionally described as '(alveo)palatal', by one speaker of Nyangumarta and two speakers of Warlpiri

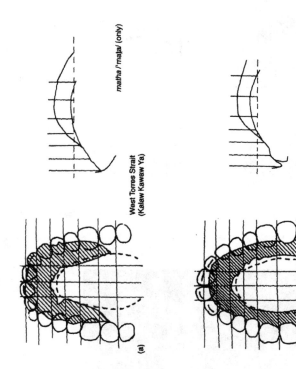

matha /'maʈa/ (only)

West Torres Strait
(Kalaw Kawaw Ya)

badjo /'baɟo/ (bush radish (sp.))

Eastern Kunwinjku

(a)

(b)

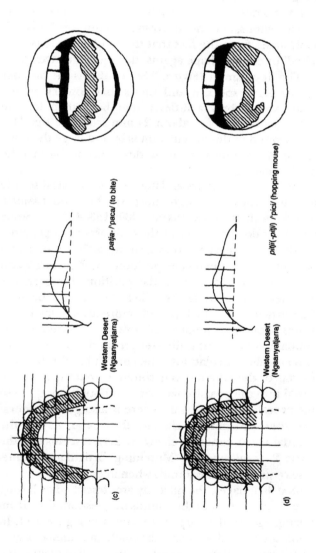

Figure 2.12 Palatograms and sagittal cross-sections of non-contrastive LAMINAL articulations: (a) and (b) realisations described as 'dental' in two different languages; (c) and (d) apparent allophonic variation between 'dental' and 'palatal' realisations within one language

Western Desert
(Ngaanyatjarra)

patja- /'paca/ (to bite)

Western Desert
(Ngaanyatjarra)

pitji(-pitji) /'pici/ (hopping mouse)

(c)

(d)

regard as the blade. Contact extends to the rim of the tongue in places, but not to the very tip. Figure 2.8b shows that the tongue tip is in fact visible, i.e. such articulations are typically interdental rather than dentialveolar, in the careful pronunciation of isolated words.

Palatograms of ALVEOPALATAL articulations in double-LAMINAL languages are illustrated in Figure 2.9. These actually tend to have *narrower* bands of contact than their DENTAL counterparts, varying from 9 to 13 mm in depth at the midline, although in the case of Arrernte and Yanyuwa contact is noticeably broader at the sides. The constrictions are confined to the alveolar and postalveolar regions, and the narrowness of the contact bands at the front presumably arises from the fact that the tongue blade is held in a somewhat 'bunched' or convex shape against the equally convex peak of the alveolar ridge. The linguagram (Figure 2.8c) confirms the broader lateral contact in the Arrernte speaker, and shows that contact on the tongue at the midline extends only a little further back than for the corresponding DENTAL articulation – i.e. about 24 mm from the tip. This indicates that the area involved in this articulation is by and large the same as that involved in DENTAL articulations, the main difference being that the tongue tip is down rather than up.

It is rather rare for a double-LAMINAL language to neutralise the distinction amongst initial stops (although most will have no LAMINAL contrast amongst final consonants – see Dixon 1980: 153–4, 169). Some speakers of Guugu Yimidhirr do appear to lack the contrast in this position, however.[7] Figure 2.10 shows palatograms from a young male speaker who produces contrasting LAMINALS in intervocalic position (cf. Figures 2.7 and 2.9), which also sound quite distinct. In initial position, however, the distinction made by other (mainly older) speakers appears to be neutralised in favour of an articulation which sounds more alveopalatal than dental. The palatograms show that the area of contact is indeed almost identical in the two initial LAMINALS but is different from that for either of the two contrastive intervocalic articulations. The contact band is broader than for either the DENTAL or the ALVEOPALATAL sound, extending from the edge of the incisors, well into the postalveolar zone, although not quite so far back as for the intervocalic ALVEOPALATAL. There is also greater lateral contact than for the ALVEOPALATAL, but less than for the DENTAL. As with the neutralisation of the initial APICAL contrast (cf. Figure 2.4), it seems that the neutralisation is of type 2, resulting in a 'Mittelding' articulation somewhere in between those required for the sounds when in contrast.

Amongst single-LAMINAL languages, the majority are described as having a predominantly 'palatal' articulation of the sounds in question. Data from speakers of two such languages in the corpus are shown in Figure 2.11. In general, the constrictions do indeed appear to be made in a similar way to those for ALVEOPALATAL articulations in double-LAMINAL languages (cf. Figure 2.9), with contact in the alveolar and postalveolar zones. However, there is, in fact, a wide range of variation in the realisation of LAMINALS in single-LAMINAL languages. The two speakers of Warlpiri whose articulations are illustrated in Figure 2.11 speak the same dialect. Although contact in both cases is centred on the same area, variation in articulatory pressure appears to lead to striking differences in the extent of contact. In the one case there is seemingly light contact just at the back of the alveolar ridge and in the other a very extensive constriction, extending from the edge of the incisors 23 mm back along the midline to cover most of the prepalatal zone. There is also extensive contact over the side teeth and, as the frontal photograph confirms, the tip of the tongue is behind the lower incisors, with the front part of the blade forced out between the front teeth.

In some single-LAMINAL languages the major allophones of the LAMINAL category are described as 'dental'. This is the case with the three speakers whose articulations are illustrated in Figure 2.12. In the case of the Western Torres Strait language, the constriction very much resembles that which we have seen for DENTAL articulations in double-LAMINAL languages (cf. Figure 2.7), although there is somewhat less contact at the sides. There is no doubt that the tongue tip is raised, and most tokens are in fact dentialveolar. LAMINAL sounds in this language never sound alveopalatal, even in the environment of an /i/-vowel. The Eastern Kunwinjku speaker, on the other hand, consistently uses a tip-down articulation. His LAMINAL sounds, although also centred on the alveolar zone, do not involve contact on the (upper) teeth, and do in fact sound more alveopalatal than dental, even in a back vowel environment. The Ngaanyatjarra speaker differs from both of these two in having a tip-down articulation which nevertheless involves dental as well as some alveolar contact. Her LAMINALS consequently sound dental when followed by a back vowel, but just a small amount of tongue raising, as in anticipation of a following /i/, causes them to sound alveopalatal. The area of contact at the front hardly changes between the two vowel environments. More extensive lateral contact on the palate and the tongue indicates that the middle of the tongue is raised in anticipation of the following high vowel, however, and this appears to be sufficient to impart an alveopalatal quality to the sound of the stop.

THE PHONETICS OF AUSTRALIAN CORONAL ARCHIPHONEMES

The question as to whether neutralisation is complete in the case of the Australian CORONALS (i.e. from the point of view of production as well as perception) is difficult to answer and perhaps of doubtful relevance. As noted earlier, claims for 'incomplete neutralisation' appear to be based exclusively on cases of final devoicing in European languages – i.e where there is a historical merger of contrasts whose original existence is still attested in the orthography. Unlike European orthographies, which are based, almost without exception, on an earlier stage of the language concerned, Australian writing systems have all been developed very recently. They thus represent the current state of the spoken language and offer no clues as to candidate pairs of words which might be investigated for partial neutralisations. More importantly, as we have seen, it is in any case highly probable that both the APICAL and the LAMINAL archiphonemes represent an original single phoneme which has failed to 'split', rather than, as in the final devoicing cases, a merging of two originally contrasting sounds. Nothing in our data contradicts the traditional auditorily based view that within-speaker variation in the realisation of these archiphonemes is purely allophonic. There is no instrumental evidence of systematic but imperceptible variation correlated with difference in meaning. It would appear that the 'standard view of neutralisation', said by Dinnsen (1985: 275) to be 'without empirical support', is not called into doubt by the Australian data, and is still only open to question in the case of historical mergers in the speech of literate speakers.

With regard to the typology of the archiphoneme representatives, on the other hand, the palatographic data do appear to contradict the auditory impressionistic descriptions found in the literature. There are, as we have seen, almost no instances of type 1 realisations, where the archiphoneme could be said to be represented by a sound corresponding to one member of the un-neutralised contrast. APICALS in initial position (and APICALS in a single-APICAL language) are indeed postalveolar, as is usually claimed, but they are only rarely (and inconsistently) sublaminal, and thus quite different from un-neutralised POSTALVEOLAR articulations. Similarly, LAMINALS in single-LAMINAL languages (and when neutralised in a double-LAMINAL language) are, with one exception, tip-down articulations, but are always alveolar rather than alveopalatal, and thus do not resemble the realisation of contrastive ALVEOPALATALS. The exception is the KKY dialect of the Western Torres Strait language, which has LAMINALS articulated with the tip up, in a very similar fashion to contrastive DENTALS in double-LAMINAL languages. But in all the mainland languages for which we have data we would classify the archiphoneme representatives as being of type 2. The vast majority of realisations are without doubt 'Mittelding' articulations, some-where between the realisations of the two phonemes when in opposition. It could be argued, especially in the case of the LAMINALS, that there is often a fair degree of allophonic variation and that therefore in some instances the archiphoneme realisation is of type 3. The palatographic evidence, however, indicates that the articulatory gesture may be relatively invariant, and the allophonic variation the perceptual consequence of co-production of the consonant with surrounding vowels. It seems likely that the contrasting sounds in post-split phonologies have exaggerated these original allophonic differences: the POSTALVEOLAR sounds have become sublaminal and the DENTALS have become tip-up articulations, whilst the

34

ALVEOLARS have become more advanced and the ALVEOPALATALS more retracted. At the same time, of course, such contrastive articulations have become more precise and less variable. Thus Dixon (1980: 184) is probably right to suggest that amongst the contrasting pairs it is the ALVEOLARS and the ALVEOPALATALS which are phonetically closer to the pre-split APICAL and LAMINAL sounds – i.e. non-retroflexed and tip-down respectively. But this has no bearing on the question of synchronic phonological *markedness* within the post-split pairs.

In fact, in view of the evidence for a type 2 realisation of the archiphoneme, it would seem there is little sense in talking in terms of *either* of the contrasting members of the opposition being marked. On the other hand, it would seem to be possible, within the framework of current theory, to characterize the CORONAL archiphonemes and the single APICAL and LAMINAL phonemes as phonologically unspecified for anteriority. The question is whether this underspecification is carried through to the phonetic level. Are such segments 'transparent' for anteriority in Keating's (1989) terms or is a target articulation specified for them which includes an intermediate degree of anteriority? The case of the Australian APICALS and LAMINALS is in fact rather different from the examples considered by Keating (1989) and by Boyce *et al.* (1991): first, the segments involved are often at word boundaries, and are therefore, at least in the case of isolated utterances, flanked by a vowel on only one side; second, the feature concerned is a tongue tip and blade feature and thus not normally involved in the specification of neighbouring vowels. Thus, on these two grounds alone, it seems quite clear that there is no sense in which the phonetic feature value of these consonants for anteriority can be the result of a trajectory from one adjoining vowel to another: adjoining vowels are not always present on both sides, and when they are, they are not specified for the feature in question anyway. The case of the Australian CORONALS is clearly one where, on the one hand, a phonological description in terms of underspecification is entirely appropriate, but where a phonetic description must recognise that these segments have characteristic articulatory targets which are both intermediate between and independent of those for the corresponding fully specified contrastive segments.

NOTES

1 These are, in fact, numbered 1a, 1b, 2, 3a, 3b and 4.
2 For an up-to-date survey of issues in Australian phonologies, the reader is referred to Evans (in press), and for a more detailed discussion of the interrelation between *place* contrasts and phonotactics to Hamilton (1989).
3 Note that labels for phonological categories appear in SMALL CAPITALS in order to distinguish them from similar or identical phonetic terms used to describe articulations.
4 This term is used in the more extended sense generally employed by American

and Australian linguists, rather than in the British sense (see Keating 1990: 37f.; Butcher forthcoming).
5   In palatograms reproduced here (such as Figure 2.4), cross-hatching descending from right to left indicates contact by the upper surface of the tongue. Sublaminal contact is indicated by cross-hatching descending from left to right.
6   It should be noted that this is not regarded as a prototypical Australian language. Certainly the phonology appears to have been influenced in some ways by that of the neighbouring (non-Australian) Eastern Torres Strait Language.
7   Haviland (1979: 37) remarks that 'there are rather few full minimal pairs between the two laminal series, and many speakers seem not to be sensitive to the difference'.

REFERENCES

Avery, P. and Rice, K. (1989) 'Segment structure and coronal underspecification', *Phonology* 6: 179–200.
Bani, E. and Klokeid, T. J. (1972) 'Kala Lagau Langus – Yagar Yagar', ms. report to AIAS, Canberra.
Boyce, S. E., Krakow, R. A. and Bell-Berti, F. (1991) 'Phonological under-specification and speech motor organization', *Phonology* 8: 219–36.
Busby, P. A. (1980) 'The distribution of phonemes in Australian aboriginal languages', *Papers in Australian Linguistics* 14: 73–139.
Butcher, A. R. (forthcoming) *The Phonetics of Australian Languages*, Oxford: Oxford University Press.
Capell, A. and Hinch, H. H. (1970) *Maung Grammar, Texts and Vocabulary*, The Hague: Mouton.
Carroll, P. J. (1976) 'Kunwinjku: a language of western Arnhem Land', MA thesis, ANU, Canberra.
Catford, J. C. (1977) *Fundamental Problems in Phonetics*, Edinburgh: Edinburgh University Press.
Chadwick, N. (1975) *A Descriptive Study of the Djingili Language*, Canberra: AIAS.
Clements, G. N. (1985) 'The geometry of phonological features', *Phonology* 2: 225–52.
Dinnsen, D. A. (1985) 'A re-examination of phonological neutralisation', *Journal of Linguistics* 21: 265–79.
Dinnsen, D. A and Charles-Luce, J. (1984) 'Phonological neutralisation, phonetic implementation and individual differences', *Journal of Phonetics* 12: 46–60.
Dixon, R. M. W. (1972) *The Dyirbal Language of North Queensland*, Cambridge: Cambridge University Press.
—— (1977) *A Grammar of Yidiny*, Cambridge: Cambridge University Press.
—— (1980) *The Languages of Australia*, Cambridge: Cambridge University Press.
—— (1983) 'Nyawaygi', in R. M. W. Dixon and B. Blake (eds), *Handbook of Australian Languages*, Vol. 3, Canberra: ANU Press, pp. 431–525.
Douglas, W. (1964) *An Introduction to the Western Desert Language* (Oceania Linguistic Monographs 4), Sydney.
Evans, N. (1985) 'Kayardild: the language of the Bentinck Islanders of north-west Queensland', Ph.D. thesis, ANU, Canberra.
—— (n.d.) 'How to write Gun-djeyhmi', ms., Australian National Parks and Wildlife Service and the Gagudju Association.
—— (in press) 'Current issues in the phonology of Australian languages', in J.

Goldsmith (ed.), *Handbook of Phonological Theory*, Oxford: Basil Blackwell.

Firth, J. R. (1957) 'Word palatograms and articulation', in his *Papers in Linguistics 1934-1951*, Oxford: Oxford University Press, pp. 148-55.

Glass, A. and Hackett, D. (1970) *Pitjantjatjara Grammar: A Tagmemic View of the Ngaanyatjara (Warburton Ranges) Dialect* (Australian Aboriginal Studies 34, Linguistic Series 13), Canberra: AIAS.

Goddard, C. (1983) 'A semantically-oriented grammar of the Yankunytjatjara dialect of the Western Desert Language', Ph.D. thesis, ANU, Canberra.

Green, I. P. (1989) 'Marrithiyel: a language of the Daly River region of Australia's Northern Territory', Ph.D. thesis, ANU, Canberra.

Hamilton, P. (1989) 'Australian phonotactics and the internal structure of the place node', MA thesis, University of Toronto.

Harvey, M. (1991) 'The glottal stop and underspecification in Arnhem Land languages', *Australian Journal of Linguistics* 11: 67-105.

Haviland, J. (1979) 'Guugu Yimidhirr', in R. M. W. Dixon and B. Blake (eds), *Handbook of Australian Languages*, Vol. 1, Canberra: ANU Press, pp. 27-180.

Hercus, L. A. (1969) *The Languages of Victoria: A Late Survey* (rev. edn 1986), Canberra: AIAS.

Hyman, L. M. (1975) *Phonology: Theory and Analysis*, New York: Holt, Rinehart & Winston.

Jagst, L. (1975) 'Ngardilpa (Warlpiri) phonology', *Papers in Australian Linguistics* 8: 21-57.

Jernudd, B. (1974) 'Articulating Gunwinjgu laminals', in B. J. Blake (ed.), *Papers in Australian Aboriginal Languages* (Linguistic Communications 14), Monash University, Melbourne, pp. 83-109.

Keating, P. A. (1989) 'Underspecification in phonetics', *Phonology* 5: 275-92.

—— (1990) 'Coronal places of articulation', *UCLA Working Papers in Phonetics* 74: 35-60.

Kennedy, R. (1981) 'Phonology of Kala Lagaw Ya in Saibai dialect', in B. Waters (ed.), *Australian Phonologies: Collected Papers* (Work Papers of SIL-AAB, A-5), pp. 103-37.

Kiparsky, P. (1982) 'From cyclic phonology to lexical phonology', in H. van der Hulst and N. Smith (eds), *The Structure of Phonological Representations*, Pt. I, Dordrecht: Foris, pp. 131-75.

Ladefoged, P. and Maddieson, I. (1986) 'Some of the sounds of the world's languages', *UCLA Working Papers in Phonetics* 64.

Ladefoged, P. and Traill, A. (1980) 'Instrumental phonetic fieldwork', *UCLA Working Papers in Phonetics* 49: 28-42.

Lass, R. (1984) *Phonology: An Introduction to Basic Concepts*, Cambridge: Cambridge University Press.

Laughren, M. (1990a) 'Another look at the stop versus flap contrast in Warlpiri', paper delivered at the Central Australian Linguistic Circle Mini-conference on Australian Languages, Institute for Aboriginal Development, Alice Springs, 23 June.

—— (1990b) 'Tracking sound changes in central Australian languages in the light of recent developments in phonological theory', paper delivered at the Australian Linguistics Society conference, Macquarie University, 28 September.

Lowe, B.M. (1975) 'Alphabet and pronunciation [Gupapuyngu]', Galiwinku, NT: Galiwinku Adult Education Centre.

Martinet, A. (1968) 'Neutralisation et syncrétisme', *La Linguistique* 1: 1-20.

McDonald, M. and Wurm, S. A. (1979) *Basic Materials in Wangkumara (Galali): Grammar, Sentences and Vocabulary*, Canberra: Pacific Linguistics, B-65.

McEntee, J. and McKenzie, P. (1992) *Adna-mat-na/English Dictionary*, Adelaide: the authors.

McGregor, W. B. (1990) *A Functional Grammar of Gooniyandi*, Amsterdam and Philadelphia: John Benjamins.

Morphy, F. (1983) 'Djapu, a Yolngu dialect', in R. M. W. Dixon and B. J. Blake (eds), *Handbook of Australian Languages* Vol. 3, Canberra: ANU Press, pp. 1–188.

O'Connor, J. D. (1973) *Phonetics*, Harmondsworth: Penguin.

O'Grady, G. N. (1963) *Nyangumata Grammar* (Oceania Linguistic Monographs 9), Sydney.

Osborne, C. R. (1974) *The Tiwi Language*, Canberra: AIAS.

Port, R. F. and O'Dell, M. L. (1985) 'Neutralization of syllable-final voicing in German', *Journal of Phonetics* 13: 455–71.

Proffit, W. R. and McGlone, R. E. (1975) 'Tongue–lip pressures during speech of Australian Aborigines', *Phonetica* 32: 200–20.

Rumsey, A. (1982) *An Intra-sentence Grammar of Ungarinjin, North-Western Australia*, Canberra: Pacific Linguistics B-86.

Slowiaczek, L. M. and Dinnsen, D. A. (1985) 'On the neutralizing status of Polish word-final devoicing', *Journal of Phonetics* 13: 325–42.

Street, C. S. and Mollinjin, G. P. (1981) 'The phonology of Murinbata', in B. Waters (ed.), *Australian Phonologies: Collected Papers* (Work Papers of SIL-ABB, A-5).

Strehlow, T. G. H. (1942) *Aranda Phonetics and Grammar* (Oceania Monographs 7), Sydney.

Taylor, P. and Taylor, J. (1971) 'A tentative statement of Kitja phonology', in B. J. Blake (ed.), *Papers on the Languages of the Australian Aborigines*, Canberra: AIAS, pp. 100–9.

Trubetzkoy, N. S. (1939) *Grundzüge der Phonologie* (Travaux du Cercle Linguistique de Prague 7), repr. 1958, Goettingen: Vandenhoeck & Ruprecht.

Wilkins, D. (1989) 'Mparntwe Arrernte (Aranda): studies in the structure and semantics of grammar', Ph.D. thesis, ANU, Canberra.

Williams, C. J. (1980) *A Grammar of Yuwaalaraay*, Canberra: Pacific Linguistics B-74.

Wordick, F. J. F. (1982) *The Yindjibarndi Language*, Canberra: Pacific Linguistics C-71.

Yallop, C. (1977) *Alyawarra: An Aboriginal Language of Central Australia*, Canberra: AIAS.

3

Some articulatory characteristics of the tap

Bruce Connell
Oxford University Phonetics Laboratory

INTRODUCTION

The most frequent means of defining or describing the type of sound referred to as a tap is with reference to its duration – the tap is similar to its cognate stop, except shorter. There has not, however, been total agreement among phoneticians as to this. Some have made reference to the nature of the gesture as well as its duration, finding it necessary to distinguish between a tap and a flap, as well as between these two on the one hand, and a stop on the other. In this paper I briefly review some of the various views contributing to the debate and then present evidence from electropalatography in an effort to arrive at a more satisfactory character-isation of this type of articulatory gesture. It is concluded that the degree of linguo-palatal contact involved is more relevant to the production of the tap than has usually been considered.

DESCRIPTIONS OF TAPS

The term 'tap' is in widespread use in the phonetic literature, normally referring to a manner of articulation involving a very brief contact between the passive and active articulators. Pike (1943: 124–5), for example, characterises the tap as the tongue making 'one rapid tap against its articulating region ... [in a] ... a single ballistic movement ... [for which] ... the stricture cannot be retained any longer than is necessary'. The term 'flap' also often appears in the literature, though very often no distinction is drawn between the two types of articulation. This is typified by J. D. O'Connor's (1973: 48) definition: 'it is the speed which characterizes flaps, which consist of a single fast closing and opening of the air passage ... one fast tap of the tongue-tip against the alveolar ridge; and uvular and bilabial taps can be made in a similar way'. Without specific mention of the 'tap' as a separate manner of articulation, we assume that for O'Connor, the two, taps and flaps, are the same.

Other authors have expressed similar opinions. Ladefoged (1982), prefers not to distinguish between taps and flaps, describing them both as 'a single contraction of the muscles so that one articulator is thrown against another. It is often just a very rapid articulation of a stop closure.' On the other hand, he had earlier (Ladefoged 1971: 50–1) drawn a distinction between the two, suggesting 'A flap is therefore distinguished from a tap by having one articulator strike against another in passing while on its way back to its rest position, as opposed to striking immediately after leaving its rest position.' He went on to suggest that the central/lateral dichotomy regarding routing of the air applies to flaps, but not taps, though we may also note here that Elugbe (1978) describes a lateral tap for Ghotuọ.

Catford (1977: 128–9) also draws a distinction, but refers to two types of flap, saying that for the one, 'the flapping articulator shoots out from its position of rest to flick lightly against the other (stationary) articulator, returning again to its original position'. This he calls a 'flick', but it appears equivalent to the tap referred to by others, and the symbol [ɾ] is used to represent it when it is apical. In the other, 'transient' type, the active articulator moves from one position to another, momentarily striking in passing the stationary articulator; this would be equivalent to the flap for those who have made the distinction. It is characterised as being retroflex, and the symbol [ɽ] is used to represent it when it is apical. Other properties are shared by the two types: both are said to be momentary (10–30 ms) as opposed to stops (minimum 50 ms), and also different from stops, in that neither can be prolonged. Catford goes on to claim that the flick type differs from a stop in that the articulatory gesture may start its motion from a point more distant from the passive articulator than it does for a stop. Finally, in a footnote citing Fujimura et al. (1972), Catford suggests that a flap (presumably either type) 'may involve a much smaller area of contact'. My own research thus far does not permit me to shed any new light on the distinction between the tap and the flap, but does allow for a contribution as to the possible ways in which a tap may be distinguished from a stop. In particular, I hope to show that Catford's final, footnoted, point regarding degree of contact, may be more crucial to an appropriate description of the nature of the tap than has previously been thought and that the role of duration may be less so. To this end, data from electropalatography are presented that show that perceptually distinct stops and taps may have more or less similar durations, but differ primarily with regard to the nature of the linguo-palatal contact.

EXPERIMENTAL METHODOLOGY

Instrumentation

As is well known, electropalatography is a dynamic technique, enabling the researcher to examine the progress of an articulation over time. Since the technique has now become relatively well known, I offer here only a brief description of the system used; further details may be gleaned from Hardcastle *et al.* (1989). The research was conducted using the EPG2 system designed at Reading University. This system uses an artificial palate (approximately 0.8 mm thick) made of acrylic, and containing sixty-two silver electrodes as contacts. A low-voltage current is introduced to the subject's body, allowing an electrical circuit to be completed whenever contact is made between the tongue and one of the electrodes. The resulting signal is sent to an electronic processing unit and is then available for storage, analysis and display using an IBM (or compatible) PC, the display taking the form of stylised charts of the artificial palate. The arrangement of electrodes on the palate and their relation to the chart is shown in Figure 3.1. As printed by the PC (see Figure 3.2 in a later section), these charts show the changes in linguo-palatal contact over time, with each individual chart representing a timeframe of 10 ms.

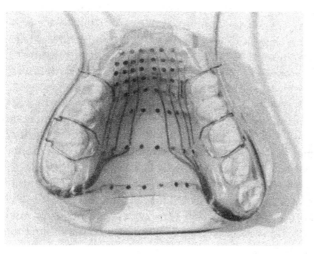

Figure 3.1 Arrangement of electrodes on the artificial palate and their representation on the EPG chart

Procedure

The work reported here is part of a much larger investigation of the consonantal phonetics of the Lower Cross languages of south-eastern Nigeria (see Connell 1991). The analysis presented is based on the speech of one person, a male native speaker of Ibibio, who was approximately twenty-eight years old at the time the recordings were done. Speech materials consisted of wordlists designed such that all stem-initial consonants of the language were found in VCV sequences using all possible combinations of the vowels [i, u, a], and in both high and low tone environments. In most cases, it was possible to use words occurring naturally in the language, and where this was not possible, nonsense VCVs were substituted; in principle, this gave a total of eighteen occurrences of each consonant.

For this paper, articulations of [d] and [ɾ] are of interest. In Ibibio, [ɾ] does not occur stem initially (i.e. in the dialect of our speaker). Many of the words used, however, did include tokens of this consonant as it occurs in ambisyllabic position – which is normally the second C in a VCVCV sequence. Nonsense sequences were added to complete the paradigm for [ɾ], but certain of these were produced unnaturally by the speaker; therefore the analysis presented here is based on tokens of [d] and [ɾ] as spoken in the vowel context [a_a], which are extracted from naturally occurring Ibibio words – a total of eight tokens of each consonant.

Measurements of these utterrances for a number of articulatory parameters were then done, using the EPG system described above. The parameters examined were duration of the onset phase (= closing gesture), of the medial phase (= complete or maximum closure) and of the offset phase (= opening gesture), and the average number of electrodes activated per frame throughout the gesture. The onset phase was delimited by the commencement of consistent movement (i.e. as represented by an increase in contact) towards the alveolar ridge and the attainment of either complete closure or maximum contact, whichever was less. The medial phase was considered achieved with activation of either a complete row of electrodes or two overlapping rows of electrodes (e.g. frame 2575 in Figure 3.2a) or maximum contact, and was considered released when this complete row was broken (e.g. frame 2579). The offset phase began at this point and was judged to be completed when movement away from the consonantal constriction had finished.

RESULTS

Temporal characteristics

Results of the durational measurements for all eight repetitions of both [ada] and [aɾa] sequences, together with their means and sample standard deviations, are presented in Tables 3.1 and 3.2. Values in these tables reveal what appear to be relatively similar temporal characteristics for Ibibio [d] and [ɾ], at least regarding the onset and medial phases. To the extent that they do differ, this actually runs contrary to expectation; i.e. while [ɾ] is normally said to be shorter in duration than the stop [d], this is true only of the onset phase; the medial phase of [ɾ] is in fact slightly longer, and both its offset phase and total duration are substantially longer. The differences in means for the onset and medial phases of the gesture are small enough to suggest that these aspects of the two gestures may be considered to be essentially the same. To check this from a statistical point

Table 3.1 Temporal measurements in milliseconds for eight tokens of [ada]

Rep.	Onset	Medial	Offset	Total
1	40	40	30	110
2	10	50	40	100
3	20	40	50	110
4	10	40	40	90
5	60	10	40	110
6	30	30	30	90
7	20	30	30	80
8	20	40	30	90
mean	26.25	35	36.25	97.5
s.d.	16.9	12	7.4	11.7

Table 3.2 Temporal measurements in milliseconds for eight tokens of [aɾa]

Rep.	Onset	Medial	Offset	Total
1	20	50	40	110
2	10	80	40	130
3	20	20	90	130
4	40	20	90	150
5	20	50	70	140
6	20	40	40	100
7	20	30	50	100
8	10	30	60	100
mean	20	40	60	120
s.d.	9.3	20	21.3	20

of view, these means were subjected to a t-test. This revealed the difference in onset phases to be not significant (p = 0.373), and the difference in medial phases to be not significant (p = 0.554). The differences in the offset phases and total duration did prove to be significant, with p = 0.01 and p = 0.16, respectively. Certainly the relatively low sample size and the relatively high standard deviations (especially for the tapped articulation), may leave the statistical analyses somewhat inconclusive; it is also pertinent to note that differences in means of only a few milliseconds also require perceptual experimentation in addition to statistical tests to establish their significance. Temporal characteristics of these consonants, then, did run counter to expectation; that is, the tapped articulation did not prove to be shorter in duration than the stop. It is therefore important to look further for features that distinguish these two consonants, and for this I present an examination of their linguo-palatal contact patterns.

Spatial characteristics

In order to compare the linguo-palatal contact patterns of the two consonants using electropalatography, a count was made of the number of electrodes activated during their medial phases. Figure 3.2 presents representative EPG charts showing contact patterns for [d] and [ɾ], excised from tokens of the Ibibio words [ádáŋà] 'boundary' and [ísárá] 'prostitute' respectively. The stop, [d], normally involves complete closure, albeit brief, and a 'rolling' or forward movement; whereas the tap, on the other hand, did not exhibit this forward movement in the eight tokens examined here, and is in general slightly retracted relative to the stop. It is possible that this movement of the tongue seen for the stop also exists for the tap, but that in the absence of sufficient contact, is not reflected on the artificial palate. However, what is more striking from the EPG charts is the difference in linguo-palatal contact between the two, with the tap involving much less contact, and never showing complete closure. The charts reveal that it is primarily contact in rows 2, 3, 4 and 5 (i.e. the alveolar-postalveolar region) that is relevant in articulating both of these consonants. The graph presented in Figure 3.3 shows the percentage of electrodes activated in this region for these two consonants, averaged across eight tokens of each. This graph, together with Figure 3.2, shows vividly the substantial difference in degree and nature of contact for the two consonants. Boundaries of the three phases of the articulatory gestures can be interpolated from Tables 3.1 and 3.2.

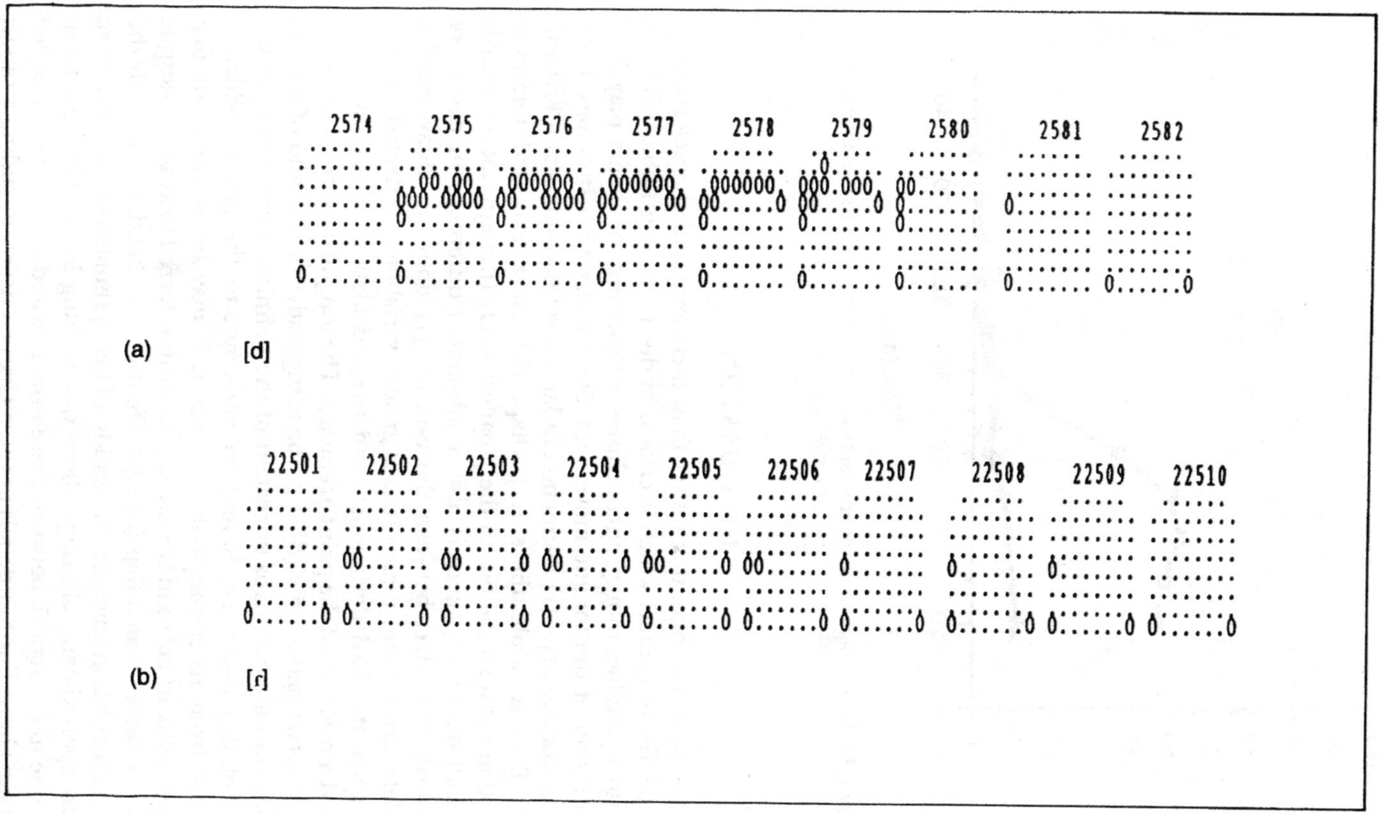

Figure 3.2 EPG charts showing representative articulations of (a) [d], from [ádájá], and (b) [ɾ], from [ísáɾá]

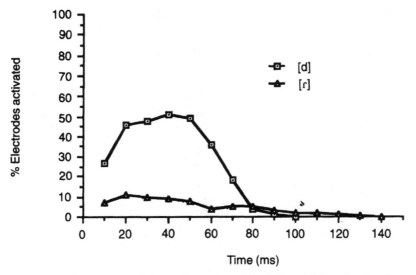

Figure 3.3 Percentage of electrodes activated for [d] and [ɾ] in the alveolar–postalveolar region

DISCUSSION

It seems apparent, then, that rather than their temporal characteristics, it is the degree of contact which is critical in distinguishing Ibibio [d] from [ɾ], with a possible, though inconclusive, supporting role being played by the direction of the tongue movement. Similar characteristics have been reported for the [d] ~ [ɾ] distinction in Japanese (Sawashima and Kiritani, 1985). That is, while there is perhaps the more expected temporal distinction between the two in the Japanese study (though not necessarily in overall duration), there is also a substantial difference in degree of linguo-palatal contact between the two, i.e. [ɾ] does not always exhibit complete closure and demonstrates greater variability (reflected here in the higher standard deviations), and the articulation of [d] involves a forward movement of the point of contact. The tongue movement reflected in the contact pattern for [d] is perhaps suggestive of the kind of motion attributed to alveolar flaps in certain of the definitions referred to at the outset of this paper, i.e. having an end-point to the gesture which is different from its starting-point. However, it may be pointed out that auditorily this articulation is more satisfactorily referred to as a stop, despite its brevity, rather than a flap (or tap). On the other hand, occasionally the tapped articulation gave the impression of being simultaneously both a tap and an approximant, although there was nothing in the EPG record to allow one to distinguish between these instances and those which sounded like a tap alone. Further details of these characteristics, including a report

46

on a listening test, are found in Connell (1991).

To the extent that other phoneticians have considered differing degrees of contact to be relevant in distinguishing stops from taps (or flaps), it has been assumed, at least implicitly, that the lesser contact associated with taps is a result of undershoot, due to their shorter duration. The temporal characteristics of the alveolar tap in Ibibio presented above show clearly that if this is to be considered an instance of undershoot, it is not a result of shorter duration. Similarly, Catford's suggestion, that for the tap, the tip of the tongue may start its motion from a point more distant from the alveolar ridge, also seems unlikely, as one would then expect somewhat greater contact for the tap, given the greater velocity required for the tongue tip to reach its target in approximately the same time as it does for the stop. Rather, I would suggest that this indeed may be considered an instance of 'undershoot', but as a result of less muscular activity involved in the gesture. This hypothesis would also account for the slower release associated with the tap. The tapped articulation should therefore be seen as a weaker gesture than that involved in the production of the stop, a notion that fits in with diachronic developments seen in Ibibio and other related languages (Connell 1989). This view also fits in with that proposed by Elugbe (1978) who, although describing them primarily in terms of their duration, relates the taps of Ghotuọ to other lenis sounds, of which lesser force of articulation is said to be characteristic.

By way of conclusion, I would like to return to O'Connor's suggestion that taps ('flaps') may also be found at other places of articulation, specifically labial and uvular. The possibility of labial and uvular taps is rarely mentioned in the general phonetic literature. However, both of these sounds exist phonetically in Ibibio (cf. Cook 1969 for Efik). While obviously neither of these is accessible to investigation by electropalatography, spectrographic work does suggest that both of them, as well, involve less contact, together with having a shorter duration, than their cognate stops. What may well prove to be consistent in the production of taps, then, is the lesser degree of contact involved in their production, and that the shorter duration usually observed by phoneticians is just one of a variety of means speakers may employ to achieve this type of contact.

ACKNOWLEDGEMENTS

I would like to thank Dr Benjamin Etuk of the University of Cross River, Nigeria, for his willing participation in the electropalatography investigation which formed the basis of this study.

REFERENCES

Catford, J. C. (1977) *Fundamental Problems in Phonetics*, Edinburgh: University of Edinburgh Press.

Connell, B. A. (1989) 'Instrumental evidence for phonetically gradual sound change', *Work in Progress*, No. 22, Dept of Linguistics, University of Edinburgh, 58–68.

—— (1991) 'Phonetic aspects of the Lower Cross languages and their implications for sound change', Ph.D., University of Edinburgh.

Cook, T. L. (1969) *The Pronunciation of Efik for Speakers of English*, Bloomington, IN: African Studies Program and Intensive Language Training Center, Indiana University.

Elugbe, B. O. (1978) 'On the wider application of the term "tap"', *Journal of Phonetics* 6: 133–40.

Fujimura, O., Fujii, L. and Kagaya, R. (1972) 'Computation processing of palatographic patterns', *Conference Record: 1972 Conference on Speech Communication and Processing (USAF)*. (Also published as Fujimura *et al.* (1973) *Journal of Phonetics* 1: 47–54.)

Hardcastle, W., Jones, W., Knight, C., Trudgeon, A. and Calder, G. (1989) 'New developments in electropalatography: a state-of-the-art report', *Clinical Linguistics and Phonetics* 3, 1: 1–38.

Ladefoged, P. (1971) *Preliminaries to Linguistic Phonetics*, Chicago: University of Chicago Press.

—— (1982) *A Course in Phonetics*, 2nd edn, New York: Harcourt Brace Jovanovich.

O'Connor, J. D. (1973) *Phonetics*, Harmondsworth: Penguin.

Pike, K. L. (1943) *Phonetics*, Ann Arbor: University of Michigan Press.

Sawashima, M. and Kiritani, S. (1985) 'Electro-palatographic patterns of Japanese /d/ and /r/ in intervocalic position', *Annual Bulletin of the Research Institute of Logopedics and Phoniatrics* 19: 1–6.

4

Assimilations of alveolar stops and nasals in connected speech

W. J. Hardcastle
Queen Margaret College, Edinburgh

INTRODUCTION

A frequently observed phenomenon in connected speech is the so-called 'instability' of alveolar consonants, the tendency for alveolars to elide or to be assimilated to the place of articulation of a following consonant. The phenomenon occurs for both alveolar plosives within words and at word boundaries. O'Connor cites as examples the *tin* in *Tin Pan Alley* produced as /tɪm/, *nutcracker* as /nʌkkrækə/ and so on (O'Connor 1973: 250). Gimson (1989) points to the instability of both nasals and plosives at word boundaries but suggests the bilabial assimilations (as in /ðæp pɜːsn̩/ for *that person*) are far less common than the velar assimilations (such as /ʃɔːk kʌt/ for *short cut* (Gimson 1989: 310). The instability of alveolars has been noted also in languages other than English (e.g. German: see Kohler and Hardcastle 1974; Kohler 1976): there is some suggestion it may be a language universal.

One question that arises is whether the assimilated form of the velar is in fact identical to a target velar or bilabial or whether there are some subtle differences often undetected auditorily. For example, is the assimilated medial stop /k/ in /'kʰækkɪn/ *catkin* identical to /k/ produced in the word *kin*. Early studies with electropalatography (Hardcastle and Roach 1977; 1979) showed how subjects produced /VtkV/ and /Vt#kV/ items with a variety of different spatial patterns. One subject produced a clearly defined alveolar closure followed by a short period of simultaneous alveolar/velar closure and then a velar release. Another subject showed some indication of an alveolar gesture but, compared to a target alveolar stop in a word like *eat* it was extremely short (approx. 20 ms) and showed incomplete or partial closure on the alveolar ridge. Still another subject produced a velar stop pattern in *eat cake* which was considerably further forward than the same subject's production of an /iki/ target sequence, and without any contact in the alveolar zone. The suggestion was that some aspects of an underlying

49

alveolar gesture may even occur in the so-called assimilated forms.

Further evidence of 'partial' or 'residual' alveolar gestures was noted in an EPG study of /l/-vocalisations in English by Hardcastle and Barry (1989) and by Wright and Kerswill (1989), who compared EPG contact patterns in pairs such as *road collapsed* and *rogue collapsed*. In the Wright and Kerswill study a professional phonetician was instructed to produce sentences containing the minimal pairs with varying degrees of assimilation. One interesting finding from this study was the suggestion that there 'may after all not be any such thing as "complete assimilation" or the possible merger of one phoneme with another in certain speech styles.' (Wright and Kerswill 1989: 56). A residual trace of an alveolar may be present in the pattern for a velar even in the assimilated form. In items such as *dig/did, leg/lead* and *beg/bed* there was a more retracted velar contact in the assimilated alveolar member than the velar member. As Wright and Kerswill say:

> This is, in fact, residual evidence of a tongue body configuration appropriate for an alveolar; as the tongue tip moves up towards the alveolar ridge, the blade and pre-dorsum become concave, which reduces the amount of lateral contact in the pre-velar area. At the same time, this tongue shape will cause the velar contact itself to be more retracted.
>
> (Wright and Kerswill 1989: 54)

A similar phenomenon was found to occur in a cross-language study of EPG patterns in /kl/ clusters (Gibbon *et al.* 1993). In these clusters all speakers manifested a more retracted place of articulation for the /k/ than when it was produced as a singleton. It seemed likely that the presence of the /l/ exerted a retracting influence on the tongue body gesture for the /k/.

A number of questions arise from these studies. How consistent are speakers in producing these types of assimilations involving alveolars? What factors constrain their production? Are alveolar plosives as susceptible to assimilation as alveolar nasals in natural connected speech? A study was carried out on the EPG patterns of alveolar–velar sequences in connected speech produced by seven native speakers of English.

METHODOLOGY

Subjects

Seven native speakers of English were chosen as subjects. A variety of different accents were represented. One speaker (BH) used a variety of General Australian English; one had a Northern English accent (HD). The others had Southern British accents. All subjects were accustomed to EPG methodology and had worn EPG palates for many hours at a time during recording in the Speech Research Laboratory for various projects.

Experimental set-up

A multi-channel data acquisition system was used which records EPG data simultaneously with acoustic airflow and laryngograph data (see Trudgeon *et al.* 1988; Hardcastle *et al.* 1989). EPG data is sampled at 200 Hz and the acoustic signal at 20,000 Hz. Oral and nasal air flow are recorded separately by a pneumotachograph (Oral Enterprises Inc., used with a hand-held Rothenberg and mask filtered to 70 Hz). Airflow is calibrated in 1/min against a rotameter. The Fourcin laryngograph records details of vocal fold vibration and is used in this experiment as an accurate indicator of voicing. Various display and editing programs allow the analysis of the multi-channel data. The acoustic waveform, for example, can be displayed along with airflow and EPG channels (see Figure 4.1). Points on the signals can be labelled using an annotation facility if required.

For the EPG records, various data reduction facilities are available (see Hardcastle *et al.* 1991). These include

1   contact 'totals' in different regions of the palate (see Figure 4.2);
2   'centre of gravity' of contact patterns plotted against the number of contacts (Figure 4.2);
3   various numerical indices including an 'asymmetry' index.

Speech material

A sentence, *Fred can go, Susan can't go and Linda is uncertain,* was chosen for analysis from a set of fifteen similar sentences in the EUR-ACCOR database (Hardcastle and Marchal, 1990). The sentence contains a number of potential assimilations, elisions and various other reduction phenomena when spoken naturally. This study will focus on the following potential assimilations:

/d/ → /g/ in *Fred can*
/n/ → /ŋ/ in *can go*
/n/ → /ŋ/ in *Susan can't*
/nt/ → /ŋ/ in *can't go*

There are five repetitions of the sentence from each speaker in the database using the combination of sensors indicated above.

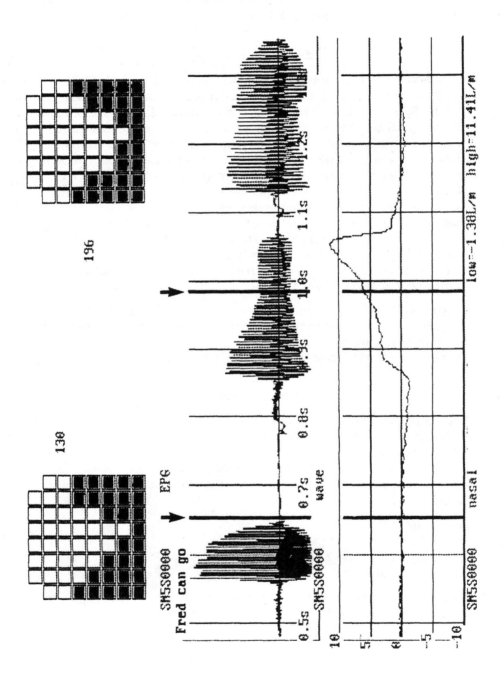

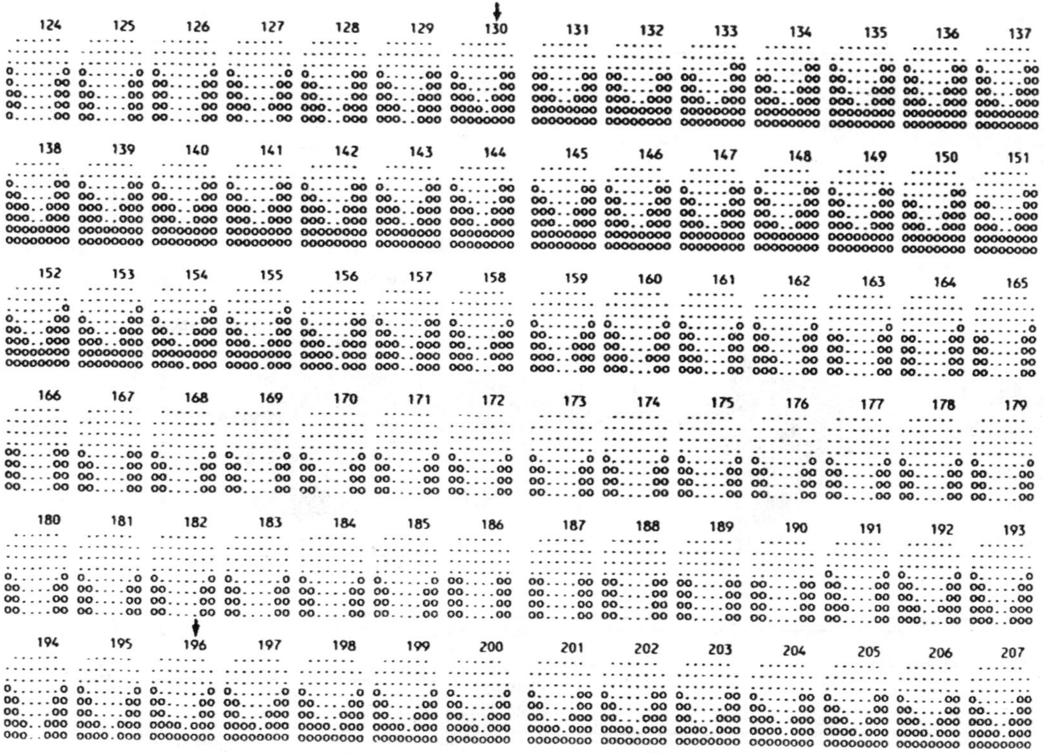

Figure 4.1 EDIT screen display of the utterance *Fred can go* showing waveform, nasal airflow (calibrated in 1/m) and EPG frames at positions of the left and right cursors (shown by arrows). A full EPG printout (sampling rate 200 Hz) of the complete utterance is provided below the screen display with the frames corresponding to the cursors indicated by the arrows (subject SN)

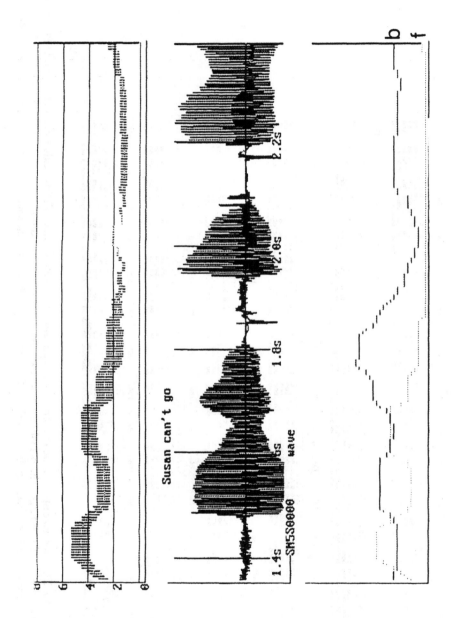

Susan can't go

wave

SM5S0000

1.4s   1.6s   1.8s   2.0s   2.2s

b
f

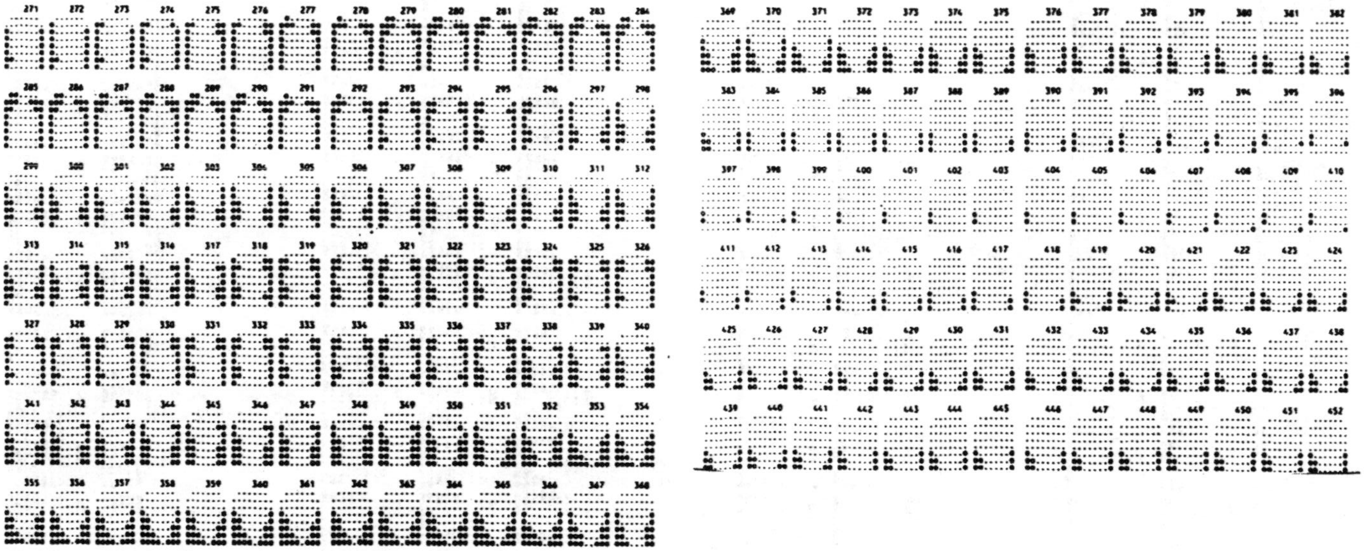

Figure 4.2 EDIT screen display of the utterance *Susan can't go* showing the 'centre of gravity' (upper window) and the contact totals for the front and back of the palate (lower window). The vertical axis on the COG trace indicates anteriority – the higher the COG, the closer to the front of the palate. The length of the vertical striations on the graph indicate total number of contacts. Full EPG printout of the utterance is shown below the EDIT screen display.

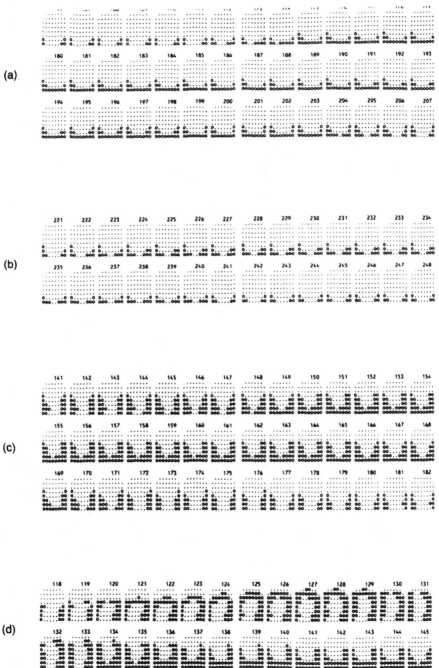

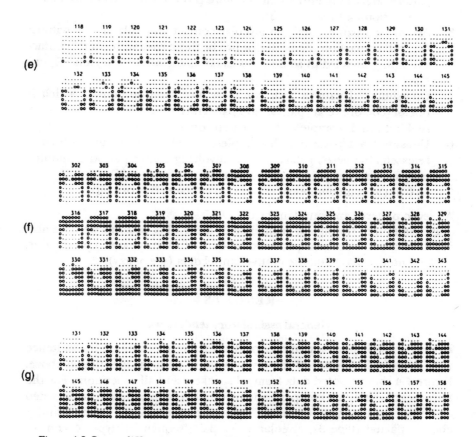

(e)

(f)

(g)

Figure 4.3 Seven different patterns of EPG contact for the alveolar–velar test
sequences (for explanation see below)

Speech variables measured

Using the EDIT speech analysis program displaying EPG patterns along
with airflow, laryngographic and acoustic waveform traces, each sentence
was analysed and EPG patterns noted for each of the four test locations in
the sentence. Initially the data were analysed on the basis of the following
main types of EPG patterns:

1   Assimilated pattern with no indication of alveolar contact and retracted
    velar stop pattern (i.e. full posterior contact in row 8, i.e. the most
    posterior row of the palate and some posterior lateral contact) (see
    Figure 4.3a).

2   Assimilated pattern with no alveolar contact and incomplete velar stop

pattern suggesting either contact more posterior than row 8 or a laxer articulation (see Figure 4.3b).

3   Assimilated pattern with no alveolar contact and palatal stop pattern (i.e. full contact on the posterior two or three rows with lateral contact extending forward in some cases as far as the alveolar region (Figure 4.3c).
4   Unassimilated pattern with complete alveolar stop contact which is released before velar/palatal stop pattern (Figure 4.3d).
5   As 4 but with incomplete alveolar stop contact (Figure 4.3e).
6   Unassimilated pattern with complete alveolar stop contact which is released after velar/palatal contact involving a short period of simultaneous or 'overlapping' double stop closure (Figure 4.3f).
7   As 6 but with incomplete alveolar stop contact (Figure 4.3g).

All seven patterns are found in the data.

In addition to noting the incidence of these EPG patterns we have also provided a more detailed phonetic account of each speaker's production of the sentence, based on the multi-channel data (see below).

RESULTS

General assimilatory tendencies

Firstly the EPG patterns that occurred at each test location in the sentence were described in terms of the seven types of patterns mentioned above. Figure 4.4 shows pooled data from all speakers and all repetitions. For the purposes of this figure complete and incomplete stop patterns are regarded as similar thus leaving four main types of patterns: velar (types 1 and 2 above); palatal (type 3); alveolar + vel/pal ('sequential' types 4 and 5); alveolar – vel/pal ('overlapping' types 6 and 7).

A number of general trends are revealed by the figure. For example, the assimilated forms (velar and palatal) are generally far more common than the unassimilated (alv + vel/pal and alv – vel/pal). The only exception to this is the location /dk/ (*Fred can*) where occurrences of the two broad types, i.e. assimilated and unassimilated, are about equal. One possible conclusion from this is that the plosives are less susceptible to assimilation than the nasals.

Within the nasal targets the /ng/ sequence (*can go*) shows the greatest difference (94.2 assimilated versus 2 unassimilated). Least susceptible amongst the nasals is the /ntg/ sequence (*can't go*), with 71.3 (assimilated) versus 28.5 (unassimilated).

Vowel effects on the place of articulation of the target nasal and oral velar stops can be seen by comparing velar with palatal categories for four different target sequences. By far the greatest difference can be seen for the /ntg/ sequence, where the predominant place is velar, reflecting the more

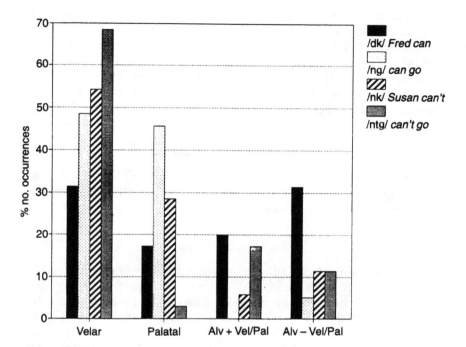

Figure 4.4 Pooled data from all seven subjects showing the incidence of each EPG contact type in the four test sequences

posterior placement of the tongue in the /a/ environment compared to a more anterior and closer position for the other sequences.

The results also showed considerable intra- and inter-subject variability. Intra-subject variability was assessed by examining differences in the five repetitions for a given item on the one hand and different assimilatory tendencies for the different sequences on the other. Most subjects showed fairly consistent patterns over the five repetitions for all items (except for the /dk/ sequence). In /dk/ five of the seven subjects had a mixture of unassimilated and assimilated versions. The next most variable sequence was the /ntg/ in *can't go*, where two out of the seven subjects produced a mixture of unassimilated and assimilated forms in the course of the five repetitions.

The different sequences encouraged different assimilatory tendencies. As mentioned above, the /dk/ sequences involved the most unassimilated forms. In fact, all subjects except one produced at least one assimilated instance out of the five repetitions. This one subject did in fact produce unassimilated forms for all his repetitions of /ntg/ as well.

Subjects were generally quite inconsistent in their general assimilatory strategies. That is, it was not generally true that if an unassimilated form was used in one sequence then it was more likely than not to occur in another sequence. Subjects were not consistent either in the type of assimilation pattern they used: for example, of the six subjects who had examples of the unassimilated form (i.e. presence of alveolar contact) for /dk/, three used the double vel/alv type, two used the sequential form and one used a mixture of both types. In the next section these inter- and intra-subject differences are examined in more detail.

Phonetic details of variability

Detailed observation of the oral and nasal airflow, EPG, acoustic and laryngographic data revealed some additional subtle differences in the subjects' productions of the test items.

/dk/ sequence in Fred can

In their production of the /dk/ sequence subjects varied considerably. Three subjects (SN, HD and PD) showed clear preference for the assimilated form while two subjects (BH and RK) showed preference for the unassimilated. Of those who assimilated, one subject (SN) showed quite anterior placement for the [k] with lateral contact as far forward as the alveolar region (row 3). Of the subjects who did not assimilate, BH preferred an overlapping pattern (type 6 above and Figure 4.3f). This subject also tended to use the unassimilated form in /ntg/ which, amongst the seven subjects, was extremely unusual. Subject RK generally spoke more slowly and deliberately and was found to favour the sequential form with the /d/ released before the /g/. The other two subjects (FG and KM) used both assimilated and non-assimilated forms during their five repetitions. Of all the non-assimilated types the overlap was by far the most common.

/ng/ sequence in can go

For the /ng/ sequence the clear preference amongst all subjects was for the assimilated forms (Figures 4.3 a, b, c). However, observation of the multi-channel data showed a number of interesting differences amongst the subjects in the way they released the velar stop in *can*. Three main patterns were found:

1   [kʰɜ̃ŋɡ̊ ...] with the nasal trace rising during the [ə] vowel and reaching a peak towards the end of the [ŋ] (as defined by velar contact on the EPG printout) (FG, SN, HD) (see Figure 4.5)
2   [kʰŋɡ̊ ...] no evidence of the [ə] vowel; EPG contact in the velar region begins simultaneously with the onset of voicing and maximum nasal flow after the [kʰ] release (KM, RK, PD) (Figure 4.6)

60

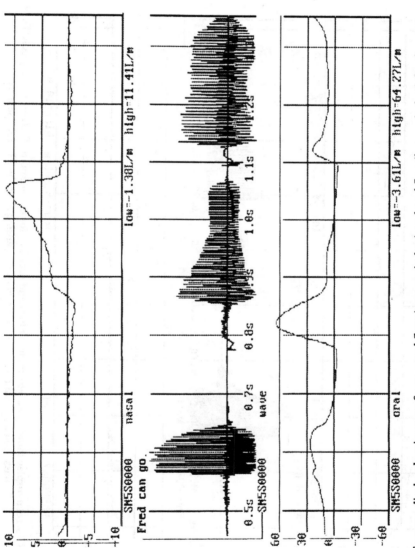

Figure 4.5 **EDIT** screen display showing waveform, nasal flow (upper window) and oral flow (lower window) for the utterance *Fred can go* (subject SN)

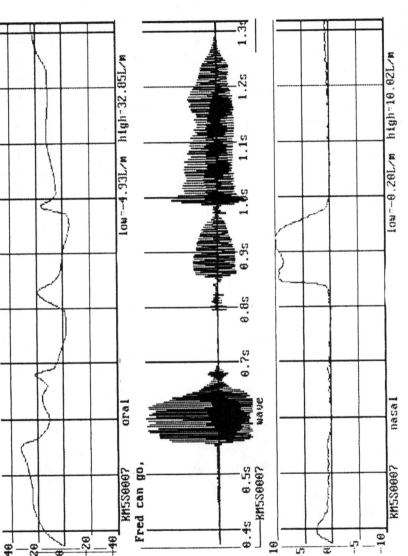

Figure 4.6 EDIT screen display showing waveform, nasal flow and oral flow for the utterance *Fred can go* (subject KM). Note maximum nasal flow beginning at onset of the periodic pulsing after the /k/ release in *can*

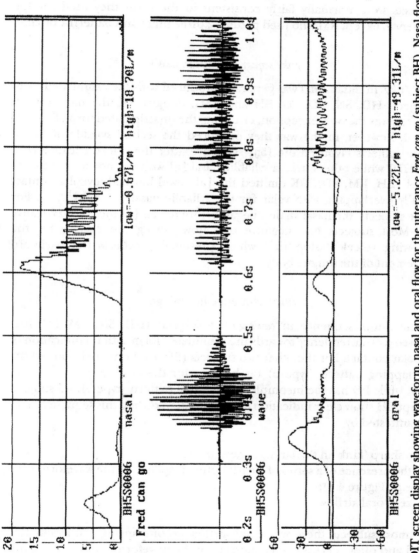

Figure 4.7 EDIT screen display showing waveform, nasal and oral flow for the utterance *Fred can go* (subject BH). Nasal flow begins simultaneously with /k/ release

3   [kʰŋɡ̊ ...]] Nasal airflow rises simultaneously with oral flow at the release of the [k]. There is no suggestion of [ə], EPG remains at the velar place throughout (BH) (Figure 4.7)

Subjects were normally fairly consistent in the form they used for the sequence, except KM who used pattern 2 three times and pattern 1 twice.

/nk/ sequence in Susan can't

The /nk/ in *Susan can't* was generally produced with the assimilated form (subjects HD, SN, PD, FG, BH and KM). Subject RK, the most careful speaker, was the only exception, favouring the unassimilated form. Subjects varied, however, in the way they produced the second syllable of *Susan.* Some subjects favoured the [ɜŋ] sequence after the voiced fricative (FG, SN, HD) while others used a syllablic nasal [ŋ] with no indication of a [ə] vowel (BH, KM, PD). RK omitted the [ə] vowel but had alveolar contact usually overlapping with velar for the syllablic nasal [... zɳ͡ŋkʰ ...]. For some subjects, the nasal airflow began before the end of the voiced fricative [z]. Most subjects had negative oral flow during the closure for the following voiceless stop [kʰ] which presumably reflects the backward movement of the tongue body.

/ntg/ sequence in can't go

In the /ntg/ sequence in *can't go* five subjects (HD, SN, KM, FG, RK) showed a clear tendency towards the assimilated form with no indication of alveolar contact. For the other two subjects (PD, BH) one, BH, showed the overlapping pattern (type 6) (as he does for the /dk/ sequence in *Fred can*), while PD has the incomplete sequential pattern (type 5). All subjects except BH show clear indication of glottalisation during this sequence. This is manifested by

1   a sharp 'kink' in the laryngograph trace;
2   the presence of a series of clearly defined 'spikes' on the waveform (see, e.g., Figure 4.8);
3   zero oral airflow.

For most subjects there was nasal airflow accompanying the assimilated nasal and often a creaky voice pattern on the waveform – thus [ŋ]. Figure 4.8 illustrates a typical nasal flow pattern for the sequence. Nasal flow begins during the preceding vowel [ɑ̃ː] then drops at the end of the vowel (probably here there is momentary glottal closure) then a rise on the nasal trace accompanied by nasal creak [ŋ]. The EPG usually indicates velar contact during the small nasal rise after the vowel. All subjects except BH

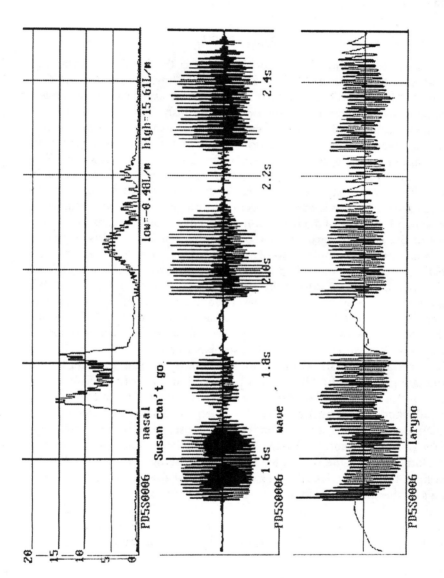

Figure 4.8 EDIT screen display showing nasal flow, waveform and laryngograph traces for the utterance *Susan can't go* (subject PD)

showed considerable nasal flow on the preceding vowel. For some subjects, e.g. SN, the nasal flow began at the onset of the vowel. Occasionally for this subject there was no evidence of [ŋ], the nasal flow being zero at the onset of the velar contact, hence [... ɑ̃ɑ̃ʔkʰ ...].

DISCUSSION

One of the interesting findings of this study is the degree of variability found in subjects' production of the test alveolar–velar sequences. The multi-repetition paradigm enabled us to examine aspects of intra-subject variability which have not been noted previously. These variations are generally rather subtle ([əŋ] instead of [ŋ] for example), although the assimilated–unassimilated alternation found in the /dk/ sequence may have salient acoustic consequences. In this sequence one speaker, RK, tended to release the /d/ before onset of the /k/ gesture. As a result a small release burst was clearly visible on the acoustic waveform trace. As mentioned above, this speaker was generally judged to be a slow deliberate speaker and this type of manifestation of the /dk/ sequence illustrated this. Most of the speakers favoured the overlapping pattern for this sequence with some using incomplete alveolar contact. One consistent feature of all speakers except one was the glottalisation present towards the end of the [ɑː] vowel in *can't* and during the assimilated nasal [ŋ]. The glottalisation was clearly visible on the acoustic waveform and the laryngograph trace as a series of sharply defined spikes and was heard as creaky voice. There was indirect evidence also of a glottal stop after the vowel. The only exception was speaker BH, who has a General Australian accent.

The results summarised in Figure 4.4 showed a clear preference for assimilating the nasals. All speakers produced at least one unassimilated form for the /dk/ sequence but the majority assimilated the nasals in both the /nk/ and /ng/ sequences. The /ntg/ sequence was complicated by the presence of an underlying [t] manifested by most speakers as a glottal stop, although one speaker (PD) had a partial alveolar contact accompanying the glottalisation. One reason for the lack of assimilation in /dk/ may in fact have been the relatively stressed position of the word *Fred*. Both the nasals in the /nk/ and /ng/ sequences occurred in relatively unstressed positions. There is ample evidence that stress will affect assimilatory tendencies although this may not be the only reason for the nasal preference regarding alveolar assimilation noted in this study.

CONCLUSIONS

The results of this limited study reveal some interesting and subtle differences in the way subjects produce alveolar–velar sequences in natural connected speech. A variety of different tongue configurations could be interpreted from the EPG contact patterns and there were some indications of subtle reduction strategies used, many of which were difficult to detect auditorily.

The next phase of this work involves a study of the spectral features associated with the /dk/ sequence and those involving the nasals. One aim of this study will be to assess the acoustic salience of the different contact types, including the partial or incomplete types.

ACKNOWLEDGEMENTS

Thanks are due to Sara Wood for assisting with the data analysis. The work was supported by the EEC (ESPRIT-BRA project ACCOR 3279) and by the NATO Scientific Affairs Division.

REFERENCES

Gibbon, F., Hardcastle, W. and Nicolaidis, K. (1993) 'Temporal and spatial aspects of lingual coarticulation in /kl/ sequences: a cross-linguistic investigation', *Language and Speech* 36: 261–77.

Gimson, A. C. (1989) *An Introduction to the Pronunciation of English*, 4th edn, London: Edward Arnold.

Hardcastle, W. J. and Barry, W. (1989) 'Articulatory and perceptual factors in /l/ vocalisations in English', *Journal of the International Phonetic Association* 15: 3–17.

Hardcastle, W. J. and Roach, P. J. (1977) 'An instrumental investigation of coarticulation in stop consonant sequences', *Speech Research Laboratory Work in Progress*, University of Reading, 27–44.

—— (1979) 'An instrumental investigation of coarticulation in stop consonant sequences', in P. Hollien and H. Hollien (eds), *Current Issues in the Phonetic Sciences*, Amsterdam: John Benjamins, pp. 531–40.

Hardcastle, W. J. and Marchal, A. (1990) 'EUR-ACCOR: a multi-lingual articulatory and acoustic database', in *ICSLP 90: Proceedings of the International Conference on Spoken Language Processing*, Kobe, Japan, 18–22 November, pp. 1293–6.

Hardcastle W. J., Gibbon, F. and Nicolaidis, K. (1991) 'EPG data reduction techniques and their implications for studies of lingual coarticulation', *Journal of Phonetics* 19: 251–66.

Hardcastle, W. J., Jones, W., Knight, C., Trudgeon, A. and Calder, G. (1989) 'New developments in electropalatography: a state-of-the-art report', *Clinical Linguistics and Phonetics* 3: 1–38.

Kohler, K. (1976) 'The instability of word-final alveolar plosives in German: an electropalatographic investigation', *Phonetica* 33: 1–30.

Kohler, K. and Hardcastle, W. J. (1974) 'The instability of final alveolars in English and German', *Proceedings of the Stockholm Speech Communication Seminar*, Uppsala: Almqvist & Wiksell, pp. 95–8.

O'Connor, J. D. (1973) *Phonetics*, Harmondsworth: Penguin.

Trudgeon, A. M., Knight, C., Hardcastle, W., Calder, G. and Gibbon, F. (1988) 'A multi-channel physiological data acquisition system based on an IBM PC and its application to speech therapy', *Proceedings of the Speech 1988, 7th FASE Symposium*, Edinburgh, pp. 1093–1100.

5

Field procedures in forensic speaker recognition

Hermann J. Künzel
Bundeskriminalamt Wiesbaden
Phonetics Institute, University of Trier

In most criminal cases involving speaker recognition (SR) tasks an expert is supposed to define the possibilities and limitations of this forensic discipline. Quite often the expert will face questions by solicitors or attorneys such as: 'Isn't there a simple solution to this problem: after all, everyone seems capable of safely recognising people by their voices, even on the phone! And why can't you use one of those computerised devices they have in detective films which can verify voices in just a couple of seconds?' Quite obviously most individuals do not realise how difficult and complex the problem of forensic SR really is. So before elaborating on different methodological approaches it is possibly useful to clarify the fundamental differences between forensic and other SR applications.[1]

PECULIARITIES AND CHARACTERISTICS OF FORENSIC SR

Today non-forensic SR, which for the sake of simplicity will be called 'commercial', is not much of a problem either scientifically or techno-logically. Quite a number of solid-state devices were or still are on the market for control of access to high-security installations such as certain military facilities, nuclear power stations, research laboratories and computer centres. More recently telephone banking and particularly tele-monitoring of individuals on probation or parole have become lucrative applications, since huge expenditures may be saved if conventional control and surveillance procedures become obsolete. One such system has been claimed capable of verifying up to 20,000 voices of clients via normal telephone channels. Table 5.1 contains only a few of the more well-known systems. The systems by Texas Instruments and Bell were developed during the 1970s and are of historical interest since they showed the way to later developments as far as acoustic parameters and statistical evaluation procedures are concerned.

Table 5.1

System name	Manufacturer	(Main) Application
Voice Bolt II	University of Trier, Germany	access control
LSRS	Electronic Warfare Associates	access control, intelligence operations
Biometrischer Sprachverifikator	Telenorma AG	bank-by-phone, office automation, pass 'word' to enter computer systems
Vericon 1	Vericon Systems	electronic monitoring for legal use, community supervision
BESSY	Messerschmitt-Bölkow-Blohm (MBB)	access control
?	Texas Instruments	access control
?	Bell Laboratories	access control
ASV 1000	Kreutler	access control, bank-by-phone

Commercial systems typically operate according to the following principle (Rosenberg and Sambur 1975; Doddington *et al.* 1976; Rosenberg 1976): after identifying him/herself with a personal number code a person entitled to enter a controlled zone, a so-called customer, is required to pronounce a test phrase chosen from a more or less limited set of possible phrases or combinations of words. After some sort of acoustical analysis, mostly based on LTAS (normalised Long-Term Averaged Spectrum) parameters, a feature vector is derived from the test signal and matched to vectors gained from earlier access claims of the person in question. A similarity index is then calculated. Recognition is affirmed if a certain threshold is exceeded; if not, the procedure may be repeated or the person will be regarded as a so-called impostor or intruder. Manufacturers claim that the performance of such systems comes close to a 1 per cent error rate for both false rejections and false identifications, or, in terms of the signal detection theory, false alarms and missed hits.

The preceding remarks will help to reinforce the principal differences between commercial and forensic SR.

1 In commercial applications an individual desires to be recognised and is thus a co-operative speaker. In a forensic situation, however, one reason for oral communication is to conceal a person's identity. Therefore a so-called non-cooperative speaker has no interest in natural, loud and clear speaking. As a matter of fact, in about 15 per cent of cases worked on at the German Federal Criminal Police Office (BKA) Speaker Identification Department there is evidence of deliberate voice disguise. Figure 5.1 shows an example. In order to make things easier for observers not familiar with

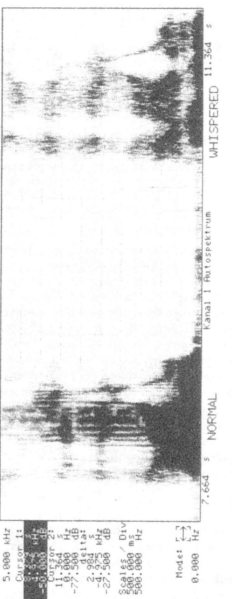

Figure 5.1a Spectra of modes of disguise (i)

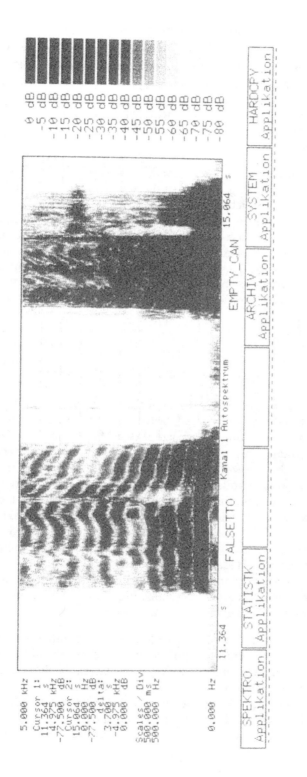

Figure 5.1b Spectra of modes of disguises (ii)

telephone-transmitted speech high quality equipment was used to record the phrase *How are you*, spoken by a male adult speaker with a mean F_0 of 120 Hz. The phrase is uttered with normal voice, whispered, with falsetto voice and with an empty mug held close to the lips. It emerges that the spectra are severely affected by the three modes of disguise which are among the most frequently used in real life.

2 In a forensic case there is no preselected or prearranged text to be produced which could be used for powerful word-to-word comparisons. In many cases there is not a single aspect of the speech sample – including its overall duration – on which the expert can exert an influence. Either suspected persons bluntly refuse to produce any speech sample at all, which of course they may do in most western legal systems, or it would be risky to openly address a person, for example in a live kidnapping case. In as many as 20 per cent of the cases questionable and/or known samples contain less than 20 seconds of what may be called 'net' speech, that is what remains of the original signal after removing speech portions of dialogue partners and badly distorted portions. Another 'advantage' of commercial SR is the severe limitation on the number of possible test words/phrases, mostly down to a dozen or two; and, facilitating the task even further, these words would contain speech sounds such as open vowels or nasal consonants which are known to contain highly speaker-specific information.

3 In more than 95 per cent of the cases worked on at the BKA telephone-transmitted material has to be dealt with; this implies a multitude of potential degradations of the speech signal (see Moye 1979 for a detailed discussion). To name only a few of them: the signal is bandpassed at 300–3400 Hertz; thus, low-frequency components containing the first formant of some sounds and, more importantly, fundamental frequency are no longer audible; also, some highly speaker-specific features such as a peculiar or defective pronunciation of high-frequency obstruents like [s] or [ʃ] become unobservable. The dynamic range of a recording is reduced to 30 dB at best; there are distortions of different degree and mathematical complexity, and last but not least, additive noise.

In most commercial systems the acoustical environment is carefully controlled; some use sound-treated rooms, high-fidelity recording equipment and high-quality lines to the computer system.

4 Perhaps the most salient theoretical difference between the two kinds of SR is the fact that for commercial applications the number of customers is relatively small, and, even more importantly, finite. Such a closed-set recognition task consisting of only one paired comparison is therefore called *verification*. In a typical forensic situation, however, it cannot be taken for granted or even assumed that the unknown speaker is among the two or perhaps twenty suspects' voices handed in for comparison. In fact, the

set of potential speakers is open: it may for example consist of all adult male native speakers of a language. This type of voice comparison is called *identification.*

As was mentioned earlier, commercial systems use thresholds on which the decisions are based. Threshold values are fixed on a cost/benefit rationale: a balance is struck between the damage which might be caused by a potential impostor and the delay and loss of working time caused by falsely rejecting a customer. Signal detection theory has made it clear that one type of error cannot be reduced without increasing the other (Green and Swets 1966; see also Hecker 1971 and Bolt *et al.* 1979). However, the better the overall performance of the system, the lower the point of intersection of the probability density functions of both errors (the so-called equal error rate, EER).

In a forensic SR environment the concept of one (general) similarity threshold value is not open to the question for two reasons. First, an error here will not result in a financial loss; rather, it will lead to the acquittal of a guilty person or to the condemnation of an innocent one. Whereas the former error is deplorable the latter is a catastrophe to any judicial system and must be avoided by all possible means, in terms of the signal detection theory: at the cost of increasing the probability of a missed hit to near certainty. Also, there is no way of having the result of a verification checked and possibly revoked by an independent controlling mechanism. If, for example, a customer is rejected by the system because his/her similarity index is affected by a sore throat or acute abuse of alcohol he/she can still be visually identified by security staff. Second, in the forensic domain we are still very far from constructing a single feature vector powerful enough to be used for standard identification tasks. This is without even considering a procedure or an algorithm for the statistical evaluation of the various speaker-specific parameters, some of which may be exploited in one case but not in another. Strictly speaking: we do not even know the totality of parameters that might be of speaker-specific value under certain circumstances.

To the background of this rather disenchanting perspective let us look at how forensic SR is carried out today. Basically there are three different approaches:

1   auditory SR, consisting of two completely different variants:
    (a) performed by non-experts, i.e. mostly victims or witnesses of an offence;
    (b) performed by a phonetician or speech scientist on scientific principles;
2   visual inspection of broad-band spectrograms;
3   semi-automatic, computer-aided SR systems.

HERMAN J. KÜNZEL

SPEAKER RECOGNITION BY NON-EXPERTS

Auditory SR has long been used and accepted in forensics as part of the testimony of a victim or witness. Prior to the inventions of the telephone and sound-recording equipment it could be the key evidence on behalf of which a suspected individual could be identified or excluded from an offence committed in the dark or when a victim had been blindfolded. Ever since the telephone has become popular as an instrument in committing crimes SR has become relevant in nearly all the kinds of offences listed in the code of law (Künzel 1987).

The introduction of voice line-ups analogous to the well-known visual line-ups was the first formalisation of the recognition task, providing an objective, controllable, even statistically analysable response from a subject. Today, a well-developed form of this procedure is performed at the request of German courts by scientists who are expected to explain in detail the underlying principles, the test format and in particular the error matrices gained from a subject's responses. In most of these cases a so-called direct identification or naming test will be used because it complies better with the conditions of a forensic application than discrimination or rating tests. For reasons of space this issue cannot be discussed any further (for details see Künzel 1988, 1990, 1994). Fundamentally, the plot consists of identical text material gained from the unknown and at least four known dummy speakers which are selected according to the results of a thorough auditory analysis of the unknown voice. Thus it is possible to obtain speakers who are closely similar to the unknown speaker as far as age, dialect, voice quality, hesitation phenomena, speech rate, etc. are concerned. The reason for this procedure is to render the subjects' task of picking out the unknown voice more difficult. Furthermore, the stimuli obtained from the dummy speakers are treated acoustically in order to reconstruct the telephone channel characteristics of the unknown recording. Finally, the set of randomised stimuli is rerecorded on a test tape. The worst kind of mistake possible with this type of auditory SR – which is beyond the control of the expert – would be to have the misfortune to use the voice of a 'suspect' who, although not the criminal, is 'identified' consistently by one or more of the subjects as the 'voice in question'. The reason would be that the 'voice in question', preselected as a result of prior investigations, exhibits a *purely accidental* similarity to one or more features of the anonymous person's voice, e.g. very high or low voice pitch, unusual dialect, etc. In such a case, which of course illustrates well the open set condition in forensic SR, it would be virtually impossible to establish an actual non-identity. To avoid this danger the legal authorities must bestow great care on the preselection of speakers to be nominated for a line-up procedure. Other factors that have to be accounted for by the expert conducting the test are:

74

differences in the classification strategies of subjects;

originality of the unknown voice;

acoustical quality and duration of the taped material;

hearing ability of subjects;

elapsed time between first contact with the unknown voice and the recognition task;

subjects' familiarity with the unknown voice;

general circumstances of the criminal situation.

Another advanced type of formalised auditory identification test or rather test series with paired comparisons and 'blind' panels of listeners has been described by Hollien (1990: 204f.). It consists essentially of paired comparisons (ABX). However, listeners do not have to respond to 'experimental' samples only, i.e. samples containing the known and unknown voices: they will also have to respond to special 'reference' material in order to assess their general ability to discriminate between voices auditorily. If performance does not meet a pre-fixed threshold for this task a subject's responses to the 'experimental' material are discarded from the test.

Although much research is still needed in order to understand the principles underlying auditory SR – particularly under forensic circumstances – it is probably justified to state that these types of SR experiments, if properly performed, may yield reliable and objective results. In principle SR by non-expert individuals (witnesses, victims) may thus be regarded as a valuable tool in cases without live recordings of a crime.

SPEAKER RECOGNITION BY EXPERT

Whenever both questioned and known speech materials have been recorded in a case, voice comparison by an expert is the method of choice. Unlike a layperson, the expert will be able to make his/her observations and analyses explicit and state the underlying scientific categories and principles. Thus it is possible for this expert, for other experts appointed to the case, and last but not least for the judge and the jury, to check and reconstruct every link in the expert's chain of arguments. An expert is able to analyse all the features of a speech signal which may carry speaker-specific information, that is linguistic, phonetic and acoustic. Doddington (1985: 1653) uses the terms 'high-level' and 'low-level information', the former comprising 'dialect, style of speech, subject matter or context' etc.; the latter 'spectral amplitude, voice pitch frequency, formant frequencies and band-widths' and other acoustic features.

Whether or not an expert equipped with such tools will achieve a better performance than naive listeners in all types of experiments and under all possible circumstances of a real-world case is another question. The experiment by Shirt (1983) which is often referred to by opponents of the auditory approach does not offer conclusive evidence for the claim that there is no essential difference between recognition rates of phoneticians (without further specifications of their native languages, duration of auditory phonetic training, specialisation, etc.) and naive listeners. Although the original speech material had been provided by a police authority, the experimental set-up contained several characteristics completely untypical of forensic situations, particularly the duration of the test items of only four seconds.[2] Unless a speaker exhibits several rare features such as speech defects, hyponasality, certain types of hoarseness, etc., and unless all these features happen to occur in such a brief sample, any responsible phonetician, particularly one with forensic experience, would altogether refuse to give a formal opinion on identity, because the minimal base for applying the analytical tools is lacking. Such a situation would remind one of a surgeon who is urged to remove an appendix in a couple of minutes, a timespan normally needed just to prepare the operational site! Speech samples are not like holograms, which contain the entire picture in every little fragment. Nolan (1983: 3) was certainly right in criticising a case in which an opinion was obviously given on such a small amount of material.

Other evidence does indeed suggest that the performance of trained observers is superior to that of naive listeners. In experiments with familiar and unfamiliar speakers Köster (1987) obtained twice recognition rates of 100 per cent from a group of five phoneticians, as against 94 and 89 per cent from thirty naive listeners. Informal evidence of this author from numerous court sessions shows that judges, attorneys or solicitors may have great difficulty in perceiving such obvious speaker-specific features as creaky voice, sigmatism and even instances of tonic or clonic stuttering. In fact, some individuals would have a demonstration tape enhancing such features replayed several times before making up their minds. Since all relevant features are also demonstrated visually through computer-based spectrograms or other forms of documentation, an expert is sometimes doubtful whether the original auditory phenomenon or perhaps the pertinent red or green spot on a multi-coloured computer printout were essential to the individuals' decisions.

Auditory expert opinions by linguists and phoneticians have long been accepted by courts in many countries. After several decades of progress in acoustics, phonetics, signal processing and pattern-recognition techniques scientists have begun to disagree as to whether or not this method is still up to date. A comprehensive discussion can be found in Baldwin and French (1990). Quite naturally, this issue has first arisen in countries like the United Kingdom where criminal jurisdiction is based on the adversarial principle which implies that there are two opposing experts in court, each appointed to one party. Many other European jurisdictions, however, require only one 'independent' expert appointed to a case by the court. In

Germany, for instance, a second opinion will be called for only if the court or one party officially declares that they consider the first expert to be biased or incompetent.

A practitioner who has repeatedly been asked by courts to express his/her personal opinion on auditory, auditory-acoustic and computer-aided reports made by other experts, will come to view the problem as follows: whenever a speaker's dialect or sociolect, individual hesitation phenomena and the like have to be analysed, the trained ear of a phonetician or dialectologist is certainly the most adequate tool, superior to any technical procedure if such is applicable at all. This is particularly important in the initial stages of a case when there are only one or more unknown voices which are to be described in as much detail as possible. An excellent example involving the English language is the analysis of the verbal behaviour of the hoaxer in the Yorkshire Ripper case by two English phoneticians (Ellis and Windsor Lewis 1994). There is no doubt either that certain auditory findings may be called objective at least in the sense that narrow phonetic transcriptions made by different individuals represent acoustical events which have been interpreted according to the same well-established categories as provided by general phonetic theory (see Kohler 1977: 150f.): In this author's experience there have been many examples of identical transcriptions performed by two or more phoneticians working independently on the same case, even when the speech samples were degraded (Künzel 1987). On the other hand it is clear that the phonetic and linguistic parameters just mentioned are only a small subset of speaker-specific parameters, although they might be critically important in some cases (Nolan 1983, 1990; Köster 1987). Therefore a view such as that expressed by Baldwin cannot be supported that an exclusively 'auditory approach' to forensic speaker identification is 'fully adequate for the task' (Baldwin and French 1990: 9). Stating the question in polemical terms: nobody would acknowledge the diagnostic strategy of a medical doctor who uses only a stethoscope for the diagnosis of a potentially life-threatening heart disease, ignoring modern achievements like ECG, computer tomography, echo cardiography and blood tests.

The procedures discussed in the next section may be considered as a way out of this dead-end approach since they include the valuable classical phonetic tools. But first, a brief comment should be made on another technique which was widely used in the United States, parts of Europe, Israel and other countries in the late 1960s and 1970s as an allegedly objective method for forensic voice comparison, namely the visual interpretation of ordinary broad-band spectrograms. Whereas in the past ten years this procedure has been losing ground in the States and was abandoned completely in Germany it is still in use in countries like Israel, Italy, Spain and Colombia; the FBI are using it for investigative purposes only (Koenig 1986 and Koenig, pers. comm.). A vast number of studies have exposed the substantial shortcomings of spectrography as a forensic tool which are quite obvious even in the latest so-called voice comparison standards issued by a 'Voice Identification and Acoustic Analysis Sub-committee' of the 'International Association for Identification' (VIAAS 1992). Here is just one characteristic example: to be an examiner, 'a minimum of high school diploma is required, but a college degree is desirable' (p. 373). In other words: a thorough scientific education is by no means regarded as a prerequisite. Furthermore, a total of twelve (*sic!*) publications are the 'required reading' for the would-be examiner, and another thirteen publications are 'suggested reading' (pp. 374–6). The most comprehensive report on voice identification by spectrographic analysis was published by a 'Committee on Evaluation of Sound Spectro-grams' which had been installed by the US Department of Justice (Bolt *et al.* 1979; see also Hollien 1974; Doddington 1985; and the controversy between Koenig and collaborators (Koenig 1986; Koenig *et al.* 1987 and Shipp *et al.* 1987).

It is difficult to state exactly which patterns or salient features of spectrograms have been used by its proponents; at least there is no exhaustive checklist to be used in casework by all the examiners. The most widely used features are formant bandwidths, centre frequencies, hubs, the spectral composition of fricatives and plosives for individual segments and transitions, and something which is termed 'peculiar spectrographic "gestalt"' without being defined or even described (Tosi 1979: 116). An individual observer's internal threshold for a decision on identity/non-identity relates to the visual similarity of these parameters, tacitly assuming that variability within subjects is smaller than between them. Many critics have shown this to be wrong. Consider, for example, spectrograms of same and different speakers in Hollien (1990: 216–19) or the spectrograms of three kinds of voice disguise as compared to the undisguised phrase from Figure 5.1 of this report. It is probably not unfair to say that the visual interpretation of spectrograms does nothing but shift the problems and pitfalls of the comparison task from the auditory to the visual domain: that is, from the ears to the eyes of a subjective human observer. The allegation of some authors (Kersta 1962; Tosi *et al.* 1972; Smrkovski 1977; Tosi 1979) that their technique attains up to 99 per cent correct results has never been supported by any independent scientist, i.e. one who did not belong to the inner circle of spectrograph analysts. Rather, error rates of more than 20 per cent occurred; auditory analysis of speech samples has been shown to be more effective than spectrogram interpretation (Stevens *et al.* 1968). Another fact to be noted is that people with commercial interests in the propagation of the technique introduced the term 'voiceprint' analysis (Kersta 1962), thus consciously alluding to the high identificational power of fingerprints which, contrary to spectrographic patterns, have indeed proved to be unique and unalterable. In summary: the visual interpretation of spectrograms cannot be considered as an adequate technique for forensic SR. Therefore it can only be deplored that some countries not only tolerate but have even recently introduced this technique.

THE STATE-OF-THE-ART APPROACH

It it clear from the preceding discussion that an adequate procedure for forensic SR must reduce the human factor as far as possible and augment the number of and speaker-specific power of objective parameters. It is also clear, however, that even the most advanced SR systems require the interaction of an expert in many ways, starting off with the selection of appropriate speech material, the setting of threshold values for filtering and other preprocessing measures, the selection or suppression of certain acoustic or linguistic parameters, the interpretation of numerical results, and, last but not least, the formulation of the final statement on identity or non-identity. The word 'expert' used here is of special significance, as can be seen from this example: in the early 1970s a sophisticated semi-automatic speaker identification system (SASIS) for forensic use was developed in the United States. It showed the way to several later projects as far as interactive segmentation of the speech signal, nature of acoustic parameters and statistical evaluation procedures are concerned (Paul *et al.* 1974). Yet, ultimately the system failed, one of the main reasons being the orderer's condition that it would be operated by police officers after some training: imagine how well or how poorly such personnel may have performed in a highly sensitive task like the phonetic segmentation of fluent, telephone-transmitted, degraded speech from an oscillogram and/ or spectrogram! If a phonetician had been consulted on this issue he/she would certainly have predicted this outcome.

One of the first phonetic-acoustic approaches to forensic SR was developed at the German Federal Criminal Police Office. It was introduced in 1980 and has since been employed in about two thousand cases. The procedure which has been fully documented elsewhere (Künzel 1987) consists of the following main steps: After preprocessing the data, a phonetician isolates speaker-specific features from the speech signal in each of the three areas of the verbal behaviour, i.e. voice, speech and what is called 'manner of speaking', the latter containing among other features articulation rate, rhythm, hesitation phenomena and intonation contours. These features, part of which are initially perceived by the trained ear of the expert, may be put on an objective physical basis through the use of modern instrumental techniques such as LTAS, traditional spectrograms with a choice of one out of seven filter bandwidths according to the nature of the acoustic features of interest (focus on temporal or frequency aspects), three-dimensional and waterfall spectra, oscillograms, cepstra and others. In a voice comparison report, the final opinion is determined by a synopsis of the results from each parameter, that is about eight to twelve on average, according to the nature of the speech material. In order to optimise the procedure, a computer-based 32-colour signal manipulation and analysis system was developed which is constantly being extended. Thanks to a very specialised hardware and firmware configuration almost all analyses can be performed in real time except for some of the more complicated filtering and jitter extraction algorithms. Figure 5.1 was created by the system, which is also being used in medical (ENT) research and certain intelligence operations. Currently a module is being tested which provides an algorithm for the quantitative assessment of certain types of hoarseness. The key feature of this module is that it works on fluent speech, which is of course the *conditio sine qua non* for its use in forensics: an unknown speaker would hardly be as co-operative as an ENT patient who is required to sustain an open vowel for several seconds on a monotone for an automatic measurement of hoarseness.

A number of speaker-specific features such as fundamental frequency (F_0), F_0 variation and acoustical characteristics of all sorts of pathological events, mainly mispronunciations and speech errors, can be evaluated using statistical background data gained from large numbers of subjects

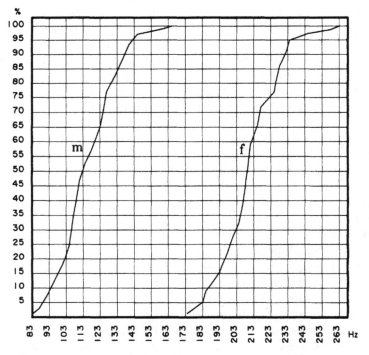

Figure 5.2 Cumulative distribution of F_0 in Hertz for female (f) and male (m) subjects

and/or real cases. Figure 5.2 shows the cumulative distribution of average F_0 for adult males and females (taken from Künzel 1989: 121). In court, such material may be of considerable value to the expert, for example when he/she states that both an anonymous caller and a defendant have about the same low F_0 of say 90 Hz, because he/she can in fact tell the jury that there is only a 3 per cent chance of two males having such a low or lower voice. Of course, this figure represents this parameter only and must not be considered as a measure for identity/non-identity in general. The aim of our team of scientists is to increase the number of parameters which can be expressed on such quantitative scales and thus broaden the objective basis for SR. In view of the tremendous amount of experimental work needed, co-operation from other researchers is welcome.

Another SR system for forensic use which relies even more on acoustic parameters has been developed at the Los Angeles County Sheriff's Office (Nakasone and Melvin 1988, 1989). After preprocessing, the speech signal is analysed for up to fourteen text-independent parameters from both the time and the spectrum domains. The so-called intensity deviation spectrum (IDS), a sort of normalised spectrum clear of transmission distortions, is particularly important. After the feature vector is established a sophisticated statistical analysis and weighting procedure is applied, resulting in what is called a proximity index. On a preliminary background database of fifty male speakers the system is claimed to reach a 98 per cent correct identification rate.

Another fairly advanced SR system called SAUSI was developed by Hollien and associates (Hollien 1990; Hollien et al. 1990). It is all the more interesting since, similar to the German concept, it basically uses 'natural speech' parameters such as F_0, number and duration of silent intervals, speech rate, vowel durations and the like (Hollien et al. 1990; see also the early approach by Holmgren 1967). Such features may be considered to parallel the mechanism of auditory SR to a certain degree and are also much easier to explain to a court than abstract parameters such as the third cepstral coefficient. SAUSI currently works on a background database of about 400 speakers to which questioned and known samples may be matched.

THE FUTURE OF FORENSIC SR

In future SR systems for forensic use the number of objective parameters will constantly increase. There will also be refined algorithms for statistical evaluation of individual parameter results according to their speaker-specific significance under the circumstances of a given case. However, the limits for progress are staked out by the forensic real-world conditions. To quote George Doddington, an outstanding expert on automatic SR: 'it is not reasonable to expect that *any* level of performance is possible, limited only by improvements in feature extraction and algorithm development. Rather ... the performance ... is dependent on the amount of control that can be exerted on the operational conditions' (1985: 1663; my emphasis). As was shown earlier, however, there is almost no such control in a normal forensic environment. Thus it is inevitable that even in the long run an automatic procedure will not be available, and for this reason experts will still be needed to perform the tasks mentioned earlier. Thus the question of who is to be regarded as competent is all the more important. The SASIS example has shown that it is not sufficient to have law enforcement personnel trained. There should be general agreement also as to the unfitness for such work of signal processing or sound engineers, or acousticians, who are able to assess only some acoustic but probably not phonetic and linguistic features. Incidentally, a British colleague was recently appointed to a case where his opponent regarded himself as qualified because he was the owner of a recording studio. Eventually, it became obvious that this individual was totally unaware of (if the matter were not so serious one should rather say 'uncompromised by') the difference between letters and sounds! Qualification as an expert in forensic SR requires a thorough education in modern speech science so that all speaker-specific features of the speech signal, in Doddington's terms both 'high' and 'low-level information', may be covered. Consequently, phoneticians and speech scientists are probably best qualified to meet this requirement. But even they should always be aware of the abyss between carefully controlled experiments in the laboratory and the intricacies of the forensic world.

NOTES

1 Extended version of an invited paper for the twelfth Congress of Phonetic Sciences, Aix-en-Provence, France, August 1991.
2 It should be acknowledged, however, that Shirt herself chose the short stimuli 'not necessarily to simulate the forensic situation ... but to avoid having too long a tape and thereby discouraging listeners from the start' (1983: 1). It goes without saying that in a forensic situation such an argument would be completely irrelevant, but unfortunately some opponents of auditory expert opinions tend to ignore this fact. The BKA Speaker Identification Department demands a minimum of 30 seconds of 'net' speech material from each unknown and known speaker for voice comparisons, but even this may be too small a base in a number of cases.

REFERENCES

Baldwin, J. and French, P. (1990) *Forensic Phonetics*, London and New York: Pinter.
Bolt, R. H., Cooper, F. S., Green, D. M. (1979) *On the Theory and Practice of Voice Identification*, Washington DC: National Academy of Sciences.

Doddington, G. R. (1985) 'Speaker recognition – identifying people by their voices', *IEEE-ASSP-Transactions* 73, 1651–64.

Doddington, G. R., Helms, R. E. and Hydrick, B. M. (1976) 'Speaker verification III', *Texas Instruments Inc. Report for RDAC,* Rome and New York.

Ellis, S. and Windsor Lewis, J. (1994) 'The Yorkshire Ripper – a case history', *Forensic Linguistics* 1, 2.

Green, D. M. and Swets, J. A. (1966) *Signal Detection Theory and Psychophysics,* New York and London: Wiley & Sons.

Hecker, M. H. L. (1971) *Speaker Recognition: An Interpretive Survey of the Literature* (Monograph 16), American Speech and Hearing Association.

Hollien, H. (1974) 'Peculiar case of "voiceprints"', *Journal of the Acoustical Society of America* 56: 210–13.

Hollien, H. (1990) *The Acoustics of Crime,* New York and London: Plenum Press.

Hollien, H., Gelfer, M. P. and Huntley, R. (1990) 'The natural speech vector concept in speaker identification', in J. P. Köster (ed.), *Neue Tendenzen in der Angewandten Phonetik III,* Hamburg: Buske pp. 71–87.

Hollien, H., Hicks, J. W. and Oliver, L. H. (1990) 'A semi-automatic system for speaker identification', in J. P. Köster (ed.), *Neue Tendenzen in der Angewandten Phonetik III,* Hamburg: Buske, pp. 89–106.

Holmgren, G. (1967) 'Physical and psychological correlates of speaker recognition', *Journal of Speech and Hearing Research* 10: 57–66.

Kersta, L. G. (1962) 'Voiceprint identification', *Nature* 196: 1253–7.

Koenig, B. E. (1986) 'Spectrographic voice identification: a forensic survey', *Journal of the Acoustical Society of America* 79: 2088–90.

Koenig, B. E., Ritenour, D. S., Kohus, B. A., Kelly, A. S. (1987) Reply to 'Some fundamental considerations regarding voice identifications', *Journal of the Acoustical Society of America* 82: 688–9.

Kohler, K. J. (1977) *Einführung in die Phonetik des Deutschen,* Berlin: Schmidt.

Köster, J. P. (1987) 'Leistung von Experten und Naiven in der auditiven Sprechererkennung', in R. Weiss (ed.), *Festschrift für H. Wängler,* Hamburg: Buske, pp. 171–80.

Künzel, H. J. (1987) *Sprechererkennung: Grundzüge forensischer Sprachverarbeitung,* Heidelberg: Kriminalistik-Verlag.

—— (1988) 'Zum Problem der Sprecheridentifizierung durch Opfer und Zeugen', *Goltdammer's Archiv für Strafrecht* 5: 215–24.

—— (1989) 'How well does average fundamental frequency correlate with speaker height and weight?', *Phonetica* 46: 117–25.

—— (1990) *Phonetische Untersuchungen zur Sprecher-Erkennung durch linguistisch naive Personen,* Stuttgart: Steiner.

—— (1994) 'On the problem of speaker identification by victims and witnesses', *Forensic Linguistics* 1, 1: 45–57.

Moye, L. S. (1979) *Study of the Effects on Speech Analysis of the Types of Degradation Occurring in Telephony,* Harlow, Essex: Standard Telecommunication Laboratories.

Nakasone, H. and Melvin, C. (1988) 'Computer assisted voice identification system', *Proceedings IEEE-ASSP,* 587–90.

—— (1989) *Project CAVIS Final Report,* Whittier, CA: Los Angeles County Sheriff's Department.

Nolan, F. (1983) *The Phonetic Bases of Speaker Recognition,* Cambridge: Cambridge University Press.

—— (1990) 'The limitations of auditory-phonetic speaker identification', in H. Kniffka (ed.), *Texte zu Theorie und Praxis forensischer Linguistik,* Tübingen: Niemeyer.

Paul, J. E., Rabinowitz, A. S., Riganati, J. P. and Richardson, J. M. (1974) *Semi-automatic Speaker Identification System (SASIS)* (Analytical Studies Final Report), Anaheim, CA: Rockwell.

Rosenberg, A. E. (1976) 'Evaluation of an automatic speaker verification system over telephone lines', *Bell Technical Journal* 55: 723–44.

Rosenberg, A. E. and Sambur, M. R. (1975) 'New techniques for automatic speaker verification', in *IEEE-ASSP-Transactions* 23: 169–79.

Shipp, T., Doherty, E. T. and Hollien, H. (1987) 'Some fundamental considerations regarding voice identification', letter to the Editor, *Journal of the Acoustical Society of America* 82: 687–8.

Shirt, M. (1983) 'An auditory speaker-recognition experiment comparing the performance of phoneticians and phonetically naive listeners', unpublished paper given at the tenth International Congress of Phonetic Sciences, Utrecht, 1983.

Smrkovski, L. L. (1977) *Voice Identificaton*, East Lansing: Michigan Dept of State Police.

Stevens, K. N., Williams. C. E., Carbonell, J. R. and Woods, B. (1968) 'Speaker authentication and identification: a comparison of spectrographic and auditory presentations of speech material', *Journal of the Acoustical Society of America* 44: 1596–607.

Tosi, O. I. (1979) *Voice Identification: Theory and Legal Applications*, New York: Academic Press.

Tosi, O. I., Oyers, H., Lashbrook, W., Pedrey, C., Nicol, J. and Nash, E. (1972) 'Experiment on voice identification', *Journal of the Acoustical Society of America* 51: 2030–43.

VIAAS (Voice Identification and Acoustic Analysis Subcommittee of the International Association for Identification) (1992) 'Voice comparison standards', *Journal of Forensic Identification* 5: 373–96.

6

Voice types in automated telecommunications applications

John Laver
Centre for Speech Technology Research
University of Edinburgh

INTRODUCTION

The rapidly growing field of speech technology is a multi-disciplinary domain whose industrial advances benefit from contributions originating in applied interests in the linguistic sciences, the information sciences and the engineering sciences. The purpose of this article[1] is to offer a brief outline of some of the factors relevant to the concept of speaker type that might be taken into account in the telecommunications industry when considering the choice of voice type to use in any given automated telecommunications application, as an example of an applied interest in phonetics.

It is becoming an increasingly commonplace experience for users of telephone services in a number of countries to find that they are speaking to computers rather than to human operators, and to hear synthetic speech in response. One example would be an automated bank account query system, where an account-holder can make a telephone call to ask questions about the current state of his/her account. In such systems, the input speech from the user is subjected to automatic speech recognition, the output speech is often produced by a text-to-speech conversion system, and the structure of the dialogue between the user and the system, while resembling true conversation only in the most limited fashion, and being possible only in the most sharply constrained task domains, can nevertheless be characterised as a rudimentary form of human–computer interaction through speech.

Not too far in the future, Ms Smith, a (fictional) customer of the (fictional) Alpha Centauri Bank, might telephone her bank computer to change a monthly standing order. The possible dialogue between the two participants, after verification of caller identity and account number, might conceivably be:

SYSTEM   Which service do you require, Ms Smith? Statement queries, transfer of funds between accounts, or standing orders?

CALLER   Standing orders.

SYSTEM   Do you want a list of your current standing orders, to change a current order, to delete one, or to add a new one?

CALLER   I'd like to change one.

SYSTEM   What is the name of the payee of that order?

CALLER   British Gas Board.

SYSTEM   What do you want the new amount for the standing order to the British Gas Board to be?

CALLER   Thirty-two pounds fifty.

SYSTEM   Do you want the new standing order for the British Gas Board to continue to be paid monthly?

CALLER   Yes.

SYSTEM   Should we start this arrangement on the first of next month?

CALLER   No, on the seventh of next month.

SYSTEM   I understand that you require a standing order for thirty-two pounds fifty to be paid to the British Gas Board each month until further notice, beginning on the ninth of next month. Are all these details correct?

CALLER   No.

SYSTEM   Which detail is wrong, the payee, the monthly amount or the start date?

CALLER   The start date should be the *seventh* of next month.

SYSTEM   Sorry. I understand that you require a standing order for thirty-two pounds fifty to be paid to the British Gas Board each month until further notice, beginning on the *seventh* of next month. Is that correct?

CALLER   Yes, thanks.

SYSTEM   Do you require any other service?

CALLER   No.

SYSTEM   Thank you for using the Alpha Centauri Telephone Banking system, Ms Smith. Goodbye.

Compared with automated telephone applications in use today, the hypothetical dialogue here is free to an unusual degree from the need for corrective recycling, and the caller is unusually co-operative and compliant. Automatic speech recognition technology needed to support such an application exists already in many university and industrial laboratories; similarly, the ability to generate continuous synthetic speech of a quality and intelligibility that is sufficiently high not to impede the conversational progress of the dialogue is already available (Laver 1990). The degree of machine understanding of the caller's utterances is also not unacceptably high, in that most of the requirement for the computer to understand the intentions of the caller is limited to the need to recognise a rather small number of key words or phrases, against a well-specified and restricted set of possibilities. The occurrence within the next few years of a task-oriented conversation between a human caller and a computer-based automated telecommunications service of the sort described above is therefore not implausible.

The point of focus of this article is the nature of some of the unspoken assumptions in the mind of the human user of such a system about the quasi-human identity of that system. The evidence of the quasi-humanity of the system is exhibited by its apparent ability to understand the caller's speech and to generate plausible replies to those utterances. The apparent knowledge displayed by the system in navigating its path through the conversational dialogue gives it a quasi-cognitive quality, and the phonetic quality of the synthetic speech invites comparison with the speech of a human speaker of particular attributes of identity.

Every transaction involving speech unavoidably brings into play deeply ingrained responses by the listener to the sound of the speaker's voice, in which the listener ascribes personal attributes of sex, age, imagined physique, personality and sociolinguistic community membership to the speaker, as well as such shorter-term attributes as state of health and fatigue levels, and current emotional and attitudinal state. The conclusions reached about such personal attributes are often stereotypic, pigeon-holing the speakers into more crude categories than their actual fine-tuned differences might justify, but no listener seems to be able to resist the tendency to classify speakers into types. Equally, the behaviour of each member of every speaker–listener pair is shaped in conversational dialogue partly on the basis of his/her perception of the other's identity as revealed through speech.

The attributional process is thus inevitable, involves many different factors of personal identity and state, and strongly influences the flavour and outcome of every conversational interaction. It is a fundamental assumption underlying this article that the above observations about the responses of listeners to a given voice seem to be as true for the perception of machine-produced speech (so long as it is linguistically intelligible) as they are for the perception of human speech.

As soon as the user accepts the possibility of holding a conversation with a computer-based system, even when the conversation is as rudimentary as in the telephone banking application described above, the attributive process seems to come into play in the user's willingness to ascribe a number of quasi-human attributes of identity to the machine. To the extent that such attributes depend on the programmable phonetic and linguistic performance of the computer-based system, strategies of vocal engineering, influencing the user's perception of those attributes of apparent identity, hence become a matter of design choice. In particular, the chief question to be approached in this article is 'What is the effect on the user of selecting one output voice type rather than another in a given telecommunications application?'.

The structure of the article will be first, in the section below, to make some comments about the framework of a general interest in the perceived identity of the output voice of automated telecommunications applications. Then the third section (pp. 91–2) will give an outline of the principal ways that speakers can differ from each other. The fourth section (pp. 92–3) will make some brief points about the attributional process of the listener. The fifth section (pp. 93–4) will outline the ways in which the conversational relationship between the speaker and the listener can differ, in response to their perception of speaker identity. The sixth section (p. 94) will set up a typology of different means of evaluating the effect of changing the voice type of an automated telecommunications application. Finally, the concluding section will offer some practical suggestions that might be considered when choosing a voice for a given telecommunications application.

GENERAL FACTORS IN VOICE TYPING IN TELECOMMUNICATIONS APPLICATIONS

There are two general cross-cutting dimensions to be taken into account in considering choices of output-voice types in telecommunications. The first concerns the choice between human versus computer-generated voices. The second general dimension is to do with whether the thinking behind the choice of voice type is oriented towards the needs of one or both of the participants in the dialogue, towards aspects of the application, towards factors relevant to the properties of the telecommunications channel being used, or towards the public projection of a particular company image to its customers.

The choice of human versus computer-generated voices is not binary, but ranges across at least four categories:

1   a finite set of messages which have been prerecorded by some chosen individual human speaker;
2   computer-controlled concatenation into variable sentences made up of individual words or phrases prerecorded by such a speaker;
3   a speech synthesis method which concatenates smaller human-speaker-recorded units such as individual syllables, demi-syllables or consonants and vowels into variable sentences;
4   a fully mechanical, rule-based method of speech synthesis where no human-generated recordings contribute in any direct way to the speech heard by the listener.

In all these methods, the listener will draw a conclusion about whether he/she believes the voice is naturally human, human but distorted, synthetic but naturalistic, or synthetic and mechanically unnatural. The conclusion drawn will have a direct impact on what the listener is prepared to believe the speaker can be held to know about. If the application is dialogue-based, the listener's conclusion about the human or mechanical identity of the speaker will sharply condition the range and type of the listener's own spoken contributions to the dialogue (not necessarily in ways which are fully predictable, when the listener believes the voice is mechanical, depending on the listener's experience of computer-based speech interfaces).

In choosing either human or computer-generated voice types, three listener-based factors apply: intelligibility, comprehensibility and acceptability. These are related, but also distinct from each other. Intelligibility of messages produced by human voices across the telephone network is well researched, and perhaps needs no further comment except to say that intelligibility is not simply speaker-specific but also dependent to some degree on the linguistic identity and experience of the listener. A voice with a Scots accent may well be discernibly more intelligible to Scots listeners than to listeners from the South of England; a Texan accent may be less intelligible to listeners from New England than from Texas. The choice by a telephone company of one single speaker for a given application regardless of the origin of the call accessing that service would carry with it the tangible risk of variable intelligibility in different parts of the country concerned.

When a computer-generated voice is chosen for a given application, issues of overall message comprehensibility loom larger. It is a not uncommon experience in speech synthesis research to find that a message whose individual words are fully intelligible is nevertheless not fully comprehensible as a whole message. Conversely, with a considerably data-reduced speech signal in synthetic speech, the cognitive task of deciphering the intelligibility of individual words is greater than with human-generated speech: losing track of the intelligibility of a single word in a synthetic sentence then often partly or completely destroys the comprehensibility of the overall message, because recovery of intelligibility of the remainder of the utterance is a harder task than in listening to human speech. This would lead to the conclusion that, other things being equal, fully mechanical synthetic speech systems should not be the first choice for applications involving a large set of cognitively complex, unpredictable messages.

Acceptability is a highly multi-dimensional concept, with factors specific to the speaker, specific to the listener, general to the interaction of the speaker and the listener, and specific to the application itself, all playing a part. Speaker-specific factors include cosmetic issues such as the need to avoid any striking idiosyncrasy of the speaker's accent and voice type, the perceived smoothness versus roughness of the speaker's phonation type, the degree of nasality, etc. Listener-specific factors include all aspects of listener preferences, somewhat unpredictably based on listeners' life-long accumulations of experience of hearing voice types but tappable by opinion research for the population at large. Interaction-general factors (often subtle and implicit, but thereby disproportionately influential on impressions of a company's image as a service provider) include the compatibility or otherwise of the speaker's and listener's accents, and the perceived social power relationship between them. Application-specific factors include the match between the functionality of the application and the voice type chosen to provide access to that service. An example might be the match (or mismatch) between the perceived authoritativeness of the apparent personality lying behind a given output voice and the nature of the information provided in an information service.

The type of voice that is acceptable in a given application has some dependence on the type of application. Where one application can tolerate the economic advantage gained by using synthetic speech for frequently updated messages (say in weather forecasts), another might find the use of a human voice more desirable because of a crucial need for guaranteed intelligibility in the particular service provided (as in the case of services providing alarm messages).

The impact of choosing a human versus a computer-generated output voice, as far as channel-oriented issues go, will be less when fully digital lines are universal. Until then, the type of line has some interaction with the type of voice chosen, in the sense that the spectral properties of the voice type will in part condition the intelligibility (and the comprehensibility and acceptability) of the voice. A female speaker with a voice characterised by low overall intensity, and whispery phonation with even a moderate degree of attenuating nasality (which is a not uncommon female voice type in Britain), would be a less desirable choice for transmission over noisy lines than one without these characteristics. Account also has to be taken of the consequences for intelligibility, comprehensibility and acceptability of interaction between any coding technology used and the particular voice type. There is some evidence that some voice types show differential intelligibility results for given coding methods.

A final general consideration is that, since listeners unavoidably allocate physical identity, personality and mood to any voice that sounds to them even remotely likely to be human in origin, then the corporate image of a telephone company is itself inevitably to some extent coloured by the apparent physical identity, personality and mood of any output voice(s) it chooses to represent its services in the range of automated applications provided. Since the nature of possible future applications covers a very wide range of types of information and service, it follows from the general attitude espoused in this article that it would be unwise for a telecommunications company to think in terms of choosing a single 'golden' voice for all such automated applications. The vocal engineering of the future, in the highly competitive telecommunications industry, will need to develop expertise and technical methods for choosing voices (or of adjusting computer-generated voice types) to reflect principled judgements about the fit of the chosen voice to the attributes of the application and the projection of a carefully considered company image.

THE PRINCIPLES OF INTER-SPEAKER DIFFERENCES

Speakers can differ from each other organically and phonetically. Organic differences are those that reflect differences of anatomy – differences of the geometry of the vocal apparatus such as the nature of the speaker's pattern of dentition, the thickness, shape and size of the lips, the shape of the palate, the size and massiveness of the lower jaw, the length of the soft palate, the overall length of the vocal-tract, the volume of the nasal cavity, the thickness of the muscular vocal tract walls, and the diameter of the pharynx. Speakers vary in these details at least as much as they do in facial appearance (facial structure and vocal anatomy obviously being anatomically linked). Organic factors are by definition genetically inherited, not capable of voluntary change and very strongly speaker-identifying.

Phonetic differences of voice type between speakers reflect the way that the individual speaker has learned, over a lifetime of habituation, to use his/her vocal apparatus. An obvious element of phonetic use is the speaker's accent, which will be partly a result of learning the mode of speaking which typifies the speaker's sociolinguistic accent community, and partly a consequence of the (usually minor) idiosyncrasies which help to identify the speaker as an individual within that community.

A less immediately obvious aspect of the phonetic differences between speakers is what phoneticians have come to call voice quality 'settings' (Laver 1980, 1991). A setting is a long-term average value of some articulatory, auditory and acoustic parameter running through the moment-to-moment variations of speech sounds. An example would be the tendency of a given speaker to maintain his/her lips in a rounded position throughout most of speech. Another would be a tendency to maintain the tongue in a slightly curled retroflex position, as the film actor James Stewart did. Another would be the tendency of a given speaker to maintain a whispery mode of phonation, as Marilyn Monroe did. Another would be the tendency of a speaker to maintain the jaw in a nearly closed, almost clenched-teeth position. Another would be the tendency to keep the larynx in a relatively raised position throughout speech. It is the combination of phonetic factors of this sort with the organic foundation that often gives a voice its distinctively individual quality.

Another way of considering the differences between speakers is to look at the linguistic, paralinguistic and extralinguistic strands that make up

91

their speech. Matters such as sociolinguistic accent constitute a linguistic strand. The tone of voice that a speaker uses throughout an utterance (such as an angry tone of voice, or a persuasive one, or an encouraging one, etc.) is usually referred to by phoneticians and linguists as a paralinguistic strand. Another contributor to paralinguistic communication is the style of speech used – formal and careful versus informal and casual. Finally, the speaker-identifying voice quality of the speaker is usually thought of as an extralinguistic strand. All three strands – linguistic, paralinguistic and extralinguistic – need to be taken into account in making appropriate voice choices for particular applications. All three colour our attributional process as listeners.

THE NATURE OF THE ATTRIBUTIONAL PROCESS BY LISTENERS

The evidence that a listener uses to reach attributional conclusions about the imputed characteristics of the speaker can be called markers. We can distinguish between three general types of markers – physical markers, psychological markers and social markers (Laver and Trudgill 1979). Physical markers tend to rely on extralinguistic aspects of speech such as the evidence of physique from the resonatory characteristics of the length of the vocal tract, or the phonatory evidence of the size of the larynx found in the pitch of the speaker's voice. Psychological markers rely more on paralinguistic tone-of-voice evidence, and social markers mostly on linguistic evidence.

In general, the most accurate conclusions are drawn about physical markers. The correlation between the average fundamental frequency of a speaker's voice and the overall size and physique of the speaker, for example, is fair. A sign of the approximate reliability of this correlation is the degree to which we are disconcerted when the association turns out to be false. When we hear a deep loud voice, we are fairly confident that we are dealing with a large adult male speaker. When this turns out to be wrong, we are surprised. In telecommunications applications, it is the listener's reaction that is prime, since the 'truth' about the real identity characteristics of the output voice is almost never relevant. What is important for telecommunications applications, then, is that listeners in general will tend to reach the same marking conclusions from the same evidence, whether this stereotyping process results in 'true' attributions or not. To make an obvious comment, the attributional process in tele-communications applications is particularly salient, since the literally disembodied voice of the system is all the listener has to go on.

As a final comment in this section, it bears repetition that every telephone-based transaction involves the attributional process, and inevitably deploys social mechanisms of constructing and sustaining a temporary social relationship for the duration of that transaction. The nature of this social relationship between the user and the person perceived through the medium of the voice of the system is explored in the next section.

THE SOCIAL RELATIONSHIP BETWEEN THE USER AND THE SYSTEM

There are two aspects of this relationship that are partly mediated through the choice of output voice type that deserve comment here. The first is to do with solidarity between the user and the 'owner' of the system voice. The second is concerned with the relative power differential between the user and the 'owner' of the system voice.

In most spoken interactions, an influential factor which governs the choice of such linguistic behaviour as address terms, greeting and parting phrases, apology strategies, repair strategies and politeness mechanisms generally, is the degree of relative solidarity – that is, the degree of relative acquaintance and social attributes shared by the two participants. Normally, the degree of relative acquaintance is irrelevant in telecommunications applications, except to the extent that customers enjoy the psychological reassurance of meeting a familiar voice on every occasion of use of some application. More important is the question of what social attributes the user and the system voice might be designed to share. It has already been remarked that using a single accent for the voice of a system used by callers throughout a given country disregards the differential social effect of the chosen accent on users of other regionally marked accents. Choosing the output-voice accent to conform to the (broadly defined) geographical origin of the caller is one way a telephone company might use of establishing increased solidarity (and hence possibly greater social identi-fication) with the caller.

Relative power is another subtle parameter of spoken interaction. This finds its formal expression most often in the politeness strategies of address terms (Laver 1981), with asymmetric use of address-term types ('Mr X' versus 'First name' for address terms between social non-equals who are acquainted). But in telecommunication operations, the system is unacquainted with the caller (at least in present system design), and is bound by obligations of politeness as a service provider to a caller who is paying for the service. To that extent, the system is conventionally bound to use a formal address term (such as 'Ms Smith'), if any is used at all, and to use formal phrases of thanks, if any are used. But an important ingredient of telephone-based information services is that the system has privileged access to information that the user wants, and to that extent the user is momentarily in the social power of the system (with access by the user being able to be theoretically even if never actually withheld). From the perspective of such social and psychological tensions, telephone transactions of an information-seeking sort (say of Directory Enquiries) are potentially uncomfortable experiences for the user, if the tacit threat of power is not mitigated by the system's use of linguistic behaviour and a voice-type that effectively restores the balance of power. By choosing linguistic and phonetic behaviour which represents lower power status (i.e. behaviour presenting a cheerful and willingly helpful acceptance of a subordinate role), the system designer could compensate to some degree for the risks of this psychological problem.

This is probably also the place to mention that for more advanced, second-generation automated systems with a degree of enhanced intelligence or interpretive knowledge, a problem that is going to arise for users of such systems is being able to construct an adequate model of what knowledge the system can be counted on to have. When hearing an apparently human voice coming from the system, it is almost inevitable that the user will conclude that the system knows more than it ever really will, opening the way to consequent frustration. Controlling the voice type of such systems to be obviously non-human might help to keep this problem within manageable bounds.

EVALUATION OF VOICE TYPES

There are several different ways of evaluating differences between types of output voices. Some of these are fairly familiar, such as the testing of the cosmetic attractiveness of a voice by Mean Opinion Score or Semantic Differential methods, or the assessment of the intelligibility of different voices by using the Diagnostic Rhyme Test or the Modified Diagnostic Rhyme Test. Perhaps less familiar are methods of acoustic profiling of long-term acoustic parameters, such as long-term-average spectrum, spectral tilt, jitter and shimmer characterisation, long-term prosodic parameters of fundamental-frequency behaviour, long-term formant-frequency means, ranges and variability. A further possibility is attributional testing, where the perceived identity characteristics of the candidates for the output voice are evaluated and matched against some conceptualisation of desired characteristics.

CONCLUSIONS

Some practical considerations to which companies might give attention in choosing an output-voice for a given telecommunications application, springing from the comments offered above, are as follows:

Choose an educated version of a local accent for relevant services as an output voice in a given region, where the origin of the call can be regionally identified, rather than using a single output voice for every region.

Choose voice types which are demonstrably intelligible and comprehensible over the telephone lines available.

Choose voice types which are acceptable to the user in the context of the type of service involved, in terms of suitable extralinguistic, paralinguistic and linguistic attributes.

Choose voice types which are consistent with the projection of a desired company image.

In order to be able to make the above choices on an informed basis, a number of areas need further research. These include: the fit between given voice types and sets of perceived attributes of identity, personality and mood; the fit between voice type and application requirements; improvements in methods of synthetic speaker characterisation; and the development of better methods of evaluating and describing voice types.

NOTE

1   The preparation of this article was supported by BT Laboratories, Martlesham, under a contract to the Centre for Speech Technology Research, University of Edinburgh. Permission by BTL to publish the text in this form is gratefully acknowledged.

REFERENCES

Laver, J. (1980) *The Phonetic Description of Voice Quality*, Cambridge: Cambridge University Press.

—— (1981) 'Linguistic routines and politeness in greeting and parting', in F. Coulmas, (ed.), *Conversational Routines*, The Hague: Mouton, pp. 289–304.

—— (1990) 'European speech technology in perspective', *Terminologie et Traduction* 1: 163–79, Luxembourg: Office des publications officielles des Communauteés européennes.

—— (1991) *The Gift of Speech: Papers in the Analysis of Speech and Voice*, Edinburgh: Edinburgh University Press.

Laver, J. and Trudgill, P. (1979) 'Phonetic and linguistic markers in speech', in K. R. Scherer and H. Giles (eds), *Social Markers in Speech*, Cambridge: Cambridge University Press, pp. 1–32; reprinted in J. Laver, *The Gift of Speech: Papers in the Analysis of Speech and Voice*, Edinburgh: Edinburgh University Press.

7

The effect of context on the transcription of vowel quality

Moray J. Nairn and James R. Hurford
University of Edinburgh

INTRODUCTION

The analysis of speech and speech perception is still plagued, to a great extent, by one of the most puzzling and frustrating problems to have faced speech scientists this century.[1] The 'Lack of Invariance' problem may be neatly summed up by considering that the vowel sounds in the words *mean* and *beat*, which to the average language user seem identical, cannot be found to be the same either in terms of acoustic measurements or in articulatory description. In fact, these sounds can be said to be the same only in so far as they are both members of the same phoneme, which is itself a psychological unit. Thus the problem of the lack of invariance is a very real one at the phonetic level – indeed, how the perceptual categories of speech are determined in the acoustic signal at all falls under the title of perceptual constancy. Just as the classification of colour under changing contexts of illumination presents the human perceptual system with a problem in constancy (Gibson 1966) so the perception of speech is essentially a constancy problem involving classification. The description of sounds in phonemic terms is a classification with respect to psychophysical parameters.

Linguists have tried to decompose speech into its constituent levels for analysis: Ladefoged (1967) proposed three levels of an utterance which he called the *what, how* and *who* – corresponding with the linguistic message, information about the communicative situation and information about the identity of the speaker. Hockett (1958) described speech as exhibiting a 'duality of patterning', i.e. that it is comprised of both meaningful and meaningless units. Morphemes are the smallest meaningful units and they, in turn, are made up from smaller meaningless units – the phonemes. (Bloomfield 1933). The transmission and reception of meaningful speech must therefore depend in part on how the speaker and hearer perceive the phonemic categories of their language.[2] An auditory analysis of the relationship between acoustic form (meaningless units) and its communicative content (meaningful forms) is often achieved by phonetic transcription. The details of the processes underlying phonetic transcription have never been comprehensively accounted for but rather assumed by many renowned phoneticians (see for example Jones 1964; Abercrombie 1967; Gimson 1980). Richter (1973) assumes that phonetic transcription is based on 'articulatorily defined symbols'. He continues by pointing out the qualitatively different processes that phoneticians adopt as compared to naive listeners when transcribing speech.

The two different processes undertaken by naive listeners and phoneticians match the two components of speech recognition which form the basis of phonetic transcription. We must all firstly recognise the utterance which is being communicated and then discover what the signal represents. In fact, these two 'separate' processes are not so separate after all. Indeed, they are interdependent. We must analyse the psychoacoustic construction of the form of the utterance in order to access the meaning, and we often have to understand the meaning before we can analyse the construction. That mechanism of the human perceptual system which listens to the meaning of an utterance (i.e. to Ladefoged's '*what*' aspect, or to Hockett's 'meaningful' items) may be termed **semantic listening**, and its complement, which focuses attention on the internal construction of the utterance (i.e. to Ladefoged's '*how*' aspect, or to Hockett's 'meaningless' items) may be termed **analytic listening** (Vieregge 1987). When attending to well-formed words from one's native language one will almost certainly be listening semantically – an untrained language user decomposes the speech signal into its constituent sounds only to the extent required to understand the content of that signal. In psychological terms, semantic listening is a top–down or concept-driven process as expectation and conceptualisation feature importantly in comprehension.

Psycholinguistic experimentation indicates that less than the whole acoustic signal is needed for a listener to identify a word. This phenomenon is due to the listener supplying some of the missing information from other sources, e.g. memory of the general language structure, knowledge of semantic context, etc.

Analytic listening, on the other hand, is the converse of semantic listening. It is the foundation of the ability of phoneticians to transcribe minute phonetic variation. Whereas the non-linguist can generally only distinguish the speech sounds which are used contrastively in his/her language, i.e. the phonemes, the phonetician must be trained to ignore the meaning to a certain extent and focus on non-distinctive variations at the phonetic level. From this point of view, analytic listening is a bottom–up process or a 'data-driven process by which the utterance is built up by means of minimally auditorily detected units (speech sounds and/or distinctive features) which constitute the utterance as a whole' (Lindsay and Norman 1977). Whilst analytic and semantic listening are contrary processes, they

97

are also complementary as successful decoding of speech under all conditions requires the operation of both. Even the best phonetician cannot listen totally analytically, however, as concept-driven and data-driven processing occur simultaneously. As Vieregge (1987) points out, 'there always remains a "semantic residue" which helps even the best trained transcriber to transcribe narrowly'. He continues by demonstrating that the phonotactic constraints of any language belong to the 'semantic' residue. Although perhaps an interference when it comes to phonetic transcription, semantic listening does contribute more usefully to analytic listening in identifying the dysfluencies widespread in conversational speech and in distinguishing phrases such as *tea meeting* and *team eating* on the basis of context (Miller 1962, 1965).

Originally it was thought that phonetic transcription had a purely physiological basis and that each phone could be acoustically defined. This theoretical belief was shattered in the 1950s and 1960s when a series of tape-splicing experiments failed to find any way of combining units smaller than about half a syllable into intelligible speech. Furthermore, the improving sophistication of spectrographic techniques only served to demonstrate that phonemic and syllabic units, which are so clear perceptually, have no obvious correlates in a spectrogram (Fant 1962). Research with synthetic speech concluded that there is no one-to-one correspondence between perceptual units and the acoustic structure of the signal. Phonemic information, it seems, must be encoded into patterns of syllabic length (Liberman *et al.* 1957, 1967).

One other finding of the above research was that, in speech, the co-articulated vowel assists in the specification of the acoustic form of the consonants. What, then, specifies the quality of the vowel? The idealised vowel is considered to be a vowel made with a steady-state vocal-tract configuration which is acoustically determined by the frequencies of the first three formants. Unfortunately, a vowel of this description occurs only very rarely in continuous speech – because of co-articulation, vowels tend not to be steady-state items but are encoded into the whole syllabic framework. Formant transitions, as well as any steady-state nuclei, are involved in the identification of vowels (Stevens and House 1963).

Second, the speech rate can affect the acoustic structure of vowels. Lindblom (1963) proposed a theory of articulatory undershoot during conditions of rapid speech production where inertia of the articulators in response to neural motor excitations prevents movement to the 'target' positions of isolated vowels. Listeners were shown to alter their acoustic criteria for vowels (phoneme boundaries) as a function of the perceived rate of articulation (Lindblom and Studdert-Kennedy 1967) – they responded to articulatory undershoot with perceptual overshoot. These experiments further indicate that formant transitions, which are known to play a part in the specification of consonants, also contribute to vowel identification.

Joos (1948), whilst discussing the non-invariance problem, raised the issue of normalisation for the first time in phonetics. As we have seen, the judgement of sameness of two vowel stimuli cannot be based wholly on their acoustic structure:

> Therefore the identification is based on outside evidence.... If this outside evidence were merely the memory of what the same phoneme sounded like a little earlier in the conversation, the task of interpreting rapid speech would presumably be vastly more difficult than it is. What seems to happen, rather, is this. On first meeting a person, the listener hears a few vowel phonemes and on the basis of this small but apparently sufficient evidence he swiftly constructs a fairly complete vowel pattern to serve as background (coordinate system) upon which he correctly locates new phones as fast as he hears them.
>
> (Joos 1948: 61)

Thus, according to Joos, the listener requires reference points by which to judge the scale and distribution of the speaker's vowels – he/she must set up a perceptual vowel space relative to a sample of the speaker's speech. It is likely that the relevant reference points are articulatorily defined. Note that, unlike the Cardinal Vowel system which is partly speaker-specific, partly universal, Joos's system involves an individual vowel pattern constructed with reference to the speaker's vowels, not to some arbitrary set of 'cardinal' vowels. This mode of normalisation would imply that syllables spoken in isolation by an unfamiliar speaker should be extremely difficult to perceive accurately. Experiments by Peterson and Barney (1952), however, do not support this position. They show that the information contained within a single syllable is generally enough for listeners to compensate adequately for individual speaker characteristics. Nevertheless, listeners are influenced by prior phonological context as shown by Ladefoged and Broadbent (1957). Ladefoged (1967) cites Helson (1948) in his interpretation of the normalisation experiments. Helson's theory proposes that perceptual constancy (of any type) is achieved as the perceiver scales his/her responses not to the absolute properties of each stimulus, but according to a weighted mean of a set of stimuli distributed over time.

More recently, the ambiguity in vowel perception due to individual differences in speakers' vowel spaces and the improvement in vowel recognition with prior phonological context were assessed by Verbrugge *et al.* (1974). It was found that, as with Peterson and Barney's classic experiment (*ibid.*), extended prior exposure to the talker's vowels is unnecessary – the relevant information for vowel identification is generally contained in the same syllable. Second, the idea that normalisation is directly facilitated by the so-called point vowels (extremes of articulation – /i/, /ɑ/ and /u/) as claimed by Joos (1948), Gerstman (1968) and

99

Lieberman (1973) is not supported (Verbrugge *et al.* 1974). An isolated syllable is not as ambiguous as was once thought.

If we accept the findings of the above studies, then we must look for the sources of information that specify a vowel *within* the syllable, and explore how the listener uses that information in the course of vowel perception. As we saw earlier, listeners might use aspects of the formant transitions to help identify the nucleus of the vowel as well as the consonants. This being so, we would expect the perception of isolated vowels to be much more difficult than it is. Fairbanks and Grubb (1961) achieved an identification rate of only 74 per cent for isolated vowels judged by 'experienced listeners'. The 'phonetically-skilled subjects' of Lehiste and Meltzer (1973) fared little better. Millar and Ainsworth (1972) found that synthetic vowels which were co-articulated (in a /h_d/ environment) were more reliably identified than vowels with identical steady-state target values presented in isolation. Lindblom and Studdert-Kennedy (1967) discovered that listeners utilised different acoustic criteria to distinguish vowel pairs depending on whether the vowels were situated in a CVC context or in isolation.

Strange *et al.* (1974) conducted a series of experiments to test the hypothesis that the consonantal environment provides critical information for the vowel independent of talker-related variation. They found that both experimental variables – consonantal context and speaker variation – had significant effects and that the decrease in accuracy of vowel identification due to the absence of consonantal context was the same whether talkers varied or not. However, whereas the variation of speakers during the experiment impaired recognition by only about 8 per cent, the absence of a consonantal environment impaired performance by more than 20 per cent. Vowels coarticulated with surrounding consonants, as in normal speech, are considerably more intelligible than isolated vowels, irrespective of speaker variation.

Amongst the substantial body of literature pertaining to the non-invariance problem there are a number of experiments which compare the identification of synthetic vowels in context with synthetic vowels in isolation, and similarly there are those which compare the identification of natural human vowels in context with those in isolation. However, the third class of studies, which would seem to capture the best parts of both approaches, is surprisingly poorly represented. Whereas the studies of synthetic stimuli can be criticised simply for their use of synthetic material and the studies of human vowels tend to compare the judgements of two acoustically different items (co-articulated vowels and isolated vowels), an experiment which compares the judgement of human vowels in context with the same *acoustic* medial vowel excised digitally from that context would bring useful new information to the perceptual constancy debate.

Fujimura and Ochiai (1963) directly compared the identifiability of vowels in context and those gated out of the CVC framework and found that the latter were less intelligible.

The experiment presented in this article pursues a similar line to that of Fujimura and Ochiai (1963) in assessing the influence of phonological context on judgements of vowel quality, but bringing the methodology up to date with the use of digital processing techniques. Furthermore, in the light of what has been discussed earlier in this introduction, the experiment will shed light on the ability of phoneticians to listen purely analytically and to negate the top–down influence of context.

METHOD

Design

Differences in judgements along the X (front–back) and Y (high–low) dimensions between two tokens of each of four vowel phonemes /ɪ/, /ɛ/, /ʌ/ and /u/ were compared under two conditions

1 vowels in isolation,
2 vowels in consonantal contexts (i.e. words),

using an Analysis of Variance with repeated measures.

Preparation of materials

Twenty different words were selected from *A Phonetic Lexicon* (Rockey 1973) such that the words were monophthongal and contained an instance of each of the vowels /ɪ/, /ɛ/, /ʌ/ or /u/ in each of the consonantal frames *p_p, p_t, b_t, b_d, d_d*. The words formed by the combinations of consonants and vowels are shown in Table 7.1.

These vowels were selected as representing areas generally towards the corners of the vowel quadrilateral which were maximally distinct and yet still generated well-formed English words when combined with the consonantal frames. The consonantal frames consisted of two marginal oral stops which, when combined with a nuclear vowel, formed a monosyllabic

Table 7.1 The test vowels in consonantal contexts

	/ɪ/	/ɛ/	/ʌ/	/u/
p_p	pip	pep	pup	poop
p_t	pit	pet	putt	put
b_t	bit	bet	but	boot
b_d	bid	bed	bud	booed
d_d	did	dead	dud	dude

word. Note that two of the frames consist of only voiceless stops, two of the frames consist of only voiced stops and one frame is a mixture of a voiced and a voiceless stop (House and Fairbanks 1953). Nasal stops were not permitted because they have assimilatory effects on the vowel. Similarly, /r/ was omitted to avoid vowel rhotacisation and /l/ was omitted to avoid vowel colouring. Each test word was repeated to give a total of forty test tokens in the final experimental corpus.

In addition to the test items, 160 'distractor' items were included to mask the intention of the experiment. These words were also drawn from *A Phonetic Lexicon*, but they were formed by combining eight vowels (/i/, /ɪ/, /ɛ/, /a/, /u/, /o/, /ɔ/ and /ʌ/) with consonantal frames chosen to exploit as much of the English consonant system as possible.

Thus, while the test items were solely [+stop] V [+stop] in structure, the distractors contained oral stops, nasals, approximants, fricatives and affricates in both voiced and voiceless combinations. While the syllable structure of the test items was only CVC, the distractors contained words with structures such as CVC, CCVC, CVCC and CCVCC.

Within each 'vowel group' of the distractor words (words with the same vowel) there were sixteen different items, four of which were selected randomly to be duplicated to give a total of twenty words. Thus, in total, there were 160 (8 × 20) items in the distractor group and forty items in the test group giving a grand total of 200 items in the whole experimental corpus.

These words were randomly ordered by computer to give the list in Appendix I. This wordlist was read aloud by the speaker and recorded directly to Digital Audio Tape.[3] This recording was subsequently copied to standard audio cassette format and represented the material for condition 2 of the experiment. To obtain the corresponding material for condition 1, the words from the master recording were digitised at a sample-rate of 16 kHz using a Sparcstation 1 running under the SunOS Unix operating system. The vowels were excised from their surrounding contexts using the Entropic Signal Processing System software (Ver. 4.0) and the Waves+ graphics interface (Ver. 2.0). The Waves+ software controls the display and the interactive segmentation and editing of the digitised speech waveform. The excision procedure was performed by a combination of visual and aural means. The time-amplitude waveform of the word is displayed visually by the Waves+ program and it is relatively simple to demarcate the boundaries of the steady-state portion of the vowel on the computer. Very fine adjustments can be made by listening to the demarcated portion and refining the positioning of the onset or offset points, as necessary. The criteria for determining 'steady-state' portions were obvious periodicity (visual) and an apparently unchanging quality (auditory).

These digitised vowel portions were then recorded directly onto audio cassette in the same ordering as the words from which they were excised.

The vowels were numbered from 1 to 200 on the tape to identify them. From these second-level master tapes, multiple copies were made using a high-speed duplicator.[4] The copies were of equally high quality.

Blank vowel quadrilaterals were required for recording responses in both conditions. These were constructed with the dimensions shown below. These measurements conform to the 2:3:4 ratio of sides as favoured by Abercrombie (1967). For the purposes of this experiment, four quadrilaterals were printed horizontally (2 × 2) on A4 paper.

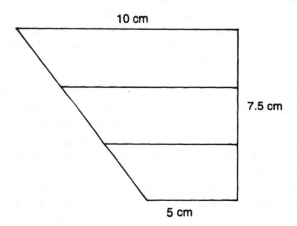

Procedure

The experiment consisted of two distinct parts. During part 1, four professional phoneticians were each sent one experimental pack for that part of the experiment. This pack contained a copy of the condition 1 tape (200 numbered, excised vowels); fifty sheets of blank vowel quadrilaterals (four quadrilaterals per sheet) and a letter of instructions.

The letter informed the subjects of what was required of them without explaining the precise nature of the experiment in case this should prejudice their responses. Subjects were asked to mark with a dot on each different quadrilateral the auditory quality of each different vowel. There were 200 vowels in total and 200 corresponding quadrilaterals, thus each quadrilateral received one, and only one, dot. It was explained that the subjects could listen to the tape as often as was necessary to form a judgement (the situation should be roughly analogous to a phonetician's use of the Cardinal Vowel system in fieldwork to transcribe an utterance by a native speaker of an unfamiliar language: he/she would ask the informant to pronounce the phone(s) several times before arriving at a phonetic conclusion). It was suggested that the whole procedure of the transcription of the 200 vowels should take no longer than about three hours, based on an estimation of roughly one minute per vowel (in fact, subjects report that the task took significantly less time than this initial estimate).

The speaker on the tape was a twenty-year-old female student from Perth, Scotland with a 'Standard Scottish English' accent. Each of the test vowels (/ɪ/, /ɛ/, /ʌ/ and /u/) were part of her phonemic inventory and the subjects were informed of the details of her age and accent in their instruction letter.

On completion of part I, the subjects were instructed to return the fifty sheets of vowel quadrilaterals and the tape immediately. Subjects were then sent an experimental pack for part II containing a further fifty sheets of blank vowel quadrilaterals; a copy of the condition II tape (200 words); a printed, numbered list of words matching the words on the tape (Appendix I) and an instruction letter. The subjects were informed that the procedure to part II was similar to that of part I: they were required to transcribe vowels from the tape to the quadrilaterals. On this occasion, however, they were to transcribe the vowels from words which they could hear from the tape and read from the list. The list was included so that on each presentation (playing) of a word from the tape, the subject would know unequivocally what that word was and there could be no danger of confusion with competing lexemes. The list also helped in matching the numbering of the words and the quadrilaterals.

To produce the raw data values, a front–back and a high–low measurement was taken from the top left corner of the quadrilateral (the position of Cardinal One) to the centre of the dot. This resulted in two figures for each judgement – a value for the position on the X-dimension (front–back) from 0 to 10 cm, and a value for the position on the Y-dimension (high–low) from 0 to 7.5 cm.

RESULTS

The main results of this study are presented summarily in tabular form in this section. They will be discussed in detail in the following 'Discussion' section. For the purposes of this analysis, the front–back judgements and the high–low judgements are being treated as varying independently and thus are measured in two separate ANOVAs. The three independent variables and their levels are: (1) **Phonetician** (Dr Ladd, Ms House, Mr Kemp and Dr Cruttenden); (2) **Context** (in isolation or in context) – these are treated in a repeated measures design; and (3) **Vowel** (/ɪ/, /ɛ/, /ʌ/ or /u/) which is a grouping variable. (See Table 7.2.)

The dependent variable is a measure of the difference between the first and second token of each test word. Thus a significant context effect, for example, would result from significant differences between the (token 1 – token 2) measure between the two contexts.

Table 7.2 Mean differences in judgement along front–back dimension (X-axis) between tokens of the same type by phonetician, context and vowel (cm) (standard deviations in parentheses)

Phonetician	Context	/ɪ/	/ɛ/	/ʌ/	/u/
Ladd	Isolation	1.18 (0.92978)	0.80 (0.58202)	0.37 (1.02078)	0.27 (1.52135)
	In context	0.03 (0.68702)	–0.26 (0.18507)	–0.36 (0.34893)	0.76 (1.15726)
House	Isolation	–0.50 (1.25449)	–0.36 (1.21264)	–0.20 (0.61135)	–0.11 (0.96268)
	In context	–0.23 (0.60477)	0.17 (0.37517)	–0.09 (1.1502)	0.23 (1.50690)
Kemp	Isolation	1.53 (1.17452)	0.07 (0.26363)	0.06 (0.29665)	0.37 (0.89972)
	In context	–0.16 (0.37316)	–0.05 (0.24769)	–0.07 (0.65822)	0.47 (1.50773)
Cruttenden	Isolation	1.02 (0.81747)	0.86 (1.27053)	–0.28 (0.94181)	–0.51 (1.61222)
	In context	–0.37 (0.39147)	–0.12 (0.73451)	0.33 (0.32711)	–0.08 (0.24393)
Grand Means		0.31250	0.13875	–0.12250	0.1750

Combining the means for each vowel across each phonetician and context gives the results shown in Table 7.3.

Table 7.3 Mean difference (cm) in judgements along the front–back dimension between tokens of the same type by phonetician and context

	Phonetician			
	Ladd	House	Kemp	Cruttenden
Context				
Isolation	0.4700	–0.2925	0.5075	0.2725
In context	0.0425	0.0200	0.0475	–0.0600

Combining the values for each of the contexts across phoneticians gives the means shown in Table 7.4.

Table 7.4 Mean differences (cm) in judgement along the front–back dimension between tokens of the same type by context

Context	
Isolation	0.2394
In context	0.0125

Combining the values for contexts and vowels across phoneticians gives Table 7.5.

Table 7.5 Mean difference (cm) in judgements along the front–back dimension between tokens of the same type by context and vowel

	Vowel			
	/ɪ/	/ɛ/	/ʌ/	/u/
Context				
Isolation	0.81	0.34	−0.20	0.01
In context	−0.18	0.07	−0.05	0.35

The results of the Analysis of Variance for the three independent variables and their interactions are shown in Table 7.6.

Table 7.6 Results of the analysis of variance for the variables and their interaction

Source of variation	Sum of squares	DF	Mean square	F-ratio	p
Vowel	3.96392	3	1.32131	0.88	0.4719
Phonetician	4.36330	3	1.45443	1.74	0.1714
Context	2.05889	1	2.05889	2.25	0.1535
Interaction (phonetician × vowel)	8.93689	9	0.99299	1.19	0.3243
Interaction (context × vowel)	10.78367	3	3.59456	3.92	0.0283
Interaction (phonetician × context)	3.96680	3	1.32227	2.22	0.0981
Interaction (phonetician × context × vowel)	6.97739	9	0.77527	1.30	0.2617

The identical analysis was used on the height dimension (Y-axis).

Table 7.7 Mean differences (cm) in judgement along height dimension (Y-axis) between tokens of the same type by phonetician, context and vowel (standard deviations in parentheses)

Phonetician	Context	/ɪ/	/ɛ/	/ʌ/	/u/
Ladd	Isolation	−0.19 (0.40835)	0.45 (0.98234)	−0.43 (0.67138)	−0.24 (0.18507)
	In context	−0.26 (0.52249)	−0.08 (0.29917)	−0.16 (0.63777)	0.11 (0.36297)
House	Isolation	−0.45 (0.7250)	0.49 (1.26165)	0.62 (0.57944)	0.26 (0.40528)
	In context	−0.23 (0.46583)	−0.16 (0.28810)	−0.01 (0.50175)	−0.16 (0.76273)
Kemp	Isolation	0.06 (0.42632)	0.11 (1.55620)	0.35 (0.34278)	0.06 (0.19812)
	In context	−0.17 (0.45634)	−0.01 (0.06519)	−0.24 (0.78930)	−0.01 (0.08216)
Cruttenden	Isolation	0.71 (1.69167)	0.93 (1.15953)	0.25 (1.24449)	1.06 (1.03706)
	In context	−0.15 (0.67082)	0.10 (0.87963)	−0.16 (0.41743)	−0.13 (0.26125)
Grand means		−0.08500	0.22875	0.02750	0.11875

Table 7.8 Mean difference (cm) in judgements along the height dimension between tokens of the same type by phonetician

Phonetician	
Ladd	−0.100
House	0.045
Kemp	0.019
Cruttenden	0.326

Table 7.9 Mean difference (cm) in judgements along the height dimension between different tokens of the same type by context and phonetician

	Phonetician			
	Ladd	House	Kemp	Cruttenden
Context				
Isolation	−0.1025	0.2300	0.1450	0.7375
In context	−0.0975	−0.1400	−0.1075	−0.0850

MORAY NAIRN AND JAMES HURFORD

Table 7.10 Mean difference (cm) in judgements along the height dimension
between tokens of the same type by context

Context	
Isolation	0.2525
In context	–0.1075

Table 7.11 Mean difference (cm) in judgements along the height dimension
between different tokens of the same type by context and vowel

	Vowel			
	/ɪ/	/ɛ/	/ʌ/	/u/
Context				
Isolation	0.0325	0.4950	0.1957	0.2850
In context	–0.2025	–0.0375	–0.1425	–0.0475

The result of the Analysis of Variance in the Height dimension for the
three independent variables and their interactions are shown in Table 7.12.

Table 7.12 Analysis of Variance in the Height dimension for the three independent
variables

Source of variation	Sum of squares	DF	Mean square	F-ratio	p
Vowel	2.13538	3	0.71179	0.71	0.5624
Phonetician	3.91163	3	1.30388	2.57	0.0648
Context	5.18400	1	5.18400	8.12	0.0116
Interaction (phonetician × vowel)	2.96700	9	0.32967	0.65	0.7479
Interaction (context × vowel)	0.46538	3	0.15513	0.24	0.8650
Interaction (phonetician × context)	3.58788	3	1.19596	2.59	0.0638
Interaction (phonetician × context × vowel)	3.15875	9	0.35097	0.76	0.6536

The diagonal distances between the two tokens of the same words were
calculated for each phonetician in each context. The value for this diagonal
difference of tokens in context was then subtracted from the value of the
difference between tokens in isolation. The results of this calculation are

Table 7.13 Diagonal distance differences (in centimetres)

Word	Cruttenden	House	Kemp	Ladd	Average
pip	2.297	0.542893	2.73084	0.990046	1.64019
pep	0.755573	1.10665	1.79445	0.809488	1.11654
pup	1.45476	0.07855	0.066425	0.36173	0.490366
poop	1.42614	−1.58776	0.33240	−0.69833	−0.131887
pit	0.87409	0.87414	−0.443983	−0.707107	0.149285
pet	2.24067	1.36014	0.026507	0.571182	1.04962
putt	1.02803	−0.589041	0.315397	1.0485	0.450721
put	2.52482	−0.673212	−0.846952	1.54146	0.636529
bit	1.23661	1.23652	0.297942	0.18424	0.738828
bet	−0.26943	0.139878	0.147398	1.81188	0.457431
but	1.12154	−0.46055	−0.157647	0.384952	0.222074
boot	2.21263	0.28528	−1.34022	1.06877	0.556615
bid	0.378479	0.8	0.858579	1.27038	0.82686
bed	−0.56407	1.92936	0.145049	0.819625	0.582491
bud	0.006318	0.53894	0.425658	0.191304	0.290555
booed	0.033777	0.144622	−0.3473	−0.45136	−0.155065
did	1.32853	−0.109017	2.2924	0.929912	1.11046
dead	2.52447	0.751665	2.30832	0.63213	1.55415
dud	0.790525	−0.028176	−1.82938	0.501961	−0.141268
dude	1.58371	−0.22472	−0.35	−0.969272	0.009929
Mean	1.14921	0.305808	0.321294	0.514575	0.572721

shown in Table 7.13 (all values in centimetres).

Note the heavy preponderance of positive values indicating that the distance between tokens of a word in isolation was generally larger than the distance between tokens of a word in context.

DISCUSSION

There are essentially two views of the greater consistency in identification of vowels in context over vowels in isolation. One is that, for two moderately well-spaced judgements of tokens, the narrowing of judgements in context reflects an improvement in transcription – a reduction of the amount of error separating the two tokens. The other view is that, for the same well-spaced token judgements, the narrowing of the transcriptions reflects a loss of discriminability – a *worsening* of the phoneticians' ability to make fine phonetic distinctions. It is the latter view, the reduction in subphonemic discriminability, that is assumed throughout this discussion. It is felt that this approach is more in keeping with the issues of semantic and analytic listening raised earlier, although without an acoustic analysis, we cannot say whether what the phoneticians are discriminating is really different or simply presents the illusion of difference.

Table 7.14 Levels of significance for each of the variables

Variable	Front–Back	Height
Vowel	N.S	N.S.
Phonetician	N.S.	$p < 0.1$
Context	N.S.	$p < 0.05$
P × V	N.S.	N.S.
C × V	$p < 0.05$	N.S.
P × C	$p < 0.1$	$p < 0.1$
P × C × V	N.S.	N.S.

From an examination of the two ANOVA tables (Table 7.6 and Table 7.12), it is clear that two of the three independent variables (PHONETICIAN and CONTEXT) show either clear significance or strong tendencies towards significance in at least one of the two analyses. Furthermore, there are some significant interactions occurring. Table 7.14 summarises the levels of significance for each of the variables in each analysis (front–back dimension and height dimension). The lack of significance in both analyses of the VOWEL variable is as expected. It indicates that there is no real difference in the discriminability of two tokens of any of the four vowels /ɪ/, /ɛ/, /ʌ/ or /u/ measured over all contexts and over all phoneticians.

The CONTEXT and PHONETICIAN variables both display the same pattern of effects – no significance in the front–back analysis and significance (or a trend) in the height analysis. As far as the CONTEXT variable is concerned, the results suggest that the presence or absence of a phonological context affects the ability to make token-to-token discriminations of vowel height. The means of the differences for all judgements (shown in Table 7.4 (front–back dimension) and Table 7.10 (height dimension)) show greater average difference in token-to-token judgements for isolated vowels than for vowels in a word. The asymmetry could be due to either of two factors. First, it is possible that the statistical difference reflects a qualitatively real difference between the front–back and height dimensions in the way context affects the discriminability between phonetically similar tokens. The overwhelming majority of the cell means indicate, however, that there is a greater degree of apparent recorded difference between tokens for vowels in isolation rather than for vowels in words for *both* front–back and height analyses, and this is borne out by the standard deviations. Second, the lack of significance in the front–back analysis, if not due to an underlying perceptual difference, may be an artefact of the design of the Cardinal Vowel quadrilateral. The amount of variability is greater over both levels of the CONTEXT variable in the front–back analysis than the height analysis (grand mean of front–back judgements = 0.12594; grand mean of height judgements = 0.0725). One possible reason for this is that subjects had a larger range of possible responses along the front–back dimension

(0–10 cm at the periphery) than along the height dimension (0–7.5 cm) because of the shape of the quadrilateral. We shall return to the Cardinal Vowel quadrilateral and some flaws in its construction later. What can be said is that the tendency to discriminate tokens of the same phoneme changes with context. It is appropriate at this point to show that this grand mean, and indeed potentially all of the means, may be ambiguous in the information they appear to convey.

Taking judgements along the front–back dimension to illustrate the point, a large value for token 1 of any vowel (i.e. judging it to be relatively far back) and a smaller value for token 2 of the same vowel (further front) will result in a positive difference, as the measure of difference is $X_{(token\ 1)}$ – $X_{(token\ 2)}$. The mean of such differences will be a positive figure representing a true arithmetical average. Similarly if $X_{(token\ 1)} < X_{(token\ 2)}$ (i.e. if token 1 is judged as being further front than token 2) then the mean of such differences will be negative and will represent a true average. If, however, a set of differences (say, for one vowel across four phoneticians and two contexts) is made up of four positive differences and four negative differences, then the arithmetical mean may be very small as the signs will tend to cancel each other out. So, to return to the grand means, there are two possible interpretations: – *one,* that there really is a larger amount of difference occurring consistently across phoneticians, contexts and vowels in the X-dimension (front–back) than in the Y-dimension (height): *two,* that the smaller mean in the Height dimension is due to more cancellation of positive and negative signs occurring in the submeans. This, in itself, is important as it indicates that there is less consistency or, in a sense, reliability in the data which comprise that specific mean. And, of course, the data which comprise the grand mean are means themselves (the eight numbers which constitute the grand mean represent the average difference between tokens value for each phonetician in each context, i.e. averaged across vowels). These means are the result of the cancellation of positive and negative values also, indeed all means right down to the lowest-level mean (the average difference between two tokens measured over five consonantal environments) are prone to this effect. It should be remembered that this mathematical artefact does not in any way invalidate the data: if phonetician A judges token 1 of a vowel as further front than token 2 of the same vowel in the 'isolation' condition, and phonetician B judges their positions exactly in reverse in the same condition then, although the differences may largely cancel themselves out when data for all the phoneticians are averaged together, there is still an important effect occurring here which will be detected in the comparisons of other means or in the ANOVA. The point to be made is that care needs to be taken before any statements can be confidently made about the variability of the data. Whereas in the initial measurements, the further a difference value was from zero, whether it was positive or negative, the greater the difference between the tokens, when averages are taken of averages it becomes harder to state that a smaller value represents less variability. The only reliable solutions are to examine the apparent tendencies in the means and compare them against the raw, unanalysed data or simply to use the absolute values of differences. These processes, in association with an examination of the standard deviations which give a fair reflection of the proportion of variability, reveal that the effect of context is indeed a true one (see also Table 7.13).

In order to determine specifically whether the reduction in discriminability of vowel tokens in context was due to the phonological effect of the surrounding consonants or to an effect of word frequency, an analysis of covariance (ANOCOVA) was carried out on the test items using the Kučera-Francis frequency value of the words as the covariable. The hypothesis was that if the deterioration in discrimination was caused by a prejudice towards an idealised vowel target then the words with the highest lexical frequency, i.e. the most commonly occurring words, would show a more marked narrowing of judgements (due to the worsening of the ability to distinguish two subphonemic sounds caused by the influence of the mental, phonological model of the word). No correlation between frequency and context effect was recorded. Thus the hypothesis that it was the lexical frequency of the word that influenced the transcription process was not supported.[5]

The PHONETICIAN variable reflects the variation in judgements that is attributable to the differences between the four phoneticians. We have already seen a significant difference between the transcriptions of the same vowels under different contexts which appears to contradict the view that phoneticians are acting in a purely bottom–up, data-driven way when transcribing sounds. A significant PHONETICIAN effect would serve to further support the idea that phoneticians are not 'transcribing machines' but are prone to individual differences. In fact, as Tables 7.6 and 7.12 show, the variable shows no significance in the front–back dimension and a strongly significant tendency in the height dimension. It is clear from Table 7.8 that Dr Cruttenden performed significantly differently from the other subjects in the judgements of differences. In particular, he transcribed the two tokens of the vowels in isolation as much more widely spread than his fellow phoneticians. A specific instance of unusually distributed data such as we have here is always likely to come to the surface when analysing interactions. In this case the interaction is between PHONETICIAN and CONTEXT and the relevant F-ratio is very nearly significant ($p < 0.1$). Table 7.9 shows the marked discrepancy between Dr Cruttenden's judgements of isolated vowels and the judgements of the other phoneticians very clearly. Table 7.3, on the other hand, shows the comparison of the same means for the front–back dimension. Although the context effect is demonstrated,[6] there is less of an interaction as the absolute differences between the means of each context for each phonetician are very similar. For an interaction of the type

A × B to achieve a significant effect, the levels of A must affect the levels of B differently.

Bearing this in mind, let us consider the interaction between CONTEXT and VOWEL. There is no important interaction occurring in the height dimension. All of the vowels except for /ɪ/ are subject to a greater discriminability in isolation than in context (see Table 7.12). If we examine the submeans which constitute the CONTEXT × VOWEL value we discover that the mean values for each of the the four phoneticians for /ɪ/ in context are close to the –0.2 point (they are all negative) and therefore an average of –0.2025 is a fair reflection of the mean difference judgement across all phoneticians. The values for /ɪ/ in isolation, however, consist of –0.19, –0.45, 0.06 and 0.71, in other words, two reasonably small negative numbers, one very small positive number and one large positive number. This is a case of signs cancelling each other out, as was anticipated earlier. Consideration of the raw judgement scores shows that, in general, the difference in judgements between tokens *was* greater in isolation than in context (see also Table 7.13). Table 7.11 therefore shows again the context effect discussed above but no interaction.

The same interaction on the front–back dimension, however, is statistically significant and theoretically interesting. The data in Table 7.5 show the familiar pattern of larger[7] values for the vowels in isolation than in context across three of the vowels – /ɪ/, /ɛ/ and /ʌ/ – but the arrangement of values for /u/ appears to be reversed. In fact the value for the judgement of the vowel in isolation (0.01) may be artificially small due to sign cancellation. The value for judgements in context (0.35), however, is substantially larger than the analogous value for other vowels and is a valid reflection of the variation in judgements. The interpretation of this result is that there is no narrowing of transcription distance between tokens of /u/ in the same words from the levels of the distances judged in isolation.

One possible explanation of this effect is that, as was suggested earlier, phoneticians use different perceptual mechanisms when transcribing items in context and items in isolation. Largely phonetic, bottom–up strategies are used in making fine subphonemic distinctions for isolated sounds, whereas partly top–down strategies involving access to stored, idealised, prototypical auditory/acoustic models are used when listening to complete contexts. As these mental representations must be based on some physical reality, it is likely that the phonetic judgements of isolated vowels and the phonological (or, at least, phonologically influenced) judgements of contextually specified vowels will be reasonably close to one another. The particular realisation of the /u/ phoneme in the experimental corpus was typical of the speech of a speaker from the social and geographical background of our speaker – i.e. [ʉ], a high, back, rounded vowel with considerable advancement of the tongue body. The judgements of [ʉ] in isolation showed the pattern of variation which one might expect of auditory, phonetic judgements; however, the vowels in context showed an unusually high amount of variation in inter-token judgements – as if the internalised phonemic representation of the vowel was missing or weakened and hence was not causing the anticipated narrowing of transcription. This explanation is somewhat unlikely as, if there are indeed idealised, perceptual targets such as we are suggesting, there is no reason why any vowel to which a phonetician has been exposed should remain unrepresented. There is another much more likely explanation which is linked to this last point: if a phonetician, say from the south of England, develops a perceptual target of the /u/ phoneme from the realisations of /u/ which he/she hears, then the advanced [ʉ]pronunciations of certain Scottish speakers may fall outside the boundaries of his/her mental vowel space which is nominated for /u/. If this is indeed the case then we would expect such a phonetician to cope normally with the vowel in isolation as it is not being compared (at least not to the degree that it is when listening in context) to any stored targets, but to have difficulty in matching the phone in context with the internal phoneme patterns. This difficulty should manifest itself in a reduction of the narrowing of difference effect which is precisely the situation which occurs with /u/.

Another possibility, which is a slight variation in the details proposed above, is that when analysing vowels in context, a phonetician will use both of the perceptual strategies discussed. He/she may first listen analytically using only the raw acoustic/auditory information available in the signal to determine his/her judgement and then, with this temporary result stored somewhere in short-term memory, may continue to perform the top–down phoneme placement process and the results from these two processes would feed an algorithm which would produce the final judgement. In the vast majority of cases a comparison of the results of these two stages ought not to reveal any large discrepancy. The case of /u/ in this experiment is a perfect example of the alternative in the above hypothetical model: the results of the phonetic/auditory analysis (front vowel) and the result of the mental representation (back vowel) conflict and so there is no narrowing of inter-token difference as is found in other more 'standard' vowels.

The fact that these odd values for /u/ are found only in the front–back dimension and not in the height dimension is easy to explain in the preceding framework. It is the front or back quality of the variant of /u/ that is in dispute, not the height. All of the phoneticians correctly judged all the instances of /u/ as being high on the quadrilateral; however, there were considerable differences between phoneticians as to whether they were hearing high back or high front rounded vowels.

The interaction between PHONETICIAN and VOWEL was not significant in either dimension. A significant result here would indicate that the portion of variance due to phoneticians was not distributed evenly over the four vowels but depended on the vowel that each was transcribing.

114

In order that the three-way interaction between PHONETICIAN × CONTEXT × VOWEL might be significant, the judgements of a particular phonetician of a particular vowel in a particular condition of context must be different enough for this source of variability to manifest itself above the 'sea of background noise' (extraneous and single-factor variability). Not unexpectedly, this does not happen in either dimension.

Earlier, we noted that there was an apparent asymmetry between the front–back and height dimensions in the effects of the PHONETICIAN and CONTEXT variables and we suggested some possible explanations for this situation. The data, however, also lend themselves to an explanation which is based on a more critical examination of the theory which underlies the Cardinal Vowel system.

In an attempt to account for the evolutionary principles on which the linguistic selection of sounds is made from the vast sound-making potential of man, Stevens (1972) developed his 'Quantal' theory of speech. The basis of the quantal theory is a selection of only those zones of articulatory performance where the results of small articulatory differences are not auditorily perceptible. This clearly would confer useful stability on a speech system used for communication.

It is possible that the significance of the context effect in the height dimension in this experiment represents the operation of a perceptual analogue to Stevens' theory – a kind of Quantal theory of perception. The point of Stevens' theory is that small variations in point of stricture, such as might occur by random variation between similar tokens, will not cause a listener to mistake one place of articulation for another and thus confuse two words. Larger variations, however, will result in the listener perceiving a different sound. A production system organised in this way helps both speaker and hearer to define the acceptable parameters of variation within and amongst phonemes. In the present experiment, a large degree of difference between tokens in isolation is being reduced significantly more in the height dimension than in the front–back dimension when the tokens are presented in context. Why is this? The Quantal theory of perception would argue that the variability of these tokens must be narrowed more in the height dimension to prevent misidentification due to competing words. Due to the construction of the Cardinal Vowel quadrilateral and the general phonetic theory which underlies it, there are four phonetic levels of vowel height (high, mid-high, mid-low and low) but only two degrees of frontness (front and back), and so a token of /u/ transcribed in context can vary up to 5 cm along the vowel chart from the top-right corner before it encroaches on the area deemed to enclose a phonetically distinct item, i.e. /i/, whereas a variation of 2.5–5 cm from the same point in the vertical dimension will result in the transcription of /o/. It would seem that sounds have more freedom to vary in safety along the front–back dimension than the height dimension (although this effect would be expected to lessen

115

with progressively lower vowels). As Hurford (1969) puts it, '[I] find it consistently difficult to judge vowel qualities "along the top" of the vowel chart, i.e. qualities anywhere between, but not including, /i, y/ and /ɯ, u/. This is probably because there are no vowel phonemes in [my] own speech regularly articulated with /ɨ/- and /ʉ/-like qualities.' Thus 'boot' will become in turn boat and bought within the same scope of variation (along a different dimension) that it will become *[byt], which of course is not a possible English word. The theory we are suggesting would compensate for this by scaling the degree of variation to within the boundaries of the mental representation of the phoneme, as discussed above.

The tendency to accede to the traditional degrees of height and frontness is almost universal now. Ian Maddieson (1984) describes vowels of 317 languages in the UCLA Phonological Segment Inventory Database using various degrees of vowel height but only two of frontness. In other words, although a language might have a number of vowel phonemes, each with different phonetic levels of height and frontness, it is the feature of height which distinguishes most of them – front vs back distinguishes only those vowels situated on the same height level. Even !Xü, with twenty-four different monophthong phonemes, is categorised with features such as ±nasal and ±pharyngeal rather than ±front and ±central which could allow up to four levels of frontness. We are not, of course, suggesting that !Xü or any other language is *incorrectly* specified, rather that the full potential of the general phonetic theory which determines the conventional vowel chart is underexploited; this must cast doubt on the vowel chart as a map of the real human possibilities.

Future studies

Constraints on time and resources unfortunately limited the number of phoneticians participating in this experiment to four rather than the twelve originally envisaged. Any future replication of this work is strongly recommended to involve more subjects to ensure that the statistical results reflect the tendencies of a representative sample of phoneticians.

It would also be useful, from a theoretical point of view, to include an acoustic measurement in the comparison of judgement differences to show whether the narrowing of judgements of items in context reflected a movement towards, away from or independently of an acoustic target.

ACKNOWLEDGEMENTS

The four phoneticians contacted whose results were available to include in this report were, Dr Alan Cruttenden, University of Manchester; Ms Jill House, University College London; Mr Alan Kemp, University of Edinburgh; and Dr Robert Ladd, University of Edinburgh. We are grateful to these, and all the phoneticians who participated in the study.

For her generous help with the complex statistical analyses of the data and patient discussion of the results we are indebted to Ellen Bard. We would also like to thank Norman Dryden, Stewart Smith, Cedric McMartin and Geoff Lindsey for technical support and, last but not least, Veronica Laing for kindly providing her vowels for analysis.

NOTES

1   The idea for this study was the second author's, intended to qualify the conclusions reached in Hurford (1969): a study supervised by J. D. O'Connor. The great bulk of the work in carrying the present study through was the first author's.

2   See Van Valin (1976) for evidence that speakers take phonemic categories into account when judging the distance between vowel stimuli.

3   The speech was recorded via a SENNHEISER MKH815T RF Condenser microphone to a SONY DTC1000 ES Digital Audio Tape Recorder. The DAT has a 90dB Signal/Noise Ratio and samples at a rate of 16 kHz with a sampling resolution of 16 bits.

4   A SONY High Speed Cassette Duplicator was used with MAXELL XLS-I C60 audio cassettes.

5   See Oller and Eilers (1975) for evidence that phonetic expectation due to knowledge of word meaning influences transcription.

6   Note that the negative value for Ms House in the isolated vowels condition is probably a contributing factor to the failure of significance of the CONTEXT variable in the ANOVA.

7   That is, larger in absolute terms: –20 is larger than –5 as it shows more displacement from a 'perfect' difference judgement value of zero.

APPENDIX I: WORD LIST USED IN EXPERIMENT

1	sneak	20	hall	39	pep	58	sum
2	pup	21	test	40	comb	59	bet
3	bead	22	dim	41	green	60	duck
4	hoof	23	love	42	talk	61	beaks
5	gift	24	sneeze	43	but	62	heave
6	pip	25	hawk	44	rag	63	back
7	did	26	sieve	45	dead	64	globe
8	booed	27	jazz	46	desk	65	test
9	Sid	28	choose	47	stall	66	stiff
10	snooze	29	pet	48	pool	67	bet
11	pub	30	raw	49	bead	68	wove
12	myth	31	taunt	50	stud	69	book
13	dad	32	desk	51	talk	70	launch
14	move	33	nut	52	dude	71	fetch
15	zone	34	keep	53	priest	72	pit
16	poop	35	pool	54	boot	73	rough
17	goose	36	stem	55	soup	74	comb
18	pet	37	code	56	peach	75	gush
19	bun	38	mat	57	putt	76	beam

77	web	108	dud	139	boom	170	cup
78	catch	109	duck	140	sin	171	fig
79	poke	110	green	141	deaf	172	smash
80	hall	111	step	142	bud	173	tanned
81	loathe	112	booed	143	fudge	174	jaws
82	wax	113	dude	144	tooth	175	pep
83	bit	114	love	145	salt	176	mesh
84	peace	115	bed	146	gang	177	launch
85	then	116	put	147	boost	178	cab
86	heave	117	did	148	groove	179	have
87	sauce	118	beg	149	note	180	hip
88	snooze	119	peace	150	bed	181	shed
89	stitch	120	have	151	dead	182	but
90	bud	121	wit	152	flute	183	bid
91	dish	122	thick	153	vet	184	Dutch
92	deck	123	mist	154	spell	185	bus
93	sheet	124	soap	155	teeth	186	fiend
94	note	125	bit	156	June	187	stove
95	both	126	Pam	157	dad	188	beg
96	nib	127	league	158	sap	189	soothe
97	caught	128	gas	159	hull	190	sum
98	poop	129	bun	160	web	191	goal
99	dim	130	watch	161	dud	192	mood
100	cab	131	cough	162	pip	193	damp
101	have	132	soap	163	hedge	194	boot
102	broad	133	thug	164	bid	195	road
103	thick	134	pit	165	hose	196	tooth
104	vogue	135	gas	166	scan	197	put
105	hip	136	pup	167	putt	198	hose
106	poach	137	cause	168	guess	199	thump
107	thief	138	dish	169	kiss	200	yawn

REFERENCES

Abercrombie, D. (1967) *Elements of General Phonetics*, Edinburgh: Edinburgh University Press.

Bloomfield, L. (1933) *Language*, New York: Henry Holt.

Chomsky, N. (1988) *Language and the Problems of Knowledge: The Managua Lectures*, Cambridge, MA: MIT Press.

Denes, P. B. (1963) 'On the statistics of spoken English', *Journal of the Acoustical Society of America* 35: 892–904.

Fairbanks, G. and Grubb, P. A. (1961) 'A psychophysical investigation of vowel formants', *Journal of Speech and Hearing Research* 4: 203–19.

Fant, G. (1962) 'Descriptive analysis of the acoustic aspects of speech', *Logos* 5: 3–17.

Fujimura, O. and Ochiai, K. (1963) 'Vowel identification and phonetic contexts', *Journal of the Acoustical Society of America* 35: 1889 (abstract).

Gerstman, L. J. (1968) 'Classification of self-normalized vowels', *IEEE Transactions on Audio- and Electroacoustics* AU16: 78–80.

Gibson, J. J. (1966) *The Senses Considered as Perceptual Systems*, Boston, MA: Houghton-Mifflin.

Gimson, A. C. (1980) *An Introduction to the Pronunciation of English*, 3rd edn, London: Edward Arnold.

Helson, H. (1948) 'Adaptation level as a basis for a qualitative theory of frames of reference', *Psychological Review* 55: 297–313.

Hockett, C. F. (1958) *A Course in Modern Linguistics*, New York: Macmillan.

House, A. S. and Fairbanks, G. (1953) 'The influence of consonant environment upon the secondary acoustical characteristics of vowels', *Journal of the Acoustical Society of America* 25: 105–13.

Hurford, J. R. (1969) 'The judgement of vowel quality', *Language and Speech* 12: 220–37.

Jones, D. (1964) *An Outline of English Phonetics*, 9th edn, Cambridge: Heffer.

Joos, M. A. (1948) 'Acoustic phonetics', *Language* (supplement) 24: 1–136.

Kučera, H. and Francis, W. N. (1967) *Computational Analysis of Present-Day American English*, Providence: Rhode Island.

Ladefoged, P. (1967) *Three Areas of Experimental Phonetics*, London and New York: Oxford University Press.

Ladefoged, P. and Broadbent, D. E. (1957) 'Information conveyed by vowels', *Journal of the Acoustical Society of America* 29: 98–104.

Lehiste, I. and Meltzer, D. (1973) 'Vowel and speaker identification in natural and synthetic speech', *Language and Speech* 16: 356–64.

Liberman, A. M., Cooper, F. S., Shankweiler, D. and Studdert-Kennedy, M. (1967) 'Perception of the speech code', *Psychological Review* 74: 431–61.

Liberman, A. M., Harris, K. S., Hoffman, H. S. and Griffith, B. C. (1957) 'The discrimination of speech sounds within and across phoneme boundaries', *Journal of Experimental Psychology* 54: 358–68.

Lieberman, P. (1973) 'On the evolution of language: a unified view', *Cognition* 2: 59–94.

Lindblom, B. E. F. (1963) 'Spectrographic study of vowel reduction', *Journal of the Acoustical Society of America* 35: 1773–81.

Lindblom, B. E. F. and Studdert-Kennedy, M. (1967) 'On the role of formant transitions in vowel recognition', *Journal of the Acoustical Society of America* 42: 830–43.

Lindsay, P. H. and Norman, D. A. (1977) *Human Information Processing: An Introduction to Psychology*, 2nd edn, New York: Academic Press.

Maddieson, I. (1984) *Patterns of Sound*, Cambridge: Cambridge University Press.

Millar, J. B. and Ainsworth, W. A. (1972) 'Identification of synthetic isolated vowels and vowels in h_d context', *Acoustica* 27: 278–82.

Miller, G.A. (1962) 'Decision units in the perception of speech', *IRE Transactions on Information Theory* 8: 81–3.

—— (1965) 'Some preliminaries to psycholinguistics', *American Psychologist* 20: 15–20.

Oller, D. K. and Eilers, R. E. (1975) 'Phonetic expectation and transcription validity', *Phonetica* 31: 288–304.

Peterson, G. E. and Barney, H. L. (1952) 'Control methods used in a study of vowels', *Journal of the Acoustical Society of America* 24: 175–84.

Richter, H. (1973) 'Grundsätze und System der Transkription', *IPA (G), Tübingen (Phonai. Lautbibliothek der europäischen Sprachen und Mundarten*, German edn, Vol. 3).

Rockey, D. (1973) *Phonetic Lexicon of Monosyllabic and some Disyllabic Words, with Homophones, Arranged According to their Phonetic Structure*, London: Heyden.

Stevens, K. N. (1972) 'The quantal nature of speech: evidence from articulatory-acoustic data', in E. E David, Jr and P. B. Denes (eds), *Human Communication:*

a Unified View, New York: McGraw-Hill.

Stevens, K. N. and House, A. S. (1963) 'Perturbation of vowel articulations by consonantal context: an acoustical study', *Journal of Speech and Hearing Research* 6: 111–28.

Strange, W., Verbrugge, R. and Shankweiler, D. (1974) 'Consonant environment specifies vowel identity', *Status Report on Speech Research,* SR37/8, New Haven: Haskins Laboratories, pp. 209–16.

Van Valin Jr, R. D. (1976) 'Perceived distance between vowel stimuli', *Journal of Phonetics* 4: 51–8.

Verbrugge, R., Strange, W. and Shankweiler, D. (1974) 'What information enables a listener to map a talker's vowel space?', *Status Report on Speech Research,* SR37/8: New Haven: Haskins Laboratories, pp. 199–208.

Vieregge, W. H. (1987) 'Basic aspects of phonetic transcription', in A. Almeida and A. Braun (eds), *Probleme der phonetischen Transkription,* Stuttgart: Franz Steiner Verlag.

8

Place of articulation features for clicks: anomalies for universals

A. Traill
University of the Witwatersrand

INTRODUCTION

The overwhelming majority of phonetic descriptions of clicks are based on articulatory features (e.g. Doke 1937; Beach 1938; Snyman 1975; Chomsky and Halle 1968; Traill 1985; Sagey 1986; Ladefoged 1989; Taljaard and Snyman 1990). These features are used only to express redundancy-free phonological contrasts. As they have no further justification, they are in a sense arbitrary since there is no linguistic evidence based on phonological processes in the click languages for the features. In this paper we shall examine data from assimilation and language change in the Khoisan languages which provide a novel perspective on the natural classes of clicks. The correct generalisations cannot be framed adequately in terms of the conventional articulatory features but require instead acoustically defined features. The acoustic features also reveal the essential relationships between clicks and non-clicks. These relationships are entirely obscured by articulatory features and as a result the Khoisan consonant inventories in Maddieson's (1984) survey of phonological inventories show a universally unprecedented lack of uniformity in the consonant systems when it comes to place-of-articulation terms.

PLACE OF ARTICULATION

In almost all the literature on clicks, the phonetic differences between them are described in terms of articulatory features. Notable exceptions are Kagaya (1978), Sands (1989) and Jakobson (1968). Jakobson's acoustically based classification for resonance and source features is given in Table 8.1 (1968: 226). A sample of articulatory-based descriptions of clicks is given in Table 2 below.

It is clear from Table 8.2 that there is not complete agreement on the correct description of the clicks, particularly for [ǂ, !]. Some of the details are minor: everyone agrees that [ǀ, ǁ] involve a noisy release and that [ǂ, !] do not, even if this is not explicitly mentioned. However, when it comes to

Table 8.1 Jakobson's acoustic features for the plain clicks [|, ǂ, ||, !]

	|	ǂ	||	!
Compact	−	−	+	+
Continuant	+	−	+	−
Checked	+	+	+	+

Table 8.2 Some articulatory phonetic descriptions of the clicks [|, ǂ, ||, !]

Source	Language	|	||	ǂ	!
Snyman (1975)	Zhu	denti-alveolar	lateral	alveolar	palatal
Sagey (1986)	Khoisan	+coronal +anterior +distributed −lateral	+coronal −anterior −distributed +lateral	+coronal +anterior +distributed −lateral	+coronal −anterior −distributed −lateral
Beach (1938)	Nama	dental affricatives	alveolar lateral affricative	denti-alveolar implosive	alveolar implosive
Bleek and Lloyd (1911)	ǀXam	dental	lateral	palatal	cerebral
Kohler (1981)	Kxoe	dental	latéral	alvéolaire	palatal-rétroflexe
Doke (1936)	ǂkhomani	dental with friction	lateral with friction	alveolar instantaneous	palato-alveolar instantaneous
Ladefoged (1991)	Khoisan/ Zulu	dental laminal affricated	lateral apical affricated	dental-palatal laminal	(postdental) apical
Maddieson (1984)	Nama	dental (lateral)	alveolar (-alveolar)	palatal	alveolar
Maddieson (1984)	Zulu	alveolar	alveolar lateral		-palatal-alveolar
Taljaard and Snyman (1990)	Zulu	apico-lamino-dental	apico-alveopalatal		apico-lamino-palatal

place-of-articulation features it is obvious that there is a lot of quite substantial disagreement.

THE PHONETIC ADEQUACY OF ARTICULATORILY BASED FEATURES

It is conventional to ask of any feature set what natural classes it predicts (or rules out). Sagey's features predict two classes, one based on the feature [anterior] (+ [ǀ, ǂ] vs −[ǁ, ǃ]), the other based on the feature [distributed] (+[ǀ ǂ] vs −[ǁ, ǃ]; Beach's features support a class based on [alveolar] ([ǁ, ǃ]) and less obviously one based on [dental] ([ǀ, ǂ]) (although [ǂ] is labelled dentialveolar) and another based on affricated vs implosive; Ladefoged's features cross-classify [ǀ, ǂ] as laminal and [ǁ, ǃ] as apical, and [ǀ, ǁ] as affricated and [ǂ, ǁ] as not. Maddieson's Nama features cross-classify [ǃ, ǁ]. In all the other proposals there are no explicit natural classes.

The question that now arises is whether Table 8.2 contains the correct description of clicks. Do clicks fall into just these natural classes, or is there something peculiar about their phonetic structure that prevents their features from cross-classifying? It happens that none of the above feature sets is explicitly formulated in order to express phonological generalisations; they are constructed with the sole purpose of expressing lexical contrasts and may therefore attain only some degree of observational adequacy at the articulatory level, although, as we shall see, not at a more general phonetic level because the acoustic properties associated with these clicks are not fully recoverable from any of the feature sets. Indeed, with the exception of the implied noisiness of the affricated releases, clicks are generally acoustically unspecified. This is a serious inadequacy.

There are two sources of evidence that throw light on the linguistic properties of clicks and thus provide a perspective on the features that could be used to classify them. The first is from a vowel assimilation rule in ǃXóõ) (a Southern Bushman language of Botswana), and the second is from the process of click replacement in certain of the Khoe (commonly referred to as Central) languages of Botswana.

In its most simple case the ǃXóõ assimilation affects the non-pharyngealised vowel /a/ when it is immediately preceded by the clicks [ǀ, ǂ] and immediately followed by /i/ (there are a handful of cases that show this effect following the non-click consonants /t, th, s/; however, the argument below is not substantially affected by this). In this environment the low vowel assimilates completely to /i/ so that, for example, /ǀai/ > [ǀiː] or /ǂai/ > [ǂiː]. However, after [ʘ, ǁ, ǃ] the assimilation may only be partial and /a/ may appear as a raised and central version of the vowel, viz. [ɐ]. Some examples of this are provided below.

/ǀa̰i/ > [ǀḭi] 'aardwolf' (Proteles cristatus)
/ǂài/ > [ǂɨi] 'steenbok' (Raphicerus campestris)

but

/ʘá'i/ > [ʘéʼi] 'abomasum' (part of a ruminant's digestive system)
/ʘá'i/ > [ʘéʼi] 'sp. of tree' (Ziziphus mucronata Willd.)
/ǁái/ > [ǁɐ̰i] 'old' (Class. 1)

It seems clear that the configuration of the anterior part of the tongue for [ǀ, ǂ] and [i] must have something in common that is missing from the configuration of the anterior part of the tongue for [ʘ, ǁ, ǃ] and [i]. Do any of the click features provide a natural way of stating these facts? The articulatory features do not in any direct sense: [laminal] and [distributed] cross-classify [ǀ, ǂ] on the one hand and [ǃ, ǁ] on the other. But neither feature is used for vowels (this lack of uniformity also applies to the non-clicks /t, th, s/). Other sets of features cross-classify the clicks incorrectly or do not cross-classify them at all. Nor do Jakobson's acoustic features cross-classify the clicks appropriately. Actually, the acoustic feature [grave] *does* cross-classify the clicks [ǀ, ǂ] vs [ʘ, ǁ, ǃ] and vowels in the appropriate way, since [ǀ, ǂ, i] are [–grave] (i.e. have a high frequency emphasis in the spectrum) and [ʘ, ǁ, ǃ, a] are [+grave] (i.e. have a lower frequency emphasis in the spectrum) (this is true for the non-clicks /t, th, s/ too), but this feature is not used by Jakobson to classify clicks. The most transparent explanation for this rule therefore appears to lie in this acoustic fact rather than in articulatory ones. The latter features are thus linguistically inadequate for the facts considered.

The Khoe dialects provide the second piece of evidence for a linguistically more revealing description of clicks. Certain of these dialects have replaced the [ǃ]-series with pulmonic airstream velars and the [ǂ]-series with pulmonic airstream palatals. Thus [ǃa] > [ka] and [ǂa] > [ca] etc.; the clicks [ǀ, ǁ] are not affected ([ʘ] is not found in these languages). See Traill (1986) for full details. Some examples of this substitution are given below:

ǃ	ǃare	kare	'cut into strips'
	ǃŋaro	ŋaro	'chameleon'
	ǃganee	ganee	'chin'
	ǃhae	khae	'pierce'
ǂ	ǂii	cii	'call'
	ǂŋu	ɲɟuu	'black'
	ǂgoa	ɟua	'ash'
	ǂhuni	chuni	'elbow'

The features in Table 8.2 that cross-classify the clicks that are replaced in these ways are [implosive] vs [affricated] (Beach), [instantaneous] vs [with friction] (Doke), and [–affricated] vs [+affricated] (Ladefoged). The other features either fail to achieve any cross-classification or do so by claimed redundancies (e.g. friction is a redundant feature of clicks for Sagey). However the problem is that with the exception of Ladefoged's feature [dental–palatal laminal], no feature sets cross-classify clicks with the cognate non-clicks to yield any predictions about the consonants that naturally replace clicks, i.e. the [ǃ]-series with [k]-series and [ǂ]-series with [c]-series This is a serious shortcoming of articulatory based classifications. The reason is that clicks are treated as *sui generis* in all the articulatorily based classifications. Any connection between clicks and non-clicks rests on the similarities of affrication (irrelevant for explaining the present

124

problem) and the secondary velar closure of clicks (also irrelevant for the present problem since all clicks have it). Even the acoustic features proposed by Jakobson fail to cross-classify the clicks and non-clicks appropriately. While the feature [continuant] cross-classifies [!] with [ǂ], i.e. those clicks that are replaced, it is irrelevant to the cognation of [ǂ] with [c]. Since [ǂ] is [–compact] in Table 8.1, it will not cross-classify with the [+compact] palatal [c]. Only [!] and [k] are appropriately cross-classified in his features as [+compact –continuant] (both are, of course, [+grave] but not in this classification).

This survey of linguistic processes involving the natural classes of clicks, the cognate non-clicks and the vowel assimilations therefore shows that the facts cannot be stated in a natural way in any of the articulatorily based feature systems available and only partially with Jakobson's acoustically defined features. Thus these features do not achieve descriptive adequacy.

ACOUSTIC FEATURES OF CLICKS

An ongoing acoustic analysis of clicks in !Xóõ (Ladefoged and Traill 1994) suggests the invariant phonetic features in the examples listed above. Average acoustic spectra of single tokens of each click are given as illustration in Figure 8.1. Although there is a great deal of acoustic variability across tokens, Figure 8.1 will give an idea of the basis of the feature specifications in Table 8.3.

The non-click features and their specifications are based on Jakobson, Fant and Halle's ([1958] 1965) definitions. They are used to classify the stops [c] and [k] and the vowels [i, a] following these definitions. The rules of vowel assimilation and click replacement may now be stated naturally:

Vowel assimilation
+grave → –grave / –grave__–grave

  [a]   [i]   [Iǂ]   [i]

Click replacement
+checked → –checked /   __
                      –affricated
                      α grave

  [!]   [k]
  [ǂ]   [c]

Table 8.3 Invariant acoustic features of the clicks [⊙, |, ||, ǂ, !], the non-clicks [c] and [k] and the vowels [i, a]

	⊙			||	ǂ	!	c	k	i	a
Grave	+	−	+	−	+	−	+	−	+
Compact	−	−	+	+	+	+	+	−	+
Affricated	+	+	+	−	−	−	−		
Checked	+	+	+	+	+	+	+		

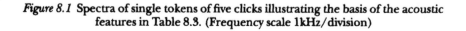

Figure 8.1 Spectra of single tokens of five clicks illustrating the basis of the acoustic features in Table 8.3. (Frequency scale 1kHz/division)

IMPLICATIONS FOR UNIVERSAL PHONETIC FEATURES

The attempt to describe clicks with conventional articulatory categories and the consequent failure to express the click and non-click cognates and consonant and vowel affinities leads directly to the postulation of bizarre consonant systems for the click languages. In Maddieson's (1984) survey of hundreds of phonological systems, the only languages that have two distinct consonant inventories are the Khoisan languages Nama (language no. 913) and !Xū (language no. 918). In each of these languages there is an inventory (a) of non-clicks and (b) of clicks (pp. 418–19 for Nama and pp. 421–2 for !Xū). This disjunction is suspicious in itself: all the other languages surveyed have a single system of consonants, including Zulu, a click-using language, and therefore it is surely an artefact of the exposition that consonants may be divided into sets. But this convention conceals a different problem, namely that the two systems of click and non-click consonants yield inventories with unprecedented kinds of place-of-articulation distinctions. Thus !Xū has the following six places of articulation for stops and clicks:

> bilabial (p) – dental (|) – alveolar (t, ǂ) – palato-alveolar (tʃ) – palatal (!, ‖) – velar (k).

Bearing in mind the acoustic interpretation given above of these articulatory categories, we may reduce them to three places under the alternative interpretation of clicks being offered here:

> bilabial (p) – dentopalatal (|, t, ǂ, tʃ) – velar (!, ‖, k). !Xóõ adds a fourth, viz. uvular (q). ([c] falls into the dentopalatal class in those languages in which it occurs).

The most startling aspect of this grouping from the articulatory perspective is the separation of the coronal sounds [|, ‖, !, ǂ] into one class that is strictly coronal and another that is velar; but, as we have attempted to show, the articulatory features obscure the linguistic patterns.

There is therefore nothing strange about the places of articulation in the Khoisan consonant inventories since the overwhelming majority of languages in Maddieson's sample have three places of articulation. And !Xóõ turns out to have an unremarkable four places of articulation.

CONCLUSION

Of course, this use of acoustic categories remains more or less phonetically opaque from an articulatory point of view; but this merely serves to underline the theme of this paper, that the most adequate account of clicks in !Xóõ and the Khoe languages must be stated in terms of their acoustic

127

properties, whatever the articulatory 'facts' may be. This does not mean one must ignore the unique articulatory and acoustic features that distinguish clicks from non-clicks; rather, it shows that undue emphasis on the differences has obscured some of their linguistically significant similarities as speech sounds.

We conclude therefore that clicks in Khoe and !Xóõ are at present best categorised with acoustic features. The articulatory features surveyed are descriptively inadequate for the task. In the present context it should be mentioned that although the acoustic phonetic descriptions will extend to Zulu or Xhosa clicks, there do not appear to be any phonological generalisations that require such a classification.

ACKNOWLEDGEMENTS

The author gratefully acknowedges a grant from the Institute for Research Development, Pretoria, for the acoustic investigation of clicks. This research benefited from the technical assistance of C. Sandrock of the Department of Linguistics, University of the Witwatersrand, Johannesburg.

REFERENCES

Beach, D. M. (1938) *The Phonetics of the Hottentot Language*, London: Heffer.

Bleek, W. H. I. and Lloyd, L. C. (1911) *Specimens of Bushman Folklore*, London: George Allen & Co., repr. 1968.

Chomsky, N. and Halle, M. (1968) *The Sound Pattern of English*, Cambridge, MA: MIT Press.

Doke, C. M. (1937) 'An outline of ǂkhomani Bushman phonetics', in J. D. Rheinhallt-Jones and C. M. Doke (eds) *Bushman of the Southern Kalahari*, Johannesburg: Witwatersrand University Press.

Jakobson, R. (1968) 'Extra-pulmonic consonants (ejectives, implosives, clicks)', *Quarterly Progress Report*, 90, MIT, Research Laboratory of Electronics.

Jakobson, R., Fant, G. M. and Halle, M. (1958) *Preliminaries to Speech Analysis*, Cambridge, MA: MIT Press, repr. 1965.

Kagaya, R. (1978) 'Sound-spectrographic analysis of Naron clicks – a preliminary report', *Annual Bulletin*, 12, Research Institute of Logopedics and Phoniatrics, University of Tokyo.

Köhler, O. (1981) 'La Langue !Xü', in G. Manessy (ed.) *Les Langues Khoisan*, Paris: Centre de la Recheche Scientifique.

Ladefoged, P. (1989) *Representing phonetic structure, UCLA Working Papers in Phonetics*, 73.

Ladefoged, P. and Traill, A. (1994) 'Clicks and their accompaniments', *Journal of Phonetics*, 22: 33–64.

Maddieson, I. (1984) *Patterns of Sound*, Cambridge: Cambridge University Press.

Sagey, E. (1986) 'The representation of features and relations in non-linear phonology', unpublished Ph.D. dissertation, MIT.

Sands, B. (1989) 'Acoustic characteristics of Xhosa clicks', *Journal of the Acoustic Society of America*, 86(S): S123–4(A).

Snyman, J. W. (1975) *Zhu|hoãsi Fonologie en Woordeboek*, Cape Town: Balkema.

Taljaard, P. C. and Snyman, J. W. (1990) *An Introduction to Zulu Phonetics*, Hout Bay: M. Lubbe.

Traill, A. (1985) *Phonetic and Phonological Studies of !Xóõ*, Hamburg: Helmut Buske.

—— (1986) 'Click replacement in Khoe', *Quellen zur Khoisan Vorschung* 5, 2: 301–20.

9

Postura: clear and dark consonants, etcetera

L. van Buuren
University of Amsterdam

This article attempts to develop and refine the long-standing concepts of clear versus dark, secondary articulation, *Artikulationsbasis* and articulatory setting. The term 'postura' is put forward as a phonetic term for the relevant vowel-type and approximant-type postures of tongue and lips.

A VOCAL EXPERIMENT

In order to get to grips straight away with the subject, I would ask the reader to do a small vocal experiment on 'Little Bo-Peep' (who has lost her sheep, and doesn't know where to find them). First, read out this nursery-rhyme in the transcription given below; then replace, as we have done in the transcription, all its vowels by *one* single vowel, first by (approximately) cardinal [i], then by [y], then by [ɑ], [ɛ], [ɯ], [æ], [ɜ], by [ʊ] as in [ə gʊd wʊmən], and finally by [ɪ] as in [mɪsɪsɪpi]. Especially when doing this *silently*, one becomes highly aware of the tension or *equilibrium* between various muscles of the lips and the tongue, and of the resulting differences in voice quality. Figure 9.1 represents the *forces* exerted on the tongue as a whole as A, B, C and D. In actual fact, A, B and C correspond directly to external 'pulling' muscles, but force D is a more complicated resultant of various pushing and pulling actions. For the present purpose, however, it is easiest to think of the tongue as a puppet suspended between four such 'strings'. The reader must of course be careful to pronounce exactly the same vowel in each syllable.

litl̩l bəʊ piipl̩l ʃi lɒst ə ʃiipl̩l ənd dɪdnnt nəʊ weə tə faɪnd
ðəml̩l liiv ðəm əleʊnl̩l ənd ðeəl kʌm həʊml̩l brɪŋɪŋ ðeə teɪlz
bɪhaɪnd ðəm‖

i	litl̩l bi piipl̩l ʃi list i ʃiipl̩l ind dɪdnnt nii wii ti fiind ðiml̩l liiv
0+12	ðim iliinl̩l ind ðiil kim hiiml̩l briŋiŋ ði tiilz bihiind ðim‖

y 0+12	lytll by pyypǁ ʃy lyst y ʃyypǁ ynd dydnnt nyy wyy ty fyynd ðymǁ lyyv ðym ylyynǁ ynd ðyyl kym hyymǁ bryŋyŋ ðy tyylz byhyynd ðym‖
a 18–12	latll ba paapǁ ʃa last a ʃaapǁ and dadnnt naa waa ta faand ðamǁ laav ðam alaanǁ and ðaal kam haamǁ braŋaŋ ða taalz bahaand ðam‖
ɛ 12+12	lɛtll bɛ pɛɛpǁ ʃɛ lɛst ɛ ʃɛɛpǁ ɛnd dɛdnnt nɛɛ wɛɛ tɛ fɛɛnd ðɛmǁ lɛɛv ðɛm ɛlɛnǁ ɛnd ðɛɛl kɛm hɛɛmǁ brɛŋɛŋ ðɛ tɛɛlz bɛhɛɛnd ðɛm‖
ɯ 0–12	lɯtll bɯ pɯɯpǁ ʃɯ lɯst ɯ ʃɯɯpǁ ɯnd dɯdnnt nɯɯ wɯɯ tɯ fɯɯnd ðɯmǁ lɯɯv ðɯm ɯlɯɯnǁ ɯnd ðɯɯl kɯm hɯɯmǁ brɯŋɯŋ ðɯ tɯɯlz bɯhɯɯnd ðɯm‖
æ 15+12	lætll bæ pææpǁ ʃæ læst æ ʃææpǁ ænd dædnnt nææ wææ tæ fæænd ðæmǁ lææv ðæm ælæænǁ ænd ðææl kæm hæ",æmǁ bræŋæŋ ðæ tæælz bæhæænd ðæm‖
ɜ 12+0	lɜtll bɜ pɜɜpǁ ʃɜ lɜst ɜ ʃɜɜpǁ ɜnd ddnnt nɜɜ wɜɜ tɜ fɜɜnd ðɜmǁ lɜɜv ðɜm ɜlɜɜnǁ ɜnd ðɜɜl kɜm hɜɜmǁ brɜŋɜŋ ðɜ tɜɜlz bɜhɜɜnd ðɜm‖
ʊ 6–9	lʊtll bʊ pʊʊpǁ ʃʊ lʊst ʊ ʃʊʊpǁ ʊnd dʊdnnt nʊʊ wʊʊ tʊ fʊʊnd ðʊmǁ lʊʊv ðʊm ʊlʊʊnǁ ʊnd ðʊʊl kʊm hʊʊmǁ brʊŋʊŋ ðʊ tʊʊlz bʊhʊʊnd ðʊm‖
ɪ 4+8	lɪtll bɪ pɪɪpǁ ʃɪ lɪst ɪ ʃɪɪpǁ ɪnd dɪdnnt nɪɪ wɪɪ tɪ fɪɪnd ðɪmǁ lɪɪv ðɪm ɪlɪɪnǁ ɪnd ðɪɪl kɪm hɪɪmǁ brɪŋɪŋ ðɪ tɪɪlz bɪhɪɪnd ðɪm‖

Apart from distinct changes in the muscular 'settings' for tongue and lips, and the effect thereof on 'voice quality', the reader may have noticed some other interesting things while carrying out the experiment. For instance, using only *one* vowel, it turns out that intelligibility is hardly affected. Indeed, some one-vowel versions sound almost natural, reminding us of certain accents or well-known speakers. In other cases only very slight adjustments to the single vowel (i.e. to the overall setting or equilibrium) will achieve that effect. An *y*-posture reminds one of the (admittedly untypical) Swedish Cook in the *Muppet Show*. An *æ*-posture is characteristic of the speech of Jean Alexander as Hilda Ogden in *Coronation Street*, an *ɯ*-posture of a Liverpool accent, an *ɛ*-posture of John Inman as the effeminate Mr Humphreys in *Are You Being Served?*, an *œ*-posture (approximately 9+12) of Peter Sellers as Inspector Clouseau, an *ʊ*-posture of English spoken with a Dutch or Afrikaans accent, and so on. An RP accent seems to require something of an *ɪ*-posture, say around vowel-placing 6+4.

These associations can be so striking that one feels inclined to actually

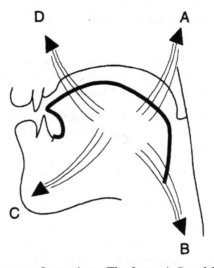

Figure 9.1 Puppet between four strings. The forces A, B and C on the tongue as a whole are exerted by 'pulling' muscles, but D is a combination of various pushing and pulling actions

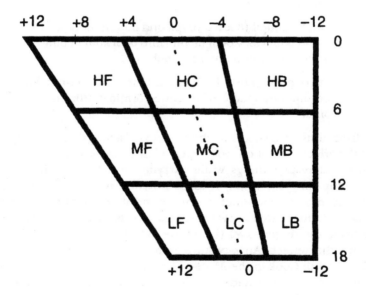

Figure 9.2 CV diagram with numerical grid. Co-ordinates are: 0 to 18 from close to open, +0 to +12 from central to front, –0 to –12 from central to back. Hf, mc, lb stand for high-front, mid-central, low-back, etc.

start talking like Hilda Ogden, Inspector Clouseau or the Swedish Cook, instead of just substituting one single vowel for all the normal ones as required by the experiment. This, of course, is not the idea – we must resist such primitive urges in serious scientific experiment. Even then, one might still feel tempted to change the overall pitch or phonation when alternating, say, between an *a*-posture and an *y*-posture. But this is also to be avoided. The experiment should be kept under control by changing only the vowel *and nothing else.*

It would appear, then, from the experiment that much (or perhaps all) speech 'pivots' around a particular vowel (= tongue-plus-lips) posture, although this is perhaps more obvious if that underlying or 'basic' vowel is on the periphery of the vowel area rather than somewhere in the middle. Indeed, such an assumption also seems to make sense from the point of view of motor-control. It is like saying that a speaker (like a puppeteer) keeps the overall tension or equilibrium between the four 'strings' holding the tongue more or less constant while making continuous small movements, rather than having a wholesale resetting of all the strings at every movement. And it is like saying that one may adopt different basic 'posturas' while making the puppet perform the *same* movements. If this is accepted, one of the first things to do in describing an accent would be to 'plot' its overall 'postura' (i.e. its underlying or 'basic' vowel setting) in a vowel diagram.

Actually, this hypothesis raises a few problems, to be discussed below. However, to put it to the test in a practical way, I would ask the reader to engage in two more phonetic experiments. The first is to read aloud from, say, *Winnie-the-Pooh*, giving different 'voices' to Pooh, Piglet, Owl, Eeyore, etc. When I ask my students of English phonetics to do this, they generally find it possible to say whether the overall postura they use is [ʌ] or [ø] or [ɤ] or whatever. Or, more conveniently perhaps, the reader may wish to say 'Little Bo-Peep' in as many 'funny' voices and accents he/she can muster, again trying to establish the 'basic' or 'underlying' vowel positioning in each case. Our final experiment consists in trying to establish, next time one finds oneself in front of the television, the overall postura of some of the numerous fascinating (and more 'normal') voice qualities one hears, not only in cartoons or commercials, but indeed in any kind of television programme. Again, all one has to do is to try and *say* to oneself the vowel that seems to be 'basic' for a particular speaker or singer and decide whether this contributes to the analysis of that type of pronunciation. I leave it to the reader to make up his/her own mind about it.

L. VAN BUUREN

CLEARNESS AND DARKNESS FOR A FIRST-YEAR
STUDENT OF ENGLISH

As a first-year student of English, in 1956, I learnt from Daniel Jones' *Outline of English Phonetics* that English had a clear and a dark [l] in a word like [leɪbəl]. Clear [l] was said (chapter XX, section 669) to have 'the resonance of a front vowel approaching i' (i.e. roughly [ɪ]?), dark [l] was said to have 'the resonance of a back vowel approaching u'. This was somewhat confusing to a native speaker of Dutch like myself, since Dutch is also known to have a clear and a dark [l] in a word like [leepəl] 'spoon'. It took me several years to realise that Dutch *clear* [l] is about the same as English *dark* [l], that Dutch dark [l] is much darker, and so on. So much for *clear* and *dark* as descriptive terms. Obviously, they are merely differentiating terms meaning no more than *relatively* clear and dark.

Ever since the first (1918) edition of the *Outline*, however, nearly forty years before that, Jones had added (chapter XI, section 235, from the third edition onwards chapter XX, section 665):

> Many varieties of l-sounds may be formed with the tip of the tongue in the lateral position against the teeth-ridge or teeth. These varieties depend on the position of the main part of the tongue and not on the position of the tip; this is a point of extreme importance. While the tip is touching the teeth-ridge or teeth, the main part is free to take up any position, and in particular, it may take up any given vowel position. The l-sound produced with a given vowel position of the main part of the tongue, always has a noticeable resemblance to the vowel in question, and may be said to have the resonance of that vowel. It is not difficult to pronounce a whole series of l-sounds having the resonance of all the principal vowels, i, e, ɑ, ɔ, u, ə, etc. These varieties of l may be represented by the notation lⁱ, lᵉ, lᵃ, lᵖ, lᵘ, lᵖ, etc.

In my view, this is indeed an observation 'of extreme importance', and it was apparently Daniel Jones' own original idea. At least, I have not been able to find any such statement in the works of his predecessors Sievers, Sweet, Storm or Jespersen, all of whom do discuss 'tongue-settings' as an element of the 'basis of articulation'. Note that Jones specifically allows front and/or open vowel positionings. Unfortunately, he does not seem to have made the link with this earlier work. In retrospect, indeed, his 'point of extreme importance' looks like somewhat of a fluke, as it never seems to have occurred to him even to work out its further implications for [l]s, nor for consonants other than [l], and certainly not for the basis of articulation. It seems quite obvious now, for instance, that Jones' 'vowel-positionings' can be similarly combined with virtually all other tip and/or blade consonants, e.g. [n, ɹ, s, ʒ, ð], with *any* labial consonant, and even with velar consonants, such as [x].

Also, by Jones' own argument, the obvious way to describe different degrees of clearness–darkness in [l] would have been to plot the '*vowel position of the main part of the tongue*' in his own Cardinal Vowel diagram, and to state the degree of lip rounding or spreading. Thus, in RP [leibəl] the vowel positioning during the initial lateral may be said to be approximately 6+4 (i.e. 6 down, 4 forward, in terms of the numerical grid shown in Figure 9.2; see also Abercrombie 1967: 61ff.), and during the final lateral about 6–9 (i.e. 6 down, minus 9). The lip posture is weakly spread. In my version of Dutch [leepəl] the vowel positioning during the initial lateral is approximately 8–10 and during the final lateral it is approximately 10–12. The lip posture is weakly rounded in the first and slightly more so in the second. More precisely still, if we classify spreading and rounding between 0 (minimum) and 6 (maximum), the [l]s in [leibəl] may be said to take approximately spreading 1, and those in [leepəl] rounding 2 and rounding 3, respectively.

Of course, positioning 6+4 is another, more precise way, of saying 'weakly palatalised', 6–9 or 8–10 of saying 'somewhat uvularised' and 10–12 of saying 'more pharyngealised'. Jones' description of RP dark [l] as 'having a resonance of a back vowel approaching u', suggests something like positioning 3–9, i.e. 'weak velarisation', plus lip rounding. But a few lines later he advises foreign learners to make dark [l] while trying 'to pronounce the vowel u *without* rounding the lips' (my italics). Moreover, as suggested by Abercrombie (1967), such velarised [l]s are more characteristic of London speech than of RP. All in all, then, Jones' treatment of clear and dark [l] seems positively sloppy. One feels, however, that this was not so much due to bad observation – on the contrary! – or to disagreement about the facts as to an inadequate general phonetic theory.

Having to work out for himself the nature of various clear and dark [l]s caused this first-year student a good deal of unnecessary trouble. But that was only a minor matter. A far bigger problem to him was: if English [l] is clear or dark, what about all the other consonants – are they clear or dark, or what? Thirty-seven years later, foreign students of English still receive no answer to this perfectly obvious and elementary question. Sometimes the customer may wonder what phoneticians are *doing*.

The answer to this question actually seems quite simple. For instance, if we pronounce words like [lɪli] and [lɒli], and then replace the [l]s by other consonants, we keep the same clearness or 'vowel positioning' in words like [hei nɒni nɒni, nɪni, mɪni, mʌni, fɪli, fɒli, sæli, sɪsi, bɪli, kɪlʊŋ], etc. But we observe various degrees of darkness around [ʃ, w, r] in [fɪʃi] vs [fɪli], in [wɪli] vs [lɪli], in [rɪəli] vs [lɪli], and in [lɒri] vs [lɒli]. Cf also *oh, I'm so* [ɡlllæd] with clearness in the [l], and: *oh, that's* [ɡrrreɪt], with darkness in the [r], etc.

In short, in (our version of) English *all consonants are clear* (6+4 postura

= weakly palatalised), exactly like clear [l]. *Except*: dark [l] takes uvularisation (approx. 6–9); [ʃ/ʒ] take mid-velarisation (approx. 3–9) and rounding 3; [w] takes mid-velarisation (approx. 3–9) and rounding 6; [r] takes prevelarisation (approx. 2–2), rounding 3 and (in my speech) labiodentalisation. One would think that a student of English pronunciation may reasonably expect this sort of information for his money.

SOME OTHER VIEWS ON TONGUE AND LIP POSTURAS

For instance, the English as it were push forward the whole of their pronunciation into the front of the mouth, speaking with a wide mouth cavity, so that their sounds are more distinct. The Germans [Germani = the Dutch, presumably], on the other hand, retract their pronunciation to the back of the mouth and the bottom of the throat.

(Wallis 1653: 209; translation Kemp)

If, as a native of Hessen, I try to speak a typically Northern German dialect like that of Holstein, then once and for all the tongue must be slightly retracted and broadened; having found the correct position, the 'Operationsbasis' so to speak, and knowing how to hold on to it during the alternation of different sounds, the sound-nuances characteristic of the dialect will follow by themselves. If I add to this 'Articulationsweise' the tendency of the tongue to cerebral articulation combined with a passive lip-posture, then I arrive without any effort at the basis for the pronunciation of English.

(Sievers 1876: 47; my translation)

It is possible to maintain, the whole time one is talking, a posture of the vocal organs that is in effect a secondary articulation, but one which is continually present instead of being confined to the duration of a segment or two. ... For example, the lips may be held in a slightly rounded position, giving a continuous over-all labialized quality to the resulting speech; or there may be palatalization, or velarization, or pharyngalization running all through it. Each one of these maintained secondary articulations gives an auditory effect which is difficult to put into words, but which is immediately recognized as familiar when demonstrated.

(Abercrombie 1967: 93)

For any dialect, the organs of the vocal tract have certain preferred positions, which may differ from those they have in the physiological state of rest. The movements away from and back into the preferred positions give a variety of speech its characteristic 'colour'. The preferred shape of the vocal tract is known as the articulatory setting.... In Scouse [Liverpool speech], the centre of gravity of the tongue is brought backwards and upwards ... The setting of the tongue effectively velarizes all consonants. This is most noticeable in voiceless apical consonants like /t, s, θ/, but certainly affects the quality of others, including /m, v, dʒ/.... Vowels – other than back ones – are incompatible with the setting, at least as vowel production is usually understood.... Corresponding vowels in Scouse and RP are recognizably similar in quality, but whether they are produced with anything like the same tongue shapes is an open question.

(Knowles 1978: 6)

Various constrictive settings result from the following radial move-ments of the location of the centre of mass of the tongue: upward towards the hard palate, and slightly forwards, to give a voice 'with palatalization', ... forwards and upwards for 'palato-alveolarization', ... forwards and slightly upwards for 'alveolarization', ...forwards for 'dentalization', ... backwards and upwards for 'velarization', ...back-wards and slightly upwards for 'uvularization', ... backwards for 'pharyngalization'.... Settings where the centre of mass of the tongue moves downward, or downward and forward, as a continual tendency, seem rare.

(Laver 1980: 46ff.)

All these authors seem to be saying that different 'vowel positionings' may be maintained through all the consonants (and through the vowels as well?), as Daniel Jones stated specifically for [l]. But none of them actually makes the connection with *vowels* or vowel places, as Jones did. Present thinking is rather in terms of consonant places, as indicated by the terminology: palatalisation, velarisation, uvularisation, etc.

The term 'secondary articulation', by the way, is particularly unfortunate in this context, since everyone seems to agree that the (long-term) settings are primary, coming before everything else. Terms like *Operationsbasis* 'basis of articulation', 'voice quality', 'articulatory setting', on the other hand, rule out *short-term* tongue-body settings as in English [l, ʃ, w, r]. We need a term to sort out this confusion, neutral between longer and shorter durations of such 'positionings' and between value judgements such as primary and secondary. As a student of Abercrombie's, in the early 1960s, I took over his term 'posture'. Later, I felt this needed a more precise definition and would be better internationalised to *postura*.

Laver is the only one who actually mentions the possibility of downward or forward tongue-settings, i.e. open and/or front vowel positionings such as [ɛ, a, ɜ]. This is probably no coincidence considering that he also studied under Abercrombie. But he then retreats from the obvious conclusions with the argument that such tongue settings seem rare.

137

The reader may wonder why I have not referred, so far, to Honikman's famous 1964 article 'Articulatory settings'. Undoubtedly, this is still the most detailed treatment of long-term settings of the tongue, lips and jaw, notably in English and French. At the time of its appearance, it also had the enormous merit of demonstrating, most convincingly, the crucial importance of long-term features, previously ignored or considered 'redundant', thereby helping to liberate linguists and teachers from the stranglehold of phoneme-based, segmental phonetics. It is deservedly regarded as a classic of the phonetic literature.

The main reason I had not mentioned it so far is that it actually says very little about 'tongue-body setting' or 'vowel positioning'. Rather, it is largely concerned with the 'lateral anchoring' of the anterior part of the tongue (the blade-front area) near the canines and premolars, 'determined, to a great extent, by the most frequently occurring sounds and sound combinations in that language'. From her description one *gathers* that, in English, the overall tongue setting is as for [ɪ], but it is not really stated what the tongue body is supposed to be doing. Since there is no mention of the difference between clear and dark consonants one *could* conclude that they are all clear, or dark, or whatever. Admittedly, Honikman's purpose was mainly to describe her own experiences as a teacher of French and English pronunciation, without any theoretical pretensions. But nevertheless, it seems a pity that she made no attempt to relate her observations to those of Daniel Jones discussed above, nor, for that matter, to the earlier literature on the 'basis of articulation'. This makes her otherwise admirable article somewhat idiosyncratic and difficult to integrate into the mainstream of phonetic thinking.

It seems a reasonable idea to reserve one term (say *postura*) for positionings associated with consonant and vowel places. Apart from vowel positionings, this could include any consonantal (approximant) positioning, such as labiodentalisation, blade-alveolarisation, uvularisation, etc. Lip-spreading and rounding, having comparable auditory effects and linguistic functions, should also be included. These are all familiar as 'secondary articulations' (a term, as suggested, that is better replaced by something less prejudicial). 'Nasalisation', usually lumped together with these 'secondary articulations' obviously does not belong here. The term 'labialisation', is perhaps better avoided as well: on the analogy of the other terms it should merely mean labial approximation, but it tends to be used quite carelessly to imply anything to do with *rounding* and/or *protrusion*.

The major tongue and lip actions would thus be accounted for under the parameters *manner*, (consonant and vowel) *placing* and *postura*. This leaves a number of smaller, more subtle tongue actions like pointing, spreading, hollowing, tensing, etc., and lip actions like drooping corners or raising/lowering, protrusion/retraction of either or both lips. All these are probably better kept apart under *tongue shape* and *lip shape*. Finally, one should consider *jaw movement*. In an article on Mrs Thatcher's pronunciation (Van Buuren 1988) I have described such features in some detail, demonstrating, I think, that they are clearly audible (in the long run, at least), and a crucial part of voice quality. This is exactly what Honikman was also saying. Indeed, we are now in a position to conclude that her article is largely about the importance of tongue shape, lip shape and jaw movement. The only posturas she deals with are lip rounding and alveolarisation/ dentalisation.

SOME PROBLEMS WITH THE HYPOTHESIS

My hypothesis then, already put forward in the first section, is that speakers maintain a certain constant equilibrium in the tongue body and lip muscles, which is best described as a vowel 'positioning' and indeed should be described before any other tongue and lip activity. At least three questions arise. (1) Is this, then, the vowel we hear during hesitations and/ or 'neutral' vowels? (2) Is this 'permanent' postura not *interrupted* during other posturas? (3) Must it not be *interrupted* during vowels, or at least during vowel positions well away from the postural positioning? The answer to all three questions, I would suggest, is a qualified 'No'.

Hesitation noises, neutral vowels

An investigation of these (which I have not undertaken) may well provide strong counter-arguments against the hypothesis; but it would have to refute arguments like the following. Hesitation noises vary, and some are not even vowels, e.g. [mm]. Some hesitation vowels, like the very open [ɜ] of RP, appear to be institutionalised, rather than 'natural' consequences of a neutral setting. The same applies to 'neutral' vowels, witness the different [ə]s in [təgeðə]. Although such noises often do seem to correspond to the basic setting (e.g. in Scots, Liverpudlian or French) there appears to be no necessary connection.

Other posturas: interruption or overlay

Going back for a moment to

1 lɪtl̩ bɪ pɪɪpll ʃɪ lɪst ɪ ʃɪɪpll ɪnd dɪdnnt nɪɪ w̱ɪɪ tɪ fɪɪnd ðɪmll lɪɪv ðɪm ɪlɪɪnll ɪnd ðɪɪḻ kɪm hɪɪmll bṟɪŋɪŋ ðɪ tɪɪḻz bɪhɪɪnd ðɪmH

etc., we decided to replace only the vowels, and nothing else. The various degrees of velarisation/uvularisation and lip rounding around the underlined consonants were therefore meant to be kept intact. The reader may now try to replace all these 'darknesses' as well, in this case with an ɪ-postura. When comparing the 'clearness only' and 'darknesses preserved' versions, the overall (clearness) tension in tongue and lip muscles feels the same. This suggests that in the latter case the clearness is *overlaid* by darknesses, not *replaced* by them. In other words, an extra tug on string A (see Figure 9.1) seems to be simply *added* to the constant tension in strings A, B, C and D rather than changing/replacing the whole configuration. Which would also be much more work, of course, so apart from *feeling* that the basic postura is maintained, it also seems more logical.

In Russian, every syllable may be said to begin and end with a *y*-prosody (palatalisation) or a *w*-prosody (velarisation), e.g. /ʸpatʸ/ 'five', /ʷspatʸ/ 'to sleep', /ʸradʷ/ 'row', /ʷsadʷ/ 'garden'. This seems to imply that palatalisation and velarisation alternate constantly in Russian. If it could be shown that this is indeed the case, it would of course destroy our hypothesis that Russians (like everybody else) speak with a single constant tongue setting, and any such evidence would therefore be most relevant. However, there is also another possibility. Recently, I was listening to the Russian politician Yegor Gaidar being interviewed in English. As with most Russians, his English sounded to me positively velarised (approx. 3–10) throughout, rather like that of Liverpudlians. So, for that matter, did his Russian. Again, this would suggest overlaying rather than replacement of one postura by another. In other words, tugging on string D, required for palatalisation, did not seem to involve relaxation of the relatively strong tension in string A, required for velarisation, or that in strings B and C. In this view, then, Russian is velarised *throughout*, with occasional *overlays* of palatalisation.

Cairo Arabic, too, might provide ammunition against the hypothesis here presented. Words like /ʸtiːn/ 'figs', /ʸmaːt/ 'he died', /ʸlaf/ 'to stroll', /ʸbenti/ 'my daughter', /ʸwaziːr/ 'minister', have a *y*-prosody, i.e. palatalisation throughout, words like /ʷtiːn/ 'soil', /ʷsaːd/ 'to hunt', /ʷtab/ 'to fall', /ʷhotti/ 'put down (imp. fem)', /ʷsamuːla/'screw', have a *w*-prosody, being said with 'pharyngealisation' (i.e. approx. postura 12–12 plus pharyngeal constriction). Again, the question is whether Cairo speakers alternate constantly between these two posturas, whether one of the two is basic or constant, with the other one superimposed on it, or whether perhaps both are superimposed alternately on a third postura, i.e. a constant one overlooked so far. My observations suggest that Cairo speakers 'pharyngealise' throughout and that palatalisation is superimposed during *y*-words only, but I shall happily be proved wrong by experts on Arabic pronunciation.

A third language that might help to falsify the hypothesis here put forward is English as spoken in Shetland. Working there for the Scottish Dialect Survey many years ago, I found minimal pairs like /ʸpen/ 'pane', /ʸtel/ 'tale', palatalised throughout, versus /ʷpen/ 'pain', /ʷtel/ 'tail', velarised throughout. To me it seemed that the dialect was palatalised throughout, with overlays of velarisation only during *w*-words.

Clear and dark vowels?

Knowles (1978) wonders whether recognisably similar vowels in Scouse and RP are produced 'with anything like the same tongue-shapes'. Having said that Scouse is velarised throughout and the tongue setting of RP is quite different (say, weakly palatalised), the implication is that the 'same' vowel may be either velarised or palatalised, etc., i.e. dark or clear. A heretical thought indeed, not to be lightly uttered. Before we burn Knowles at the stake, however, let us first think back to our experiment with 'Little Bo-Peep'.

While replacing all the vowels by a single vowel, [æ], [ɯ] or [y], we felt a strong temptation to actually start talking like Hilda Ogden, Harold Wilson or the Swedish Cook. In order to do this, the major adjustment one has to make is to aim at all one's 'normal' vowel placings, while *hanging on* to the *æ*, *ɯ* or *y*-postura, respectively. Perhaps this is the moment to go back to the exercise and try out all the posturas with one's *normal* vowel placings.

Our experiments seem to show that it is indeed perfectly possible to pronounce the same (sets of) vowels with quite different posturas. And why not? Surely, one can make the same gestures from different basic positions. Auditorily, such 'recognisably similar vowels' may in fact be quite different, of course, but articulatorily they are indeed the same, at least if we think of articulation as gestures at targets rather than as the targets themselves. When one thinks of it, such vowel placings are indeed no different from the short-term posturas combining with long-term posturas discussed in the previous paragraph, only more varied, more frequent and perhaps a little faster. So perhaps one may conclude that any postura may be *overlaid* by the complete range of vowels, and that Knowles should be reprieved for the time being.

One reason why this idea appears so heretical is its implications for vowel theory, more precisely for Daniel Jones' Cardinal Vowel system. Phoneticians, including Daniel Jones himself, have never quite been able to make up their minds whether the Cardinal Vowels (or any other vowels, for that matter) are first of all sounds or articulatory positions. We are now suggesting that they are neither, but merely *gestures* at these articulatory positions. It would follow that the set of Cardinal Vowels can be said with different posturas, and will sound different each time. If some readers find this an outrageous idea, it may perhaps be pointed out that nobody minds very much whether we say the Cardinal Vowels on a different pitch than the note F natural, with voice, creaky voice, breathy voice or even creak or whisper, sounding quite different each time, and that certainly no-one will object to the Cardinal Vowels being said by a woman. In this view, then, the Cardinal Vowel system is quite an abstract concept, with Jones' CV recording no longer to be regarded as *the* set of Cardinal Vowels, but only as an exemplification of it, with a particular pitch, phonation-type, degree of nasality, jaw setting and tongue/lip postura, in a male voice.

Tense and lax posturas

One final problem we run into, although not such a crucial one, may be mentioned briefly.

When saying 'Little Bo Peep', for instance with an ɯ-postura, the gestures towards the vowel targets may be comparatively large or small. Much depends on the stiffness or tenseness of the muscular configuration, and again I may mention jaw setting as a comparable case. If the tension in the strings A, B, C and D is great, naturally the effect will be that the tongue body is virtually immobilised, so that a tug on string C, for instance, will have little or no effect on the position of the tongue. On the other hand, if the tension is minimal, the same tug on string C (i.e. the same vowel gesture or placing) will displace the tongue far further down and forward. Normally, perhaps, we speak in a fairly relaxed way, but as every actor knows, some speaking styles, like angry or very precise speech, require great muscular tension. Therefore, it seems appropriate, when stating a speaker's overall postura, also to state its degree of tenseness, say between 0 (minimal) and 6 (maximal).

REFERENCES

Abercrombie, D. (1967) *Elements of General Phonetics*, Edinburgh: Edinburgh University Press.

Buuren, L. Van. (1988) 'Margaret Thatcher's pronunciation: an exercise in ear-training', *Journal of the International Phonetic Association*, 18, 1: 26–38.

Honikman, B. (1964) 'Articulatory settings', in D. Abercrombie, D. B. Fry, P. A. D. MacCarthy, N. C. Scott and J. L. M. Trim (eds), *In Honour of Daniel Jones*, London: Longman.

Jones, D. (1918) *(Outline of) English Phonetics*, Leipzig and Berlin: Teubner; 3rd and later edns Cambridge: Heffer.

Knowles, G. (1978) 'The nature of phonological variables in Scouse', in P. Trudgill (ed.), *Sociolinguistic Patterns in British English*, London: Edward Arnold, pp. 80–90.

Laver, J. (1980) *The Phonetic Description of Voice Quality*, Cambridge: Cambridge University Press.

Sievers, E. (1876) *Grundzüge der Lautphysiologie*, Leipzig: Breitkopf & Härtel.

Wallis, J. (1653) *Grammatica linguae anglicanae*, ed. J. A. Kemp, 1972, London: Longman.

Part II

PITCH, INTONATION AND RHYTHM

10

Spelling aloud: a preliminary study of idiomatic intonation

Patricia D. S. Ashby, University of Westminster
Michael G. Ashby, University College, London

INTRODUCTION

The description of English rhythm and intonation must obviously be concerned with 'connected speech' (this being in contrast, presumably, with single words spoken in isolation); but a particular conception of what constitutes connected speech – speaking in complete and grammatical sentences, and most typically in a dialogue – has dominated most descriptions. As a result, there is a large class of examples of English expressions whose rhythm and intonation are largely undescribed; examples are prices, telephone numbers, exchange rates, credit-card numbers, addresses, postcodes, flight numbers, times. Many of these have their own characteristic rhythmic and intonational treatments, which are important to the listener in processing the information conveyed. In this paper we describe a study of one such neglected 'connected speech' activity, that of spelling aloud. Seven subjects were recorded spelling aloud fifty-six words varying in length from four to fourteen letters. The recordings were analysed auditorily to identify word-group boundaries. Though there were differences between speakers in the way in which words were split into groups, there was also remarkable uniformity in the general pattern and in average length of groups. On the basis of these findings, we are able to propose an algorithm which generates an acceptable phrasing. The algorithm shows that a realistic word-group division (including idiomatic handling of the use of 'double' for double letters) can be produced by a mechanism which works from left to right looking at the word to be spelled through a window just three letters wide.

TYPES OF CONNECTED SPEECH

For many years, practice material for intonation has been almost exclusively 'conversational', where this has been interpreted to mean short, chatty exchanges and rapid alternation of turns. The drills in O'Connor and Arnold (1973: 106) start in typical fashion:

Can you come tomorrow?
Yes.

Exactly the same style is found in the most recently published intonation practice book (Bradford 1988). As soon as two tones have been introduced, the practice begins like this (p. 18):

LISA Hello Tony. Did you go for your interview yesterday?
TONY Hi Lisa. Yes, I did.

(The accompanying cartoon shows the participants standing in a rather bored-looking bus queue.) Though relaxed chat is certainly one of the uses of speech, there are other uses, equally 'colloquial', in which considerable quantities of important information are exchanged: for instance, speakers are often called upon to identify themselves, make transactions, arrange appointments, and so on. The expressions involved (addresses, numbers, times, etc.) have not generally been systematically described; perhaps they have somehow fallen between the grammar book and the dictionary. Kingdon (1958) includes a short section (pp. 187–9) on the stressing of initials and numerals, while J. Windsor Lewis introduced tonetic stress marks in various numerical expressions as part of his reorganisation of the treatment of pronunciation in the third edition of the *Oxford Advanced Learner's Dictionary*; an appendix on 'Numerical expressions' appears as pages 1522–8 of the current (4th) edition.

Though it would be too much to claim that there are specific rules of grammar for each of these types of expression, there are clearly widely agreed conventions and idioms which include the use of characteristic rhythm and intonation. Consider the example of London bus numbers (similar patterns are probably found worldwide). Numbers up to and including 100 are spoken in full: the bus number 73, for example is spoken as *seventy-three*; but numbers over 100 are spoken as digit strings; a 121 is always *one two one*; the string of digits is spoken as a single word group, with a head accent on the first item and nucleus on the last. The learner of English who does not know these conventions is almost as likely to be misunderstood as one who cannot pronounce the English names of the digits intelligibly.

The expressions we are directing attention to – and they are a type increasingly spoken to us by machines as well as human talkers – typically contain a large amount of information, and a very small degree of redundancy (for instance, no digit in a telephone number is entirely predictable). Generally there is little or no choice about rhythm or intonation in speaking expressions of this type; to that extent, the intonation may be termed 'idiomatic'. The role of rhythm and intonation is not directly meaningful in the sense of clarifying otherwise ambiguous expressions; but the listener relies upon familiar rhythm and intonation patterns to indicate the packaging of information and ease the processing burden. For instance if a ten-digit London telephone number such as 071–387 7050 is spoken with anything other than the expected pattern, the listener may find great difficulty in remembering it even long enough to note it down, and is much less likely than usual to notice an error such as omission or addition of a digit.

SPELLING ALOUD

This paper is concerned specifically with the skill of spelling aloud-naming in sequence the letters which spell out one's name, for example. It is a skill which learners of English will often be called upon to exercise, though it is surprising how many relatively advanced learners hesitate even over the English names of letters of the alphabet. Spelling aloud is also the last recourse of the speech synthesis system whose text-to-speech rules cannot cope with an unknown word or name, or when a user requests clarification of an unintelligible word or phrase. Under these circumstances, it is clearly important that the spelling aloud itself should be carried out in a way that eases the listener's task.

When spelling aloud has been treated at all in EFL texts, it has been as an example of listing, each letter being given a separate word group. Thus an earlier work of one of the authors (Sheldon 1978: 141) contains the exchange:

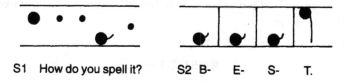

S1   How do you spell it?   S2   B-   E-   S-   T.

It seems clear, though, that most examples of spelling aloud (certainly by adults) are not simply sequences of letter names spoken with listing intonation. This treatment would imply as many word groups (in the sense of O'Connor and Arnold 1973: 2–4) as letters in the word. Our intuitions were that for words up to a certain length (perhaps four or five letters) the letter names would probably be spoken as a single word group with nuclear accent on the last letter name. It seemed likely to us that longer words (six letters or more) would be chunked into word groups, either on the basis of the number of letters, or possibly according to syllable or morpheme structure.

RECORDINGS

An experiment was designed specifically to investigate chunking (division into word groups) as a function of word length. A list of fifty-six words was prepared, covering lengths from four to fourteen letters; the words were all related to the educational context: *polytechnic, student, book, dissertation*, etc. There were six examples each of lengths 4 and 5, seven examples for lengths 6–10, and smaller numbers for lengths 11–14. The words were typed singly onto cards and randomised by shuffling.

Seven subjects – all of them polytechnic lecturers – were recorded. The experimenter held the cards, and read each word aloud in turn. The subject repeated the word once, and then spelled it aloud. The subject could not read from the card, so the task of spelling aloud included recalling the spelling and monitoring one's output. The subjects were not discouraged from believing that the experimenter's interest was primarily in the spelling itself.

ANALYSIS

The recordings, consisting of sequences of letter names (together with the item *double*, which was employed by six of the seven speakers) were analysed auditorily to identify word-group boundaries. The criteria were those implicit in the O'Connor and Arnold description of English intonation: real pause, apparent pause (cued by stretching of group-final syllable), and completion of a tune (cued by identification of one of the nuclear tones). Word groups were classified according to length, expressed as the number of letters they include.

RESULTS

Figure 10.1 shows the number of occurrences of groups of different lengths. Leaving aside a very few long examples, groups spanned a range of one to five letters, with only groups of two, three and four letters being at all common. The distribution shows a clear peak, with two being the favoured length.

Division into groups did not, however, affect words of different lengths equally. Figure 10.2 shows the average number of groups as a function of word length. From this it is apparent that words of four letters are hardly ever divided, while those of five letters almost always are. There is thus a threshold word length of about five letters which must be passed before chunking begins. Once word length exceeds five letters, the number of groups is a function of the length of the word.

Figure 10.3 shows there is no systematic relationship between average length of group and word length: the size of the group remains remarkably

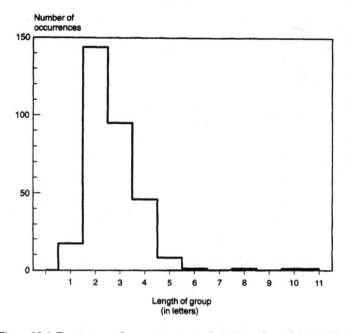

Figure 10.1 Frequency of occurrence as a function of word-group length

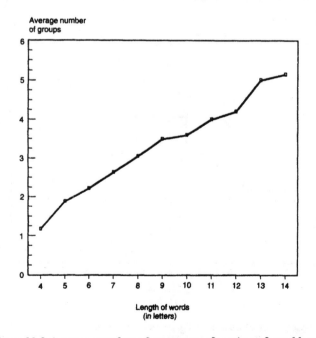

Figure 10.2 Average number of groups as a function of word length

149

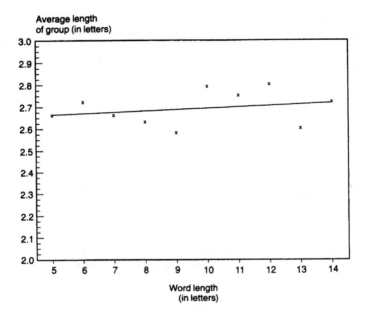

Figure 10.3 Average length of group as a function of word length

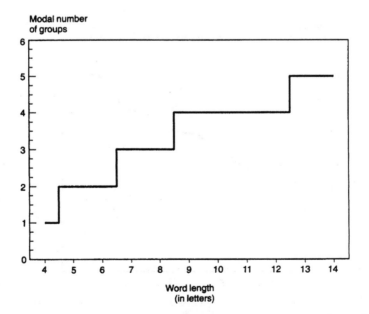

Figure 10.4 Most frequent number of groups into which words of different lengths are divided

constant around an average 2.7 letters, regardless of the length of the word. There is thus no tendency to use longer groups in longer words, for instance.

The manner in which the number of groups varies with increasing word length is displayed very clearly in Figure 10.4, which shows the modal number of groups as a function of word length.

THE ROLE OF RHYTHM

It seems very probable to us that the need to impose acceptable English rhythm upon what is spelled aloud is a factor controlling the length of spoken groups; a group of three letter names, for instance, resembles three-letter abbreviations of the type *BBC, CIA*, which are generally stressed on the first and last syllables (see Kingdon 1958: 187). The first-and-last rule applies also to four components (*RSVP, LRAM*) and it is noteworthy that relatively few groups with more than four elements were found in our data. On the whole, then, our subjects spelled aloud in such a way as to produce groups which require two stresses, first and last.

SOME ASPECTS OF A PERFORMANCE MODEL

It is unlikely that the planning of the rhythm and intonation of spelling a word aloud can involve a complete preview of what is to be spoken, especially in the case of a longer word. Speakers are much more likely to work from left to right, producing acceptable rhythm and intonation even though at no time is the whole utterance available for planning. On the other hand, speakers clearly do not proceed on a letter-by-letter basis; at least two considerations point to at least a limited amount of look-ahead:

The use of *double* for adjacent identical letters shows that speakers must look ahead by at least one letter; if this were not so, the first of two identical letters would be named aloud before it was realised that a second identical letter was to follow.

Speakers do not produce groupings such that single letters, or even pairs of letters are left to be completed at the end; on the contrary, the final group which completes the word is more likely to be somewhat longer, perhaps of four letters. This suggests a limited (perhaps two- to three-item) look-ahead mechanism enabling the end of the word to be detected.

ALGORITHM

Shown below is an algorithm for inserting tone-group boundaries in spelling aloud. This has been derived empirically to match many of the

151

patterns followed by the subjects, and turns out to give realistic results. The parameters X and Y are integers which determine the precise behaviour of the algorithm; the discussion below assumes that X = 3 and Y = 2.

> begin
>> do this until all letters have been output
>>> if (1) = (2), output 'double (2)' and move the window 2 steps; otherwise output (1) and move the window 1 step;
>>>
>>> if the number of letters output so far in the current word group is equal to or greater than X and the number of letters left is equal to or greater than Y, output a non-final word-group boundary;
>>>
>>> output a final word-group boundary;
>> end.

The word to be spelled is scanned in a single left-to-right pass with a window three letters wide; the three positions are referred to as (1), (2), (3). At the start of the algorithm, the window is at the beginning of the word; the first letter of the word occupies (1). The algorithm has very restricted power; it can

advance the window one step at a time, so that (2) replaces (1), (3) replaces (2), and a fresh letter (or blank if the end of the word is encountered) enters position 3;

determine whether letter (1) and letter (2) are identical, and distinguish a letter from a blank;

replace the letter in position (1) with the word 'double'.

Letters (and the word 'double') are spoken aloud as they leave the window to the left. When a word-group boundary is output, it is placed to the immediate left of the window.

EXAMPLES OF OUTPUT

Examples of output from the algorithm are given below.

applicant	→	A double P l L I C l A N T l
assessment	→	A double S l E double S l M E N T l
school	→	S C H l double O L l
syllabus	→	S Y double L l I A B U S l

The word groups which are generated are suitable for first-and-last stress treatment in every case.

As an illustration of the operation of the algorithm, we give below the contents of the window at each stage during the scanning of the word *applicant*, with the output which is determined at each step shown to the left.

Output		Window	
		APP	
A		PPL	
		dPL	(d = double)
double P ǀ		LIC	
	L	ICA	
	I	CAN	
	C ǀ	ANT	
	A	NT	
	N	T	
	T ǀ		

HUMAN AND COMPUTATIONAL IMPLEMENTATION

Our algorithm would make a useful addition to speech synthesis-by-rule systems. Obviously, an equivalent output could be obtained computationally in a somewhat more efficient fashion; for instance, there is no need for the search for doubles to be within the procedure effecting word-group division; instances of *double* could be inserted very simply in a separate pass through the word. But we have attempted to formulate the algorithm in human terms, and memory limitations make it highly improbable that a human speaker could operate with two passes. The task of unprepared reading aloud is another in which the performer may be thought of as scanning material through a window which is just a few items wide; reasonably acceptable rhythm and intonation can nevertheless be produced under these circumstances. In view of their potential value to the learner of English, it seems to us that there may be some general advantages in seeking accounts of rhythm and intonation which are compatible with highly restricted models of performance.

APPENDIX: LIST OF WORDS EMPLOYED

4 letters	5 letters
unit	class
form	essay
test	paper
dean	group
exam	enrol
book	tutor

6 letters

school
thesis
theses
relief
folder
cohort
degree

7 letters

courses
diploma
contact
lecture
entrant
seminar
library

8 letters

syllabus
register
registry
computer
academic
tutorial
lecturer

9 letters

committee
executive
timetable
interview
registrar
applicant
education

10 letters

university
department
assessment
blackboard
evaluation
sabbatical
monitoring

11 letters

polytechnic
directorate
examination

12 or more letters

departmental
dissertation
registration
documentation
administrative
administration

REFERENCES

Bradford, B. (1988) *Intonation in Context*, Cambridge: Cambridge University Press.
Kingdon, R. (1958) *The Groundwork of English Stress*, London: Longman, Green.
O'Connor, J. D. and Arnold, G. F. (1973) *Intonation of Colloquial English*, London: Longman.
Oxford Advanced Learner's Dictionary of Current English (4th edn, 1989), Oxford: Oxford University Press.
Sheldon, P. D. S. (1978) 'Reference appendix on intonation', in L. G. Alexander (ed.), *Mainline Beginners A*, London: Longman.

11

Rises in English

Alan Cruttenden
University of Manchester

INTRODUCTION

O'Connor and Arnold (1961, 1973) was the culmination at the same time both of that type of intonational analysis conveniently called nuclear tone analysis and of the description of the attitudinal meanings associated with nuclear tones and their preceding 'heads' in Received Pronunciation (RP). Pike (1945), on the other hand, is a detailed analysis of General American (GA) intonation (indeed it is the only thorough analysis of GA), written in terms of four pitch levels, and associating meanings with primary pitch contours beginning on a stressed syllable and consisting of a sequence of pitch levels. Yet the overall impression conveyed by the two analyses is that in some sense we are dealing with the same system, particularly as regards the meanings associated with tunes. For example, Pike (p. 45) says that contours falling to pitch level 4 tend to have the meaning of finality and that possibly the most frequent for the majority of English speakers is the one beginning at pitch level 2 – the contour °2–4; similarly O'Connor and Arnold (1973: 53, 73) describe patterns using the High Fall as involving definiteness and completeness. Both imply that the unmarked pattern for declaratives is a fall (beginning on the last accented syllable) — the term 'unmarked' is employed more formally for this tone by Halliday (1968). Yet there are a number of reports that suggest a greater use of rises in a number of English dialects and hence also suggest a system very different from either RP or GA. Cruttenden (1986) attempted to survey in five and a half pages the extent and type of rises in such dialects. This to my knowledge was the first attempt at an overview of intonational variation in English. The intention of this article is to expand on those few pages by looking in detail at those dialects which use more rises than RP or GA. The assumption will be that those dialects of English which I do not mention will roughly follow RP and GA in their distribution of falls and rises; sometimes this has actually been confirmed by report, e.g. Burgess (1973) on Australian English, Haldenby (1959) on Lincolnshire and Bilton (1982) on Hull.

I make very little attempt to deal with stylistic and sociolinguistic variation

ALAN CRUTTENDEN

between English dialects, basically because descriptions of stylistic and sociolinguistic intonational usage within dialects are themselves limited. Reports on stylistic usage in English intonation are almost totally limited to RP (e.g. Crystal and Davy 1969) and reports on sociolinguistic usage are limited to Tyneside (Pellowe and Jones 1978) and to Australia and New Zealand (McGregor 1980; Horvath 1985; Guy *et al.* 1986; Britain 1992). Basic assumptions made in this article regarding such variation are that any regional intonational habits will of course show up most prominently in the basilect of the area (but this is called into doubt in the discussion of the Pacific Rim in the later part of this article) and in what can loosely be called the conversational narrative style, i.e. that sort of style where a speaker is telling a story or recounting an experience even though this may be subjected to frequent interruptions by a listener. In the final section of this article, it will become clear that stylistic or sociolinguistic (in particular, dialect mixing) factors may actually be fundamental in interpreting the theoretical import of those dialects with a greater use of rises.

There are two broad areas where wider use of rises has been reported: northern British cities (in particular, Belfast, Derry, Glasgow, Newcastle, Liverpool and Birmingham), henceforth urban north British (UNB) and the Pacific Rim (henceforth PR) – in particular Australia and New Zealand (where it has been referred to as use of high rise tone or HRT), California and Canada. In the following sections I review the evidence from these two areas, and attempt to show that rise use within each area is homogeneous. I then discuss two possible explanatory hypotheses for more extended rise use and suggest that one hypothesis is more relevant to UNB and one to PR.

URBAN NORTH BRITISH (UNB)

In this section I review the evidence on those cities in the north of Great Britain which have been reported as having more use of rising tunes than RP. For some cities there is fairly detailed and reliable evidence; in other cases there is little more than a preliminary report.

Belfast and Derry

The intonation of Belfast was described briefly in Jarman and Cruttenden (1976); Derry was more fully described in McElholm (1986), using both auditory and instrumental data. The same framework (based on Halliday 1968) was used on both occasions and McElholm related his findings systematically to the earlier work by Jarman and Cruttenden. What I present here is therefore a composite of the two articles. Basically three tones predominate in both Belfast and Derry:

1 'Low rise': the pitch of the voice is low on the main accent of the sentence and rises from that low to remain on a mid-level plateau for the rest of the intonation group, e.g. (all the examples are from McElholm):

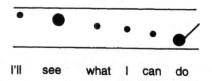

I'll   see   what   I   can   do

This tone is the unmarked tone for declaratives and for *wh*-interrogatives and for rhetorical tag interrogatives. (In RP a simple fall is of course the unmarked tone for these types of sentence.)

2 'High rise': for this tone the pitch of the voice is low to mid on the nucleus and rises from that mid pitch to remain on a level high pitch for the remainder of the intonation group, e.g.:

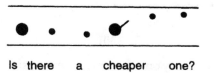

Is there   a   cheaper   one?

This tone is the unmarked tone for *yes/no* interrogatives. It is also used for 'involved' declaratives and *wh*-interrogatives.

3 'Rise–fall': for this tone the voice is low on the nucleus, rises to the very top of the pitch range before falling gradually downwards to the end of the intonation group (i.e. it does not, like the RP rise–fall, go rapidly down to the baseline), e.g.:

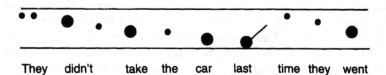

They   didn't   take   the   car   last   time   they   went

This tone is used for contrast and reservations. The only other tone which is at all frequent is a compound tone involving a sequence of tones 1 and 2. Both Jarman and Cruttenden (1976) and McElholm (1986) report the rare use of a further tone which does involve a rapid fall (in the case of the latter, an 'extra-high rise–fall') for surprise or exclamation. Jarman and Cruttenden state that, overall, rises account for 70 per cent of the intonation groups and McElholm implies that the figure is much higher. Moreover the principal informant used by Jarman and Cruttenden and the two informants who supplied the majority of McElholm's data were in higher education, confirming an as yet unproven impression that the intonation here described is not limited to the lower end of the educational spectrum.

Glasgow

Impressionistically the intonation of Glasgow is very similar to that of Belfast (not surprisingly, given that the two accents are in general similar). Yet there is very little in the way of solid evidence. There have consistently been hints in the literature, e.g. Samuels (1972) suggests that the west of Scotland (by which he seems to mean primarily Glasgow) has neutralisation of statement and question patterns. The only firm evidence comes in Currie (1979). She reports that in Glasgow English 'each unit ends with a rise on the final stressed word of the unit' (p. 389) and thus 'the contour unit [with two stressed syllables] in Glasgow English is realized' as follows:

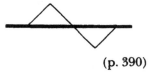

(p. 390)

For example, the fundamental frequency on one contour unit was:

the   way   he   spoke
180   250   180   170–185 Hz. (p. 389)

So 'the final "peak of prominence" [compared with Edinburgh] is "reversed", with the result that the final stressed element is low and not high' (p. 391). From the unconditional way in which Currie talks of this contour it appears that, as in Belfast, final rise is by far the most frequent pattern for many speakers and that it is not constrained by any sort of stylistic variable. Currie's report is made from instrumental measurements of data based on a short extract of a conversation between herself and a woman in her forties. Unfortunately we are not told the educational or social background of the woman; because of the possible existence of an Edinburgh 'standard', which involves a predominance of falling patterns, it is very likely that the consistent use of rising patterns is more limited sociolinguistically than in Belfast (indeed I have a number of recordings of Glasgow speakers who almost never use a rise on declaratives). Moreover, although Currie describes basically a simple rising tune, Ladd and Lindsay (1991) found in unscripted dialogues among Glaswegians that the most common intonation pattern was that best described as rise–plateau–slump.

Newcastle

Anyone with a reasonable listening ear has always known that Tyneside, like Glasgow, has its own special tone. For example, Strang (1964) in a discussion of a lecture by Bolinger on intonational universals asserted that Tyneside regularly used a final rise 'for positive affirmative statements, for non-yes–no questions, in short, for finality'. But, again like Glasgow, there has been little objective confirmation of this tone and its use. The Tyneside Linguistic Survey included intonation among much other linguistic material; Pellowe and Jones (1978) presented from this survey a detailed intonational report on informants from Gateshead (aged between 17 and 70 and mainly from the lower socio-economic classes). The proportion of various nuclear tones was compared with RP data from the Survey of English Usage (Quirk *et al.*, 1964); the figures were as follows, based on 4,066 intonation-units (20 speakers – 11 men, 9 women) from Tyneside and 1,880 intonation-units (10 speakers – all men) from RP:

	RP (%)	Tyneside (%)
Fall	51	28
Rise	25	18
Fall+Rise	8	9
Fall–rise	5	7
Rise–fall	3	4
Level	2	20
Rise+Fall	1	1

From this it is clear that there are many more rise–falls and levels in the Tyneside data. The level tone is frequently preceded by a jump-up in pitch, i.e. it is a high level. We are not given information on the exact nature of the rise–fall but impressionistically rise–falls in this dialect have a long rise followed by a slight fall. There are also a smaller number of rises in the Tyneside data. However Pellowe and Jones make clear that use of rises was very variable from speaker to speaker; some speakers, particularly younger women, and women from low socio-economic classes, used a larger number of rises which often appeared to take over from level. Unfortunately we are given no information on syntactic, discoursal, or attitudinal uses of the tones (although there is information on differing correlations with form classes in Tyneside and RP; and Local (1986) shows that some rises and levels can 'act as exponents of utterance-finality' (p. 187)). The overall situation, compared with RP, seems to involve more high levels, more rise–falls where the fall is slight, and more rises from some speakers (Local (1986) states that rises on Tyneside involve rise–level rather than a continuous rise from the nucleus.) In short, the number of tones which do not involve a fall to the baseline would appear to be very much greater than in RP. But the situation is plainly not as clear-cut as in the previously

159

discussed cities: falls certainly do occur and the rising tones of Belfast, Derry and Glasgow are on Tyneside outnumbered by high levels or rises with a slight fall at the end of them.

In Cruttenden (1986: 139) I wrote 'It must surely be no accident that in most of the areas involved [in the greater use of rises] there is a strong Celtic influence ... an indirect influence in cases like Liverpool and Tyneside, where the influence is dependent on an influx of people from Ireland or Scotland, who usually do not speak a Celtic language.' Knowles (1975: 221ff.) supports the claim of Irish influence on Scouse intonation very strongly (24.5 per cent Irish in 1861). However, E. Clavering (personal communication) has pointed out to me that (a) there were never very many Irish on Tyneside – almost none before 1830 and reaching a limited peak of 7.9 per cent of the population in 1851 (see Cooter 1975: 18) and that, although there were rather more Scots in the nineteenth century, these were usually from Lowland areas on the East Coast and were easily assimilated; and (b) that there is documentary proof of the existence of the Tyneside Tone well before the nineteenth century. Clavering has sent me the following interesting quotation about two boys who, in 1789 at the ages of six and nine, were sent away to a preparatory school in High Wycombe. Their father complained that after four terms their speech was still local, and the head replied:

> It was impossible their manner of reading should have escaped you; it has been long a subject of conversation here, sometimes of mirth, at other times we have treated it very seriously, particularly to Master Ellison [i.e. the elder boy]. He can inform you that he has hardly ever said a lesson or read an English book to me without my talking a great deal to him about it. I have only observed that he generally spake the last syllable in a sentence nearly a third above the last but one. I have made him repeat the concluding syllables after me and have sunk my voice which he exactly imitated and therefore doubt not but we shall acquire a correct cadence in time.
>
> (Ellison Collection, Gateshead Library, quoted by Hughes 1956: 363)

Clavering also suggests that the present extent of the Tyneside Tone is roughly co-extensive with the pre-1750 coalfield. Whether this is true or not, the evidence from 1789 does throw very considerable doubt on the theory which explains the increased use of rises in northern urban areas as due to a Celtic substrate. An alternative would be to assume that the use of rising tones is a case of urban spread, well documented sociolinguistically.

Liverpool

Scouse intonation is thoroughly described in Knowles (1975) with some additional theoretical comments in Knowles (1978) and (1981). Two tones in particular are identified as very common in Scouse. (1) What Knowles calls the 'step'. This involves a step-up from a low-mid accented syllable to a high-mid plateau followed optionally by a slight slump in pitch at the very end of the intonation group, e.g. (I put GOK after those examples taken from Knowles and AC after those examples which are my own):

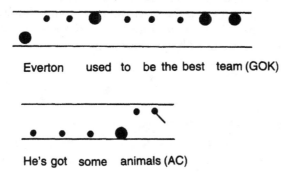

Everton   used to   be the best team (GOK)

He's got   some   animals (AC)

And (2) what Knowles calls the 'drop'. This involves a high-mid level pitch followed by a low-mid level pitch (i.e. it is almost the reverse of the 'step'):

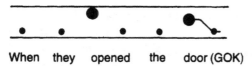

When   they   opened   the   door (GOK)

In Scouse, whose intonational usage Knowles systematically distinguishes from middle-class Liverpudlian speech, the step (which Knowles analyses as a narrowed rise–fall) replaces most of the RP uses of the simple fall, and the 'drop' (which Knowles analyses as a simplified fall–rise) replaces most of the RP uses of the simple rise. So declaratives and *wh*-interrogatives commonly take the step, while non-final groups and *yes/no*-interrogatives commonly take the drop.

Although Knowles analyses the step as a type of rise–fall (and at some sort of 'deep' level I would not wish to quarrel with this analysis) superficially and physically it clearly leads to an increase in the number of rises compared with RP. On the other hand, the position as regards the drop is the reverse: superficially and physically there is an increase in the number of falls, even if, at a deeper level, the drop is to be analysed as a type of fall–rise. So it could be argued that systemically the introduction of the step and the drop merely leads to a tit-for-tat situation. Nevertheless textually the superficial and physical sound of Scouse will produce more rises, simply because declaratives are most common (in conversation they are probably numerically greater than non-finals and *yes/no*-interrogatives put together).

Birmingham and Manchester

The only (brief) work on Birmingham intonation was carried out over fifty years ago (Wilde 1938). It gives a short discussion of the intonation of two humorous stories spoken in the dialect as entertainment by a comedian named Graham Squires. A kymograph tracing of one part of one of the two stories (the wedding) is appended to the discussion. My own re-analysis of this tracing divides it into 107 intonation groups, and shows an above-average number of rises in sentence-final position, e.g.:

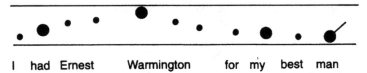

I   had Ernest   Warmington   for my best man

There are also a large number of rise–levels and rise–falls, many of them made up of the long rise and the short fall already familiar from the discussion of other dialects, e.g.:

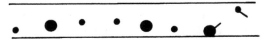
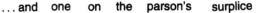

...and one on the parson's surplice

Wilde himself is certain about the dialect's uniqueness: 'Der Birminghamer Industriedialect hat eine auffallende Tonbewegung, die sich z. T. auch in der Birminghamer Hochsprache so eingebürgert hat, dass der Birming-hamer Gebildete geradezu an seiner intonation erkannt wird' (The industrial dialect of Birmingham has a striking contour, which has partly been adopted in middle-class speech, so that the culture of Birmingham is almost recognisable by its intonation). My own preliminary acquaintance with a large body of recently collected data from both both north and south Birmingham suggests that use of the rise–levels and rise–falls mentioned above (and which are of course very like those already detailed for Liverpool) is common on question-word interrogatives and occasional on declaratives and polar interrogatives but by no means the unmarked pattern which it is in, for example, Belfast. Much the same is the case for Manchester, where this intonation can often be overheard in conversations but is difficult to obtain in elicited recordings. Here it is also difficult to estimate the degree to which this pattern is a recent import from Liverpool, which is only thirty miles away.

There is clearly a greater use of rising intonation patterns (including rise–falls where the rising element is dominant) in UNB than in RP (or, for that matter, GA). One possible origin, a Celtic substrate, suggested by Knowles as the origin of Scouse intonation, was discounted as a more general theory in the discussion of Newcastle above. Another folk etymology suggests that it arises from the habitual ironic outlook of these urban populations (conditions being such that this outlook has been required to survive, particularly in the nineteenth century). It is certainly true that the effect of the UNB rise–fall (and also the Liverpool 'drop') is sarcastic to southern British listeners, and many of the inhabitants of these areas are proud of their 'humour'. All this is indeed folk etymology, virtually incapable of any sort of remotely scientific confirmation. In the final section of this article I discuss at greater length more general 'explanations' for the greater use of rises in some dialects; but before that I wish to discuss rises in another part of the world – the Pacific Rim.

THE PACIFIC RIM (PR)

Australia

There has been much popular discussion within Australia in the past ten years over the use of a high rising tone (generally and henceforth referred to as HRT) at the end of declarative sentences. Visiting linguists are often asked to comment on it on television (Crystal, personal communication). According to a footnote in McGregor (1980) the earliest written reference to HRT was in the *Sydney Morning Herald* on 19 February 1974, when J. R. L. Barnard referred to 'the rising intonation which is unfortunately becoming more and more common on declarative statements (not only among broad speakers)'. On the other hand, in Mitchell and Delbridge (1965) the only report of rising tones on statements concerns the use of a 'high head plus low rise' which they call the 'interview tune' and which carries a self-justificatory attitude when questioned (in fact this seems little different from RP); moreover, there are only 0.3 per cent HRTs in Mitchell and Delbridge's data, according to Guy *et al.* (1986). So it is evidently a relatively recent innovation. The main reports concern Sydney (Britain (1992) reports a further discussion in the *Sydney Morning Herald* in 1992), although Allan (1984) reports it from Melbourne also, and my own informal listening confirms this.

In the last ten years HRT has become the focus of the most detailed investigations of any dialectal intonational feature. The first was indeed that of McGregor (1980), who surveyed the use of HRT among 115 adolescent schoolchildren (interviewed in school) and 120 adults ('approached in public places'!). Informants were asked to relate the story of a book they had recently read or a film they had recently seen and were categorised as HRT users or non-users according to whether they used any instance of HRT in their first 47 seconds of speech. HRT usage was correlated with age, sex, occupational status (presumably of fathers in the case of the adolescents) and residential area; and, for the adolescents only, with type of school, intelligence and variety of Australian English. For the adolescent sample type of school was the most significant variable, state schools showing far more HRT usage; there were lesser correlations with occupational status and intelligence, and a weak correlation with type of English. For the adult sample, the strongest correlations were with age (few over the age of twenty-five used HRT), and occupational status. For both samples, a non-significant majority of users were women, and there was virtually no correlation with residential status. 56.5 per cent of the adolescents and 35.8 per cent of the adults were HRT users; actual community usage is likely to be very much higher because, for example, the numbers in the survey from each occupational group were equal, whereas in the community at large they are not.

Guy *et al.* (1986) investigated 130 speakers (drawn from Horvath's 1985 corpus) divided according to age, sex, class and ethnicity. The speakers produced 107,685 intonation-groups, of which 1,724 were HRTs (1.6 per cent). Teenagers used HRTs ten times more frequently than adults; females used HRTs twice as much as males; working-class speakers three times as much as middle-class; and Italians two and a half times and Greeks one and a half times as much as those of British descent. Guy and Vonwiller (1984) used a matched guise subjective reaction test to investigate listeners' understanding of the meaning of the tone. Two recorded passages were used from three female speakers, one containing an HRT and one no instances of HRT (the recordings were mixed with other sentences irrelevant to the experiment). Thirty informants stratified for age and sex, and 67 linguistics students (47 male, 20 female) were asked to rate the passages on various scales: (i) a seven-point job suitability scale (Labov 1966); (ii) an estimate of the speaker's age in five categories; (iii) five different semantic differential scales: (a) confident–uncertain, (b) forceful–yielding, (c) attentive–indifferent, (d) friendly–unfriendly, and (e) dull–expressive. Initial studies showed no difference between the two groups of students so the results were pooled. With some limited exceptions HRT passages were heard as more uncertain, more yielding (= 'deference'), and more friendly and attentive (= 'checking'); HRTs were more associated with young people and with low-status employment. Guy and Vonwiller go on to discuss the meanings of uncertainty, deference and checking in more detail, in the light of the content and situation of the sorts of passages where speakers use HRT. They conclude that there is no sign of uncertainty or deference in such content (speakers are typically telling listeners about a series of events) or situation (HRT is typically used between peers) and that therefore the primary meaning of HRT is 'to seek validation of the speaker's comprehension' (i.e. the 'checking' meaning). This is reinforced by HRT's use most commonly in narrative and descriptive texts, rather than in statements of fact or opinion. There is thus to some extent a mismatch between speaker's intention and listener's reaction, a situation not uncommon in language. Guy and Vonwiller suggest that the mistaken judgements concerning uncertainty and deference arise from stereotyping – those who most use it are young and female, therefore they must be uncertain and deferential.

Allan (1984), whose data includes recordings from Melbourne and who regards high fall–rise as a variant of high rise, confirms that the speaker is always presenting information to which the listener could not be privy, that the speaker is not uncertain and that there is never any sign of deference on the speaker's part. However Allan takes issue with Guy and Vonwiller by suggesting that mistaken judgements of HRT as deferential and uncertain do not stem from the stereotyping of those who use it but from general, universal, meanings of intonation (which may be genetic): deference is generally associated with high pitch and rising tones are generally associated with uncertainty. Moreover, the correctly inferred meaning of checking arises from another universal association in intonation, that of rising tone and non-finality (particularly involved in sentence-medial position). Additionally, continual checking that the listener is listening and understanding may itself quite reasonably imply uncertainty and deference.

There is no reason why all three factors, stereotyping, universal meanings associated with rising tones, and implications from checking to deference and uncertainty, should not work together to produce the mistaken effects.

New Zealand

Britain (1992) analysed a corpus from sixty working-class speakers, varied in age, sex and ethnicity, from the Wellington suburb of Poirua. Of 14,844 intonation groups, 612 involved HRT, i.e. 4.12 per cent (two and a half times the Guy *et al.* (1986) figure for Sydney). HRT was used by more younger than older speakers and by more Maoris than Pakehas. However, unlike the findings in Guy *et al.*, Britain's showed no correlation between social class and the use of HRT and he found more women users only among the Pakehas. Like Guy *et al.*'s study, opinion texts disfavoured HRT while narratives favoured them. Britain and Newman (1992) found HRTs frequently used in 'evaluation clauses', which display the involvement of the speaker and which heighten the interest of the listener in the narrative; they often occurred in series and frequently in the climactic part of narratives.

North America

Similar use of HRT has been reported informally from North America, in particular from California. Bolinger (1979: 510) writes:

Many speakers of American English, in giving a running account of something, will use exactly this kind of terminal rise at the end of practically every sentence – clearly a channel-clearing device, that says, in effect, 'Are you listening?' for unless someone gives a sign of attention, the monologue comes to a halt. It would not be hard to imagine such a habit becoming a contagion, after which, with the interlocutor weary of giving the countersign, the language could be said to have a rising intonation as a mark of clause terminals in general.

Similarly Lakoff (1975: 17): 'There is a peculiar sentence intonation pattern, found in English so far as I know only among women, which has the form of a declarative answer to a *yes/no* question, and is used as such, but has the rising inflection typical of a *yes/no* question, as well as being especially hesitant.' Ching (1982) collected examples of the use of the 'question intonational contour' by fourteen speakers from Memphis, Tennessee, either recorded on tape or on notecards. Among the meanings she suggested were the speaker craving the indulgence of the listener, the need for re-assurance, deference, and politeness. In a recent book Raban (1990: 243), talking of the residents of Gunnersville, Alabama, claimed to be 'picking up an accent that turned every statement into a question'. Evidently the use of HRT is common in parts of the Deep South as well as in California. In a popular thriller (Francis 1988: 104), set on a trans-continental train in Canada, the conductor is said to have 'had the widespread Canadian habit of turning the most ordinary statement into a question'. James *et al.* (1989), quoted in Britain (1992), report more academically on the growing use of high rise in Toronto. In another popular novel by Lodge (1991: 130), set in Hawaii, the following exchange occurs between a waitress and her customer:

'Tonight we have a special?' she said.
'I don't know, I'm sure,' said Bernard, examining the menu.

But apparently the girl's rising intonation did not signify a question for she proceeded to tell him what the special was: spinach lasagne.

A footnote in Allan (1984: 20) refers to *Time*, South Pacific edition, 27 November 1982, p. 76, where HRTs were said to be found in the Valley Girl dialect of the San Fernando Valley in the foothills adjacent to Los Angeles. This was not a dialect in the usual sense of the word, being just a cult way of speaking ('Valley-speak') among the affluent teenagers of the region, exemplified in a hit single of 1982 made by Moon Zappa called 'Valley Girls' (see the report in *The Peninsula Times Tribune* on 21 July 1982, pp. 4–5). In the same year (July 1982) I was given (by Marilyn Vihman) a recording of a teenager growing up in northern California (in Palo Alto) which clearly indicates use of HRT. The teenager involved was a girl aged 15 and in the recording she is talking to a family friend aged 31 about her school friend (I have changed the names in the quoted passages); this is interspersed with discussion about the preparation of a meal. The excerpt which I analysed lasted 10 mins, 54 secs and most of the speech was from the informant rather than the older friend. The informant's speech contained 408 intonation groups (from which it can be gathered that she spoke very fast). Of the 408 groups, 381 were declaratives (declarative is here a catch-all category defined negatively to include all groups which were not marked grammatically or lexically as interrogatives or exclamatives). In the declarative groups, 23 were clear cases of HRT (including one wide HRT, i.e. where the rise started lower than in the other cases), 11 were cases of what I labelled a mid rising tone, i.e. where the rise did not reach quite as high as in the clear HRT cases, and 6 involved a high level (cf. the varieties of HRT mentioned in Britain 1992). There were thus 40 instances of variants of HRT on declaratives out of a total of 381, i.e. 10.5 per cent or 1 in 10. There were also ten instances of HRT on tags following declaratives (which corresponds to a similar use in RP), e.g. 'but her PE teacher says she has a 'B /in P'E /which is really im'possible /'right?' (tonetic stress marks are used in the traditional way, e.g. '= high fall, '= high rise, ₌ = low fall, > = mid level). If the HRTs on tags are included, there are 50 out of 394, i.e. 12.6 per cent, or 1 in 8. Additionally there were four instances of HRT on interrogatives, one on a polar interrogative, one on a question word interrogative and two on elliptical interrogatives, e.g. 'Want me to 'help you?'. There are thus 54 HRTs out of a total of 408, i.e. 13.2 per cent or 1 in 7.

Almost all the instances of HRT were in the narrative portions of the text. Some typical stretches were:

So we're both trying to avoid Mary 'looking at us /so we wouldn't have to 'say anything /so >finally like /Robert ₍told her

So we stand there and talk for a long 'time/ and then wander into the class about five minutes 'late / and we're just standing there outside the 'door /and the whole class is kind of 'talking /and >then

But then Julie had an N.C. [= no credit] in her 'class /when the teacher raised her to a 'C /and she wrote that Julie was getting a ₍C.

But her P.E. teacher says she has a 'B/ in P'E /which is really im'possible /'right?/ Obviously her teacher is just trying to be 'nice.

(What school does she want to go to next year?)
Sunnyvale Christian 'High.

HRT is in this excerpt clearly being used in the same way as reported for the Australian texts. It is used in the narrative passages as a 'check' that the listener is attending and understanding (although it could be misinterpreted as uncertain and deferential). The user is young and female, and other informal reports suggest that this is typical.

This completes the descriptive survey of the various evidence of the greater use of rises around the Pacific Rim. As noted at various points in this article, HRT frequently gets the attention of newspapers, either in articles or in letters to the Editor. *The Sydney Morning Herald, The Peninsula Times Tribune* and *Time* have already been mentioned. During January 1992, a correspondence took place in *The Times* following an article by Charles Bremner on 3 January, which in turn was a response to an article by Lynne Sharon Schwartz in *The New York Times*. This article was particularly interesting in its perception of the meaning of HRT: it was entitled 'Uneasiness out there: Charles Bremner studies timid-talking America'. I quote two pieces from the article:

> Novelist Lynne Sharon Schwartz has called this epidemic of rising inflections ominous and Orwellian. It implies, she says, that Americans are no longer sure of anything, not even their own names ('Hi, I'm Jim Smith?' is a common self-introduction, inviting the reply 'Yes, of course you're Jim Smith'). Writing in *The New York Times*, Ms Schwartz concludes that, when they open their mouths, Americans seem to be saying 'Here's what I think, but if you don't agree I can easily change my mind.'

> Since British speech has always sounded diffident to Americans, the tentative tone will probably not join the eastward flow of slang across the Atlantic. British visitors, however, should make a mental translation. Arriving at Kennedy airport, the man in uniform may say 'I'm a customs officer?' Offering reassurance is not appropriate.

Note that, although reassurance may not be appropriate here, it was listed as one of the suggested meanings by Ching (1982: 104).

Does usage in the various dialects represent a similar or different phenomenon? And how does it relate to a theory of intonational meaning? I attempt to answer these two questions in the final section.

STYLE, SYSTEM AND THEORY

All intonologists are agreed that intonational meanings are universally less arbitrary than those associated with segmental phonology (for a more detailed summary than here, see Cruttenden 1986). Syntactically, there is, for example, a universal tendency for declaratives to have falls and polar interrogatives to have rises. Although there are various types of exception to this tendency, one type of absolute exception never occurs: no language is reported where declaratives regularly have rises and polar interrogatives regularly have falls. Attitudinally, there is a universal tendency for certainty to be shown by falls and doubt by rises – try, for example, answering questions with a simple 'certainly' or 'possibly'; the former will be said with a fall and the latter with a rise. A language in which doubt was shown by a fall and certainty by a rise is inconceivable. Discoursally, there is a universal tendency for finality to be shown by a fall and continuance to be shown by a rise, e.g. Lehiste (1980) showed that in reading aloud the ends of paragraphs are indicated by a fall which falls to a very low level; it is inconceivable that a language will be found where a rise would indicate the end of a 'paratone'.

Despite the universal aspects of intonation there is nevertheless variation from language to language. First, there is of course variation in the type(s) of rise and the type(s) of fall which a language may use, e.g. the falling–rising nuclear tone which is typical of English (and which counts as a type of rise, tones generally being classified by the direction of their final movement) is uncommon in most other European languages. Second, and it is this that is most relevant in the present discussion, the frequency of falls and rises may vary from one language to another, or, as in the present case, from one dialect to another. That such differences in frequency are common between languages is of course implied by saying that the correlations between tones and meanings mentioned above are tendencies and not absolutes. These differences in frequency present a real problem for any theory of the universality of meanings in intonation.

There are at least two explanations which might be hypothesised to account for frequency differences. The first is that there is in some way a difference in the systems of any two languages or dialects (I call this the 'systemic hypothesis'). A systemic difference would involve some of the universal semantic tendencies mentioned in the first paragraph of this section not being applicable in one particular language or dialect. Syntactically a language might not make a tonal distinction between declaratives and polar interrogatives; both might regularly have falls or both might regularly have rises. Attitudinally a language might show no difference between the tone of certainty and the tone of doubt. Discoursally a language might have no way of showing continuance. If all the putative distinctions were unused in a particular language, then the language would make no distinction of (intonational) tone at all. If only a limited number of the distinctions are realised in any one language, then the frequency of falls and rises will be different from some other language which realised all the distinctions.

The second hypothesis is that there is a conceptual–stylistic difference between the speakers of any two languages with tonal frequency differences (the 'conceptual–stylistic' hypothesis). By this hypothesis speakers of the two languages (or at least some speakers of the two languages) use different cognitive styles. Syntactically speakers of one language may not be in the habit of reinforcing the syntactic distinction between declarative and polar interrogative with a tonal difference. Attitudinally speakers of one language may be in the habit of appearing more certain or more doubtful than speakers of some other language or dialect. Discourally it may be the habit in one language not to signal continuance by tone (although it is of course likely to be signalled by some other means). Moreover the realisation of such distinctions by tone may be quantifiably variable. Speakers of a language (or some speakers of a language) may only tonally differentiate a polar interrogative from a declarative on rare occasions. Speakers of a language may be in the habit of showing doubt by means of tone only on rare occasions. Speakers of a language may choose to show finality only rarely – maybe, for example, never just at a sentence end but only at the end of a read-aloud paragraph or a turn.

From the reports presented in the earlier sections of this article, can we decide which of the two hypotheses fits the dialects of English which have more rises than RP or GA? Before we can answer this question, we have to have some sort of criterion or criteria which would help us to decide this question. The difference between the two hypotheses would seem to be shown by the way in which the difference in frequency is manifested. If a tonal difference is used to make a particular semantic distinction in both languages or dialects, but is used more regularly to do so in the one language or dialect than in the other, then it seems clear that we are dealing with a conceptual-stylistic difference. If, on the other hand, a tonal difference is never used to make a certain semantic distinction in one language, then it is likely that a systemic difference is involved.

Considering first the dialects of the Pacific Rim, in this case it is clear that the conceptual-stylistic hypothesis best fits the facts of HRT usage. HRT is used primarily as a 'check'; a similar high rise is used as a check in RP (see, for example, O'Connor and Arnold (1973: 201), where its use on statements is described as 'questioning, trying to elicit a repetition, but lacking any suggestion of disapproval or puzzlement'). What differentiates HRT usage in PR is the more frequent use of this tone for checking.

Turning now to UNB, the present evidence (and it must be emphasised again how limited it is) does not so clearly support one explanation or the other. At least some speakers from Newcastle, Birmingham and Manchester evidently use more rises than RP, although it is not clear with what meaning. Unless the extra rises are used for an extra meaning not present in RP, which seems *prima facie* unlikely, there is apparently a greater use of rises with the same meanings as in RP, which again suggests that the conceptual-stylistic hypothesis is the better explanation (although of course it would not in this case be the checking meaning which is differentially present – indeed it is not clear what meaning would be involved). Alternatively the data from these cities may represent a case of dialect mixing (i.e. the mixing of two systems) in ways not yet obvious. In this case we might be dealing with a different system but one which is rarely realized in an unadulterated form.

The evidence from Liverpool does indeed suggest dialect mixing;

Knowles (1975) suggests two varieties of Liverpool intonation; that associated with broad Liverpool speech or Scouse, and that associated with middle-class Liverpool speech; the latter being more like RP. Thus the fact that individual speakers mix the Scouse 'step' (= (superficially) a type of rise) and 'drop' (= superficially a type of fall) with middle class RP-like fall and fall–rise is more easily accounted for by dialect mixing than by an increased use of falls or rises for particular functions. If the step and the drop are the unmarked tones for declaratives and polar interrogatives in Scouse when there is no admixture from middle-class Liverpool, then a systemic distinction is involved.

The data from Belfast and Derry presented above clearly support the systemic hypothesis; in this case rises are the ubiquitous tone with a distinction between low rise and high rise replacing the distinction between fall and rise. Data recently collected from Belfast by me and not yet fully analysed do show more use of falls among the still more common rises; but such data can of course be explained by dialect mixing, as in the case of Liverpool above. The paucity of the data from Glasgow (where superficial observation suggests that rises are not as common as in Belfast) makes it impossible to decide between the two hypotheses.

In sum the PR evidence supports the conceptual–stylistic hypothesis, while much of the UNB evidence rather less strongly supports the systemic hypothesis. In the one case rising tones are a stylistic habit; in the other case they are incorporated into the system. We can finally hypothesise that there may be a connection between tone as a stylistic habit and tone as systemic. An earlier quotation from Bolinger (at the beginning of the section on North America) talked of 'a habit becoming a contagion', and imagined a situation whereby the checking high rise simply became 'a marker of clause terminals in general'. Fónagy (1979) reports that the usual polar interrogative intonation in Hungarian (similar to the RP rise–fall) began to be used by train-drivers and shop assistants as a polite imperative; nowadays it is the unmarked imperative for young people. By the same means the Australian stylistic HRT might one day become a systemic HRT like the Belfast low and high rises. Yet despite this type of potential for intonational change, there remain the universal (and non-arbitrary) semantic tendencies mentioned at the beginning of this article; at some stage intonational changes are blocked (or even reversed) to prevent intonational meanings becoming as arbitrary as those associated with segmental sequences. But that is another story.

REFERENCES

Allan, K. (1984) 'The component functions of the high rise terminal contour in Australian declarative sentences', *Australian Journal of Linguistics* 4: 19–32.

Bilton, L. (1982) 'The phonology of the accent of Hull', *Journal of the International Phonetic Association* 12: 30–5.

Bolinger, D. L. (1979) 'Intonation across languages', in J. Greenberg, C. A. Ferguson and E. A. Moravcsik (eds), *Universals of Language*, Vol. 2: *Phonology*, Stanford: Stanford University Press, pp. 471–524.

Britain, D. (1992) 'Linguistic change in intonation: the use of HR terminals in New Zealand English', *Language Variation and Change* 4: 77–104.

Britain, D. and Newman, J. (1992) 'High rising terminals in New Zealand English', *Journal of the International Phonetic Association* 22: 1–11.

Burgess, O. N. (1973) 'Intonation patterns in Australian English', *Language and Speech* 16: 314–26.

Ching, M. (1982) 'The question intonation in assertions', *American Speech* 57: 95–107.

Cooter, R. J. (1975) 'On calculating the nineteenth century Irish population of Durham and Newcastle', *Northern Catholic History* 2: 16–25.

Cruttenden, A. (1986) *Intonation*, Cambridge: Cambridge University Press.

Crystal, D. and Davy, D. (1969) *Investigating English Style*, London: Longman.

Currie, K. L. (1979) 'Intonation systems in Scottish English', unpublished Ph.D. thesis, University of Edinburgh.

Fónagy, I. (1979) 'Structure et aspects sociaux des changements prosodiques', in E. Fischer-Jørgensen, J. Rischel and N. Thorsen (eds), *Proceedings of the Ninth International Congress of Linguists*, Vol. 2, University of Copenhagen, Institute of Phonetics, pp. 204–11.

Francis, D. (1988) *The Edge*, New York: Fawcett Crest.

Guy, G. and Vonwiller, J. (1984) 'The meaning of an intonation in Australian English', *Australian Journal of Linguistics* 4: 1–17.

Guy, G., Horvath, B., Vonwiller, J., Disley, E. and Rogers, I. (1986) 'An intonational change in progress in Australian English', *Language in Society* 15: 23–52.

Haldenby, C. (1959) 'Characteristics of Lincolnshire dialect intonation', unpublished MA thesis, University of Leeds.

Halliday, M. A. K. (1968) *Intonation and Grammar in British English*, Mouton: The Hague.

Horvath, B. (1985) *Variation in Australian English: The Sociolects of Sydney*, Cambridge: Cambridge University Press.

Hughes, E, (1956) *North Country Life in the Eighteenth Century*, Vol. 1: *The North-East 1700–1750* (University of Durham Publications), London: Oxford University Press.

James, E., Mahut, C. and Latkiewicz, G. (1989) 'The investigation of an apparently new intonation pattern in Toronto English', *Information Communication* (Speech and Voice Society and Phonetics Laboratory, University of Toronto) 10: 11–17.

Jarman, E. and Cruttenden, A. (1976) 'Belfast intonation and the myth of the fall', *Journal of the International Phonetic Association* 6: 4–12.

Knowles, G. O. (1975) 'Scouse: the spoken dialect of Liverpool', unpublished Ph.D. thesis, University of Leeds.

—— (1978) 'The nature of phonological variables in Scouse', in P. Trudgill (ed.) *Sociolinguistic Patterns in British English*, London: Edward Arnold, pp. 80–90.

—— (1981) 'Variable strategies in intonation', in D. Gibbon, and H. Richter (eds), *Intonation, Accent and Rhythm*, Berlin: de Gruyter, pp. 236–42.

Labov, W. (1966) *The Social Stratification of English in New York City*, Washington, DC: Center for Applied Linguistics.

Ladd, D. R. and Lindsay, G. (1991) 'Theoretical consequences of Glaswegian intonation', paper presented at the York meeting of the Linguistics Association of Great Britain.

Lakoff, R. (1975) *Language and Women's Place*, New York: Harper & Row.
Lehiste, I. (1980) *Phonetic Characteristics of Discourse*, Tokyo: Acoustical Society of Japan.
Local, J. (1986) 'Patterns and problems in a study of Tyneside intonation', in C. Johns-Lewis (ed.), *Intonation in Discourse*, London: Croom Helm, pp. 181–97.
Lodge, D. (1991) *Paradise News*, Harmondsworth: Penguin.
McElholm, D. D (1986) 'Intonation in Derry English', in H. Kirkwood (ed.), *Studies in Intonation* (Occasional Papers in Linguistics and Language Learning, 11), University of Ulster, pp. 1–58.
McGregor, R. L. (1980) 'The social distribution of an Australian English intonation contour', *Working Papers*, Vol. 2, No. 6, 1–26. Macquarie University, School of English and Linguistics.
Mitchell, A. G. and Delbridge A. (1965) *The Speech of Australian Adolescents*, Sydney: Angus & Robertson.
O'Connor, J. D. and Arnold, G. F. (1961, 1973) *Intonation of Colloquial English*, London: Longman.
Pellowe, J. and Jones, V. (1978) 'On intonational variability in Tyneside speech', in P. Trudgill (ed.), *Sociolinguistic Patterns in British English*, London: Edward Arnold, pp. 102–21.
Pike, K. L. (1945) *The Intonation of American English*, Ann Arbor: University of Michigan Press.
Quirk, R., Svartvik, J., Duckworth, A. P., Rusiecki, J. P. L. and Colin, A. J. T. (1964) 'Studies in the correspondence of prosodic to grammatical features in English', in H. G. Lunt (ed.), *Proceedings of the Ninth International Congress of Linguists*, The Hague: Mouton, pp. 679–91.
Raban, J. (1990) *Hunting Mister Heartbreak*, London: Pan.
Samuels, M. L. (1972) *Linguistic Evolution*, Cambridge: Cambridge University Press.
Strang, B. (1964) 'Comments on D. L. Bolinger, intonation as a universal', in H. G. Lunt (ed.), *Proceedings of the Ninth International Congress of Linguists*, The Hague: Mouton, p. 845.
Wilde, H.-O. (1938) 'Der Industrie-Dialekt von Birmingham: Intonation und Sprachvariante; Tonbewegung, Lautqualität und Lautquantität', *Studien zur Englischen Philologie* 94, Halle: Niemeyer.

173

12

Documenting rhythmical change

David Crystal
University of Wales, Bangor

It has often been remarked that the essential auditory identity of a language, the immediate impression conveyed upon a first or a passing encounter, derives from the character of its prosody (in a broad, Firthian sense). Evidence on the point comes from the way young children (before the end of the first year) are able to differentiate prosodic features from the auditory soup which surrounds them and to introduce them into their own discourse, long before segmental distinctions come to be discriminated and used. The evidence is somewhat mixed, as regards the role of intonational features, but is substantial with respect to rhythm. For example, the latest study I have seen (Levitt and Aydelott Utman 1992) compares the syllable durations of French and American infants, and shows that the French-learning infant produced more regularly timed non-final syllables and showed significantly more final syllable lengthening than the English-learning infant. In other words, there was evidence of the emergence of the 'machine-gun' rhythm typical of French syllable-timing, while the English child maintained the 'morse code' rhythm typical of English stress-timing (see Lloyd James (1940: 25) for the former pair of terms, Pike (1945: 35) for the latter pair).

The persistence with which this distinction is still referred to testifies to the value of the original insight, which continues to motivate research in such fields as child language acquisition, speech pathology and foreign-language teaching. None-the-less, the value of attempting to classify the languages of the world into two main rhythmical types has been questioned several times (e.g. Mitchell 1969; Roach 1982). A particular problem in carrying out studies of comparative rhythm is the subjective nature of the task, which is apparently much influenced by the mother tongue of the speaker. This is a problem which concerned Abercrombie (1967: 97):

We talk, for convenience, about 'hearing' rhythm, but in fact we *feel* it, entering empathetically into the movements of the speaker, to which the sounds we hear are clues. But in order to have this immediate and intuitive apprehension of speech rhythm it is necessary, of course, that the speaker and hearer should have the same mother-tongue – otherwise 'phonetic empathy' will not work: the sounds will not be recognized as accurate clues to the movements that produce them.

The notion of rhythmical empathy is intriguing. Of particular interest would be a language which manifested both stress-timing and syllable-timing, as native speakers could try out their intuitions against both types, and some interesting experiments could be devised to bear on the issue. Such 'mixed' situations may be more common than is often realised. Roach, in fact, after a study in which inter-stress intervals were measured for a range of languages of both types, concludes 'there is no language which is totally syllable-timed or totally stress-timed – all languages display both sorts of timing ... [and] different types of timing will be exhibited by the same speaker on different occasions and in different contexts' (1982: 78). This is fair comment, but I do do not think the conclusion has been followed up by appropriate empirical observation. Just how much syllable-timing is there in English, for example?

If we go looking (I restrict my search to British English), we shall certainly find it. For example, I have heard it recently in the following range of contexts:

It can be heard when adults use baby-talk to very young children or animals. The 'Isn't he a lovely little baba, then?' type of speech, typically produced with much articulatory simplification and much labialisation, is also typically isosyllabic. Of course, a great deal of infant speech (at least, until the fourth year) itself demonstrates this rhythm, especially when children are trying out new structures. It is not surprising, therefore, to find it when adults adopt a comic infantile speech style, such as the character of Bluebottle in BBC Radio's *Goon Show* or of Frank in BBC Television's *Some Mothers Do 'Ave 'Em.*

Syllabic rhythm is common in speech which is expressive of several emotions, such as irritation and sarcasm. 'Oh we are in a bad mood today', with a clipped stress on each syllable.

Several children were heard playing Dr Who and the Daleks – the latter efficiently using the syllabic rhythm characteristic of their (and much other alien) speech.

Many cartoon characters are given a syllable-timed mode of speech, especially those representing monsters, aliens, bad guys and other stereotypes.

A great deal of popular music is syllable-timed. A clear example is the rhythm of ABBA's 'Money, money, money'.

Speech standards for the air and sea services (known as Airspeak and Seaspeak), because they need to articulate with extra clarity, often tend towards syllable-timing, with grammatical words made prominent and an even rhythm throughout. Public announcements generally move in this

175

direction as is often (though not always consistently) heard at bus
stations, railway stations and other such locations.

Various television and radio commercials adopt a staccato or spiky rhythm
in their slogans which is moving in the direction of isosyllabicity. 'Drinka
pinta milka day' is one of the most famous. Several media presenters
(especially news reporters, such as BBC Television's Martin Bell) also
adopt a somewhat isosyllabic style of delivery, the clipped manner of
presentation presumably striving to convey an impression of control,
crispness and precision.

Doubtless there are several other such contexts which could be usefully
collected and analysed, and conclusions drawn about the perception and
empathy of native speakers, as they respond to different types of rhythmical
utterance. In aggregate, however, these contexts do not amount to a great
deal. It is still the case that British English as a whole would give the general
auditory impression of being stress-timed.[1] Is it possible to conceive of a
single language in which stress-timing and syllable-timing are both present
in significant proportions and in comparable speech situations?

There is such a language. And it is in fact English – or, to be precise,
World English. This language has in recent years, in certain of its dialects,
been undergoing a prosodic development of considerable potential significance – comparable in its importance, possibly, to the prosodic change
which affected the language in its earliest days, when stress-shifting was a
factor in the loss of inflections. The situation is probably unique, arising out
of the unprecedented status of English as a world language, within the last
hundred years or so, which has brought it into contact with a range of
languages of diverse structural types, most of which have rhythms of a
broadly isosyllabic character. These situations have resulted in varieties of
modern English in which the syllable-timing has been transferred from the
contact languages, producing a natural variety of isosyllabic English spoken
as a mother tongue by large numbers of people, and viewed as a local
spoken standard.

This situation is most dramatic in the subcontinent of India, where one
of the most noticeable features of Indian English – and the one which
contributes most to the difficulty British speakers have in understanding
Indian speech – is the failure to preserve traditional stress distinctions
because of the isosyllabic rhythm. Syllable-timing is a noticeable feature of
the native languages of India, and is a characteristic of the official language,
Hindi. The importance of this particular variety of English lies in the
number of people who speak it. In India alone, with a current population
of about 850 million, and assuming some 3 per cent are fluent in English
(Kachru 1982: 378), there are over 25 million speakers – nearly half the size
of the English-speaking population of Britain. Less conservative estimates
double that figure.

To what extent could the syllable-timed speech of India influence other varieties, such as Standard British English? This is unlikely, because Indian English has a low-prestige value in Britain; however, not all regional varieties are in this position. The second most noticeable area where syllable-timing is normal is the creole English spoken throughout many of the islands of the Caribbean, and now (through immigration) in several parts of Britain. This culture has a much higher prestige rating, especially among the young, thanks mainly to its popular music, and the rhythms of reggae and rapping. I recently observed a rapping competition in this country, where most of the participants were not of West Indian ethnic origin. All participants, however, rapped using the isosyllabic rhythms characteristic of that style of performance. Whether such teenage imitative ability is likely to have any permanent effect on their speech, or on the speech of others, I cannot say: but their fluency in this alien rhythmicality was certainly impressive.

There is a syllable-timed English emerging all over the world. It is noticeable in South Africa, where it is a dominant feature of Afrikaans-influenced English, and of the English of many black people. Most other African varieties of English are syllable-timed. The phenomenon is also a noticeable feature of pidgins and creoles all over the world, such as Krio in West Africa and Tok Pisin in Papua New Guinea. It is noticeable in the United States, especially in those areas where mixed varieties of Spanish and English (such as Tex-Mex) have developed. There are millions in Florida, Texas, California and New Mexico who speak a variety of English which displays the syllable-timed rhythms of Spanish. Many in the cities of the north are second- or third-generation Italian immigrants whose speech is distinctively Italian in rhythm, and other isosyllabic languages display similar influence. It is too early to say what is happening in the corridors of power of the European Community, but according to several local observers a form of 'Eurospeak' is already emerging. I would not be surprised to find it characterised by a tendency towards isosyllabism in due course. Decades of experience of teaching English as a foreign language tells us that most learners have considerable difficulty mastering the weak vowel system in the language, and the most usual residual deficiency in a fluent learner's accent is likely to relate to this area. Given a community of English-using foreigners where this deficiency is shared, it would not be surprising to see it emerge as a standard feature in due course.

As we move into a world where British and American speakers of English are outnumbered by the totals of those learning English as a second language, intriguing questions arise. What will we begin to listen out for in the new dispensation? Will we cease to feel the need to pay attention to word-stress rules altogether? And will this matter? Many phoneticians and teachers have spent hours working with foreigners on their aberrant word stress, but we seem to know very little about the extent to which native speakers encounter a genuine problem of listening comprehension if such patterns are not followed. How many ambiguities actually arise within Indian English as a consequence of isosyllabism? And then with reference to phonetic empathy: what will happen to our intuitions, when the majority of the English-speaking world use varieties of English which are to varying extents isosyllabic?

There are many such unanswered questions, but one thing is plain. The linguistic situation is far more fluid than our early attempts at prosodic classification would lead us to expect. It is also – at least in respect of English – more rapidly changing than at any time in recent centuries. There is an urgent need to carry out some empirical studies of the range of rhythmical expression found in the new Englishes, and of the nature of the diffusion which is currently taking place. Perhaps the lack of stress in the new varieties is being compensated for by other kinds of contrastivity, such as changes in vowel quality, pitch or duration. Perhaps some kind of rhythmical bidialectism will emerge, as the varieties come increasingly into contact with each other. Or perhaps the whole question of rhythmical types has been overrated and nothing of consequence will take place in the language, while it develops its new rhythmical dimension. As Doc himself put it, at the end of an account of rhythmical types in his Pelican *Phonetics*: 'indeed there is no reason why there should be any rhythmical basis at all, in the sense of some feature recurring at regular time intervals' (p. 239). A breathtaking comment which I never fully grasped until now.

NOTE

1   Some accents display a noticeable tendency towards syllable-timing – certain varieties of Welsh English, for example. It is actually possible to be momentarily confused between Welsh and Indian speakers (see further below) – an observation which from time to time motivates local amateur linguists in Wales to conclude that Welsh was the original language of the Indo-Europeans!

Jack Windsor Lewis reminds me that a comic exaggeration of the fact that at least residual traces of a typical Welsh accent can occasionally be confused with a non-retroflex type of Indian English accent was made the subject of a review sketch on the London stage in the early 1960s (probably by Peter Cook for *One Over the Eight*). A darkened stage represented apparently a cageful of Welsh miners. The joke was that only when the pit cage ascended from the darkness into the light were the miners able to realise that one of their number was an Indian.

REFERENCES

Abercrombie, D. (1967) *Elements of General Phonetics*, Edinburgh: Edinburgh University Press.

Kachru, B. B. (1982) 'South Asian English', in R. W. Bailey and M. Gorlach (eds), *English as a World Language*, Cambridge: Cambridge University Press, pp. 353–83.

Levitt, A. G. and Aydelott Utman, J. G. (1992) 'From babbling towards the sound systems of English and French: a longitudinal two-case study', *Journal of Child Language*, 19, (1): 19–49.

Lloyd James, A. (1940) *Speech Signals in Telephony*, London: Pitman.

Mitchell, T. F. (1969) Review of Abercrombie, *Elements of General Phonetics*, *Journal of Linguistics* 5: 253–63.

O'Connor, J. D. (1973) *Phonetics*, Harmondsworth: Penguin.

Pike, K. L. (1945) *The Intonation of American English*, Ann Arbor: University of Michigan Press.

Roach, P. (1982) 'On the distinction between stress-timed and syllable-timed languages', in D. Crystal (ed.), *Linguistic Controversies*, London: Edward Arnold, pp. 73–9.

13

The social distribution of intonation patterns in Belfast

E. Douglas-Cowie, R. Cowie and J. Rahilly
The Queen's University of Belfast

INTRODUCTION

This paper describes social variation in intonation in Belfast.

There has been rather little research on either regional or social varieties of intonation in English. Regional varieties have been studied by Brown *et al.* (1980), Guy and Vonwiller (1984), Guy *et al.* (1986), McGregor (1980) and Pellowe and Jones (1978). Jarman and Cruttenden (1976) have written on Belfast intonation. In the social domain Pellowe and Jones (1978) considered the effects of age and socio-economic status on intonation, and there are a few studies of sex differences in intonation patterns (Elyan 1977; McConnell-Ginet 1988; Pellowe and Jones 1978).

There are two reasons for wanting to extend knowledge about social and regional variation in intonation: the first is that intonational variables may carry important signals about social origins and attitudes; the second is that theoretical analyses of intonation are often based on a limited body of descriptive knowledge. We make use of tunes as our units of analysis. Tune-based analysis has been found useful in other contexts (e.g. Armstrong and Ward 1926; O'Connor and Arnold 1973; Sag and Liberman 1975; de Pijper 1979, 1983; Bolinger 1982, 1986). Our data suggest that it may be particularly relevant to the social domain.

METHOD

Twenty-three people from Belfast were studied. There were twelve males and eleven females, with comparable distributions of age between the sexes. Subjects were selected to give a cross-section of Belfast society. They were assigned to three broad social groups – professional, working class and intermediate – on the basis of their education, occupation and income. Subjects were tape-recorded speaking in a range of styles. We analysed relatively informal speech which was produced by asking them to describe a day in their lives.

Each subject's speech was divided into tone groups. Each tone group was then subdivided into head, nucleus and tail, and each component was classified in terms of its general pitch movement (e.g. rise, fall, rise–fall or level). This leads to an overall description in which a tune might be categorised as, for instance, RF+R+L (i.e. rise–fall head + rising nucleus + level tail). A zero (Ø) in any of the labels means that one of the elements was missing, i.e. there was no head or no tail. The sample contained a total of 220 tone groups.

In addition to the social variables of the speaker's class and sex, each tone group was also labelled according to its grammatical function and the attitude which it expressed. The grammatical variables explored were clause type (dependent or independent) and clause position (terminal or non-terminal).

RESULTS

Links among the variables emerged only at a relatively abstract level. There were no convincing associations between simple frequency of component types (e.g. rising nuclei, falling tails, etc.) and any social variables, or between grammatical variables and any intonational variables. Some suggestive relationships between attitude and intonational variables were found, but they were far from conclusive.

The approach which did reveal systematic links involved organising tunes into higher-order families, each defined by a simple underlying pattern

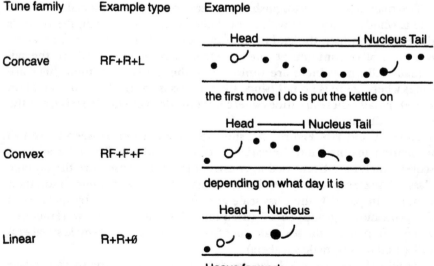

Figure 13.1 Examples of the tune families which were identified

with many different variations. Three broad families of tunes were distinguished. These are referred to as the concave family, the convex family and the linear family. The names convey the general shape which tunes in the family share. Figure 13.1 illustrates these families.

This grouping of tunes is motivated by the fact that it allows an orderly system of social marking to emerge. Each family shows its own form of social marking. The concave family is marked for both class and sex; the convex family is marked for sex; and the linear family is primarily class-marked.

The concave family

This is the largest of the three families. It contains more tune types than any other and also far more individual tone groups (approximately half of all the tone groups were in this family). All the tunes in the family have a fall or a rise–fall in the head, followed by a rising nucleus. The simplest version of the concave shape is the F+R+Ø tune. More elaborate versions are the F+R+L and RF+R+L tunes with their continuation past the rise into a level tail. Other tunes with a similar pattern of continuation past the rising nucleus are F+R+R and RF+R+R.

Most types of concave tune are shared by speakers of high and low status. Some tunes, though, tend to be associated with higher-status speakers. There is no individual concave tune that is purely or mainly associated with low-status speakers. There are also concave tunes that are more strongly male than others.

Two main features distinguish the concave tunes that are socially marked: one is whether they start with a rise–fall or with a simple fall; the other is the extent to which the end of the tune rises or falls. This second feature is a kind of continuum: at one extreme, there are tunes where the tail actually falls; next there are tunes where the tail is level; then there are tunes where there is no tail (since the nucleus is rising, these tunes end on a rise). Finally, there are tunes where not only does the nucleus rise, but the tail rises after it.

Panels 1 and 2 of Figure 13.2 show the relationship between these two intonation features and the variables of class and sex. The class and sex scores which have been used to construct the graphs measure the average class or sex respectively of the speakers who showed these intonation features. In panel 1, the class scale goes from 1 (used only by speakers in the professional group) to 2.5 (used only by speakers in the working-class group). In panel 2, the sex scale goes from 0 (used only by female speakers) to 1 (used only by male speakers).

Panel 1 shows that social class tends to be reflected in the way a concave tune ends. The downward trend on the graph shows that as a tune goes from a falling end to a very marked rising end, it becomes more likely to

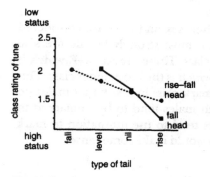

Panel 1: Concave tune endings and status

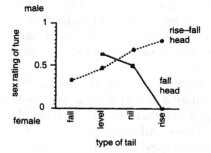

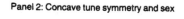

Panel 2: Concave tune symmetry and sex

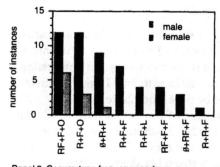

Panel 3: Convex tune frequency and sex

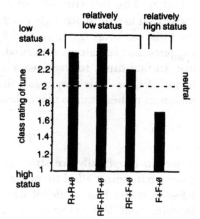

Panel 4: Tailless linear tunes and class

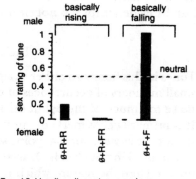

Panel 5: Headless linear tunes and sex

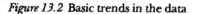

Figure 13.2 Basic trends in the data

be associated with high-status speakers. This is true however the tune begins, so long as it is concave.

Sex is reflected in a more abstract feature of concave tunes, shown in the crossover pattern in panel 2 of the graph. Males tend to begin and end a concave tune with the same pitch direction, i.e. their patterns tend to be symmetrical. This is not a particularly intuitively satisfying finding, and it is reasonable to treat it with some scepticism.

An interesting observation emerges when sex and class are considered together. The two concave tunes that are most strongly female are also those that are most strongly marked for class. These are RF+R+F, which is the most working-class tune, and F+R+R, which is the most upper class. This suggests that females use intonation to mark class in a way that males do not. In fact tunes strongly associated with males tend to be unmarked in terms of class. This may mean that males tend to use intonation to mark maleness rather than to mark class, which would make some sense.

The convex family

Tunes in this family are strongly marked for sex. Panel 3 in Figure 13.2 shows that almost all of them are very strongly male. The commonest tune, RF+F+Ø is the least male of the family. It is a regular pattern in all the families that the commonest tunes are not strongly marked for any variable.

There seems not to be much marking for class within the convex family. This fits the idea that males may use intonation to signal their maleness rather than their class. The data also suggest that there may be a kernel of rather similar tunes which are used by all classes, and that departures from this basic kernel tend to be used by high-status speakers. This is plausible, but the evidence for it is not clear cut.

The linear family

Tunes in this family go either straight up or straight down. There are rather small numbers of occurrences of some tunes, and so it would be unwise to make too much of them; but the family is none the less rather interesting. It is primarily class-marked, but it also has links with sex. It may be linked to attitude as well, but that point will not be developed here.

The marking of class is clearest in the case of tunes that have heads but no tail. Here the feature which relates to class is whether one starts with a rise or a fall. Panel 4 of Figure 13.2 shows the mean class scores for tunes in this subfamily. There seems to be a fairly sharp break with respect to class distribution: starting with a fall is markedly higher class than starting with a rise.

A second subfamily consists of tunes which have tails but no heads. They are generally marked for status in the sense that they tend to be working-class tunes; but within that they are marked for sex. The headless tunes that are rise-dominated are very much female, while the fall-dominated tune is exclusively male (see panel 5 of Figure 13.2).

CONCLUSION

The thrust of this paper can be expressed in terms of predictions. The existence of sex and class differences suggests that a Belfast listener would be able to discriminate the sex and social standing of a Belfast speaker from a tape which had been filtered to remove spectral components above F_0, and normalised to eliminate male–female pitch differences. The importance of tunes as a whole suggests a second likelihood, that the discrimination would survive if tone groups were separated and presented out of sequence, but break down if the individual components of tone groups were separated and presented out of sequence.

We have some confidence in these predictions. They are consistent with experience (such as hearing voices through walls or against noise) as well as with our particular data. The existence of social markers at this level is well worth asserting, and it appears to be a significant omission that sociolinguistics concentrates so heavily on segmental markers.

It is another matter entirely whether the details of our descriptive system are optimal. We do not claim that they are, only that they capture enough of the truth to be a useful starting-point for enquiry into social variation in prosody. The general strategy of distinguishing tune families seems likely to be a useful one, though it would clearly be better to have a theoretical motivation for the choice of families.

It is also another matter why the observed variations occur. Several obvious options exist. Some variation may occur because different groups use different surface forms to express the same underlying content and intention. Some may be a consequence of social differences at deeper levels, for instance in the content that different social groups tend to express or in the syntactic and conversational means which they use to express it. A possibility that particularly interests us is that speakers monitor prosodic attributes of their speech and adjust them to maintain a balance that fits the image they want to convey. That would be consistent with the way acquired deafness disrupts stylistic variation in intonation (Cowie and Douglas-Cowie 1992) as well as with the data described here.

Exploring these options is an interesting task with wide-reaching implications; however, it is well beyond the scope of this paper.

REFERENCES

Armstrong, L. E. and Ward, I. C. (1926) *A Handbook of English Intonation*, Leipzig and Berlin: B. G. Teubner.

Bolinger, D. (1982) 'Intonation and its parts', *Language* 58, 3: 505–33.

—— (1986) *Intonation and its Parts*, London: Edward Arnold.

Brown, G., Currie, K. and Kenworthy, J. (1980) *Questions of Intonation*, London: Croom Helm.

Cowie, R. and Douglas-Cowie, E. (1992) *Postlingually Acquired Deafness: Speech*

Deterioration and the Wider Consequences, Berlin: Mouton de Gruyter.

de Pijper, J. R. (1979) 'Close copy stylisations of British English intonation contours', *IPO Annual Progress Report.*

—— (1983) *Modelling British English Intonation*, Dordrecht: Foris.

Elyan, O. H. (1977) 'Sex differences in speech style', paper read at the First European Conference on Sex-Role Stereotyping, Cardiff.

Guy, G. R. and Vonwiller, J. (1984) 'The meaning of an intonation in Australian English', *Australian Journal of Linguistics* 4, 1: 1–17.

Guy, G. R., Horvath, B., Vonwiller, J., Disley E. and Rogers, I. (1986) 'An intonational change in progress in Australian English', *Language in Society* 15, 1: 23–51.

Jarman, E. and Cruttenden, A. (1976) 'Belfast intonation and the myth of the fall', *Journal of the International Phonetic Association* 6: 4–12.

McConnell-Ginet, S. (1988) 'Language and gender', in F. J. Newmeyer (ed.), *Linguistics: the Cambridge Survey*, Vol. 4: *Language: the Socio-cultural Context*, Cambridge: Cambridge University Press, pp. 75–99.

McGregor, R. L. (1980) 'The social distribution of an Australian English intonation contour', *Macquarie University Working Papers* 2: 1–26.

O'Connor, J. D. and Arnold, G. (1973) *Intonation of Colloquial English*, London: Longman.

Pellowe, J. and Jones, V. (1978) 'On intonational variability in Tyneside speech', in P. Trudgill (ed.), *Sociolinguistic Patterns in British English*, London: Edward Arnold, pp. 101–21.

Sag, I. and Liberman, M. (1975) 'The intonational disambiguation of indirect speech acts', *Papers from the Eleventh Regional Meeting, Chicago Linguistic Society*, 487–97.

14

Principles of intonational typology

Anthony Fox
University of Leeds

INTRODUCTION

That intonational features of languages may differ from one language to another is evident from even a casual analysis; such differences have been documented in numerous contrastive studies, and foreign-language learners – especially those learning English – are often given training in intonation on the assumption that there is something for them to learn. But it is also frequently asserted that intonation may actually be rather similar across different languages, and there have been discussions of intonational 'universals' (Bolinger 1964, 1978; Cruttenden 1981, 1986; Ladd 1981; Ohala 1983; Vaissière 1983); the assumption behind such assertions is that all languages must do rather similar things with intonation, and that they have rather similar means of doing them, the differences being superficial and rather insignificant.

The apparent contradiction here is clearly not unique to intonation; a similar problem arises wherever the search for abstract general principles of 'universal grammar' conflicts with observable linguistic diversity. One solution, which represents something of a middle way between unconstrained variety on the one hand and complete uniformity on the other, is to accept the reality of diversity, but to set limits to it in the form of a typology: languages may differ from one another, but only in certain clearly defined ways. This might perhaps be formalised, as in much recent work in syntax, by assuming that choices are limited to specific 'parameters', which may be set differently in different cases (see e.g. Chomksy 1981: 6ff.)

The present paper[1] presents some preliminary findings of an investigation into the intonational features of a number of languages from a typological perspective. Despite the many cross-language investigations of intonation, our detailed knowledge of the intonation of any but a few languages is unfortunately very patchy, and not especially reliable (see Cruttenden 1986: 144ff.). There is also the problem, more acute here than in segmental phonology, that there is no single established theory or mode of description, so that an attempt to compare the intonational features of different languages on the basis of published accounts also entails comparison of the descriptive and theoretical frameworks that they adopt. Since these frameworks are rarely articulated in an explicit manner, it is small wonder that little substantive progress has been made in this area.

In the absence of generally accepted parameters for the description of intonation it is clear that the collection of large amounts of data from a wide range of languages, though desirable in itself, would be unlikely to yield satisfactory results. More important at this stage of the investigation is the clarification of principles and the formulation of hypotheses, though it is obviously desirable that such principles and hypotheses should be based on as representative a range of observations as possible. One initial assumption of the present investigation is that intonational differences correlate closely with different kinds of overall prosodic organisation – tone language vs non-tone language,[2] languages with and without various kinds of accentual features, and so on – and it is important, therefore, to examine languages displaying a variety of such types of prosodic organisation. Remarks in the remainder of this paper will therefore draw on data taken not only from some well-known European languages – English, French, German – but also from a number of languages with quite different prosodic structures: Chinese (both Mandarin and Cantonese), Japanese, Mende (West Africa) and Zulu (South Africa). It must be stressed, however, that investigation of the intonation of a large number of languages for its own sake is not the aim here; the intention at this stage is rather to address – in a preliminary and rather informal way – a number of central questions that arise in the attempt to establish an intonational typology.

THE CHARACTERISTICS OF INTONATION

In considering the characteristics of intonation we must make a decision at the outset about what is, and what is not, to be regarded as 'intonation' and, more specifically, whether we take intonation to be a matter of pitch alone or to include other features such as 'stress' or 'accent'. This question pervades the 'classical' literature on the subject, but rarely surfaces explicitly: for instance, American structuralists separated the various features of prosodic structure as independent 'phonemic' systems, with 'pitch phonemes', 'stress phonemes', etc. (see Trager 1941; Trager and Smith 1951; Hockett 1955). More 'functionally' based approaches, including the British school, have been happy to include accentual and rhythmical features in their intonation systems along with pitch; the British tradition (e.g. Palmer 1922; Armstrong and Ward 1926; Kingdon 1958; Schubiger 1958; O'Connor and Arnold 1961) sees the accentual 'nucleus' as an integral part of the intonation pattern. Similarly, Pierrehumbert (1980) envisages a succession of 'pitch accents' in her description of English intonation. As will be seen from the conclusions presented in this paper, the question of what to include as 'intonation' is crucial for discussions of intonational typology, since these other features may vary across languages and be considered independently from a typological point of view. Hence the inclusion or exclusion of specific features from our definition of intonation has obvious implications for the typology of intonation itself. For the purposes of the initial exposition in this paper, we shall be concerned primarily with features of pitch alone, though with some reference to the prosodic context in which these features appear; the question of the scope of 'intonation' will be touched on again below.

As a starting-point of the investigation it was possible to identify in all the languages investigated a comparable unit of prosodic structure which could be regarded as an *intonation unit*. (This is not to say, however, that this unit is exclusively intonational, even in a broader definition of this term which includes accentual features. There is considerable evidence that units of intonation also serve as the domains of other prosodic features, and are not, consequently, intonation units as such. We return to this question below.) This unit can no doubt be interpreted as a basic unit of 'information' in the sense of Halliday (1967) and others, but since our investigation was concerned only with the strictly phonological aspects of prosodic structure, the semantic or communicative character of the unit will not be explored systematically here. There is also certainly some correlation – however inconsistent – between intonation units and syntactic groupings, but this again is not central to our investigation and will not be considered further. The units themselves could be identified partly on the basis of pauses and other junctural phenomena, partly on the basis of their internal structural integrity, for example, unity of pitch movement, consistency of rhythm, subordination to a single accentual peak, and so on. Their length was found to vary widely, but this variation was found in all the languages examined, and hence we cannot use the length or scope of intonation units as a typological criterion. There was also clear evidence for at least some degree of hierarchical ordering of intonation units, with the individual units forming part of larger structures, again characterised by consistent features throughout, for example with a progressively lower initial pitch in each unit within the structure. This kind of phenomenon was consistently encountered in all the languages examined, and it can therefore with some justification be considered a universal. Where languages differ, therefore, is not in the nature or scope of the units themselves but in the internal organisation of these units and of the features which characterise them.

As noted above, the categories used in the description of the intonation of different languages vary from case to case; it is therefore necessary to devise more general categories which will not necessarily coincide, or indeed even be compatible, with the familiar categories found in other descriptive work. Concepts such as 'nuclear tone', 'pitch accent', etc., are too typologically restricted for our present purposes, and also include other prosodic features besides pitch itself. In the present investigation, a different, and more generally applicable scheme will be used. The features of the intonation unit that occurred with reasonable consistency in the languages examined were found to fall loosely into three types, which it is proposed to designate as follows:

1 'envelope' features;
2 'prominence' features;
3 'modality' features.

By envelope features is meant the pitch features which characterise the intonation unit as a whole, notably the overall pitch height, the pitch range and the pitch slope.[3] These features form the setting for the more specific and more localised features of 'prominence' and 'modality'. Prominence features are those which pick out a specific point or points in the intonation unit, often, though not necessarily, correlated with some form of linguistic 'accent'. Modality features involve local variations in the pitch pattern itself, e.g. to give a 'rising' or 'falling' intonation, traditionally associated with 'sentence types' or the 'attitude of the speaker'. In the discussion which follows, these sets of features will be considered in turn, with appropriate exemplification and justification from the languages investigated. On the basis of this, conclusions can then be drawn about the possible status and scope of an intonational typology.

ENVELOPE FEATURES

Instrumental analysis confirms that both the overall height and the range of the pitch pattern can vary considerably between utterances in all the languages examined, though this appears to depend to a considerable extent on the place of the unit in a more complex intonation structure, as discussed above. Units occurring early in the sequence tended to display both a higher pitch and a wider range than later units. That such factors are not completely automatic, but can to some extent be manipulated by the speaker, is evident from the differences in isolated intonation units. When asked to produce more 'animated' or 'emphatic' forms of utterances, for example, speakers consistently raised the average pitch level and increased the range, along with other modifications, both segmental and supra-segmental. A general rise in pitch level was also encountered in utterances with certain functional roles, especially questions, in a number of languages.

In Mende, for example, questions were regularly accompanied by, among other things, an overall rise in the pitch level (Figure 14.1), while

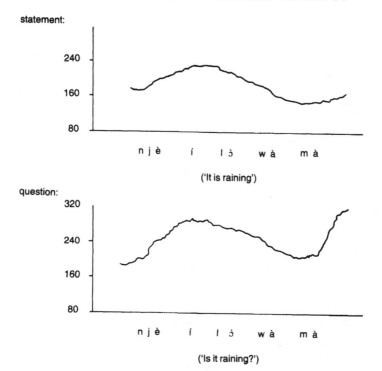

statement:

('It is raining')

question:

('Is it raining?')

Figure 14.1 Envelope features in Mende: statement and question

exclamatory utterances tended to have increased range (Figure 14.2). A comparable situation was found in Zulu (Figure 14.3). (Note: F_0 values, where given, are taken from recorded utterances.) The pitch range was also not always consistent throughout the unit itself. It was noticeable that larger pitch excursions tended to occur in the earlier part of the unit than in the later part. This is no doubt due to the effects of declination, which becomes more marked as the unit progresses, and which, by lowering the top line of the pattern, restricts the available range.

Declination (pitch slope, downdrift) is the most complex, and most variable envelope feature (see Hombert 1974; Pierrehumbert 1980; Vaissière 1983; Ladd 1984). Some form of declination is widely reported for very many languages, and it was certainly encountered in all the languages investigated in this research, though not in every utterance. However, unlike the envelope features considered so far, its mode of manifestation differed from language to language. Consider as a simple example the case of French, where declination may take the form of a progressive lowering from syllable to syllable. In Figure 14.4, the pitch drops gradually after the initial rise until the onset of the final sentence accent (Hirst 1983: 96).

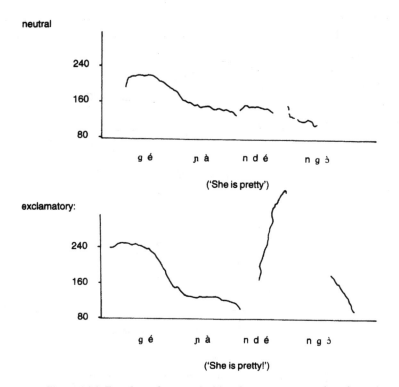

Figure 14.2 Envelope features in Mende: statement and exclamation

The situation in Japanese appears to be comparable; here each intonation unit is also an accent phrase, usually characterized by pitch prominence on the 'accented' mora[4] but with no other accentual features comparable to 'stress'. We find that declination is realised as a steady fall from mora to mora, though the presence of the phrase accent often inhibits the declination, the pitch remaining on a high plateau until the accented mora (Figure 14.5).

The complications created by the interaction between declination and accentual structure are also familiar from better-known non-tone languages such as English or German (Fox, 1978, 1984). In both cases there is a clear downward tendency throughout the intonation unit, but this is not manifested in a simple way as a fall from one syllable to the next, but must take account of accentual units (feet), giving a regular fall from foot to foot . Figure 14.6 gives a typical instance from German. Incidentally, though the principles are analogous in English and German, the details are different: the pitch of an English foot tends to fall initially and rise at the end; in German the opposite pattern is observed (see Fox 1978, 1984).

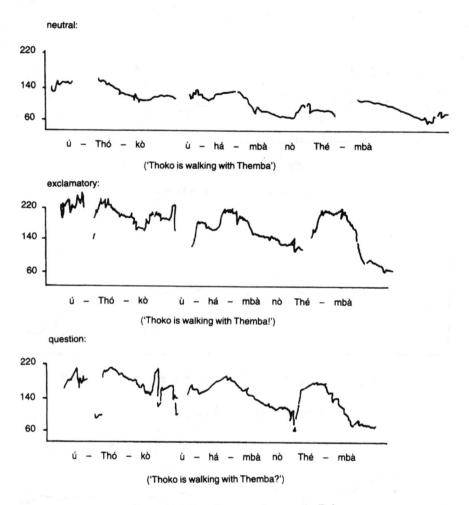

Figure 14.3 Development features in Zulu

Declination was also observable in the African languages investigated, though here with other impediments to its implementation in the form of tone. A simple example from Mende, spoken by a female speaker, is given in Figure 14.7. It can be seen that both the sequence of high tones and the final sequence of low tones are characterised by a gradual downdrift which does not, however, endanger the distinctiveness of the tones.

It has often been observed in languages of this type that downdrift is more marked where a high tone follows a low tone, giving the impression of a series of 'terraces' (Wellmers 1959). In Figure 14.8 it

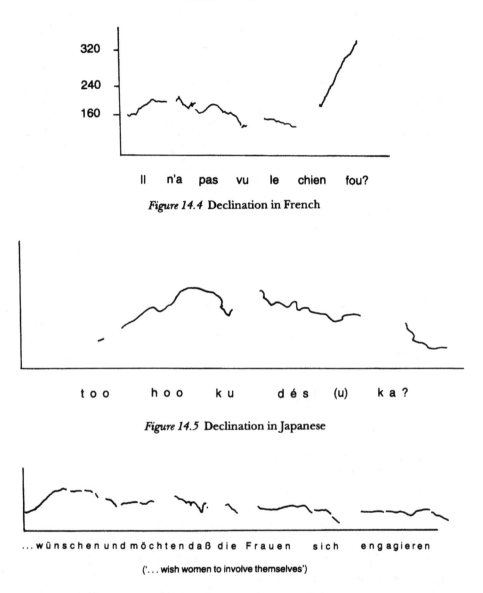

Figure 14.4 Declination in French

Figure 14.5 Declination in Japanese

Figure 14.6 Declination in German

will be noted that the high tones become progressively lower until they are no higher than the earlier low tones. Nevertheless, declination does not obscure the tonal distinctions here, as each high tone is still higher than the preceding low, and any upward movement is sufficient to identify it as a high tone.[5] A comparable situation is found in Zulu,

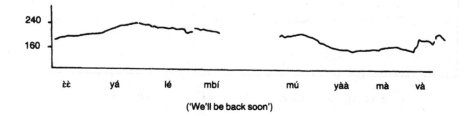

('We'll be back soon')

Figure 14.7 Declination in Mende

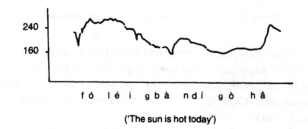

('The sun is hot today')

Figure 14.8 Tonal terraces in Mende

('The boys are taking out cattle from the fold')

Figure 14.9 Declination in Zulu

though with some added complications. In addition to its tones, Zulu also has an accentual structure, with one high syllable of the word treated as accented, and subject to lengthening. Although declination is found to operate as consistently in Zulu as in Mende, it is evidently constrained by this accentual structure. The pitch of high tone syllables is, as expected, progressively lowered after low tones, giving utterances such as those of Figure 14.3; but the downward trend is also often counteracted

195

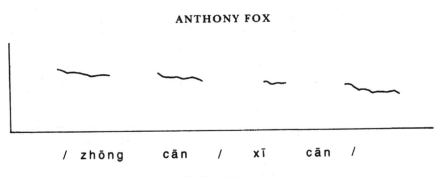

/ zhōng   cān   /   xī   cān   /

(tā dōu chī)

('(He eats both) Chinese food and Western food')

Figure 14.10 Declination in Mandarin Chinese

by an upward tendency on the accented syllables, as in Figure 14.9. Here, declination is not only inhibited by a sequence of high tones, but it is also completely suspended within each accentual unit, so that a rising trend predominates. Only in the final accentual unit does declination take its normal course.

Interaction between declination, accentuation and tone can also be observed in Mandarin Chinese. Mandarin (unlike Cantonese) has an accentual structure with feet comparable to those of English, and declination is noticeable in the progressively lower pitch both of successive feet and of successive syllables within the foot: for example, the phrase *Zhōng cān, xī cān, (tā dōu chī)* ('(He eats both) Chinese food and Western food') contains only high-level lexical tones, but in a recorded utterance the pitch fell throughout (see Figure 14.10 – foot boundaries are marked by '/').

The examples given here serve to demonstrate two things: first, the universality of the downward pitch tendency; and second, the variety of ways in which this tendency is actually manifested in specific languages. In all these cases it is evident that the manifestation is directly dependent on the prosodic structure of the language in question: features of this structure, either accentual or tonal, may restrict the realisation to certain parts of the intonation unit, or ensure that this realisation may take place only in certain ways and under certain conditions. Of course, not all details of the realisation can be explained in terms of these basic parameters of variation (tone vs non-tone language, different kinds of accentual structure), the differences between English and German noted above being a good example; but it is nevertheless clear that many of the most fundamental intonational divergences can be ascribed to these parameters.

PROMINENCE FEATURES

By 'prominence features' we mean those pitch features which serve to single out specific points in the utterance. The term 'prominence' must be used with care, as it does not necessarily imply greater loudness but merely that the syllable or syllables in question have some pitch feature which distinguishes them from their context. The functional role of such prominence is also not at issue here. Pitch prominence is a common feature of most languages, though its role within prosodic structure is somewhat variable. In English we are accustomed to two basic kinds of phonological pitch prominence: that associated with the 'nucleus' and that associated with the non-nuclear accented syllables.[6] In Japanese, however, there are no 'stressed' syllables in the English sense; one mora within the intonation unit is generally 'accented' (though there are also accentless units), but this accentuation is realised exclusively by pitch: the accented mora is high, as are all preceding moras except the first, and it is followed by a pitch drop. Investigations suggest that it is possible to boost two points in the accent phrase in order to achieve greater prominence: the second mora (the first mora is generally low and the second high, but the amount of the rise is adjustable) and the accented mora itself, though this latter possibility is not available in 'accentless' phrases. As we have already noted, declination tends to be deferred until after the accented mora.

Of the African languages examined, Mende had no accented syllables in the normal sense, but individual words could be picked out by slightly raising or lowering the pitch of their syllables. The low tones of an emphasised word tended to become lower, and the high tones higher, and there was often increased length, as in the example given in Figure 14.2. Of more interest, however, is Zulu. As noted above, the intonation units of Zulu are characterised not just by contrastive tone but also by an accentual system. Within each word group forming an intonation unit, several syllables can be regarded as accented, and one of these can be seen as especially prominent. This invariably appears to have a high tone, with the highest pitch of the unit. As we saw above, the accented syllables have an important role in relation to declination, with the tendency of the pitch to rise towards the accent. In cases where the pitch of the whole unit is raised, for example in interrogative or exclamatory utterances, it is this syllable whose pitch is raised the most.

Oriental languages of the 'contour' type are also variable in the use made of pitch prominence. In Cantonese the possibilities seem to be limited in the same way that they are in Mende, as there are, in this language, no accented syllables. As in Mende, however, pitch prominence can here be achieved by boosting any high tone syllable, or increasing the rise on a rising tone; syllables with low tone seem not to be susceptible to this kind

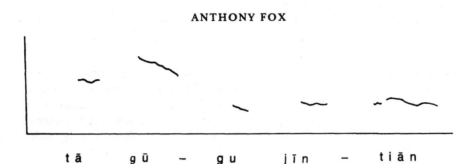

t ā   g ū   –   g u   j ī n   –   t i ā n

(kāi–zhe xīn chē)

('His aunt (was driving a new car) today')

Figure 14.11 Pitch prominence in Mandarin Chinese

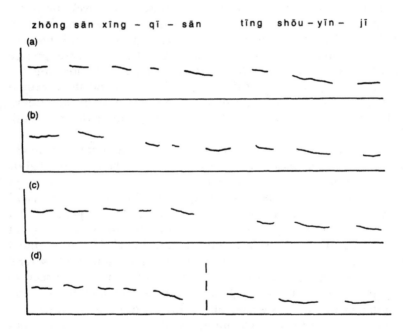

('Zhong San listens to the radio on Wednesdays')

Figure 14.12 Deferred declination in Mandarin Chinese

of modification. In Mandarin Chinese there are accented syllables analogous to those of English, and greater prominence can be achieved by boosting their pitch, though in the case of the low (third) tone by lowering it. In Figure 14.11, the syllable 'gū' is raised above the level of surrounding syllables (the lexical tones here are either high level or 'neutral').

Another method of giving pitch prominence to syllables is, as we have encountered in other languages, deferring declination: declination begins only after the prominent item (cf. the case of Japanese, discussed above). The four utterances of Figure 14.12 are renderings of the 'same' utterance *Zhōng Sān xīngqīsān tīng shōuyīnjī* ('Zhong San listens to the radio on Wednesdays'), in which contextual cues were given to elicit a different focus in each case. Note that all the lexical tones are high level. Apart from (a), where no such cues were given, the focus was on (b) *Zhōng Sān*, (c) *xīngqīsān* and (d) *shōuyīnjī* (the postponement of the focus to the end in example (d) led the speaker to split the utterance into two intonation units). The results here show no particular modification of the tone in the different versions, but simply a delay to the start of the declination, resulting in a high level plateau before the focus. This would suggest a kind of two-part structure to the Mandarin intonation unit, the first being relatively level, the second being subject to declination. It is not clear, however, whether the pivot of this structure should be regarded as a 'nucleus' in the English sense, since this syllable is not characterised by any significant pitch modification as such.

The question of the existence of a 'nuclear accent' is a complex one, and not merely in Mandarin Chinese. Some descriptions of languages with a prosodic structure similar to that of English have dispensed with a 'nucleus' (e.g. Thorsen 1983, on Danish). Moreover, even in the case of English doubt has been cast on the validity of this category (Brown *et al.* 1980: 138ff.; Currie 1980, 1981). Against this, Bolinger (1978) treats the variable location of a central pitch feature as one of the universals of intonation.

Some of the difficulty here is caused by a failure to distinguish 'prominence' from 'modality' features. The English 'nucleus' tends to combine both of these: it has an accentual role, but also carries distinctive pitch patterns. It is clear from our investigations, however, that this unity is not universal. In Japanese, for example, as we shall see below, the two are kept entirely separate, with the accent having no possibility for the realisation of intonational modalities. Languages do not, therefore, need to have a 'nucleus' in order to have modality features, and this would appear to be the case with, for example, Mende and Cantonese. But even in English the 'prominence' and 'modality' features are not always combined: a 'rising tone', for instance, does not necessarily involve a rise on the nucleus itself (which may well be simply low and level) but more commonly only at the end of the utterance. Those cases in English (and Danish) where the nucleus has proved hard to identify would seem to be largely those where there is this separation. The fact that 'modality' features are not located where the intonational 'nucleus' is assumed to be does not, therefore, invalidate the accentual role of the 'nucleus'; in some languages this is the norm. The problem is, however, that in cases where modality features are not associated with the accentual peak (the 'nucleus') of the intonation unit, this peak may be difficult to identify, unless, as in Japanese, it has consistent pitch features of its own. This makes it difficult to decide whether Mandarin Chinese, for example, which, at the lower level, has an accentual system similar to English, can be said to have a 'nuclear' accent, since such an accent is not associated with modality.

It is possible to conclude, nevertheless, that all languages are able to employ pitch prominence, but it is again evident that the significance of this prominence, and the manner in which it is implemented, varies with the prosodic structure of the language.

MODALITY FEATURES

Modality features involve modifications of the pitch pattern to distinguish what are traditionally called 'attitudinal' meanings and 'sentence types'. All the languages investigated made use of pitch for this purpose, but sometimes in a rather limited way. As before, the main interest is in the manner in which such features can be manifested, given the constraints of the different prosodic systems. Although the term 'modality' suggests the nature of the characteristic functions of this kind of intonational feature, the intended use of this term here is a little more restricted, referring only to certain *local* modifications of the pitch. Some of the 'envelope' features reflect functions of this sort, for example declination may be inhibited in questions, resulting in a high final pitch, or there may be a general raising of the overall pitch level in such utterances. But in addition there are more specific and more localised features associated with particular intonational meanings, and it is these to which the term 'modality' is intended to refer. Our concern here is also purely with the phonological organisation of intonation, and hence the use of traditional labels such as 'question intonation', etc., is for convenience only, and is not to be taken as indicating endorsement of their accuracy.

The major difficulty with the implementation of such local features of intonation is clearly that pitch details of this kind are frequently pre-empted

ʃ   t u   m a   d e   d e   s (u)   k a?

('Until when are you studying here')

Figure 14.13 Final modality in Japanese

200

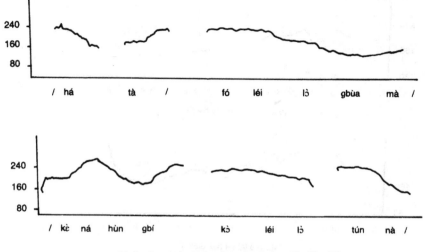

('Today the sun is shining, but nevertheless it is still cold')

Figure 14.14 'Continuative' intonation in Mende

for other purposes, especially lexical or grammatical tone, but also pitch accent. Though Japanese is not a tone language, it has a phrase accent, and this is characterised by a specific pattern, a falling pitch, immediately following the accented mora. This means that the potential for other modalities – such as a rising pattern – is excluded at this point in the utterance. In this language, therefore, intonational modalities are implemented not at the accented mora but at the end of the phrase. In many cases, such a final modality accompanies a modal particle, such as *yo, ka* or *ne*. In all cases, the pitch movements are confined to the final mora, and thus in no way disturb the pitch of the rest of the utterance, with its obligatory high-pitched plateau and falling pitch accent. This is illustrated in Figure 14.13.

In tone languages proper, the implementation of intonational modalities could in principle conflict with distinctive tones. In the majority of cases, the modality features of intonation are regularly implemented at the end of the intonation unit, but without any implication of accentuation. Consider the sentence from Mende given as Figure 14.14. There are three intonation units here (separated by '/'), all of which end in a low tone, but the first two, being non-final, have what might be called a 'continuative' intonation, consisting of a rise. The rise is attached to the low tone in each case; only in the final intonation unit does the final low tone maintain its low pitch. Consider further some examples of 'attitudinal' intonation patterns. The 'same' sentence is given a variety of different intonations in Figures 14.15 and 14.16, which have

201

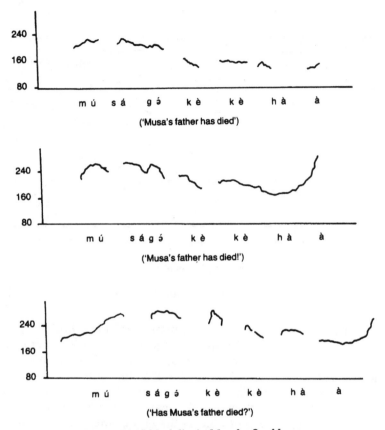

Figure 14.15 Modality in Mende: final low tone

a final low tone and a final high tone respectively. (These intonational modifications may also often be accompanied by changes in length and voice quality.) Figure 14.1 gives a further example.

A similar principle was also found in Chinese, both Mandarin and Cantonese, where the intonation contour can similarly interact with the lexical tone. In 'neutral' utterances, for example, for which a final falling modality is likely, the final syllable will have a lower pitch level than usual, with a downward slope. This can be illustrated with final high level tones from both Mandarin and Cantonese, given in Figure 14.17.

The intonation may also be combined with the lexical tone to form a composite pitch pattern. The Cantonese expression *hoey kei ma* ('go horse-riding'), for example, ends in a low-rising lexical tone, but the pitch of the final syllable when in final position was rising–falling, the rise being the residue of the lexical tone, the fall being the intonational feature. Where tone and intonation agree, for example a

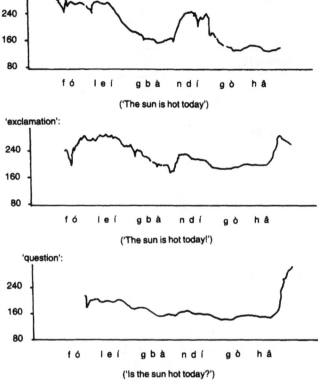

'neutral':

('The sun is hot today')

'exclamation':

('The sun is hot today!')

'question':

('Is the sun hot today?')

Figure 14.16 Modality in Mende: final high tone

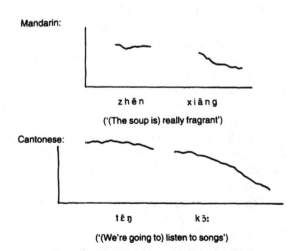

Mandarin:

zhēn   xiāng

('(The soup is) really fragrant')

Cantonese:

tɛ̄ŋ   kɔ̄:

('(We're going to) listen to songs')

Figure 14.17 Modality in Chinese

203

'neutral':

'excitement':

'doubt':

'astonishment':

'surprised acceptance':

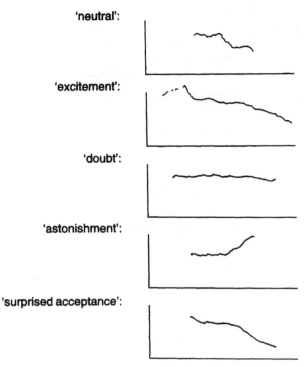

Figure 14.18 Some modalities with Cantonese 'a'

rising tone and a rising intonation, we may find an exaggerated tonal movement, with a longer or higher rise than usual. A final falling tone may be barely noticeable as such, because of the narrow range at the end of the unit, though the fall may be more obvious where the intonation also demands a clear falling pattern. But we may also find a similar strategy to that of Japanese: the addition of a final particle as the bearer of the intonation. Conventionally, and in citation form, such particles (e.g. Mandarin *ma, a, ne, ba,* etc.) are assigned a lexical tone, but in practice they are, in Mandarin at least, toneless, and thus are free to take a variety of intonational modalities; *a* in particular occurs with a wide variety of such patterns. The particle *a* may likewise take a variety of intonation patterns in Cantonese, of which those given in Figure 14.18 are examples (the labels are for identification purposes only, and have no systematic status).

In Zulu, however, there did not appear to be modifications or additional pitch movements at the end of the intonation unit. Consider the utterances of Figure 14.3, which are comparable to those given for Mende and Chinese, above. As can be seen, intonational modality here consists in adjustment of the pitch levels of individual syllables (especially

204

accented ones) rather than in changing or adding to the basic shape.

These examples again show the universality of intonational modalities but also demonstrate that a number of different strategies are employed in their implementation in different languages. The major location for such features is clearly at the end of the intonation unit, especially where they would otherwise interfere unacceptably with pitch features associated with tone or pitch accent, but even here the other characteristics of the utterance, notably the tonal features, need to be taken into account. Accentual features play a variety of roles here; they are not associated directly with modality in Japanese, Mandarin Chinese or Mende, but seem relevant in both English and Zulu (neither of which necessarily relegates its modality features to the end).

CONCLUSIONS

The aim of the present paper was to consider the possibility of establishing a typology of intonation in order to satisfy the demands of both universality and observable variety. On the one hand we have seen that a wide range of intonational phenomena can be brought under a relatively small number of headings: 'envelope', 'prominence' and 'modality' features. It is at least arguable, therefore, that these constitute a universally valid framework for the description of intonational features. At the same time, it is clear that some of the widely used categories for the description of individual languages – such as 'nuclear tone' – are unsuitable as universals.

On the other hand we have also seen considerable variety in the realisation of these basic intonational categories. The universality of envelope features is perhaps to be expected, since these would appear ultimately to reflect the physiological constraints of the speech process itself, but even here we find variety. Though probably a universal phenomenon, declination is implemented in remarkably different ways in different languages. As far as features of pitch prominence are concerned, these are similarly variable, since the possibilities for such prominence are differently constrained in different cases. Modality features are the most variable, not merely in the details of individual patterns (which is to be expected) but also in how and where such features can be used.

As argued above, however, the variety of intonational features is for the most part not intrinsic to intonation itself in the sense that it is intonational variables as such that are involved. Most of the differences illustrated in this paper have been cases where the intonational variety derives from differences in other features of prosodic structure, particularly accentuation and tone. Accentual differences determine the manner of declination (different in, say, English and French, or Mandarin and Cantonese), the possibilities for pitch prominence (since it is usually accented syllables that may carry prominence in languages which have an accentual feature), and the location of modality features (which may be associated with accented syllables). The presence or absence of tone is also a significant factor for intonation, since the necessity of preserving tonal distinctions severely limits the use of pitch for other purposes. Tone thus imposes limits on declination, and we find that modality features typically have to be separated from the tonal pattern in languages with distinctive tone.

All this clearly has implications for a typology of intonation. If the major differences in the intonational features of languages are not the result of different parameters within intonation itself, but depend on differences found in other prosodic features, then it is extremely doubtful if we can establish a typology of intonation as such at all. A typology of intonation will turn out to be a typology of the other features with which intonation interacts. This does depend, of course, as discussed at the beginning of this paper, on what we take 'intonation' to be. Inclusion of features of accentuation in the definition of intonation, as in, for example, the British descriptive tradition, would naturally mean that typological differences in accentuation are also intonational, and hence an intonational typology is possible, even if based on accentual features. However, this has the disadvantage of precluding the kinds of generalisation about intonation that have been made in this paper.

It must be said, of course, that not all differences in the intonation systems of languages (in the narrower sense of pitch features alone) can be attributed directly to differences in other prosodic features. English and German, for example, cannot be said to differ significantly in the basic organisation of their prosodic structures, yet they are by no means identical in their intonation (see Fox 1984). Differences can be found in, for example, the set of possible intonational modalities ('nuclear tones'), as well as in the details of their realisations. In claiming that apparently typological distinctions in intonation are the result of distinctions else-where we evidently cannot exclude all purely intonational variation. However, a corollary of this claim is that such differences as remain will be of a less significant kind, less important, that is, in a typological sense. They lie below what may be called the 'typological threshold'. There may of course be some room for difference of opinion as to where this threshold should be located, but any typological classification of linguistic phenom-ena has in any case to select particular features as typologically significant at the expense of others. The claim here is that intonational features which are not dependent on the rest of prosodic structure are not significant enough to justify a meaningful typology of intonation.

The implication of this is that a typology can be established for at least some of the other features of prosodic structure. The literature on typologies of accentuation and tone is, in fact, quite extensive (see Fox 1985), and it has received new impetus from discussions of the nature of accent and tone within a non-linear framework (e.g. Goldsmith, 1982). It can be no part of the present paper to attempt such a typology or typologies,[7] but some light may be thrown on this question by a brief consideration of how intonational features interact with other prosodic features.

Various models can be envisaged for the assignment of intonational features to utterances. There is first the 'bottom–up' model, which entails the derivation of intonation contours by means of the progressive inter-action of constituent parts of the utterance, in the manner in which stress contours were derived in classical generative phonology (see Chomsky and Halle 1968). This model was used, for example, by McCawley (1968) in the specification of Japanese pitch contours. An alternative is the 'left-to-right' model, which assigns pitch in a linear fashion. This is implicit in the analysis of English intonation given by Pierrehumbert (1980), who envisages a finite-state grammar for the generation of contours. The model that has proved to be most successful in this area, however, especially in the synthesis of artificial intonation contours, and which appears to be the most suitable for the present purpose, is the 'top–down' approach, in which a generalised contour is successively modified by its interaction with 'lower-level' features, be they accentual or tonal. This is the model adopted, for example, by Fujisaki in Japanese (e.g. Fujisaki and Nagasami 1969) and more recently in the extensive work by Gårding and her associates (e.g. Gårding 1983). This approach is also compatible with those models which postulate a hierarchy of prosodic units, since the intonation contour can be applied as a feature of the highest unit and modified by features of lower units (which would include accent and tone). Such a hierarchy was part of a number of structuralist models of prosodic structure, e.g in Tagmemics (Pike 1967) and Systemic Grammar (e.g. Berry 1977), and it is also found in more recent models, e.g. those of Selkirk (1980, 1984) and Giegerich (1984), and especially that of Nespor and Vogel (1983, 1986).[8]

From a typological perspective, therefore, intonational variety can be ascribed to the way in which the envelope, prominence and modality features of intonation interact, in a top–down process, with typologically different organisations of prosodic structures. These differences may be in the hierarchy of prosodic units itself (for example, languages without an accentual structure will lack a metrical foot), or they may be in the prosodic features associated with specific units: tone languages have tonal features at syllable- or foot-level which must be superimposed on the features of intonation associated with the higher units of prosodic structure.

These remarks suggest a means by which intonation can be incorporated into a model of prosodic structure in a typologically neutral fashion. Apparently typological distinctions in intonation can be filtered out of the intonation patterns themselves and ascribed to the structures with which these patterns interact.

These remarks are clearly speculative and programmatic and they need further elaboration. In particular, the nature of these typological distinctions in prosodic structure needs to be clarified, although this task cannot be undertaken in the framework of the present article. Also to be explored are the implication of this approach for the teaching of intonation, which was alluded to in the first paragraph of this article. Clearly, if the major differences between the intonation patterns of different languages lie not in the intonation patterns themselves but in the prosodic structures through which they are realised, then the effort expended in teaching intonation might be better directed towards the teaching of prosodic structure, where this differs typologically from that of the native language.

NOTES

1 This research was supported by an award from the ESRC (grant no. C00232182).
2 Pike (1945: 25; 1948: 16), asserts that tone languages cannot have intonation, at least in the sense of a structured set of contours. That view is not adopted in the present paper; indeed, ample evidence is adduced to the contrary.
3 These labels can be given informal definitions as follows: by *height* is meant the difference between the average pitch of the contour and that of some notional baseline; *range* refers to the average difference between the top and bottom values of the contour, while *slope* is the overall upward or downward trend in height.
4 The mora, rather than the syllable, is the basic unit of Japanese prosody.
5 One further complication is 'downstep', consisting in a lowering of pitch comparable to declination, but involving only adjacent high tones and often having grammatical, or even lexical, significance. This phenomenon is clearly distinct from declination, but it has considerable affinities with it, differing primarily in its obligatory nature and in the functions it has acquired. In view of this, we may not wish to regard downstep as strictly intonational, but it nevertheless forms part of the pitch 'envelope' of the relevant utterances. It may also be noted that Pierrehumbert (1980) includes 'downstep' in her description of English intonation.
6 It is sometimes asserted or implied that the 'nucleus' is in some way more prominent than the other accented syllables, an impression that is reinforced by such terms as 'primary stress' (= nucleus) and 'secondary stress' (= nonnuclear stress). This depends, of course, on what is meant by 'prominence'. There is certainly a sense in which the 'nuclear stress' is more important than the 'non-nuclear' stresses: for example in rapid speech, where the number of stresses is reduced, the 'nuclear stress' is the only stress in the intonation unit which cannot disappear (if it does then the intonation unit ceases to exist). The 'nuclear'/'non-nuclear' distinction, and all the various 'degrees of stress' postulated in the literature, involve a hierarchy of *stressability* in this sense, but not a hierarchy of physical prominence as such. Failure to recognise this often vitiates discussions of 'degrees of stress' in the literature.
7 A more detailed discussion of prosodic typologies is in preparation; earlier attempts at typologies are summarised in Fox (1985).
8 Much recent work in the non-linear framework, especially Metrical Phonology, uses a hierarchical model, but usually postulates a recursive strong + weak structure rather than a set of distinct prosodic units (see Hogg and McCully

1987; Goldsmith 1990). For a summary of hierarchical models in phonology see Fox (1986).

REFERENCES

Armstrong, L. E. and Ward, I. C. (1926) *A Handbook of English Intonation*, Cambridge, Heffer.

Berry, M. (1977) *Introduction to Systemic Linguistics*, Vol. 2: *Levels and Links*, London: Batsford.

Bolinger, D. L. (1964) 'Intonation as a universal', in *Proceedings of the Ninth International Congress of Linguists*, The Hague: Mouton, 833–44.

—— (1978) 'Intonation across languages', in J. Greenberg, C. A. Ferguson and E. A. Moravcsik (eds), *Universals of Human Language*, Vol. 2, Stanford: Stanford University Press, pp. 471–524.

Brown, G., Currie, K. and Kenworthy, J. (1980) *Questions of Intonation*, London: Croom Helm.

Chomksy, N. (1981) *Lectures on Government and Binding*, Dordrecht: Foris.

Chomsky, N. and Halle, M. (1968) *The Sound Pattern of English*, New York: Harper & Row.

Clements, G.N. and Goldsmith, J. (eds) (1984) *Autosegmental Studies in Bantu Tone*, Dordrecht: Foris.

Cruttenden, A. (1981) 'Falls and rises: meaning and universals', *Journal of Linguistics* 17: 77–91.

—— (1986) *Intonation*, Cambridge: Cambridge University Press.

Currie, K. (1980) 'An initial search for tonics', *Language and Speech* 23: 329–50.

—— (1981) 'Further experiments in the search for tonics', *Language and Speech* 24: 1–28.

Cutler, A. and Ladd, D. R. (eds) (1983) *Prosody: Models and Measurements*, Berlin: Springer.

Fox, A. (1978) 'A comparative study of English and German intonation', unpublished doctoral dissertation, Edinburgh University.

—— (1984) *German Intonation: an Outline*, Oxford: Clarendon Press.

—— (1985) 'Aspects of prosodic typology', *Working Papers in Linguistics and Phonetics* (University of Leeds), 3: 60–119.

—— (1986) 'Dimensions of prosodic structure', *Working Papers in Linguistics and Phonetics* (University of Leeds), 4: 78–127.

Fujisaki, H. and Nagasami, S. (1969) 'A model for the synthesis of pitch contours of connected speech', *Annual Report of the Engineering Research Institute* (Faculty of Engineering, University of Tokyo), 28: 53–60.

Gårding, E. (1983) 'A generative model of intonation', in A. Cutler and D. R. Ladd (eds), *Prosody: Models and Measurements*, Berlin: Springer, pp. 11–25.

Giegerich, H. (1984) *Relating to Metrical Structure*, Bloomington: Indiana University Linguistics Club.

Goldsmith, J. A. (1982) 'Accent systems', in H. van der Hulst and N. Smith (eds), *The Structure of Phonological Representations*, Vol. I, Dordrecht: Foris, pp. 47–63.

—— (1990) *Autosegmental and Metrical Phonology*, Oxford: Blackwell.

Halliday, M. A. K. (1967) *Intonation and Grammar in British English*, The Hague: Mouton.

Hirst, D. (1983) 'Structures and categories in prosodic representations', in A. Cutler and D. R. Ladd (eds), *Prosody: Models and Measurements*, Berlin: Springer, pp. 93–109.

Hockett, C. F. (1955) *A Manual of Phonology*, Bloomington: Indiana University Press.

Hogg, R. and McCully, C. B. (1987) *Metrical Phonology: a Coursebook*, Cambridge: Cambridge University Press.

Hombert, J. M. (1974) 'Universals of downdrift: their phonetic basis and significance for a theory of tone', *Studies in African Linguistics* 5: 169–83.

Kingdon, R. (1958) *The Groundwork of English Intonation*, London: Longman.

Ladd, D. R. (1981) 'On intonational universals', in T. Myers, J. Laver and J. Anderson (eds), *The Cognitive Representation of Speech*, Dordrecht: North Holland, pp. 389–97.

—— (1984) 'Declination: a review and some hypotheses', *Phonology Yearbook* 1: 53–74.

McCawley, J. D. (1968) *The Phonological Component of a Grammar of Japanese*, Cambridge, MA: MIT Press.

Nespor, M. and Vogel, I. (1983) 'Prosodic structure above the word', in A. Cutler and D. R. Ladd (eds), *Prosody: Models and Measurements*, Berlin: Springer, pp. 123–40.

—— (1986) *Prosodic Phonology*, Dordrecht: Foris.

O'Connor, J. D. and Arnold, G. F. (1961) *Intonation of Colloquial English*, London: Longman.

Ohala, J. J. (1983) 'Cross-language use of pitch – an ethological view', *Phonetica* 40: 1–18.

Palmer, H. E. (1922) *English Intonation with Systematic Exercises*, Cambridge: Heffer.

Pierrehumbert, J. B. (1980) 'The Phonology and phonetics of English intonation', Ph.D., MIT Press.

Pike, K. L. (1945) *The Intonation of American English*, Ann Arbor: University of Michigan Press.

—— (1948) *Tone Languages*, Ann Arbor: University of Michigan Press.

—— (1967) *Language in Relation to a Unified Theory of the Structure of Human Behaviour*, The Hague: Mouton.

Schubiger, M. (1958) *English Intonation, its Form and Function*, Tübingen: Niemeyer.

Selkirk, E. O. (1980) *On Prosodic Structure and its Relation to Syntactic Structure*, Bloomington: Indiana University Linguistics Club.

—— (1984) *Phonology and Syntax: the Relation between Sound and Structure*, Cambridge, MA: MIT.

Thorsen, N. (1983) 'Two issues in the prosody of Standard Danish', in A. Cutler and D. R. Ladd (eds), *Prosody: Models and Measurements*, Berlin: Springer, pp. 27–38.

Trager, G. L. (1941) 'The theory of accentual systems', in L. Spier, A. I. Hallowell and S. Newman (eds) *Language, Culture, and Personality: Essays in Memory of Edward Sapir*, Menasha, WI: Sapir Memorial Publication Fund.

—— (1964) 'The intonation system of American English', in D. Abercrombie, D. B. Fry, P. A. D. MacCarthy, N. C. Scott and J. L. M. Trim (eds), *In Honour of Daniel Jones*, London: Longman, pp. 266–70.

Trager, G. L. and Smith, H. L. Jr, (1951) *An Outline of English Structure*, Washington: American Council of Learned Societies.

Vaissière, J. (1983) 'Language-independent prosodic features', in A. Cutler and D. R. Ladd (eds), *Prosody: Models and Measurements*, Berlin: Springer, pp. 53–66.

Welmers, W. E. (1959) 'Tonemics, morphotonemics, and tonal morphemes', *General Linguistics* 4: 1–9.

15

Intonational stereotype: a re-analysis

Jill House
University College London

INTRODUCTION

The use of special intonation patterns to denote situations which are in some way stereotyped has been the subject of much debate in the phonological literature. Discussion has particularly centred on what Ladd (1978a) characterised as 'stylised' contours, where the melody is composed of a series of sustained pitches, rather than falling or rising pitch glides. A typical example is given in (1):

(1)   _Come and –get –it
         L–   H– M–

where we perceive a formal pattern which starts with sustained low pitch (L–), jumps up to a sustained high pitch (H–), and then down to a sustained mid pitch (M–). The coherence of this tune, and its association with calls to attract attention, usually from a distance, or with routine, predictable situations, has often been observed (Liberman 1975, for instance, describes it as the 'vocative chant'). The question has been how best to incorporate patterns like this into the intonational phonology, capturing formal and functional generalisations.

A rich source of natural examples of stereotyped intonation – including stylised examples – may be found in telephone enquiry service dialogues. Here, a caller (C) interacts with an agent (A) whose job it is to supply information in some specialised area. It is A's contribution which is most likely to contain stereotyped patterns: she is answering the telephone as a matter of routine throughout the working day, and many of her exchanges with C follow a predictable path.

Some recent research[1] into the modelling of natural language dialogues has focused on examples of this type. The objective has been a techno-logical one: the development of an automated telephone information service, in areas such as flight enquiries or home banking. In an automated system with spoken output, A's role is taken over by a message planner and language generator, and her/his voice supplied by a rule-based speech synthesiser.[2] The acceptability of this synthetic voice is likely to be enhanced if the intonation is appropriate to the context. In the first instance, we have therefore looked to natural speech as a source for suitable intonation patterns to implement in the system.

Having identified a range of relevant natural patterns, we cannot simply assume that whatever is found in natural examples will necessarily be suitable in the context of a person–machine dialogue. For one thing, the linguistic structures and expressions available to an automated A will be considerably constrained compared with those of his natural counterpart; for another, C may have very different ideas about what is acceptable and suitable coming from a synthetic rather than a natural voice. Simulation-based research is needed before we can answer these questions satisfactorily, and they will not be addressed further here. In the meantime, our observations of natural dialogues raise interesting questions for intonational theory. The main part of this paper will concentrate on investigating some of the theoretical issues raised by the observed stereotype patterns.

THE USE OF INTONATIONAL STEREOTYPE IN TELEPHONE DIALOGUES

House and Youd (1991) reported on a study of natural dialogues in the flight enquiries domain, in which we found a widespread use of apparently stereotyped intonation patterns associated with particular components of the dialogue. In the Conversation Analysis tradition, summarised in Levinson (1983), dialogues of this type have three major components of overall structure:

1   opening section;
2   topic-oriented slots;
3   closing section.

To this we added an optional 'absence' section, embedded within 2, in cases where the agent needs to ask the caller to hold the line, while information is being looked up or checked. In more detail, a typical dialogue structure would be as follows:

opening section
*identification
*greeting
*task elicitation
topic-oriented section
*request formulation
*information transfer
absence section
*temporary disconnection

*reconnection
topic-oriented section
*information transfer
*request resolution
closing section
*pre-closings
*terminal exchanges

Exchanges during the opening, absence and closing sections were concerned with the phatic management of the conversation rather than the transfer of information. They represented the recurrent, routine components of the dialogue, where speakers in the A role were most likely to adopt stereotyped tunes, including the stylised contours.

We did not adopt a strict criterion of stylisation, based on 'steady level pitch' (Ladd 1978a) or 'monotone' (Johnson and Grice 1990) in order to recognise stereotype; rather, we followed Fónagy *et al.* (1984) in identifying intonational 'clichés',[3] patterns with a simplified, highly predictable melodic component which recurred regularly in the routine contexts, and which seemed to be stored as prefabricated, holistic tunes. An important subset of these tunes involved the pitch sustention on final syllables associated with stylisation, and some also showed the apparent rhythmic adjustments in the direction of isochrony discussed by Johnson and Grice (1990), but these were not defining. Within the set of stereotyped tunes, a true, chantable stylisation seemed to be just one extreme of a gradient of realisational possibilities. What really marked these tunes as a natural class was the sequential arrangement of two or more well-defined pitch levels mapped over the syllables in the phrase. Two tunes, each involving three pitch levels, were particularly common, and can be described as follows:

Tune I: Low + High + Mid (LHM)
For example:

(2)   Flight information
        L   H M

(3)   British Airways
        L   H M

(4)   Good afterno-on
        L   H M

(5)   Can I help you
        L   H   M

(6)   Hold the li-ine, I'll just che-eck
        L   HM L   H   M

In the above examples, L, H and M are used purely descriptively, and have been aligned with the syllables on which the new pitch level begins; they do not have any theoretical status as pitch accents. There were some more or less trivial differences in the realisation of tune I. Non-stylised (or less stylised) variants allowed an upglide in pitch from the final mid-level (M^) (Ia), and a somewhat 'scooped' version showed an upglide from both the high and the mid levels (H^ M^) (Ib). If the pitch on H and M remained level, there was no necessary prolongation of the relevant syllables (Ic). Finally, this pattern lent itself readily to stylisation, realised as sustention at each successive pitch (L– H– M–), and lengthening of the H and M components (Id). The initial low pitch (L–) was maintained until the jump to high was made, regardless of the presence or absence of upglides in the high and mid components. Frequently, particularly during openings, the tune would be repeated over successive phrases, as in a sequence of (2)–(5). The different variants seemed more or less interchangeable, reinforcing the impression that they constituted a natural class, apart from a tendency for the upglide versions to be produced turn-finally. (House and Youd (1991) analysed these rising variants as involving an overlay on an underlyingly stylised form, indicating a turn-giving cue.)

Tune II: High + Low + Mid (HLM)
Examples:

(7)   Flight information
        H   L   M

(8)   British Airways
        H   L M

(9)   Good morning
        H   L   M

(10)   Can I help you
        H   L   M

(11)   Hold on a moment
        H   L   M

Again, there were jumps between well-established pitch levels, but a conventional analysis would not have described these as 'stylised': the final mid tone was never prolonged, was regularly mapped on to the very last syllable, and often, but not always, displayed an upglide; however, the high and low components maintained a flat pitch over the relevant text.

According to our observations, neither of these tunes was idiosyncratic to an individual speaker; speakers could, and did, switch between different stereotype tunes, though some showed a tendency to prefer one tune for, say, the opening section over a number of successive calls. We found no gender-based differences in their usage.

THE PHONOLOGY OF STEREOTYPED INTONATION

If we try to fit the two basic tunes described above, with their variants, into an existing phonological analysis of English intonation, we soon encounter problems. It is usually possible to fit individual exemplars into a given descriptive framework, but it is not so easy to find an underlying representation which makes explicit the natural class to which they belong. This is a long-standing problem in intonational analysis; for example, analysts of the stylised contour illustrated in (1) have tended to adopt one or more of three strategies:

1 to propose a simple addition to the inventory of pitch configurations available (Fox 1969, 1970; Pierrehumbert 1980);
2 to propose that certain configurations fall outside the 'normal' tonal phonology (Windsor Lewis 1970; Johnson and Grice 1990);
3 to analyse this and other stylised tunes as variants of something in the regular tonal phonology (Crystal 1969a; O'Connor and Arnold 1973; Ladd 1978a, 1983; Gussenhoven 1983).

The favoured approach will reflect the analyst's priorities in establishing formal difference or functional generalisation. Taking the third approach implies some kind of hierarchical arrangement among tone patterns – that there are 'families' of contours with characteristics in common, within which specific variants may be categorially distinct, but none the less more closely related than contours from some different 'family'.[4] This is essentially the approach adopted here.

The analyst's priorities will also tend to be reflected in the label attached to the tune. It may be characterised by its association with a 'calling' or 'vocative' function (e.g. Pike 1945; Liberman 1975), by its phonetic shape, e.g. 'step-down' (Fox 1969; Johnson and Grice 1990), or by its perceived relationship to some major category, e.g. 'stylised fall' (Ladd 1978a; Gussenhoven 1983), or 'stylised fall–rise' (Pierrehumbert 1980; Ladd 1983). What we have identified above as tune I bears a clear relation to this step-down contour, analysed here as Id.

I shall not attempt a detailed evaluation of all the different analyses of stylisation here. Johnson and Grice (1990) demonstrated a number of problems, both formal and semantic, arising from the proposals by Ladd, Pierrehumbert and Gussenhoven to account for the step-down contour as a type of fall or fall–rise. My concern will rather be to account for what I have perceived as natural classes of stereotype contours analysed as tune sets I and II above, where stylisation represents just one of the options available for tune I. It seems important to be able to capture the formal similarity of the variants as much as their differences, particularly since their functional equivalence and virtual interchangeability has been attested in the context of the telephone dialogues. Rightly or wrongly, this paper assumes the assignment of the contours into natural classes as a starting-point.

In the following subsections, I shall consider how these tunes with their variants might fit into some existing analyses, and how far these analyses can succeed in making the similarities between the variants of each tune transparent. I shall then propose a way of adapting the pitch accent (PA) notation developed by Pierrehumbert (1980) in an autosegmental framework to exploit class similarities.

Analyses of tune I

There are various options available for the patterns classified as tune I in a contour-based analysis. All analyses assume that the initial L component is in some way optional (because prenuclear) and that only the H and M components can be relevant to the nuclear tone itself.

If the final M component shows any upglide (Ia), the H M sequence must presumably be treated as some rather high variety of fall–rise. In (12),

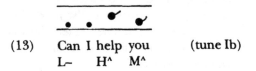

(12)   Can I help you   (tune Ia)
         L–   H– M^

we would therefore say that *help* carried a fall–rise nucleus, preceded by a low head (if *can* was stressed), or a low prehead. The combination of low head + fall–rise does not form part of one of the tone groups detailed in O'Connor and Arnold (1961 or 1973) – but this may be taken to indicate that it was not considered important for the foreign learner. An upglide on the H component as well (Ib) would make the nuclear tone a rise–fall–rise:

(13)   Can I help you   (tune Ib)
         L–   H^ M^

Among more recent analyses using the autosegmental framework, Gussenhoven's (1983) theory would see both (12) and (13) as involving fall–rises (H*LH) with the modification of 'half-completion', with (13) presumably having the additional modification of 'delay'. Pierrehumbert's (1980) H*+L H⁻ H% accent would be consistent with (12) and L*+H H⁻ H% with (13). A similarity between the two patterns is implicit only from the combination of phrase accent and boundary tone.[5]

If there is no final rise, and no obvious pitch sustention, or prolongation of the final syllable (Ic), we have to account for some fall-to-mid, or arrested fall, assuming that we still identify *help* as the nucleus:

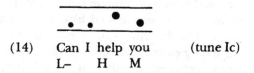

(14)	Can	I	help	you	(tune Ic)
	L–		H	M	

This can be accommodated by Crystal (1969b) as a fall interacting with the prosodic systems of pitch height and pitch width; it is not explicitly included in the O'Connor and Arnold inventory. In Gussenhoven's analysis, this comes out as a half-completed fall, H*L, and in Pierrehumbert's as H*+L H⁻L%.

Examples like (15),

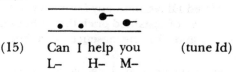

(15)	Can	I	help	you	(tune Id)
	L–		H–	M–	

consistent with the step-down contour, involving the pitch sustention of stylisation (Id), are the type which moved Fox (1969) to write his note about a 'forgotten' English tone. He assumes that the nucleus coincides with the H component, and his accurate observations of the formal properties of the pattern are worth quoting in detail:

> the nuclear syllable takes the high pitch and the step-down occurs at the first prominent syllable of the tail. If no prominent syllable follows, a normally weak syllable will be made strong for the purpose, or, if there is no tail at all, the nucleus will be split into two, thus: ⁻Da-vid, ⁻Jo-ohn. The pretonic is low to mid and is level: _Come and ⁻get –it, _where _are –you.
>
> (p. 13)

This relationship between pitch contour and prominence marks the pattern as unusual (both in a nuclear tone and a PA framework); so much so that Crystal (1969a) tried to force an analysis of the step-down as a variant of the level tone, proposing that the nucleus should coincide with the M component, even if this meant giving nuclear status to a normally weak syllable. His solution was not favoured by Fox (1970) or Windsor Lewis (1970), though curiously it seems to have been taken up by O'Connor and Arnold (1973), who include (p. 89):

(16) |Thank >you
(17) |Dinner's >ready

as exemplifying a high head + mid-level nuclear tone on the second word. They have nothing to say about single-word examples of step-down, and

217

consider the pattern of little importance to the foreign learner. Windsor Lewis (1970), who sees the sustained step-down as properly belonging to the relatively minor tonal system of 'remote speech', also observes that the 'fall–level' – a step-down from unsustained high pitch to a sustained mid pitch – often replaces the fall–rise, and is used in hailing, in routine acknowledgements, apologies and leave-taking. This supports the view that the different patterns grouped together as tune I have something in common.[6] For Gussenhoven, this tone is the H*L fall with stylisation, whereas for Pierrehumbert and for Ladd (1983) it is better seen as a type of fall–rise; Pierrehumbert sees it as formally equivalent to H*+L H⁻ L% (the fall to mid), and explicitly notes its semantic relatedness to H*+L H⁻ H% (the high fall–rise), a 'variant of the vocative contour with a rise at the end' (p. 62). Ladd's (1983) reanalysis of the contour using his simplified PA model makes it a stylised HL without any boundary tone, since stylisation is viewed as '(a) a feature[7] of sustained pitch throughout the transition that follows a given tone, and (b) the absence of a final boundary tone' (p. 744).

There would appear to be no formal mechanism in a traditional contour-based nuclear tone analysis for analysing the variants in tune I as anything other than separate, independent tones. Any similarity between them, such as the fact that they all end in a non-low pitch, may be expressed informally, but would appear to be purely coincidental. Furthermore, the fall-to-mid (Ic) and stylised step-down (Id) seem to have been regarded as 'marked', and peripheral to the regular system. The L component must be viewed as an optional prenuclear constituent, presumably commuting with a high level head, or the pattern found in Pike's spoken chant (with extra high pitch on *a*):

(18)   ⁻Susie –is ⁻a ⁻tattle –tale

A componential, nuclear tone analysis cannot include the initial low pitch of tune I as part of a holistic contour, as Liberman (1975) sees it, for instance. The PA analyses, assuming a tonal sequence model, fare little better in this respect, but at least have some mechanism for relating tones to each other transparently: contours may be classed according to their shared PAs, or modifications, or features, or boundary tones, or even phrase accents, depending on the model chosen. In that sense, Pierrehumbert, Ladd and Gussenhoven can all show the relatedness between the variants of tune I, but not in a consistent way. Ladd (1983) comes closest, in that all would be seen as sharing the basic HL PA; but this would not differentiate them from numerous other examples of HL, such as the fall-to-low, because the boundary tone specification is free to differ.

Analyses of tune II

There are different problems with the analysis of tune II. The issue is not so much how to account for formally distinct minor variations, as how to come up with a common analysis for essentially the same melody realised over different texts. If we look again at examples (7)–(11) (repeated below for convenience as (19)–(23), with stressed syllables capitalised), we find that the individual tokens can be analysed perfectly easily. But apart from (21) and (22), which share the same analysis, they all have to be treated differently. In (19), for instance, in O'Connor and Arnold terminology, we are dealing with a fall-rise nucleus on *flight*, with the rising part of the tail initiated by the *ma* of *information*.

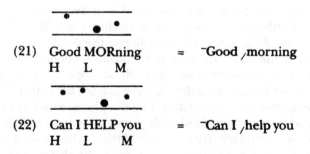

(19)   FLIGHT inforMAtion = ˅Flight infor₀mation
       H   L   M

In (20), we must identify a high head, followed by a low rise nucleus + rising tail:

(20)   BRITish AIRways   =   ꞌBritish ₍Airways
       H   L   M

In (21) and (22), we still have a low rise nucleus, but this time preceded by a high prehead:

(21)   Good MORning   =   ⁻Good ₍morning
       H   L   M

(22)   Can I HELP you   =   ⁻Can I ₍help you
       H   L   M

while in (23), we have to propose a low rise nucleus on the *mo* of *moment*, preceded by high prehead and low head:

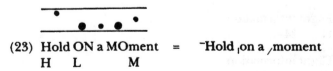

(23)   Hold ON a MOment   =   ⁻Hold ₍on a ₍moment
       H   L   M

The PA models will encounter similar problems, since they will tend to identify the nucleus as falling on the same syllables as in the traditional analyses. The full fall–rise nucleus in (19) would fit with Pierrehumbert's H* L⁻ H%, Ladd's (1983) HL H% and Gussenhoven's unmodified H*LH. In (20)–(23), the low rise nucleus would be consistent with Pierrehumbert's L* H⁻ H% or L*+H H⁻ H% (seemingly neutralised here where the tail is monosyllabic), Ladd's LH H%, and Gussenhoven's L*H. As before, the problem lies in characterising the prenuclear portion consistently, and in identifying the relationship between (19) and the rest. An alternative analysis of (23) with the nucleus on *on* could be represented in Ladd's model as a simple low L tone, sustained at a low level until the high H% boundary tone, or in Gussenhoven's system as L*H with delay.

A RE-ANALYSIS

Accent placement

As we observed on pages 213–14, both tunes I and II were used repeatedly over pieces of dialogue serving a routine, discourse management function. The linguistic expressions used were stereotypes or clichés, and the tunes themselves jumped predictably between three pitch levels. Transfer of information was not an issue. Whether produced with true stylisation or not, both tunes would seem to be functioning in the way that Ladd describes as typical of stylised intonations: 'to signal that an utterance is in some way part of a stereotyped situation or is otherwise more predictable or less informative than a corresponding utterance with plain intonation' (1978b: 185). It follows that the location of accents in the text has little to do with information focus, but will still be underpinned by metrical prominences. Furthermore, it was argued in House and Youd (1991) that the requirements of the tune itself may dictate the distribution of accents over the text. If the tune is stored as a holistic sequence of three level pitches, then some adjustment will be made as necessary to ensure that, provided there are enough syllables, all three pitches are realised. Take, for example, the opener *flight information*. This is a phrase which is ambivalent between a reading as a compound, with primary stress on *FLIGHT*, or as a noun phrase, with primary stress on *inforMAtion*. When tune I was being used, nearly all realisations were phrasal, as in (2) above, with the high pitched nucleus on -*MA*-, to accommodate the low pitch on preceding syllables. Examples with the compound stress pattern, like (24a) or (24b)

(24) a. Flight information
         H   M–

     b. Flight information
         H–   M–

did exist, but were much less common. Conversely, when tune II was being used, the compound stress pattern was preferred, allowing the analysis with a fall–rise nucleus on *FLIGHT* in (19) above. Another possibility for tune II would have been to sustain the high pitch over the first three syllables:

(25)   Flight information
   (?)   H–   L M

This would have made it consistent with the low rise analyses of the other tune II examples (20)–(23), but the pattern was not observed. Presumably the compound interpretation was preferred, and could be readily used since it did not conflict with the requirements of the tune.

If we analyse these stereotyped contours as holistic units, then we would seem to be marking them as exceptions to a tonal sequence model, since they would be operating on a contour interaction basis. It is none the less plausible that within the intonation system, some phrase-length contours should have a fixed pattern, whereas others should be built up componentially in the traditional manner. But can such holistic units be represented in the same way as the freely combining PAs, or must they have an alternative representation?

A common representational format can be found within a framework which assumes that prosodic phenomena have a hierarchical structure. For a start, if one accepts that individual PAs are dominated by an intonational phrase, or tone group (see Ladd 1986):

(26)

then some marker (treated here for convenience as a feature, though its apparently gradient properties make its status unclear) for phenomena such as stereotype will apply at the level of the TG node itself, and will affect the realisation of any PAs dominated by such a node. In the metrical hierarchy, it is likely that this characterisation also applies at phrase level, affecting prominence relations in the metrical grid, perhaps leaving them underspecified. Further, if we adopt the proposals made in the following section, we shall find it possible to account for both tunes I and II in terms of a single PA, dominated by an intonational phrase marked for stereotype, and mapped on to a convenient metrically strong syllable.

Internal structure of PAs

One way of representing tunes like I and II using a standard PA notation, and which also captures generalisations about natural classes, would be to exploit the internal structure of the PA itself. The following proposals sketch out how this might be done. The analysis is very partial at this stage, since much detail would need to be worked out to extend it to provide a complete account of English intonation.

Beckman and Pierrehumbert (1986) talk about the 'starred (or metrically strong) tone of the pitch accent', which may be interpreted, following Grice (1992), as implying that the star is not just a device for linking a tone to a prominent syllable in the metrical hierarchy, but that it has an intrinsic strength value of its own, with bitonal accents represented thus:

(27)

English PAs, it would seem, are typically s–w, or left-headed. Traditional British-school contour analyses of accent types are similarly left-headed, with the nucleus always located on the accented syllable, and the nuclear tone always characterised by what occurs on and after the nuclear accent. Head accents have a similar description. Any pitch movement which takes place between adjacent constituents such as head and nucleus is accounted for in terms of some kind of transition; for example, a jump up or down to the nuclear syllable is not seen as intrinsic to the nuclear tone itself, though an appeal to such a jump may be used informally as a criterion for distinguishing between 'high' and 'low' falls and rises (e.g. Cruttenden 1986).

Exceptions to this approach include Bolinger (1986 and elsewhere) and Pierrehumbert (1980), who explicitly allow the pitch preceding an accent to play a part in its definition. Pierrehumbert, for instance, includes in her inventory of accents L+H* and H+L*, bitonal accents which are apparently right-headed, with a leading tone rather than a trailing one. Rationalisations of Pierrehumbert's analysis (Ladd, 1983; Lindsey 1985) and alternative proposals in the autosegmental framework (Gussenhoven 1983) have tended to revert to the left-headed approach, analysing the leading tone as belonging properly to some preceding constituent. Though this more traditional approach scores highly for consistency and simplicity, there is a price to be paid: intuitively, the pitch movement towards an accented syllable is often felt to be an integral part of it, and to contribute to any 'meaning' associated with it,[8] and some patterns can only be accommodated clumsily within a strictly left-headed analysis, even in RP-style English. PAs in other languages or other varieties of English may also be better analysed as right-headed. Grice (1992) presents persuasive evidence for a right-headed analysis of certain intonation patterns in regional Italian, as well as for some English contours. Beckman and

Pierrehumbert (1986) defend the H+L* and L+H* accents, partly on the grounds that they reflect the phonetic facts, partly because of the role attributed to bitonal accents in triggering downstep, or 'catathesis'. The latter (possibly circular) argument is not pursued here, since the proposals in this paper have nothing to say about downstep or accent scaling.

We can accommodate leading tones, while preserving the notion that English PAs are normally left-dominant, if we allow the accents to have a more complex internal structure. At the same time we can capture some useful generalisations and natural-class characteristics amongst related contours. Let us propose the following principles:

1 The minimum structure of a PA is monotonal, as in (28):

(28)
                               PA
                                |
                               T*

This PA node, the 'core' of the accent, may branch in binary fashion, as in (27) above, with the starred tone associated with the strong branch.

2 Leading tones may be represented as weak branches dominated by a projection of the PA core, PA':

(29)

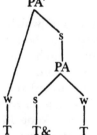

The domain of such a leading tone will normally be restricted to the syllable immediately preceding the metrically strong syllable bearing the starred tone.

3 Starred tones inside the PA core spread only when dominated by a node marked for a feature such as [stereotype]; unstarred tones spread rightwards.

4 There will be a boundary tone (T%) at either end of each tone group, dominated directly by the TG node. These are unstarred and therefore an initial boundary tone spreads rightwards.

5 Features applying to a node at a higher level will percolate down to the units they dominate.

223

There would seem to be no need at this stage for a Pierrehumbert-style phrase accent, which would be accounted for by the unstarred trailing tone of a bitonal PA core.

Representing tunes I and II

The underlying representation of tune I is proposed as in (30), where a single pitch accent L + H*L is associated with a metrically strong syllable:

(30)

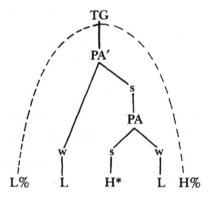

There is a low initial boundary tone, which spreads rightwards up to the leading tone of the PA. The high final boundary tone ensures that there is no final fall to low, and the high pitch may itself be realised on the final syllable, depending on the tune variant.

Tune Ia will then be the unmodified version of this PA, with the high boundary tone effecting a final rise. Tunes Ic and Id will be marked for [stereotype] at TG level, where tune Id will be additionally marked for [stylisation]. The effect of [stereotype] will be to flatten the H and L tones in the PA core, and to 'crowd out' the final H% boundary tone (in a fully specified representation, this would mean delinking the H% from the skeletal tier). The feature [stylisation], only present in conjunction with [stereotype], will introduce the phonetic properties of monotone, laryngeal precision and isochrony described in Johnson and Grice (1990).

Rather more problematic is tune Ib, the version with a scooped high tone on the nuclear syllable. We can follow Ladd (1983) in proposing a feature [delay], which we can apply to the PA' node; this extra layer of structure now allows us a formal mechanism for the rightward shifting of the tone: it will change the prominence relations immediately dominated by the PA' node, making the leading tone the terminal element, and assigning to it the star which will make it map on to the metrically strong syllable, thus:

(31)

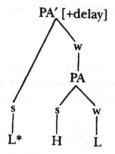

PA′ [+delay]

This solution is equally applicable outside the field of stereotyped intonation, to account for rise–fall and rise–fall–rise tones as modifications of high falls and fall–rises respectively. The implication would then have to be that the representation of the unmodified falls and fall–rises also involved a leading L tone.

The details of the phonetic alignment of individual tones and the relative scaling of the pitches requires further investigation. The relationship between tune I and a 'normal' fall–rise is also unclear; it is likely that they would share the tonal structure of (30), but that tune I would also involve a feature analogous to Gussenhoven's 'half-completion', to stop the final L tone from dropping below mid-level.

There are several advantages for tune I with this structured representation. First of all, there is an underlying high boundary tone in all variants, whether it is explicitly realised or not. The boundary tone would appear to be a useful device for capturing the major division between the family of tones which falls to the baseline (all the 'falls' in a traditional analysis, asociated with 'completion') and those which do not (the rises and level tones associated with 'incompletion'). A weakness of Pierrehumbert's analysis is that she loses this generalisation by allowing the boundary tone to differ for patterns like Ia and Ic, whereas Ladd's solution for stylised contours – to have no boundary tone – removes the possibility of relating them to either category. Second, all variants of tune I share the core PA specification of HL. Third, the use of a leading tone allows us to represent the initial low pitch which seems to be an integral part of the tune, without having to have recourse to additional prenuclear accents. For a holistic tune to be expressable as a single PA seems to be an advantage, particularly when the accentual function of the prominent syllables appears to be negligible.

Grice (1992) presents additional evidence for leading tones by recalling the phenomenon described by Kingdon (1958) as 'homosyllabic preheads'. Kingdon proposes that there is an emphatic device to suggest a pitch contrast before a stressed syllable when there are no prehead syllables available to carry the pitch,

> by pronouncing the beginning of the stressed syllable on a pitch
> which will contrast with the tone and its accompanying stress for a

length of time sufficient to allow the initial unstressed contrasting pitch to be felt.

(p. 53)

Sonorant consonants are particularly good at carrying this initial, contrasting pitch: for example, the word *yes* produced as a monosyllabic realisation of tune Id would plausibly include a quite marked initial on-glide from a low pitch:

(32)

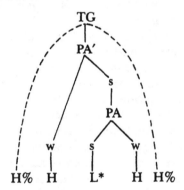

y‾e-ess

It could be argued that as far as tune I is concerned, the initial L% boundary tone would serve the same purpose. The phenomenon needs to be further investigated, to see if it can be identified within a tone group, far from any boundary tone, rather than group-initially.

Tune II's representation has a similar format, but this time the core PA has a branching L*H tone. There is a high leading tone, and there are high boundary tones at each end:

(33)

A bitonal representation for the PA core is proposed[9] to allow differentiation between variants with an actual rise (between H tones) on the final syllable, and those which step up to a final steady high pitch; these would be the ones marked for the feature [stereotype], which once again applies at TG level, allowing spreading of the tones in the PA core, and the delinking of the final boundary tone. This will allow a common representation for the different textual mappings given in (20)–(23) above, if we assume that the PA is associated with the syllable on which low pitch begins in each case (i.e. the nucleus would fall on *on* rather than *mo-* in (23)).

The problematic example would seem to be (19), where our traditional analyses would identify the nucleus as falling on the first syllable. Again, we can appeal to the prominence relations operating within the PA to save our common representation, but this time motivated by a difference in the metrical representation rather than by any [delay] feature. Again, we will be dealing with a switch from w–s to s–w at the level dominated by PA':

(34)

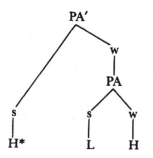

The leading tone will now be associated with the metrically strong syllable consistent with the noun compound reading, *flight*. Even though it is dominated by a [+stereotype] TG, it remains a leading tone within the PA, and cannot spread beyond a single syllable.

CONCLUDING OBSERVATIONS

The above analysis of intonational stereotype has attempted to account for a very restricted set of data within a pitch–accent theory. There will doubtless be problems with the details of the analysis when it is extended to the wider context of English intonation generally. Nevertheless, the proposals concerning the internal structure of the PA have wide-ranging implications: they allow the pitch preceding an accent to have formal status; they provide a common representation for patterns which empirical evidence would suggest are related; they promise to be revealing about inter-language differences in intonation structure; and they assign a structure to the pitch accent which is consistent with the binary, branching structures currently adopted for syllables and units in the metrical hierarchy. The driving force behind it all has been the continuing need to provide a systematic account of intonation which is phonetically explicit, captures phonological generalisations, and is functionally revealing.

NOTES

1   Specifically, within SUNDIAL, Speech UNDerstanding and DIALogue, a European project supported by Esprit; UK collaborators include Logica Cambridge Ltd and the University of Surrey.
2   For British English, the spoken output in SUNDIAL is provided by an adaptation of the Infovox text-to-speech system.
3   The 'clichés mélodiques' in French and Hungarian discussed by Fónagy *et al.* are given a double characterisation: high regularity in their 'micro-structure' – the fundamental frequency within syllables – which in turn enhances the melodicity of their 'macro-structure'.

4   See Gussenhoven and Rietveld (1991) for an attempt to compare the success
of two theories of the structure of English intonation in predicting the semantic
relatedness of individual tones.
5   In Windsor Lewis's (1977, 1979) terminology, tune Ia would be classed as an
'Alt-Rise', and tune Ib as a 'Climb-Rise'.
6   That the high pitch need not be sustained fits in with our observations of F_0
traces plotted for some of our natural examples; even when the high pitch was
perceived as relatively level, it was often the case that the F_0 peak was only
achieved late in the H syllable.
7   The formal status of stylisation is left rather unclear in Ladd's paper; though
it is described here in terms of a 'feature of sustained pitch', this is not
proposed as a formal feature comparable with [delayed peak], [downstep] and
[raised peak].
8   Anyone teaching introductory courses in the structure of English intonation
will have had to justify this approach, which for some students, who find it
counter-intuitive, proves to be a major problem.
9   Arguably, a monotonal L tone is all that is required within the PA, with high pitch
accounted for by the boundary tone. However, this would mean that in a
[+stereotype] phrase, the boundary tone was delinked for tune I, but not for tune
II, an inconsistency which makes the more abstract bitonal analysis preferable.

REFERENCES

Beckman, M. and Pierrehumbert, J. (1986) 'Intonational structure in Japanese and
English', *Phonology Yearbook* 3: 255–309.
Bolinger, D. (1986) *Intonation and its Parts*, London: Edward Arnold.
Cruttenden, A. (1986) *Intonation*, Cambridge: Cambridge University Press.
Crystal, D. (1969a) 'A forgotten English tone: an alternative analysis', *Le Maître
phonétique* 84: 34–7.
—— (1969b) *Prosodic Systems and Intonation in English*, Cambridge: Cambridge
University Press.
Fónagy, I., Bérard, E. and Fónagy, J. (1984) 'Clichés mélodiques', *Folia Linguistica*
17: 153–85.
Fox, A. (1969) 'A forgotten English tone', *Le Maître phonétique* 84: 13–14.
—— (1970) 'The forgotten tone: a reply', *Le Maître phonétique* 85: 29–31.
Grice, M. (1992) 'The intonation of interrogation in Palermo Italian: implications
for intonation theory', Ph.D. dissertation, University College London.
Gussenhoven, C. (1983) *A Semantic Analysis of the Nuclear Tones of English*, distributed
by Indiana University Linguistics Club.
Gussenhoven, C. and Rietveld, A. (1991) 'An experimental evaluation of two
nuclear-tone taxonomies', *Linguistics* 29: 423–49.
House, J. and Youd, N. (1991) 'Stylised prosody in telephone information services:
implications for synthesis', *Proceedings of the Twelfth International Congress of
Phonetic Sciences* 5, Aix-en-Provence, pp. 198–201.
Johnson, M. and Grice, M. (1990) 'The phonological status of stylised intonation
contours', *Speech, Hearing and Language: Work in Progress* 4, University College
London: 229–56.
Kingdon, R. (1958), *The Groundwork of English Intonation*, London: Longmans,
Green.
Ladd, D. R. (1978a) 'Stylised intonation', *Language* 54: 517–41.
—— (1978b) *The Structure of Intonational Meaning: Evidence from English*,
Bloomington: Indiana University Press.

—— (1983) 'Phonological features of intonational peaks', *Language* 59, 4: 721–59.
—— (1986) 'Intonational phrasing: the case for recursive prosodic structure', *Phonology Yearbook* 3: 311–40.
Levinson, S. (1983) *Pragmatics*, Cambridge: Cambridge University Press.
Liberman, M. (1975) *The Intonational System of English*, MIT dissertation; published 1980, New York: Garland.
Lindsey, G. (1985) 'Intonation and interrogation: tonal structure and the expression of a pragmatic function in English and other languages', Ph.D. dissertation, UCLA.
O'Connor, J. D. and Arnold, G. F. (1961, 1973) *Intonation of Colloquial English*, 1st and 2nd edns, London: Longman.
Pierrehumbert, J. (1980) 'The phonology and phonetics of English intonation', MIT dissertation; distributed 1987, Indiana University Linguistics Club.
Pike, K. (1945) *The Intonation of American English*, Ann Arbor: University of Michigan Press.
Windsor Lewis, J. (1970) 'The tonal system of remote speech', *Le Maître phonétique* 85: 31–6.
—— (1977, 1979) *People Speaking*, Oxford: Oxford University Press.

16

Speech fundamental frequency over the telephone and face-to-face: some implications for forensic phonetics[1]

Allen Hirson
City University, London
Peter French
University of Birmingham
David Howard
University of York

INTRODUCTION

In well over 90 per cent of cases, speaker identification for forensic purposes involves the comparison of a disputed speech sample recorded off a telephone line with reference speech samples elicited in face-to-face interviews with suspects.[2] Routinely, the two sets of speech samples are compared, *inter alia*, with respect to their fundamental frequency (F_0), the main physical correlate of perceived pitch. Although F_0 does not have a one-to-one mapping with its corresponding percept, measurements of the former may be a useful objective indication of pitch range and pitch distribution of an individual speaker (Braun 1994).

In the vast majority of forensic cases, F_0 measurements from recorded telephone conversations appear to be higher than those measured from reference samples recorded in face-to-face interviews with suspects. Further, this appears to be the case even when there is overwhelming independent (i.e. non-phonetic) evidence that the suspect made the call. However, these results from forensic phonetic casework run against the accepted doctrine that the fundamental frequency profile of an individual is a 'robust variable' that is relatively resistant to communication channel and affective situation (see McGonegal *et al.* 1979; Nolan 1983). The aim of this study is to examine this variability of F_0 in a controlled series of experiments.

We have directed our attention to three questions arising from this apparent pattern:

1   Can the apparent shift observed in forensic speech material be replicated under experimental conditions? This question derives from the fact that the identity of disputed telephone speakers in real cases is only rarely resolved with certainty. Our experimental set-up removes any such uncertainty about speaker identity.

2   Does the difference result from variations in the affective situation, i.e. does a shift reflect different pitch profiles as a result of different types of speech used in face-to-face and telephone situations? Our experiment controls for this as far as possible by keeping the type of speech material constant in the two situations.

3   Does a shift derive in some way from the recording apparatus, pitch estimation device, or from the telephone transmission itself?

In this chapter we present F_0 data from telephone speech and equivalent material elicited face-to-face. The experimental method provides reliable F_0 data from direct laryngographic measurements of vocal-fold vibration (Fourcin and Abberton 1971; Hess and Indefrey 1984) from each individual speaker at one end of the telephone. In addressing 3, we attempted to compare these direct measurements with those from acoustic recordings at the 'far' end of the line.

METHOD

The twenty-four participants in this experiment were all students or lecturers in the Department of Electronics at York University. They were all males aged between 21 and 37 (mean: 24;8) and they were not informed of the purpose of the investigation. All subjects had no known hearing problems and answers to a questionnaire did not result in any subjects being excluded for factors likely to influence their voices, e.g. excessive smoking or alcohol consumption. Four speech samples were rejected owing to recording quality, and the ages above refer to usable samples only.

The speech material used in the current study was of two types:

1   A sample of 'free' speech elicited from the subjects by one of the researchers.

2   A reading of a text (*The Story of Arthur the Rat*) chosen so as 'to cover as many of the phonetic and phonological points of variation of the English-speaking world as possible' (Abercrombie 1964: 38).

Each of these two tasks was performed under two conditions: in a face-to-face context, and via a telephone line. Possible 'precedence effects' were avoided by randomising the conditions for each participant.

Figure 16.1 shows how the face-to-face recordings were made. Each participant in the experiment was recorded both laryngographically (Lx) and acoustically (Sp) using a cardioid microphone, a laryngograph

231

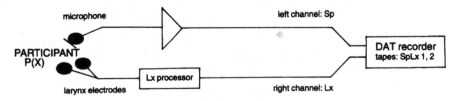

Figure 16.1 Speech and Lx recording setup involving two speech tasks: face-to-face
and read speech (no telephone)

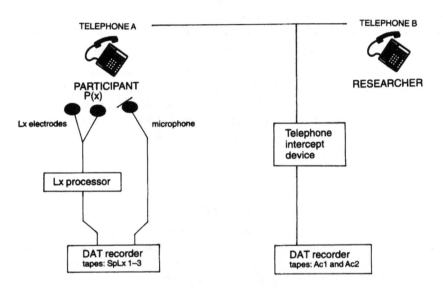

Figure 16.2 Simultaneous speech and laryngographic recordings during telephone
transmission of (a) 'free' face-to-face conversation, and (b) reading of a text

processor and two channels of a DAT recorder (CASIO DA7). These
recordings were referenced SpLx(1–3).

In the telephone link-up (via the local exchange) the speaker was
recorded acoustically and laryngographically but in addition an acoustic
recording was made at the 'far end' of the line at telephone B. As shown
in Figure 16.2, the transmitted speech was recorded onto a DAT recorder
connected to the telephone line via a hard-wired link. Recordings of the
transmitted speech were referenced Ac(1–2).

The laryngographic data from each speaker recorded on the SpLx tapes
was analysed using the PCpitch module of the PCLx laryngograph
processor. This provides statistical measures of the fundamental frequency,
including the form of distribution, its range, central tendency (averages)
and the degree of 'regularity' of vocal-fold vibration.

As shown in Figure 16.3, the distribution of fundamental frequency can

PC Pitch Analysis

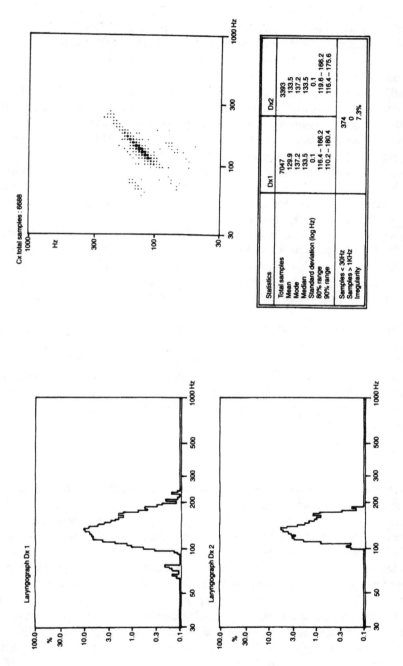

Cx total samples : 6688

Laryngograph Dx 1

Laryngograph Dx 2

Statistics	Dx1	Dx2
Total samples	7047	3393
Mean	129.9	133.5
Mode	137.2	137.2
Median	133.5	133.5
Standard deviation (log Hz)	0.1	0.1
80% range	116.4 – 166.2	119.6 – 166.2
90% range	110.2 – 180.4	116.4 – 175.6
Samples < 30Hz	374	0
Samples > 1KHz	0	
Irregularity	7.3%	

Figure 16.3 F_0 distribution data (Dx and Dx2) from a normal sample, and the corresponding scatter plot, Cx

be graphically displayed using the first-order (Dx1) and second-order (Dx2) distributions as described in Abberton *et al.* 1989. These graphs display fundamental frequency from individual larynx periods against percentage occurrence, and provide statistical data on F_0 for each individual.

Pitch glides such as rising intonational contours are usually relatively smooth, that is, one would expect each period to be slightly greater than its predecessor. As a consequence, each F_0 plotted against the subsequent F_0 aligns on the X–Y axis of the Cx graph or cross-plot (Abberton *et al.* 1989; Kitzing 1990). Creaky voice and electrical noise are shown as points some distance to the diagonal on the Cx plot (see Ball *et al.* 1990; Hirson and Duckworth 1993). In the Dx2 analysis which we have used here, such irregularities are excluded and the resultant filtered data provide a clearer image of modal voice F_0 distribution.

A subset of the acoustic recordings (eight subjects) was analysed using the PC-based Microspeech Laboratory program, MSL-pitch, developed by the University of Victoria, Canada. This is a 'peak-picking' program for the determination of F_0, with adjustment settings for analytical parameters, including variable thresholds for avoiding pitch-doubling ('octave errors').

The MSL-pitch program was used in an attempt to analyse the recordings made at the 'far' end of the telephone line. The purpose of this was to enable comparisons to be made with the F_0 averages established from the same material from the direct, non-telephone-transmitted recordings. By this means, one could establish whether or not the telephone transmission apparatus itself caused any measurable modifications to the F_0 of the speech signal.

RESULTS

Attempts to analyse the telephone-transmitted speech were rather unsuccessful using MSL-pitch, most likely as a function of the bandpass filtering effect of the telephone line. The program plotted spurious values for voiceless fricative consonants for some speakers, and also values for 'line noise'. In addition, apparent octave-halving and octave-doubling required *ad hoc* editing, and results of such 'tweaked' data are therefore not presented here. A separate follow-up study will aim to analyse this data and compare F_0 estimation devices for telephone-transmitted speech.

The speech analysed in this experiment involved two tasks, free conversational speech and reading *The Story of Arthur the Rat*, under two conditions: face-to-face and over the telephone. Results of the F_0 analyses together with the overall means and standard deviations (SD) are shown in Tables 16.1 and 16.2 below.

The results of the acoustic analyses of both the face-to-face and the

Table 16.1 Mean F_0 values from laryngographic (Lx) data (SpLx tapes) analysed with the laryngograph peak-picker (20 subjects)

Task: Channel: Subject	Read Telephone (Hz)	Read Face-to-face (Hz)	Free Telephone (Hz)	Free Face-to-face (Hz)
P1	137.2	133.5	141.0	133.5
P2	133.5	141.0	123.0	126.4
P3	123.0	130.0	107.2	102.0
P4	129.9	129.9	116.4	113.3
P5	101.5	99.0	82.0	79.3
P6	133.5	126.4	104.3	101.5
P7	119.6	123.0	116.4	116.4
P8	129.9	129.9	119.6	113.3
P9	107.2	104.3	93.5	91.0
P10	126.4	119.6	113.3	110.2
P11	98.8	96.1	98.8	98.8
P12	107.2	101.5	98.8	96.1
P13*	141.0	137.2	113.3	107.2
P14*	107.2	110.2	91.0	91.0
P15	126.4	126.4	110.2	107.2
P16	129.9	133.5	107.2	110.5
P17	141.0	144.9	137.2	126.4
P18	113.3	116.4	107.2	116.4
P19	101.5	104.3	96.1	96.1
P20	116.4	123.0	101.5	101.0
Mean	121.2	121.5	108.9	106.9
SD	(13.7)	(14.6)	(14.6)	(13.4)

Note: *Averaged from two samples

telephone recordings from the 'near' end of the line show a similar tendency to the laryngographically estimated data: an upward shift in F_0 for the telephone condition.

One-tailed t-tests and analysis of variance (ANOVA) performed on the raw data give an indication of statistical significance. The conversational (free) speech over the telephone has a higher F_0 than comparable speech face-to-face, with a statistical significance provided by the ANOVA of $F:(1,7)$ = 5.304, $p < 0.0547$ for the Sp data. The Lx data of this effect fall short of statistical significance.

Considering the read and 'free' speech (Lx and Sp data) independently, the effect (raising F_0 in telephone speech) is not apparent for read speech. In other words, speech read over the telephone does not have a significantly higher fundamental frequency than the same speech read face-to-face.

However, the strongest trend demonstrated by the ANOVA on both the Lx and Sp data is that the read speech (for this particular text) has

Table 16.2 Mean F_0 values from speech acoustic (Sp) data (SpLx tapes) analysed with the MSL peak-picker (8 subjects)

Task: Channel: Subject	Read Telephone (Hz)	Read Face-to-face (Hz)	Free Telephone (Hz)	Free Face-to-face (Hz)
P1	141.0	142.3	152.0	137.3
P2	145.0	147.0	123.3	123.3
P2a*	93.3	97.0	92.3	91.8
P3	124.3	131.0	110.8	103.0
P4	130.5	131.3	115.0	112.0
P5	103.8	100.8	85.0	79.8
P6	132.8	125.0	108.0	103.3
P7	126.3	116.8	115.0	111.0
Mean	124.6	123.9	112.7	107.7
SD	(17.7)	(18.0)	(20.3)	(17.8)

Note: *This subject was excluded from the laryngographic analysis but included in this acoustic pitch estimation.

a significantly higher F_0 than free speech, face-to-face and over the telephone $(F:(1,19) = 48.66, p < 0.0001$ for Lx; $F:(1,7) = 16.077, p < 0.01$ for Sp$)$.

DISCUSSION AND CONCLUSIONS

The variability of F_0 within and between speakers makes it impracticable to identify speakers using this parameter alone. F_0 in a single native English speaker varies in response to emotional state, exposure to background noise, conversational task and so on (French and Local 1983, 1986; Summers *et al.* 1988; Hollien 1991).

Other variables which have been shown to affect measurements of voice fundamental frequency also include the type and duration of speech samples; free vs read speech; the duration of the sample, and even the time of day that the speech is elicited (Barry *et al.* 1990). The current study demonstrates that F_0 from read speech is consistently and significantly higher than that from free speech.

We might have predicted that read speech would have a lower mean F_0 than the 'free' speech. However, dramatic reading by the participants, particularly those parts of the passage which are direct speech (highlighted in the appendix to this chapter) may account for a skewing of the results. When the relevant passages are edited from the recording, the mean figures calculated from the remaining speech material are very close to those from the free (conversational) speech. This skewing of the results suggests that future studies of a similar kind should consider using a different text.

Variation of F_0 is constrained by several factors. Mean F_0 for adult male speakers of English from the same age range as that in this study is approximately 117 Hz (averaged from 448 studies cited in Krook 1988). Also averaging data from a number of studies of males in this age group, Aronson (1985) quotes an overall mean of 128 Hz. Using laryngographic data, Barry *et al.* (1990) cite means of 123 Hz for free monologue, and 126 Hz and 132 Hz for two reading tasks using different texts.

The overall means from the Lx data presented here show a similar relationship between read and spontaneous speech, with means of 121 Hz and 108 Hz for the reading and free speech recordings respectively. Equivalent values from the acoustic data are 124 Hz and 110 Hz respectively. Measurements of F_0 range vary in different studies, but 1.08 octaves (Graddol 1986) and 0.64 octaves (Barry *et al.* 1990) suggest that the standard deviation figures in Table 16.2 are consistent with other research in the field.

One question which requires review is the application of various F_0 estimation devices (see Rabiner *et al.* 1976; Howard *et al.* 1993) for forensic phonetics. The present study employs the MSL 'peak picker' operating on the acoustic waveform, and a similar algorithm built into the Lx processor. The 'peak-picker' analysis is a time domain technique based on identifying the major peaks in each cycle of the acoustic waveform during voiced speech when the vocal folds are vibrating. Howard (1989) gives a review of its operation, and compares its output with that from the laryngograph and two acoustically based techniques: cepstral (frequency domain) and Gold Rabiner algorithm (time domain). There is no single acoustically based device which produces reliable results for any speaker in any acoustic environment (see Hess 1983). The particular limitations of F_0 extraction from the acoustic recordings were highlighted by the difficulty in obtaining reliable results from the far end of the telephone line.

Comparison of F_0 distributions between speakers often involves significant overlap, particularly if speakers are the same sex, similar age, etc. If, as this study suggests, a small upward shift may be expected when a speaker is recorded from the telephone, such channel effects may be taken into consideration in speaker identification. Furthermore, since recorded telephone conversations requiring forensic phonetic analysis are often emotionally charged, one may expect an accentuated pitch shift in the disputed call. For the purposes of speaker identification, we suggest that in cases where F_0 from a disputed telephone caller is *lower* than that from a reference speech sample from an interview, this should be interpreted as a relatively strong indication that *different* speakers are involved.

Telephones convey only a restricted band of the speech signal. In Britain, the system typically transmits sound between about 340 Hz and 3,400 Hz effectively acting as a bandpass filter between these two frequencies. This of itself would not be expected to alter the fundamental frequency, although the effect of selective frequency attenuation on some lines does deserve investigation. However, to control for any effects of telephone transmission, the speech of each speaker is recorded at both ends of the telephone line. Difficulties in carrying out an F_0 analysis of band-limited speech have prevented this analysis to date, but this does not affect the measurable differences in speech behaviour by subjects on the telephone compared to face-to-face conversation.

The findings in this study are mainly descriptive, and although they may have some practical significance, they lack explanatory power. In other words, we have not addressed the question: Why? One possible explanation for the rise in F_0 may be similar to an effect described in the early part of this century by Etienne Lombard. In this early study he theorises that speakers:

> increase their vocal effort in the presence of noise in the environment … [and] attempt to maintain a constant level of intelligibility in the face of the degradation of the message by the environmental noise source.
>
> (cited in Summers *et al.* 1988: 917)

In the case of telephone speech, the loss of high and low frequencies may be formally (and perceptually) equivalent to a compromised speech signal in noise, reducing both intelligibility and the perceived overall loudness of the speech signal. The narrower the bandpassed signal, the greater this effect may be expected to be. Although the telephone speaker in the experiment does not *hear* very much transmitted speech, experience of telephones, and the audibility of the interlocutor may prompt the speaker to adjust features of his output. Further studies with naïve subjects (e.g. children), and examining the effects of systematic variations in background noise and bandpass range will test this hypothesis.

Extending the current dataset to include female speakers is the next stage of this research. Such data will provide a valuable database, not only for F_0 studies, but in the wider research programme on the relative stability of speech transmitted by various means and under adverse conditions of background noise. It will also provide a further test of the current finding that telephone 'free' speech tends to be higher pitched than equivalent speech face-to-face.

NOTES

1 Paper originally presented to the International Association for Forensic Phonetics Conference, University College of Ripon and York St John, York, England, Summer 1992.
2 Based on examination of 100 case records in 1991–2, J. P. French Associates, New York.

APPENDIX

Below is reproduced *The Story of Arthur the Rat* (Sweet 1890). Direct speech is marked in italics. This aspect of the passage appears to skew the F_0 results, readers tending to inflect and raise their voices when play-acting individual characters in the story.

The Story of Arthur the Rat

There was once a young rat named Arthur, who would never take the trouble to make up his mind. Whenever his friends asked him if he would like to go out with them, he would only answer, '*I don't know.*' He wouldn't say '*Yes*,' and he wouldn't say '*No*' either. He could never learn to make a choice.

His aunt Helen said to him, '*No-one will ever care for you if you carry on like this. You have no more mind than a blade of grass.*' Arthur looked wise, but said nothing.

One rainy day the rats heard a great noise in the loft where they lived. The pine rafters were all rotten, and at least one of the joists had given way and fallen to the ground. The walls shook and the rats' hair stood on end with fear and horror. '*This won't do,*' said the old rat who was chief. '*I'll send out scouts to search for a new home.*'

Three hours later, the seven scouts came back and said, '*We've found a stone house which is just what we wanted. There's room and good food for us all. There's a kindly horse named Nelly, a cow, a calf and a garden with an elm tree.*' Just then the old rat caught sight of young Arthur. '*Are you coming with us?*' he asked. '*I don't know,*' Arthur sighed, '*the roof may not come down just yet.*' '*Well,*' said the old rat angrily, '*We can't wait all day for you to make up your mind. Right about face! March!*' And they went off.

Arthur stood and watched the other rats hurry away. The idea of an immediate decision was too much for him. '*I'll go back to my hole for a bit,*' he said to himself, '*just to make up my mind.*'

That night there was a great crash that shook the earth, and down came the whole roof. Next day some workers rode up and looked at the ruins. One of them moved a board, and under it they saw a young rat lying on his side, quite dead, half in and half out of his hole.

ACKNOWLEDGEMENTS

The authors wish to acknowledge the subjects at York University for their co-operation, and Dr Tim Pring of City University for his assistance with the statistical analysis of results.

REFERENCES

Abberton, E. R. M., Howard, D. M. and Fourcin, A. J. (1989) 'Laryngographic assessment of normal voice: a tutorial', *Clinical Linguistics and Phonetics* 3, 3: 281–96.

Abercrombie, D. (1964) *English Phonetic Texts*, London: Faber & Faber.

Aronson, A. E. (1985) *Clinical Voice Disorders: An Interdisciplinary Approach*, 2nd edn, New York: Thieme.

Ball, V., Faulkner, A. and Fourcin, A. (1990) 'The effects of two different speech-coding strategies on voice fundamental frequency control in deafened adults', *British Journal of Audiology* 24: 393–409.

Barry, W. J., Goldsmith, M., Fourcin, A. J. and Fuller, H. (1990) 'Larynx analyses of normative reference data', *Alvey Project MMI/132: Speech Technology Assessment.*

Braun, A. (1994, in press) 'Fundamental frequency – how speaker specific is it?', in J.-P. Köster and A. Braun (eds) *Neue tendenzen in der angewandten phonetik: Forensischephonetik*, Trier: University of Trier Press.

Fourcin, A. J. and Abberton, E. (1971) 'First applications of a new laryngograph', *Medical and Biological Illustration* 21, 3: 172–82.

French, J. P. and Local, J. (1983) 'Turn competitive incomings', *Journal of Pragmatics* 7, 1: 17–38.

—— (1986) 'Prosodic features and the management of interruptions', in C. Johns-Lewis (ed.), *Intonation in Discourse*, London: Croom Helm, pp 000–00.

Graddol, D. (1986) 'Discourse specific pitch behaviour', in C. Johns-Lewis (ed.), *Intonation in Discourse*, London: Croom Helm.

Hess, W. (1983) *Pitch Detection of Speech Signals*, Berlin: Springer.

Hess, W. and Indefrey, H. (1984) 'Accurate pitch determination of speech signals by means of a laryngograph', *Proceedings of the IEEE International Conference of Acoustics and Speech Signal Processing*, ICASSP-84: 1–4.

Hirson, A. and Duckworth, M. (1993) 'Glottal fry and voice disguise: a case study in forensic phonetics', *Journal of the Biomedical Engineering Society* 15: 193–200.

Hollien, H. (1991) *The Acoustics of Crime: the New Science of Forensic Phonetics*, New York: Plenum Press.

Howard, D. M. (1989) 'Peak-picking fundamental period estimation for hearing prostheses', *Journal of the Acoustical Society of America* 86, 3: 902–9.

Howard, D. M., Hirson, A., French, J. P. and Szymanski, J. E. (1993) 'A survey of fundamental frequency estimation techniques used in forensic phonetics', *Proceedings of the Institute of Acoustics – Reproduced Sound* 15, 7: 207–17.

Kitzing, P. (1990) 'Clinical applications of electroglottography', *Journal of Voice* 4, 3: 238–49.

Krook, M. I. P. (1988) 'Speaking fundamental frequency characteristics of normal Swedish subjects obtained by glottal frequency analysis', *Folia Phoniatrica* 40: 82–90.

McGonegal, C. A., Rosenberg, A. E. and Rabiner, L. R. (1979) 'The effects of several transmission systems on an automatic speaker verification system', *Bell System Technical Journal* 58: 2071–87.

Nolan, F. (1983) *The Phonetic Bases of Speaker Recognition*, Cambridge: Cambridge University Press.

Rabiner, L. R., Cheng, X., Rosenberg, A. E. and McGonegal, C. A. (1976) 'A comparative performance study of several pitch detection algorithms', *IEEE Transactions Acoustics and Speech Signal Processing*, ASSP-24, 5: 399–418.

Summers, Van W., Pisoni, D. B, Bernacki, R. H., Pedlow, R. I. and Stokes, M.A. (1988) 'Effects of noise on speech production: acoustic and perceptual analysis', *Journal of the Acoustical Society of America* 84, 3: 917–28.

Sweet, H. (1890) *A Primer of Spoken English*, Oxford: Clarendon Press.

17

The effect of emphasis on declination in English intonation

Francis Nolan
University of Cambridge

INTRODUCTION

The synthetic creation of speech by computer has been a goal which has given considerable impetus to the testing and refinement of phonetic models. Developments in the specification of acoustic segments, and of their temporal integration, have led to increases in the realism and intelligibility of synthetic speech; but no less important have been advances in the description of intonation. Perfecting the segmental aspects of synthetic speech is of little value if its intonation is such as to misdirect listeners away from the informationally important parts of the utterance, or to antagonise them through undesirable attitudinal cues, such as those to hostility or impatience.

Historically much of our knowledge about intonation has been embodied in impressionistic models based on careful listening and intuition. O'Connor and Arnold (1973), which is oriented towards teaching intonation to foreign learners, draws on and contributes to a tradition of intonation analysis within which are also found, for instance, Palmer (1922), Kingdon (1958) and Crystal (1969). Impressionistic models provide many valid insights about the phonological structure and the semantic function of intonation patterns, but in general they lack the degree of precision and quantification at the phonetic level which is required in speech synthesis. More recently, this shortfall has been redressed by researchers such as Pierrehumbert (e.g. 1980, 1981), Silverman (1987) and Cooper and Sorensen (1981). As well as measuring the physical dimensions of intonation, these researchers have also concerned themselves with its representation, and have revised and extended the terms in which the phonological structure of intonation is expressed.

A major source of controversy in the quantitative modelling of intonation has been the treatment of declination. This is an aspect of intonation which received little explicit discussion in the impressionistic literature. Declination, broadly, is the tendency for fundamental frequency (F_0)[1] to become lower throughout the course of an utterance. In English, for instance, successive high pitch accents will tend to follow a downward sequence.

Beyond this broad definition there exists a variety of views about the nature and causes of declination. Ladd (1984) provides a wide-ranging discussion. Least controversially, declination can be seen as a statistical abstraction from F_0 contours. Measure enough utterances, calculate means, and a downward trend in F_0 will emerge. This is not to say, of course, that all individual utterances must conform to the statistical abstraction. Particular types of utterance, as long as they are in a minority in the corpus analysed, may systematically deviate from the norm. Questions are an utterance type which sometimes behave differently with respect to declination. And individual utterances of a type which are normally characterised by declination are quite free to deviate from the statistical norm. Speakers of English, for instance, appear to have considerable latitude to adjust the height of accents on individual words to reflect their semantic weighting in the utterance, so that an accent late in an utterance may be higher than an earlier one. But at the level of the individual utterance the concept of declination is still perhaps useful, because it functions as a default or unmarked case, a reference from which individual utterances can deviate to signal marked informational properties.

In what follows, a brief outline is given of the aspects of two contrasting approaches to modelling declination which are relevant here. The outline will be worded as far as possible in terms familiar in traditional intonation analysis, at the risk of oversimplifying some of the technical aspects of the approaches. After this an experiment will be reported which tests a specific version of one of those approaches.

CONTOUR INTERACTION AND TONE SEQUENCE MODELS

Although the notion of declination may provide a partial description of the intonation of an utterance, it is clearly insufficient by itself. Any auditory or acoustic analysis reveals complexities of pitch movement – particularly those associated with accented syllables – which are incompatible with a simple line or curve extending over the whole utterance. To account for the details of intonation patterns using only a 'global' contour would require an ever-expanding inventory of such contours to accommodate different numbers of accents and of syllables within accent units, and different accent types. The generalisation of associating a particular global contour with a particular function or class of functions would be lost.

In practice, the solution is to view the global contour as merely one of a hierarchy of domains, whose constituents interact to produce the observable pitch contour. Thus, for instance, the hypothetical global downslope of an unmarked statement has, superimposed on it, the shorter contours of successive accent units within the utterance. This is

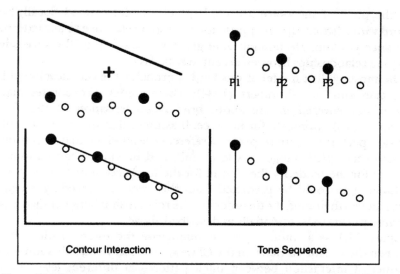

Figure 17.1 Schematic representation of the 'Contour Interaction' and 'Tone Sequence' approaches to modelling declination

schematised in the left half of Figure 17.1, adapted from Thorsen (1983: 32), who presents arguments based on data from Danish in favour of such an approach. In Figure 17.1, the global contour is shown as the sloping line. Below this, accented syllables are shown as large filled circles. An accented syllable together with any unaccented syllables (shown as small open circles) is taken to comprise an accent unit, which has a pitch contour associated with it (in Figure 17.1, a fall). The contour for a particular accent unit finds its proper place in the pitch scale by 'latching onto' the sloping utterance contour. Models of this kind are referred to by among others Ladd (1983) as *Contour Interaction* (CI) models.

A contrasting view discards the notion of an utterance contour. Instead, the downtrend over an individual utterance, if there is one, is largely the cumulative effect of relationships between the pitch of successive accents. The relationship between successive accents is a phonological variable, and may differ from utterance to utterance. A common pattern for English, however, is a stepping pattern, where each successive accent is lower than the preceding one. This relationship will automatically produce a down-trend over the accented syllables of the utterance.

To model this, the pitch of each accent is calculated with reference only to the pitch of the preceding accent – for instance, as a fixed percentage of its pitch. Thus, in the right half of Figure 17.1, the pitch of the second accent (P2) is calculated with reference purely to that of the first (whose determination need not be of concern here) – perhaps $P2 = P1 \times 0.7$. Likewise, P3 is calculated with reference purely to P2 ($P3 = P2 \times 0.7$). In this way the pitch of successive accented syllables is determined 'locally', in accord with a 'strict adjacency principle', without reference to any external utterance contour. Declination emerges principally[2] from the successive stepping relationships between accented syllables.

The most explicit model of this kind is probably the one developed by Liberman and Pierrehumbert (1984). Their model incorporates many aspects not covered in the above brief characterisation of the Tone Sequence (TS) approach; for instance, it assumes that the accent calculations are performed with respect to a reference level which may be sensitive to the overall pitch range of a tone unit, and provides a mechanism to account for the tendency they found for the final accent of a tone unit to be lower than could be predicted from the trend of preceding accents. Nevertheless their model's treatment of the relationship between successive accents appears to be essentially as described above.

Figure 17.1 as a whole serves to summarise the essential differences between the CI and TS views. In the CI view, the observed declination is the product of interaction between pitch patterns at different levels in an intonological hierarchy. In the TS view, declination is a by-product of relationships between successive elements (accents) at their own level.

TESTING THE TONE SEQUENCE APPROACH

Liberman and Pierrehumbert (1984: 166) cite a number of factors emerging from their experiments which lead them to favour a TS model:

> we find no clear evidence for phrase-level planning of F_0 implementation. The major factors shaping F_0 contours appear to be local ones. Potential long-distance effects are erratic and small at best. All of our model's computations are made on pairs of adjacent elements

The experiment reported in the following section aims to test the associated claim that all relevant calculations 'fall within the scope of the two pitch-accent window' (1984: 166).

The experiment is essentially the one originally proposed in Nolan (1984: 4.6). Crucially it focuses on the case where, in a sequence of descending accents, one of those accents is 'boosted' – moved up out of the trend of the other accented syllables – in order to give particular prominence or emphasis to the linguistic element containing the accented syllable. Crystal (1969: 144–5), from whom the term 'booster' is taken, has a rather complex categorisation of boosters, but in the present context an accent will simply be regarded as boosted if its pitch is higher than that of the preceding accent. Crystal implicitly acknowledges declination in suggesting (1969: 144) that the norm for an English syllable is to be 'slightly lower than the preceding (stressed or unstressed) syllable', but his description of boosters, and their relatively common occurrence in his

244

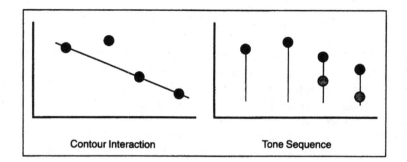

Figure 17.2 Schematic representation of the predictions of CI and TS approaches for the pitch of accented syllables following a boosted accent

transcriptions, underlines the point that a regular declination of accented syllables is a default which can be overridden, rather than a well-formedness condition on tone units.

The criterial question is this: what happens to the pitch of accents *after* the boosted syllable? A CI model would, presumably, predict that after the local deviation of the boosted accent from the utterance contour, subsequent accents would dutifully return to that contour – as schematised in the left of Figure 17.2, where the second of four accented syllables is shown as boosted. On the other hand a TS model which incorporated a strict adjacency principle would have to calculate the post-booster accent with reference to the pitch of the booster, and thus a 'resetting' of the declination trend would occur, as schematised in the right half of Figure 17.2 (the grey circles show where the third and fourth accents would have been, had the boosting of the second accent had no effect on them).

To summarise, it seems that the CI approach and the TS approach make distinct predictions for accents following an instance of boosting. The CI approach predicts that these accents will ignore the boosting, whereas the TS approach predicts that the raising of pitch associated with the boosting will feed down the line of subsequent accents. The experiment to test these predictions is reported below.[3]

THE EXPERIMENT

The experiment is based closely on the 'berry name' task reported in Liberman and Pierrehumbert (1984). In order to observe declination in as pure a form as possible, those researchers used semantically bland and linguistically minimally structured reading material consisting of lists of (American English) berry names, for instance 'Blueberries bayberries raspberries mulberries and brambleberries.' Because they were interested in the effect of changes in pitch range, Liberman and Pierrehumbert required their readers to produce their utterances with one of three different degrees of 'overall emphasis' – indicated for a given token by a number from 1 to 3.

The crucial difference in the present experiment is that local, rather than global, pitch range effects were controlled. This was done by underlining one item in the list and asking subjects to emphasise that item in their reading of the list. This ensured a 'boosted' accent on the appropriate syllable of that item.

There is an intonological property of lists which is not commented on explicitly by Liberman and Pierrehumbert but which is crucial to the present enterprise. Specifically, they inhibit nucleus fronting. Given a text such as 'He admired Kathy's singing enormously' the default reading would place the nucleus on -norm-. For a speaker asked to give particular emphasis to *Kathy*, one very natural strategy is to move the nucleus to the appropriate syllable of that word (*Kath-*), in functional terms focusing that name and backgrounding the following material, and in intonological terms de-accenting -*sing*- and -*norm*-. Clearly if declination is inferred from high accented syllables, the effect on declination of a boosted accent will be hard to assess if no further accents follow. One of two methods must be adopted: either to give subjects a tutorial on nucleus placement and ask them to achieve emphasis without changing nucleus placement; or to find a type of utterance which inhibits nucleus fronting. Lists appear to do this; it is very unnatural to put the nucleus on the middle item of a list and de-accent the remainder. Instead, the relevant later syllables retain their accent.

Materials

The materials for this experiment consisted of lists of musical note-names. Despite being lists, these constitute a fairly plausible class of utterance, as for instance when naming the sharps or flats in a particular key. The phonetic motivation was to achieve a list where all items were rhythmically identical and had the same vowel. The latter was to ensure that vowel-intrinsic pitch differences were controlled for, which reduced the need to use, as Liberman and Pierrehumbert (1984) did with their berry names, all possible orderings of items in the list in order to neutralise the effects of intrinsic vowel F_0. To this end only the note names B C D E and G (all with the vowel /iː/) were used. A subset of four of the possible orderings of the items was used, with a view to controlling for any intrinsic F_0 effect which might persist from the voiced, voiceless or zero syllable-initial consonant as far as the measurement point in the middle of the vowel.

In this experiment the note names were combined with the suffix -*sharp*, written #, yielding lists of the form

C# B# G# D# E#

The choice of a suffix with an initial voiceless fricative permitted crisp segmentation in the acoustic analysis and, it may be hoped, a consistency in the choice of F_0 measurement point, as discussed under 'Acoustic analysis' below.

Each of the five ordered lists occurred in four emphasis conditions: no particular emphasis, and emphasis on the second, third or fourth item, indicated by underlining of that item. It was not considered helpful for the purpose of the experiment to obtain emphasis on the first or last item, since the F_0 of the accented syllable of these would itself be crucial to establishing the declination trend before and after boosting.

The material thus consisted of five-item lists, in 4 orders × 4 emphasis conditions. This material, together with similar lists of varying lengths for other experiments, was subject to five separate randomisations, so that each list would be read five times, once in each of five randomised blocks.

Subjects

The subjects were four speakers of General Australian English, two male and two female, aged between 25 and 35. All were phonetically sophisticated, and were experienced at making recordings of controlled material, but none was aware of the purpose of the experiment.

In the case of declination, a phenomenon which has been shown to recur across prosodically diverse languages, it was reasonable to expect General Australian speakers to behave in a way similar to speakers of other dialects of English, notably the most-measured General American. This expectation was borne out where results were directly comparable to those of previous studies.

Recording

The recordings were made in the sound-treated studio of Macquarie University's Speech, Hearing and Language Research Centre. Each token was read from a typed card. Subjects were instructed to read each list, giving emphasis to any item underlined. No further instructions on the manner of reading were given, with the exception that if the experimenter, who was monitoring the productions, was unable to perceive unambiguously the location of emphasis in a token with emphasis, the speaker was asked to repeat the token with more marked emphasis at the appropriate point. Such problems only arose with one speaker, at the beginning of the recording session. The procedure in the present experiment was rather more *laisser faire* than in the original 'berry name' experiment (Liberman and Pierrehumbert 1984); there, 'the desired intonation pattern was demonstrated to [the two] subjects other than the authors, and the subjects' ability to produce it naturally was checked' (1984: 177).

Table 17.1 Mean time and F_0 values of accented syllables in four emphasis conditions for speaker CH

	No emphasis		Emphasis 2		Emphasis 3		Emphasis 4	
	time	freq.	time	freq.	time	freq.	time	freq.
Accent 1	0.00	196	0.00	197	0.00	199	0.00	200
Accent 2	0.63	182	0.63	205	0.63	183	0.63	184
Accent 3	1.27	176	1.31	177	1.27	197	1.28	180
Accent 4	1.87	171	1.91	169	1.88	172	1.90	194
Accent 5	2.52	166	2.56	166	2.54	167	2.60	167

Table 17.2 Mean time and F_0 values of accented syllables in four emphasis conditions for speaker JV

	No emphasis		Emphasis 2		Emphasis 3		Emphasis 4	
	time	freq.	time	freq.	time	freq.	time	freq.
Accent 1	0.00	242	0.00	220	0.00	233	0.00	241
Accent 2	0.44	210	0.46	251	0.46	204	0.45	211
Accent 3	0.91	194	0.95	197	0.92	260	0.94	193
Accent 4	1.37	183	1.41	182	1.39	178	1.39	243
Accent 5	1.86	176	1.90	173	1.88	170	1.91	167

Table 17.3 Mean time and F_0 values of accented syllables in four emphasis conditions for speaker PK

	No emphasis		Emphasis 2		Emphasis 3		Emphasis 4	
	time	freq.	time	freq.	time	freq.	time	freq.
Accent 1	0.00	194	0.00	190	0.00	192	0.00	197
Accent 2	0.52	173	0.54	197	0.52	175	0.52	172
Accent 3	1.03	164	1.09	165	1.06	189	1.04	163
Accent 4	1.54	155	1.58	151	1.59	156	1.57	183
Accent 5	2.10	152	2.13	153	2.15	152	2.18	154

Table 17.4 Mean time and F_0 values of accented syllables in four emphasis conditions for speaker RM

	No emphasis		Emphasis 2		Emphasis 3		Emphasis 4	
	time	freq.	time	freq.	time	freq.	time	freq.
Accent 1	0.00	124	0.00	125	0.00	126	0.00	128
Accent 2	0.45	117	0.44	142	0.45	119	0.44	121
Accent 3	0.90	115	0.93	112	0.90	140	0.89	119
Accent 4	1.33	113	1.38	110	1.38	111	1.34	136
Accent 5	1.81	114	1.87	107	1.87	109	1.86	108

(a)

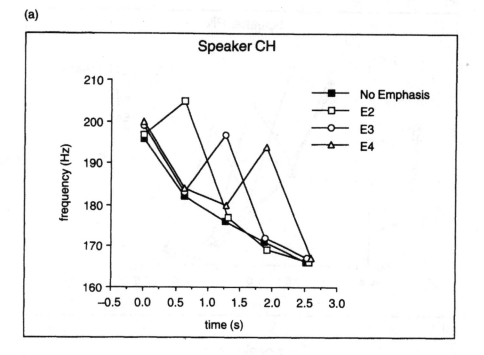

(b)

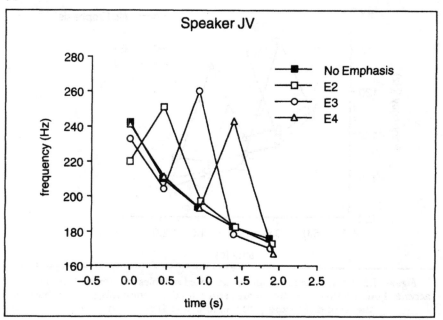

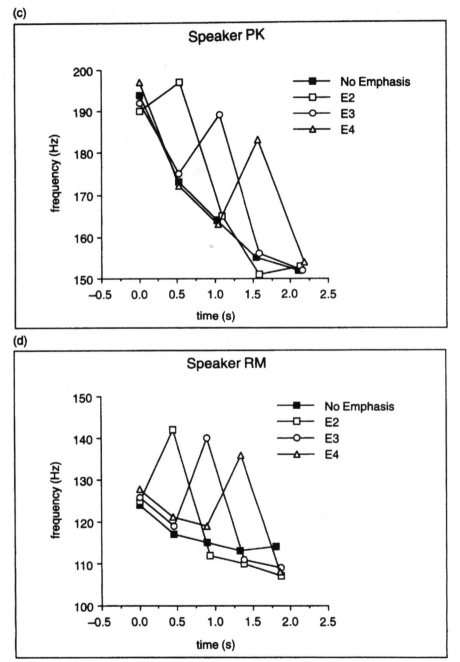

Figure 17.3 Mean F_0 against time for accented syllables in utterances with five accents. Four emphasis conditions are represented: no emphasis, and emphasis on the second (E2) and (E3) and fourth (E4) accented syllable

Acoustic analysis

The first step in the analysis of the recordings was the production of expanded scale (0–1 kHz) narrowband (45 Hz) spectrograms, using a Voiceprint spectrograph. Such displays reveal clearly the lower harmonics of voiced portions, allowing measurement of F_0. Because of the diametrically opposed spectral properties of /iː/ and /ɑː/ (in e.g. *C sharp E sharp*...), and the crisp discontinuity caused by the voiceless postalveolar fricative (/ʃ/) and the other (stop) consonants, phonetic segmentation was (by design) possible with a high degree of confidence.

The quantification of F_0 was carried out using a digitiser table with crosshair cursor, and computer software for taking time–frequency measurements from spectrograms.[4] F_0 was measured by placing the cursor on a harmonic and entering its frequency into the computer. Normally the second, or sometimes the third, harmonic was used, being the highest reliably present in the 0–1 kHz range in the /iː/ vowels of interest.

Five measurement points were defined for each utterance, at the durational mid-point of each accented vowel. F_0 was in general relatively level on accented vowels, and so F_0 estimated at this mid-point would differ little from a peak estimate. Exceptions were the emphasised accented syllables, where F_0 typically rose sharply through the syllable and where therefore a mid-point measurement results in a value lower than would a peak measurement. An advantage of mid-point measurements is that their durational indices provide a more consistent synopsis of the temporal structure of the utterance than would peak measurements, where minor F_0 perturbations could displace the point of measurement considerably in a relatively level portion. No attempt was made to measure an utterance-final low F_0 since all speakers frequently dropped into creak at this point.

Results

Mean F_0 values for accented syllables in the four emphasis conditions are shown for the four speakers in Tables 17.1–17.4. Each value represents a mean based on twenty measurements, that is, five tokens by a speaker of each of four orderings of the note names for a given emphasis condition. The values in Tables 17.1–17.4 are presented graphically in Figure 17.3(a–d). In these graphs each point represents a value for an accented syllable, and the lines joining the points are for visual continuity only. 'No emphasis' indicates values for the condition where no item received special emphasis; 'E2', 'E3' and 'E4' relate to the conditions where respectively the second, third and fourth item were emphasised. Note that the points are plotted on a 'real' time axis, rather than merely at equidistant points for successive accented syllables as in the somewhat comparable Figures 26–28 in Liberman and Pierrehumbert (1984).

251

Discussion

It is immediately clear from Figure 17.3 that all four speakers mark emphasis on a given syllable by an appreciable increase in fundamental frequency relative to other syllables, which is not surprising. The finding which is important for evaluating CI and TS models, however, is what happens after this boosted syllable. The outcome of the experiment is strikingly clear: F_0 drops back to where it would have been had the previous syllable not been boosted. This is so whether the comparison is made with the equivalent syllable of the 'No emphasis' condition, or with the trend of unboosted syllables in the particular emphasis condition. In terms of the predictions schematised in Figure 17.2, the results of the experiment unequivocally match the prediction of the Contour Interaction model and not that of the Tone Sequence model.

It is noticeable that the timing pattern of the utterances is little affected by boosting an accent. This is perhaps surprising, and, together with the very regular F_0 behaviour seen, might motivate the objection that the task in this experiment is somewhat remote from natural speech production and leads to mechanical, repetitive production. This can be countered in part by the fact that subjects were not reading only five-item utterances, but a randomised list including a variety of utterance lengths. A more narrowly based defence against the objection is that this experiment was deliberately modelled on Liberman and Pierrehumbert's (1984) 'berry names' experiment, the results of which are used to support the TS approach. To use an experiment of the same general type (but including a new condition, local emphasis) allows for the most direct comparison, which in this case turns out to bring the TS approach into question.

The regularity of the timing pattern may help to rule out one alternative interpretation of the data. It might be argued that in emphasising syllable *n*, speakers were in fact introducing a tone unit boundary after it (or making the emphasised item into a separate intonational phrase). Since the context for discussing declination is normally the tone unit, and resetting would be expected to occur after a boundary, the presence of such a boundary would make conclusions about the correct modelling of declination within a tone unit impossible to draw. However, intonational boundaries are normally associated with durational effects such as lengthening of preceding syllables, and so the absence of appreciable durational variation between conditions makes it unlikely that the intonational structure at the level of the tone unit is being altered.

Furthermore, the F_0 behaviour after the boosted syllable is not what would be expected at the start of a new tone unit, where a return to a higher level, a 'resetting' of the declination trend, would be normal. The 'Tone Sequence' pattern of Figure 17.2, had it been found, might have been ambiguous between a single tone unit and two tone units (with the

252

boundary after the boosted syllable), but the 'Contour Interaction' pattern, to which the F_0 patterns of Figure 17.3 so clearly correspond, unambigously supports a single tone unit with a unifying declinational trend which is deviated from only to achieve boosting on the relevant syllable.

CONCLUSION

A major disagreement in the modelling of intonation has been whether there is a 'global' intonation component associated with a tone unit, responsible at least in part for observed declination, or whether instead declination is simply the cumulative effect of the relation of each accent to its immediate predecessor. These views have been characterised as the Contour Interaction and Tone Sequence approaches. The experiment reported here took as its starting-point the 'berry name' experiment of Liberman and Pierrehumbert (1984), which appeared to fit the predictions of the TS approach. The present experiment involved a minimal enrich-ment of the intonational system elicited from speakers; namely, it required in the reading of lists of items that one of the items should be emphasised. The possibility of 'boosting' an accent to achieve emphasis is well recognised in traditional intonation analysis. The reason for eliciting boosted accents was that the CI and TS approaches appear to make crucially different predictions as to what should happen to the pitch of accents following a boosted accent. The CI approach predicts that the boosted accent will have no effect on subsequent accents, whereas the TS approach seems to predict that subsequent accents will be rescaled upwards because the pitch height of each is calculated with respect to its immediate predecessor.

Assuming that the predictions of the two approaches have been correctly interpreted, the results of this very narrowly constrained experiment unambiguously supported the CI approach. This does not necessarily mean that the CI approach can be regarded as a correct description of speakers' behaviour in spontaneous natural speech. It may be that the kind of reading task tested here provides the optimal conditions for the use of an 'utterance contour'. Furthermore, it is possible that a relaxation of the 'strict adjacency principle' would enable the effects of boosting to be accommodated within a TS model. What is clear from the experiment, however, is that the debate between the two approaches is far from being settled in favour of the TS approach, and that to pursue the matter, declinational behaviour will have to be explored in a richer variety of intonational contexts.

NOTES

1 'Fundamental frequency' is the rate of repetition of a waveform, expressed in Hz (or cycles per second). It is therefore a physically measurable quantity. 'Pitch', strictly, is the perceptual sensation which is more closely dependent on fundamental frequency. At times, however, I shall use 'pitch' ambiguously to cover both percepts and their physical correlates.

2 Such an account does not exclude the possibility that other factors, such as physiological ones, also contribute to declination.

3 The experiment included in this paper was carried out while I was a Visiting Fellow at the Speech, Hearing and Language Research Centre (SHLRC), Macquarie University, Sydney in 1987. I am particularly grateful to John Clark for making the visit possible, and for discussing declination and the design of the experiment.

4 The software was written by Harry Purves of SHLRC, Macquarie University.

REFERENCES

Cooper, W. E. and Sorensen, J. M. (1981) *Fundamental Frequency in Sentence Production*, Berlin: Springer.

Crystal, D. (1969) *Prosodic Systems and Intonation in English*, Cambridge: Cambridge University Press.

Kingdon, R. (1958) *The Groundwork of English Intonation*, London: Longman.

Ladd, D. R. (1983) 'Peak features and overall slope', in A. Cutler and D. R. Ladd (eds), *Prosody: Models and Measurements*, Berlin: Springer, pp. 39–52.

—— (1984) 'Declination: a review and some hypotheses', *Phonology Yearbook* 1: 53–74.

Liberman, M., and Pierrehumbert, J. (1984) 'Intonational invariance under changes in pitch range and length', in M. Aronoff and R. T. Öhrle (eds), *Language Sound Structure*, Cambridge MA: MIT Press, pp. 157–233.

Nolan, F. (1984) 'Auditory and instrumental analysis of intonation', *Cambridge Papers in Phonetics and Experimental Linguistics* 3: 1–26.

O'Connor, J. D. and Arnold, G. F. (1973) *Intonation of Colloquial English*, 2nd edn, London: Longman.

Palmer, H. E. (1922) *English Intonation, with Systematic Exercises*, Cambridge: Heffer.

Pierrehumbert, J. B. (1980) 'The phonology and phonetics of English intonation', Ph.D. dissertation, Massachussetts Institute of Technology.

—— (1981) 'Synthesising intonation', *Journal of the Acoustical Society of America* 70: 985–95.

Silverman, K. (1987) 'The structure and processing of fundamental frequency contours', Ph.D. dissertation, University of Cambridge.

Thorsen, N. (1983) 'Two issues in the prosody of standard Danish', in A. Cutler and D. R. Ladd (eds), *Prosody: Models and Measurements*, Berlin: Springer, pp. 27–38.

18

Nucleus placement in English and Spanish: a pilot study of patterns of interference

Héctor Ortiz-Lira
Universidad Metropolitana de Ciencias de la Educación,
Santiago

INTRODUCTION

My starting-point will be the assumption that intonation involves choices in three different areas, viz. division into intonation groups, location of the nuclear accent and choice of tune (Halliday 1967: 18; Cruttenden 1986: 35).[1] In my particular experience as teacher of English prosodies to Spanish-speaking students, I am among those who believe that mistakes in nucleus placement are responsible for more serious problems of inter-ference than mistakes in the choice of tune. Experimental evidence to prove one or the other position is badly needed, but to my knowledge it has not yet been presented.

The problem of nucleus placement was taken up by the two most representative treatments of British intonation addressed to the EFL audience – and also the two most widely used in Latin-American universities – i.e. Kingdon (1958) and O'Connor and Arnold (1973) – but both left important questions unanswered when it came to explaining cases of de-accenting. For instance, the page-and-a-half long account by O'Connor and Arnold (1973: 5–7) on the varying degrees of 'importance' contributed by words was certainly insufficient for the reader to understand why practically *half* the approximately thirty 'word groups' containing at least one lexical item in dialogue 1 (at p. 275) have an early nucleus, as in the opening exchange:

(1)   Did you see OTHELlo on television last night?

O'Connor and Arnold's massive corpus provides countless examples of de-accenting which their theory of accent does not account for.

On the other hand, descriptions of nucleus placement in Spanish (e.g.

Bolinger 1954–5; Contreras 1976; Suñer 1982; Silva-Corvalán 1983), which might help explain the origin of some of our students' mistakes in English, contain crucial omissions, the most important being the fact that given information in Spanish can be, and in fact normally is, accented, as simple observation of facts attests. Kingdon's long residence in Spanish-speaking countries helped him to realise that 'Spanish speakers have a habit of repeating a kinetic stress on a word that has already had one in the same utterance', a practice that is relatively rare in English: e.g.

(2)   Tra₁baja de ₁noche en el 'cine, y ₁hoy no hay 'cine.

(1958: 264–5)

In order to obtain some kind of experimental evidence of differences and similarities between the English and Spanish sentence accent systems, I conducted a series of five tests with two groups of Spanish-speaking subjects of Chilean nationality: one made up of linguistically naive informants, and another of speakers with both practical and theoretical knowledge of English and Spanish phonetics. This paper is an account of the last of these tests.

APPROACH, OBJECTIVES AND METHOD

This test was devised with the specific aim of looking into the exceptions to the Last Lexical Item (LLI) rule (Halliday 1967: 22) in English utterances in both broad and narrow focus (Ladd 1980: 74ff.; Cruttenden 1986: 81ff.). The investigation set out to provide empirical evidence, in the form of recordings, concerning how many of the exceptions analysed constitute a problem in the teaching of spoken English to Spanish speakers. Errors in nucleus placement in this test would reveal that English and Spanish are governed by different, language-specific rules. The first assumption is that in Spanish the nuclear accent tends to fall on the last content word not only of constituents and sentences in broad focus, but also very often of sentences which are in narrow focus, as is the case of utterances containing given information. The second assumption is that in English the LLI rule does not apply to constituents and sentences in narrow focus and does not always apply in utterances in broad focus.

There were nine areas under research. The number in parentheses indicates the number of times each area was tested: 1 final adverbial (3); 2 non-pronominal subject+intransitive predicate (4); 3 final vocative (3); 4 restrictive relative clause in definite NP (2); 5 (final) given information (5); 6 post-modifying infinitive clause (2); 7 softening phrases (3); 8 object of general reference (3); and 9 reporting clauses (3).[2]

In the main, the test postulates the hypothesis that the exceptions to the LLI rule in utterances in broad and narrow focus constitute a problem area for Spanish-speaking students, and in the second place, that Spanish speakers will experience more difficulty when dealing with accentual patterns which are more unlike the corresponding Spanish ones. This tendency will manifest itself in wrong nucleus placement in comparable contexts.

To design the test, it was considered advisable to resort to conversational exchanges which provided not only a suitable compilation and random distribution of the areas listed above, but also realistic, communicative contexts. Eighteen mini-dialogues were written and then given to five native speakers to read and record in order to test their validity. So as to limit the scope of the investigation, a homogeneous group of students able to take the test under similar conditions was chosen. The group consisted of a random selection of 35 subjects from a total of 48 Chilean students of English who had done a course covering the theory and practice of word and sentence accent as part of a teacher-training course. The test was given to the students in a written form for them to read aloud and record on tape after five minutes of prereading. The complete version of the test is given in the appendix.

RESULTS

Table 18.1 summarises individual results, showing total number of readings, number of correct and incorrect readings and corresponding percentages. The figures in Table 18.1 reveal the existence of two clearly distinct tendencies concerning subjects' performance: the first group comprises final vocatives, softening phrases and reporting clauses, all of which score in the region of 79–89.5 per cent correct nucleus placement, and the second group contains the remainder, which ranges between 15.7 and 54.3 per cent.

Table 18.1 Individual results

Problem area	Total readings	Number of correct patterns and percentage		Number of incorrect patterns and percentage	
Adverbial	105	34	32.4%	71	67.6%
Subject + intransitive predicate	140	22	15.7%	118	84.3%
Final vocative	105	94	89.5%	11	10.5%
Relative clause in definite NP	70	16	22.9%	54	77.1%
Given information	175	69	39.4%	106	60.6%
Post-modifying infinitive clause	70	38	54.3%	32	45.7%
Softening phrase	105	83	79.0%	22	21.0%
Object of general reference	105	27	25.7%	78	74.3%
Reporting clause	105	87	82.9%	18	17.1%

DISCUSSION

The two hypotheses put forward proved to be correct. As predicted, Spanish speakers performed fairly well in those areas where the nuclear accent patterns are comparable in English and Spanish, but had varying degrees of difficulty in those areas where usage diverges. The discussion will be organised around these two areas.

Final vocatives, reporting clauses, softening phrases

Final vocatives comprised the area where informants reached the highest scores. This is not surprising, since Spanish final vocatives are normally appended as tails to the nuclear accent whenever they function as true, colourless vocatives.[3] All three examples in the test translate fairly literally into Spanish, e.g.

(3)   How do you like this BLOUSE, honey?

(4)   ¿Te gusta esta BLUsa, amor?

Reporting clauses and softening phrases in Spanish behave in quite a similar way to their English counterparts. This accounts for the high proportion of correct answers, as exemplified by (5)–(8):

(5)   'What did you SAY?', Bill asked John.

(6)   '¿Qué diJIste?', Bill le preguntó a John.

(7)   She'll give it back on MONday, I think.

(8)   Lo va a devolver el LUnes, creo.

The relatively few cases of wrong nucleus placement appeared to be due to a hesitant, slow reading. Failure to produce an immediate, smooth link between the two clauses often caused the intrusion of an artificially long pause, which in turn called for an extra pitch movement on the wrong word. This was judged as an additional nuclear accent.

The remainder

The area of postmodifying infinitive clauses was one in which students still scored over 50 per cent correct, with a much higher score for (9) than for (10):

(9)   I have some BOOKS to read.

(10)   I still have some TOPics to cover.

The structure in (9) does not translate neatly into Spanish, which prefers the reverse word order, with both the argument and the nuclear accent in

258

final position, as in (11). On the other hand, (10) translates more fluently (as in (12)), and it is therefore significant that there were more errors on this item:

(11)   Tengo que leer algunos LIbros.

(12)   Me quedan algunos temas por cuBRIR.

The last five areas proved to be the most difficult ones. In this group, correct nucleus placement ranged approximately between 23 and 40 per cent. They were, in descending order of incorrectness: given information, final adverbial, object of general reference, relative clause in definite NP, and subject + intransitive predicate. In the case of givenness, the lowest results (between 37 and 23 per cent) were the following, (13), which contains inferred information (Prince 1981):

(13)   (A: They say that most of the subjects are too difficult to cope with.)
         B: I KNEW that would happen.

The English text has a perfect word-for-word Spanish translation, and the pattern fluctuates in Spanish between accent on the last lexical item (14) and early nucleus (15), a version which conveys B's greater involvement:

(14)   Yo sa'BIa que eso iba a pa'SAR.

(15)   Yo sa'BIa que eso iba a pasar.

Example (16), where informants also scored 37 per cent correct, shows the reluctance Spanish speakers feel to alter the accentual pattern of prefixed antonyms in order to highlight the contrast, as can be seen in the normal Spanish version (17):

(16)   A: I think German people are FRIENDly.
         B: Come on! For me they're absolutely uNfriendly!

(17)   A: Yo creo que los alemanes son amisTOsos.
         B: ¿Qué? Para mí son totalmente inamisTOsos.

The lowest score (23 per cent correct answers) corresponds to example (18), which involves shifting the accent onto a function word. The normal Spanish version (19) prefers a repeated accent on the last lexical item *atrasados* (*late*):

(18)   (A: But we're already LATE.)
         B: I don't care if we ARE late.

(19)   (A: Pero si ya estamos atrasAdos.)
         B: No me importa si estamos atrasAdos.

Students' performance on final adverbials was dissimilar. Whereas item

(20) was correctly read by almost 70 per cent of the informants, item (24) barely reached 6 per cent. The Spanish version of the first one may have a number of possibilities, ranging from a pattern similar to English, as in (21), to a nuclear adverbial, of either place or time, as in (22) and (23):

(20)   It's rather HOT in here today.

(21)   Hace caLOR hoy día aquí.

(22)   Hace caLOR hoy día aQUI.

(23)   Hace caLOR aquí hoy DIA.

The low results obtained for the second item (24) can be found in the interference of the Spanish version (25), where *together* (*juntos*) would normally take an accent. Practically all mistakes consisted in making *together* nuclear, rather than the last, time adverbial, as in (26), which is probably a marked version in Spanish, since it reinforces the immediateness of the action:

(24)   We went SHOpping together the other day.

(25)   Estuvimos comprando JUNtos el otro día.

(26)   Estuvimos comprando juntos el otro DIA.

Objects of general reference constituted an area where informants reached consistently low percentages, in that they tended to give them nuclear accent, as a result of Spanish interference. The highest score was for the item in (27), with 40 per cent correct answers, but the other two did not get more than 20 per cent each. The item in (29) does not have a direct translation into Spanish because the structures are not completely parallel. The normal Spanish versions for the other two are provided in (28) and (31):

(27)   She must have DROPPED something.

(28)   Se le debe haber caído ALgo.

(29)   He's OUT somewhere.

(30)   Let's ASK somebody.

(31)   Preguntémosle a ALguien.

The next most difficult area was that of final relative clauses, with a final score of just under 23 per cent. Item (32) scored 9 correct answers, and (34) only 7 out of 35, respectively. Both translations are the neutral, unmarked Spanish versions, the accentual patterns of which were misused by the informants in 77 per cent of the cases:

(32)   You live opposite the PUB we used to go to.

(33)   Tú vives frente al bar donde solíamos ɪʀ.

(34)   Where's that sᴡᴇᴀᴛᴇʀ I gave you?

(35)   ¿Dónde está ese suéter que te ʀᴇɢᴀʟᴇ?

Non-pronominal subject + intransitive predicate (i.e. the so-called 'event sentences') was the area where the group of 35 Spanish-speaking students of English obtained the lowest results: out of a total number of 140 readings, correct answers hardly reached 16 per cent. In most cases informants applied the LLI rule of accentuation, thus making the intransitive verb nuclear, or in item (37), the final adverb. The target sentences are (36)–(39):

(36)   I think we need the wɪɴᴅow open.

(37)   The ʀᴏʙɪɴson's are coming tonight.

(38)   My ᴄᴀʀ broke down.

(39)   My ᴡᴀᴛᴄʜ has stopped.

The corresponding Spanish versions would normally have a different word order, with the nuclear subject in final position, e.g.

(40)   Creo que necesitamos abrir la venᴛᴀna.

(41)   Esta noche vienen los ʀᴏʙɪɴsons.

(42)   Se me echó a perder el ᴀuᴛo.

(43)   Se me paró el ʀᴇʟᴏᴊ.

A second-best option for a simple event sentence such as (42) and (43) would consist of a similar word order to the English versions, e.g.

(44)   El auto se me echó a peʀᴅᴇʀ.

(45)   El reloj se me paʀᴏ.

CONCLUSIONS

The following main conclusions emerge from the above results:

1   Spanish-speaking students of English who may have become fairly proficient in the segmental aspects of the target language normally transfer nucleus placement rules from their mother tongue into English.

2   English and Spanish differ in the way they signal given information intonationally. In Spanish, unlike English, information already present in the discourse is normally accented. A shift of accent to convey givenness is possible in Spanish, but not necessary. (The results

obtained in the other tests support this view, but they have no place in the present discussion.)

3   English and Spanish differ in the way they consider arguments and predicates in their capacity as accent carriers. In Spanish, unlike English, neither arguments nor predicates take prevalence in carrying nuclear accent. This would probably have become more evident if the present discussion had taken into account other accents apart from the nucleus.

4   Closely connected with the above, in Spanish there is a strong tendency for final lexical items to carry the nuclear accent (irrespective of whether they are nouns or verbs, etc.). Word order adjustments are sometimes necessary to allow this rule to come into operation, but the implications of this variable have not been considered here.

5   There tend to be no significant differences between English and Spanish in the accentual treatment of final vocatives, reporting clauses and softening phrases. The accentual tendencies of final adverbials seem to vary, and further research is necessary.

6   Whereas English prefers to leave objects of general reference unaccented in certain contexts, Spanish does not. (More evidence was found in the other tests, but that is beyond the scope of this discussion.)

The patterns of interference discussed here have certainly not exhausted the issue. Important differences will emerge from the analyses of other patterns in narrow focus, such as English sentences with the nuclear accent on operators and prepositions, and others which have not attracted the linguists' attention but still puzzle the advanced students, such as (46) and (47), which Spanish learners will normally accent as in (48) and (49), respectively:

(46)   I've only ˈBEEN here once.

(47)   I've only ˈBROUGHT a thin sweater.

(48)   I've ONly been here ONCE.

(49)   I've ONly brought a thin SWEATer.

Since the publication of the first edition of *Intonation of Colloquial English* (1961), a lot of discussion has been carried out on nucleus placement that urgently needs to be fed into EFL textbooks. This 'practical handbook', as it was subtitled, has been widely reviewed and criticised and has in recent years been out of print. Yet the fact that thirty years later no one has taken up the challenge of replacing it with anything that will compare with the richness and variety of its corpus and the exhaustiveness of its drills is perhaps the most eloquent tribute we could pay to its authors.

NOTES

1   This article is based on one of a series of tests conducted as part of a Ph.D. thesis for the University of Manchester.
2   For detailed treatments of these notions, under these or different names, see Halliday (1970), Crystal (1975), Schmerling (1976), Ladd (1980), Bing (1985), Cruttenden (1986), Gussenhoven (1986) and Faber (1987).
3   There exists (at least in Chilean Spanish) a type of vocative which can take the nuclear accent. This occurs when the speaker feels the need to establish a close relationship with the hearer.

APPENDIX: THE TEST

Capitalisation shows the problem areas tested and the expected answers.

1   (It is summer time. Two friends are talking after lunch.)
    TOM   It's rather HOT in here today.
    DAVID   I agree. I think we need the WINdow open.
2   (A couple is going out for dinner. The wife is looking for a top for her skirt.)
    WIFE   How do you like this BLOUSE, honey?
    HUSBAND Not much really, dear.
    WIFE   Oh, what shall I wear then?
    HUSBAND Well, let's see. Where's that SWEATer I gave you?
    WIFE   I lent it to Susan. She'll give it back on MONday, I think.
3   (Two hours later the same couple are still at home.)
    HUSBAND If we hurry we can get there in no time.
    WIFE   You can hurry if you like, I'm not going to.
    HUSBAND But we're already late!
    WIFE   I don't care if we ARE late.
4   (Two friends are talking about a newly married couple.)
    PETER   By the way, have you heard from Betty and Andrew?
    TOM   Oh, yes. Betty and I went out SHOPping together the other day. They're getting on like a house on fire.
5   (It is breakfast time. Husband and wife are talking.)
    WIFE   Oh honey! I forgot to tell you. The ROBinsons are coming tonight.
    HUSBAND Oh gosh! I can't stand them.
    WIFE   Come on! They're not THAT bad, David.
6   (Kathy and Jack are talking on the phone.)
    JACK   Are you free this weekEND, Kathy?
    KATHY   No, I'm afraid not. I have some BOOKS to read. I'm taking my FInals, you know.
7   (A tutor is talking to his student.)
    TUTOR   Do you think you could possibly hand in your final report by the end of the week?
    STUDENT No, I'm afraid I can't. I still have some TOPics to cover.
8   (Two girls are at a party.)
    SUSAN   What TIME is it, Rose?
    ROSE   (looking at her watch) Oh no! My WATCH has stopped!

9   (Two tourists are trying to find their way to the station.)
    TOURIST 1 I wonder where the station is. Can you find it on your map?
    TOURIST 2 No, I can't. Let's ASK somebody.
10 (Liz and Mary have just been introduced.)
    LIZ So you live in Park Street.
    MARY No, Park Avenue.
    LIZ Oh, I remember now. You live opposite the PUB we used to go to.
11 (Two friends are talking about their likes and dislikes.)
    MIKE And you're interested in CLASsical music, I believe.
    BOB Yes, I am. Aren't you?
    MIKE Well, not much, really. I like pop music.
12 (Two tourists are in Germany.)
    JAKE I think German people are friendly.
    TED Come on! They're absolutely UNfriendly.
13 (Mike is knocking at Peter's door.)
    MIKE Isn't Peter in?
    TOM No, he's OUT somewhere. He should be back by three.
14 (Miss White is late for work. Mr Parker is her boss.)
    MR PARKER Miss White, you know you are supposed to be here at eight o'clock. Not at ten PAST eight.
    MISS WHITE I'm sorry, Mr Parker, but my CAR broke down.
15 (Two lecturers are discussing class problems.)
    LECTURER 1 A lot of first year students have already dropped out. They say that most of the subjects are too difficult to cope with.
    LECTURER 2 I KNEW that would happen.
16 (Tony and John are in the livingroom and a loud noise comes from the kitchen).
    TONY What was that?
    JOHN Helen's in the kitchen. She must have DROPPED something.
17 (Bill couldn't hear what John said about Liz.)
    'What did you SAY?', Bill asked John.
    'I said she has a SCREW loose', John replied.
    'Yes, I'm afraid you're RIGHT', Bill agreed.
18 (Sally and Janet are talking about Lucy's plans for this summer.)
    SALLY Lucy is going to BraZIL this summer.
    JANET What about her trip to Europe?
    SALLY She said it had been called off.

REFERENCES

Bing, J. M. (1985) *Aspects of English Prosody*, New York and London: Garland.

Bolinger, D. B. (1954–5) 'Meaningful word order in Spanish', *Boletín de Filología* (Universidad de Chile) 8: 45–56; repr. in J. H. Silverman (ed.) (1991), *Essays on Spanish: Words and Grammar*. Newark, DE: Juan de la Cuesta, pp. 218–30.

Contreras, H. (1976) *A Theory of Word Order with Special Reference to Spanish*, Amsterdam: North-Holland.

Cruttenden, A. (1986) *Intonation*, Cambridge: Cambridge University Press.

Crystal, D. (1975) 'Prosodic features and linguistic theory', in D. Crystal, D. *The English Tone of Voice*, London: Edward Arnold, pp. 1–46.

Faber, D. (1987) 'The accentuation of intransitive sentences in English', *Journal of Linguistics* 23: 341–58.

Gussenhoven, C. (1986) 'The intonation of "George and Mildred": post-nuclear generalizations', in C. Johns-Lewis (ed.), *Intonation in Discourse*, London: Croom Helm; pp. 77–123.

Halliday, M. A. K. (1967) *Intonation and Grammar in British English*, The Hague: Mouton.

—— (1970) *A Course in Spoken English: Intonation*, London: Oxford University Press.

Kingdon, R. (1958) *The Groundwork of English Intonation*, London: Longman.

Ladd, D. R. (1980) *The Structure of Intonational Meaning*, Bloomington: Indiana University Press.

O'Connor, J. D. and Arnold, G. F. (1973) *Intonation of Colloquial English*, London: Longman (1st edn, 1961).

Prince, E. F. (1981) 'Toward a taxonomy of given–new information', in P. Cole (ed.), *Radical Pragmatics*, New York: Academic Press, pp. 223–55.

Schmerling, S. F. (1976) *Aspects of English Sentence Stress*, Austin: University of Texas Press.

Silva-Corvalán, C. (1983) 'On the interaction of word order and intonation: some OV constructions in Spanish', in F. Klein-Andreu (ed.), *Discourse Perspectives on Syntax*, New York: Academic Press, pp. 117–40.

Suñer, M. (1982) *Syntax and Semantics of Spanish Presentational Sentence-Types*. Washington, D.C.: Georgetown University Press.

19

Rhythm and duration in Spanish

G. E. Pointon
BBC Pronunciation Research Unit

In an article published some years ago (Pointon 1980), I cast doubt on the placing of Spanish among the syllable-timed languages, re-analysing the results of experiments carried out by other investigators, sometimes many years before.

It seemed to me that languages which have sets of lexical items minimally distinguished by stress placement – e.g. English and Spanish – should have more in common with each other, at least rhythmically, than either would have with languages such as French, which do not have such sets.

Word stress may be fixed, or it may be free, depending on the language we are discussing: sometimes it may be both. In Finnish, for instance, it is fixed for each word, on the first syllable; in Polish, with very few exceptions, it is fixed on the penultimate syllable. In English and Spanish the word stress is fixed for each word, but its placement within the word varies: 'photograph, pho'tography, photo'graphic, photogra'vure; 'cántara ('water jug'), can'tara ('he would sing'), canta'rá ('he will sing').

Both English and Spanish exhibit shifts in stress for what appear to be rhythmical reasons: Picca'dilly but 'Piccadilly 'Circus; Jo'sé but 'José An'tonio; but English also permits contrastive stress: the deliberate stressing of a normally unstressed syllable: I said "conformed' not "deformed', while Spanish does not: Dije 'confor'mar', no 'infor'mar'.

Traditional Spanish verse structure is different from both English and French types. While English verse counts stresses per line, and French counts syllables, Spanish does both: lines are classed by their number of syllables: 'octosyllables' or 'Alexandrines' (with fourteen syllables), for instance, but all octosyllables do not have eight syllables, nor do Alexandrines all have fourteen. The important syllable in these particular types of line is the seventh, or thirteenth, which must be stressed. The nominal total is then reached by simply adding one. Many words have penultimate stress, so many lines do have the requisite number of syllables, but there are also many words with final-syllable stress, and also many with antepenultimate stress. There are even a few with pre-antepenultimate stress. Thus a nominal octosyllable may have any number of syllables from seven to ten, and still be metrically correct, provided the seventh syllable is stressed.

This last characteristic in particular does not seem to me to be one which would be appropriate for a conventional syllable-timed language: in most traditional verse patterns, line lengths exhibit some regularity, but if Spanish syllables are approximately equal in duration, then this cannot be so.

Six recordings of the Spanish text of *The North Wind and the Sun* were measured for segment duration, for syllable duration, and also for the duration from the onset of each stressed syllable up to but excluding the next stressed syllable onset: the inter-stress interval.

The recordings all differed from one another in some way: for instance, in no two did the informants coincide in all their pauses for breath. However, the whole text may be divided into twelve units, corresponding to groups at the end of which all the informants paused. Within these twelve units, pauses, for breath or hesitation, occurred at varying locations.

If we deal with the units measured in descending order of size, the first is the inter-stress interval, which in a stress-timed language would be called a 'foot'. The first syllable of the passage, /el/, precedes the first stressed syllable, and so is not included in the count at this level. Similarly, the last stressed syllable of the passage, /sol/, is excluded because there is no point to measure to (i.e. another stress onset). The figures for durations between the onsets of stressed syllables varied a lot: the shortest duration was between three and five times shorter than the longest, for every speaker. In four cases a speaker's longest inter-stress interval occurred in a stretch of speech which was interrupted by a pause in the version as recorded by at least some of the other informants. If we accept the concept of the silent stress, we might be justified in such cases in assuming that two 'feet' have been telescoped into one, and a silent stress subsumed. Even allowing for this, however, it is clear that isochrony is not operating at this level. The inter-stress interval increases in direct proportion to the number of syllables it contains – as one would expect of a syllable-timed language. In fact for stress groups of one to three syllables, the increase in duration is exactly as predicted for syllable-timing: 23.0 cs, 32.5 cs, 48.0 cs. As there were altogether 97 examples of two-syllable groups, and 93 of three-syllable groups, the ratio seems quite reliable. The greater-than-predicted duration of one-syllable groups may be accounted for by the general tendency for stressed syllables to be lengthened, and this may be further exaggerated when the following syllable is also stressed. Above three syllables, however, there is some evidence of compression, but the number of such stress groups is much smaller and so less reliable. Four-syllable groups (twenty-four examples) averaged 57.5 cs; five-syllable groups (five examples), 68.5 cs; and six-syllable groups (six examples), 64.0 cs.

The stressed syllable remains remarkably stable, averaging 18.5 cs whether in two-, three- or five-syllable groups (accounting for 276 out of a total of 353 groups). As already noted, in one-syllable stress groups it was considerably longer: 23.0 cs before another stressed syllable, and as much as 29.0 cs before a pause. Is this all accounted for by position, or may structure be involved?

The passage contained ten different syllables forming one-syllable stress groups, giving eleven non-prepausal tokens, and thirty-five prepausal ones. Remarkably, given the supposed tendency for Spanish syllables to be simply CV structures, nine of the ten were CVC and the other CVvC. (I am using v to represent a semi-vowel.)

In fact, among the six recordings, there were 353 stressed syllables. They were distributed among nine different syllable structures: V, VC, CV, CvV, CVv, CCV, CVC, CvVC and CVvC, of which CV and CVC occurred 112 times each. The durations increased with the 'size' of the syllable, according to the number of segments in it. V syllables (twenty occurrences) averaged 9.5 cs, while CVvC syllables (six occurrences) averaged 25.0 cs. The differences in duration of the stressed syllable according to the number of segments were significant at the 0.01 level when subjected to an Analysis of Variance, and the variance ratio was greater on this analysis, 58.7, than when syllable structure was analysed, 24.3.

Almost twice as many unstressed syllables were measured in the same passage – 642 – but remarkably similar variance ratios were discovered: 58.2 by number of segments and 25.0 by syllable structure.

As stress-timing had to be rejected because the inter-stress interval increased with an increase in the number of syllables it contained, so syllable-timing should also be rejected as the duration of the syllable, whether stressed or unstressed, also increases with an increase in the number of segments.

We are led once again to suggest that a third type of timing is present: segment-timing. There is no theoretical reason why there should not be temporal organisations of speech other than stress- and syllable-timing: there may even be a case for arguing that there may be languages with no rhythmical organisation at all. Indeed, segment-timing may offer such a possibility!

It is often stated that all infant language is syllable-timed, and that even children learning a stress-timed language initially speak in syllable-timed rhythms, later learning to organise their speech into 'feet'. Is it not at least possible that, in fact, the initial patterns of infant speech are segment-timed, as they try out the articulatory possibilities and learn to control their muscular gestures, first of all not regulating the durations very well, and only later, when the necessary patterns are well established, organising them into temporal patterns which may be either syllable- or stress-timed? Syllable-timing, after all, demands a considerable amount of organisation, and to suggest that infants acquire this, only to abandon it in favour of another set of even more highly structured rhythmical patterns if they are learning a stress-timed language, implies a very heavy load on them. Additionally, how would they acquire syllable-timing when there are no adult models for them to copy? The hypothesis of segment-timing seems far more likely to me.

Rhythm 'is a relation of successive events in time' (Sonnenschein 1925: 15). These events must be similar enough to be perceived as 'the same' or no rhythm is evident. Rhythm is not necessarily concerned with isochrony, but beats, as in music, should be isochronous. Thus a linguistic rhythm may not be concerned with isochrony: it may not have beats, as stress- and syllable-timing are assumed to have, but if it is to be truly called a rhythm, it must have some reference points from which a copy can be made. A random sequence of sounds, governed by extraneous forces, is not replicable, and is not therefore rhythmical: by its nature it has no pattern. Segment-timing fits this description: the sequence of sounds is governed by an extraneous feature (meaning) and is not replicable except by someone specially trained (i.e. either a speaker of the language, who can repeat the meaning, and hence secondarily the sounds, or a phonetician – but would even a phonetician produce the same durations?).

A lot of work remains to be done on the nature of rhythm in language. Matters are improving, but it is still the case that very few languages have been investigated, and that the investigators themselves need to come from more diverse linguistic backgrounds.

REFERENCES

Pointon, G. E. (1980) Is Spanish really syllable-timed?, *Journal of Phonetics* 8, 3: 293–304.
Sonnenschein, A. E. (1925) *What is Rhythm?*, Oxford: Blackwell.

20

The boundaries of intonation units

Paul Tench
University of Wales, Cardiff

In this paper I hope to show that O'Connor's description of rhythm is a more effective means of establishing boundaries than Halliday's (and Abercrombie's, from whom Halliday derived his theory of rhythm).

If an utterance consists of a single intonation unit, then the boundaries are preceded and followed by silence. If an utterance consists of two or more units of intonation with clearly identifiable pauses which exactly coincide with sentence or clause boundaries, then the unit boundaries can be unproblematically identified. But any other case is problematical, that is if we compare analyses of different linguists: 'One major problem is that it is at times difficult and sometimes impossible to decide where one tone unit ends and the next begins' (Brazil *et al.* 1980: 7).

For some, the issue is not one of great importance. Brazil *et al.* maintain this as a virtue of their analysis:

> Whatever description of intonation one uses to analyse recorded speech, there are inevitable difficulties in deciding where to put the tone unit boundaries in a small number of cases. One significant advantage of our description, which suggests that all intonational meaning is carried by the *tonic segment* [= head + tonic syllable], whose boundaries *are* perfectly clear, is that it gives us a principled reason for saying that *tone unit boundaries are not in fact of great importance*. We have argued that the proclitic and enclitic segments contain no prominent syllables and are thus equally uninforming. It is therefore of no great significance which tone unit they are attached to, though in fact the boundary is usually unproblematic and marked by a slight pause or hesitation.

> (*ibid.* 1980: 45–6; their italics)

Their view is not dissimilar from Halliday's:

> The fact that since a tone group boundary must be also a foot boundary, it does not necessarily coincide exactly with the boundary of the clause is immaterial; it is always clear whether or not there is an

equivalence of clause and tone group. In any case it must be insisted
that the location of the tone group boundary is a theoretical decision:
the best description is obtained if a new tone group is considered to
begin at the foot boundary immediately preceding the first salient
syllable of its tonic or pretonic, as the case may be. But what matters
is that the boundary between any two tone groups can be shown to lie
within certain limits, so that it is clear how many tone groups there are
in any stretch of utterance, and where – that is, in association with
which elements of grammatical structure – their contrasts are made.

(Halliday 1967: 19, footnote)

The difficulty, and, occasionally, impossibility in deciding on boundaries is
well illustrated in Brown *et al.* (1980): 'We cannot consistently identify tone
groups by intonational criteria.' They admit that in many cases 'one is able to
assign tone group boundaries with some confidence' (p. 41), but 'in a very
substantial number of cases' problems were encountered. The problems
were due mainly to hesitation phenomena or to cases where a phrase could
either belong to a preceding intonation unit or a following one.

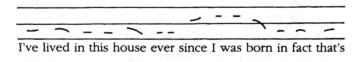

I've lived in this house ever since I was born in fact that's

for well sixty years   (13 TE)

The problem here arises with the phrase *in fact*. Auditory and
spectrographic analyses show no pauses bounding *in fact*, and there is
no perceptible pitch change preceding or following it. Pitch movement on *house, born* and *years* suggest that we have at least three tone
groups here. We seem to have three plausible analyses: (i) to suppose
that *in fact* is included within the second tone group (*I've lived here ever
since I was born in fact*), (ii) to suppose that it is included within the
third tone group (*in fact that's for well sixty years*) or (iii) to decide that
in fact constitutes a separate tone group. Appeal to semantic criteria
obviously does not help – indeed, we might have supposed that the
phonetics would have sorted out the semantic analysis for us here and
made it clear what in fact is modifying, but, as happens frequently in
our data, the ambiguity is unresolved.

(Brown *et al.* 1980: 42)

The fact that Brown *et al.* had so much more difficulty in this aspect of
their intonation analysis than Brazil *et al.* encountered is accounted for

entirely in the kind of material that formed the basis of their investigations. The latter were using material drawn largely from teachers' talk, the context of which is mostly thought out before talk is employed; furthermore, there is a clear distinction of roles in classroom talk and there is usually a high degree of familiarity between participants. The former, however, were using material drawn from spontaneous, unrehearsed, informal conversations between strangers, whose participant roles were sometimes in doubt; spontaneous speech in such situations is often far from fluent (see Brown *et al.* 1980: 47), whereas teachers in a familiar setting are usually very fluent. Non-fluent speech is, understandably, much more difficult to analyse than fluent speech.

Similarly, Crystal claims that hurried speech is more difficult to analyse than unhurried speech (Crystal 1969: 205). Crystal (pp. 204–7) has the most complete discussion of the phonetic features which act as clues to the identification of intonation unit boundaries. His remarks are treated as a basis for description by Gibbon (1976), Brown *et al.* (1980) and Jassem *et al.* (1984).

Crystal claims that in English there seem to be 'regular definable phonological boundaries' for intonation units in 'normal (here meaning mainly 'not too hurried') speech' (p. 205). There are two 'phonetic features' that manifest such a boundary *after* a tonic syllable:

> Firstly, there will be a perceivable pitch-change, either stepping up or stepping down, depending on the direction of nuclear tone movement – if falling, then step up; if rising, then step down; if level, either, depending on its relative height ... there is always a pitch-change following a nuclear tone, and this may be taken as diagnostic.
>
> The second criterion is the presence of junctural features at the end of every tone-unit. This usually takes the form of a very slight pause, but there are frequently accompanying segmental phonetic modifications (variations in length, aspiration, etc.) which re-inforce this.
>
> (Crystal 1969: 205–6)

Crystal notes a number of exceptions in the first case, which may lead to ambiguity, and two occurrences, admittedly very rare, where the combination of tonic syllable with a following pause would be inconclusive. Nevertheless, Crystal is bold enough to assert that 'These phonological criteria suffice to indicate unambiguously where a tone-unit boundary should go in connected speech in the vast majority of cases' (p. 206). He concedes that in a small minority of cases, an analyst may have no alternative but 'to have recourse to grammatical or semantic criteria to place the boundary' (p. 207).

Pike would no doubt concur. On the one hand, in a well-known clash of theory in the 1940s and 1950s, Pike protested against the lack of realism in

272

the form of structuralist theory in which information from one component of language was deliberately excluded from a consideration of description problems in another component; in other words, he was prepared to allow grammatical or semantic criteria to help decide on problematical issues in phonology which the 'compartmentalists' would not allow. But also in the realm of junctural features, Pike would concur. He described two types of pauses, tentative and final (Pike 1945: 3–2). The final pauses are not at issue here, since they would be uncontroversial. The tentative pauses are accompanied by two other factors, which either together or separately help to identify the placement of the tentative pause itself. The two factors are a sustaining of the 'height of the final pitch of the contour' (p. 31), i.e. there is not the same dropping of pitch as associated with final pauses, and second, there is a change in the degree of quantity of prepausal and/or postpausal syllables: 'In general, it may be that any departure from the normal length of the elements of a primary contour contributes to the recognition of a following pause as tentative, provided that the full height of the pitch is sustained at the end of the contour' (p. 31).

Gibbon (1976: 66) reminds us that 'The issue of boundaries, then, is a secondary issue as far as the problem of segmentation is concerned.' The primary issue is the recognition of the essential internal structure, and as Pike has noted elsewhere (Pike 1943), the edges of other phonological units (e.g. syllables) are fuzzy by virtue of the fact that it is a continuum that is being segmented. Gibbon seems to downgrade the importance of Crystal's description of boundary criteria as being optional and 'thus not defining'. However, in defence of Crystal, one might add that criteria that decide the 'vast majority' of cases are hardly optional; they may not be 'defining', but they are relatively regular. Such regularity gives the criteria a certain status in a descriptive mechanism. They do not work in absolutely all cases, e.g. the problem of *in fact* in the earlier example, but they provide the regular pattern.

Halliday's description of boundaries and his transcriptions indicating tonality division do call for further comment in the light of such remarks as 'These tone-group boundaries seem counterintuitive if they are really to be regarded as the direct encoding of the boundaries of information units in speech' (Brown and Yule 1983: 159) and 'Many peculiar tone group boundaries may be found in Halliday 1970' (Jassem *et al.* 1984: 223). The examples of peculiar boundaries the latter give are (1) and (2) (their examples (11) and (12)):

(1)   he was // grey and he was woolly and his // pride was inordinate. He // danced on an outcrop in the // middle of Australia and he // went to the Big God Nqong

(2)   on the Isle of Man you can // still ride in a horse-drawn tram

Their peculiarity is that they appear to defy the strongest cases of syntactic cohesion – breaking into the middle of close-knit noun and verb phrases and dividing off an unaccented subject pronoun from its verb. Furthermore, the boundaries do not coincide with the beginnings and ends of pieces of information.

The reason for this peculiarity of description and transcription is not hard to find: Halliday took over somewhat uncritically a view of rhythm that Abercrombie had developed from Steele (1779), the basis of which was the metre of poetry. Abercrombie's theory involved a rhythm unit, the foot, which by definition had always to begin with a stressed syllable; consequently any unstressed syllable follows a stressed one within the same foot. If any utterance begins with an unstressed syllable, a 'silent stress' is posited, i.e. no sound is materialised objectively but is felt to be real psychologically. The boundaries of the foot are assigned mechanically by the occurrences of accented syllables. This system operates without much difficulty in poetry and in what Halliday calls 'rhythmic prose narrative' which is a 'framework of a maximally regular rhythm' (Halliday 1970: 120). However, it is much more difficult to assess 'accent-worthiness' of a whole host of items in spontaneous, informal speech (see Brown *et al.*'s difficulty in identifying boundaries in such speech). Stress-timing is also very much more difficult to recognise in such speech.

Other theories of rhythm units are not necessarily based on metre, but on more detailed phonetic observations of the speed with which unstressed syllables are produced. O'Connor (1973) explains that utterances are broken up into groups of syllables each containing one and only one stressed syllable. Unstressed syllables cluster around stressed ones. How can one tell whether a given unstressed syllable that occurs somewhere between two stressed ones belongs to the preceding or to the following one? The answer is: 'unstressed syllables which precede the stress are said particularly quickly' (O'Connor 1973: 198), which implies that post-stress unstressed syllables are said relatively more slowly. That is the case of English: 'In the group // ɪt wəz *betə // there are two unstressed syllables before the stress and one after it. The first two are said quickly, the last one not so quickly, taking the same amount of time as /be-/' (O'Connor 1980: 97).

Pike (1962) gives more detail and is able to relate that detail to a wider range of languages. The junctural features of feet (which he calls 'stress-group rhythm waves') can be summarised in Table 20.1. The purpose of this table is to aid the recognition of borders of feet by noting the more common prejunctural and postjunctural features. It is the upper row that is most relevant to English: prenuclear unstressed syllables are marked by a rapidly increasing level of loudness (crescendo) as well as by relative shortness as opposed to postnuclear unstressed syllables which are characterised by relative lengthening, lenis articulation (including

Table 20.1 Normal rhythm wave

	Pre-nucleus	*Nucleus*	*Post-nucleus*
Frequent (often non-contrastive)	Crescendo (tŏ)	Long (to·) Loud ('to)	Descrescendo (tò) Long but lenis (to·, tos·) Devoicing (toh)
Less frequent (often non-contrastive)		High pitch (tō) Fortis contoids (tob̰)	Down glide (to) Lenis contoids (tob̥) Glottal stop (to?)

Frequent (often contrastive)	Long vs short
	High vs low tone,
	  etc.
		Long vs short
		High vs low
		Ballistic vs
		  controlled
			Long vs short
			High vs low tone,
			  etc.
			Ballistic vs controlled

Source: Pike 1962: 150.

devoicing) and decrescendo. All this means that for Pike, and O'Connor, feet do not necessarily *begin* with a stressed syllable; they must *contain* one but it may be preceded by unstressed syllables which are significantly characterised by a relative swiftness of articulation and crescendo.

Jassem's description of rhythm units is broadly similar (see Jassem *et al.* 1984: 206–8). He distinguishes two kinds of rhythm units: 'narrow rhythm units' in which the only or first syllable is accented, and 'total rhythm units' which include an anacrusis preceding the accented syllable. An anacrusis consists of a syllable, or a sequence of syllables, 'which is characterized by being as short as possible', i.e. as short as is compatible with sufficiently distinct articulation of the constituent phones. Jassem thus concurs with O'Connor's and Pike's observations on the distinctive significance of speed of articulation. He also noted that unaccented syllables following the accent are roughly equal in length to the accent and are therefore significantly longer than the unaccented syllables preceding the accent. In other words, Jassem asserts that feet do not necessarily begin with an accented syllable but may 'accrue' preceding unaccented syllables.

O'Connor, Pike and Jassem identify the borders of feet on observable phonetic grounds. When their rhythm structure is combined with Pike's and Crystal's observations on pause and other junctural features, then it becomes apparent that intonation units do not have to begin with accented syllables. The first foot, or unit of rhythm, in an intonation unit may be an instance of what Jassem calls a total rhythm unit with its initial anacrusis. The examples, given earlier, of peculiar intonation unit boundaries would be transcribed, on this basis, as follows:

(1') he was grey / and he was woolly / and his pride was inordinate /
      he danced on an outcrop / in the middle of Australia / and he
      went to the Big God Nqong

(2') on the Isle of Man / you can still ride in a horse-drawn tram

The placement of boundaries now conforms not only with syntactic and
semantic boundaries but also with observable phonetic features of pause
and pitch change (which incidentally Halliday himself produced as the
narrator recorded in the accompanying tapes) and also with the structure
of rhythm units that take the relative speed of anacrusis into account. The
first, longer, example is taken from an illustration of rhythmic prose
narrative, in which regular rhythm is maximally present; one would expect
Abercrombian feet to be particularly manifest in this genre, but taking
pause and pitch change into account, this is in fact not the case. This
discrepancy is even more noticeable in spontaneous monologue (e.g.
Halliday 1970: 133–4, in which apparently Halliday reads from a transcript
of an original spontaneous monologue). Here is a comparison of (13),
Halliday's transcription of the first part of the recorded monologue (*ibid.*,
p. 133, with tone numbers omitted) and (13a), a transcription that takes
overt junctural features into account:

(3)   // from / Scarborough to / *Whit*by is a
          // very / pleasant / *jour*ney with
          // very / beautiful / *coun*tryside . . .
          // in / fact the / Yorkshire / coast is / *love*ly
          // all a/ *long*. ex
          / cept the / parts that are / covered in / *cara*vans
          of / course. and
          // if you / go in / *spring*
          // when the / *gorse* is / out
          // or in / *sum*mer
          // when the *heath*er's / out
          // it's / really / one of the / most de/ *light*ful /
          *a*reas in the
          // whole / *coun*try //
(NB // = Halliday's tone group boundaries; / = his foot boundaries)

(3')   From 'Scarborough / to ' *Whit*by
          is a 'very / 'pleasant / '*jour*ney
          with 'very / 'beautiful / '*coun*tryside . . .
          in 'fact / the 'Yorkshire / 'coast / is '*love*ly
          'all / a' *long*
          ex'cept / the 'parts / that are 'covered / in
          ' *cara*vans / of 'course
          and 'if / you 'go / in ' *spring*

when the '*gorse* / is 'out
or in '*summer*
when the '*hea*ther's / 'out
it's 'really / 'one / of the 'most / de'*light*ful /
areas
in the 'whole / '*coun*try
(NB / = O'Connor's foot boundaries).

As Jassem would point out, his own model of English rhythm as illustrated in the second transcription has 'a simpler relation to syntax and does not result in such disconcerting discrepancies between the phonological and the syntactical structure of running speech' (Jassem *et al.* 1984: 223). I would agree, and so, I am sure, would O'Connor and Pike and Crystal, and many, many more.

REFERENCES

Brazil, D., Coulthard, M. and Johns, C. (1980) *Discourse Intonation and Language Teaching*, London: Longman.
Brown, G and Yule, G. (1983) *Discourse Analysis*, Cambridge: Cambridge University Press.
Brown, G., Currie, K. L. and Kenworthy, J. (1980) *Questions of Intonation*, London: Croom Helm.
Crystal, D. (1969) *Prosodic Systems and Intonation in English*, Cambridge: Cambridge University Press.
Crystal, D. and Davy, D. (1975) *Advanced Conversational English*, London: Longman.
Gibbon, D. (1976) *Perspectives of Intonation Analysis*, Bern: Peter Lang.
Halliday, M. A. K. (1967) *Intonation and Grammar in British English*, The Hague: Mouton.
—— (1970) *Intonation*, London: Oxford University Press.
Jassem, W., Hill, D. R., and Witten, I. H. (1984) 'Isochrony in English speech : its statistical validity and linguistic relevance', in D. Gibbon and H. Richter (eds), *Intonation, Accent and Rhythm*, Berlin: de Gruyter, pp. 203–25.
O'Connor, J. D. (1973) *Phonetics*, Harmondsworth: Penguin.
—— (1980) *Better English Pronunciation*, 2nd edn, Cambridge: Cambridge University Press.
Pike, K. L. (1943) 'Taxemes and immediate constituents', *Language* 19: 65–82.
—— (1945) *The Intonation of American English*, Ann Arbor: University of Michigan Press.
—— (1962) 'Practical phonetics of rhythm waves', *Phonetica* 8: 9–30.
Steele, J. (1779) *Prosodia Rationalis*, London: Nichols.

21

Stylisation of the falling tone in Hungarian intonation

László Varga
Eötvös Loránd University, Budapest

So-called 'stylised' intonation became a renewed talking point when Robert Ladd (1978, 1980) suggested that from each 'plain tone' of English intonation (the fall, the low rise and the high rise) a corresponding 'stylised tone' could be derived and that the meaning of stylisation was 'routine'. Basically similar views have also been expressed by Gussenhoven (1983, 1985), Bolinger (1986, 1989), and others. The contour which Ladd calls the stylised fall is probably the best-known stylised tone of English: it is the intonation used for calling children home, e.g.:

(1)   John–   Din–
            ny–   ner–   (Ladd 1980: 169)

This kind of tone also exists in Hungarian, and it shows remarkable similarities with its English counterpart in both form and function. The Hungarian stylised fall consists of two terraces: the first one is high, the second one is lower but not low, it remains well above the baseline (i.e. the lower limit of the speaker's normal voice range). The first syllable of the carrier phrase is stressed; we shall regard this syllable as primary-stressed.

In the one-syllable variant of the contour both terraces are realised in one syllable:

(2)   ‾‾Zsolt!   Zso–
            (a male first name)   olt–
                                           ‾‾‾‾‾‾‾‾‾

(The symbol ‾‾ stands for the stylised fall and also for the primary stress on the syllable which initiates the contour. In the melodic diagram the letter o has been doubled to accommodate the stepdown between the two terraces; the dashes are meant to show the 'horizontality' of the terraces; and the line below the diagram represents the baseline.)

In the more-than-one-syllable variant the higher terrace continues up to the last syllable and the lower terrace occurs on the last syllable:

(3)　¯¯Kati!　　　　　　　　　　　Ka–
　　　　　　　　　　　　　　　　　　　ti–
　　　Katie　　　　　　　　　　　　———
　　　'Katie'

(4)　¯¯Szamosi úr!　　　　　　　Szamosi–
　　　　　　　　　　　　　　　　　　　úr–
　　　Szamosi sir　　　　　　　　———
　　　'Mr Szamosi'

Secondary stresses (i.e. non-initial stressed syllables) do not influence the shape of the tone. In (5) below, the syllable *meg-* (a perfective prefix) is secondary-stressed; but the lower terrace is still restricted to the final syllable:

(5)　¯¯Úgyse　　　　　tudsz　　　megfogni!
　　　by-no-means　can-you　catch
　　　'You can't catch me!'

　　　　　　　　　　　　　Úgyse tudsz megfog–
　　　　　　　　　　　　　　　　　　　　　　　　ni–
　　　　　　　　　　　　　　　　　———————————

It is here that the English stylised fall differs slightly from its Hungarian counterpart. If the English contour contains a secondary-stressed syllable, the second terrace will be realised not on the last syllable alone but on the sequence of syllables starting with the secondary-stressed one (see Gussenhoven 1985: 123–4).

When the Hungarian stylised fall is utterance-final, its last syllable can be considerably lengthened (cf. (2), (3) and (4)). If the penultimate syllable in the utterance-final stylised fall contains a long vowel, that syllable can also be lengthened, with or without lengthening the last syllable. Thus in (6), lengthening can occur on both, or either, or neither of the syllables *né-* and *ni*:

(6)　¯¯Kati　　néni!　　　　　　Kati né–
　　　　　　　　　　　　　　　　　　ni–
　　　Katie　aunt　　　　　　　———
　　　'Aunt Katie'

Apart from (5), the examples presented so far have been vocatives. Hungarian vocatives take the stylised fall if the person being addressed is not seen by the speaker, or if the speaker is not seen by the addressee; i.e. if there is no eye contact between speaker and hearer. The contour is the same as the 'vocative chant' of descriptions of English (see Leben 1976; Liberman 1978).

Vocatives belong to a group of utterances that have an imperative force

279

and a form which is neither imperative nor interrogative. I shall call such utterances 'declarative imperatives', to distinguish them from 'interrogative imperatives'. (Interrogative imperatives are utterances with the intonation of a *yes/no* question but with the force of an imperative, e.g. *Kinyitnád az ablakot?* 'Would you open the window?')

Declarative imperatives are not only vocatives; they include other kinds of utterances, too, which also can take the stylised fall when there is no eye contact between the speaker and the addressee. For instance, greetings are also declarative imperatives. If you enter your neighbour's home but you cannot see anybody there, you may call:

(7)　　⁻⁻Jó　　reggelt!　　　　　　　Jó reg–
　　　　　　　　　　　　　　　　　　　　　　　gelt–
　　　　good　morning-acc.　　　　　———————
　　　　'Good morning.'

Or, if you see your friends in front of you in the street, you can call to them:

(8)　　⁻⁻Sziasztok!　　　　　　　　Sziasz–
　　　　　　　　　　　　　　　　　　　　tok–
　　　　⁻⁻hello-2nd pl.　　　　　　　———————
　　　　'Hi, folks.'

Declarative imperatives also include various kinds of announcements. You can use (9) to let your family know that you are back home, while you are taking off your coat in the hall:

(9)　　⁻⁻Megjöttem!　　　　　　　Megjöt–
　　　　　　　　　　　　　　　　　　　　tem–
　　　　perf.-came-I　　　　　　　　———————
　　　　'I'm come home.'

And this is how you can call for people's attention in a public place:

(10)　　⁻⁻Figyelem!　　　　　　　　Figye–
　　　　　　　　　　　　　　　　　　　　lem–
　　　　attention　　　　　　　　　———————
　　　　'Attention, please.'

You can use (11a) and (11b) to wake someone up:

(11) a.　⁻⁻Ébresztő!　　　　　　　　Ébresz–
　　　　　　　　　　　　　　　　　　　　tő–
　　　　waken-er　　　　　　　　　———————
　　　　'Wake up.'

b. ⁻⁻Hét   óra!   Hét ó–
                                            ra–
                                         ———————
seven   o'clock
'It's seven o'clock.'

The following utterances are warnings that the door has been left open and should be closed, the lights have been forgotten and should be switched off, or that the phone is ringing and should be answered:

(12) a. ⁻⁻Ajtó!   Aj–
                                       tó–
                                    ————————
door
'Close the door.'

b. ⁻⁻Villany!   Vil–
                                     lany–
                                  ——————————
electricity
'Switch off the light.'

c. ⁻⁻Telefon!   Tele–
                                     fon–
                                  ——————————
telephone
'The phone's ringing.'

The next two examples show informal ways of calling people to dinner:

(13) a. ⁻⁻Asztalhoz!   Asztal–
                                        hoz–
                                     ——————————
table-to
'Come to the table.'

b. ⁻⁻Kész a ⁻⁻vacsora!   Kész– vacso–
                                         a–   ra–
                                      ——————————————
ready the dinner
'Dinner's ready.'

(In (13b) there are two primary-stressed syllables: *kész* and *va-*, and both initiate a stylised fall.)

The following is an example of how you can warn someone that their favourite television programme is starting:

(14)   ⁻⁻Kezdődik a ⁻⁻tévé!   Kezdődik– té–
                                               a–   vé–
                                            ——————————————
starts   the TV
'The TV-programme is starting.'

The Hungarian stylised fall can, however, appear not only in declarative imperatives but also in some arrogant expressions, especially the boasting utterances of small children. I shall call these 'infantile boasts':

281

(15) a. ⁻⁻Én győztem!   Én győz–

                              tem–
                            ———————

    I   won
    'I've won.'

b. ⁻⁻Új ruhám   van!   Új ruhám–

                              van–
                           ———————

    new dress-my   is
    'I have a new dress.'

c. ⁻⁻Úgyse   tudsz   megfogni!   Úgyse tudsz megfog–

                                            ni–
    by-no-means   can-you   perf.-catch   ————————————
    'You can't catch me.'

d. De   ⁻⁻igen!   i–
                         De ge_n–

    but   yes   ————
    'Yes, I can.'

e. ⁻⁻Első!   El–

                              ső–
    first   ————
    'I'm the first.'

f. ⁻⁻Indulunk ⁻⁻Keszthelyre!   Indu–   Keszthely–

                                lunk–   re–
                                ————————————————
    start-we   ⁻⁻Keszthelely-to
    'We're leaving for Keszthely.'

Such infantile boasts constitute the second area of Hungarian where the stylised fall is used.

In addition to its basic, two-terraced form, the Hungarian stylised fall can have two special modifications. The first of these can appear on declarative imperatives; it increases the imperative effect. In this modification the first terrace is replaced by a rising tone (cf. (16a, b)), or the last syllable of the first terrace steps up (16c, d). The symbol ⁻⁻ will represent this variety:

(16) a. ⁻⁻Zsolt!   o
                          Zs olt–

                              ————

b. Kati!   a
                          K ti–

                              ————

c. ⁻⁻Asztalhoz!

tal
Asz   hoz–
_____

d. Szamosi úr!

si
Szamo   úr–
_____

The second modification is possible on infantile boasts, etc.: the last (rightmost) stylised fall of the utterance is replaced by a high monotone. The final high monotone sharpens the boasting and tinges it with an element of mockery. It will be marked with the symbol ⁻.

(17) a. ⁻Én győztem!

Én győztem–
_____

b. ⁻⁻Indulunk ⁻Keszthelyre!

Indu–   Keszthelyre–
      lunk–
_____

c. Én ⁻⁻igen, de te ⁻nem!

igen de–   nem–
Én   te–
_____

I   yes   but you   not]
'I do but you don't.'

Syllables in the modifications can be lengthened in the same ways as in the unmodified form of the stylised fall.

The English stylised fall is often associated with the physical distance between speaker and hearer or with lack of eye contact between them and is thus often looked upon as a feature of loud calls (see e.g. Pike 1945: 187; Abe 1962: 520; Liberman 1978: 19). Gibbon (1976: 280–1) considers distance metaphorical and claims that the function of this contour is establishing contact between speaker and hearer. Ladd (1980: 172–9) does not think that distance (real or metaphorical) has a critical role to play; he claims that the function of the stylised fall in English is 'to signal an element of predictability or stereotype in the message' (1980: 173). This element can be referred to as 'routine' (see Gussenhoven 1985: 123–5; Bolinger 1986: 226–34). 'Routine' is the cover term for natural, normal, everyday, predictable matters which do not cause any excitement.

Physical distance is not crucial for the stylised fall in Hungarian, either. We can produce a stylised fall at normal (or even less than normal) volume, right into the ears of someone we want to wake up, for instance. This can be explained away by reference to metaphorical distance. When one is asleep, one is 'a long way away'. Lack of eye contact can result from physical distance, but also from the speaker and hearer not facing each other. The latter case is a subtype of metaphorical distance again.

Overcoming distance (physical or metaphorical) is undoubtedly a frequent motive for using the stylised fall at least in the case of declarative imperatives. But not in the case of infantile boasts, which need neither real nor metaphorical distance for them to be realised with a stylised fall: they can occur with a stylised fall right in the middle of a face-to-face conversation.

But if the aim of overcoming distance is not a common feature, what is common to the examples considered so far? What is the stable component of the meaning of the stylised fall in Hungarian? I think the answer is: 'routine', just like in English. This will become clear if we consider a few utterance pairs.

If it is the stylised fall that we use for warning, there is hardly any serious danger. This is how a waiter carrying plates will probably warn people to get out of his way:

(18)   ⁻⁻Vigyázat!   Vigyá–
                                          zat–
                                     _____
        care
        'Be careful.'

When there is real danger (a car coming at high speed, for instance), we use a plain falling tone:

(19)   'Vigyázat!   Vi
                                      gyázat
                                   _____

(where the symbol ' represents the plain fall).

When we are waking someone at an hour which is considered usual or has been previously agreed on, we use a stylised fall:

(20)   ⁻⁻Gyerekek! ⁻⁻Hét óra!   Gyere–   Hét ó–
                                          kek–   ra–
                                       _____
        ⁻⁻children ⁻⁻seven o'clock
        It's seven o'clock, children.'

But if someone ought to have got up at six and is still asleep at seven, we would prefer a plain fall:

(21)   'Gyerekek! 'Hét óra!   Gye   Hét
                                       rekek   óra
                                    _____

This is also how I call my wife out of her room when her friend who lives next door pops in to see her about a recipe:

(22) ⁻⁻Marika!   (Az Etus van itt.)   Mari-
                                                        ka-
                                                      ‾‾‾‾‾‾
      Mary-dimin. the Etus is here
      'Mary. Etus is here to see you.)'

But I would probably use a plain fall if it was the police who wanted to see
her:

(23) ‘Marika!   (A rendőrség van itt.)   Ma
                                                       rika
                                                     ‾‾‾‾‾
      Mary-dimin. the police is here
      'Mary. (The police are here.)'

The stylised fall sounds all right in the next example because it is used
for announcing an everyday domestic event:

(24) ⁻⁻Gyerekek! ⁻⁻Kezdődik a ⁻⁻tévé!
      children   starts   the TV
      'The TV-programme is starting, children.'

                    Gyere-   Kezdődik-   té-
                         kek-   a-   vé-
                    ‾‾‾‾‾‾‾‾‾‾‾‾‾‾‾‾‾‾‾‾‾‾‾‾‾‾‾‾‾‾‾‾

But the same contour would be comic and grotesque in this utterance:

(25) * ⁻⁻Gyerekek! ⁻⁻Felrobbant a ⁻⁻tévé!
        children   exploded   a   TV
        'The TV-set has exploded, children.'

                    *Gyere-   Felrobbant-   té-
                         kek-   a-   vé-
                    ‾‾‾‾‾‾‾‾‾‾‾‾‾‾‾‾‾‾‾‾‾‾‾‾‾‾‾‾‾‾‾‾

The examples show, of course, that whenever a declarative imperative is
uttered with a stylised fall, tthe meaning is: 'This is routine.' But what about
infantile boasts? After all, the object of boasting is something unusual,
something extraordinary, something non-routine. Though this is true,
when we choose a stylised fall for our boast, we pretend that the
extraordinary thing we announce is merely routine for us. When a child
says (26) to a playmate, the child wants to create the impression that in this
family it is commonplace to get such expensive presents:

(26) ⁻⁻Villanyvasutat is kaptam!
      electric train-acc. too received-I
      'I was given an electric train, too.'

285

Villanyvasutat is kap–

                              tam–

With a plain fall the same announcement would sound serious and non-boasting:

(27) ⁻⁻Villanyvasutat is kaptam!
      Vil
        <u>lanyvasutat is kaptam</u>

'Routine' (real or pretended) is undoubtedly part of the meaning of the stylised fall in Hungarian. (In addition to 'self-contained', which is the general meaning of all kinds of falls.) Ladd's statement about the meaning of the stylised fall (1978, 1980) is valid for Hungarian too and is probably of universal force.

I do not think, however, that 'routine' and 'self-contained' are the only components of the meaning of the Hungarian stylised fall. The contour also says that the speaker is expecting something from the hearer. The speaker expects the hearer either to do something (as in the case of declarative imperatives) or to be impressed by what is said (as in the case of infantile boasts). Let us call this the 'mobilising' meaning of the stylised fall: for instance, (28) is a routine utterance, but at the same time it has a mobilising effect either as a declarative imperative (28a) or as an infantile boast (28b):

(28)   ⁻⁻Esik az ⁻⁻eső!   Esik–   e–
                                       az–   ső–

      starts the rain
      'It's raining.'

a. 'So let's go to the cinema: you've promised to take us to the cinema if it rains.' (declarative imperative)

b. 'How clever of me! I knew it would rain and I told you so.' (infantile boast)

It seems then that the full meaning of the Hungarian stylised fall is: 'self-contained + routine + mobilizing'.

REFERENCES

Abe, I. (1962) 'Call-contours', in *Proceedings of the Fourth International Congress of Phonetic Sciences, Helsinki*, The Hague: Mouton, pp. 519–23.
Bolinger, D. (1986) *Intonation and its Parts*, London: Edward Arnold.
—— (1989) *Intonation and its Uses*, London: Edward Arnold.

Gibbon, D. (1976) *Perspectives of Intonation Analysis* (Forum Linguisticum, 9), Bern: Lang.

Gussenhoven, C. (1983) *A Semantic Analysis of the Nuclear Tones of English,* reproduced by the Indiana University Linguistics Club, Bloomington.

—— (1985) 'Intonation: a whole autosegmental language', in H. van der Hulst and N. Smith (eds), *Advances in Nonlinear Phonology,* Dordrecht Cinnaminson: Foris, pp. 117–31.

Ladd, D. R. (1978) 'Stylised intonation', *Language* 54: 517–40.

—— (1980) *The Structure of Intonational Meaning,* Bloomington and London: Indiana University Press.

Leben, W. (1976) 'The tones of English intonation', *Linguistic Analysis* 2: 69–107.

Liberman, M. (1978) 'The Intonational System of English', doctoral dissertation, MIT, distributed by Indiana University Linguistics Club, Bloomington.

Pike, K. L. (1945) *The Intonation of American English,* Ann Arbor: University of Michigan Press.

22

The teaching of English intonation

Jack Windsor Lewis
Leeds

The term intonation is difficult to delimit precisely but its narrowest sense of the melodic aspect of the language, excluding the question of which syllables may be stressed and which unstressed in words or higher linguistic units, is the one intended in this paper. Admittedly most writers on English intonation have treated 'sentence stress' as part of intonation. EFL difficulties with tonic placement are very numerous, probably responsible for making more utterances unidiomatic than any other feature. However, many teachers seem to believe that intonation proper (i.e. excluding tonicity) is an area of great difficulty for them, some apparently imagining as great as or even greater than tonicity. To dispel this false impression is a main aim of the present paper.[1]

O'Connor and Arnold (1961, 1973: 1) were right to say that the pitch patterns of another language may sound wrong if they are applied to English' but it strikes me as likely to induce unwarrantable apprehension to say that 'they very often do'. I was more at home with the opinion expressed by the late A. C. Gimson in his Introductory Address to the first Leeds University Conference on the Teaching of Spoken English in 1977 when he remarked:

> We mustn't be led astray into thinking that every intonation in English is
> different from every other intonation pattern in any other language....
> I've heard in foreign countries teachers teaching an English intonation
> pattern which is identical with the intonation pattern for that type of
> sentence in the native language of the learners.

In fact the suggestion that pitch-pattern forms and semantic effects of such forms in English bear a relationship to other languages which can properly be summarised by saying only that there may be resemblances here and there seems excessively gloomy in an EFL context. One wonders also about the suggestion that native speakers of English are so much less able to make ... allowance for mistakenly used tunes than for imperfect sound-making. Such assertions have often been made but as they remain largely untested, it is questionable how far they are worth repeating. As Gimson (1977) again suggested: 'There's room for a study of the errors which people make when they use the wrong intonation pattern. Do ordinary people notice these errors? How important are they from the point of view of meaning?'

What is perhaps also relevant to the evaluation of pitch patterns as a subject for EFL practice is the attitude to wrong intonations observable when one of two mother-tongue speakers (whether or not they have exactly the same type of accent) uses a wrong intonation. It is no very uncommon thing according to my observations for a speaker to experience a 'slip of the tongue' in which it is obvious that the wrong intonation, and nothing else inappropriate, has quite accidentally been employed. I have never in such circumstances heard any speakers correct themselves nor have I ever heard anyone draw attention to the falseness of the tone choice of their interlocutor. Nor have I ever observed a grown-up correct a child's intonation.

Yet another probable witness to the relative universality and essential simplicity of intonational features is the fact that, whereas accentuation (especially word stress) and segmental matters yield plentiful examples of social shibboleths in the south-east of England from which the most general British form of educated English speech has spread, there are virtually no intonational features to be found there which are different in demotic from what they are in sophisticated speech. (One suggestion of such a possibility was made in Windsor Lewis 1977: 69.)

With the honoured exception of the late Roger Kingdon, who was responsible for so much of the best and most original work on English intonation, writers in the British EFL field have written about the most general kinds of usages without so much as a sidelong glance at the other mother-tongue English speech communities. The departures from these usages to be heard from the vast majority of EFL users are relatively slight, rarely if ever causing breakdown of communication. The often strikingly different intonational usages of a great many Irish and Scottish people are far more removed from the Anglo-American mainstream than these EFL departures. And yet who would claim that Irish or Scottish pitch patterns in themselves have any serious effect on comprehensibility? In referring to the Anglo-American mainstream I have in mind the fact that the intonations employed by General American speakers correspond extensively to those used in southeast England. As Gregory (1966: 1) said cautiously of the two varieties, they 'probably use the same intonation contours more frequently than different contours'. Another American writer on intonation matters, the late Dwight Bolinger (1972: 315), made a comment germane to our theme that *the general characteristics of intonation seem to be shared more broadly than those of any other phenomena commonly gathered under the label of 'language'.*

Research into the relative importance of pitch patterns to other linguistic features is very difficult to carry out and understandably has been

very little attempted: however, occasionally evidence presents itself for-
tuitously. I should like to mention two examples of this, both of which
concern what tonologists seem to agree is one of the most fundamental
semantic contrasts of the mainstream English intonation system, that
between the fall and the fall–rise.

On listening to the recordings accompanying Halliday 1970 one noticed
quite a few discrepancies between what was to be heard on the tape and
what the transcriptions indicated. Another shrewd Gimson (1977) comment, by the way, was 'How often do we look at a notation which one of our
respected colleagues has made and then check the actual recording and
find there are great discrepancies?' At any rate, at the 'Spontaneous
Monologue' Study Unit 35, in five places within two dozen lines of text, the
speaker (not Halliday himself) used falls in situations where one would
have been inclined to predict that a person with his (General British)
accent would favour fall–rises, as in 'once a train gets into a section' and
both halves of 'much more fun than going up the M1 or the main line from
King's Cross'. Although the recording was a good one which was listened to
with high-fidelity equipment, it was perfectly clear that the speaker's falling
tone each time was not followed by any rising one even though the
transcription in each case wrongly represented the expected fall–rise tone
as being used. Despite the relative unexpectedness of his tone choices, the
speaker, one felt very clearly, did not sound at all unnatural.

The other illuminating occurrence that I should like to mention
happened on an occasion when I and my colleague Luke Van Buuren were
listening to a recording of Margaret Thatcher, with no particular attention
to her intonations, for convenience through the quite low-fidelity built-in
loudspeaker of a very small cassette player. At a point where we decided that
the loudspeaker's quality was becoming a disadvantage, we plugged in some
high-quality headphones. We then detected in the phrase we were examining, much to our surprise, a perfectly clear, not notably narrow but
previously quite inaudible, rise immediately following a fall which we had
heard. The interesting evidence this constituted in relation to intonation
semantics was that, heard either way, no difference of effect was felt. Things
like this cause one to wonder whether the importance of mere pitch-
direction contrasts on which so much of EFL attention to prosodic features
has been focused is of less importance (always excepting tonicity matters)
than other features that have had less attention.

The comments quoted earlier from O'Connor and Arnold (1961, 1973)
were taken from it because it is the premier text of its kind, containing an
extremely generous repertoire of authentic contemporary British English
expressions presented with intonations that are thoroughly appropriate
and indicated in a generally excellent notation. It is an admirable set of
texts for students to use for practice in acquiring English rhythms. However,
in regard to the problem of just how urgently or extensively EFL teachers

should apply themselves to the study of pitch patterns, there is an important question to be asked: if intonation errors were so frequent and so serious as seems to have been suggested, should one not expect textbooks to abound in examples of pitch-pattern blunders? Yet in O'Connor and Arnold (1961, 1973: 2), as also in O'Connor (1980: 108), only one and the same single illustration is to be found, the 'danger' that the phrase *Thank you* may be made to give a *rather casual* impression when a *genuinely grateful* one is called for (by substitution of a low-to-high tone for the required high-to-low type, as only the 1980 text makes really clear).

I find myself, although a quite careful observer of such matters for three or four decades, unable to recall actually encountering any instance of this kind of blunder. The occasions of unease I can attest to regarding *Thank you* in terms of its pitch values have related to disagreeably narrow pitch movement and seem to have been experienced more often from native speakers of English than from EFL users! I have had plenty of regular contact with non-mother-tongue users of English in Britain and have spent more than a decade abroad in half a dozen different countries where I heard such English daily. I am in the habit of noting down (as unobtrusively as possible!) any unusual intonations I hear yet the only really remarkably 'wrong' tone choice that comes to mind is that I once heard the expression 'Nice day, isn't it?' spoken with a high rising tone on the tag question. When I did so, from a Russian teacher of English on a course in Cambridge, I strongly suspect he chose the tone not from natural bent but on the basis of an imperfect mastery of intonation theory.

An examination of the literature of EFL advice on intonation reveals astonishingly few specific examples of observed errors attributed to EFL speakers. Tonicity aside, there are none at all in Palmer (1922), Armstrong and Ward (1926), Halliday (1970), O'Connor and Arnold (1961, 1973), Brazil *et al.* (1980) or Gimson (1980). This last (at p. 282) does give general warnings against unintentional impressions that might result from an over-use of rises or from too many falls but offers no illustrations of the possibilities even though attention is drawn later (at p. 315), perhaps puzzlingly for many thoughtful readers, to the necessity for the ambitious student to note that 'frequent use of falls on pre-nuclear accented syllables is a common feature of natural discourse'. Gimson (1980: 305, 307), by the way, clearly excluded intonation, 'accentuation patterning' aside, from those 'characteristics of pronunciation which ... constitute a priority for the great majority of learners.

The most important reason why specific genuine problems are so rarely to be found dealt with is, one can hardly doubt, that there are so few of them. The first book ever to mention any was the Daniel Jones *Outline of English Phonetics* which in 1918 at section 742ff. gave (after eight French and five German types of mis-accentuations) an example of a German use of rise instead of a normal level tone and a Swedish use of a falling tone which, though non-accenting in Swedish, would be likely to strike any English speaker as a false accentuation (e.g. of the second syllable of *London* as well as the first). The 1932 revision added a second German problem of substituting high-level for low-rise tones within complex sentences and the Norwegian one of substituting rising for what in General British usage would be final (and prefinal) descending tones. The only other point made was that most learners find 'great difficulty in learning to make a fall–rise on a single syllable'.

From this sparse collection of only five items he wisely removed in 1932 the Swedish one, which is so gross that Swedes very rarely ever commit it. It was not considered worth inclusion in Windsor Lewis 1969 at pp. 68–71 where, in reference to all three Scandinavian languages, barely a dozen points could be made, some of them attributed only to restricted regions. There is at the end of Kingdon (1958a), his admirable *Groundwork of English Intonation*, a section on 'Comparative tonetics' which has various valuable specific mentions of intonation transfers into English and a number of hints at other possibilities in sketches of the main intonation characteristics of other languages. The points include the essentially accentual one regarding the Spanish habit of incorporating end-adverbials in the main tune, the common (e.g. French, German and Swedish) tendency to ask most question-word questions with high rising tones, the Hindi use of rising–falling tones more than would be normal in General British usage (though not, for example, among the English-mother-tongue speakers who constitute the large majority of the population of Wales) and two structural points about the Swedish use of low-rising and falling–rising tone types. (Compare the endnote to the Crystal paper in this volume.)

Crystal (1975) reported a valuable comparison of Brazilian Portuguese intonational habits with English ones in regard to a dozen sentence types with closely parallel grammatical structures in the two languages. This included references to rhythmic and pitch-range variations of tones, tone selection in specific situations and in quantitative terms, and various tone distribution points concerning rising tails, vocatives, final and initial adverbials, initial noun, appositional subordinate and final-comment clauses (again accentual matters in many cases). The only other specific intonation fault warning I can recall was not in a book but in an American film on language teaching which represented a Japanese speaker of English as ending a closed-list alternative question with an inappropriate rise. Again not a problem that I can recall having met.

The evidence of Crystal (1975) seemed to suggest that some of the lack of treatment of intonation problems is simply due to neglect of the topic, but much of that neglect clearly stems from the relative triviality of the problems. There is also the fact that many of the problems that might be expected do not materialise or do so only to a negligible extent. We have mentioned the example of the very rare transfer of the Swedish double-fall tone into Swedes' English. Another example is the Finnish speakers' great success with employing a low-rise tone type which is apparently quite absent from their native repertoire of tones. Even speakers of complex toneme languages like Cantonese seem to find that their having fixed pitches on most of their syllables on the whole ... does not make English intonation more difficult [for them] than it is for speakers of other languages (O'Connor 1980: 141). I find this comment closer to my own impressions than the Gimson (1980: 320) suggestion of difficulties, in the comment that 'learners whose mother tongue is a tone language may find the concept of intonation's functions as they occur in English ... entirely novel'. Though the warning on the same page of the need of care by those whose native language makes use of such devices as particles for signalling questions, without any significant pitch variation, no doubt a timely one.

What then, if one can find little or nothing in the way of advice on the problems of one's particular pupils, is the teacher to do about intonation? It of course very much depends on the level of achievement of the pupils, but one should certainly ignore the alarmist comments of some of the theorists. Most of what pupils are likely to do which is different in pitch-patterning from the usage of English mother-tongue speakers is likely only to be trivially so compared with the very many matters of sound-making, tonic-placing, rhythm, lexis and grammar that can go awry.

Those who in their study and practice of English intonation are so ambitious as to aspire to native-like performance, perhaps especially in drama or the reading aloud of literature, will find most practically valuable the study of O'Connor and Arnold and Kingdon (1958a and 1958b). They can extend this knowledge most effectively by looking also at some phonetic readers as for example O'Connor (1971), Crystal and Davy (1975) and Windsor Lewis (1979). They should be warned, or perhaps encouraged, by noting that it is only the exceptional native English speaker who has the ability to consistently produce the most thoroughly appropriate intonations in reading aloud.

Subsequently to the work of Kingdon and O'Connor and Arnold, Halliday (1970) has dazzled many by its brilliant but too arbitrary and not really well thought out handling of the subject (cf. Tench in this volume). Brazil *et al.* (1980), is currently the treatment in vogue. It purports mystifyingly to be directed especially to the EFL audience. Where it is genuinely at variance with more traditional analyses in substance its claims do not in the main appear to be well founded. For a fairly detailed appraisal of it see Windsor Lewis (1986). In addition to the texts recommended above, two grammars are well worth noting: viz. Kingdon's (1969) under-rated reworking of Palmer's *Grammar of Spoken English*, and *A Communicative Grammar of English* by Geoffrey Leech and Jan Svartvik (1975), which comes very near to being adequate in its quite full information using only four tonal distinctions. Quite a lot of theoretical works on English intonation have appeared in recent years which have had no orientation towards, and are not likely to be found to be of any help in, the EFL world.

The most effective way of identifying idiomatic uses of intonations is broadly to relate them to syntactic units. The most fruitful generalisations are those quite simple ones that can be made about different kinds of questions, commands, statements, etc., as Henry Sweet showed over a hundred years ago. The refinements upon this basis made in Kingdon (1958a) and in O'Connor and Arnold (1961, 1973) are still the most commendable reading on tone semantics. Many have been all too inclined to overlook the fact that both of these books were offered to the EFL public as demonstrations of what are typical idiomatic uses of intonation of the most general types to be heard in England. As such they are unimpeach-able, yet critics have persisted in referring to them as if they were primarily analytical works when their clearly avowed intentions were prescriptive. If, as was suggested in Windsor Lewis (1971: 78), O'Connor and Arnold could have ratcheted its wording just one notch away from talking about what intonations 'convey' to claiming only to identify what they correlate with, this 'essentially practical text-book ... for the foreign learner' might have been spared much of the criticism levelled at it.

The problem with tone semantics is, I have become progressively more convinced over many years, that tones have meanings so elemental – so vague if you like – that ordinary language lacks terms broad enough to convey them suitably. Tones are highly ambiguous but such differences as there are between them can, I have suggested, (e.g. 1977: 9), be captured by comparing them for just two elemental features – what I have best been able to identify as 'animation' and 'continuity'. Anything more specific semantically is doomed to futility. The upshot of this is that teachers should not waste time speculating on just what quota of meaning pitch features contribute to spoken English but should accept any intonations from their pupils in spontaneous speech that they do not consider to be grossly unnatural – a pretty unusual finding.

What is perhaps desirable for teachers to be able to do is to recognise readily (when they are boldly made) and demonstrate clearly the half dozen most basic English tones, high and low rises and falls, high level and the high-fall-low-rise (even when it occurs on a monosyllabic word). They should not be discouraged if they find identification of many tones baffling in ordinary speech. It is the natural thing for a speaker's intonational performance to be highly imprecise. They should not expect that even a thorough knowledge of the tones prescribed in books like O'Connor and Arnold will equip them to analyse the tonal performance of speakers they hear. Again as Gimson (1977) commented:

People have accused O'Connor and Arnold of being over-complex although [their intonation notation] system is so simplified that we

THE TEACHING OF ENGLISH INTONATION

can't use it with native speakers because native English speakers use tunes which don't occur in the O'Connor and Arnold system.

Even when it comes to tones included by O'Connor and Arnold, its rising–falling tone, for example, although very commonly used by many native speakers, is a difficult luxury in terms of what most learners need actively to use. Kingdon showed very clearly that he recognised this in his arrangement of practice materials. Teachers, even those specialising in such matters, should not be discouraged if they find identification of many tones baffling in ordinary speech. It is natural for speakers' intonational performances to be imprecise: so often, in fact, as their attitudes are less than clearcut.

If you have ever listened to something like the recording of an O'Connor and Arnold dialogue muffled, for example, by an intervening wall, you will know that it takes only seconds to realise when the prosodies alone can be detected that one is not hearing spontaneous conversation. Which is only as it should be. They sound reasonably 'natural' but genuinely spontaneous dialogue would make a very unsatisfactory and difficult model for an EFL student to set out to imitate.

It may be of interest that Windsor Lewis (1977) adopted a 'fine' tone notation (by contrast with the 'coarse' notation deliberately and wisely adopted by O'Connor and Arnold) because it was offered not simply as a practice book but equally as an expository reader. Many of the later items in it were never intended for wholesale imitation. Its fifty-odd passages were graduated. They began with the kind of slightly wooden, dynamically very even, prosodies that actors perfectly understandably adopt for EFL dialogues. They know that total comprehensibility must take precedence over anything like naturalism in the ordinary run of such materials. In conducting the recording sessions I accepted this manner initially but subsequently asked for progressively greater realism. The last items in the book were a mixture of totally spontaneous monologues and bits of the actors' personal conversation recorded with their prior agreement but relying on their forgetting the presence of a live microphone. Much more material was recorded than was ultimately used. Users of the book were meant to accept the challenge to see if they could detect when the transition came from the scripted to the unscripted matter. This represented a totally different aim from that of O'Connor and Arnold and so the finer notation was necessary. It was the most fine that has been used for any published collection of intonation-marked passages. The recordings on which Crystal (1969) and Crystal and Davy (1969) were based have never been published and Crystal and Davy (1975) used a fairly coarse notation.

Finally, in all probability the unease with intonation matters I seem to have detected among very many teachers of English as a foreign language is most probably largely based on the failure to realise that, in spontaneous speech, even though the intonational choices they and their pupils may make will sometimes not be exactly the ones that native speakers of English would favour in the same linguistic situations, yet they will generally be within the range of choices open to English-mother-tongue speakers. They should realise that they are able to circumvent the problem of producing purely English-language intonation usages because of the circumstance that many markedly different tonal strategies can arrive at the same semantic effects. Making a selection of tones based on the intonational choices they would have made had the utterance been couched in their native language, they will be usually very likely to produce intonations that give no difficulties of comprehension or of acceptability. They should take heart at the thought of the goodwill that mainstream native English speakers have no difficulty in exercising constantly in daily communication with the rich variety of other mother-tongue English speakers they may encounter.

NOTE

1   This article was partly based on a paper given in April 1982 at a conference at the Paris-Nord University, France, the proceedings of which were published by its university press in 1984 as *Deuxième Colloque d'Avril sur l'Anglais Oral* (pp. 13–19).

REFERENCES

Armstrong, L. E. and Ward, I. C. (1926) *A Handbook of English Intonation*, Cambridge: Heffer.
Bolinger, D. L. (1972) *Intonation*, Harmondsworth: Penguin.
Brazil, D., Coulthard, M. and Johns, C. (1980) *Discourse Intonation and Language Teaching*, London: Longman.
Crystal, D. (1975) *Prosodic Systems and Intonation in English*, Cambridge: Cambridge University Press.
—— (1975) *The English Tone of Voice*, London: Edward Arnold.
Crystal, D. and Davy, D. (1969) *Investigating English Style*, London: Longman.
—— (1975) *Advanced Conversational English*, London: Longman.
Gimson, A.C. (1962, 1980) *An Introduction to the Pronunciation of English*, London: Edward Arnold.
—— (1977) Unpublished Introductory Address to the First Leeds University International Conference on the Teaching of Spoken English.
Gregory, O. D. (1966) 'A comparative description of the intonation of British and American English for teachers of English as a foreign language', D.Ed. thesis, Columbia University.
Halliday, M. A. K. (1970) *Intonation*, London: Oxford University Press.
Jones, D. (1918, 1932, etc.) *An Outline of English Phonetics*, Leipzig: Teubner, and Cambridge: Cambridge University Press.
Kingdon, R. (1958a) *The Groundwork of English Intonation*, London: Longman.
—— (1958b) *English Intonation Practice*, London: Longman.
—— (1969) *Palmer's Grammar of Spoken English*, Cambridge: Heffer.

Leech, G. and Svartvik, J. (1975) *A Communicative Grammar of English*, London: Longman.

O'Connor, J. D. (1967, 1980) *Better English Pronunciation*, Cambridge: Cambridge University Press.

—— (1971) *Advanced Phonetic Reader*, Cambridge: Cambridge University Press.

O'Connor, J. D. and Arnold, G. F. (1961, 1973) *Intonation of Colloquial English*, London: Longman.

Palmer, H. (1922) *English Intonation*, Cambridge: Heffer.

Sweet, H. (1885) *Elementarbuch des gesprochenen Englisch*, Oxford: Clarendon Press.

Windsor Lewis, J. (1969) *A Guide to English Pronunciation*, Oslo: Scandinavian Universities Press.

—— (1971) An Examination of *Intonation of Colloquial English* (1961) by O'Connor and Arnold, *Phonetics Department Report*, University of Leeds, pp. 51–82.

—— (1977, 1979) *People Speaking*, London: Oxford University Press.

—— (1986) Review article on Brazil *et al.* (1980), *Journal of the International Phonetic Association* 16: 54–62.

Part III

THE PHONETICS OF MOTHER-TONGUE ENGLISH

Part III

THE PHONETICS OF
MOTHER-TONGUE
ENGLISH

23

A 'tenny' rate

John Baldwin
University College London

As a postgraduate UCL student in the Department of Phonetics, as it then was, I had the pleasure of attending lectures given by J. D. O'Connor (Doc) on a wide variety of topics. Though I remember with gratitude all my teachers of those years, and recall many of their academic dicta, the one thing I retain, in addition, of Doc's sayings is his favourite expression at that time, *at any rate*, which he repeated several times in each lecture. I registered the expression as 'a tenny rate', so Doc must have produced the /t/ with the degree of affrication/aspiration appropriate to the context of initial in a stressed syllable. Furthermore, I must have found this pronunciation sufficiently unusual for it to have struck me at the time as amusing, and for me to have remembered it for more years than either Doc or I would care to count. The process whereby a consonant or more than one consonant at the end of one word is transferred in connected speech to the beginning of the next word if it has a vowel onset, has many wider implications, and I would like to consider some of them here. I shall use the customary term 'consonant capture' to refer to that process.

In, probably, most languages this is the default case in the syllabification process: CVCVC(C)#VCV → CVCV#C(C)VCV. The purpose of consonant capture, as I understand it, is to produce open syllables wherever feasible, this being the more natural structure in terms of linguistic universals. In theory we would expect to find three categories of effects:

1   instances in which the process does not lead to any phonetic re-adjustment, save, perhaps inevitably, that of duration;
2   instances in which all those segmental changes that in principle could occur are actually brought about, with the concomitant requirement of some kind of phonological explanation;
3   instances in which only some of the phonetic effects are present, and where any phonological or other explanations are likely to be more problematical.

With the exception of a few common expressions like *at all, it isn't* and so on, English is generally considered to be a language in which consonant

301

capture across word boundaries does not normally occur, hence the title of this article. However, in my everyday work at UCL, in my forensic practice and as a phonetically aware observer of my speech environment I have encountered dozens of native English speakers who do precisely the thing they are supposed not to. For example, I mention in *Forensic Phonetics* (Baldwin and French 1990: 114), in the Goodwin case, the policeman who pronounced ... *and eliminated* ... as '... an-deliminated ...', and ... *brought out* ... as '... brough-tout ...'. In the first example the syllable division was very clear auditorily, and related to durational factors, principally the slight lengthening of /n/ in *and* (category 1). In the second example there was strong affrication of the first /t/, and reduced clipping of the preceding vowel. However, that vowel did not resemble in the least any of its realisations in word-final open syllables in that idiolect, but was produced as an almost pure vowel quite close to Cardinal Vowel [o]. In the latter example we have an instance of category 3: although /t/ has all the characteristics expected of it initially in a stressed syllable, it is not easy to explain why the process fails to produce an appropriate word-final realisation of the vowel. Given the nature of human behaviour I would expect this category, i.e. the one which presents us with problems of explanation, to turn out to be the most common.

A more spectacular example, from a different case, is 'What happened? He was thrown out.' This was realised as two word groups, with a high head on 'What', a high rise nuclear tone on 'happened', a high head on 'thrown' and a high fall on 'out'. Thus far there is nothing unusual, but the speaker did not make a silent pause between the word groups, introduced marked lengthening of the /n/ of 'happened' and transferred the /d/ to the beginning of the next word group, triggering /h/-deletion in the process. (It must be 'deletion' because the speaker produced the /h/ in 'happened'.)

The omission of a silent pause in the above example, though relatively unusual, is by no means unheard of. In my study of a corpus of unscripted Russian conversation (Baldwin 1966), for which, incidentally, Doc was my supervisor, I found that out of 137 sentence-final word groups, roughly 17.5 per cent were not followed by (silent) pauses; however, in the case of the 164 word groups which were not sentence-final, slightly over 60 per cent were not followed by pauses. The study offered a definition of 'hesitation' in phonetic terms, one of which was the kind of marked lengthening of segments noted in 'happened', and this was one of the criteria used to delimit word groups. Seventeen per cent of non-final but only 5 per cent of final word groups were delimited by hesitation. No formal boundaries were observed in the case of 43.3 per cent of non-final and 12.4 per cent of final word groups. I would expect a conversational, i.e. unscripted and unprepared, corpus in any language to produce comparable figures.

The examples chosen so far might give the impression that the process only affects stops. That is far from being the case, though. On another occasion I was reading through an orthographic transcript of a conversation made by an employee of a police force, and came across the words 'A number of things can be done to be ... the England squad.' The transcript-writer had left blank the utterance after 'be', obviously being unable to interpret it. When I listened to the tape, though, it was clear that the speaker, a Londoner who did not speak Received Pronunciation (RP), had been using the expression *beef up*, but with a syllable division uninterpretable to that transcript-writer: 'be-fup'. It is interesting to note, in passing, that he was unable to guess *beef up* from the context, something I find hard to understand; presumably he was unfamiliar with that expression. I have encountered, too, many speakers who produce forms like *It was only right* ... as 'It wa-zonely right...' with a clear stress onset before /z/.

As in other areas of phonetics, pronunciations heard from foreign speakers can be of interest, and the more advanced the speaker, the more sophisticated the version is likely to be. The best example of consonant capture I have noted within a word is the rendering by a bilingual speaker of Brazilian Portuguese/Ukrainian of the word *workload* with rhythmic clipping of the first vowel and virtually full devoicing of /l/. I do not recall actually having heard this pronunciation from a native speaker of English, but, given the common pronunciation of *Atlantic* as 'A-tlantic' (with fully devoiced /l/) and the kind of examples I shall be quoting below, I would not be all that surprised if I did.

Another example which I noted from a foreign speaker of English, this time Bulgarian, was in ... *complex interrelationship* ..., which he produced as '... complek-sinterrelationship ...', with a clearly audible release of /k/ and a marked secondary stress at the beginning of the second word. Again, I would not be surprised to find such a pronunciation in some English idiolect.

Given the widespread occurrence of consonant capture, it would seem reasonable to look for some kind of distributional explanation in terms of either regional or social background, or perhaps both: for example, I have the impression, and it is only an impression, that consonant capture, in England at any rate, is rather more likely amongst people from an Afro-Caribbean background than otherwise. However, it would clearly be unwise to place any great reliance on that impression since none of the examples in this paper is taken from that community. Fellow phoneticians have informed me, and I have noted myself, that Scots speakers, including Scots/Irish speakers, regularly carry out consonant capture, and with no observable distinction between people of differing social backgrounds. It is even, apparently, usual for such speakers to produce *as well* as 'a-swell', with the change of /z/ to /s/, presumably to avoid the absolute prohibition of */zw/ as any kind of initial cluster, whether of the word or of the syllable. I have observed the same pronunciation in England, but have been unable to discover any distributional characteristics there. In the English context it is, for example, by no means unknown to hear *Biggleswade* pronounced as 'Biggle-suede', with the same switch of /z/ to /s/. To be sure, the functional load of the *s/z* contrast is not at its highest here, but the fact that it can be ignored at all in order to gain open syllables, is, to my mind, of the greatest significance. Given the possible vocalisation of /l/, many people achieve the maximum number of open syllables in these words.

The explanation I suggested, though without any great conviction, in *Forensic Phonetics*, that of a Huguenot substratum (since French is well known as a consonant capture language), might just about be true for some Londoners, particularly those from families with a long history of residence in the East End, and I know there are such families. However, this will not help us explain its sporadic nature, since no London speaker I have ever heard produces consonant capture on every theoretically possible occasion. We also cannot explain why, say, one of two sisters does it frequently and the other virtually never, or why one of a team of local police officers does it occasionally, and his colleagues, apparently, not at all.

The recently formed (1991) International Association for Forensic Phonetics has as its aims:

1   to provide a forum for phoneticians working actively in forensic phonetics;
2   to foster basic research in forensic applications of phonetics.

One such research project might well be to investigate the incidence of consonant capture at word boundaries in a given population of native speakers of English. In the forensic context, i.e. (usually) where speech samples are being compared for the purposes of speaker identification, the phonetician as expert consultant might express the opinion that, since the process seems to be rare, it should be rated as a strong point of positive identification if it is found in both a contested and an admitted sample, and a strong point of negative identification if it is found in one but not in the other. In the absence of statistical data the 'rarity' or otherwise must be an impression; however, that impression is not a figment of the phonetician's imagination, but is the product of his/her professional experience. As such it can properly be presented in a court of law as evidence of expert opinion, on a par with opinions expressed by medical practitioners, handwriting experts and so on. The impression of rarity is the best indicator we have at the moment, but statistical data, if such existed, would allow the forensic phonetician to express his/her conclusions on a higher level of probability. Of course, all evidence of a phonetic character, even the most statistically supported, must be expressed in terms of opinions about probabilities rather than certainties.

As stated above, the purpose of consonant capture is to achieve a more natural syllable structure, and it might be possible to regard what is happening in English as a tendency in that direction. We already have instances of this within words like *postponement*, where there are often conflicting indications: the absence of aspiration in the medial /p/ in the speech of many people would require a syllable division before the cluster /sp/, which, given the deletion of the medial /t/, achieves an initial open syllable. However, the presence of, probably, more marked clipping of the diphthong in the first syllable than could be explained by rhythmic factors alone would lead one to suggest that the /s/ belongs to the first syllable and not the second. This is category 3 again, and I would suggest that, when there is conflict, matters of aspiration should take precedence over clipping in the determining of syllable division.

It might be interesting to note that some or all of the syllable divisions I propose in this paper are to be found in Wells (1990a) and Windsor Lewis (1972), but none in Gimson (1988).

Similarly, in *sixteen* the syllable division would be /k-st/, because of the unaspirated /t/. However, in *fifteen* the usual, or at least very common, pronunciation is also without aspiration of the /t/. I would argue that the resulting stressed syllable-initial cluster /ft/ is acceptable because

1   we cannot account for the absence of aspiration of /t/ in any other way;
2   it fits better into the universal expectation of open syllable structure.

We note, however, that */ft/ is disfavoured as a word-initial cluster. Acceptance of such a syllable-initial cluster in the word *safety* would enable us to explain why, discounting possible vowel and rhythm differences, 'Safe T First' (a commercial heading) sounds quite different from *Safety First*.

As was intimated above, I believe there is often an association of aspiration with affrication, in that /t/ and /k/, when aspirated in RP, are usually associated with a measure of affrication: a brief fricative interval can be heard upon the release of the stop and before the onset of the effect of devoicing. My experience of teaching English pronunciation to foreigners provides, I believe, some interesting evidence of the association of affrication with aspiration in the native English speaker's mind. In most Slavonic and Romance languages /p/, /t/ and /k/ have no aspiration, but many native speakers produce /k/ with slight affrication. When those speakers are trying to pronounce RP unaspirated stops, the substitution of their own sounds usually produces acceptable forms, at least as far as aspiration is concerned. However, if they fail to suppress the affrication of /k/, the resulting form could be identified by a native English speaker as aspirated, with the possible consequence that the foreigner's attempt at, say 'skewer' might be perceived as 'secure', with a devoiced vowel in the first syllable.

Some accents of English have unaspirated /p/, /t/ and /k/ where other accents would have aspiration, and it is precisely in those accents that I perceive pronunciations of the affricate at the beginning of words like *cheap* to have such a brief fricative interval that the word comes close to sounding like RP *jeep*. If we accept the specification of affrication as a frequent phonetic concomitant of phonological 'aspiration', we could suggest that the English regional accents in question have both unaspirated (voiceless) stops and an unaspirated (voiceless) affricate.

The possibility that the RP voiceless affricate might, like /p/, /t/ and /k/ be realised with or without aspiration depending on its phonetic context, would enable us to distinguish in a principled way between affricate realisations that I perceive to be quite different, such as that in *discharge* (verb) as opposed to those in *exchange* and the non-standard *mischievious*. To my ear at least the affricate in the first word has a relatively long fricative interval, suggesting the syllable division 'dis-ch', whereas in the other two words the reduced, or 'clipped' fricative duration would suggest the divisions 'ek-sch' and 'mi-sch'.

As in the case of *fifteen*, the above revisions of syllable structure result in syllable-initial clusters which have traditionally been regarded as unacceptable, to say nothing of *Atlantic* mentioned above. The following forms, noted from different RP speakers, require the modification of accepted notions (Wells 1990b) of vowel distribution in RP:

(1)   look after → loo-kafter
(2)   set out → se-tout
(3)   back up! → ba-ckup!

In each example there was an auditorily clear stress on the second syllable, the onset of which included the transferred stop. In each instance the stop had the degree of affrication/aspiration appropriate to it in its new location: initial in a stressed syllable. There seems to be no alternative but to accept the occurrence of short, strong vowels in open syllables in these sorts of RP idiolect. Again we see that open syllables have been achieved at the expense of complications in the phonotactic statement. Taking the main argument of this paragraph in conjunction with that of the unaspirated realisation of the voiceless affricate, I would feel it appropriate to divide the word *question* as 'que-stion'.

This tendency to open syllables, and it seems reasonable to suppose that that is what it is, might well find its counterpart in the common deletion of a final stop in the context of a following word beginning with a consonant or a consonant cluster, as in *Mark Cox*, where the final /k/ was, when he was a regular topic of conversation, often elided to give 'Ma Cox', and the ever-present 'Flea Street' for *Fleet Street*. I can be neither the first nor the only phonetician to have been invited, by RP-speaking cabin crew before take-off, to fasten my 'sea-belt'. This could be explained as an elegantising avoidance by the speaker of a word-final glottal stop, and this would certainly seem to explain the operation, by an RP speaker, to change *Camp David* to 'Cam David', and a near-RP speaker to pronounce *that day* as 'tha-day'. Indeed, in any accent in which the glottal stop occurs at all widely, this would be a consideration: for example, in the area of the person who said 'brough-tout' it would be usual to hear both /t/s realised as glottal stops instead of only the second one, and it is quite likely that he was trying to elegantise his speech by this means. However, this could not be offered as an explanation of the RP examples 'loo-kafter', 'se-tout' and 'ba-ckup', since no glottal stop would be expected in that accent; it would also not explain the (barrister) RP speaker's 'work-tout' for *worked out* (with all the expected phonetic re-adjustments). It is clear that some other explanation(s) must be sought for such cases.

Looking again at some of the examples discussed above, many fall into the category verb + affix:

(Non-ethnic east London) brought out, beef up
(RP) look after, set out, back up, worked out

Avoidance, conscious or otherwise, of glottal stops can account for the east London speakers' forms: they omit the glottal stop, (over)emphasise the obstruent, and transfer it to the beginning of the next word. However, no such explanation can be offered for the RP speakers' forms; they really do appear to be examples of pure consonant capture. By nature distrustful of 'unique' explanations, I am inclined to believe that, in fact, both groups share the tendency to consonant capture. The first of the east London speakers did not realise all the theoretically possible /t/s in the substantial sample of his speech as glottal stops, but had some alveolar articulations. On the face of it, therefore, he might equally well have opted to give this /t/ an alveolar realisation too, and simply omit the glottal stop. For the second east London speaker there was an equally obvious solution: he could simply have omitted the glottal stop, as he usually did, in fact, in a large sample of his speech. It is not clear, I think, why they chose on these occasions to carry out consonant capture, i.e. their less favoured elegantising strategy.

In the case of *worked out*, consonant capture cannot be attributed to the speaker's fear of pronouncing a glottal stop. Similarly, there is obviously no expectation on his part of achieving an open syllable. The remaining consideration, if an open syllable is impossible, must be the pressure to simplify the syllable coda as far as the phonotactics allow: *worked out* → 'work-tout' → *'wor-ktout'. This principle could be part of the motivation for the suggested syllable division in words like *exchange* → 'ek-schange', where *ksch* would not be a possible sequence in English.

In the case of noun nhrases, i.e. *that day, Camp David, Mark Cox, Fleet Street* and *seat-belt*, we seem to have examples of over-reaction to the fear of producing a glottal stop, which results in the deletion both of the glottal stop and of the oral stop, a 'baby and the bathwater' solution if ever there was one!

I believe it is usually the case in languages (e.g. Baldwin 1966, which was also supervised by Doc) that word-initial consonant clusters are more complex than word-final clusters. In looking at English consonant clusters (e.g. O'Connor and Trim 1953) one can readily perceive that word-final clusters could be candidates for simplification, and, if a measure of congruence might be expected between word-final and syllable-final clusters, such simplification might also be appropriate for the latter. All the process examples discussed above show that tendency.

Two final examples will complete this paper, both of which I heard fairly recently. The first was spoken by a non-RP, non-ethnic, south London speaker. In saying the words *Scott's Dad* (with both syllables stressed, but the nucleus on *Dad*) he realised the /t/ as a glottal stop and transferred the word-final /s/ to the beginning of *Dad*. I would not claim that I expected to hear such an example of consonant capture, but, given the neutralisation of the *d/t* contrast in this position, I was not exactly startled by it. The second example was spoken by a young man with a, to me, unidentifiable Scottish accent to his girlfriend on a London bus. In saying the words *That sounds good to me* (with stresses on *That* and *good*, and the nucleus on *me*) he elided the /d/ of *sounds*, slightly lengthening the /n/, and transferred the final /z/ to the beginning of the word *good*, in the process changing the /z/ to an /s/. The switch of /z/ to /s/ is well attested in other idiolects, where any cluster beginning with /z/ is rigorously avoided. Again, I think that neutralisation of the *g/k* contrast makes this admittedly fleeting observation believable.

It seems to me, in conclusion, that the most important point to emerge from the above discussion is the very strong tendency of many native English speakers to carry out various processes: consonant capture, consonant deletion, cancelling of the /s~z/ contrast, etc., all of which have as a single outcome the simplification of the codas of the English syllable. It has become clear that this process of coda simplification is not without constraints. The clusters /ft/ and /s/ + *ch*, for example, have been shown to occur initially in syllables which are within words, but not initially in words. However, the clusters */zw/, */zg/ and */kt/, for example, have proved to be disfavoured in any context. Where the simplification process would generate clusters of the kind just mentioned, the speakers avoid them by not making a cluster at all, as in the case of: */kt/ → /k/-/t/, or by ignoring the *z/s* contrast in the case of */zw/ → /sw/. In both */zg/ and */sd/ the fricative has to be /s/, and the stops are probably best analysed as archiphonemes: /s/ + {G} and /s/ + {D}.

It is my impression that coda simplification of English syllables is occurring with ever greater frequency, although I am aware of the danger that that impression might be a function of the greater attention I am now giving to the question. I am also inclined to believe that we are witnessing the first stages of a long-term historical change, as opposed to an ongoing, relatively stable situation of free variation, whether within or between idiolects. It could be argued that such a change would be in the expected direction of a simpler syllable structure for English, though the further, detailed consequences of the change are not easy to predict.

REFERENCES

Baldwin, J. (1966) 'Alternative analyses of the structure of consonant clusters in modern Russian, and their implications for phonological transcription' unpublished MA thesis, University of London.

—— (1979) *A Formal Analysis of the Intonation of Modern Colloquial Russian* (Forum Phoneticum, 18), Hamburg, Helmut Buske.

Baldwin, J. and French, P. (1990) *Forensic Phonetics*, London and New York: Pinter.

Gimson, A. C. (1988) *Everyman's Pronouncing Dictionary*, revised by Susan Ramsaran, London: Dent.

O'Connor, J. D. and Trim, J. L. M. (1953) 'Vowel, consonant and syllable: a phonological definition', *Word* 9: 103–22.

Wells, J. C. (1982) *Accents of English*, Cambridge: Cambridge University Press.

—— (1990a) *Longman Pronunciation Dictionary*, London: Longman.

—— (1990b) 'Syllabification and allophony', in S. Ramsaran (ed.), *Studies in the Pronunciation of English*, London and New York: Routledge.

Windsor Lewis, J (1972) *A Concise Pronouncing Dictionary of British and American English*, London: Oxford University Press.

24

Pronunciation and the rich points of culture

Nikolas Coupland
University of Wales College, Cardiff

PHONETICS AND SOCIOLINGUISTICS

At the time when sociolinguistics *was* Labovian studies of social and stylistic stratification (Labov 1966), there was an unbroken chain of mutual influence from descriptive phonetics through dialectology to mainstream sociolinguistics.[1] Given Labov's explicit favouring of phonological as opposed to syntactic, lexical or discourse variation in quantitative studies – on the practical grounds that phonetic variants were at least frequent and often relatively easy to code, plus the theoretical grounds that they allow us to meet the requirement of sameness needed in variationist research (Lavandera 1978; Coupland 1983) – modern sociolinguistics was founded on the already rich analyses of geographically and socially varying phonetic forms and phonological systems (Wells 1982). And it was largely in phonological terms that researchers developed theories about how linguistic systems were organised in the competences of individuals and communities, and about how these changed over time.

Priorities in sociolinguistics have, however, shifted. Part of this re-alignment has been the progressive strengthening of the cognitive 'wing' of sociolinguistics, for example through the work of Tajfel, Lambert and Giles. Perhaps the dimension of sociolinguistic variation that Labov called 'stylistic' or 'contextual' (Halliday's 'diatopic') was better analysed in terms of human motivations and perceptions, and with reference to the cluster of affective and strategic goals that drive relationships. Might there be, as Giles and others have argued, *accommodative* processes at work in dialect interviews which would at least refine the usual Labovian interpretations of the findings and might possibly vitiate the basic assumptions of paradigm itself (Giles and Coupland 1991; Giles *et al.* 1991)? Later studies, including one by Trudgill (1981), showed that speech accommodation was indeed an important piece of the puzzle and was detectably at work in at least some of the most influential pronunciation-based sociolinguistic surveys.

It was social psychologists who suggested that sociolinguists tended to say naive things about the 'reality' of linguistic data and that we generally put too much faith in correlating pronunciation phenomena with gross social dimensions such as social class (which we thought we were measuring objectively), gender and social situation. In fact, the social psychology of language was leading sociolinguistics into the *anti-determinist* perspective and the concern for strategic analysis of talk in context that are now so widely accepted. Slowly it became possible to reconceptualise variation in pronunciation as driven by micro interactional concerns as well as macro social processes. The best example of this integration is certainly Trudgill's (1986) *Dialects in Contact* – a thorough reworking of our understanding of linguistic change through appreciating specifically accommodative processes at work at dialect boundaries, also invoking the social psychological construct of salience. Bell's influential (1984) paper on audience design is also an important instance.

But another very general trend within sociolinguistics (and within the social sciences generally) has been the move to discourse and conversation analysis and typically to qualitative interpretations of 'talk' in social situations. We must add to this the ever-increasing influence of ethnographic, cross-cultural approaches, stemming from Hymes' seminal analyses of 'ways of speaking' and communicative competence. Together, these tendencies have produced an array of contemporary approaches that at least agree on the need for text-based and thoroughly contextualised approaches to sociolinguistics. And this has probably tended to weaken its historical links with phonetics. Sociolinguistics has rapidly been catching up with the observation that the social meaning of language use resides every bit as much in what is said, and why, as in how, where, when and by whom it is said.

The aim of this paper is to argue that a discourse-based and sociopsychological sociolinguistics *still needs* an explicit phonetic dimension and can still build the contextual analysis of pronunciation variation into its frameworks. Seen from the other side, we can very valuably take up the analysis of variation in pronunciation in more context- and content-sensitive ways than has typically been the case. I shall illustrate this claim by introducing some ideas about variation in pronunciation and cultural identity, mainly relating to English in Wales.

PRONUNCIATION AND DISCOURSE

Looking back on what the Labovian and attitudes/accommodation paradigms have allowed us to know, it seems that we are still some considerable distance from answering some of the most fundamental questions to do with sociolinguistic variation in what we call 'accent' and 'dialect'. We still have only a limited understanding of how, and why, dialect variation is implemented in the ways that it is in everyday speech events. What is certain is that the macro-level patterning of variation through the speech community and through social situations that Labov-inspired sociolinguistic surveys have repeatedly shown us *and* the cluster of motivational, attitudinal and evaluative factors in social psychological studies are all relevant. But we have relatively little idea about how to put these two dimensions – the macro and the micro – together in an explanatory framework.

In a couple of very small-scale studies in the 1980s I tried to show how, in individual speaking situations, group-level and intra-individual factors can conspire to generate accent performances – that is, trying to develop an interpretive 'dialect stylistics' (Coupland 1988). I would like to suggest this approach, based as it has to be on very small data-sets and often case studies of the relational and identity significance of dialect in interactions (my own work has studied radio disc-jockey performances and travel agency work settings). In the future, there will be some key emphases for this sort of work:

1   To integrate the analysis of pronunciation forms with that of *content*. It seems remarkable to me that our work in dialect has almost never explored how variation in pronunciation is integrated as part of a speaker's 'meaning potential' (in Halliday's phrase), and hence available to speakers as a semiotic resource *within* the meaning-generating system. We have tended to hive off 'dialect' as contributing a dimension of 'social meaning' at one remove from other aspects of phonology and the semantics of lexico-grammar and discourse.
2   To be alert to the strategic use of pronunciation variation, for example in the symbolising of ethnic, class, regional and other identities, in the articulation of cultural experiences generally, and in the negotiation or modification of social relationships.
3   To take a more critical and interpretive stance rather than try to isolate individual social factors and control out others in survey designs. In the spirit of a stylistic textual enquiry, we must be prepared to take what comes and respond to whatever social and psychological factors are interpretable at any one point in talk.

This agenda is in fact very different from the established one. As is well known, within quantitative sociolinguistics, it became conventional (following Labov's seminal studies in New York and Martha's Vineyard) to follow a definite and very revealing procedure for the quantification of phonetic variation. Sociolinguistic 'variables' were established as abstract entities which represented a textual locus for meaningful social variation (class/status-related or situation-related or both) within a particular speech community. Variant forms of the variable, often including a zero form, were identified and ranked on a scale of standard/non-standard. The occurrences of variants could then be charted within a corpus of recorded speech which had already been assigned to some contextual type (e.g. working class, male speakers reading from a passage of written text). The end-product was a numerical index of standardness for that speaker or group of speakers in a named context.

This procedure has been discussed and re-evaluated many times (see Milroy 1987 for an excellent review). One less frequently discussed facet of the procedure, however, is its insensitivity to the stylistic impact of *particular* variant selections in *particular* discursive contexts. Since the procedure aggregates scores for a particular variable across many occurrences, any interest in local occurrences is of course designed out. Also, beyond the need to respect and measure the impact of certain restricted aspects of linguistic context, such as the position of a variable within a word and relative to other categories of phonemes (see Mees 1990 for a careful analysis of linguistic context constraints on phonological variables), the procedure does not try to capture the interaction between variant selections and lexical/discourse choices.

PRONUNCIATION AS A SEMIOTIC RESOURCE

Yet pronunciation is a very powerful resource for meaning generation, and at many levels. Sociolinguistics has regularly recognised the symbolic power of accents in expressing national or local identities or aspirations to group membership (Fishman 1977), degrees of solidarity or antipathy and status difference in relationships (Giles and Powesland 1975), etc. In fact, it is in just these terms that Labov's findings of the co-variation of pronunciation and class, of hypercorrection or of linguistic change need to be *explained*. But there have been relatively few explicit studies of the details of how pronunciation functions in cultural signification, however well recognised this association is in general.

Agar (1991) has written very provocatively about the cultural implications of bilingualism. He argues that our experience of second-language learning can be thought of in modified Whorfian terms. Whorf is often taken to have argued that a language presents us with a uniformly insurmountable barrier because, locked into our own world-view, we have no access to its cultural 'frames'. In Agar's view, 'Frames are structures of interrelated expectations into which a particular expression fits. Frames provide a context in terms of which an expression makes sense, knowledge in terms of which the expression can be discussed, and links in terms of which ... poetic echoes ... can be made explicit' (1991: 176). But Agar sees these frames and the cultural 'barriers' to second-language learning that they represent as highly variable. In most respects, we may find few such barriers, because of the cultural knowledge and assumptions shared by our first and second languages. But then we will run across local but often intractable problems, because 'the problematic bit of language is puttied thickly into far-reaching networks of association and many situations of use.

313

When one grabs such a piece of language, the putty is so thick and so spread out that it's almost impossible to lift the piece of language out' (*ibid.*).

Agar's conclusion is that languages have their 'rich points', relative to others, and this is the notion I want to borrow. These are precisely those 'problematic' areas in language-learning terms, but the term 'rich' is used to convey how they are also the points at which cultural context is most amply embedded in linguistic forms, and of course vice versa. And it seems to me that the metaphor is every bit as applicable to intralinguistic codes and varieties as it is to languages themselves. The popular fascination of dialectology, after all, does not lie in the fact of organised linguistic variation alone but in the interplay between this variation and cultural distinctiveness. Weinreich insisted that the study of 'folk speech' should be linked to that of 'folk life' in all its aspects (1954: 397; see also Wakelin 1977: 10). But accents and dialects, I want to suggest, are themselves replete with rich points which have a special responsibility for carrying the cultural 'stuff' that we (perhaps wrongly) take to be defined by the variety as a whole.

Agar suggests that particular rich points will probably have some special significance within the speech community generally, not only when the variety is contrasted with another: 'rich points are also areas that native speakers recognize instantly and then disagree over when they discuss them' (p. 177). I take this to mean that they will be recognisable through their richness and power to encapsulate subjective experiences of cultural belonging, but that the precise cultural content, *because* it is so richly represented, will always be a matter of inconclusive debate. When ingroup cultural members cannot fully analyse the cultural meaning of a rich point, it will of course prove doubly inaccessible to outgroup members. Giles *et al.* (1977) have developed the notion of 'ethnolinguistic vitality' and, within it, the perception of inter-group boundaries being either 'hard and closed' or 'soft and malleable' (see also Giles and Coupland 1991: 136ff.). In this connection it would be useful to explore, in future studies, how perceptions of inter-group boundaries may in fact be based on members experiencing multiple 'problematic' rich points in their dealings with an outgroup's language variety.

PRONUNCIATION AND CULTURAL RICH POINTS

At what linguistic levels, then, might a dialect community's rich points be recognisable? We might turn most readily to lexis, since it is clearly true that ideational 'fields' (in Halliday's sense) are commonly culture-specific. To say this is partly to echo traditional dialect geography's interest in culture mapping through charting the distribution of regional vocabulary. But regionally restricted vocabulary items will not all be rich points in Agar's sense. The example he discusses at length is 'schmah', as it surfaces in

Vienna. He tries to define 'schmah' as 'a view of the world ... that rests on the basic ironic premise that things aren't what they seem, what they are is much worse, and all you can do is laugh it off' (Agar 1991: 179).

The example is such a strong one since the referent of 'schmah' is itself a cultural experience. Terms *for* culturally restricted events or customs might be similarly direct in their functioning as rich points, for example the Welsh *eisteddfod* (the competitive arts festival), *gymanfa ganu* (choral singing). But more typical instances would be referents *within* everyday cultural experience, perhaps mundane objects or events, or conventional expressions realising speech acts like greetings or toasts. Semiotically, the 'richness' of an item need not be inherent, but in the cultural significance *attributed* to it contextually, and this is where pronunciation can have its effect. For example, it is interesting that Trudgill and Hannah (1982: 30) mention *eisteddfod* and *llymru* (a porridge dish) as Welsh lexical items found in *English* discourse. And in Wales there is certainly a tradition of preserving Welsh-language-derived items, often anglicised phonetically and/or orthographically (see below). This can happen, even in the English of the anglicised south-east of Wales. Windsor Lewis lists variants of the oath *Duw* (God), including *jiw, jawch* and *jawl*, also *cariad* (darling), *bach* (small), *crach* and *crachach* (the elite), *didorath* (shiftless), *milgi* (a whippet) and *shwmai* (a greeting), and some other forms as occurring in the *Cymric* (i.e. non-Cardiff) spoken English of Glamorgan (Windsor Lewis 1990: 110). Despite varying degrees of anglicisation that are possible in producing these forms, many of them necessarily involve English speakers in *phonological* as well as lexical language-crossing, and it is a reasonable supposition that it is partly the phonological non-Englishness of many of the items that allows them to signify cultural Welshness. *Crachach* expresses a derogatory standpoint *vis-à-vis* 'refined' or 'posh' classes, but where the standpoint is necessarily culturally Welsh. Therefore the expression as a whole exudes ethnopolitical significance which 'posh' cannot precisely achieve. (Are the 'crachach' the English, or perhaps those in Wales who endorse or represent English influence?)

More specifically, I want to suggest that the perceptible richness of such forms (to some Welsh people and probably not to non-Welsh people) hinges on the *interaction* between their referential semantics and their phonetic semiosis. The sociolinguistic effect of an item like *bach*, translatable as 'small' (see above) but used, for example, as an endearment in addressing a child or a vulnerable intimate, can be very different from that of *love*, a near-equivalent from the English cultural experience. *Bach* can be a gesture within the cultural context of ingroup Welsh solidarity; it connotes a parochial closeness and a protective but not patronising intent within these confines. So, its most literal ideational sense 'small' is indeed central to the meaning of *bach* in this usage, but it is a Welsh smallness, redolent with imagery of maternalism and homeliness. It is not possible to

315

imagine the semiotic effect being achieved so fully, in Welsh or in English, without an appropriately Welsh phonological form. To put this punitively, if you cannot achieve the phonology you are unlikely to be able to invoke the ethnic symbolism; even if you can invoke the symbolism, you cannot legitimately employ it.

In an earlier analysis of the pronunciation of Welsh place-names in Cardiff (Coupland 1988: 40 ff.) I was interested to trace the extreme degree of phonological anglicisation that is common when Cardiffians pronounce the names of their own city districts and streets. For the most part, this was a straightforward descriptive exercise, though it did raise questions about ethnolinguistic identity in the capital city of Wales. Place-names are of course potentially *highly* rich points in any language, often through their etymologies as well as through the historical associations of places. In Wales, Welsh-language place-names are a Welsh cultural resource even to people who call themselves monolinguals (English speakers), and it is not surprising that the campaign for bilingual road-signs, public notices and official forms was fought and decisively won during the 1970s and 1980s despite a falling roll of Welsh speakers – now about half a million.

We could use Thomas's (1984) term 'the Welsh substrate' to refer to this sort of residual competence that many English speakers in most parts of Wales clearly show. In the Cardiff data, however, what is striking is the systematic annihilation of this potential for Welsh ethnolinguistic identi-fication through the vernacular anglicisation of 'Welsh' place-names. Realisations of *Cyncoed* (Welsh /kɪn kɔɪd/) as /kɪŋ kʊəd/, or *Heol-y-Berllan* (Welsh /heʊl ə bɛrɬan/) as /hiəl bəleɪn/, or *Pen-yr-heol* (Welsh /pɛn ər heʊl/) as /peni rɔɪəl/ are common (see Coupland 1988: 46). These pronunciation norms give Cardiff people a means of *not* engaging *at all* with Welsh-language phonology, and they certainly preclude cultural associa-tions that would have been available through the etymologies of these names.

One interesting side issue is that the broadcast media in Wales are involved in a tacit campaign of de-anglicisation of Welsh place-names through their preferred pronunciation norms. That is, even where a community has firmly and consensually adopted an anglicised version of its own name (examples would be *Beddau* (locally /beɪðə/] or *Pencoed* (locally /pɛn koːd/)), media versions resolutely follow pronunciation norms for 'Standard Welsh' (/pen kɔɪd/ and /beðaɪ/, respectively). The stakes in this conflict are alternative cultural formations, grossly 'Welsh-Welsh' versus 'Anglo-Welsh', though implicitly both camps recognise that there is a sociolinguistic rich point that defines the battleground.

The processes we are considering are not exclusive to ethnic or national identities. Many urban communities are able to express aspects of their distinctiveness, with a strong tinge of class loyalty superposed, through lexico-phonetic rich points. Local working-class Cardiff culture makes good

316

use of its stereotyped long /aː/ in the pronunciation of a range of culturally key expressions: *the Arms Park* (the Welsh rugby ground in the city), *dark* (a prized local dark beer) and of course the name *Cardiff* itself. We do not need to believe that these referents have *become* identifiable emblems of the city through their phonetic form, or that long /aː/ *achieved* its stereotypic meaning through association with these forms: but it is the conjunction of pronunciation and ideational reference that is culturally so potent.

Further instances are all around us. It is well known that long/short variability in the lexical set BATH (Wells 1982: 133ff.) corresponds with a rather fundamental set of social factors. In the English context, short /a/ is decidedly northern rather than southern (perceptually as well as distributionally) and, in the terms of most analysts, non-standard rather than standard. Wells says that 'the local accents of the north are ... flat-BATH accents' (p. 353). But the cultural force of this phonological distinction is most noticeable in conjunction with specific lexical items, producing expressions that are cultural mini-icons of northernness.

Within Wells' lexical set BATH, we find, for example, the items *daft, class, brass; nasty, aghast*; but for propriety, we could have found *bastard.* Subjectively, all of these are class-salient words. I once heard it said, though not in a north of England context, that an adversary was not only 'a /baːstəd/' but was 'a real /bastəd/'; the short /a/ was necessary to articulate true hostility towards a superior-acting type. It is difficult to locate a class context for the expression /daːft baːstəd/, though the RP-like /baːstəd/ form (alone) is associable with the 'standard' meaning of 'a parentless child'. On the other hand, /daft bastəd/ is eminently locatable as an ingroup working-class insult or a cross-class jibe. *Aghast* lacks credibility as an element of a working-class utterance, though with the long vowel it denotes and connotes easily enough. (Is it a pompous reaction by a character in a romantic thriller?) Of course, the term *class* itself, pronounced with either long or short vowel, internally marks its own class alignment; with the long vowel it is perhaps 'a comment about a social configuration not fully believed in any more', or perhaps an academicised notion; with the short vowel it is more readily a felt oppression. The two pronunciations of *brass* in their unmarked forms may differentiate two fairly independent referents, the metal and money. 'Where there's /mʌk/ there's /braːs/' is a self-denying aphorism; an RP pronunciation (as Agar would put it) shreds the puttying that fixes the expression as culturally rich.

At present, observations on the stylistics of pronunciation, like my own above, remain unsubstantiated. I would want to defend this position, since we have arguably overinvested in quantitative and purportedly objective studies of style in sociolinguistics. While quantification is required by survey designs for investigating the large-scale distribution of language forms, stylistic analysis can easily be asphyxiated by experimental controls. On the other hand, social-psychological research could very well be designed to take this line of study forward, systematically eliciting people's responses to ingroup and outgroup rich points. Critical studies could examine spoken and written representations of cultural distinctiveness and document appeals to rich points. Sociolinguistic studies might follow Preston's (1989) lead in 'perceptual dialectology' and explore lay perceptions of dialect differences and distributions, and record the terms in which people represent sociolinguistic differences inside and outside their own communities. Studies of spontaneous accent mimicry (as Preston again suggests) can make a serious contribution to our understanding of the forces that make up language stereotypes and allegiances. Few will disagree that *explanatory* studies must complement descriptively rigorous phonetics. And this in turn forces us to be more inventive in our studies of the 'social meaning' of pronunciation, and more open to interdisciplinary exchange.

NOTE

1 This paper is an elaboration of one section of a paper read at the fourth International Conference on Social Psychology and Language, Santa Barbara, California, August 1991: The Social Psychology of Language and Socio-linguistics' 'Big Questions'.

REFERENCES

Agar, M. (1991) 'The biculture in bilingual', *Language in Society* 20, 2: 167–82.
Bell, A. (1984) 'Language style as audience design', *Language in Society* 13, 2: 145–204.
Coupland, N. (1983) 'Patterns of encounter management: further arguments for discourse variables', *Language in Society* 12, 4: 459–76.
—— (1988) *Dialect in Use,* Cardiff: University of Wales Press.
Fishman, J. (1977) 'Language and ethnicity', in H. Giles (ed.), *Language, Ethnicity and Intergroup Relations,* London: Academic Press, pp. 15–57.
Giles, H and Coupland, N. (1991) *Language: Contexts and Consequences,* London: Open University Press.
Giles, H. and Powesland, P. (1975) *Speech Style and Social Evaluation,* London: Academic Press.
Giles, H., Bourhis, R. Y. and Taylor, D. M. (1977) 'Towards a theory of language in ethnic group relations', in H. Giles (ed.), *Language, Ethnicity and Intergroup Relations,* London: Academic Press, pp. 307–48.
Giles, H., Coupland, J. and Coupland, N. (eds) (1991) *Contexts of Accommodation: Developments in Applied Sociolinguistics,* Cambridge: Cambridge University Press.
Labov, W. (1966) *The Social Stratification of English in New York City,* Washington, DC: Center for Applied Linguistics.
Lavandera, B. R. (1978) 'Where does the sociolinguistic variable stop?', *Language in Society* 7, 2: 171–82.
Mees, I. (1990) 'Patterns of sociophonetic variation in the speech of Cardiff schoolchildren', in N. Coupland (ed., with A. R. Thomas), *English in Wales: Diversity, Conflict and Change* Clevedon: Multilingual Matters, pp. 167–94.
Milroy, L. (1987) *Observing and Analysing Natural Language,* Oxford: Basil Blackwell.

Preston, D. R. (1989) *Perceptual Dialectology: Nonlinguists' Views of Areal Linguistics*, Dordrecht: Foris.

Thomas, A. R. (1984) 'Welsh English', in P. Trudgill (ed.), *Language in the British Isles*, Cambridge: Cambridge University Press, pp. 178–94.

Trudgill, P. (1981) 'Linguistic accommodation: sociolinguistic observations on a sociopsychological theory', in C. Masek (ed.), *Papers from the Parasession on Language and Behavior*, Chicago Linguistics Society. Chicago: Chicago University Press.

—— (1986) *Dialects in Contact*, Oxford: Basil Blackwell.

Trudgill, P. and Hannah, J. (1982) *International English: A Guide to Varieties of Standard English*, London: Edward Arnold.

Wakelin, M. (1977) *English Dialects: An Introduction*, London: Athlone.

Weinreich, U. (1954) 'Is a structural dialectology possible?', *Word* 10: 388–400.

Wells, J. (1982) *Accents of English*, Vols 1, 2 and 3, Cambridge: Cambridge University Press.

Windsor Lewis, J. (1990) 'Syntax and lexis in Glamorgan English', in N. Coupland (ed., with A. R. Thomas) *English in Wales: Diversity, Conflict and Change*, Clevedon: Multilingual Matters, pp.109–20.

25

Spelling pronunciation and related matters in New Zealand English

Laurie Bauer
Victoria University of Wellington

O'Connor (1973: 145) defines spelling pronunciation as 'bringing pronunciation into line with the orthography'. Strang (1970: 33) explains why it is so much a nineteenth- and twentieth-century phenomenon: since the requirements of universal education in 1870, she says,

> we have been producing young people who through written material are exposed to a far wider range of experience than their familial background ... afforded. Reinforcing the tendencies which result is a general sense of the authority of written forms.

New Zealand English has developed entirely in this kind of environment, and consequently affords the kind of laboratory conditions in which spelling pronunciation has been able to flourish. I shall suggest below, however, that Strang's reasons, while valid in New Zealand, are not the only reasons which have led to the spread of spelling pronunciations here.

PRESCRIPTIVISM AND SPELLING PRONUNCIATION

What neither O'Connor nor Strang makes clear in the passages cited above (since it is not relevant to their general aims) is the way in which spelling pronunciation has become yet another target of prescriptivists. A good example is provided by the Fowlers' Preface to the first edition of *The Concise Oxford Dictionary*, (1911: vii), in which they say that 'warnings are freely given' against 'the undue influence of spelling'; their reason is enlightening: 'in view of certain ignorant or pedantic tendencies'.

Where New Zealand English is concerned, such normative influence is clearly felt in the work of Arnold Wall. Wall was Professor of English language and Literature at Canterbury University College in the University of New Zealand between 1898 and 1931, and a commentator on the state of the English Language in the colony. Although he does not use the term 'spelling pronunciation' (to judge from the *Oxford English Dictionary* it does not appear to have gained wide acceptance until the 1940s), the comments in Wall (1938) are, in a number of cases, clearly critical of what we should today call spelling pronunciations. Toponyms and personal names receive much attention in this respect, comments under the following entries being predictably anti-spelling: *Birmingham, Glamis, Greenwich, Heathcote, Holyrood, Inglis, Keswick, Malvern, Marlborough, Palma, Reading, Rolleston, Trentham, Wellesley, Westmoreland*. In the few of these that are New Zealand names, as well as British ones, the spelling pronunciation is now standard in New Zealand. Wall also carries the banner against spelling pronunciation in his discussion of a number of other words, *appreciation, bade, forehead, handkerchief, leaflet, nephew, quoit, vaudeville, voyage* and *Wednesday*. Some of these have been as much affected by the pronunciation which Wall deplores at Home (as he would have put it) as in New Zealand.

Less prescriptive comments on New Zealand English spelling pronunciations can also be found in the literature, for example in Bennett (1943: 71) and Bauer (1986: 253), but there too, names are particularly commented on.

SOME DATA FROM NEW ZEALAND ENGLISH *CA* 1990

In this section I shall present some spelling pronunciations from speakers of New Zealand English in the last few years. All the examples given come from the prestigious National Programme of Radio New Zealand, most of them from news broadcasts. I have not distinguished the status of the speaker (news-reader, public figure, member of the public), the sex of the speaker, nor the ethnicity of the speaker (Maori or *pakeha* – a *pakeha* is a Caucasian, a New Zealander of European descent), although clearly any of these or other variables might be relevant to a full study of the distribution of spelling pronunciations. Nor have I made distinctions between isolated pronunciations and widespread pronunciations (partly because it is difficult to tell how widespread some of these pronunciations are, partly because such pronunciations are, in any case, symptoms of a wider phenomenon). Furthermore, the data collection was not at all systematic. None the less, some patterns can be discerned.

First, there is considerable instability in the voicing of fricatives in medial or final position in New Zealand English. Unfortunately, it is not always clear to what extent this is a matter of spelling pronunciation, rather than a general tendency towards devoicing (which on some occasions is hypercorrected – in the traditional, not the Labovian, sense). A case like /eksɪbɪtəd/ for *exhibited* looks like spelling pronunciation, since the normal value for ‹x› is probably /ks/. But while it might be possible to argue that forms such as /prɪsent/ *present* (V), /pɒsɪtɪv/ *positive* and /presɪdənt/ *president* show ‹s› being pronounced /s/, the claim for this as a spelling pronunciation is severely weakened by the fact that ‹s› is also regularly pronounced /z/ in English. Examples of change in the other direction, such as /dɪzɪʒənz/ *decisions* or /pezɪmɪzm/ *pessimism*, suggest that spelling is not the overriding cause of such pronunciations. This conclusion is also borne out in the case of some examples which were not heard on the radio, and where it was possible to ask the speaker what was intended. The speaker who, on separate occasions, produced [rɪsʌlts] and [blaɪθli] said that these were /rɪzʌlts/ and /blaɪðli/ respectively. This makes it seem as if a process of fricative devoicing is at work here, rather than purely spelling pronunciation, although clearly there is some overlap.

Second, it is frequently the case in New Zealand English that a full vowel is used in place of what, in many other varieties, is a reduced vowel. This tendency was mentioned in Bauer (1986: 251) with particular reference to words which usually occur in weak forms. It also extends into less common words, where the full vowel provided is determined by the spelling. Examples are /bəʊtænɪkəl/ *botanical,* /estɪmeɪt/ *estimate* (N), /əʊbeɪ/ *obey,* /əʊfɪʃəli/ *officially,* /pleɪkeɪt/ *placate,* /serɪməʊni/ *ceremony,* /træpiːz/ *trapeze.*

As a special case of this type, there is the pronunciation which aims to retain morphophonemic transparency. That is, the pronunciation of the base of a complex word is retained as it would be if that base were pronounced in isolation, and ignoring any morphophonemic changes which take place in other varieties of English, both within and outside New Zealand. In most cases this is tantamount to a spelling pronunciation, although it does seem that spelling is not the primary motivation for such variants, as I shall argue below. In Bauer (1986: 251) I gave the example of /ekspleɪnətɔːri/ *explanatory.* Others relatively frequently heard retain the vowel /ɜː/: /dɪtɜːrəns/ *deterrence,* /əkɜːrəns/ *occurrence,* and /rɪkɜːrəns/ *recurrence.* Other examples include /eɪmiːreɪts/ *Emirates,* /eksplɔːrətri/ *exploratory,* /gləʊbjʊlə/ *globular,* /kənfaɪdənt/ *confidante* and possibly /ziːlɒts/ *zealots.*

The difficulty with terming all of these examples spelling pronunciations is that many of them do not, in fact, reflect the regular relationship between orthography and pronunciation in English. Given the ‹rr› in *occurrence,* there is no way it can have a regularly derived pronunciation /əkɜːrəns/. But there is a problem with this word: many educated speakers do not know how it is spelled, a single ‹r› being a common 'spelling mistake'. That being the case, there is a stronger link between the pronunciation and the actual orthography than might otherwise appear, though whether it is a spelling pronunciation or a pronunciation spelling is not clear. In other cases, which are apparently parallel, pronunciation spellings are so common as to verge on the normal. The spelling ‹pronounciation›, which reflects the very common pronunciation /prəʊnaʊnsieɪʃən/ is one such. In fact, I have even heard this from a member of the Broadcasting Standards Tribunal in a discussion of undesirable pronunciations in the media. This example suggests that morphophonemic transparency is the primary aim of such changes, and spelling pronunciations are an incidental by-product where they occur.

My next category of examples is made up of those words which show variation between /ʌ/ and /ɒ/ representing the letter ‹o›. Examples I have noted include /əkɒmpənid/ *accompanied*, /əkɒmplɪʃ/ *accomplish* (but see the note in the *Oxford English Dictionary* on this word), /kɒmpəs/ *compass* and /kɒndʒə/ *conjure*. Wall (1938) comments on /kɒmbæt/ *combat*, /kɒmreɪd/ *comrade* (surely lost causes, even by the 1930s), /kɒndjuːt/ *conduit*, /kɒnstəbəl/ *constable*, /kɒvənənt/ *covenant* but prescribes /kɒvənt gɑːdən/ *Covent Garden* and /kɒvəntri/ *Coventry*. It appears that the preceding /k/ is accidental in these examples, since I have heard /wɒriz/ *worries* (this is quite widespread), /wɒndəz/ *wonders* and /slɒvənli/ *slovenly*, and Wall (1938) also comments on /kənfrɒnt/ *confront*, though this form is not familiar to me. I have also heard /kʌnstənt/ *constant*, apparently as a hypercorrection.

Finally, I have a mixed category that depends largely on a confusion of long and short pronunciations for the same vowel letter. Examples are /dɪplɒməsi/ *diplomacy*, /aɪdəl/ *idyll*, /pæθɒs/ *pathos*, /pɒspəund/ *postponed*, /prəʊdʒuːs/ *produce* (N) and /sæŋgwaɪn/ *sanguine*.

All the examples I have cited are ones I have heard in the years 1989–92, but I have similar examples going back to 1979–80 in all these categories, frequently forms which can still be heard today: /ɪnveɪʃən/ *invasion*, /əʊblɪvɪən/ *oblivion*, /hævɒk/ *havoc*, /prestiːdʒəs/ *prestigious*, /æfədævɪt/ *affidavit*. Some of these may, of course, like my other examples, also be heard outside New Zealand. Indeed, the possibility can't be excluded that some of the examples I have cited are borrowings from other varieties of English: for instance, /træpiːz/, /prəʊdʒuːs/, /pleɪkeɪt/ and /serɪməʊni/ can all be heard in American English (Kenyon and Knott 1953).

DISCUSSION

The examples I have cited above should be sufficient to make the point that spelling pronunciation is not a unified phenomenon. What may super-ficially appear to be a spelling pronunciation may actually arise from any one of a number of underlying causes. Despite this, it does seem that spelling pronunciation is a force which must be taken into account in any discussion of the way in which New Zealand English is developing, since it has implications which go far beyond the obvious ones. I shall go on to consider these.

The cases leading to morphophonemic transparency and the confusion of long and short qualities for vowel letters appear to arise for the reasons outlined by Strang: the words concerned are met in writing not in speech and are pronounced (accurately or inaccurately) on the basis of the orthography. That the common correspondences between orthography and pronunciation are sometimes ignored in this process (as was the case with *occurrence* cited above) should not mask the fact that such pronunciations are based on orthography, though there may be a case for a new category here of spelling mispronunciations. Where full vowels in unstressed syllables are concerned, though, another explanation is possible.

In Bauer (1994) I comment that one result of this is that New Zealand English sounds more syllable-timed than, say, RP does. I also comment that so-called 'Maori English' is more syllable-timed than other varieties of New Zealand English. This might be expected, since Maori itself is mora-timed. The result is that we find the classic pattern of variationist studies, whereby an innovation is present to a more extreme degree in the language associated with the lower social or ethnic group. But while those in the low social and ethnic groups are generally the least educated members of the society, spelling pronunciation affects those with more than minimal education (since they have to know and want to use words which are outside 'the range of experience [of] their familial background'), and continues to affect those with much higher levels of education (a Ph.D. is no guarantee that you will never produce a spelling pronunciation). There is an apparent conflict here. The conflict is made all the more striking by the fact that the replacing of reduced vowels by full vowels is a fortition, not a lenition, and as such is the kind of process we would expect to find particularly in clear speech, speech which is oriented towards the need of the listener. This, like education beyond a legal minimum, is basically a middle-class phenomenon.

I should like to suggest a solution to this paradox based on the analysis of a similar New Zealand English phenomenon by Meyerhoff (1991). Meyerhoff considers the use of the tag question *eh* in the interviews collected for a social dialect survey of Porirua, a satellite city to Wellington (see Holmes *et al.* 1991). She found that *eh* was used most by Maori males, but was used more by *pakeha* females than by *pakeha* males, and suggests that *pakeha* females have been quick to adopt this feature because 'as a positive politeness marker, *eh* appeals to women's generally more affiliative goals in conversation'. In other words, we have a linguistic feature which fulfils two different goals simultaneously: for Maori males it signals solidarity, what Meyerhoff calls 'likeness' between interlocutors, based primarily on ethnicity; for *pakeha* females it signals politeness. The result is an increase in the use of *eh* coming from two different directions. The same may be true of the high rising terminal intonation pattern in New Zealand English (and possibly Australian English too). In one sense it typifies 'Maori English', yet it is stereotypically used more by *pakeha* females than by *pakeha* males. In the case of the use of full vowels for what were earlier reduced vowels, the phenomenon strengthens the tendency towards syllable-timing that comes from Maori, but simultaneously indicates education and concern for the listener. It can thus be seen both as a change from below and a change from above simultaneously. Although a detailed analysis of actual instances of the use of full vowels would be required in order to confirm this hypothesis, if this is what is happening, spelling pronunciations are bound to increase in the foreseeable future. In the long term this could have the desirable effect of making orthography less opaque to English speakers and reducing the need for spelling reform.

REFERENCES

Bauer, L. (1986) 'Notes on New Zealand English phonetics and phonology', *English Word-Wide* 7: 225–58.
—— (1994) 'English in New Zealand', in R. W. Burchfield (ed.), *The Cambridge History of the English Language*, Vol. 5, Cambridge: Cambridge University Press.
Bennett, J. A. W. (1943) 'English as it is spoken in New Zealand', *American Speech* 18: 81–95; repr. in W. S. Ramson (ed.), *English Transported*, Canberra: Australian National University Press, 1970, pp. 69–83.
Fowler, H. W. and Fowler, F. G. (1911) Preface, in *The Concise Oxford Dictionary of Current English*, Oxford: Clarendon Press; 8th impression, 1920.
Holmes, J., Bell, A. and Boyce, M. (1991) *Variation and Change in New Zealand English: A Social Dialect Investigation*, project report to the Social Sciences Committee of the Foundation for Research, Science and Technology, Wellington: Department of Linguistics, Victoria University.
Kenyon, J. S. and Knott, T. A. (1953) *A Pronouncing Dictionary of American English*, Springfield, MA: Merriam.
Meyerhoff, M. (1991) 'Sounds pretty ethnic, eh? – a pragmatic particle in Porirua speech', unpublished paper, Victoria University of Wellington.
O'Connor, J. D. (1973) *Phonetics*, Harmondsworth: Penguin.
Strang, B. M. H. (1970) *A History of English*, London: Methuen.
Wall, A. (1938) *New Zealand English: How It Should be Spoken*, Christchurch: Whitcombe & Tombs; 2nd revised and enlarged edn, 1941.

26

Quantifying English homophones and minimal pairs

John Higgins
University of Stirling

In *Phonetics* (1973: 251), J. D. O'Connor wrote:

> A language can tolerate quite a lot of homophones provided they do
> not get in each other's way, that is provided that they are not likely to
> occur in the same contexts. This may be a grammatical matter: if the
> homophones are different parts of speech they are not likely to turn
> up in the same place in a sentence. ... If they are the same part of
> speech, e.g. *site, sight; pear, pair* they can be tolerated unless they occur
> in the same area of meaning and in association with a similar set of
> other words. *Site* may be ambiguous in *It's a nice site*, though a wider
> context will usually make the choice plain. ... If homophones do
> interfere with each other the language may react either by getting rid
> of one and using other terms or by modifying one.[1]

One of the main justifications for ear-training exercises using minimal
pairs is that a failure to distinguish two phonemes will overload a learner's
language with a number of new and false homophones. But how many
constitute an overload? O'Connor himself says that we can tolerate 'quite
a lot' without suggesting a figure. Until recently the process of counting the
number of homophones in a language would have been unacceptably
tedious and there has been no attempt hitherto, as far as I know, to count
or list all the homophones of English or the single-word minimal pairs that
exist for any two English phonemes in contrast.

Like many tedious processes this is an obvious task for a computer,
though it could conceivably be done by manually sorting index cards. The
required input is a dictionary supplying a pronunciation for each entry and
capable of being resorted using the pronunciation field. Such a dictionary
exists and is readily accessible in the form of the wordlist derived from the
Oxford Advanced Learner's Dictionary of Current English (Hornby 1974)
deposited by Roger Mitton in the Oxford Text Archive. The original list
comprised 35,000 headwords. Mitton refers to having greatly extended the
list by making separate entries for inflected forms, and adding 2,500 proper

nouns consisting of common forenames, names of English towns with populations over 50,000, countries and nationalities, and 2,000 other words, mainly derived forms of existing entries, which he noted occurring in the Lancaster–Oslo–Bergen (LOB) corpus but not in the dictionary. The whole list is now 70,637 items. It can be freely downloaded from the Oxford Text Archive and used for educational purposes. It contains no definitions, but it has separate fields for spelling, pronunciation, syllable count, syntax tagging, a rarity tag and verb-pattern usage.

Pronunciation is given for each entry in the machine-readable phonetic transcription created by John Wells for the Alvey project.[2] The system uses upper-case letters and special symbols like the ampersand to augment the normal alphabet; thus T and D represent the dental fricatives and N the velar nasal, while t and d represent the alveolar plosives and n the alveolar nasal.

This paper describes a project by the present author and undergraduate students at Bristol University to derive lists of homophones and minimal pairs from this dictionary. The students were from several different countries, each working on recognised problem pairs for speakers from their home country. The program to identify minimal pairs was written in Microsoft Basic 7.1 using ISAM (indexed sequential-access method) extensions. The wordlist is first copied to an ISAM database and indexed on the pronunciation field. Any adjacent words with identical pronunciations have to be flagged. (These are either homophones or variant spellings of the same term.) To generate the minimal-pairs lists a second copy of the pronunciation field is added to the database. On each subsequent run two sounds are selected and both symbols are replaced with the same dummy character in the second pronunciation field. The whole list is now re-indexed on this new form of the pronunciation. All the additional pairs of homophones caused by the stripping can be identified and printed out. The program needs a fairly powerful microcomputer, since sorting long lists demands a great deal of the processor. Working with a 486 DX/25, I find each list takes about twenty minutes to generate. Given that there is usually a need for a good deal of manual editing, one list makes an evening's work.

The first product of the project was a list of RP homophones. This required manual editing of the list of words flagged as having the same pronunciation in order to eliminate those which seemed to be merely variant spellings, such as *maharaja/maharajah, realize/realise, czar/tsar,* and so on. There were a number of borderline cases, including those pairs distinguished only by capitalisation when used as a proper noun, such as *Jack/jack, China/china, Barking/barking, Art/art,* or *Welsh/welsh.* Do these meet the definition of homophone (same sound, different spelling, different meaning) when the spelling difference will be neutralised in sentence-initial position or in upper-case lettering? Even more marginal are women's names which are also flower names or abstract nouns, such as *Rose/rose* and *Prudence/prudence*. In the end I retained these but with misgivings.

The homophones so identified included one quintuple, *air Ayr e'er ere heir,* and eighteen quadruples:

ay aye eye I
ayes ays eyes i's
c's seas sees seize
cawed chord cord cored
ewe U yew you
ewes U's use yews
misses missies Mrs missus
o'er oar or ore
p's peas pease pees
pause paws pores pours
raise rase rays raze
right rite wright write
rights rites wrights writes
roes Rose rose rows
sew so soh sow
t tea tee ti
t's teas tease tees
Ware ware wear where

Not all of these cases involve four semantically distinct items rather than variant spellings. The *misses* etc. set, for instance, seems to involve only two sememes. In addition there were 104 sets of triples, of which the following is a selection:

adds ads adze
aisle isle I'll
braes braise brays
buy by bye
cent scent sent
Chile chilli chilly
cite sight site
cited sighted sited
coarse corse course
Czech check cheque
Di die dye
for fore four
frees freeze frieze
Hugh hew hue
knows noes nose

328

masseurs masseuse masseuses
meat meet mete
pair pare pear
Pole pole poll
pries prise prize
rains reigns reins
road rode rowed
their there they're
toad toed towed
vain vane vein
we'll weal wheel
whirled whorled world
yore your you're

Apart from *Chile* etc., *cited* etc. and *masseurs* etc., all the words involved in these higher multiple sets are monosyllables. This is what one might expect, as one is unlikely to find three or more words in a homophone set which belong to the same part of speech and can be inflected in the same way (*cite* etc. is the only case in this set of data) or three or more long words which are true homophones. Among the homophone pairs, of which there were 1,200, there were numerous polysyllables arising from inflecting the members of the pair and a few genuine polysyllabic homophones such as:

allowed aloud
bolder boulder
cereal serial
complement compliment
councillor counsellor
elicit illicit
fallacies phalluses
formally formerly
gorilla guerrilla
humerus humorous
literal littoral
mustard mustered
pervade purveyed
populace populous
principal principle
stationary stationery
summary summery
veracious voracious

The grand total of words in the homophone list was 2,814, though the accuracy suggested by that figure is spurious since it conceals numerous editorial decisions. Two categories of homophone seemed problematical and were listed separately. The first was loanwords and phrases from French in which a gender or number distinction is seen but not heard, such as *fiancé/fiancée, nouveau riche/nouveaux riches* or *coup d'état/coups d'état*; there were sixteen of these. The second category was compounds with *-man/-men* in which the singular/plural distinction has been neutralised. There were 115 of these, including *airman, bandsman, clergyman,* etc. The particular problem here was that a number of similar pairs showed up in the minimal-pair list for the HAD/HEAD distinction, such as *barman, bogeyman* and *businessman.* Comparing the electronic list with the paper edition of the dictionary, it seems that the handling of pronunciation alternatives in the wordlist is rather arbitrary, perhaps ignoring some of the principled decisions that went into the compilation of the paper edition.

As already mentioned, the process of creating minimal-pair lists involves stripping out selected characters in the pronunciation field (replacing them with a dummy character) and seeing what new homophone pairs are created by this process. Those words which have already shown up within sets of homophones cannot all be flagged out; if they were, then they would never appear as minimal pairs with other such words. For example, if *for/ fore/four* and *fur/fir* had all been flagged as existing homophones, then *for/ fur* could not show up as a minimal pair in a BOARD/BIRD list. Therefore there has to be one word out of each set left unflagged in order to allow it to pair with other words in the minimal-pair searches. Computers sort according to the ASCII code which places all upper-case letters ahead of all lower-case letters, so that *Czech* will be placed ahead of *check.* A consequence of this is that a minimal pair will sometimes include a proper name where there is a perfectly good common word available to complete the pair. If one notices this while editing, then one can make a change manually, but it is easy to miss these items.

The twenty vowel phonemes of RP provide in theory 190 possible contrasts. In practice very few of these constitute a pronunciation problem; who is likely to confuse *heed* with *hard*? Similarly the twenty-four consonant phonemes allow in theory 300 contrasts, once again including many which, like *fish* and *dish*, would never lead to a pronunciation problem. However, I hope eventually to produce lists for all the contrasts simply to make statistical comparisons and to see what this shows us about the structure of the language. In the limited amount of work done so far (eight minimal-pair lists and the homophone list), very large numeric differences have emerged. The largest minimal-pair set is LOCK/ROCK, with 1,182 words (591 pairs), and the smallest is THIGH/THY with just sixteen words (eight pairs). Among the vowels, both FEET/FIT and HAD/HEAD have yielded about 700 words, while PULL/POOL provided just forty words.

To estimate the importance of any pair for intelligibility and the consequent need to include it in remedial pronunciation work, it will be necessary to do several further things: first, to use a distinctive-feature matrix to measure the degree of difference between the sounds; second, to identify parts of speech within each pair of words so that one can judge how likely it is that the sounds would be misheard in context; and finally, to include some frequency information so that we can downgrade those everyday words which contrast only with archaic or technical terms. In addition we will need to take account of distributional variants: for vowel pairs we shall need to separate stressed and unstressed environments, and for consonants initial, medial, final and within-cluster exponents. It will be necessary to decide how to handle problems of juncture where there are non-phonemic differences, such as *overate/overrate* from the homophones list or *plating/plaything* from the TIN/THIN minimal-pair list. This is the work which will be undertaken by the students engaged in this project. However, none of these steps can begin until one has catalogued the pairs that exist in the word-stock.

In the appendix below are examples of the lists that have emerged so far. At the time of writing only nine lists have been generated, but it is hoped that preliminary versions of all the lists will exist by the time this paper is published. All the lists are being deposited in the archive of TESL-L at CUNY and at other sites as they are created, and may be freely downloaded by anybody with access to electronic mail on the Internet.

NOTES

1 An example of such modification is what has happened to the word *aural.* While English speakers at large treat this as a homophone of *oral,* linguists and applied linguists tend to make the first vowel into a diphthong to keep the two terms apart.
2 Mitton references a paper by John Wells which I have not seen, 'A standardised machine-readable phonetic notation', given at the IEEE conference, London 1986.

APPENDIX

1 FEET–FIT (628 words)

axes axes	beans bins	bleeps blips
bases basses	beat bit	breaches breeches
beach bitch	beaten bitten	bream brim
beached bitched	beater bitter	Caesars scissors
beaches bitches	beaters bitters	ceased cyst
beaching bitching	beef biff	ceases cissies
bead bid	beefed biffed	cervices services
beading bidding	beefing biffing	cheap chip
beads bids	beefs biffs	cheat chit
beaker bicker	bees biz	cheats chits
beakers bickers	bleats blitz	cheek chick
bean bin	bleep blip	cheeks chicks

cheeped chipped
  cheeping chipping
  cheeps chips
Chris crease
click clique
  clicks cliques
Colin colleen
creak crick
  creaked cricked
  creaking cricking
  creaks cricks
cynic scenic
  cynically scenically
deal dill
dean din
  deans dins
deed did
deem dim
  deemed dimmed
  deeming dimming
  deems dims
deep dip
  deeper dipper
deeps dips
defuse diffuse
dilettante dilettanti
e'en in
ease is
eat it
eats it's
eel ill
  eels ills
ellipsis ellipses
feast fist
  feasts fists
feat fit
  feats fits
feel fill
  feeling filling
  feelings fillings
  feels fills
fees fizz
field filled
fleet flit
  fleeting flitting
  fleets flits
forefeet forfeit
freely frilly
frees frizz
freezes frizzes
  freezing frizzing
gelatin gelatine

gene gin
  genes gins
glebe glib
greased grist
greed grid
green grin
  greens grins
greet grit
  greeted gritted
  greeting gritting
  greets grits
grip grippe
  grippes grips
gyp jeep
  gyps jeeps
he'd hid
he'll hill
he's his
heals hills
heap hip
  heaps hips
heat hit
  heater hitter
  heats hits
  heating hitting
keel kill
  keeled killed
  keeling killing
  keels kills
keen kin
keep kip
  keeper kipper
  keepers kippers
  keeping kipping
  keeps kips
keyed kid
knit neat
  knitter neater
lead lid
  leads lids
leafed lift
leak lick
  leaked licked
  leaking licking
  leaks licks
leap lip
  leaped lipped
  leaps lips
least list
leave live
  leaves lives
  leaving living

  leavings livings
lever liver
  levers livers
lied lit
litre litter
  litres litters
Liz leas
Lynn lean
mead mid
meal mill
  meals mills
measles mizzles
meat mitt
  meats mitts
Mick meek
Millie mealie
neap nip
  neaps nips
Neil nil
peace piss
peach pitch
  peached pitched
  peaches pitches
  peaching pitching
peak pick
  peaked picked
  peaking picking
  peaks picks
peal pill
  peals pills
peat pit
peeler pillar
  peelers pillars
peep pip
  peeping pipping
  peeped pipped
  peeps pips
penis pinnace
  penises pinnaces
pick pique
  picked piqued
  picking piquing
  picks piques
pieced pissed
  pieces pisses
  piecing pissing
pill peal
queen quin
  queens quins
reach rich
  reaches riches
read rid

reading ridding
ream rim
reap rip
   reaped ripped
   reaping ripping
   reaps rips
reason risen
recede reseed
   receded reseeded
   recedes reseeds
   receding reseeding
reef riff
   reefs riffs
reefed rift
reek rick
   reeks ricks
   reeked ricked
   reeking ricking
reel rill
   reels rills
remark re-mark
   remarks re-marks
   remarked re-marked
   remarking re-marking
Rheims rims
schemas skimmers
scheme skim
   schemed skimmed
   schemer skimmer
   schemes skims
   scheming skimming
Scyllas sealers
seals sills
seat sit
   seater sitter
   seats sits
   seating sitting
seek sick
   seeking sicking
   seeks sicks

sheen shin
sheep ship
sheet shit
   sheeting shitting
   sheets shits
Sid cede
skeet skit
   skeets skits
ski'd skid
sleek slick
   sleeker slicker
   sleekest slickest
   sleeks slicks
sleep slip
   sleeper slipper
   sleepers slippers
   sleeping slipping
   sleeps slips
   sleepy slippy
sleet slit
   sleeting slitting
   sleets slits
sneak snick
   sneaked snicked
   sneakers snickers
   sneaking snicking
   sneaks snicks
speak spick
steal still
   stealing stilling
   steals stills
   steeled stilled
   steely stilly
steeple stipple
   steeples stipples
streaked strict
teal till
teases tizzies
teats tits
teenier tinnier

teeniest tinniest
teeny tinny
teeter titter
   teetered tittered
   teetering tittering
   teeters titters
Tim team
treacle trickle
Turin tureen
'tween twin
tweet twit
   tweeted twitted
   tweeter twitter
   tweeters twitters
   tweeting twitting
V's viz
we'll will
weak wick
weaker wicker
weald willed
weals wills
wean win
   weaner winner
   weaning winning
weaned wind
weeks wicks
weeny whinny
weep whip
   weeping whipping
   weeps whips
wees whiz
wheat wit
wheeling willing
wheeze whiz
   wheezed whizzed
   wheezes whizzes
   wheezing whizzing
Winnie weeny

2 PULL–POOL (40 words)

bull buhl
could cooed
full fool
hood who'd
hooray hurray
looker lucre
look Luke

pull pool
   pulled pooled
   pulling pooling
   pulls pools
should shooed
skewers skuas
soot suit

sooted suited
sooting suiting
soots suits
stoep stoop
   stoeps stoops
wood wooed

JOHN HIGGINS

3 THIN–TIN (218 words)

Bart bath
Bert berth
boat both
Cath cat
clot cloth
cloths clots
dearth dirt
death debt
deaths debts
eater ether
faith fate
faiths fates
fort fourth
forts fourths
Gareth garret
girt girth
Goth got
groat growth
groats growths
hart hearth
harts hearths
hat hath
heart hearth
hearths hearts
heat heath
heats heaths
kit kith
maths mats
mitt myth
mitts myths
naught north
nothing nutting
oat oath
part path

Perth pert
pit pith
pithy pity
plating plaything
quote quoth
rate wraith
rates wraiths
rot wrath
Ruth root
saith set
sheath sheet
sooth suit
tank thank
tanked thanked
tanking thanking
tanks thanks
taught thought
tawny thorny
team theme
teams themes
teat teeth
tent tenth
tenths tents
term therm
terms therms
thaws tors
thick tic
thicker ticker
thicket ticket
thickets tickets
thigh tie
thighs ties
thinker tinker
thinkers tinkers

third turd
thirds turds
thong tong
thongs tongs
thorn torn
thought tort
thrall trawl
thralls trawls
thrash trash
thread tread
threading treading
threads treads
three tree
threes trees
threw true
thrice trice
thrill trill
thrilled trilled
thrilling trilling
thrills trills
throat troth
throve trove
thrust trust
thrusting trusting
thrusts trusts
thug tug
thugs tugs
tilt tilth
tilths tilts
toot tooth
wealth welt
wert worth
whit withe

4 THY–THIGH (16 words)

loath loathe
mouth mouth
wreath wreathe

sheath sheathe
sooth soothe
teeth teethe

thigh thy
with withe

REFERENCES

Hornby, A. S. (1974) *Oxford Advanced Learner's Dictionary of Current English*, 3rd edn, Oxford: Oxford University Press.
O'Connor, J. D. (1973) *Phonetics*, Harmondsworth: Penguin.

27

Consonant-associated resonance in three varieties of English

John Kelly
University of York

Speech articulations are complex things, even when conceptualised as 'postures': and articulatory chains or 'gestures' are more complex still. Descriptive orders in phonetics such as that presented by Pike (1943) are attempts to deal systematically with some of this phonetic complexity; but when operating as phonologists phoneticians have tended on the whole to ignore a large part of it in the attempt to produce phonologies that are word-based, segmental and, given these two, economical. Statements referring subsequently to phonetic properties refer to such properties as have been previously selected as phonologically relevant to segments – and what has been ignored is gone for ever. I want here to discuss the workings of some properties of English utterances which, if heeded at all, are deemed to be of little importance – at least in the great majority of approaches to English phonology. I shall suggest that, for all that, there are reasons for their being regarded as of interest from the phonological – and not just the phonetic – point of view. I use the term 'sound-complex' in this paper in place of the more usual 'sound' or 'speech-sound' for reasons that will, I hope, become self-evident.

In an earlier paper (Kelly 1989) I devote attention to some aspects of a phenomenon there called 'resonance' and exemplify it with observations on my own spoken English, complementing the discussion with instrumental (electropalatographic) records. This present paper will extend part of that discussion. It differs from the earlier paper in that it draws on material from other varieties of English as well as my own, and also in that the discussion here is based only on impressionistic observations. In the purely descriptive domain my aim is to show that the phenomenon at hand is of wide applicability in the description of English and, more importantly, that the detail of its operation differs from one variety to another; and my more theoretical aim has been stated at the end of the preceding paragraph.

The word 'resonance', like many others in phonetics and phonology, shows a range of use and meaning. I use it here in an auditory sense at one time well established in descriptive phonetic theory, particularly of the 'London' school, and one which has a long pedigree. Grant (1914: 33) uses it in exactly the way it is understood here. Writing of laterals (in Scots English), he says 'The *l* has a resonance akin to the vowel *i* and the dark variety approaches the acoustic effect of the vowel *u*.' At about the same period Boas (1911: 17) uses, as well as this term, the expression 'the vocalic tinge of consonants' to refer to the same thing, and proposes the useful notational device of raised and reduced vowel letters $^{a\,e\,i\,o\,u}$ following consonants to show it. Especially noteworthy in Boas's treatment is the sophistication of recognising five possible resonances and of applying this variable to all consonants. Other later writers to use the term 'resonance' in this sense are Jones (1957), who replicates Boas's notation, and Boyanus (1955). A related idea, but put now in corresponding articulatory terms, is there too in Armstrong (1933, 1934), Doke (1931) and Ward (1933), in such comments as '[Luganda] f and v are velarised, i.e. their articulation is accompanied by a simultaneous raising of the back of the tongue' (Armstrong 1933: 191). In later years Jones (1957), reverting to a term in the auditory domain, points out that German final [n] is typically 'clear', and Henderson (1966) mentions the 'darkness' of initial [f] and [t] in Thai. But these later statements all share what I would regard as limitations. First, the features concerned are usually treated as dichotomous: things are either 'clear' or they are 'dark', and a more extensive set of possibilities as envisaged by Boas is seldom recognised. Sovijärvi (in Kaiser 1955: 313) is an exception here when he says 'The lateral *l* [*sc.* in Finnish] is not so clear as in German, but not so dark as the variants found at the end of syllables in English' – and even here the comparisons being made are across languages rather than within them. Second, there is an implication that the sound-complexes involved include one or the other of these characteristics in *all* of their occurrences. Whether these are two valid comments or not is, of course, an empirical matter; but the English material discussed below leads me to treat them with, at the very least, caution.

As time went by the use of the word 'resonance' for this phenomenon seems to have died out, as the relative antiquity of these references shows. More recent writers on phonetic theory, such as Heffner (1960), O'Connor (1973) or Clark and Yallop (1990), prefer to restrict the term to the discussion of the physics of speech, whilst others, such as Catford (1988), avoid its use altogether. But for what is under discussion in this paper 'resonance' is a useful and apposite term – at least for provisional use – and it will be used without quotation marks in what follows. It is useful because it is a term which relates in a unified way to an auditory effect for which separate terms and notations have to be used in an articulatory description. Boyanus (1955), for instance, has different articulatory descriptions and diagrams for the Russian consonants that in articulatory terms he calls, sensibly, 'non-palatalised'; but from the auditory and phonological points of view, where it is the resonance that counts, they are all classed as 'dark'. A unified auditory label is all the more desirable for the 'overall' resonances, resonances, that is, of whole syllables or longer stretches, which will occupy us here, since these are multiply complex in articulatory terms. In what follows I shall use 'dark' and 'clear' as labels for relative auditory effects situated at opposite ends of a scale. Various articulatory concomitants have to be recognised; frontness of vowels and degrees of palatalisation of consonants are amongst those for 'clearness', for example, whilst for 'darkness' pharyngeal activities may have to be included along with those of the back of the tongue. As I concentrate in this paper on what is to be heard, I have avoided the use of conventional transcriptions in the IPA system, which is not designed to show resonance effects in any simple or systematic way.

An essentially segmental approach to the question of resonance, alluded to above, has to develop a strategy to deal with the fact that the borders of various components of sound-complexes are in reality *not* co-incident – one component may persist whilst others change. This – let us call it 'the extent phenomenon' – is occasionally noticed by some of our earlier observers. Armstrong (1933: 191) writes, again for Luganda, that 's and z are very "clear" before i and e'. She is already using the strategy, in that the frontness of these syllables is taken to be the frontness of [i] being shared by preceding [s] and [z]. For her what I have called 'the extent phenomenon' is being construed as 'the sharing phenomenon'. This is *prima facie* a good development, since extent is only an observation, whereas sharing is a process; and the introduction of processes into our phonologies may make them both more concise and more explanatory. But various oddities in the matter of 'sharing' are to be found in this literature. There is, for instance, no comment on the darkness of [f] and [v] to correspond to that for clearness in [s] and [z]; [f] and [v] appear not to be involved in 'sharing' in Luganda. But in Russian they are: Boyanus (1955) tells us that non-palatalisation associated with consonants extends beyond word boundaries, and cites such cases as [ɪvan ɨvanɪtʃ], in which the dark resonance of the nasal at the end of [ɪvan] is shared with the vowel following, to give here [ɨ] and not [i]. It is striking here that in each case it is the extent of a phonologically relevant feature that is remarked upon – frontness of front vowels in Luganda, velarisation of consonants in Russian – whereas the velarisation of consonants in Luganda, not a phonologically relevant feature in the given phonology of that language, attracts no such comment. This is all the more striking when one remembers that these were scholars whose phonetic training was of a high standard and who were able to demonstrate great phonetic acuity on certain occasions. My caveat above about the validity of this kind of statement being an empirical matter holds again – perhaps there actually is no extent of velarisation to be observed with intial [f] and [v] in Luganda. But another conclusion lies to hand –

that when dealing with matters of 'sharing' phoneticians dealt in an 'allophonic' mode, attending exclusively to the highly determinate 'spread' of one or other of the small, usually triadic, feature set already deemed phonologically important. It is not particularly surprising given the preoccupation of the time with the eradication of what was taken to be 'irrelevant detail' that phonological theory and its related literature has tended to deal with resonance by means of devices such as that of the allophone. Indeed, this is probably the main device that has been used; and we have seen above that there is reason to suspect that this device serves out rough justice to the phonetic material of utterances. As Henderson (1977: 259) wrote of a similarly eradicated area, phonatory quality, 'It is interesting that the very number and nature of the variables involved has enabled linguists by and large to dodge the issue by selecting one feature as "phonemic" and treating the rest as "redundant"'.

The actual use made of the concept of resonance in the phonetic literature is, then, extremely limited, subjected as it was to theoretical requirements; only those portions that could be subsumed under allophonic variation could be taken into account. Henderson's (1966) work referred to above is one case of an exception in that she was prepared to utilise the darkness feature of the two Thai initial consonants in a phonological statement – but she was a writer working in an approach that incorporated no allophone concept. The upshot of it all was that the introduction of this sharing process into phonology was not as illuminating or helpful as might have been anticipated, and researchers moved on from this phonological model to other things.

Textbooks frequently make the point, correctly, that articulatory events are phonetic complexes the parts of which are (a) in constant flux and (b) independent one of another. This being so, a large number of complexes can be recognised having quite a wide range of constituency; but very few of these are ever commented on. Boas, who, as we have seen, allows five resonances for, theoretically, all consonants, puts this variable to little use in his practice. And the tendency has been for observations on matters of resonance to have fallen more and more into disuse – so that for one recent writer resonance characteristics are to be usefully associated only with certain sound types. Jassem (1983: 211) holds that in some cases things such as clearness and darkness operate vacuously. Writing of laterals, he says:

> Apart from the apical ... contact, the rest of the tongue is free to adopt positions that are like those for vocoids. ... This is also true of allophones of /n/ and /m/. However, these variations, co-occurrent with nasal articulation, are not perceptible and therefore they do not result in separate allophones.

In Jassem's submission here (which nicely highlights the 'allophonic strategy') Jones could not have heard the German clear final [n] that he remarks on!

The notion of 'sharing' is captured too in the use of the (already long-established) term 'co-articulated' to describe one kind of allophone, as by Ladefoged (1971) and by Clark and Yallop (1990: 126) in their reminder to us that 'many [sc. allophones] are due to coarticulatory effects'. Instances, in addition to those above, are nasalisation of vowels adjacent to nasal consonants, and, for English, the dental varieties of apicals that occur before [θ] and [ð]. These observations serve to introduce a link between the ideas of 'co-articulation' and 'allophonic variation' that may be unfortunate in that it could both restrict and prejudice the study of the articulatory aspects of sound-complexes. Indeed, 'co-articulation' is still often presented as a 'two-segment' phenomenon, for all that Öhman (1965) shows how co-articulation effects associated with vocalic elements may not be confined to just an adjacent element and, more dramatically, Fowler (1984) has shown that the perception of a consonant at the end of a syllable is dependent on the syllable beginning.

There are, then, various limitations of allophone theory that make it less than entirely useful for handling resonance: first, there frequently appears to be an implicit assumption that these effects are automatic and predictable; second, the effects that are entertained as 'allophonic' are generally only those over two contiguous segments (where, for 'segments', 'phonemes' can usually be read). But neither of these conditions actually obtains. As Clark and Yallop also remind us, allophonic effects are often not what might be expected. Polish *sukienka* 'dress', for instance, like all words with *-nk-* in Polish, has [n] rather than [ŋ] (Schenker 1980); and the situation involving velar contoids and front vocoids in Hausa (Kelly 1991) is another case in point, as is the complex resonance situation associated with the vocoid [u] which is reported on for Guyanese Creole in Kelly and Local (1989). In one interesting case, exceptional for the earlier literature, Jones (1957) points out that English Vowels 3 and 4 (as in *bed, bad*) are retracted before final (i.e. 'dark') [l]. In this case the 'dark' quality of the accompanying velar or velarised articulations is shared; but this is itself an 'allophonic', contextual, feature, and not, in phonemic phonology, one of the defining features of /l/. Jones' interest in this and his mention of it arise out of the pedagogical intent of the book in which they are found, a work on the pronunciation of English; and the case would not be at all exceptional in the kind of work in phonology suggested in this paper. In the matter of extent, too, there has come to be a good deal of evidence reported in the literature, in both experimental and impressionistic studies, that such effects can in fact extend over more than two adjacent segments (e.g. Amerman and Daniloff 1977). More recent developments in phonology have taken note of and attempted to accommodate findings of this kind, though not as yet with complete success (see e.g. the comments in Keating 1990).

The work reported on in Kelly (1989) takes neither of the limitations given above as being necessities. Rather it sees resonance as a continuum and, unlike Jassem's work, for instance, allows for the association of significant resonance characteristics with *any* other articulatory event, so, for instance, with stops and fricatives. It recognises the long-domain manifestation of the phonetic effects associated with resonance and, focusing particular attention on the *independence* of the components of utterance, takes the co-occurrences of resonances and other articulatory events as both conventional and mutable. So, for instance, in Kelly and Local (1986) attention is drawn to the association of clearness and darkness with English [ɹ] and [l] being different for the varieties of the two writers. The difference attended to is of reversal of polarity, as it were; the one (south Lancashire) variety has, generally speaking (but not invariably), clear [ɹ] and dark [l], the other (Tyneside) vice versa. These associations are, then, not universal for English, but conventional. It is some of the conventions involved that will make up the matter of the remainder of this paper. In this preliminary work attention will be concentrated on the 'L'-element (see below) in the three varieties of English under examination; and it must be borne in mind that the findings are – given what has been said above – without prejudice for the resonance phenomena associated with any other consonantal element.

The material to be considered here is drawn from the speech of three young educated adult native speakers of English, one each from Epsom in Surrey, Haltwhistle in Northumberland and Stockport in Cheshire (henceforth E, H and S). These are the three 'varieties' of this paper's title. The H speaker was female, the other two male. The localities were chosen partly on the purely practical grounds that the speakers were available, all being students in the university; but there was a rational element in the choice: these three localities in particular were chosen because they are well separated and are distributed in such a way as to represent a substantial part of England. In addition, casual observations made on these speakers had suggested that resonance conditions lay differently for the three. Finally, the S speaker was chosen to provide a link with the earlier observations made on myself, as his English is virtually identical with my own. Work of a similar kind has also been carried out on other varieties of English spoken in England and on a Scottish variety, but this will not be reported on here in any great detail.

The methodology employed involved some preliminary informal listening to live utterances by the three speakers, after which each of them was recorded reading a list of some twenty specially devised sentences. For each speaker two recordings of the sentences were made, separated by a period of six months (in December 1985 and June 1986), and from these detailed transcriptions were made. These listenings and transcriptions are the source of the observations on which I base what follows.

For the three varieties under description here the associations corresponding to those above are in the structure -VLV* where 'L' is a general notation for [ɹ] and [l] and V* is a short non-prominent vowel

	Haltwhistle	Stockport	Epsom
[ɹ]	dark	clear	dark
[l]	clear	dark	clear

It will be noted that the arrangement for H is the same as that for Local's Tyneside variety, that of S the same as that for Kelly's south Lancashire. This is not surprising given the geographical proximity to each other of the places in each of these pairs; but it is only a small part of the picture, as can be seen from the fact that E has the same display here as H – for all that, Haltwhistle speakers do not sound like Epsom speakers.

A new dimension is added by the important observation that, though these resonances are crucially associated with 'L', their effects are auditorily perceptible over considerable stretches of utterance. For all three speakers the appropriate resonance was to be observed, for instance, over considerable portions of such utterances as

(1) ramp as against (2) lamp
(3) It's 'Terry as against (4) It's 'Telly

The *portions involved* may be different for the different varieties. In utterances (1) and (2) the two resonances can be heard for all three speakers throughout the LVN- part of the utterance (where N = nasal): but, whereas for E and S they extend quite distinctly into the hold and release of the final plosive, for H they do not. In the second pair (uttered with prominence, shown by ', at *Te-*) the resonance difference is to be perceived for all three speakers throughout the -VLV* portion of the utterance (see Kelly and Local 1986). Differences of resonance were also perceptible for E and S, but not for H, in the 'C- ([t]) of (3) and (4). They were, to the best of my judgement, not present for any speaker in the preceding non-prominent introducer *It's*. With regard to the overall effect of resonance in these utterances, then, there is no case in which all three varieties agree. E and S have the same extents, but different resonances; and E and H have the same (relative, i.e. phonological) resonances, but different extents. We might use simple diagrams to show how the extent of perceived resonance is disposed with regard to the remaining constituency of these utterances (represented as configurations of C(onsonant) and V(owel)). C and V are used here merely to simplify the presentation by generalising over various sets of the consonants and vowels of English.

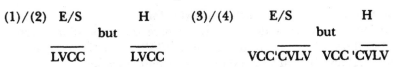

These extent diagrams must not be taken too literally. They are meant to give only an indication of the portions of utterances over which resonance effects could be perceived; they indicate areas where something, however vestigial, could be perceived as against areas where it could not. The auditory effects are generally at their least prominent towards the ends of the portions over which they occur.

Given these preliminary phonetic observations and the theoretical presuppositions set out above, a number of interesting enquiries are suggested:

1 as to the physical extent of the manifestation of resonances linked to 'L' as they occur
    a in different structures, and
    b under different conditions of accentuation (see Kelly 1989);
2 as to the interplay of the resonances of the two subcategories of 'L', [ɹ] and [l], when they are contiguous or in close proximity;
3 as to 1 and 2 in different varieties of English.

The answers to these enquiries should ideally provide the raw material for the elaboration of any theory of the workings and the role of resonances of these kinds in the phonological structure of English, i.e. of *how* they work and *what* they do. The study of these phenomena might be of very wide applicability, too, since other consonants than those subsumed under L may (and, on the strength of my own daily observations, do) have what I have elsewhere (Kelly 1989) called *conventional associations* with particular resonances. For instance, two of the present speakers, E and H, have slightly different resonances over portions of (5) and (6):

(5)   It was 'havoc   as against   (6)   It was 'haddock

utterance (6) being for each the clearer of the two, though the portions are different, being -VCVC for E and -VCV- for H. S seems to have no corresponding clear/dark opposition here.

At this stage the answer to none of the above questions is predictable; each is in the realm of investigation. My aim in this paper is to undertake some very small part of this investigation and thereby to go some little way towards demonstrating how unpredictable (and probably complex) the answers are going to be.

Returning to the English material under discussion we move to cases where, as specified at 1 above, two opposed L-resonances appear in close proximity as in, for instance:

(7)   Let 'Terry do it   (8)   Let 'Telly do it

Here the resonances respectively associated with the [ɹ] and [l] of *Terry* and *Telly* are perceptible in the final vowel of the two utterances for H, but not for E or S. The extent diagrams are:

H	E and S
LVC 'CVLV CV VC	LVC 'CVLV CV VC

In the case of the H speaker the resonance associated with [ɹ] (namely 'dark') was not perceptible in the lateral consonant of (7) above; for her the resonance difference between (7) and (8) begins at the first vowel. But in (7) for E and S the two initial laterals, and what follows, show resonance effects associated with the later L, being darker (than in *Telly*) for E, and clearer (than in *Telly*) for S. All of these observations begin to suggest that the matter of extent is not to be thought of as decided in any automatic or predictable way – an initial clear [l] does not, in one of our varieties of English (H), share, in (7), the darkness of the surrounding zone which we might say, in figurative language, to be under the dominance of the [ɹ] of *Terry*; but in variety (S) a dark [l] in the same circumstances *does* share clearness associated with the same source. It is to be noted in connection with this that all the vowels involved ([ɛ] [ɛ] [ɪ]) in the relevant portions (*Let Terry/Let Telly*) are 'front', and that the resonances are operating independently of that. Equally striking is the observation that the resonance obtains over the whole of the utterance from the first vowel on for H, but ceases after the third vowel for E and S. An analogous situation is provided by the utterances (9) and (10):

(9)   'Harry came over   (10)   'Sally came over

where for H darkness in (9) and clearness in (10) extend over the initial consonant of *came* but no further. The [k] of utterance (10) has for this speaker perceptibly fronter resonance than that of utterance (9). The front vowel of *came* has, as far as I can judge, the same phonetic quality in both cases for H, as does the whole of the utterance from that point on. The darkness associated with [ɹ] has no manifestation beyond the initial [k] of *came*. We might present this in an extent diagram as

'CVLV CVC VCV

In this same utterance both S and E share a situation different from H's. For them the integrating resonance embraces *Harry* and *Sally* only. The velar plosives are the same in each utterance for each of these two speakers (though not exactly the same articulation for S and E). The diagram here is (both utterances for both these speakers):

'CVLV CVC VCV

The next examples show different accentual arrangements, to meet the situation specified at 1(b) above:

(11)   'Terry 'read it   (12)   'Telly 'led it

The extent diagrams for all three speakers are similar, though not identical. They look like this

E and S   H

'CVLV 'LVC VC   'CVLV 'LVC VC

Here the overall resonance associated with utterance (11) is darker for both E and H within the limits indicated in the extent diagram, and that of utterance (12) clearer. It will be noted, though, that whilst these correlations are the same for E and H, the extent differs slightly for the two. E and S share their extent, but the polarity is reversed, so that the overall phonetic make-up in resonance terms is different for each variety in these utterances.

I have mentioned above the undesirability of viewing matters such as resonances, and their articulatory correlates, 'secondary articulations', as phonetically dichotomous; they are best treated, rather, as scales. Phonological categories, on the other hand, have to be taken as discrete. This can frequently mean that a *range* of phonetic elements has to be referred to one phonological category, and that what holds this range of elements together for referral might be its possession, as a set, of some property or other. This statement holds true of phonemic theory and is, I take it, unexceptionable – though it brings its difficulties in practice. But the approach here goes on to hold that a phonological property may be offset against some other property in a way that is, from the phonetic point of view, *relative*.

An example will make this clearer. For S the last two tokens of [l] in (13) are both clearer than the token at the beginning of the same utterance and than the single token in, for instance, (4) *It's 'Telly*.

(13)   Let 'Telly lead it

and the second of the two, that of *lead*, is slightly clearer than the first, that of *Telly*. This pattern is matched for this speaker by the impression in (11) of more clearness and of greater lip activity (probably rounding) in the second [ɹ] of the utterance, that of *read*, than in the first, that of *Terry*. For this speaker there is, in the matter of these articulatory components, a cumulative effect throughout these utterances. But the third and clearest of the three laterals in (13) is still not maximally clear, even given its 'front' surroundings. This, and the fact that both representatives of L take part in this build-up, means that even when each is at its clearest, before *read* and

344

lead respectively, there is still a resonance difference between them that can be appropriately labelled, from a phonological point of view, 'clear' versus 'dark'. Things then that are phonetically verging on the clear are assigned to the dark category phonologically, because there is still a systematic contrast at this point with a phonologically clear category. There seem to be comparable phonetic observations to be made for the E variety but not for H. The basic phonological distinction between one clear and one dark category remains parallel for all three varieties. In a similar way, though I have talked above of E and H having the 'same' resonances, that is clear [l] and dark [ɹ], this does not mean that the sounds involved, either at L or at other adjacent places in the 'portion', are the same, since what is clear and what is dark is a matter of relativity.

A last observation will throw into even greater relief the complexity of resonance relationships over utterances. It addresses the question presented at 1(a) above and will introduce the possibility of a close connection between various consonantal articulations (other than those associated with L) and degrees of resonance at points in the utterance other than that where that resonance is centred. In (14),

(14)   Let 'Corin do it

as pronounced by S there is a greater degree of clearness to be perceived at the initial CV- than in utterance (7). The initial [l] of (14) is, that is to say, clearer for S than the initial [l] of (7). This can only be put down to the presence in these items of a following velar rather than an alveolar occlusion, giving a different overall set of articulatory gestures for the relevant resonance to co-occur with.

What conclusions can be drawn from this survey of some of the resonance particulars in this handful of English utterances? Given the limitations imposed by the scope of the enquiry and by the rather artificial nature of the material under investigation, they can only be tentative. It seems reasonable, though, to suppose that at least part of the work done by resonances of this type has to do with holding a portion of an utterance together, whilst demarcating it from other portions. We might find 'resonance group' a useful working term in observation and discussion. It is in keeping with the idea of portions being held together that we should find one striking difference between varieties of English to be what happens at the margins of utterances. H, particularly, allows utterance margins to fall outside the specification for the resonance group, as in utterance pairs (1) and (2), (5) and (6), (11) and (12) above, where the final -C falls outside the resonance group, and in the pairs (7) and (8), (13) and (15):

(15)   Let 'Terry read it

where the initial C- is in the same case. For E and S the initial and final Cs of these utterances are in the resonance group.

When looking at these relationships we are immediately reminded that it was the H variety also that differed in its treatment of utterance pair (9) and (10), where there was once again a lack of agreement between borders of resonance group and word boundaries. There is a connection between these two situations in that the non-participation of an utterance-marginal C in a resonance group is the mirror-image, as it were, of its allying freely with another one, as in utterance pair (9) and (10). In addition, it is in H that we find one resonance group aligned with (7) and (8), as against the two resonance-groups for these utterances for E and S. The contrast here with the utterance pair (13) and (15) is not a direct one, as all speakers produced different accentual conditions for each of the two sets; and it may indeed be the accentual conditions that are involved in the different resonance 'piecings' found for E and S in (7) and (8). If this is the case the same 'piecing' arrangement appears not to hold for H. And, finally, H is the variety of English in which there appears to be no cumulation of dark or clear effect in resonance groups aligned to utterances such as those in the pair (13) and (14).

This bundle of differences in resonance effects seems to set off E and S against H, that is, the Southern and the Midlands varieties against the Northern; but this division is crossed by the other fundamental division of basic resonance distribution with regard to [l] and [ɹ], which allies H with E, two Eastern varieties. But this is what is to be expected; for any variety to be distinct (to *be* a 'variety') it must have its own unique combination of characteristics – one of which will be the organisation of its resonance systems. Some preliminary examinations of the Scots material (a speaker from Greenock) show that the resonance conditions are quite different from those in the material examined here, all varieties spoken in England. On the basis of the line taken here, that resonance arrangements are in part responsible for the fact that one variety sounds different from another, this finding is predictable. They were also much more marked, i.e. more readily appreciated by the ear. With regard to this second difference it is to be remembered that the three English speakers were educated adult persons who had spent some years away from their home environment and had been subjected, no doubt, to the various smoothing-out effects of speaking Standard English, which for many speakers include that of moving towards a less regionally marked version of their native variety. Speakers of Scots likewise move towards Standard Scots; but, since the phonetic and phonological differences between the varieties of England and those of Scotland are quite marked, such a move still leaves a lot of appreciably different phonetics.

The study of resonance effects is an area of some interest, and one that will need to be explored systematically and with great care – certainly more systematically than I have been able to do in this brief preliminary study. My paper is experimental and speculative and, over and above this, very limited in the range of its observation – no more than three speakers. Ideally, too, these observations would be complemented by a set of instrumental records. But I may have said enough to have borne out my earlier suggestion about the status of resonance as a variable component of sound-complexes that is both essentially independent of its co-variables and wide-ranging in its values.

At least two important things follow. First, having these properties, it should be available to play a role in the phonological functioning of language. As a possible instance, the matters discussed for S above with regard to (4) and (13) may be the phonetic manifestation of a phonological junction system ('close' junction perhaps?) which has no counterpart in H, or one which is manifested differently.

Second, a decision to treat resonance as having this role has, naturally, important repercussions for phonological statements of the kinds now in currency. To give an example: in H, in the *haddock/havoc* pair mentioned above, the second vowel of the first word is relative to the same vowel of the second, fronter and closer. This quality, which is associated with the clear resonance in H of medial [d] as opposed to the dark of medial [v], suggests that here we have the vowel of *bit.* The relationship between this variety of English and others (say S, which has *haddock* with [ə] in the second syllable) with regard to this word would be captured in most types of phonology in terms of the distribution of phonological elements. In these terms the vowels [ə] and [ɪ], two separate and essentially unrelated vocalic elements, are distributed differently in these two varieties of English *vis-à-vis* the final syllable of this word; and the difference is a phonological one. In the approach sketched in this paper, both of these non-prominent syllables have the same phonological vowel element; the difference would be a phonetic one, arising from a phonological statement of resonance associa-tion, which would have corresponding to it a statement of phonetic manifestation involving, amongst other things, extent. This description has the following advantages:

1   bringing together these two varieties of English phonologically:
2   possibly treating the vowel discussed here as one outcome of resonance-grouping alongside junctural effects that are another out-come of the same grouping;
3   binding intimately together the phonological categories of the lan-guage and the phonetic material that relates to them.

The result could be a 'several birds with one stone' analysis, in which a degree of congruence is combined with an economy of means.

There are also links between what is written here and the present preoccupation in the literature with co-articulation; but the links are not simple ones to make. There is in the present paper no definitive phonological statement. What I have tried to do, rather, is to draw attention

JOHN KELLY

to what may be a set of systematic differences amongst varieties of spoken
English and to speculate on their potential phonological relevance. Should
they actually be so relevant, they would take their place in an abstract
Firthian phonology of the sort envisaged here as terms in, say, a Resonance
System, and related to the phonetics of utterance by a statement of
exponency. The basic abstract elements involved might be ^{y} and ^{w},
associated with L, for the [ɹ] and [l] cases considered here. But in other
present-day models these few relatively simple observations on the phonetics of English might sit less comfortably, since most of these other
models are segmental in the way they see co-articulation as working.
Keating's (1992) simple introduction to the topic makes this clear. As a
result, degrees of, for instance, clearness, which I suspect to be at least
potentially important, are not easily recognised – segments either do have
this property or do not. In a similar case are clearness or darkness that are
associated with, say, the first part of an otherwise stable auditory complex,
but not the second – for example, an alveolar nasal in which a stable stretch
of nasality + alveolarity + voice corresponds to a resonance stretch in which
clear resonance moves into dark. And, of course, the situation mentioned
above where 'things that are verging on the clear are assigned to the dark
category phonologically' would be problematical too. So, although what I
write about is a category of co-articulation in a broad sense of that word, the
discussion here will not slot easily into the more general debate. There may
be cause for the debate to be widened.

REFERENCES

Amerman, J. D. and Daniloff, R. G. (1977) 'Aspects of lingual coarticulation',
    Journal of Phonetics 5, 107–13.
Armstrong, L. E. (1933) 'Luganda', in D. Westermann and I. C. Ward, *Practical
    Phonetics for Students of African Languages*, London: Kegan Paul, pp. 188–97.
—— (1934) 'The phonetic structure of Somali', *Mitteilungen des Seminars für
    orientalische Sprachen zu Berlin* 37: 116–61.
Boas, F. (1911) *Introduction to the Handbook of American Indian Languages*, repr. 1963,
    Washington: Georgetown University Press.
Boyanus, S. C. (1955) *Russian Pronunciation*, London: Lund Humphries.
Catford, J. C. (1988) *A Practical Introduction to Phonetics*, Oxford: Oxford University
    Press.
Clark, J. and Yallop, C. (1990) *An Introduction to Phonetics and Phonology*, Oxford:
    Blackwell.
Doke, C. (1931) *A Comparative Study in Shona Phonetics*, Witwatersrand: Witwa-
    tersrand University Press.
Fowler, C. A. (1984) 'Segmentation of coarticulated speech in perception',
    Perception and Psychophysics 4: 359–68.
Grant, W. (1914) *The Pronunciation of English in Scotland*, Cambridge: Cambridge
    University Press.
Heffner, R. M. S. (1960) *General Phonetics*, Madison: University of Wisconsin Press.
Henderson, E. J. A. (1966) 'Marginalia to Siamese phonetic studies', in D.

Abercrombie, D. B. Fry, P. A. D. MacCarthy, N. C. Scott and J. L. M. Trim (eds), *In Honour of Daniel Jones*, London: Longman, pp. 415–24.

—— (1977) 'The larynx and language: a missing dimension', *Phonetica* 34: 256–63.

Jassem, W. (1983) *The Phonology of Modern English*, Warsaw: Państwowe Wydawnictwo Naukowe.

Jones, D.(1957) *An Outline of English Phonetics*, Cambridge: Heffer.

Keating, P. A. (1990) 'The window model of coarticulation: articulatory evidence', in J. Kingston and M. E. Beckman (eds), *Papers in Laboratory Phonology 1*, Cambridge: Cambridge University Press, pp. 451–70.

—— (1992) 'Coarticulation', in *International Encyclopedia of Linguistics*, New York: Oxford University Press.

Kelly, J. (1989) 'On the phonological relevance of some "non-phonological" elements', *Magyar fonetikai füzetek* 21: 56–9.

—— (1991) 'Xhosa *isinkalakahliso* again', *York Papers in Linguistics* 16: 19–35.

Kelly, J. and Local, J. (1986) 'Long-domain resonance patterns in English', *Proceedings of the IEE Conference on Speech Input/Output*, London, pp. 304–8.

—— (1989) *Doing Phonology*, Manchester: Manchester University Press.

Ladefoged, P. (1971) *Preliminaries to Linguistic Phonetics*, Chicago: Chicago University Press.

O'Connor, J. D. (1973) *Phonetics*, Harmondsworth: Penguin.

Öhman, S.(1965) 'Coarticulation in VCV utterances', *Journal of the Acoustic Society of America* 38: 151–68.

Pike, K. L. (1943) *Phonetics*, Ann Arbor: University of Michigan Press.

Schenker, A. (1980) 'Polish', in A. Schenker and E. Stankiewicz, *The Slavic Literary Languages*, Columbus: Slavica, pp. 195–210.

Sovijärvi, A. A. I. (1957) 'The Finno-Ugrian languages', in L. Kaiser (ed.), *A Manual of Phonetics*, Amsterdam: North Holland, pp. 312–24.

Ward, I. C. (1933) *The Phonetic and Tonal Structure of Efik*, Cambridge: Heffer.

28

Syllabification and rhythm in non-segmental phonology

John Local
University of York

INTRODUCTION

In a paper entitled 'Vowel, consonant, and syllable – a phonological definition' O'Connor and Trim write: 'Generally, however, there is a choice of syllable division. In the word /ekstrə/, for instance, only the possibilities /elkstrə/and /ekstrlə/are excluded. The divisions /eklstrə/, /eksltrə/, /ekstlrə/ all yield a permitted final + a permitted initial combination' (1953/73: 257). They summarise their analysis of English syllable structure by suggesting that:

> the syllable may be defined as a minimal pattern of phoneme combination with a vowel unit as nucleus, preceded and followed by a consonant unit or permitted consonant combination. All longer sequences are to be analysed as a succession of syllables, the relative frequency of occurrence of various syllable-initial and syllable-final consonant combinations furnishing a basis for determining the point of syllable division.
>
> (O'Connor and Trim 1953/73: 259)

In this paper I describe an approach to syllable structure and syllabification in a non-segmental phonology based on Firthian prosodic principles (Firth 1948, 1957). I try to show that a version of the compositional principle described by O'Connor and Trim, if enhanced with syllable structure sharing, provides a central means of handling the representation and phonetic interpretation of rhythm in such a phonology. The approach to syllable structure and syllabification which I outline will, in contrast to O'Connor and Trim's, be situated within a strictly linguistic rather than a frequency/statistical framework and will show that the choice between different possible syllabic analyses of forms like *extra* is considerably more constrained than their account suggests.

Syllabification and rhythm in phonology have proved to be long-standing issues of contention (for concise reviews of the central issues see Fudge

1987 and Selkirk 1982). The principal cause of problems in these areas can be attributed to the adherence by researchers to representations which are based on concatenated strings of consonant and vowel segments and allocate those segments uniquely to a given syllable. In the approach sketched here, such string-based data structures are rejected in favour of hierarchically structured, non-segmental representations which admit structure sharing. In order to focus what I have to say, discussion will be confined to a consideration of disyllabic words. I will consider how syllables are joined together to create phonological representations for such words, and show how those representations can be given an explicit and consistent phonetic interpretation. In order to provide a validation measure for my arguments I will discuss these issues within the context of a non-segmental approach to speech synthesis the output of which will be used to instantiate the analyses I provide. I hope to show that the structures proposed provide for the felicitous expression and representation of relationships necessary to generate synthetic versions of polysyllabic utterances which faithfully mimic the rhythmic organisation of natural speech.

STRUCTURE AND TIMING IN NON-SEGMENTAL SYNTHESIS

Before considering the phonological and phonetic consequences of syllabification it is appropriate to discuss briefly the implementation of the non-segmental phonology which will be used as the test-bed for the analytic claims. For a number of years colleagues and myself at York have been engaged in constructing and testing a restrictive theory of phonology. Using insights and techniques from Unification grammar (Shieber 1986; Pollard and Sag 1987), we have developed a computational implementation of a formally accountable version of Firthian prosodic phonology. The speech generation system is called YorkTalk and is a Prolog-based computer program which creates synthesis parameter files from non-segmental phonological representations (Coleman 1992; Local 1992; Ogden 1992).[1] In accordance with Firthian prosodic principles, a strict distinction is made between phonological and phonetic representation. Phonological representations are constructed by means of phonotactic and metrical parsers and their representations are then given explicit phonetic interpretation. The non-segmental phonological representations constructed by the parsers are structured, labelled acyclical graphs, rather than the more usual strings of segment symbols. Figure 28.1, provides a simplified example of a such a graph which reflects our non-segmental analysis of generalised English monosyllables (Whitley 1955–69): [heavy/light] represents the structural distinction between syllables with branching rimes and/or branching codas and those with non-branching rimes and codas. The phonological units [back +/–] [round +/–] together

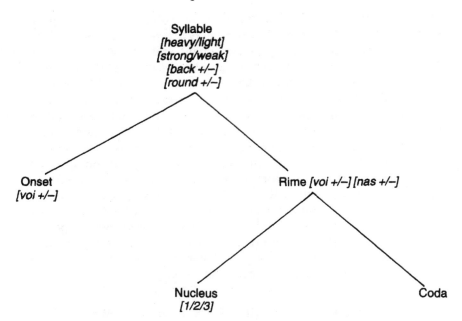

Figure 28.1 Partial phonological representation for generalised English monosyllables

represent the phonological syllable distinctions between forms such as *geese*
and *goose*; the features *[voi +/–]* represent the onset distinction between
forms such as *fan* and *van*, and at rime between forms such as *bat* and
bad. *[nas +/–]* represents the distinction between the rimes of forms such
as *bet* and *bent*; *[1/2/3]* represent terms in the 'height' contrastivity system.
One important feature of such graphs is that the constituents are
unordered and that phonological information is distributed over the
entire structure and not concentrated at the terminal nodes (see also
Vincent 1986; Goldsmith 1990: 123ff., though the phonological and
phonetic interpretation of the features in these treatments is different
from that proposed here). A graph of this kind makes it possible to
represent phonological contrastivity wherever it is needed in the structure
– at phrase domain, at word domain, at syllable domain, or at constituent
of syllable (onset, rime, etc.) for instance. These graphs, being abstract
relational structures, must be phonetically interpreted in order to generate
parameter files for synthesis.

In the YorkTalk model phonetic interpretation is of two kinds: temporal
and parametric. Temporal interpretation establishes timing relationships
which hold across the constituents of the graphs. Parametric interpretation
instantiates time-value parameter strips for any given piece of structure (any
feature or bundle of features at any particular node in the graph). These

parameters are ones which provide the information necessary to drive the Klatt cascade-parallel formant synthesiser (Klatt 1980). This parametric, rather than the cross parametric–segmental, approach is yet another respect in which YorkTalk adopts the tenets of Firthian prosodic phonology (Kelly and Local 1989).

The non-segmental representations allow in a straightforward fashion for a rather different approach to matters of timing and parameter instantiation than do typical distinguished unit or segment-sequence approaches (Chomsky and Halle 1968; Clements and Keyser 1983; Goldsmith 1990). The conventional approach to timing might be represented thus:

Concatenative timing of syllable constituents

Syllable		
Onset	Rime	
	Nucleus	Coda
C	V	C

By contrast, in the non-segmental approach proposed here, we treat the phonetic interpretation of some parts of structure as dependent on the phonetic interpretation of some other parts of structure (for instance, onsets on rimes). This leads us to propose a rather different view of the timing relationships thus:

Overlaying or 'co-catenative' timing of syllable constituents

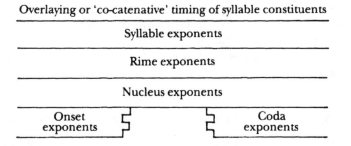

In this approach the temporal interpretation of the constituents of syllable structure is modelled so that they are not concatenated, but 'co-produced'. The implications of this are that the phonetic parameters which expone various parts of structure are not concatenated but 'overlaid' in time. The co-production model of speech (Firth 1948; Öhman 1966; Fowler 1980) accounts, amongst other things, in a straightforward way for the so-called co-articulatory effects observed between onsets and rimes.

JOHN LOCAL

BUILDING POLYSYLLABIC STRUCTURES

In YorkTalk, single-syllable structures of the kind pictured above in Figure 28.1, are defined straightforwardly by means of phonotactic phrase structure grammar of English (Coleman 1992). But what happens when we want to build larger structures such as disyllabic words? How are the syllable-timing relations and the parametric phonetic interpretation extended to handle multi-syllabic structures? The approach to phonology outlined here is declarative (non-derivational) and constrained by the principle of compositionality, which states that the 'meaning' of a complex expression (e.g. a syllable) is a function of the meanings of its parts and the rules whereby the parts are combined. Phonetic interpretation is compositional and consistent. This means that any feature, or bundle of features, at a particular place in a phonological representation is always interpreted in the same way. Therefore, it should not be necessary to invent novel, independent categories to deal with polysyllabic words. These larger structures should be composable from existing smaller ones. Thus, if intervocalic consonantal portions can be analysed as the concatenation of possible onsets and codas it should be possible to build polysyllabic words simply by concatenating well-formed monosyllabic structures. However, apparently not all combinations of codas and onsets are permitted: for instance, in non-compound words we do not find intervocalic consonantal portions such as -lfθfr-. Although monosyllables such as *twelfth*, with -lfθ at their ends exist, as do monosyllables such as *frown* with *fr-* at their beginnings these clusters do not seem to occur intervocalically in English. This 'exceptional' intervocalic portion is misleading, however, because there are no well-formed codas in English such as -lfθ. Such structures are to be treated as binary branching codas with an 'appendix', i.e. an additional piece of (morphological) structure which is immediately dominated by the word node.

SYLLABIFICATION AND AMBISYLLABICITY

With the machinery of a phonotactic parser of the kind referred to above, it is possible to determine structured representations for well-formed monosyllables. However, even with this resource, there are clearly a number of ways in which syllabification of words greater than a single syllable could be achieved. Syllabifications may, for instance, differ depending on whether we are dealing with a phonotactic structure with (a) a single intervocalic consonant, (b) more than one intervocalic consonant and/or (c) whether or not the first syllable has a phonologically long or short nucleus. To illustrate this consider possible syllabifications of the word *hammer* (the subscript numbers at the edges of the brackets indicate syllable affiliation; see Anderson and Jones 1974):

354

1   $[_1$ham $]_1$ $[_2$ ə$]_2$ (maximal coda);
2   $[_1$ha $]_1$ $[_2$ mə$]_2$ (maximal onset);
3   $[_1$ha $[_2$ m $]_1$ ə$]_2$ (maximal coda and maximal onset: ambisyllabicity).

Of these 1 is likely to be deemed the least problematic (Wells 1990), though there are problems with the interpretation of the phonetic parametric join of the intervocalic consonant and the final vocalic portion. Syllabification 2 is phonologically problematic in that it runs counter to the observation that stressed monosyllables with 'short' nuclei must be of closed syllable types in English (Lass 1987). The syllabification in 3 might also be deemed problematic in that it countenances what has been referred to as 'ambisyllabicity', wherein the intervocalic consonant is taken to be at one and the same time the coda of the first syllable and the onset of the second (see, for example, the critiques in Kahn 1976 and Selkirk 1982). However, as I demonstrate, this final syllabification is well motivated and provides the key representational mechanism within YorkTalk for ensuring that the phonetic interpretation of polysyllables is appropriate.

Anderson and Jones (1974) were perhaps the first phonologists to explore seriously the phonological and phonetic implications of allowing thoroughgoing ambisyllabicity. Largely as a consequence of their work, the concept has found widespread, if not universal, acceptance in phonological analyses. Many writers (Kahn 1976; Selkirk 1982; Wells 1990; Giegerich 1992) regard ambisyllabicity as essentially a resyllabifying process. In the approach sketched here ambisyllabicity is treated as an integral part of parsing well-formed syllables. Ambisyllabicity is a structural way of treating syllables in contact. An important part of its motivation derives from observations about the nature and variability to be found in portions of utterance. Ambisyllabic portions may have characteristics which differ from 'the same' phonological unit in initial or final position or which mix exponency characteristics of both initial and final position (e.g. the *tr* cluster in *petrol*, where the intervocalic closure portion may have coincident glottal closure (as in final position) while the postalveolar release portion may have the voicing, temporal and other characteristics associated with its co-occurrence (syllable-initially) with voiceless apicality and plosivity (Higginbottom 1964). However, the most compelling motivation for the recognition of ambisyllabicity is that it does away with the need to posit novel objects in the phonological analysis; it removes the need to formulate a phonotactic subgrammar specifically for word-internal clusters. (I am not claiming that *all* word-internal clusters can be accounted for by ambisyllabicity. We need to allow for concatenation as well as structure sharing. We require concatenation of codas and onsets in order to provide an appropriate representation for words such as *athlete* (where there is no permitted coda cluster θl or permitted onset cluster θl).)

Ambisyllabicity within the YorkTalk non-segmental model explicitly

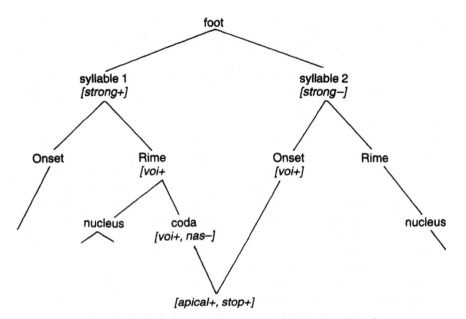

Figure 28.2 Partial graph representation of the word *hardy*

involves *structure sharing* rather than simply the sharing of some terminal (segmental) element(s) typical of segment-based approaches. This allows (a) the avoidance of syllabifications which would violate the short nucleus plus open syllable constraint; (b) the preservation of a thoroughgoing compositional account of the building of polysyllables; and (c) provides for appropriate phonetic interpretation of the medial consonantal portions of polysyllables (e.g. timing, resonance affiliations, aspiration, glottalisation as well as the appropriate exponents of syllable rhythm and quality).

As I indicated earlier, the phonological representations employed here are abstract graph structures. One important characteristic of unification-based formalisms which employ such structures is their ability to share structure. This is referred to as re-entrancy (Shieber 1986), and provides a formal means of handling structure sharing in ambisyllabicity. This is illustrated in Figure 28.2 by the partial representation of ambisyllabic voiceless plosivity in a word such as *hardy*.

RHYTHM IN ENGLISH DISYLLABIC FEET; SYLLABLE COMPRESSION

Up to this point in the discussion I have presented the description as if all the syllables under consideration had the same duration irrespective of whether they appeared in monosyllabic or polysyllabic structures and irrespective of their accented status. It is clear that this is not an adequate characterisation of the phonetics of naturally occurring speech. Temporal variability in the exponents of syllables is relatable to the different kinds of metrical structures in which they occur.

Abercrombie (1964) provides a seminal description of rhythmic-quantity configurations in disyllabic feet in English. His analysis is used as the basis for the computation of rhythmic-quantity relationships in YorkTalk. Abercrombie draws particular attention to two different kinds of rhythmic patterns which can be observed in initially accented disyllables. The first, which he labels 'short–long', is found in disyllabic structures where the first syllable can be analysed as 'light' (i.e. a Rime with a phonologically short nucleus and non-branching coda). The second kind of rhythmic patterning, 'equal–equal'– is found in disyllabic structures having a 'heavy' first syllable (i.e. a Rime with a phonologically short nucleus and branching coda or a phonologically long nucleus irrespective of coda structure). This analysis accounts for the observed differences in word pairs such as *windy* versus *whinny* and *filing* versus *filling*. Notice that the first pair of words allows us to see that the phonetic exponents of a syllable's strength and weight (which in large part determine its rhythmic relations) include many more features than traditional 'suprasegmentals' and are not simply local to that syllable. Not only are the durations of the final syllable different, but the final vocalic portions in these words have noticeably different qualities depending on whether the first syllable is light or heavy (Local 1990).

Clearly, if the exponents of ambisyllabic structures *are* compositionally constructed, we need to take account of the rhythmic and temporal characteristics of the syllables of which the Coda and Onset form part. The non-segmental structures in the YorkTalk model are parsed for syllable weight and strength, which makes it is possible to implement directly Abercrombie's analysis of syllable-quantity relations. A detailed account of how this is accomplished within the YorkTalk approach would be out of place here; however, we can briefly characterise how different syllables may be given different relative durations by reference to the notion of 'squish'. In the approach described here, rhythm is taken to be a property of metrical *feet*, not of strings of syllables or of terminal (segmental) elements (see the chart on p. 353). In YorkTalk, rhythmical effects such as those discussed above are primarily modelled by the temporal interpretation function 'squish', which is a unit of temporal compression. Squish is a means by which the system can determine the duration of any given kind of syllable in a given context. It depends on the structural piece in which the syllable occurs: for instance, its position in the metrical foot and its relationship to other syllables within a word or phrase. So, for example, in strong syllables (in disyllabic words), the value of the squish function depends, in part, on the weight of the syllable; in foot-final syllables, on the distribution of the [voice] feature in the Rime, and contents of the

Rime. The appropriate temporal interpretation of final weak syllables depends on having available information about the weight of the preceding syllable.

THE PHONETIC INTERPRETATION OF AMBISYLLABICITY

Having considered a range of structural motivations for ambisyllabicity and having provided a general outline of temporal phonetic interpretation, we can now move on to consider the phonetic interpretation of intervocalic consonantal portions. Given the partial graph representation in Figure 28.2 of the word *hardy*, how is the ambisyllabic piece of structure to be phonetically interpreted?

Although ambisyllabicity has been considered by a number of authors and a range of phonetic evidence adduced to support the construct, to date no one has been able to demonstrate empirically that it does indeed accomplish what it is intended to. The 'empirical demonstration' undertaken here employs the output of the YorkTalk speech generation system. The utility of speech synthesis for testing hypotheses about speech perception has long been recognised, and the pioneering work of the researchers at the Haskins Laboratories (see, for instance, many of the papers in Fry 1976) has demonstrated the power of such an approach. Typically, speech synthesis has been employed to test what we might regard as psycho-acoustic rather than strictly linguistic hypotheses. The YorkTalk synthesis system, however, was explicitly designed to test the feasibility of a computational implementation of Firthian prosodic phonology. This linguistic orientation allows it to be used to test specific claims concerning phonological or linguistic-phonetic analyses.

What then do we need to take into account in order to implement and test the phonetic interpretation of ambisyllabicity? One important aspect of ambisyllabic portions is that if the utterance is to sound natural the portion must be appropriately integrated with its flanking vocalic portions. In the non-segmental approach to phonetic interpretation employed in the YorkTalk model, co-articulation is not treated as some kind of 'automatic' phonetic effect which arises from some kind of automatic 'smearing' of features from 'neighbouring segments'; rather, it is treated as an integral part of the phonetic interpretation of the phonological domains Onset and Coda. For intervocalic consonantal portions to co-articulate with their flanking vocalic portions it is necessary to ensure that they are interpreted like codas with respect to the preceding portion, and like onsets with respect to the following portion. As well as providing them with the right acoustic percept, this allows for the use of the existing definition of the exponency function to generate intervocalic consonantal portions using appropriate parts of the parametric data for codas and appropriate parts for onsets, thus preserving strict compositionality in the phonetic interpretation.

However, it is not simply a matter of interpreting intervocalic consonants as a sequence of phonologically similar coda and onset, for the phonetic interpretation of non-ambisyllabic codas includes characteristics appropriate for a syllable-final release (for instance, particular kinds of durational, amplitude and resonance characteristics). It is necessary to ensure that the phonetic interpretation of the intervocalic consonant begins like a coda and ends like an onset (see Fujimura and Lovins 1982). In a segmental model implementation of such an interpretation is unlikely to be straightforward. In the non-segmental YorkTalk model, where the phonetic interpretation is parametric exponency of partial phonological structures, the process is tractable. Ambisyllabic plosivity represents a relatively simple case. A straightforward way of instantiating the parametric exponents of these ambisyllabic pieces of structure is to construct the relevant first-syllable parameters up to the coda closure, construct those for the second syllable from onset closure and then to overlay the parameters for the second syllable on those of the first at an appropriate point. (Compare the general use of parameter overlaying in the temporal and phonetic interpretation of syllables described earlier. See the chart on p. 353 above.) By doing this it is unnecessary to invent new parametric exponents and we can preserve the thoroughgoing compositional phonetic account of ambisyllabicity. The same general principle holds for other kinds of coda structures. Figure 28.3 gives a schematic representation of syllable overlaying.

The pair of spectrograms in Figure 28.4 illustrate the results of this parametric composition of ambisyllabic consonants. This figure shows two synthetic versions of the word *hardy* with different amounts of overlap (in

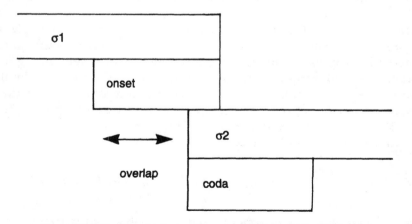

Figure 28.3 Temporal relations between two overlaid syllables

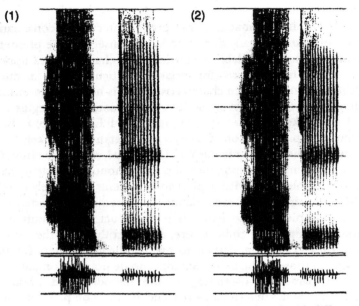

Figure 28.4 Spectrograms of two synthetic versions of *hardy* with different amounts of syllable overlap

the second version the amount of second-syllable overlaying is greater than in the first). There are a number of things to be noticed about the acoustic-phonetic interpretation of coda and onset parameters and their composition under ambisyllabicity (overlap). The parameters are not simply 'stuck together' or abutted somewhere in the middle, but show the consequences of their bidependence on Coda and Onset (for instance, the resonance affiliations of the coda and onset exponents are preserved). These spectrograms also demonstrate rather nicely that overlaying accomplishes more than the simple concatenation of coda and onset parameters. In the overlaying approach, the excitation parameters observed during the closure (e.g. low-frequency larynx pulsing) are not 'overwritten' by the onset closure, which, not being prevoiced, exhibits zero values for these parameters. This detail, which is required to model natural speech (Klatt 1975; Figure 3 in Lindsey *et al.* 1986), would be lost if a simple concatenative/abutting approach were employed.

MAXIMUM AMBISYLLABICITY AND APPROPRIACY OF PHONETIC INTERPRETATION

With intervocalic structures more complex than those illustrated up to this point there may be a number of ways of syllabifying even if we admit

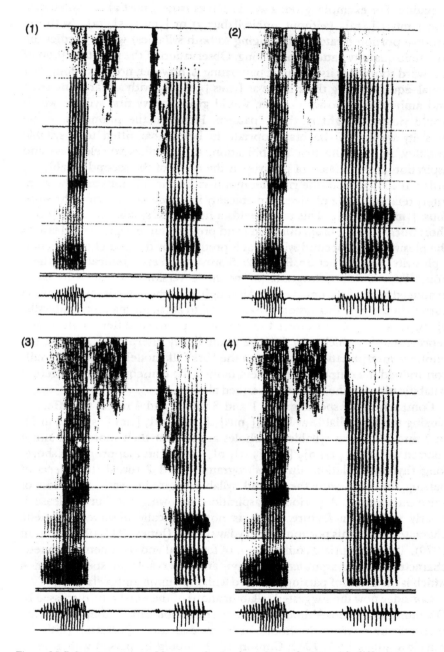

Figure 28.5 Spectrograms of four synthesised versions of *mister* with different parses

ambisyllabicity. However, the different syllabifications may make different predictions in terms of both temporal and parametric phonetic interpretation. For example, given a word such as *mister* ['mɪstˉə] the syllabification [₁mɪs]₁ [₂ tə]₂ (without ambisyllabicity) or [₁mɪ [₂ s]₁ tə]₂ (with the fricative portion treated as belonging to both syllables) would predict the rhythmic-quantity pattern short–long. Observation of the pronunciation of this word shows that its rhythmic patterning is, however, not short–long, but equal–equal. Parsing the syllable as [₁mɪs [₂ t]₁ ə]₂, with a branching coda and ambisyllabic plosive portion, would give a heavy first syllable which would yield the right rhythmic pattern. However, the phonetics of the plosivity would still be inappropriate in being that fitted to a syllable initiality. As with the first syllabification, this predicts voicelessness and aspiration at the release of plosivity in the onset of the second syllable. In order to achieve both the right temporal–rhythmic relations and the right interpretation of the plosivity and apicality it is necessary to parse the word thus: [₁mɪ [₂ st]₁ ə]₂. This parse yields a heavy first syllable consisting of a short nucleus and a branching coda and provides an unaspirated release of the plosivity in the second syllable as is predicted by the branching (friction + plosivity) onset structure. Figure 28.5 provides an exemplification of these possibilities with spectrograms of synthetic versions of the word *mister* produced with different parses. Although the phonotactic and metrical parsers in the YorkTalk system are designed to parse for maximal ambisyllabicity, it is possible to direct the system to produce different structural representations which may then be phonetically interpreted. Because the phonetic interpretation function on the YorkTalk model is compositionally constrained the output of the system models the consequences of different syllabifications in the manner described above.

Comparisons of spectrograms 1 and 3 with 2 and 4 reveal the effect of parsing the first syllable as light ([₁mɪs]₁ [₂ tə]₂ in 1, [₁mɪ [₂ s]₁ tə]₂ in 3). In 1 and 3 the first syllables as wholes are shorter than those in 2 and 4 (parsed as [₁mɪs [₂ t]₁ ə]₂ [₁mɪ [₂ st]₁ ə]₂) giving an inappropriate short–long rhythmic relationship. Spectrograms 1 and 2 reveal the effects of parsing the word with the second syllable beginning with a portion of voiceless plosivity. A period of aspiration, following the burst release is clearly visible – a feature which is not a typically observed phonetic characteristic of this portion in everyday speech (Jones 1947, 1963; Gimson 1970). The appropriate combination of temporal and parametric phonetic characteristics (unaspirated plosivity) are observable in spectrogram 4 which is the result of parsing the word with maximum ambisyllabicity.

Consider now the suggested syllabifications of the word *extra* discussed by O'Connor and Trim. Although the range of syllabifications they suggest are theoretically possible, it should be clear that *extra*, ['ɛʔkstɹə] (with [ɹ] voiceless: Jones 1947, 1963; Gimson 1970) should be parsed with a heavy first syllable in order to reflect the temporal (equal–equal) rhythmic

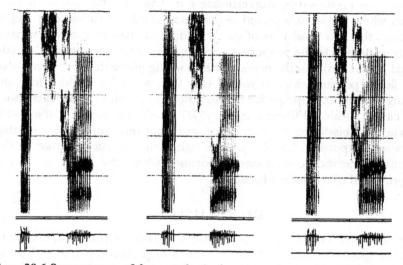

Figure 28.6 Spectrograms of three synthesised versions of *extra* with different parses

pattern observed in natural speech. Of the possible syllable divisions discussed by O'Connor and Trim (1953) only two '/eksltrə/, /ekstlrə/' yield a heavy first syllable (given a short nucleus, we require a branching coda for a heavy first syllable here). Of these, '/ekstlrə/' provides for an inappropriate interpretation of the beginning of the second syllable. The absolute initial syllabification of /r/ in the onset yields a voiced (rather than a voiceless) liquid portion. That this is so can be seen from the spectrograms in Figure 28.6. As with those in Figure 28.5, these synthetic versions were produced by the YorkTalk speech generation system employing compositional phonetic interpretation. They illustrate the results of parsing *extra*:

first as '/eklstrə/' $[_1 ek]_1 [_2 strə]_2$ with a light first syllable (notice this syllabification cannot be construed ambisyllabically as there is no possibility of a *ks* portion with *k* shared as coda + onset);

then as /ekstlrə/' $[_1 ekst]_1 [_2 rə]_2$ with a heavy first syllable (again with no ambisyllabicity. For the second syllable to begin with *r*, the only possible ambisyllabic parse would have to be *kstr* as coda with the *r* as exponent of the shared structure. Such a parse does not yield a possible coda + onset);

and finally as '/eksltrə/' $[_1 ek [_2 st]_1 rə]_2$ with maximal ambisyllabicity (with *st* as the shared piece of structure).

Comparison of the first of the spectrograms in Figure 28.6 with the other two again shows clearly the effect of parsing *extra* with a light first syllable.

The duration of the first syllable is short in comparison with the second syllable (as predicted by Abercrombie's analysis). In the second spectrogram, where the word is parsed as consisting of a heavy followed by a light syllable, the first syllable is of greater duration than in the first version (corresponding to the proportions appropriate for Abercrombie's 'equal-equal' quantities), but the parse results in wrong phonetic interpretation of the liquid portion which is voiced (the first, second and third formant configurations appropriate for the liquid portion, with periodic excitation, are clearly visible (O'Connor *et al.* 1957)). The third version (parsed with maximal ambisyllabicity), in contrast, gives not only appropriate syllable duration proportions but also just the right phonetic interpretation of the complex intervocalic consonantal portion (where the liquid portion is co-produced with voiceless friction).

CONCLUSION

One of the central problems which arise in any non-segmental approach to phonological statement and its phonetic interpretation is that of how to handle timing and rhythm. Surprisingly little work has addressed this issue. (But see the attempted reconstruction of timing in autosegmental phonology proposed in Bird and Klein 1990.) For instance, though there is a large body of work within the theory of metrical phonology which offers a number of interesting possibilities for the characterisation of rhythmic and associated effects (see Liberman and Prince 1977; Selkirk, 1986), the phonetic exponents of metrical representations have not received any serious consideration. This paper has attempted to address this lacuna by examining some aspects of timing and rhythm which arise from a consideration of word-syllabification and ambisyllabicity in a non-segmental phonology. I have presented a partial description of the phonological representation and phonetic interpretation of polysyllabic words in a non-segmental, declarative speech generation system and have tested the validity of the phonological claims by employing the non-segmental phonological theory to drive a laboratory speech synthesiser.

NOTE

1   The work on synthesis reported in this paper is supported by a grant from British Telecom Plc.

REFERENCES

Abercrombie, D. (1964) 'Syllable quantity and enclitics in English', in D. Abercrombie, D. B. Fry, P. A. D. MacCarthy, N. C. Scott and J. L. M. Trim (eds), *In Honour of Daniel Jones*, London: Longman Green, pp. 216–22.
Anderson, J. M. and Jones, C. (1974) 'Three theses concerning phonological

representation', *Journal of Linguistics* 10: 1–26.

Bird, S. and Klein, E. (1990) 'Phonological events', *Journal of Linguistics* 26: 35–56.

Chomsky, N. and Halle, M. (1968) *The Sound Pattern of English*, New York: Harper & Row.

Clements, G. N. and Keyser, S. J. (1983) *CV Phonology* (LI Monograph Series, No. 9), Cambridge, MA: MIT Press.

Coleman, J. (1992) ' "Synthesis-by-rule" without segments or rewrite-rules', in G. Bailly and C. Benoit (eds), *Talking Machines*, Amsterdam: North-Holland, Elsevier, pp. 43–60.

Firth, J. R. (1948) 'Sounds and Prosodies', *Transactions of the Philological Society*, 129–52.

—— (1957) 'A synopsis of linguistic theory', in *Studies in Linguistic Analysis* (Special Volume of the Philological Society), Oxford: Basil Blackwell, pp. 1–32.

Fowler, C. A. (1980) 'Coarticulation and theories of extrinsic timing', *Journal of Phonetics* 8: 113–33.

Fry, D. B. (1976) (ed.) *Acoustic Phonetics: A Course of Basic Readings*, Cambridge: Cambridge University Press.

Fudge, E. (1987) 'Branching structure within the syllable', *Journal of Linguistics* 23: 359–77.

Fujimura, O. and Lovins, J. B. (1982) *Syllables as Concatenative Phonetic Units*, Bloomington: Indiana University Linguistic Club (written in 1977).

Giegerich, H. J. (1992) *English Phonology*, Cambridge: Cambridge University Press.

Gimson, A. C. (1970) *An Introduction to the Pronunciation of English*, London: Edward Arnold.

Goldsmith, J. A. (1990) *Autosegmental and Metrical Phonology*, London: Basil Blackwell.

Higginbottom, E. (1964) 'Glottal reinforcement in English', *Transactions of the Philological Society*, 129–42.

Jones, D. (1947) *An Outline of English Phonetics*, 6th edn, Cambridge: Heffer.

—— (1963) *Everyman's English Pronouncing Dictionary*, 12th edn, London: J. M. Dent.

Kahn, D. (1976) *Syllable-based Generalizations in English Phonology*, Bloomington: Indiana University Linguistic Club.

Kelly, J. and Local, J. K. (1989) *Doing Phonology*, Manchester: Manchester University Press.

Klatt, D. H. (1975) 'Voice onset time, frication and aspiration in word-initial consonant clusters', *Journal of Speech and Hearing Research* 18: 686–706.

Klatt, D. H. (1980) 'Software for a cascade/parallel formant synthesiser', *Journal of the Acoustical Society of America* 67: 971–95.

Lass, R. (1987) *The Shape of English*, London: J. M. Dent.

Liberman, M. and Prince, A. S. (1977) 'On stress and linguistic rhythm', *Linguistic Inquiry* 8: 249–336.

Lindsey, G., Davies, P. and Fourcin, A. (1986) 'Laryngeal coarticulation effects in English VCV sequences', in *International Conference on Speech Input/Output; Techniques and Applications* (IEE Conference Publication No. 28), London: Institute of Electronic Engineers, pp. 99–103.

Local, J. K. (1990) 'Some rhythm, resonance and quality variations in urban Tyneside speech', in S. Ramsaran (ed.), *Studies in the Pronunciation of English: A Commemorative Volume in Honour of A. C. Gimson*, London: Routledge, pp. 286–92.

—— (1992) 'Modelling assimilation in a non-segmental, rule-free phonology', in D. J. Docherty and D. E. Ladd (eds), *Papers in Laboratory Phonology II*, Cambridge: Cambridge University Press, pp. 190–223.

O'Connor, J. D. and Trim, J. L. M. (1953) 'Vowel, consonant, and syllable – a phonological definition', *Word* 9, 2: 103–22; repr. in W. E. Jones and J. Laver (eds), *Phonetics in Linguistics: A Book of Readings*, London: Longman, 1973, pp. 240–61.

O'Connor, J. D. and Gerstman, L. J., Liberman, A. M., Delattre, P. C. and Cooper, F. S. (1957) 'Acoustic cues for the perception of initial /w, j, r, l/ in English', *Word* 13: 24–43; repr. in D. B. Fry (ed.), *Acoustic Phonetics*, Cambridge: Cambridge University Press, 1976, pp. 298–314.

Ogden, R. (1992) 'Parametric interpretation in YorkTalk', *York Papers in Linguistics* 16: 81–99.

Öhman, S. E. G. (1966) 'Coarticulation in VCV utterances: spectrographic measurements', *Journal of the Acoustical Society of America* 39: 151–68.

Pollard, C. and I. A. Sag (1987) *Information-based Syntax and Semantics*, Vol. I, *Fundamentals*, CSLI Lecture Notes 13, Stanford: Center for the Study of Language and Information.

Selkirk, E. (1982) 'The syllable', in H. van der Hulst and N. V. Smith (eds), *The Structure of Phonological Representations (Part II)*, Dordrecht: Foris, pp. 337–83.

—— (1986) *Phonology and Syntax: The Relation between Sound and Structure*, Cambridge, MA: MIT Press.

Sharp, A. (1960) 'Stress and Juncture in English', *Transactions of the Philological Society*, 104–35.

Shieber, S. M. (1986) *An Introduction to Unification-Based Approaches to Grammar* (CSLI Lecture Notes Series), Stanford: Centre for the Study of Language and Information.

Vincent, N. (1986) 'Constituency and Syllable Structure', in J. Durand (ed.), *Dependency and Non-Linear Phonology*, London: Croom Helm, pp. 305–19.

Wells, J. C. (1990) 'Syllabification and allophony', in S. Ramsaran (ed), *Studies in the Pronunciation of English: A Commemorative Volume in Honour of A. C. Gimson*, London: Routledge, pp. 76–86.

Whitley, E. (1955–69) Unpublished lecture notes on English phonology, York Prosodic Archive, Department of Language and Linguistic Science, University of York.

29

The vowels of Scottish English – formants and features

J. Derrick McClure
Aberdeen University

The fundamental fact which gives rise to most of the characteristic features of the vowel system of Scottish Standard English (SSE: the initials do not stand for 'Standard Scottish English') is the radical modification, approaching complete loss, of the common Germanic system of long and short vowels which affected Scots at an early period. This has had results which are readily visible in modern Scots dialects (for the most complete account to date see Aitken 1981), and SSE has been notably affected by this as well as by other aspects of its Scots substratum. It is not the purpose of the present article to examine the respective contributions of Scots and the London–Oxford–Cambridge-accented English of the eighteenth century to the form, at first a hybrid but shortly acquiring its present status as a fully autonomous dialect, now referred to as SSE (see Hewitt 1987 for an account of the historical and cultural background to the linguistic change)[1] nor to elucidate the complex issue of the manner in which Aitken's Law is manifest in present-day SSE:[2] in what follows the existence of a readily identifiable and recognisable Scottish accent will be taken as 'given', and the results of an instrumental examination of the monophthongs of a number of SSE speakers will be presented and discussed.

For detailed descriptions of the phonetics and phonology of SSE, see Abercrombie 1979 and Wells 1982 (Vol. 2). Assumed here is a system of monophthongs consisting of the 'basic' inventory of /i/, /ɪ/, /e/, /ɛ/, /a/, /ʌ/, /ɔ/, /o/, /u/; with a theoretical maximum of four possible additions. Three of these consist of distinctions corresponding to those heard in such words as *Sam–psalm, cot–caught, pull–pool* in some non-Scottish accents. A definite hierarchical order can be seen to govern the appearance of these distinctions: a *Sam–psalm* contrast is not uncommon, *cot–caught* much less frequent and only found in accents which also have the contrast in the low vowels, *pull–pool* very rare, always accompanied by the other two contrasts, and normally found only in accents which show marked features of anglicisation (e.g. diphthongisation of /e/ and /o/, weakening or loss of postvocalic /r/) – accents, that is, which are not to be regarded as exemplifying the phonetic/phonological system of SSE. The fourth possible addition is of another member /ɛ/, typically represented by a half-open front-central vowel and exemplified in such words as *never, clever, earth, shepherd*.[3] It will be observed that whereas the other three possible additions represent reversions in SSE to an older and more general feature of the common English vowel system, this last represents an innovation arising within the Scottish system and highly distinctive to it. (It was stated a few lines back that the additions totalled a theoretical maximum of four. The qualification is because the author has never observed a Scottish speaker in whose system /ɛ/ co-exists with all three of the other contrasts; nor, since the successive addition of *Sam–psalm, cot–caught* and *pull–pool* distinctions makes the accent approximate more to an RP-type English model whereas /ɛ/ is markedly Scottish, would such a combination seem intuitively likely.)

A group of eleven male speakers, including the investigator, made recordings of a list consisting of the following words: *beat, bit, bait, bet, bat, but, cot, boat, boot.* If preliminary questioning by the investigator revealed that any informant had an /ɛ/ or made a *Sam–psalm* or a *cot–caught* distinction, the list was augmented with the words *breadth, psalm, caught.* No informant made a distinction of the *pull–pool* type. All the speakers at the time the recordings were made were members of staff or students in the English Department at Aberdeen University. Spectrograms were then made of the recorded utterances of seven of the informants, on the apparatus in the Phonetics Laboratory at Edinburgh University or the Marine Research Institute in Torry, Aberdeen, with the kind co-operation of the technical staff at those institutions. (The seven recordings chosen were judged by the investigator to provide the clearest examples in the corpus of the distinctive systems represented.) Figures for the first three formants of the vowels as pronounced by those seven speakers are now presented.

Informant 1: born Kilmarnock, Ayrshire; parents Kilmarnock; all primary and secondary education at Ayrshire schools.

Basic system

/i/	/ɪ/	/e/	/ɛ/	/a/	/ʌ/
250	375	300	500	700	500
1900	1750	2100	1850	1200	1000
2800	2325	2625	2500	2650	2500

/ɔ/	/o/	/u/
500	350	400
750	700	1125
2300	2150	2000

368

Informant 2: born Argyll, parents Perthshire; primary and secondary education Argyll and Dumbarton.

Basic system

/i/	/ɪ/	/e/	/ɛ/	/a/	/ʌ/
250	375	400	500	700	650
2200	2000	2000	1900	1600	1000
2750	2500	2700	2500	2500	2500

/ɔ/	/o/	/u/
450	400	250
800	1000	1100
2600	2100	1800

Informant 3: born Ayr, parents Ayr and Stirling; primary and secondary education Ayr.

Basic system + /E/

/i/	/ɪ/	/e/	/ɛ/	/E/	/a/	/ʌ/
350	400	400	500	500	650	700
2500	1850	2325	2050	1750	1450	1450
3150	2550	2700	2550	2550	2600	2300

/ɔ/	/o/	/u/
600	450	500
1100	850	1050
2250	2250	2100

Informant 4: born Thurso (Caithness), parents Glasgow; primary and secondary education Thurso and Oban.

Basic system + /E/

/i/	/ɪ/	/e/	/ɛ/	/E/	/a/	/ʌ/
300	375	400	650	500	750	600
2500	1850	2250	1800	1550	1300	1000
3300	2500	3300	2500	2400	2600	2700

/ɔ/	/o/	/u/
300	250	300
800	600	1200
2400	2300	2000

Informant 5: born Turriff, Aberdeenshire, parents Turriff; primary and secondary education Turriff.

Basic system + /ɛ/

/i/	/ɪ/	/e/	/ɛ/	/ɛ/	/a/	/ʌ/
300	375	375	450	500	600	500
2300	1750	1900	1700	1625	1350	1150
3200	2500	2375	2400	2200	2200	2200

/ɔ/	/o/	/u/
450	375	300
1000	750	900
2250	2300	2200

Informant 6: born Glasgow, parents Glasgow and Newcastle; primary and secondary education at a Glasgow academy serving a largely professional-class area.

Basic system + /aː/ and /ɔː/

/i/	/ɪ/	/e/	/ɛ/	/a/	/aː/	/ʌ/
325	450	375	500	675	600	600
1850	1650	1750	1700	1375	1000	1100
2500	2375	2400	2350	2200	2400	2400

/ɔ/	/ɔː/	/o/	/u/
500	500	400	375
900	900	750	1100
2250	2250	2000	1800

Informant 7: born Lincoln but family moved to Paisley before informant's first birthday; parents Clarkston (Glasgow) and Paisley; early primary education at an English school in Singapore, later primary education Paisley, secondary education Aberdeen.

Basic system + /ɛ/, /aː/ and /ɔː/

/i/	/ɪ/	/e/	/ɛ/	/ɛ/	/a/	/aː/
250	350	300	500	600	750	800
2100	1700	2100	1750	1700	1350	1250
2850	2375	2600	2500	2350	2550	2550

/ʌ/	/ɔ/	/ɔː/	/o/	/u/
650	450	450	300	250
1150	850	850	750	1200
2550	2375	2375	2250	2000

Immediately obvious from these figures is that for the two informants who distinguished between *cot* and *caught* the difference is not one of vowel quality. The formant pattern as revealed by the spectrograms is virtually identical for the two words. A duration difference, however, is clearly visible: the actual length in centiseconds cannot be measured from the spectrograms, but the ratio of the length of the vowel in *cot* to that in *caught* is approximately 5:7 for informant 6, 5:9 for informant 7. Both informants show a quality difference for /a/ and /aː/; but a duration difference is also conspicuously present: the length ratio in this case is 7:10 for informant 6, 2:3 for informant 7. It is observable that informant 6's /aː/ and his /ʌ/ are very similar acoustically: the length ratio for the two vowels on his spectrograms is 5:2. Since /ɛ/ has not arisen through any re-emergence of an older length distinction but for other reasons, it is to be expected that this vowel would be clearly distinguished acoustically from all other vowels by speakers whose systems contain it; and this is indeed seen to be true of all informants.

The numerous and striking variations in acoustic quality shown in the various informants' realisations of the systemic items will not be discussed in detail. In many cases they are readily associated with regional accents: informants 1 and 2, for example, in whose speech phonemes comprising the same inventory show very considerable differences both in absolute realisation and in relative positioning (so to speak) in the phonetic space, have respectively a North Ayrshire and a West Highland accent, unmistakably different to any ear. The presence in an individual's speech of some or others of the additional items to the basic system, incidentally, cannot be predicted on a regional basis: informants 3, 4 and 5 were born and received at least their primary education in parts of Scotland about as mutually remote as any in the country, and their accents, on the phonetic level, are readily distinguishable. The remainder of the article will embody an attempt, on the basis of the spectrographic data, to devise a distinctive feature system appropriate for SSE.

Figures 29.1 to 29.7 show, for the various speakers' vowels, the first formant plotted against the difference between the first and second formants (cf. Ladefoged 1976). Despite obvious dissimilarities in detail, some general patterns emerge. Considering first the universal feature [back],[4] it is observable that in four cases out of the seven /u/ is further 'forward' than /a/, confirming the often-observed fact that /u/ in Scottish accents is typically realised by a vowel far advanced of Cardinal [u] and often approaching a central or even a front rounded value. This justifies the assigning of the feature [+back] to /a/, and therefore the separation of the vowels into a [+back] group consisting of /a/ /ʌ/ /ɔ/ /o/ /u/ and if present the phonemically long vowels of *psalm* and *caught*, and a [−back] group including all the others. The potentially multi-valued feature [high] presents a less simple picture. Though predictably the vowels on each informant's

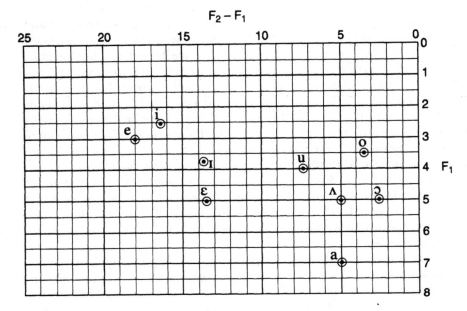

Figure 29.1 Informant 1

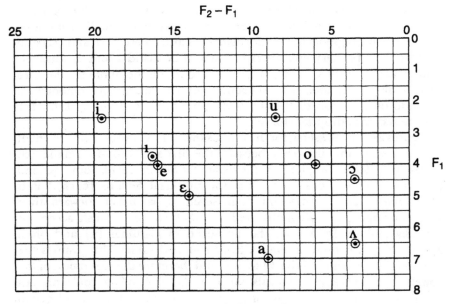

Figure 29.2 Informant 2

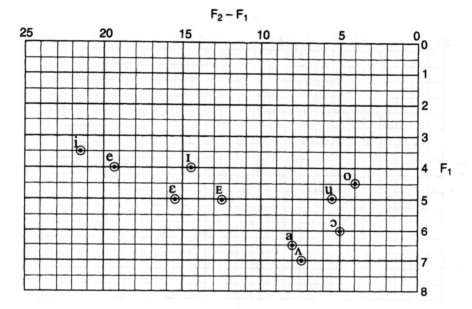

Figure 29.3 Informant 3

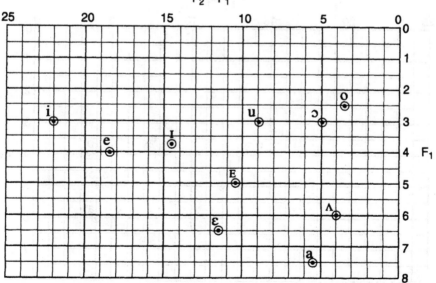

Figure 29.4 Informant 4

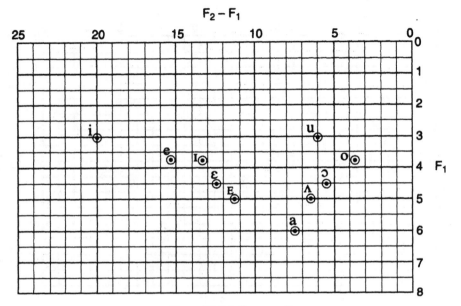

Figure 29.5 Informant 5

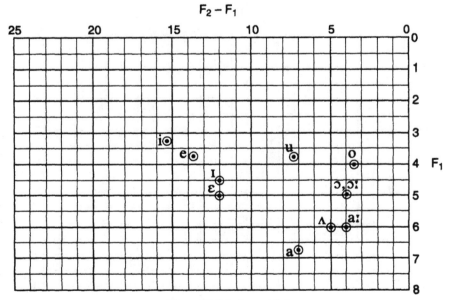

Figure 29.6 Informant 6

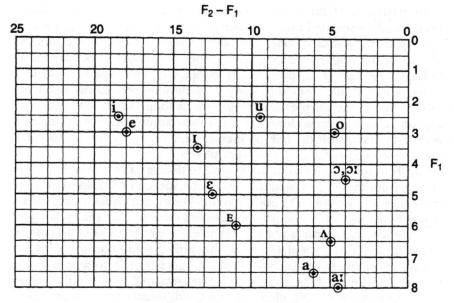

Figure 29.7 Informant 7

chart show anything from five to nine degrees of actual height (equating 'height' with the inverse frequency of formant 1), informants 2, 3 and perhaps 5 show a pattern in the [−back] vowels which suggests that three degrees of height are sufficient for classification along this dimension; and the same could be said of most of the informants, the clearest exceptions being 4 and 7, regarding their patterns for the [+back] vowels. Provisionally we will postulate three values for the feature [high] in SSE. Conspicuously, there can be no justification for regarding /u/ and /o/ as distinguished by different values of the feature [high]: for three informants the realisation of /u/ is actually lower than that of /o/, and only in the speech of informant 2 is it considerably higher. (Indeed, the question suggests itself whether the phonetic quality and systemic position of this item make the symbol u appropriate for it at all. For convenience u will continue to be used in the present study, but the appropriateness of using a different symbol, perhaps that for Cardinal Vowel 15, might be considered.)

Another point suggested by the charts is that both the [+back] and the [−back] vowels show something of a habit of grouping themselves into pairs on the horizontal dimension. The following vowels, in some at least of the speakers examined, show this tendency: /e/ and /ɪ/ (informants 3, 4, 5, 7); /ɛ/ and (when present) /E/ (informants 3, 5); /ɔ/ and /ʌ/ (informants 1, 5); /o/ and /u/ (informants 1, 3, 4, 6, 7). Lindau (1978) proposes a feature [peripheral], the acoustic correlate of which is the amount of centralisation shown on a formant chart. Her discussion focuses on the appropriateness of this feature for categorising the quality differences (traditionally associated with the descriptive terms 'tense' and 'lax') which accompany the so-called 'long' and 'short' vowels in German and in most accents of the English-speaking world other than those of Scotland and Ireland. The pairing of vowels into [+peripheral] and [–peripheral] sets which would result from this analysis in those speech-forms bears no relationship to the pairings emerging from its adoption for SSE; none the less, on acoustic criteria alone, there is a clear argument for invoking this feature to distinguish the SSE phonemes /e/, /ɛ/, /ɔ/, /o/ – [+peripheral] – from /ɪ/, /ɛ/, /ʌ/, /u/ – [–peripheral].

Finally, it is necessary to find a feature to distinguish the vowels of *Sam* and *cot* from those of *psalm* and *caught* in the speech of SSE speakers who make these distinctions. The obvious one is [long], since quality differences between the vowels of those pairs, on present evidence, are relatively slight or non-existent. Length is not a distinctive feature for users of accents of SSE with the 'basic' vowel system or this with the addition of /ɛ/. One striking exception to this last statement emerges from the present data: the realisation of /e/ and /ɪ/ in the speech of informant 2. Acoustically the two vowels he uses are virtually identical, and the difference is one of duration, the ratio as estimated from the spectrograms being roughly 8:5. (While the spectrograms were being made, the nonce experiment was conducted of using the computer program Macrecorder Analog Interface to extend the duration of the recorded word *bit* to that of *bait,* and shorten the *bait* to the length of *bit.* A staff member of Edinburgh University Linguistics Department, asked without an explanation to listen to the result, identified the true *bit* and the shortened *bait* as utterances of the same word, and similarly for the true *bait* and the lengthened *bit,* though suggesting that two speakers with slightly different accents had produced the words.) In this particular informant's accent, it could be suggested that [long] must be regarded as part of his feature inventory for the unique purpose of distinguishing /e/ and /ɪ/: uneconomical and counter-intuitive as such an analysis would undoubtedly be.

The foregoing discussion suggests that the 'basic' vowel system of SSE, and the system augmented by /ɛ/, can be conveniently described in terms of three features only: [high] (1, 2, 3), [back] (+, –) and [peripheral] (+, –). There is no need for [round] as a member of the feature inventory, though of course it is necessary in phonetic description to specify that /u/, /o/ and /ɔ/ are realised by rounded vowels. The fact that the realisation of /u/ is invariably under-rounded in SSE as compared to Cardinal [u] or the corresponding vowel in, for example, German becomes less noteworthy when it is accepted that /u/ is not distinguished from /o/ by a higher value of the feature [high]. The classification of the vowels in terms of the feature inventory suggested is as follows:

	−back		+ back	
	+peripheral	−peripheral	−peripheral	+peripheral
1high	i		u	o
2high	e	ɪ	ʌ	ɔ
3high	ɛ	E		a

Which value of [peripheral] is assigned to /i/ and /a/ is in effect immaterial, as these vowels do not contrast with any others in this dimension. Acoustic facts clearly suggest the plus value for /i/, and it may also be assigned to /a/ for symmetry.

Obviously this system does not correspond exactly to all acoustic facts for every speaker. The major area in which certain of the informants' systems clearly conflict with it is in the acoustic structure of the [>1high] back vowels (i.e. the back vowels other than /u/ and /o/): /ʌ/ is in several cases realised by a vowel so much lower than /ɔ/ that there is no warrant for considering those vowels as exhibiting the same value of the feature [high]. This could be accommodated without departing from the feature inventory suggested by assigning to /a/ the values [3high], [+back], [−peripheral] and to /ʌ/ [3high], [+back], [+peripheral] (since /ʌ/ is almost invarably further back than /a/). Among speakers with this pattern, /ɔ/ ([2high, +back, +peripheral]) would have no [−peripheral] counterpart.

This feature analysis is, clearly, very unlike any other proposed for 'English'. However, the word 'English' in phonetic literature has generally been taken to mean RP-accented English; and even if it is extended by courtesy to include the US Mid-Western accent sometimes referred to as 'American English' as well, those two accents are much more alike in their phonemic structure than either is to SSE. It is not to be expected that the distinctive feature inventory of RP should provide a revealing or an economical analysis of an accent which is both phonetically and phonologically as distinctive as SSE. The present paper should illustrate, on one particular level, the danger of using language names without qualification as if statements made of one particular form of a language were true of all forms.

NOTES

1 Investigation of this enormously complex issue has, in fact, hardly begun. For treatments of primary sources see Kohler (1966), Douglas (1991, a presentation and further examination of the same evidence), and Pollner and Rolfing (1986).

2 See for example McClure (1977), Agutter (1988) and the discussion thereof in McClure (1992).

3 The only published account of this vowel is Abercrombie (1954); the only published attempt at a historical discussion of it is a brief comment in Kohler (1966); the most complete examination of it is in McClure (1970).

4 The discussion is based on the feature inventory proposed by Lindau (1978).

REFERENCES

Abercrombie, D. (1954) 'A Scottish vowel', *Le Maître phonétique*, 23–4.

—— (1979) 'The accents of standard English in Scotland', in A. J. Aitken and T. McArthur (eds), *Languages of Scotland*, Edinburgh: Chambers, pp. 68–84.

Agutter, A. (1988) 'The not-so-Scottish vowel-length rule', in J. M. Anderson and N. MacLeod (eds), *Edinburgh Studies in the English Language*, Edinburgh: John Donald, pp. 120–32.

Aitken, A. J. (1981) 'The Scottish vowel-length rule', in M. Benskin and M. L. Samuels (eds), *So Meny People Longages and Tonges: Philological Essays in Scots and Mediaeval English Presented to Angus McIntosh*, Edinburgh: Edinburgh University Press, pp. 131–57.

Douglas, S., ed. C. Jones (1991) *A Treatise on the Provincial Dialect of Scotland*, Edinburgh: Edinburgh University Press.

Hewitt, D. S. (1987) 'James Beattie and the languages of Scotland', in J. Carter and J. Pittock (eds), *Aberdeen and the Enlightenment*, Aberdeen: Aberdeen University Press, pp. 251–60.

Kohler, K. J. (1966) 'A late eighteenth-century comparison of the "Provincial dialect of Scotland" and the "Pure dialect",' *Linguistics* 23: 30–69.

Ladefoged, P. (1976) 'The phonetic specification of the languages of the world', *UCLA Working Papers in Phonetics* 31: 3–21.

Lindau, M. (1978) 'Vowel features', *Language* 54: 541–63.

McClure, J. D. (1970) 'Some features of Standard English as spoken in South-West Scotland', unpublished M.Litt. dissertation, Edinburgh University.

—— (1977) 'Vowel duration in a Scottish accent', *Journal of the International Phonetic Association* 7, 1: 10–16.

—— (1992) Section on language in *The Year's Work in Scottish Literary and Linguistic Studies 1988*.

Pollner, C. and Rohlfing, H. (1986) 'The Scottish language from the 16th to the 18th century: Elphinstone's works as a mirror of Anglicisation', in D. Strauss and H. W. Drescher (eds) *Scottish Language and Literature, Medieval and Renaissance*, Frankfurt am Main: Lang, pp. 125–38.

Wells, J. C., (1982) *Accents of English*, Cambridge: Cambridge University Press.

30

A neglected feature of British East Midlands accents and its possible implications for the history of a vowel merger in English

J. A. Maidment
University College London

INTRODUCTION

In the area of the East Midlands where the author grew up, South Derbyshire, there is, or at least was, a traditional-dialect pronunciation feature which seems to have been largely ignored by the literature. This feature involves words such as *shirt, worse, burnt,* which in most English accents contain the vowel phoneme /ɜ/, usually realised as a mid-central or mid-centralised front unrounded long vowel. In parts of the East Midlands these words were traditionally pronounced with an open or half-open back rounded vowel of the type which usually realises the /ɒ/ phoneme. This resulted, for example, in *shirt* and *shot* being homophones at least for some traditional-dialect speakers of the area.

That this is a well-known traditional pronunciation of the area is evidenced by the existence of jokes which depend on it for their effect. One example, which also depends on the fact that the /aʊ/ diphthong is often realised as an [ɛː]-type vowel in traditional-dialect pronunciations while in the current local accent this sound, or something like it, realises the /ɜ/ phoneme, is the following about a traditional-dialect-speaking husband from Ilkeston on the borders of Derbyshire and Nottinghamshire and his wife, who obviously has social aspirations:

HUSBAND (in hurry to get ready for work):   Where's me [ʃɒt]?
WIFE (downstairs):   I've told you before – [ʃɛːt]
HUSBAND: I am [ʃɛːtɪn]! Where's me [ʃɒt]!?

From now on this feature will be called NURSE-Backing (NB), using Wells' keyword for the /ɜ/ vowel (Wells 1982). NB is probably almost dead in Derbyshire, but the current situation in other parts of the area (Lincolnshire,

379

Leicestershire, the eastern parts of Cheshire, Nottinghamshire, Stafford-shire) is unknown.

Although moribund, it is still remembered, witness the joke above, and the spellings still found in dialect literature and in popular accounts of language and folklore. There are two examples of NB in the following extract from a traditional-dialect account of work in a colliery in the 1940s by Raymond Huthwaite of Cotmanhay near Ilkeston (Scollins and Titford 1977: 5):

> Wey'd o'must a threy mile traipse te'd pit top frum dairn t'scair wokin's, an on top o'that, it wor all up 'ill gooin' frum t'uther side o' Strolley Choch.

> (*wokin's* = 'workings' and *Choch* = 'church')

Two questions are addressed here: the first is the geographical distribution of NB; the second is the lexical or phonological distribution of the phenomenon.

GEOGRAPHICAL DISTRIBUTION OF NB

As there is no mention of NB in accounts of accents such as Wells (1982), the only readily available source of information on the geographical distribution of this feature is *The Survey of English Dialects*, Volumes 2 and 3 (Orton *et al.*, 1969, 1970; henceforth *SED*). A surprisingly small number of items in the *SED* questionnaires provided the opportunity for NB to show itself. These are listed in Table 30.1, together with count of the occurrences of NB in different counties. The counties are arranged from east to west with north having precedence over south at the same longitude. The dates at the head of each county column indicate when the *SED* fieldworkers recorded the responses. The entry in each cell consists of a binomial X.Y, where X is the number of occurrences of NB for that lexical item for the county concerned and Y is the number of responses which would have the NURSE vowel in RP. This latter figure is not always the same as the number of localities from which responses were recorded because often informants used a word which gave no opportunity for NB: for example, many informants used *dry* rather than *thirsty* in response to item VI.13.10 of the *SED* questionnaire.

From Table 30.1 it may be seen that, except for a few lexical items, NB is confined to Lincolnshire, Nottinghamshire and Derbyshire. Although this is not evident from the table, it is worth noting here that the vowel in items affected by NB was recorded as [ɒ] almost exclusively in Nottinghamshire and Derbyshire. Outside these counties, [ɔ] was the preferred quality.

While it is admitted that the data in Table 30.1 is rather sparse and can give only a very rough idea of the geographical distribution of NB, it seems

Table 30.1 Evidence of NURSE-backing from the *Survey of English Dialects*

Lexical item	SED Reference	Li. 51–60	Nt. 56–7	Db. 55–6	Le. 51–60	Ch. 51–7	St. 53–4
curbstone	I.3.9	0.7	0.3	0.0	0.1	0.1	0.2
overturn	I.11.5	1.1	1.1	0.0	0.1	0.0	0.1
turd	II.1.6	1.2	2.2	1.2	0.0	0.1	0.5
turds	III.13.15	5.6	1.1	1.3	2.3	0.1	0.2
turf	IV.4.3	0.5	0.0	0.1	0.10	0.2	0.2
urchin	IV.5.5	5.5	0.0	0.0	0.0	0.1	0.2
birds	IV.6.1	11.15	4.4	2.6	0.10	0.4	0.10
perch	IV.6.3	1.15	0.4	0.7	0.10	0.6	0.10
bird	IV.7.1	1.1	1.1	1.3	0.0	0.5	0.0
worms	IV.9.1	7.15	1.4	1.7	1.10	0.6	0.10
birch	IV.10.1	0.13	0.4	0.7	0.10	0.6	0.11
fern	IV.10.13	0.14	0.4	0.7	0.10	0.6	0.11
dirty	V.2.8	2.3	2.2	0.2	0.3	0.1	0.10
churn	V.5.5	6.15	3.4	2.7	0.10	0.6	0.11
curdle/turn	V.5.7	1.9	0.2	0.6	0.10	0.5	0.11
curds	V.6.7	1.12	0.3	0.5	0.10	0.4	0.10
burnt	V.6.7	13.15	4.4	2.5	0.10	0.4	0.9
girdle	V.7.4	0.3	0.1	0.2	0.6	0.0	0.2
worse	VI.12.3	10.15	4.4	3.7	0.10	5.6	0.11
worst	VI.12.5	7.15	4.4	2.7	0.10	5.6	2.11
hurts	VI.13.3	12.15	4.4	1.7	0.10	0.5	0.11
thirsty	VI.13.1	7.10	4.4	2.6	0.10	0.6	0.11
shirt	VI.14.8	8.15	3.4	1.7	0.10	0.6	0.11

Key: Db. = Derbyshire, Ch. = Cheshire, Le. = Leicestershire, Li. = Lincolnshire, Nt. = Nottinghamshire, St. = Staffordshire.

clear that the phenomenon is largely confined to the north and east of the Midlands with a few sporadic occurrences in localities further south and west.

LEXICAL INCIDENCE OF NB

Turning now to the lexical distribution of NB, the evidence supplied by an examination of the *SED* responses will be supplemented by evidence from Scollins and Titford (1976, 1977). This is a three-part collection of traditional-dialect literature, folklore and local history of Ilkeston and the Erewash Valley area of east Derbyshire. It contains poems and prose writings in dialect by local writers and a number of glossaries of dialect words, phrases and idioms compiled by the authors. There follows a list of all the words in the traditional dialect pieces and glossaries which in RP would contain the NURSE vowel. The original dialect spellings are given: *bod-tod* ('bird-turd' i.e. birdlime), *bods* (birds), *bon* (burn), *bost* (burst), *choch*

(church), *coss* (curse), *cottins* (curtains), *dosst, dost* (durst), *dot* (dirt), *flairt*
(flirt = flick or throw), *fost* (first), *fother* (further), *Kok* (Kirk, a place-name
element), *lont* (learnt), *norrot* (won't hurt), *occaired* (occurred), *ollin*
(hurling), *ot* (hurt), *pairfect* (perfect), *pearly* (pearly), *pairpose* (purpose),
poss (purse), *sair* (sir), *Shairwood* (Sherwood), *tairn* (turn), *thod* (third), *thost*
(thirst), *thoty* (thirty), *Thozdee, Thozdi, Thosdee* (Thursday), *tockey* (turkey),
tonip (turnip), *tonn* (turn), *tonned* (turned), *vairsion* (version), *wod* (word),
wok (work), *wokkin* (working), *wold* (world), *woled* (whirled), *worrum*
(worm), *woss* (worse), *woth* (worth).

A number of tentative generalisations can be made about the occurrence
of NB in these data:

1 *NB does not occur in word-final open syllables.* The item *sir* is the only direct
evidence of this. However, it is interesting to note that Scollins and Titfield,
in a brief discussion of this phenomenon (part 1, p. 16), explicitly mention
items where it does not occur. The two examples they give are *perfect* and
occurred. It does not occur to these authors to mention items like *purr, fur,
fir, stir,* as if it were self-evident that these are not affected. The author has
no recollection of hearing words like these produced with NB. The
question of whether NB can occur in any open syllable must remain
undecided. There are a number of items where it is possible that the
relevant syllable is open, but these all have single consonant interludes and
the syllabification must remain doubtful. Examples are: *thirty, curtains,
turnip.* The only item where a non-final syllable is definitely open is
Sherwood, but this cannot undergo NB for another reason, as explained at
4 below.

2 *NB is a lexical phenomenon not a postlexical phonological process.* Again the
evidence for this is rather slim. The item *occurred* does not show NB, even
though the syllable concerned is closed by a consonant. It would seem from
this that the addition of an inflectional suffix to a word does not trigger NB.
Again the author's recollection is that words like *stirs* and *purrs* were never
pronounced with NB.

3 *NB is disfavoured before labial consonants.* There is one exception to this,
the word *worm.* It is interesting, however, that most of the *SED* informants
used a disyllabic form for this word, [wɔɹəm] or something similar, and that
the spelling of the word in the Scollins and Titford material, *worrum,*
suggests a similar pronunciation.

4 *NB occurs with words spelled with 'ir', 'or' and 'ur' and not with words spelled
'er' or 'ear'.* *Sherwood, version, perfect* and *pearly* from Scollins and Titford and
fern from *SED* are examples of this. There are two definite counter-
examples: the word *learnt* from Scollins and Titford and the response of one

informant from Lincolnshire to the *SED* item *perch.* It is certainly the author's recollection that words such as *earth, earn, certain* were never produced with NB. The items 'worrit' and 'worree', which occur a number of times in Scollins and Titford, are problematical. Scollins and Titford gloss these as 'was it' and 'was he' respectively. If this is right then we have an otherwise unknown [z] → [ɹ] rule in operation. However, it seems much more likely that we should gloss these as 'were it' and 'were he'. Then we have another example of a word spelled with an 'e' that is susceptible to NB.

IMPLICATIONS

Generalisation 4 is interesting because it has possible implications for the history of this process and perhaps for the history of what Wells has called the NURSE Merger (see Wells 1982, Vol. 1: 199–203). Unless we are to entertain the possibility that the orthography has played some part in the different treatment of 'er/ear' words and the rest, it seems reasonable to assume that at the time NB began to occur words like *earth, fern* and the rest (the E-set) were still distinct in pronunciation from the others (the IOU-set). Wells dates the beginning of the NURSE Merger in the fifteenth century and, interestingly, locates this beginning in the north and east of England. He gives a rule (p. 201) which captures what he calls the First NURSE Merger. This is:

$$\text{ɪ, ɛ, ʏ} \rightarrow \quad / \underline{\quad} r \left\{ \begin{matrix} C \\ \# \end{matrix} \right. \qquad \text{First NURSE Merger}$$

The details of this rule need not concern us here. The important thing is that it treats [ɛ] in the same way as the other short vowels of Middle English, whereas the different treatment of E-set words by NB in just the area where the NURSE Merger is thought to have originated suggests that the process may have proceeded in at least two stages with [ɛ] at first being unmerged and then merging later, after NB had begun in IOU-set words in certain environments. The rule representation of this state of affairs may have been something like:

$$\text{ɪ, ʏ} \rightarrow \text{ə} \quad / \underline{\quad} r \left\{ \begin{matrix} C \\ \# \end{matrix} \right. \qquad \text{First NURSE Merger}$$

$$\text{ə} \rightarrow \text{ɒ} \quad / \underline{\quad} \text{[–labial]} \qquad \text{NURSE backing}$$

$$\text{ɛ} \rightarrow \text{ə} \quad / \underline{\quad} r \left\{ \begin{matrix} C \\ \# \end{matrix} \right. \qquad \text{Second NURSE Merger}$$

$$r \rightarrow 0 \quad / \underline{\quad} \left\{ \begin{matrix} C \\ \# \end{matrix} \right. \qquad \text{r-drop}$$

After the first of these rules began to take effect the situation in the north east Midlands would have been strikingly similar to what has happened in some Scottish accents where E-set words are pronounced with [ɛr] (for example *berth* [bɛrθ]) and IOU-set words are pronounced with [ɕr] (*birth* [bɕrθ]). Scottish accents, of course, have developed differently since this partial NURSE Merger in that the E-set words have remained distinct and *r*-dropping has not taken place. Nor has NB taken place in Scotland. In north-east Midlands accents the vowel in E-set words has merged with that in IOU-set words which were not affected by NB and in only the last century in traditional dialect in this area has the NURSE Merger begun to be as far-reaching as it is in many other accents of English as NB has begun to die.

REFERENCES

Orton, H. with (in turn) Halliday, W. J., Barry, M. V., Tilling, P. M. and Wakelin, M. F. (1962–71) *Survey of English Dialects*, Leeds: Arnold.

Scollins, R. and J. Titford (1976, 1977) *Ey Up Mi Duck: An Affectionate Look at the Speech, History and Folklore of Ilkeston, Derbyshire and the Erewash Valley*, Parts 1–3, Ilkeston: Scollins & Titford.

Wells, J. C. (1982) *Accents of English*, 3 vols, Cambridge: Cambridge University Press.

31

Mixing and fudging in Midland and Southern dialects of England: the *cup* and *foot* vowels

Clive Upton
Centre for English Cultural Tradition and Language,
University of Sheffield

Among the most fruitful users of the findings of *The Survey of English Dialects* (*SED*) have been Peter Trudgill and J. K. Chambers. Rightly critical of the *Survey* on various points in the light of later, especially social dialectological practice, they have nevertheless used its material to good effect to provide evidence of various linguistic phenomena. It is two of these, the pronunciation compromise phenomena which they call 'mixing' and 'fudging', which are the subjects of this essay.

The concepts of mixing and fudging were first discussed by Chambers and Trudgill (1980: 132–7), and were later taken up by Trudgill alone (1983: 49–51; 1986: 60–2). Their concern is what occurs in transitional zones between regions with different phoneme systems, where speakers may possess 'mixed' lects, distributing sounds from the various systems to individual tokens in a variety of ways, or 'fudged' lects, in which speakers render the tokens using a sound which is in some way a compromise between the conflicting sounds of the systems around them.

Chambers' and Trudgill's exploration of mixing and fudging in part involves the classic variable (u) divide in England between 'northern' /ʊ/ and 'southern' /ʌ/ in such words as *cup* and *dust*. Succinctly describing this variable, O'Connor has observed that 'in broader Northern accents /ʌ/ is not distinguished from /ʊ/ as in *put* so that *cud* and *could* are identical' (O'Connor 1973: 158), and again that 'from Birmingham northwards to the Scottish border /ʊ/ and /ʌ/ are not distinguished in the broadest accents' (p. 162).

For their analysis, Chambers and Trudgill take a set of sixty-five relevant tokens from *SED* and examine their vowel representation in thirty-two *SED* localities in the East Midlands and East Anglia. By assigning an index score to each locality based on the occurrences of /ʊ/ and /ʌ/ in pronunciations

385

of the tokens, the authors are first able to show 'northern' (index 100, all /ʊ/) and 'southern' (index 0, no /ʊ/) lects and also those mixed lects which are 'more northern' (indices closer to 100) and 'less northern' (indices closer to 0). The mixing is taken to exemplify sound change taking place. This analysis is followed by an investigation of those lects with non-northern features (i.e. those below index 100), which are seen to exhibit either [ʌ] or [ɤ]. (An apparent printer's error results in SCV 7 [ɤ] being replaced by the similar velar fricative symbol [ɣ] on p. 135 and elsewhere in the book.) [ɤ] has the unrounded characteristic of [ʌ]; it has the height of [ʊ]: as such

> it might seem to be a nearly perfect realisation of (u), combining some properties of both of the other phonetic realisations. In other words, it is a fudge between the contending phone types of this change in progress, a way, as it were, of being at neither pole on the continuum or conversely of being at both poles at once.
>
> (Chambers and Trudgill 1980: 135)

The result of the quantified mixing and fudging investigation is a map of eastern England, showing a northern dialect area stretching down from south Lincolnshire, a southern dialect area stretching north and west from Suffolk, and a transitional zone between them containing mixed and fudged lects with either a northern or a southern bias (Chambers and Trudgill 1980: 136; Trudgill 1983: 50). The whole is a masterly example of what can be done with *SED* findings when unease over a simplistic interpretation of individual tokens prompts an exercise in the rigorous quantification of complex data.

A question arises, however, as to what happens beyond the area investigated and mapped by Chambers and Trudgill. It is quite understandable that the data should have been drawn from this eastern area of England: Trudgill has well-known expertise in the field of East Anglian English, and it is this area which exhibits all but a very few of the [ɤ] reflexes of (u) in *SED*. Nevertheless, the transition zone detailed by the investigation is left suspended, running out into unknown territory in the eastern part of Norfolk and in the whole of England west of the Fens.

It is just possible, of course, that mixing and fudging in (u) are phenomena restricted to the eastern England study area, but this should not be assumed to be the case. It would seem to be sensible to scrutinise the areas beyond that of the original enquiry for evidence of occurrences of the same or similar phenomena, if only to show that the first study does indeed cover all the relevant ground; and of course it might be that something more of mixing and fudging might come to light during such an exercise, as Chambers himself has readily acknowledged (personal communication).

Immediately one begins to study that set of tokens which is the subject of

Chambers' and Trudgill's enquiry, 'words which have the unrounded vowel [ʌ] in southern England (and elsewhere throughout the English-speaking world) but which retain the rounded vowel in the north of England' (Chambers and Trudgill 1980: 129), one transcription practice in particular provides reason enough to carry the investigation further. This is the widespread practice of several fieldworkers to transcribe (u) as [ʌ̞], that is raised SCV 6. In the analysis of *SED* transcriptions [ʌ̞] is normally taken as a variant of /ʌ/, indistinguishable in significance from [ʌ] and [ɪ̈] which also of course appear in the record. However, if, as has been ably demonstrated, a case is to be made for [ɤ] to have a special place in the rendering of (u), a case can also be presented for [ʌ̞] both on grounds of a most singular commonness of occurrence and of phonetic distance.

[ʌ̞] is a feature of *SED* transcriptions over a wide area of south and central England. Four *SED* fieldworkers, Ellis, Parry, Playford and John Wright, operating in the west and east Midlands and the south of England, repeatedly transcribe [ʌ̞] for (u), suggesting some regular deviation from the normal 'southern' sound. In addition the detailed phonetic notes accompanying another fieldworker's (Barry's) *SED* records for Berkshire, Kent and Hampshire indicate that in four localities what he broadly transcribes as [ʌ] is in fact [ʌ̞]. The transcriptions for these localities – 33Brk.2/3, 35K.6 and 39Ha.7 – can on this evidence be taken to be [ʌ̞], as, on the same evidence, can others by two of the previously named fieldworkers at 27Bd.1 and 32W.3. It must be acknowledged that the [ʌ~ʌ̞] distinction is at times the subject of a fieldworker boundary, as in Monmouthshire, where 23Mon.1-3/6, surveyed by one fieldworker, never exhibit [ʌ̞], whilst the remaining localities, surveyed by another, regularly do. However, although the evidence of only one fieldworker might very reasonably be questioned, the fact that five of *SED*'s eleven fieldworkers independently and to varying degrees recognise the occurrence of [ʌ̞] over large areas of their territories is most worthy of note.

To this important fact of the frequency of occurrence of [ʌ̞] in the *SED* data should be added the fact that the phonetic distance between [ʌ̞] and [ɤ] is of course very small. Recognition of this closeness increases when it is seen that Playford, one of the two fieldworkers whose [ɤ] provides Chambers and Trudgill with their fudging data, also uses [ʌ̞] and that she, as the one for whom detailed phonological data are provided in *SED*, indicates her [ɤ] to be in fact regularly lowered [ɤ̞]. In her case at least the auditory difference between the two sounds [ʌ] and [ɤ] is minute: indeed, it is somewhat surprising that under dialect fieldwork conditions *any* distinction could be perceived.

The case for being wary of imposing rigid sound distinctions based on phonetic symbols is in fact well made by Trudgill in the preamble to his discussion of mixing and fudging in *On Dialect*. Criticising map isoglosses as 'something of a fiction or distortion', he writes:

In the L[*inguistic*] A[*tlas of*] E[*ngland*] [Orton *et al.* 1978] ... there are a number of isoglosses separating [ɒ] from [ɔ]; [uː] from [ʉː]; [ei] from [ɛi]; and so on. The suspicion must be, however, that vowel quality actually changes gradually from location to location and that the placing of isoglosses is therefore arbitrary and a simple artifact of the transcription system. The isogloss between [ɒ] and [ɔ] is drawn where it is simply because the symbols [ɒ] and [ɔ] have been assigned particular phonetic values.

(Trudgill 1983: 47)

Although Chambers and Trudgill cannot be criticised for ignoring the regular occurrence of [ʌ] outside their study area, its occurrence alongside [ɤ] inside that area could be taken to have significance, especially, given her [ɤ] transcription, in the interpretation of Playford's data for Leicestershire and Rutland. Fieldworkers' preferences notwithstanding, we have reason to suspect some significance in the differentiation between [ʌ] and [ʌ̞] in the *SED* record, and to debate whether their distributions can shed any further light on the fudging issue.

In order to investigate any widespread mixing in realisations of (u), and the occurrence of a 'midpoint' vowel [ɤ~ʌ̞] between [ʊ] and [ʌ] which might be regarded as fudging as described by Chambers and Trudgill, the record of nine tokens has been studied in the *SED* West Midland, East Midland, and Southern volumes (Orton *et al.* 1967–71). The number of tokens studied has been restricted to many fewer than those handled by Chambers and Trudgill both because the investigation now involves records from all 238 localities covered by those volumes and because, as will be seen, keeping the number of tokens in single figures facilitates the presentation of data. The tokens selected for investigation are *brother, butter, cousins, ducks, dust, gums, mushrooms, suck* and *thumb*. These were chosen principally because all are asterisked in *SED* as being sought for phonological purposes and so can be expected to be the responses recorded in most localities. They also of course exhibit (u) in a number of different environments.

For each token at each locality the response vowels have been allocated to one of three groups. These groups are as follows: the 'northern' group /ʊ/, with any varieties howsoever modified by diacritics; the posited 'intermediate' or 'fudged' group [ʌ~ɤ]; and the 'southern' group /ʌ/, with modified varieties other than raised, and including [ə]. Other transcriptions such as [ɪ] and [ɤ] (Devon and Cornwall), [ɒ] (the South-east), and diphthongs (Somerset and Wiltshire) are ignored. The decision to include /ə/ with /ʌ/ has been taken in the light of the fact that southern /ʌ/ is an advanced variety and is generally regarded as such by *SED* fieldworkers, who often mark it as centralised in the notes accompanying their records. Apart from a few isolated occurrences, the incidence of stressed [ə] in the tokens studied is restricted to the Gloucestershire and Sussex areas.

388

The number of response vowels for each vowel grouping have been totalled for each locality. It is thus possible for a locality to display a total score of 9 in any one group: in such a case all nine tokens would be pronounced using a vowel from that group. By presenting the findings as a three-digit number for each locality, the digits representing 'northern', 'intermediate' and 'southern' vowels in order, it is possible to indicate the relative strength of support for pronunciations falling into the different groupings at those localities. Thus a figure of 900 indicates all /ʊ/ responses, and 117 represents one /ʊ/, one [ʌ~ɤ], and seven /ʌ/. When, as occasionally happens, the sum of the digits is greater than nine, the inference to be drawn is that one or more alternative pronunciations were given at the locality concerned. Thus 208 implies that for one token both /ʊ/ and /ʌ/ were recorded. Cases where responses were not recorded or where responses fall outside the three groupings being considered result in scores which total less than nine. Of course, in studying the scores obtained for each locality it is the *prominence* of each digit relative to its neighbours which is of real significance, rather than its nearness to 9.

The scores calculated for each locality are shown below, presented county by county. The *SED* county code and name-abbreviation are given after the county name. The identification number which each locality is given within its county is shown before the locality's three-digit score, separated from it by a colon.

Cheshire (7Ch) 1:900, 2:900, 3:900, 4:900, 5:900, 6:900

Derbyshire (8Db) (91) 1:900, 2:900, 3:900, 4:900, 5:900, 6:900, 7:900

Nottinghamshire (9Nt) 1:900, 2:900, 3:800, 4:900

Lincolnshire (10L) 1:900, 2:900, 3:900, 4:900, 5:900, 6:900, 7:900, 8:900, 9:900. 10:900, 11:900, 12:900, 13:900, 14:900, 15:901

Shropshire (11Sa) 1:306, 2:900, 3:009, 4:008, 5:900, 6:008, 7:108, 8:900, 9:009, 10:009, 11:207

Staffordshire (12St) 1:900, 2:900, 3:900, 4:900, 5:900, 6:900, 7:900, 8:900, 9:900, 10:900, 11:801

Leicestershire (13Lei) 1:900, 2:900, 3:900, 4:900, 5:900, 6:900, 7:900, 8:810, 9:550, 10:820

Rutland (14R) 1:900, 2:812

Herefordshire (15He) 1:009, 2:009, 3:900, 4:207, 5:405, 6:800, 7:307

Worcestershire (16Wo) 1:900, 2:900, 3:900, 4:900, 5:900, 6:900, 7:900

Warwickshire (17Wa) 1:900, 2:900, 3:811, 4:900, 5:900, 6:900, 7:900

Northamptonshire (18Nth) 1:900, 2:900, 3:900, 4:216, 5:702

Huntingdonshire (19Hu) 1:073, 2:009

Cambridgeshire (20C) 1:604, 2:009

Norfolk (21Nf) 1:035, 2:018, 3:036, 4:054, 5:045, 6:009, 7:063, 8:024, 9:054, 10:045, 11:018, 12:036, 13:045

Suffolk (22Sf) 1:018, 2:008, 3:018, 4:018, 5:018

389

Monmouthshire (23Mon) 1:009, 2:900, 3:009, 4:090, 5:090, 6:009, 7:021
Gloucestershire (24Gl) 1:900, 2:800, 3:009, 4:900, 5:801, 6:009, 7:207
Oxfordshire (25O) 1:306, 2:407, 3:217, 4:900, 5:009, 6:406
Buckinghamshire (26Bk) 1:900, 2:009, 3:702, 4:108, 5:009, 6:004
Bedfordshire (27Bd) 1:180, 2:009, 3:009
Hertfordshire (28Hrt) 1:208, 2:009, 3:008
Essex (29Ess) 1:009, 2:009, 3:008, 4:008, 5:009, 6:008, 7:009, 8:009, 9:009, 10:009, 11:009, 12:009, 13:009, 14:009, 15:009
Middlesex/London (30MxL) 1:009, 2:106
Somerset (31So) 1:252, 2:171, 3:270, 4:051, 5:180, 6:090, 7:080, 8:090, 9:080, 10:090, 11:090, 12:090, 13:090
Wiltshire (32W) 1:180, 2:090, 3:090, 4:360, 5:080, 6:080, 7:054, 8:090, 10:090
Berkshire (33Brk) 1:009, 2:360, 3:450, 4:108, 5:007
Surrey (34Sr) 1:009, 2:009, 3:009, 4:009, 5:009
Kent (35K) 1:005, 2:009, 3:302, 4:134, 5:205, 6:050, 7:316
Cornwall (36Co) 1:060, 2:070, 3:170, 4:180, 5:270, 6:270, 7:180
Devon (37D) 1:060, 2:050, 3:050, 4:070, 5:070, 6:060, 7:070, 8:080, 9:240, 10:270, 11:160
Dorset (38Do) 1:009, 2:180, 3:171, 4:090, 5:090
Hampshire (39Ha) 1:090, 2:090, 3:090, 4:009, 5:270, 6:090, 7:180
Sussex (40Sx) 1:009, 2:009, 3:009, 4:109, 5:108, 6:009

Presented in map form (Map 31.1), the raw data which these figures represent assume some marked order. Areas designated 1 on the map, with or without a secondary number, exhibit dominant /ʊ/: lone 1 contains those localities showing a 900-type index, where exclusive /ʊ/ is found; 1-1 and 1-2 show respectively mixing of /ʊ/ and /ʌ/ with an /ʊ/ bias and fudging of [ɤ~ʌ] with /ʊ/. Areas designated 2, with or without a secondary number, exhibit dominant /ʌ/: lone 2 contains those localities showing a 009-type index, where exclusive /ʌ/ is found; 2-1 and 2-2 show respectively mixing of /ʌ/ and /ʊ/ with an /ʌ/ bias and fudging of [ɤ~ʌ] with /ʌ/. (For reasons of history and comparison with the work of Chambers and Trudgill I have chosen to retain in the key the terms 'northern' for /ʊ/ and 'southern' for /ʌ/, even though, as can be seen, this results in the extreme south-west being given a 'northern' label.) One large distributional area carries the label 3: this is that area in which the majority of localities return a 090-type score, indicating exclusive use of a fudged variety. Most exceptions within distributional areas are indicated by symbols (the same symbols that are used by Chambers and Trudgill in their maps for mixing and fudging, with the exception of □, which is new to this map). A few localities, whose indices are worthy of special note, are indicated by their index scores.

The 1 area of the map, indicating all-[ʊ], carries no surprises. This

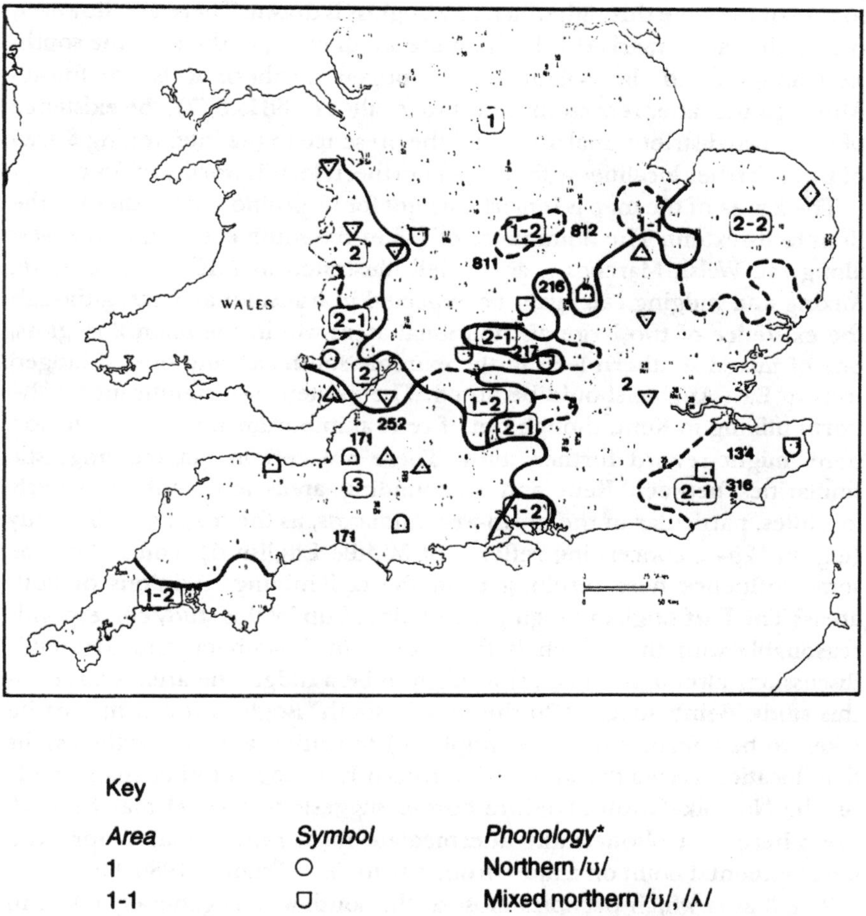

Key

Area	*Symbol*	*Phonology**
1	○	Northern /ʊ/
1-1	⊔	Mixed northern /ʊ/, /ʌ/
1-2	⌂	Fudged northern [ɤ ~ ʌ], /ʊ/
2	◇	Southern /ʌ/
2-1	▽	Mixed southern /ʌ/, /ʊ/
2-2	△	Fudged southern [ɤ ~ ʌ̣], /ʌ/
3	□	Fudged [ɤ ~ ʌ̣]
(171, 134 etc.		Scrambled /ʊ/, [ʌ̣], /ʌ/)

* /ʌ/ excludes [ʌ̣]
(Base map from
LAE)

Map 31.1 (u) lectal varieties, Midland and southern England

distribution is well known from such maps as Ph50 and Ph51 in *LAE*. The presence of mixed and fudged northern lects in small areas or isolated pockets at or near the isogloss is also not surprising, given the transitional nature of the zone through which any isogloss is drawn. There are, however, two further areas marked 1, both on the south coast, in the extreme south-west and around the Solent, where fudged northern lects are found. Although the latter represents only two localities (39Ha.5/7), the existence of these two distributional areas and the presence in the intervening 3 area of three further localities with fudged northern lects is worthy of note.

The 2 area of the map is remarkable not for its position but rather for the limit to its extent. The dominance of [ʌ] in the south-east and in the west along the Welsh Marches is again well illustrated in *LAE* and elsewhere. Mixing and fudging can again be expected in transitional areas, although the existence of two large distributional areas within the main 2 isogloss, one of mixed southern lects in the extreme south-east and one of fudged lects in East Anglia, should be noted. The existence of significant south–north mixing in Kent, though not of central importance to our discussion here, might reward further study. There are certain marked linguistic similarities between Kent and surrounding areas and more northerly localities, particular in the north-west Midlands, as the maps of *LAE* testify (e.g. Ph125–8, concerning reflexes of Middle English ǫ̣): could there be some influence here resulting from the coal-mining traditions of both areas? The East Anglian fudging area pointed up by this study corresponds reasonably with that which is the subject of Chambers' and Trudgill's discussions although, since [ʌ] is taken to be a fudge, the area is larger in this study. Being adjacent to the 'north/south' isogloss, it can in part be taken to be a feature of a (geographical) transition area. Nevertheless, its firm location across the whole of northern East Anglia rather than simply on the Norfolk–Cambridgeshire border suggests that [ɤ~ʌ] may be *established* here as a phonetically intermediate form rather than simply as a developmental point on a move from /ʊ/ to /ʌ/ (Trudgill 1986: 60).

The 3 area which occupies most of the south-west is generally taken in descriptions to be one with the 2 area, that of the 'southern' /ʌ/ of the south-east, but it surely deserves to be considered separately. The raising which leads to the drawing of this homogeneous area is largely a feature of the extensive fieldwork carried out by John Wright. To this fact should be added other observations. First, the isoglosses drawn here do not constitute a fieldworker boundary, since Wright's localities include some in the 1–2 distributional areas surrounding the 3 area. Second, recordings made by another fieldworker, Parry, support Wright in testifying to a regular [ʌ] within the area. Yet another, Barry, records exclusive [ʌ] in Kent at 35K.6. Third, as we have seen, [ʌ] is a sound held as significant in other areas where /ʊ/ and /ʌ/ interact. A possible explanation for the existence of this distributional area is that it illustrates a change in progress from /ʊ/ to /ʌ/

– the 1–2 (fudged northern) area in Cornwall and south Devon testifies to a 'northern' rather than 'southern' presence, albeit with weak northern scores typically of 270 or 180, and all of the south-west could indeed be judged to be moving towards /ʌ/. We should not assume, however, that [ʌ] would be found to be a recessive feature if it were to be investigated in the area today. O'Connor attests to its raising in northern English speech, remarking that 'in educated Yorkshire and much other Northern speech … the vowel [SCV 6] is central and above half-open' (O'Connor 1973: 158). We may with some reason suggest that the development of a fudged [ʌ] in response to a culturally dominant /ʌ/ existing alongside a remarkably resilient /ʊ/ is an established feature of much modern Received Pronunciation.

One further feature of the mapping should be noted. A very few localities, nine in all, show digits in all three positions, giving, for example, indices of 811 or 316. Such figures indicate that both the processes of mixing and fudging are taking place at the localities concerned. These localities are seen to display that phenomenon which Chambers and Trudgill, in their discussion of (a) – the /a/–/aː/ north–south split – call 'scrambling' (Chambers and Trudgill 1980: 141). The findings here support those writers' assertion that mixed and fudged elements can co-occur in a single lect, at the same time suggesting by their sparse and scattered nature that incidents of such co-occurrence are unusual.

The phenomena of mixing and fudging, and of associated scrambling, are clearly complex in their operation. By studying the record for a quite restricted geographical area, Chambers and Trudgill are able to demonstrate that they are features which occur widely in transition zones between localities possessing different phonemic systems. Extending the view to a larger area confirms that fact, instances of both showing quite clearly where transition is to be expected. Substantial occurrences of mixing and fudging away from transition zones, however, must lead us to be wary of making an assumption that such phenomena are the result of a purely spatial juxtaposition of opposing phonemic systems, or that their products are necessarily transitory. It is possible that both mixing and fudging, and especially the latter, may be long-term features of a region's phonology, rather than being stages on the route to the dominance of one system over another. Real-time study building on the *SED* recordings used here would do much to show whether this is in fact the case.

REFERENCES

Chambers, J. K. and Trudgill, P. (1980) *Dialectology*, Cambridge: Cambridge University Press.

O'Connor, J. D. (1973) *Phonetics*, Harmondsworth: Penguin.

Orton, H. with (in turn) Halliday, W. J., Barry, M. V., Tilling, P. M. and Wakelin, M. F. (1967–71) *Survey of English Dialects* Leeds: Arnold.

Orton, H., Sanderson, S. and Widdowson, J. (1978) *The Linguistic Atlas of England*, London: Croom Helm.

Trudgill, P. (1983) *On Dialect: Social and Geographical Perspectives*, Oxford: Basil Blackwell.

—— (1986) *Dialects in Contact*, Oxford: Basil Blackwell.

32

The low vowels of Vancouver English

Henry J. Warkentyne and John H. Esling
University of Victoria, Canada

INTRODUCTION

Canadian English exhibits a ten-vowel system, excluding diphthongs and rhotic vowels. Its distinguishing characteristic lies in the merger of the two low back vowels \ɔ\ and \ɑ\, which neutralises oppositions present in other varieties of English. Thus, *caught* and *cot* are homophonous and *father* and *bother* are a perfect rhyme. This is the vowel system described by William Moulton (1990) which he designates SAE 4, and is not unique to Canadian English but may be found in areas of the United States. such as northeastern New England and western Pennsylvania extending into Ohio. The source of this phenomenon in Canadian English might be traceable to the heavy influx of Scotch-Irish into Canada in the early years, combined with influences of early American immigrants from the areas in which the merger had already taken place. It is reported that the merged vowel is spreading in the United States (Wells 1982: 473–6).

In Canadian English, the back vowels before /r/ have not participated in the merger; which sometimes makes phoneme assignment problematic; *are* remains as [ɋ ɹ] and *or* as [ɔɹ]. Robert Gregg (1984: 26–7) suggests that in the cases where speakers have the rounded variant [ɒ], the [ɋ] be assigned to \æ\; and where the unrounded variant occurs in non-rhotic contexts, the [ɋ] of *are* be assigned to the \ɑ\ phoneme. Gregg's proposal may be influenced by the fact that, in some eastern Canadian communities, the ‹ar› sequence is pronounced with a fully fronted vowel [æ̞ ~ æ]; e.g., *car* [kæɹ]. To avoid such conflicts, it may perhaps be preferable to treat the rhotic vowels as a separate system.

The front checked vowel \æ\ functions as in most varieties of English. In American varieties of English, there is a widespread tendency for the phonetic quality of \æ\ to be raised, resulting in realisations such as [ɛə] , [eə] , and as high as [iə] in some instances (Wells 1982: 477–8). Canadian English does not appear to participate in that kind of change. There is some evidence that there may be a trend towards retraction of \æ\, [æ̠], rather than raising (Esling and Warkentyne 1993).

The present study represents part of a larger project, the aim of which was to make a full study of the ten-vowel system of Vancouver English. Diphthongs and rhotic vowels were excluded. An initial instrumental analysis has been completed (see Esling 1991, 1993). An auditory analysis was then undertaken and some of the results are reported here.

THE DATA

The data are derived from the Survey of Vancouver English (Gregg *et al.* 1981) which comprised a random sample of 240 subjects covering the Greater Vancouver area. More specifically, the reading passage from the interviews was selected to obtain the items for analysis. Subjects in the survey are divided into three age groups, four socio-economic status (SES) divisions, and male and female groups. The SES groupings from lower to higher are: I Middle Working Class (MWC), II Upper Working Class (UWC), III Lower Middle Class (LMC) and IV Middle Middle Class (MMC). Eliminating poorest quality recordings or those with missing data, for this study the number of subjects for each cell was reduced from ten to eight, leaving us with samples from 192 speakers.

The items selected from the reading passage for \æ\ were ask, *Saturday, fantastic, cast, fractured* and *graduated*; and for \ɒ\, *bought, caught, possibly, bother, father, bottles, talking* and *lot.* The reading passage was written in an informal style, replete with dialogue, approximating colloquial usage. It also provided comparable contexts of speaking and identical vowel tokens within those contexts.

FINDINGS

Vancouver \æ\

Reference has already been made to a widespread tendency in American English to raise \æ\, even in localities where this might not be expected. In Boston, for example, except for certain words in which the opener (or retracted) variant [a] is lexicalised (e.g. *aunt, laugh, bath* and *path*), raising is increasingly displacing opener or retracted variants, at least amongst young people (Laferriere 1977). The 'backed' [a] has become stigmatised in certain social groups. In the Vancouver sample, there is no indication of a raising trend. On the contrary, the incidence of the retracted variant increases in the youngest age group (to 67 per cent). The oldest and middle-age male groups show no significant occurrence of backing, but the retracted variant [æ] occurs in about 25 per cent of the tokens examined. The female subjects' retracted usage begins with the oldest, middle-class group (36 per cent), increases through the middle-age group (47 per cent) and reaches 67 per cent in the youngest age group (84 per cent in the young middle-class division). If one subscribes to the 'apparent time' hypothesis, it would appear that the women are leading a change in the realisation of \æ\.

Vancouver \ɒ\

In our Vancouver sample, the variations in the realisation of the low back vowel are grouped into two variants, [ɒ] and [ɑ], rounded and unrounded. The rounded allophones may vary in the degree of rounding and in height. The tongue height ranges between a position just below near-open [ɔ̞] to open [ɒ]. There is always the possibility that the impression of rounding is achieved more by tongue root retraction than by labial protrusion. The vowel quality in *caught* may be the same for Vancouver speakers as it is for General American speakers (Moulton's SAE 3). When the tongue reaches a fully open position, the vowel becomes unrounded. For a majority of speakers using the unrounded variant, it was judged to be fully back, i.e. close to Cardinal Vowel 5. In some cases, the variant [A] was slightly advanced, and only in a few instances was it advanced to a position approaching an open centralized vowel [ɑ].

The distribution of the two variants of \ɒ\ for the Vancouver subjects is presented in Tables 32.1–32.3. Where either [ɒ] or [ɑ] appears alone in a row of the tables, the frequency of occurrence for that variant is at least 67 per cent for the group designated. A higher than 33 per cent incidence of a competing variant is marked by a tilde (signifying alternation) and enclosed in parentheses. A still higher alternation of a competing variant (greater than 40 per cent) is indicated by only a tilde (~), without parentheses.

Table 32.1 Distribution of variants for vowel /ɒ/ by age – all subjects

Age group	Variants		Numerical values	
All women over 60	(ɑ ~)	ɒ	99	157
All women 35–60	(ɑ ~)	ɒ	92	164
All women 16–34	ɑ ~	ɒ	112	144
	Overall		39.5%	60.5%
All men over 60	ɑ	~ ɒ	148	104
All men 35–60	(ɑ ~)	ɒ	94	161
All men 16–34		ɒ	82	174
			42.5%	57.5%
	Overall		41%	59%

Table 32.2 Distribution of variants for vowel /ɒ/ by SES group – female subjects

Age/SES group		Variants		Numerical values	
Over 60	MWC (I)		ɒ	17	47
Over 60	UWC (II)	(ɑ ~)	ɒ	22	42
Over 60	LMC (III)	ɑ	~ ɒ	34	30
Over 60	MMC (IV)	ɑ ~	ɒ	26	38
				39%	61%
35–60	MWC (I)	ɑ ~	ɒ	29	35
35–60	UWC (II)		ɒ	21	43
35–60	LMC (III)		ɒ	13	51
35–60	MMC (IV)	ɑ ~	ɒ	29	35
				36%	64%
16–34	MWC (I)	ɑ ~	ɒ	30	34
16–34	UWC (II)	ɑ ~	ɒ	28	36
16–34	LMC (III)	(ɑ ~)	ɒ	25	39
16–34	MMC (IV)	ɑ ~	ɒ	29	35
				44%	56%

Table 32.3 Distribution of variants for vowel /ɒ/ by SES group – male subjects

Age/SES group		Variants		Numerical values	
Over 60	MWC (I)	ɑ	(~ ɒ)	41	22
Over 60	UWC (II)	ɑ	~ ɒ	36	26
Over 60	LMC (III)	ɑ		46	17
Over 60	MMC (IV)	(ɑ ~)	ɒ	25	39
				59%	41%
35–60	MWC (I)		ɒ	19	45
35–60	UWC (II)	(ɑ ~)	ɒ	25	39
35–60	LMC (III)	(ɑ ~)	ɒ	23	40
35–60	MMC (IV)	ɑ	ɒ	27	37
				37%	63%
16–34	MWC (I)	ɑ ~	ɒ	28	36
16–34	UWC (II)		ɒ	13	51
16–34	LMC (III)	(ɑ ~)	ɒ	20	44
16–34	MMC (IV)	(ɑ ~)	ɒ	21	43
				32%	68%

As shown in Table 32.1, the usage of the two variants is divided: [ɒ] 59 per cent and [ɑ] 41 per cent. Women have a slightly higher incidence of [ɒ] (60.5 per cent) than do men (57.5 per cent). This can be accounted for by the high frequency of [ɑ] in the over-sixty male category (59 per cent). Tables 32.2 and 32.3 show the distribution of variant usage in all categories of the sample population. Female subjects (Table 32.2) show a small increase from oldest to middle-age categories, but then a sharp decrease in [ɒ] usage in the youngest age group. Thus, no clear progressive change is in evidence.

Male subjects (see Table 32.3), on the other hand, show a clear progression, by age group, of an increasing incidence of the [ɒ] variant: old-age, 41 per cent; middle-age, 63 per cent; young-age, 68 per cent. It is difficult to reconcile this with the statistics shown for female subjects, unless one speculates that the young women are initiating a reverse trend.

Canadian English appears to be following a different trend from many reported varieties of American English. In the analysis of the present data, there is no obvious trend towards unrounding or fronting of\ɒ\, or fronting or raising of\æ\. In fact, quite the opposite.

The discussion above has taken into account only variation over age groups. A close examination of the SES factors might cast a different light on the problem of variation in the realisation of \ɒ\ in Vancouver English.

REFERENCES

Esling, J. H. (1991) 'Sociophonetic variation in Vancouver', in J. Cheshire (ed.), *English around the World: Sociolinguistic Perspectives*, Cambridge: Cambridge University Press, pp. 123–33.

—— (1993) 'Vowel systems and voice setting in the Survey of Vancouver English', in G. de Wolf (ed.), *The Survey of Vancouver English, 1976–1980: A Sociolinguistic Study of Urban Canadian English*, Kingston, ON: Queen's University, Strathy Language Unit.

Esling, J. H., and Warkentyne, H. J. (1993) 'Retracting of\æ\in Vancouver English', in S. Clarke (ed.), *Focus on: Canadian English*, Amsterdam: John Benjamins.

Gregg, R. J. (1984) *Canadian English*, Monograph translated into Japanese in Y. Matsumoto (ed.), *Varieties of English: Commonwealth English Series*, Tokyo: Kenkyusha.

Gregg, R. J., Murdoch, M., Hasebe-Ludt, E. and de Wolf, G. (1981) 'An urban dialect survey of the English spoken in Vancouver', in H. J. Warkentyne (ed.), *Papers from the Fourth International Conference on Methods in Dialectology*, Victoria: University of Victoria, pp. 41–65.

Laferriere, M. (1977) 'Boston short *a*: social variation as historical residue', in R. W. Fasold and R. W. Shuy (eds), *Studies in Language Variation: Semantics, Syntax, Phonology, Pragmatics, Social Situations, Ethnographic Approaches*, Washington, DC: Georgetown University, pp. 100–7.

Moulton, W. (1990) 'Some vowel systems in American English', in S. Ramsaran (ed.), *Studies in the Pronunciation of English: A Commemorative Volume in Honour of A. C. Gimson*, London and New York: Routledge, pp. 119–36.

Wells, J. C. (1982) *Accents of English*, (vol. 3), Cambridge: Cambridge University Press.

33

New syllabic consonants in English

J. C. Wells
University College London

The topic of this paper is the unexpected syllabification behaviour of certain English liquids and nasals, which results in the formation of syllabic consonants that appear to be new to RP. Typical examples include 'bɪtḷi for *bitterly*, 'kætḷɒg *catalogue* (for the traditional 'kætəlɒg) and 'detn̩eɪt *detonate* (for the traditional 'detəneɪt).

SYLLABIC CONSONANTS

I begin by considering the nature and phonological status of ordinary familiar syllabic consonants, such as the [ḷ] in *bottle* ['bɒtḷ], *people* ['piːpḷ], and the [n̩] in *button* ['bʌtn̩, 'bʌʔn̩], *garden* ['gɑːdn̩]. These consonants are called 'syllabic' because the words quoted have two syllables each (as shown *inter alia* by their rhythm and also by their treatment in versification). They therefore contain two syllabic segments: the first in each case is the vowel, [ɒ, iː, ʌ, ɑː], and the second must be the final sonorant (nasal or liquid). (In Pike's terminology, [ḷ] and [n̩] would more precisely be termed 'syllabic contoids', since they have syllabic function while being articulated with an obstruction in the oral cavity.) Syllabic consonants have greater duration, other things being equal, than their non-syllabic counterparts, just as vowels have greater duration than the corresponding semivowels.

Phonological status

I would argue that the correct analysis of syllabic sonorants is to treat them as constituting a phonetic manifestation of an underlying sequence of schwa plus an ordinary consonant. Thus *bottle* is phonemically /'bɒtəl/ and *button* is phonemically /'bʌtən/. Similarly, the rarer [ɽ], as in one pronunciation of *fishery* ['fɪʃɽi], and [m̩], as sometimes heard in *organism* ['ɔːgənɪzm̩] or *Clapham* ['klæpm̩], are realisations respectively of /ər/ and /əm/.

What are the grounds for this analysis? There might seem to be two other plausible possible phonological treatments.

401

1 They could all be accorded separate phonemic status. This solution we must reject as uneconomical, since it requires the recognition of four additional phonemes, /l̩, n̩, r̩, m̩/, in the inventory. In any case it can be demonstrated that the syllabic sonorants are not in contrast with the sequences [ən, əl, ər, əm].

2 They could be regarded as realisations of ordinary /l, n, r, m/, with syllabicity imposed by rule. This solution is adopted explicitly or implicitly by various writers. It has a certain attraction: if *bottle* is /'bɒtl/, then the rules of English phonotactics prevent /l/ being part of a final cluster, so that in this word-final position it has to be made syllabic. Many words such as *rattling*, formed with *-ing* attached to a stem which in isolation ends in a syllabic consonant, are pronounced indifferently with syllabic [l̩] or with non-syllabic [l] (so that the two possibilities might be regarded as allophones in free variation). This is the analysis implied by Jones' notation, in *EPD* (1917) and elsewhere, whereby *people* is transcribed simply as ['piːpl] or *garden* as ['gɑːdn].

There are, however, various cases where a syllabic consonant contrasts with the corresponding non-syllabic consonant (as in many of the examples cited in this paper), so that this solution is ultimately rendered unworkable. (Jones (1959) discusses this question at length.) Note that there are minimal pairs such as *finally* ['faɪnl̩i] (or ['faɪnəli]) vs. *finely* ['faɪnli], *Hungary* ['hʌŋgr̩i] or ['hʌŋgəri]) vs. *hungry* ['hʌŋgri]: my student Won Choo (work in progress) has demonstrated that in listening tests these distinctions are perceived categorically, in the way classically expected of phonemic distinctions.

The /əC/ analysis

Jones (e.g. 1950) would not even have been able to consider the analysis for which I argue. His phoneme theory required him to assign speech sounds (segments) to one or another 'family' of sounds (phoneme). It made no provision for a segment to be assigned to a sequence of phonemes. Thus he would have felt forced to assign [n̩], for example, to some specific single phoneme; he could not have 'assigned' it to the phoneme sequence /ən/. Nowadays, however, even the most conservative phonological theories take such a possibility as obviously available. Even over half a century ago, it was adopted without discussion by Trubetzkoy (1939). Gimson canvasses it in a somewhat guarded fashion (1980: 58). In fact there are several arguments in its favour.

1 English has many words that exhibit fluctuation between a syllabic consonant and [ə] plus a non-syllabic consonant: for example, *sudden* is

usually ['sʌdn̩], but is sometimes ['sʌdən]; although *garden* is most often pronounced ['gɑːdn̩], it may on occasion be heard as ['gɑːdən]. The pronunciation with [ə] is characteristic particularly of very deliberate speech in conditions of noise or interruption (for example, on a bad telephone line), and also seems to be commoner among children than among adults. Under such circumstances virtually any word usually pronounced with [n̩] may be said with [ən] instead. In passing, we may note that the two possibilities are clearly different from the articulatory point of view: in [dn̩] the tongue tip remains firmly against the alveolar ridge as the soft palate falls to effect nasal release and thus convert the plosive into a nasal, while in [dən] the plosive has ordinary oral release as the tongue tip moves away from the alveolar ridge, returning to make a renewed alveolar contact after the articulation of [ə] and the lowering of the soft palate.

2 Unlike the cases just considered, there are certain other phonetic environments in which it may be very difficult to determine whether a speaker has uttered a syllabic consonant or the corresponding sequence of schwa plus consonant. This may apply, for example, after a fricative. There may be instances when *seven* is clearly ['sevn̩], and others where it is clearly ['sevən]; but there are others again where it is difficult or impossible to judge between them by ear. Nor do physical measurements on a spectrogram make it any easier to identify which has been said. Indeed, there are cases where human auditory judgement is in conflict with the record of the acoustic signal. Barry and Grice (1991) analyse several cases where trained phoneticians identified [ə] plus a consonant, although analysis of the speech signal showed no acoustic segment corresponding to any [ə].

3 The identification of an underlying /ə/ in all syllabic consonants immediately accounts for the distributional peculiarity of their absence from stressed syllables, since /ə/ itself is exactly so restricted.

Syllabic consonant formation

Phonology since the generativist revolution has enabled us to use write rules to account for the relationship between the surface phonetics and the posited underlying phonological representation. Syllabic consonants fit readily into this framework: we need a rule or rules that selectively convert an underlying string of /ə/ plus a sonorant consonant into a single phonetic segment consisting of the sonorant consonant in question with the additional feature [+syllabic]. It thus has the form of a coalescence rule, converting two segments into one:

[ə] [+son C] → Ø [+syll]

   1   2   2

This rule is subject to probabilistic constraints, both phonological and phonostylistic. It would appear that phonological environments can be ranked by the degree to which they favour or disfavour the rule. They range from environments where it is highly probable, e.g. (for [n̩])

[strong V] [alv plos] __ *button, sudden*

through those where there is intermediate probability, e.g.

[weak V] [alv plos] __ *hesitant, accident*

to those where the probability of a syllabic consonant is low, perhaps approaching zero, e.g.

[sonorant C] __ *sullen, common*

– though even here, as Jack Windsor Lewis points out (p.c.), a schwa-less version of *common* is not impossible in the phrase *common-or-garden*.

There are evidently different probabilities for different syllabic consonants, since there are environments in which [l̩] is usual but [n̩] unusual, e.g.

n d __   *sandal* ['sændl̩], in RP rarely ['sændəl]
         abandon [ə'bændən], in RP rarely [ə'bændn̩]

SYLLABIFICATION

A further constraint on the rule of syllabic-consonant formation just discussed is arguably this: that the two input segments, [ə] and the sonorant consonant, must be not only contiguous but also within the same syllable. We note that where they are clearly in different syllables a syllabic consonant is not an available option: thus *allow* [ə 'laʊ] does not become *[l̩aʊ] (at least, not in postpausal position), nor does *annoy* [ə 'nɔɪ] become *[n̩ɔɪ].

To pursue this line of thought further, we need a theory of syllabification. In a recent article (Wells 1990b) I argued that English syllabification is governed by a principle we may call the 'stress attraction' or coda-maximising model. It can be summarised as follows:

Where permitted by morphology and phonotactics, consonants are syllabified with the more strongly stressed of the adjacent vowels. Between weak vowels, they go leftwards.

Thus I take *happy* to be /'hæp i/, *candy* to be /'kænd i/, and *quality* to be /'kwɒl ət i/. I adduced various arguments in favour of this syllabification principle, all relying on the greater elegance of allophonic statement that it makes possible. In the *Longman Pronunciation Dictionary* (Wells 1990a), the entire English vocabulary is phonetically transcribed and syllabified in accordance with this principle.

Implications for syllabic consonants

An interesting consequence of coda-maximising syllabification is that it correctly predicts the possibility of [l̩] internally in certain words, for example

Italy   'ɪt əl i → 'ɪt l̩ i
gluttonous   'glʌt ən əs → 'glʌt n̩ əs
monotony   mə 'nɒt ən i → mə 'nɒt n̩i
vigorous   'vɪg ər əs → 'vɪg ɹ̩ əs
fishery   'fɪʃ ər i → 'fɪʃ ɹ̩ i
redolent   'red əl ənt → 'red l̩ ənt

The syllabic-consonant versions of the first three of these are duly recorded by Jones in his *EPD* (1917); those of the latter three are not, although nowadays they are frequently heard (as indeed in my own usual pronunciations of these words). In fact Jones recognises no more than a handful of cases of possible syllabic [ɹ̩], though there can be little doubt that it exists in current RP as an option both in a large number of words such as those quoted and also in cases involving linking /r/ such as

hammer out   'hæmər 'aʊt → 'hæmɹ̩ 'aʊt
better off   'betər 'ɒf → 'betɹ̩'ɒf

The ending -*ly*

Some morphological boundaries override the syllabification rule, others are overridden by it. In general, the morphological boundary between elements of a compound word is preserved, thus *wide-eyed* per ˌwaɪd ˌaɪd (not ˌ*waɪ ˈdaɪd), *warlike* 'wɔː laɪk (not *'wɔːl aɪk). However, this is often not the case with the boundary before the ending -*ly*, since the /l/ may be resyllabified with the preceding syllable in accordance with the coda-maximising syllabification principle. Thus *daily* seems regularly to be 'deɪl i rather than 'deɪ li; *freely* may indeed be 'friː li, but it may also be 'friːl i . (The difference between the two possibilities here admittedly depends on a quite subtle question of timing.)

When -*ly* is attached to a stem ending in /ə/, the possibility arises of syllabic-consonant formation. This may make the matter of possible resyllabification immediately detectable, because of the co-articulatory implications. Thus *bitterly*, composed of 'bɪt ə plus li, yields an expected 'bɪt ə li. But this is often resyllabified to 'bɪt əl i, as is proved by the possibility of 'bɪt l̩ i – a possibility that is perhaps by now predominant in phrases such as *bitterly cold*. The lateral release of the /t/ in [-tl̩-] makes the difference between this and [-tə-] very evident to the phonetician's ear. The existence of [ɹ] in other accents (and at an earlier period in all accents), as signalled by orthographic *r*, is clearly no bar to the formation of a syllabic consonant incorporating the [ə] that would otherwise be its residue in RP.

Further examples include:

utterly	'ʌtl̩i (as well as 'ʌtəli)
Chatterley	'tʃætl̩i (as well as 'tʃætəli)
westerly	'westl̩i (as well as 'westəli)
sisterly	'sɪstl̩i (as well as 'sɪstəli)
orderly	'ɔːdl̩i (as well as 'ɔːdəli)
elderly	'eldl̩i (as well as 'eldəli)
mannerly	'mænl̩i (as well as 'mænəli)

Compare also such items as *Sunderland* 'sʌndl̩ənd (as well as 'sʌndələnd). Examples involving preceding fricatives (where, as we have seen, the distinction between syllabic consonant and schwa plus non-syllabic consonant may not be so clear-cut) include *northerly* 'nɔːðl̩i ('nɔːðəli), *fatherly* 'fɑːðl̩i ('fɑːðəli), and *miserly* 'maɪzl̩i ('maɪzəli).

The ending -*ily*

Among the English weak vowels we must include not only /ə/ but also the /i/ found at the end of words such as *happy*, which represents the neutralisation of the /iː–ɪ/ opposition (Wells 1990a: 476; Windsor Lewis 1990). Most speakers have a rule switching i to ə in certain pre-l environments. (For speakers of traditional RP, i is identical with ɪ, so that this means possibly switching from /ɪ/ to /ə/. Others, who may use tenser [i]-like qualities in word-final position, virtually always switch, if not all the way to [ə], then at least to an [ɪ]-like quality before /l/.) Thus the i of *angry* typically becomes ə in *angrily* 'æŋgrəli, while *verily* is typically 'verəli (as correctly observed for both these words by Gimson in his revision of *EPD*, 1977, where the forms with ə appear as first choice; Jones did not acknowledge these forms).

The nature of the environment constraint on the rule

i → ə / __ l

depends on both phonological and phonostylistic factors, as well as differing considerably from one speaker to another. A preceding /r/, as in *angrily, articulatorily* seems to be the phonological environment that favours it most highly. Other coronal consonants seem also to favour it, as in *prettily, readily, funnily, healthily, worthily, messily, easily*. Non-coronal consonants disfavour it, although there are plenty of speakers who apply the rule even here, in cases such as *happily, shabbily, clammily, scruffily, heavily, patchily*, *stingily, luckily, foggily,* for all of which Gimson's revision of *EPD* records variants with [ə].

The resultant string [əl] is naturally a candidate for syllabic-consonant formation, in environments which favour the latter process. As usual, this can be most dramatically demonstrated after [t], [d] or [n], where the co-articulatory effects of [l̩] and [əl] are quite different. Thus we find *steadily* quite frequently pronounced ['stedl̩i], with lateral release of the [d]. Similarly we get *mightily* 'maɪtl̩i, rhyming perfectly with *vitally*, and likewise *prettily* 'prɪtl̩i, *readily* 'redl̩i, *bodily* 'bɒdl̩i, *funnily* 'fʌnl̩i. Less immediately obvious to the ear, but certainly very widespread, are the forms 'helθl̩i, 'wɛːðl̩i, 'mesl̩i, 'iːzl̩i, for the words quoted in the previous paragraph; and indeed sometimes also 'hæpl̩i, 'ʃæbl̩i, 'klæml̩i, 'skrʌfl̩i, 'hevl̩i, 'pætʃl̩i, 'stɪndʒl̩i, 'lʌkl̩i, 'fɒgl̩i. The consonant cluster preceding the ə in 'æŋgrəli is generally sufficient to block the formation of a syllabic consonant in that word, but in cases such as *merrily* 'merəli there is a variant 'merl̩i. (In Windsor Lewis 1972, separate entries were accorded to *bodily, easily, heavily*, so that the possibility of a syllabic consonant could be explicitly shown: not so *steadily*, though.)

Corresponding pronunciations may sometimes also be heard involving *-less*, as in *penniless* 'penɪləs → 'penələs → penl̩əs, *pitiless* 'pɪtɪləs → 'pɪtələs → 'pɪtl̩əs, *mercilessly* 'mɜːsɪləsli → 'mɜːsələsli → 'mɜːsl̩əsli.

ANOMALIES

What our syllabification rule does *not* lead us to expect is a syllabic l in words such as *catalogue* or a syllabic n in words such as *detonate*. Yet the pronunciations 'kætl̩ɒg and 'detn̩eɪt are undoubtedly widespread in the RP of speakers born since the 1930s, and may even be displacing the traditional 'kætəlɒg, 'detəneɪt.

Further examples include the following (first the conservative form, then the newer form with a syllabic consonant: the latter being my own usual pronunciation of the words in question).

satellite	'sætəlaɪt → 'sætl̩aɪt
analyse	'ænəlaɪz → 'ænl̩aɪz
fraternise	'frætənaɪz → 'frætn̩aɪz
commissionaire	kə,mɪʃə'neə → kə,mɪʃn̩'eə
impersonation	ɪm,pɜːsə'neɪʃn̩ → ɜːsn̩'eɪʃn̩
Chattanooga	,tʃætə'nuːgə → ,tʃætn̩'uːgə
anorak	'ænəræk → 'ænɾæk

There are also various words where a conservative pronunciation, still widespread, has a weak /ɪ/, but a newer variety has /ə/, with the expected possible consequences when followed by a sonorant:

intellectual	ˌɪntɪˈlektjuəl → ˌɪntəˈlektʃuəl → ˌɪntl̩ˈektʃuəl
co-ordination	kəʊˌɔːdɪˈneɪʃn̩ → kəʊˌɔːdəˈneɪʃn̩ → kəʊˌɔːdn̩ˈeɪʃn̩
cardinality	ˌkɑːdɪˈnælɪti → ˌkɑːdəˈnæləti → ˌkɑːdn̩ˈæləti

Sonorant left capture

The reason these syllabic consonants are unexpected is that we expect the syllabification rule to put the ə and the following sonorant consonant in different syllables, so that syllabic-consonant formation would be barred. In *catalogue* /ˈkætəlɒg/ the vowel /ə/ is weak, while /ɒ/ is strong. Hence we expect to syllabify as ˈkæt ə lɒg. Even more strikingly, in *co-ordination* /kəʊˌɔːdəˈneɪʃn̩/ the consonant is straddled by a weak /ə/ and an /eɪ/ that is not only strong but bears the primary word stress, so that we expect the syllabification kəʊ ˌɔːd ə ˈneɪʃ n̩. If the ə and the following l or n are in different syllables, how can they coalesce to form l̩ and n̩?

To account for such forms, what we need is a SONORANT LEFT CAPTURE rule which resyllabifies a sonorant leftwards: taking it away from a following strong vowel, and attaching it instead to a preceding ə. The newly constituted syllable thus provides an input for possible syllabic-consonant formation. Using the symbols σ, O, R to stand for syllable, onset and rhyme, we have

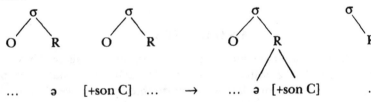

We thus have the following derivation for *catalogue*:

underlying representation	ˈkætəlɒg
syllabification	ˈkæt ə lɒg
sonorant left capture	ˈkæt əl ɒg
syllabic consonant formation	ˈkæt l̩ ɒg

The resyllabification rule, sonorant left capture, is presumably variable, depending upon style of speech and individual factors. We have already seen that the rule it feeds, syllabic-consonant formation, is probabilistic as well as phonostylistic.

In American English, unlike RP and most British English, syllabic-consonant formation readily applies to /ən/ when preceded by the cluster /nt/. Thus for *Clinton* we usually have AmE ˈklɪntn̩, but RP ˈklɪntən; for *accountant*, AmE əˈkaʊntn̩t, RP əˈkaʊntənt. Hence when sonorant left capture affects a word such as *continental*, the result is AmE ˌkɑːntn̩ˈentl̩; but in RP, even though ə nowadays sometimes displaces conservative ɪ in the second syllable, there is unlikely to be syllabic-consonant formation after the first nt, and (as a citation form, at least) we get only ˌkɒntə'nentl̩.

Morphological boundaries

There are several examples to hand that demonstrate the possibility of the sonorant left capture rule operating across morphological boundaries. Opinions will differ as to whether the name *Waterloo* involves any morpheme boundary; whatever the answer, my own pronunciation of the name (the London railway station through which I pass every day) is certainly ˌwɔːtl̩'uː. I am not alone in this, although ˌwɔːtə'luː probably remains the predominant form. When I say, however, that I am 'not alone', what I actually pronounce is ˌnɒtl̩'əʊn; and this certainly involves sonorant capture across a word boundary.

Other examples include (a) across a morpheme boundary within a word:

borderline	'bɔːdl̩aɪn ('bɔːdəlaɪn)
interlude	'ɪntl̩uːd ('ɪntəluːd)

and (b) across a word boundary:

get along	'getl̩'ɒŋ (ˌget ə'lɒŋ)
write another	ˌraɪtn̩'ʌðə (ˌraɪt ə'nʌðə)
better not	ˌbetn̩'ɒt (ˌbetə 'nɒt)
had a lot	ˌhædl̩ 'ɒt (ˌhæd ə 'lɒt)

– these examples also demonstrating that there may be a boundary either before the ə (*get along, write another*), or after it (*better not*), or both (*had a lot*).

In isolation, as is well known, *an aim* ən 'eɪm sounds different from *a name* ə 'neɪm: the difference of syllabification is reflected in the different allophones of /n/ triggered by syllable-final and syllable-initial position respectively. It follows logically from the nature of sonorant left capture that it effaces this distinction. Thus if we choose the option of syllabic-consonant formation in *got an aim* and *got a name*, we find that the two are homophonous: ˌgɒtn̩'eɪm. Similarly, *had an ice(d)* drink 'hæd ən ˌaɪs 'drɪŋk is distinct from *had a nice drink* 'hæd ə ˌnaɪs 'drɪŋk; but with syllabic consonants the two phrases tend to become homophonous as 'hæd n̩ ˌaɪs 'drɪŋk.

A NEW PHENOMENON IN RP?

It might seem to be a bit of a mystery why such variants are virtually absent from Jones (and those few found in Gimson wrongly analysed). Has RP changed in this respect?

409

Jones' account

The easiest way to check whether these syllabic consonants were known to Daniel Jones is to examine his *English Pronouncing Dictionary* (1917). In his transcriptions prevocalic syllabic consonants are mostly restricted to inflectional forms (*-ing, -er*) of stems ending in syllabic consonants (e.g. *settling, threatening*; see Jones 1959). He has a few cases involving *-y* and *-ous* (*gluttony, monotonous, scandalous*) and two involving *-aire* (*commissionaire, concessionaire*). Beyond this, there are very few instances; among those that I have noted are *Italy, litany*, and *satellite* (all as subsidiary variants). Indeed, it is striking that even in the later revisions by Gimson and Ramsaran the apparent inconsistency remains of a possible ļ in *satellite* but not in the comparable *catalogue* or *analyse*.

Jones uses italic symbols to denote a sound that is 'sometimes pronounced and sometimes omitted', the two possibilities 'appear[ing] to be of approximately equal frequency'. Thus his notation at *vigorous* ('vɪɡərəs) and *liberal* ('lɪbərəl) does not imply a possible ɾ, merely the possibility of trisyllabic and disyllabic versions ('vɪɡərəs, 'lɪbərəl; 'vɪɡrəs, 'lɪbrəl, 'lɪbrļ) – i.e., in terms of Wells (1990a), without and with compression.

The interesting pair *formerly* and *formally* are shown by Jones as homophones, but only with -məl–, not with -mļ-.

Since Jones was a meticulous observer, the increased use of syllabic consonants by RP speakers at the present time must constitute one of the ways in which RP (and English English in general) has changed during the present century.

What is the origin of the change? Is it possible that it comes from American English? Kenyon and Knott (1953) show only syllabic-consonant pronunciations for *analyse*, in their transcriptions 'ænļˌaɪz, *catalogue* 'kætļˌɔɡ, *intellectual* ˌɪntļ'ɛktʃuəl and the like, and as one of two possibilities at words such as *readily* 'rɛdļɪ, 'rɛdɪlɪ. They do not cater for a syllabic consonant at *detonate* 'dɛtəˌneɪt. The intervening /r/ of course prevents syllabic-consonant formation in cases such as AmE *bitterly, interlude*.

It seems, therefore, that if the English borrowed this new pronunciation habit from the Americans, it was a matter of borrowing a rule (sonorant left capture), rather than borrowing the pronunciations of individual words. Having borrowed the rule, it was natural for us, as speakers of a non-rhotic variety, to apply it to cases such as *bitterly* and *interlude* to which it could not apply in American English. In fact it may be that we must look not to American but rather to Scottish or Irish English for the source of the borrowing. They are not well enough described to permit any firm conclusion. Nevertheless, they too, like General American, are rhotic; so the point made in the preceding paragraph stands.

Gimson's account

In his widely used textbook A. C. Gimson (1980: 293, in the section on 'The word in connected speech, elision') notes some examples of what we have identified as sonorant left capture across word boundaries. His transcription and phonemic analysis, however, must be regarded as idiosyncratic, if not outright faulty.

> *not alone* 'nɒtl̩ 'ləʊn, *get another* 'getn̩ 'nʌðə,
> *run along* 'rʌnl̩ 'lɒŋ, *he was annoyed* hɪ wəzn̩ 'nɔɪd

Comparison with the phrase *is the bottle low?* (-'bɒtl̩ 'ləʊ) shows *that not alone* is more usually 'nɒtl̩ 'əʊn, with but a single lateral segment. Similarly, we can contrast Gimson's other examples with such phrases as *threaten nothing, Is the tunnel long?, He wasn('t) noisy.* In each case there is a clear phonetic difference at the crucial point.

In London there is a bicycle shop with the punning name *Cycle Logical.* But, *pace* Gimson, the pun is not a perfect one: the shop is 'saɪkl̩'lɒdʒɪkl̩, while *psychological* (with sonorant left capture feeding syllabic-consonant formation) is 'saɪkl̩'ɒdʒɪkl̩. The rule involved in *not alone* and *psychological* is not a segment-copying rule but a resyllabifying segment movement rule (left capture).

Final note

In my syllabification article (Wells 1990b), I commented that I found the predicted syllabification of *accelerate* as ək 'sel ə reɪt and *memorize* as 'mem ə raɪz to be counter-intuitive. Now I can see why: the /r/s are candidates for left capture, which accounts for my own usual pronunciations ək'selr̩eɪt, 'memr̩aɪz. Anomalous or not, I felt uneasy about left-uncaptured sonorants.

REFERENCES

Barry, W. and Grice, M. (1991) 'Auditory and visual factors in speech database analysis', in *Speech Hearing and Language: Work in Progress*, Vol. 5, University College London Dept of Phonetics and Linguistics.

Gimson, A. C. (1980) *An Introduction to the Pronunciation of English*, 3rd edn, London: Edward Arnold; 1st edn, 1962; 4th edn, ed. S. Ramsaran, 1989.

Jones, D. (1917) *English Pronouncing Dictionary*, London: Dent; 12th edn, 1963; 14th edn, ed. A. C. Gimson, 1977; reprinted with revisions and supplement by S. Ramsaran, 1988, 1991, Cambridge: Cambridge University Press.

—— (1950) *The Phoneme, its Nature and Use*, Cambridge: Heffer; 2nd edn, 1962; 3rd edn, 1976.

—— (1959) 'The use of syllabic and non-syllabic *l* and *n* in derivatives of English words ending in syllabic *l* and *n*', *Zeitschrift für Phonetik und allgemeine Sprachwissenschaft* 12: 1–4.

Kenyon, J. S. and Knott, T. A. (1953) *A Pronouncing Dictionary of American English*, Springfield, MA: Merriam (1st edn: 1944).

Trubetzkoy, N. S. (1939) *Grundzüge der Phonologie* (TCLP 7), repr. 1958, Göttingen: Vandenhöck & Ruprecht.

Wells, J. C. (1990a) *Longman Pronunciation Dictionary*, Harlow: Longman.

—— (1990b) 'Syllabification and allophony', in S. Ramsaran (ed.), *Studies in the Pronunciation of English: A Commemorative Volume in Honour of A. C. Gimson*, London: Routledge, pp. 76–86.

Windsor Lewis, J. (1972) *A Concise Pronouncing Dictionary of British and American English*, London: Oxford University Press.

—— (1990) 'HappY land reconnoitred: the unstressed word-final -y vowel in General British pronunciation', in S. Ramsaran (ed.), *Studies in the Pronunciation of English: A Commemorative Volume in Honour of A. C. Gimson*, London: Routledge, pp. 159-167.

Part IV

THE PHONETICS OF
NON-MOTHER-TONGUE
ENGLISH

34

Approaches to articulatory setting in foreign-language teaching

Beverley Collins
University of Leiden
Inger M. Mees
The Copenhagen Business School

INTRODUCTION

O'Connor (1973: 289–90) emphasises the importance of articulatory setting (henceforth AS), i.e. the overall manner in which the speech organs are held and which underlies all articulatory movements superimposed on them. In this paper, we shall discuss how a knowledge of setting can help the Danish learner to acquire convincing American English pronunciation, and compare the pedagogic approach needed with that appropriate for other types of learner.[1]

The idea of AS can be traced back a long way (Knowles 1978: 89; Laver 1978) but the concept appears to have been clearly stated first in the classic work of Henry Sweet (1890: 69), under the heading of 'organic basis':

> Every language has certain tendencies which control its organic movements and positions, constituting its organic basis or the basis of articulation. A knowledge of the organic basis is a great help in acquiring the pronunciation of a language.

Similar notions are expressed in Zwaardemaker and Eijkman (1928: 305–7), which contains a notable contrastive section on *articulatiebasis*, i.e. 'basis of articulation'; but the credit for reviving the idea in relatively recent times goes to Honikman (1964: 73), who coined the term 'articulatory setting' and redefined it as 'the overall arrangement and manoeuvring of the speech organs necessary for the facile accomplishment of natural utterance'. Like Sweet, Honikman (1964: 74–6) emphasised that 'all languages do not have identical settings'. She also distinguished between 'external setting', in particular lips and jaw, and 'internal setting', i.e. tongue, velum and pharynx. Her description of the latter concentrates on tongue setting at the expense of the larynx but subsequent work, notably

415

that of Laver (1968; 1980: 24–31, 93–135), has revealed that the setting of the vocal folds is a crucial differentiator of voice quality, both for whole speech communities and for individuals (see also Van Buuren 1988).

DESCRIPTIONS OF SETTING

Various descriptions have been made of the AS of British English (RP), e.g. Honikman (1964), mainly in relation to French; Collins and Mees (1984: 189–90) in relation to Dutch (see Jenner 1987 for a subsequent expanded analysis on very similar lines). In addition, outlines of the AS of at least three British regional accents of English have been published: Norwich (Trudgill 1974: 185–93). Liverpool (Knowles 1978: 88–90) and Cardiff (Collins and Mees 1990: 88–9); however, to our knowledge, only one description of the AS of General American (GA) English is widely available (Esling and Wong 1983) whilst Danish AS has been described (briefly) only in Mees and Collins (1987: 101–2; 1992: 98–9).[2]

DANISH ARTICULATORY SETTING

In Danish, the lips show considerable activity in the production of vowels, this activity being utilised, in particular, as a feature distinguishing the series of front rounded and front unrounded vowels. On the other hand, lip rounding is insignificant in consonants, arising only as a result of contextual assimilation from adjacent vowels. The jaw setting is relatively tight.

The front of the tongue is tense and raised towards the palate (palatalisation) thus giving an [i]- or [j]-like colouring to sounds, discernible in the obviously 'clear' quality of Danish /l/ and /n/. Palatalisation also affects other consonants in the context preceding close front vowels or /j/, in the former case giving rise to a [j]-like off-glide, e.g. *firma* 'company' ['fʲiɒmæ], *tirsdag* ['tʲiɒʔsdæ] 'Tuesday', *kirke* ['kʲiɒɡə] 'church', *kjole* ['kʲjoːlə] 'dress'. The Danish palatalised setting is in some respects similar to that described by several writers for French (e.g. Honikman 1964: 78–9; Laver 1980: 47–8).

The root of the tongue is tense and drawn down towards the lower pharynx wall producing the laryngo-pharyngealisation characteristic of Danish /r/, found both in word-initial approximant allophones and in postvocalic contexts when /r/ is realised as an open back vowel. Vowels adjacent to /r/ are also affected by this type of pharyngealisation; the quality of the non-pharyngealised allophone in *kat* [kæɖ] 'cat' is strikingly different from that of the pharyngealised realisation in *rat* [ʁɑɖ] 'steering wheel'.

If one takes a diagram like Figure 34.1 (slightly modified from Laver 1980: 45) showing an array of possible radial directions of movement in lingual settings as illustrated below, it would be possible to characterise

416

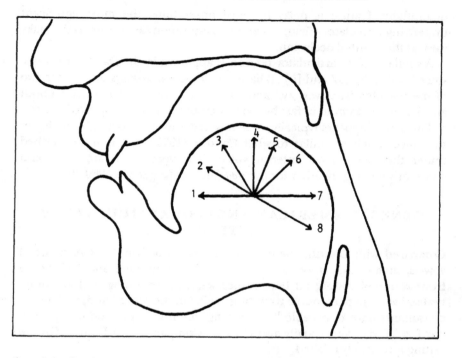

1	dentalisation	5	velarisation
2	alveolarisation	6	uvularisation
3	palato-alveolarisation	7	pharyngealisation
4	palatalisation	8	larnygo-pharyngealisation

Figure 34.1 Diagram to illustrate a possible range of lingual tongue settings (after Laver 1980: 45, with modified numbering)

Danish as having a 4 + 8 type of lingual setting (i.e. palatalisation plus laryngo-pharyngealisation).

The phenomenon of aspiration in languages like Danish, English and Standard German can also be explained in terms of an AS attribute of lack of tension, rather than being treated solely as a feature of voice onset time. In Danish, the body of the tongue is lax and there is a noticeable lack of tip firmness in the apico-alveolar closure for Danish /t/, producing the aspirated or – increasingly in the present-day language – affricated realisations of this phoneme, e.g. *time* ['t^{s}iːmə] 'hour' . Likewise, the velar closure for /k/ is loose, giving rise to the leak of air and voiceless onset to the following vowel: *kime* ['k^{h}iːmə] 'to chime'; whilst the slack labial contact for Danish /p/ also results in a similar 'leaky' effect: *pine* ['p^{h}iːnə] 'pain'. In all these instances, one might surmise that although the most easily quantifiable feature is delay in voice onset time, the most significant underlying articulatory feature leading to aspiration/affrication is the leaky valve at the point of occlusion.

A similar lack of articulator tension is apparent in the Danish fricatives, since Danish /f, v, s/ and [ð] all have very loose narrowings. As a result, two of the so-called fricatives, /v/ and [ð], are almost always realised without any friction and would in fact be more logically considered approximants.

The larynx appears typically to be lowered and there is a tight quality to the voice which is similar to what Catford (1977: 102–3) has described under the heading of 'anterior voice'. The vocal folds are tense and constantly moving together for the *stød* (Fischer-Jørgensen 1989: 8).

GENERAL AMERICAN ENGLISH ARTICULATORY SETTING

Compared with Danish, there is much less lip activity for GA rounded vowels, such as /uː, ʊ, oʊ, ɔː/. These are few in number and include no front rounded vowels; all have rather weak lip rounding and are often realised with no perceptible rounding at all. On the other hand, certain GA consonants have noticeable lip rounding, often with protruding lips, e.g. /w, ʃ, ʒ, tʃ, dʒ/ and usually also GA /r/. Compared with Danish, GA jaw setting is relatively relaxed.

GA also has areas of tenseness and laxness in the vocal tract but in different locations from those of Danish. The tip/blade of the tongue has more tension than in Danish and this portion of the tongue articulating against the teeth/alveolar ridge forms the centre of activity for many consonant sounds, e.g. /θ, ð, s, z, t, d, n, l/. In general, GA has somewhat tighter closures for stops and closer narrowings for fricatives.

Esling and Wong (1983: 91–2) describe American English as palatalised, citing in evidence the raising of front open vowels. Such raising, incidentally, would appear to be more noticeable in non-standard American English, such as New York City, and many Southern accents (Wells 1982: 477–9; 510–14; 531–3; 535–6) than in mainstream GA. We cannot detect in standard General American anything analogous to the overall palatalisation effect heard in Danish, and should prefer to regard the characteristic anterior tongue setting of American English as alveolarised, i.e. with the tip/blade of the tongue poised to be raised towards the alveolar ridge.

Additionally, GA is characterised by strong *r*-colouring affecting not only vowels preceding /r/ but also adjacent consonants; for example, in *partner* not only are the two vowels influenced, but also the /t/ and /n/. Given the high frequency of /r/ in rhotic accents such as GA, it is not surprising that it has a considerable overall influence on pronunciation. GA /r/ is pronounced with what has frequently been termed a 'bunched' tongue-shape (Higgs 1980: 114; Mackay 1987: 107; Kreidler 1989: 42), i.e. a characteristic configuration with the body of the tongue hollowed, the sides of the back of the tongue raised in contact with the molars, and the tongue root drawn back. Catford (1988: 206) describes American /r/ thus:

> The body of the tongue is bunched up into roughly the position of an [ɤ] vowel. At the same time the root of the tongue is slightly retracted into the pharynx (slight deep pharyngalization) and there is a short longitudinal furrow in the dorsal surface of the tongue roughly opposite the uvula, or a little forward from there.

Elsewhere, in his description of the r-coloured vowel in *bird*, Catford (1988: 170) refers to this concavity opposite the uvula as 'sulcalisation'.[3]

It is possible to see a connection here with another similar semi-continuous feature involving the raising of the back of the tongue – but with no concavity – namely the uvularisation involved in the articulation of GA /l/ and /n/. This gives rise to what is generally termed the 'dark' quality of these consonants, particularly in postvocalic contexts. Here the body of the tongue is hollowed and the back raised towards a point somewhat in advance of the uvula.

On the basis of Figure 34.1 above, GA tongue setting could be characterised as 6 + 2, i.e. uvularisation combined with alveolarisation. By contrast, RP might be considered as 2 + 5, i.e. predominantly alveolarisation plus a degree of velarisation.

One further very important influence on GA is a quality of nasalisation. The velopharyngeal valve appears never to be completely closed, permitting a constant leak of air which adds resonance from the nasal cavity.[4] Nasalisation is clearly heard if a vowel is adjacent to a nasal consonant, but not only there; it is semi-continuous, seeming to colour the whole of most American speech (Moulton 1962: 59; Strevens 1972: 78; Esling and Wong 1983: 92).

The vocal folds are laxer in GA than in Danish. Glottal reinforcement although frequent is not as all-pervasive a feature as Danish *stød* (see Fischer-Jørgensen 1989 for a detailed discussion of the phonetic correlates of glottal stop, creaky voice, creak and *stød*). Furthermore, less tension is transmitted to adjacent phonemes. In contrast to Danish, GA speakers typically do not appear to have the 'tight' voice quality associated with anterior voice. GA – especially in its prestigious varieties – seems often to be characterised by a degree of larynx lowering; this is, for example, very commonly heard from newscasters (see Esling and Wong 1983: 92).

PRACTICAL APPLICATION OF ARTICULATORY SETTING

Previous writers (see, for example, Sweet and Honikman above) have considered AS in relationship to second-language acquisition. Mees and

Collins (1987: 10–12) applied contrastive AS description to pronunciation training for Danes learning RP English, whilst Mees and Collins (1992: 98–100) attempt the same for the Danish learner of GA on the lines set out below.

Speakers of Standard Danish learning an American model of English should modify their AS in the following ways:

1 Adopt generally tenser setting of the body of the tongue, with firmer closures and narrowings for stops and fricatives and use of the tongue tip for alveolar consonants.
2 Avoid palatalisation in favour of uvularisation plus bunched tongue shape to produce /r/ and provide r-colouring for r-adjacent segments.
3 Adopt semi-continuous nasalisation.
4 Adopt laxer lip setting to facilitate weak rounding and protrusion for certain consonants.
5 Adopt relaxed larynx setting for weaker glottalisation and avoidance of anterior voice.

A DIFFERENTIATED APPROACH

Since AS varies from language to language and from accent to accent, advice to learners acquiring a second language will depend crucially on the differences between the AS of the particular variety of their first language and the pronunciation model of the target language.

Different and apparently contradictory instructions may sometimes have to be suggested to learners with different language backgrounds. To illustrate this, we may contrast the AS strategies required for students of American English who are from (1) Danish-speaking and (2) Dutch-speaking backgrounds.

DUTCH SETTING AND THE DUTCH LEARNER

In contrast to Danish, Dutch setting is notable for firmly held closures for stop consonants, using large areas of the articulators. As might be expected (see p. 417 above), therefore, aspiration in the fortis plosives is minimal. The tongue setting is characterised by inactivity of the tip; the tip is, in fact, usually lowered, being held behind the bottom front teeth during rest and even for coronal articulations. Many articulations involve the blade/front area of the tongue in contact (or near-contact) with the rear of the alveolar ridge/anterior portion of the palate. The root of the tongue is drawn back to approach the pharynx wall. This root retraction is apparent in the strong pharyngealisation of dark [l] (Mees and Collins 1982: 7–8) and also affects /n/, which – as in American English – is considerably darker than its counterpart in most other languages (Fischer-

420

Jørgensen and Talma-Schilthuis 1948: 7). The high-frequency vowel /ɔ/ as in *mot* 'moth' is also strongly pharyngealised (Mees and Collins 1983: 66). There is considerable activity in the uvular/velar area in the articulation of /x/, and (for many Dutch speakers) also /r/. Using the system outlined above (pp. 416–18 and 418–19), Dutch tongue setting might be categorised as 6/7 + 3.

Velic closure tends to be lax, with semi-continuous nasalisation as a feature of connected speech. The glottis has a tight setting, with raised larynx and very little use of creaky voice. For further detail of Dutch setting, see Collins and Mees (1984: 189–90); cf. Jenner (1987); for contrast of Dutch and GA settings, see also Collins and Mees (1993: 95–6).

In contrast with the Danish learner, who would be asked to make firmer and tenser closures, the Dutch student of GA would be prescribed looser contacts for plosives, particularly in order to achieve aspiration for initial [p, t, k]. In respect of lingual setting, the Dutch student will be required to adopt a less pharyngealised AS; the Dane, on the other hand, would be instructed to remove palatalisation and acquire a degree of uvularisation. Any instruction to adopt tongue bunching (i.e. side-tongue raising) for /r/, whilst essential for the Danish learner of GA, would be superfluous for the typical Dutch student, who already has an AS which in this respect is suitable for American English. Because of the frequent occurrence of *stød* in Danish, the Danish learner has a glottal setting which is readily adaptable to the articulation of the glottal reinforcement found in GA syllable-final stops. The Dutch learner, on the other hand, has a larynx setting which is quite inappropriate for the adoption of this feature.

Additionally, advice on AS will depend on the model of pronunciation chosen as a target: for example, the requirement above to adopt tongue bunching for postvocalic /r/, so important for GA, will be quite out of place for the student of British English. Again, the prescription of a somewhat nasalised setting would be more appropriate for American English than for RP.

PEDAGOGIC ADVANTAGES OF AN ARTICULATORY SETTING APPROACH

By definition, AS phenomena extend over more than a single segment (Laver 1980: 2–3); that is to say, they are essentially prosodic in character. As a result, AS prescriptions given with the aim of correcting the articulation of one segment are also likely to improve the neighbouring vowels or consonants. As O'Connor (1973: 289) puts it, 'better results are achieved when the learner gets the basis of articulation right rather than trying for the foreign sound sequences from the basis of his own language': for example, the adoption of tongue bunching will improve not only realisations of GA /r/ but also vowels and consonants adjacent to them.

Furthermore, in terms of pronunciation teaching strategy, an AS approach has advantages of economy since AS phenomena generally have application to several phonemes of the target language. Thus a recommendation to work towards a less palatalised AS will assist a Danish learner with the articulation of a whole range of English consonants, i.e. /ʃ, ʒ, tʃ, dʒ, w, n, l/, together with any adjacent vowels. Such a strategy is likely to be more effective than piecemeal attacks on each individual speech sound. *Mutatis mutandis*, the same goes for the Dutch student.

Just as in any other form of articulatory pronunciation training, the ease of providing effective AS teaching prescriptions varies greatly according to the location within the vocal tract. Here, Honikman's categorisation of internal and external AS marks an important dichotomy. Lip and jaw settings are easy to demonstrate and it is not difficult for students to obtain corroborative evidence from their own observations. The aspects of internal AS are less straightforward and the difficulty for the instructor and the student obviously increases as one moves further back within the vocal tract. Instructions based on the apical and laminal settings of the tongue in the anterior portion of the oral cavity are relatively uncomplicated for the student, since there is good proprioceptive sense in this region. Dorsal tongue settings make greater demands on the student, whilst velopharyngeal, pharyngeal and, especially, laryngeal settings are far more problematical. In these areas, one must rely to a large extent on imitation and imitation labels.

CONCLUSION

Whilst AS prescriptions cannot ever replace all traditional teaching techniques based on segmental contrastive analysis, we believe that they can nevertheless be a very valuable aid to expediting such procedures. However, it has frequently been stated that the range of AS phenomena has been inadequately explored and described (see, for instance, Wells 1982: 91). Although great progress has been made in the last two decades in general phonetic research on voice quality and related phenomena (e.g. Laver 1980), contrastive studies of AS are few, and the application of these to practical teaching is still in its infancy. At the moment, much of the description of AS features – including our own – is largely impressionistic. What O'Connor (1973: 289) stated over two decades ago remains largely true at the time of writing:

We know a good deal more about the detailed articulatory movements in a language than we know about the general articulatory background on which they are superimposed, and with greater knowledge we might be able to explain in these terms a great many differences in sound between languages, which at present puzzle us.

422

NOTES

1 A preliminary version of the ideas presented here has appeared in *POET* (1992), the departmental publication of the English Department of the University of Copenhagen and a paper on this topic was read at the 1992 Amsterdam Symposium on the Acquisition of Second-language Speech.

2 Some details in the present description of Danish setting supersede those to be found in Mees and Collins (1987: 101–2).

3 There is some variation in the assignment of place articulation – for example, Higgs terms American /r/ as prevelar as opposed to Catford's uvular. However, all quoted scholars (with one exception, see below) are in agreement in regarding GA /r/ as being typically a back tongue articulation, rather than tongue-tip 'retroflex' as previously thought. Esling and Wong's (1983: 92) description of 'retroflexion of the tongue tip' in the setting of American English would seem, surprisingly, to retain the traditional view of American /r/.

4 It has been considered for many years (for fuller discussion, see, for example, Laver 1980: 68–92) that the effect of nasalised speech has additional and more complex factors involved than merely the nature of the velopharyngeal closure.

REFERENCES

Abercrombie, D., Fry, D. B., MacCarthy, P. A. D., Scott, N. C. and Trim, J. L. (eds) (1964) *In Honour of Daniel Jones*, London: Longman.

Catford, J. C. (1977) *Fundamental Problems in Phonetics*, Edinburgh: Edinburgh University Press.

—— (1988) *A Practical Introduction to Phonetics*, Oxford: Clarendon Press.

Collins, B. and Mees, I. M. (1984) *The Sounds of English and Dutch*, 2nd edn, Leiden: Brill/Leiden University Press.

—— (1990) 'The phonetics of Cardiff English', in N. Coupland and A. R. Thomas (eds), *English in Wales*, Clevedon and Philadelphia: Multilingual Matters, pp. 87–103.

—— (1993) *Accepted American Pronunciation*, Apeldoorn: Van Walraven.

Esling, J. and Wong, R. (1983) 'Voice quality settings and the teaching of pronunciation', *TESOL Quarterly* 17, 1: 89–95.

Fischer-Jørgensen, E. (1989) *A Phonetic Study of the Stød in Standard Danish*, Turku: Turku University, Dept of Phonetics.

Fischer-Jørgensen, E. and Talma-Schilthuis, J. G. (1948) 'Specimen of Dutch', *Le Maître phonétique* 3, 89: 5–8.

Higgs, J. (1980) 'The American /r/ is advanced velar not post-alveolar', *Work in Progress 13*, Edinburgh University Dept of Linguistics, 112–6.

Honikman, B. (1964) 'Articulatory settings', in D. Abercrombie, D. B. Fry, P. A. D. MacCarthy, N. C. Scott and J. L. Trim (eds), *In Honour of Daniel Jones*, London: Longman, pp. 73–84.

Jenner, B. R. A. (1987) 'Articulation and phonation in non-native English: the example of Dutch-English', *Journal of the International Phonetic Association* 17, 2: 125–38.

Knowles, G. O. (1978) 'The nature of phonological variables in Scouse', in P. Trudgill (ed.), *Sociolinguistic patterns in British English*, London: Edward Arnold, pp. 80–90.

Kreidler, C. W. (1989) *The Pronunciation of English: A Course Book in Phonology*, Oxford/New York: Blackwell.

Laver, J. (1968) 'Voice quality and indexical information', *British Journal of Disorders of Communication* 3: 43–54.

—— (1978) 'The concept of articulatory settings: an historical survey', *Historiographia Linguistica* 5: 1–14.

—— (1980) *The Phonetic Description of Voice Quality*, Cambridge: Cambridge University Press.

Mackay, I. R. A. (1987) *Phonetics: The Science of Speech Production*, Boston, Toronto and San Diego: Little, Brown.

Mees, I. M. and Collins, B. (1982) 'A phonetic description of the consonant system of Standard Dutch (ABN)', *Journal of the International Phonetic Association* 12: 2–12.

—— (1983) 'A phonetic description of the vowel system of Standard Dutch (ABN)', *Journal of the International Phonetic Association* 13: 64–75.

—— (1987) *Sound English*, Copenhagen: Nyt Nordisk Forlag Arnold Busck.

—— (1992) *Sound American*, Copenhagen: Nyt Nordisk Forlag Arnold Busck.

Moulton, W. G. (1962) *The Sounds of English and German*, Chicago and London: University of Chicago Press.

O'Connor, J. D. (1973) *Phonetics*, Harmondsworth: Penguin.

Strevens, P. (1972) *British and American English*, London: Collier-Macmillan.

Sweet, H. (1890) *A Primer of Phonetics*, Oxford: Clarendon Press.

Trudgill, P. (1974) *The Social Differentiation of English in Norwich*, Cambridge: Cambridge University Press.

—— (ed.) (1978) *Sociolinguistic Patterns in British English*, London: Edward Arnold.

Van Buuren, L. (1988) 'Margaret Thatcher's pronunciation: an exercise in ear-training', *Journal of the International Phonetic Association* 18.1, 26–38.

Wells, J. C. (1982) *Accents of English*, Cambridge: Cambridge University Press.

Zwaardemaker, H. and Eijkman, L. P. H. (1928) *Leerboek der Phonetiek*, Haarlem: De Erven F. Bohn.

35

The English accent of the Shilluk speaker

Y. M. L. Le Clézio
University College London

The data presented here derive from an investigation into Shilluk, a Nilotic language spoken in southern Sudan. During the period of my research a number of reasons, in particular the war in southern Sudan, made it impossible for me to stay for any long period of time in Shilluk-speaking areas. As a result, the collection of data took place instead principally in Khartoum. During the early stages it was essential that my informants should have a reasonably good command of English and therefore I relied on several university students and a few Shilluk Catholic priests and Protestant ministers; later I also obtained information from people with a lower level of education or none, conducting the interviews in Khartoum Arabic, Southern Sudanese Arabic (Janûbî) and Shilluk.

As Shilluk is a tone language, in order to study its tonal system I needed to take account of the pitch variations used by each informant during the interviews. So whenever possible I asked them to say in English or in Arabic the equivalents of the words and sentences which they were giving me in Shilluk, all of which I recorded on tape. The items in English supplied the data for the present study.

Like so many African countries, Sudan presents a vast array of cultures and languages. Unfortunately, history has gradually created a deep cultural division and considerable antagonism between the northern part of the country, where Khartoum lies, and the south. Islam is the religion of most northerners, who speak various local colloquial Arabics (of which Khartoum Arabic is just one variety, although it is what is usually meant when people refer to Sudanese Arabic) either as their first languages or in order to communicate with other ethnic groups. On the other hand, in the south, Christianity and traditional animist religions prevail and, although Janûbî is spoken to some extent in the towns, its use is not very widespread and the various peoples speak a great number of largely unrelated languages.

During the period of the Anglo-Egyptian Condominium, English and Arabic were used as administrative languages in the north by the dual colonial authorities, but the British tended to make the south a separate area in which English was the main language of administration and education. The local languages played a minor role in the process and Arabic was virtually eliminated. Since then, by a change of policy initiated in the dominant northern Sudan after independence, Arabic has become the official language of the whole of the country and in particular the language of education in the south. This policy is not at all to the taste of the southerners, who still prefer to use English rather than Arabic whenever possible. As a result, among the Shilluk one finds that many people aged thirty-five or over have a fairly good knowledge of English but among the children and adolescents the level of knowledge is much lower. Consequently, it was inevitable that at the time of my research I should have found the range of proficiency in English among the Shilluk to vary considerably. At one end of the scale there was very little knowledge of the language and a general inability to communicate in it. Because my research was into Shilluk I have no recordings of this type of English. At the other end of the scale, a couple of persons turned out to be highly fluent no doubt on account of constant contacts with the English-speaking world. Between these extremes the majority of those I approached had a fairly good command of English, even if this command varied somewhat according to task and circumstances, but with a very noticeable accent.

For our present purposes we can for two reasons ignore the fact that Shilluk is divided into three main dialects. First, these dialects seem to share roughly the same sets of phonemes and tonemes, differing chiefly in their stock of lexical items and in various features of the words they have in common: for example, a particular word with a high level tone in one dialect has a mid-low falling tone in another. Second, my informants were able to use the standard form of Shilluk, which is based on the central dialect and can be heard in certain, often formal, circumstances all over Shilluk territory. As happens in many similar situations, transfer to English may well have been on the basis of this sort of Shilluk rather than their particular dialects.

Those who have taught English to the Shilluk have been of very diverse origins. Before independence schoolteachers came mainly from the United Kingdom, but there were also American, Italian and Central European missionaries. Since then Arabic-speaking teachers, chiefly from northern Sudan but also from Egypt, have taken over and therefore some influence of their accents is not impossible. English is used in Khartoum among the educated Sudanese to discuss certain topics. When this happens northerners mix it with Arabic whereas in general the Shilluk do not do so. One should perhaps mention also the possible contributory role of radio broadcasts.

Although there may be some influence of Sudanese English, by contrast with Ethiopia, American usages are not really perceptible. And, although a few features of Shilluk English may recall Scottish accents, there is no reason to suppose that Scottish schoolmasters and missionaries, of whom there were indeed a few, would have had an important role in fashioning the Shilluk English accent – by contrast with what, according to Wells (1982: 634), may well have happened in Malawi.

THE SOUND SYSTEM OF SHILLUK

The sound system of the Shilluk language has been described in Tucker (1955), Tucker and Bryan (1966) and Le Clézio (1990). Only a very brief synopsis will be given here.

Consonants

Pre-vocalic

	Labial	Dental	Alveolar	Palatal	Velar
Voiceless plosives	p	t̪	t	c	k
Voiced plosives	b	d̪	d	ɟ	g
Nasals	m	n̪	n	ɲ	ŋ
Approximants etc.	w		l, r	j	

Post-vocalic
Opposition between voiceless and voiced is not found, resulting in archiphonemes which are transcribed here, quite arbitrarily, as /p t t̪ c k/ with respectively [+voice and/or –tense] or [–voice and/or +tense] realisations according to whether the preceding vowel is long or short.

Three aspects of this consonantal system deserve mention There are no fricative or affricate phonemes, and the plosive phonemes can be realised as plosives, fricatives, affricates or approximants with places of articulation within the catchment areas of each phoneme. As for the modes of articulation, not all phonemes have all the four possibilities, but it seems that approximant variants are always possible. Thus /t/ → [t] or [t̪]. Such variants will not be specified below.

/p/ → [p], [ɸ] or [f]; /b/ → [b], [β] or [v]; /t̪/ → [t̪], [θ] or [t̪θ]; /d̪/ → [d̪], [ð] or [dð]; /t / → [t]; /d/ → [d]; /c/ → [c], [ç] or [tʃʲ]; /ɟ/ → [ɟ],[j] or [dʒʲ]; /k/→ [k]; /g/ → [ɣ] or [gɣ].

It can be seen from the above that /t/ cannot be realised as [s] or [ts] and /d/ cannot be realised as [z] or [dz]. The normal adaptation into Shilluk of the alveolar fricatives from loanwords, in particular from Arabic, is /t̪/ and /d̪/.

The opposition between the dental and alveolar orders is not based on total independence. There is dependence in so far as no co-existence is possible within the same morpheme between dentals and alveolars. Because of this Colloquial Arabic /nuṣ / 'half' is /nut̪/. Colloquial Arabic

/s/ → Shilluk /t̪/. Nowadays the increased amount of borrowing from Arabic results in the gradual naturalisation of /s/ and /z/, especially in the speech of the educated Shilluk.

Vowels

Shilluk has a basic system of ten vowels, five of which are realised with a creaky voice quality and five with a breathy voice quality:

Creaky:	ɪ	ɛ	a	ɔ	o
Breathy	i	e	a	o	u

The 'semi-mute' vowels ɪ and o which can be easily elided occur chiefly in word-final positions. The two sets of five vowels differ phonetically from each other not merely in voice quality. The audible difference between a creaky vowel and its breathy counterpart results from multiple adjustments of the articulatory tract which seem to involve different tongue positions and, further back, a complex modification of the shape and length of the pharynx. Vocalic length is phonemically relevant; in particular, the realizations of the plosive archiphonemes mentioned above depend upon it.

Tones

Each syllabic summit has a level, rising or falling tone: for example, /nut/ 'half' has a high level tone whereas /nut/ 'is present' has a falling high-to-mid tone. Tonal variations may mark substantive and verb inflection but often seem to provide only additional information for the identification of lexical units and their roles in sentences.

Syllabic and word structures

No consonantal clusters other than /Cw/ and /Cj/ can be found at the beginnings of syllables; syllables can end only with one consonant or semi-consonant. The most frequent type of syllable is CVC. Words of two syllables can therefore have a CVCCwVC or CVCCjVC structure. Semi-mute vowels are V-type syllables.

Below we describe a level of pronunciation which fulfils broadly the requirements of minimum general intelligibility defined in Gimson (1980: 303).

SHILLUK ENGLISH CONSONANTS

As we saw on page 427, there is often variation in the realisation of Shilluk plosives. The effect of this is frequent confusion between the English plosives, fricatives and affricates. Presence or absence of voice corresponds very much to the rules of Shilluk; in postvocalic positions this depends on the length of the preceding vowel in its Shilluk English realisations.

Plosives

Prevocalic voice onset delay ('aspiration') does not occur in Shilluk English. ShE /p, t, k / are often realised as in Shilluk: for instance, I have noted on several occasions 'paper' pronounced [ɸɛɸa], i.e. with two (rather weak) bilabial fricatives. ShE /t, d/ are realised indifferently like either Shilluk /t̪ d̪/ or /t, d/. Dental realisations may also be due to the influence of Arabic teachers of English because Sudanese and Egyptian Colloquial Arabic /t, d/ are dental. Alveolar realisations tend to occur if the plosive is followed by /j/ as in *tube*. In this case one may sometimes hear also a plosive, fricative or affricate palatal. Finally, [s] or [z] can be found as occasional Shilluk English realisations of /t, d/ so that *ten*, for example, can be [sɛn].

Fricatives and affricates

As can be deduced from the previous section, ShE /f, v/ and /p, b/ are often confused with one another because of the fricative and approximant realisations of the plosive phonemes. In general fricatives and affricates are not realised as plosives.

The realisations of ShE /t/ and /d/ are often similar to the laxer realisations of Shilluk /t̪/ and /d̪/; but sometimes they are also realised like [s] and [z], with a resulting homophony between *think* and *sink.*

Confusion occurs frequently between English /ʃ, ʒ/ and /tʃ, dʒ/ and even also between them and /k, g/. In the latter case this is due to occasional realisations of /k, g/ as palatal fricatives or approximants. Thus for example *sheep* and *keep* may sound alike.

/h/ tends to be elided, e.g. *hard* → [aːd].

Nasals

The nasals /m / and /n / are very much as in English. It may well be that /n/ is realised sometimes as [n̪] , but the difference between a dental and an alveolar nasal is not easily perceptible to a European ear.

/l/, /r/ and the semi-consonants

The semi-consonants are very much as in English but /l/ is 'clear' in all contexts and /r/ is always an alveolar tap or roll. Because English is acquired to a large extent through books one often hears a postvocalic /r/ where the orthography suggests its existence (see p. 431).

SHILLUK ENGLISH VOWELS

English vowel sets are referred to by the key-words used in Wells (1980). The vowels discussed here represent an extremely simplified English vocalic system, with much overlapping of the units.

Peripheral vowels	i	e	a	o	u
Central vowel	ɜ				
Diphthongs		aɪ		aʊ	ɔɪ and sometimes iə

It is obvious that the Shilluk English monophthongs cannot be explained by a simple process of transfer from the Shilluk vocalic system. Neutralisation of voice quality occurs usually but not always. It seems that the ten vocalic phonemes of Shilluk are accommodated into the five non-centralised monophthongs of Shilluk English as follows: /i/ → i~ɪ, /e/ → e~ɛ, /a/ → creaky [a], /o/ → creaky ~ breathy o, /u/ → u; /ɜ/ may correspond in part to Shilluk breathy /a/ but its realisations often turn out to be closer than those of the Shilluk vowel which are in the range of [ɐ].

The following account will focus on the vowels: ShE /i/ corresponds usually to both the KIT and FLEECE vowels of English. Differences of length appear in its realisations but are not systematic.The same is true of all the other vowels. Although the quality of /i/ ranges between [i] and [ɪ], this does not imply that KIT words are always realised with [ɪ] nor that FLEECE words are necessarily realised with [i]: for example, *be* may well have [ɪ] in Shilluk English just as *sit* may have [i].

ShE /e/ corresponds to the DRESS, FACE and SQUARE vowels, with realisations ranging indiscriminately from about Cardinal 2 to Cardinal 3: for example, I have noted on three occasions *a face* as [ɛ ɸɛs]. ShE /a/ is the normal reflex of the TRAP, BATH, PALM and START vowels. ShE /o/ corresponds to the LOT, CLOTH, THOUGHT, GOAT, NORTH and FORCE vowels and, as in the case of /i/ and /e/, it is impossible to predict what form any one of these English vowels will take within the range of possible realisations of the Shilluk English phoneme. ShE /u/ corresponds to the FOOT, GOOSE and CURE vowels. ShE /ɜ/ corresponds to the STRUT and NURSE vowels.

ShE /aɪ, aʊ/ and /ɔɪ/ correspond respectively to the PRICE, MOUTH and CHOICE vowels. The existence of ShE /iə/ as a reflex of the NEAR vowel is not totally certain. It seems to be under strong competition from ShE /i/ + /r/ if the postvocalic r is word-final or followed by CV inside the word or the sentence, e.g. *beer* [βir], *near me* [nir mi], and from /i/. Thus *feared* can be homophonous with *feed*. ShE /ir/ matches closely the Sudanese Arabic realisation of the NEAR vowel and it is quite possible that the influence of native Arabic-speaking teachers has determined the choice of this solution in Shilluk English.

All these correspondences of course suppose a good knowledge of English orthographical conventions and idiosyncrasies which not all reasonably fluent Shilluk speakers of English may have: for example, I have noted on several occasions an initial [βw] in *build* which was undoubtedly due to the influence of orthography.

CONSONANTAL CLUSTERS

Because they are possible in Shilluk, English VCCV structures are not difficult. On the other hand, VCCCV, word-initial CCV and word-final VCC structures are more problematic. And so are, *a fortiori*, VCCCCV, word-initial CCCV and word-final VCCC structures. In these circumstances a glide vowel is inserted somewhere in the cluster if the latter is intervocalic or word-initial; and often a consonant is elided when the cluster is word-final, e.g. *explain* [ɛksəɸlen], *try* [tərɑɪ] , *acts* or *axe* [akɪs]. Finally, if one of the consonants in a Shilluk English cluster is a voiced fricative, usually /z/, it may become syllabic, e.g. *smile* [ʐmɑɪl].

STRESS

Stresses often seem to be very weak. Sometimes this may be due to lack of fluency but usually more probably it comes from the fact that Shilluk has no stress contrasts. Listening to informants who read or speak English gives the frequent impression that the tonal variations of Shilluk have been reduced to some kind of mid tone level from which no syllable emerges much more strongly than its neighbours.

REFERENCES

Gimson, A. C. (1980) *An Introduction to the Pronunciation of English*, 3rd edn, London: Edward Arnold.

Le Clézio, Y. (1990) 'The phonetic impact of Arabic on Shilluk', *Speech, Hearing and Language – Work in Progress* 4: 257–72, London: University College Department of Phonetics and Linguistics.

Tucker, A. (1955) 'The verb in Shilluk', *Mitteilungendes Instituts für Orientforschung* 3: 421–62.

Tucker, A. and Bryan, M. A. (1966) *Linguistic Analyses: The Non-Bantu Languages of North-Eastern Africa*, London: Oxford University Press for the International African Institute, pp. 402–42.

Wells, J. C. (1982) *Accents of English*, 3 vols, Cambridge: Cambridge University Press.

36

Segmental errors in the pronunciation of Danish speakers of English: some pedagogic strategies

Inge Livbjerg and Inger M. Mees
The Copenhagen Business School

INTRODUCTION

This paper[1] is concerned with certain segmental pronunciation errors which are typical of advanced Danish students of English.[2]

We do not aim to provide here an exhaustive treatment of Danish errors, but to concentrate on the following:

1   areas which have previously received excessive or misplaced attention from teachers and the writers of textbooks, thereby creating unnecessary problems for the learner;
2   areas which have either been neglected or where instruction has been based on false assumptions;
3   areas where teaching strategies have not proved successful, especially cases where students have been reluctant to accept that there is a problem at all.[3]

Our selection of errors is chiefly based on two corpora of taped material:

1   Tape-recordings of a set of pronunciation lessons given in the mid-1970s by J. D. O'Connor to one of the authors (IL) and a colleague.
2   Taped material from pronunciation courses offered to our Business School students from 1984 to 1991. These students were advanced learners of English who had completed seven or eight years of English classes and who were aiming at careers as secretaries, teachers or interpreters.

Choice of labels for consonants

The descriptive labels for consonants in Livbjerg and Mees (1988: 68–9, 114) have been chosen for pedagogical reasons. The terms voiceless/voiced, often employed in textbooks on English pronunciation (e.g. Jones

1977; Roach 1983; Knowles 1987), have not been used by us for the English obstruents. In the case of the plosives, this is because the term 'voiced' is meaningless to the Danish learner since all Danish plosives are voiceless. In the case of the fricatives, the term 'voiced' has led to unfortunate teaching approaches, especially with respect to final /z/ (see pp. 439–40). We have chosen to use strong/weak (as in O'Connor 1967) rather than fortis/lenis (e.g. Wells and Colson 1971; Gimson 1989) for the English obstruents because the terms are instructive to any Danish learner, whereas the Latin labels may not mean anything to him/her.

The Danish plosives have been termed aspirated/unaspirated, since this is the only distinction between Danish /p, t, k/ and /b, d, g/, all Danish plosives being lenis and voiceless. For the Danish fricatives, however, we have retained the term voiceless/voiced, since this is the only relevant distinction. Note that Danish only possesses one pair of fricatives, viz. /f~v/.

We could have chosen to class Danish /v/ and /ð/[4] as approximants rather than fricatives, since they are almost always realised without friction (Grønnum and Thorsen 1991: 140–1). Because of the pedagogical benefits of being able to compare the consonant systems in the two languages, we have decided to class them as fricatives.

PRONUNCIATION ERRORS WHICH HAVE RECEIVED TOO MUCH ATTENTION

In some cases, existing textbooks or schoolteachers have dealt with problems which would appear to be of minor importance; for instance, older Danish books on the pronunciation of English (e.g. Jespersen 1950: 60–4) and even a recent publication like Steller and Sørensen (1988: 33) devote a disproportionate amount of space to explaining that Danish /p, t, k/ are more strongly aspirated than English /p, t, k/. Learners are recommended to 'start from [p], [t], [k] in unstressed syllables in their own language and use those sounds in stressed syllables in English' (Jespersen 1950: 64). Whilst it is true that Danish /p, t, k/ have somewhat more noticeable aspiration than the corresponding English sounds, the difference never results in a breakdown of communication. It is much more important to point out that Danes replace English /p, t, k/ by /b, d, g/ in medial and final position so that *lacking* sounds identical with *lagging* and *lack* the same as *lag* (see p. 438). This point is also made by Jespersen, but less space is devoted to explain this crucial area than to the minor error of over-aspiration. Davidsen-Nielsen (1983: 40–1) rightly chooses to ignore the problem of over-aspiration and instead focuses on the problem of neutralisation of /p, t, k/ and /b, d, g/.

Another area where Davidsen-Nielsen has managed to remove an unnecessary complication found in older textbooks is that of /sp, st, sk/

clusters. Jespersen (1950: 51) states that 'the English sounds [p], [t], [k] remain practically unaltered when preceded by [s]'.[5] Hence his recommendation to Scandinavians to practise aspirating these sounds after /s/ (cf. Jones, 1977: sections 497 and 501). Consequently, teachers have taken great pains to teach learners to say *spy, stone, school* as [sp^{h}aɪ], [st^{h}əʊn], [sk^{h}uːl]. But as pointed out by Davidsen-Nielsen (1970: 59) and Jacobsen (1974: 59), there is no aspiration in this context since both English and Danish here have [b, d, g]. The Danish learner has no problem whatsoever in this area, and thus from a pedagogical point of view it is best not to mention it at all.

However, in some other cases Davidsen-Nielsen continues to deal with pronunciation problems which in our opinion could be given a much lower priority: for example the emphasis which he places (Davidsen-Nielsen 1983: 56) on making learners perceive and make the difference between English /ʃ ~ sj/ as in *shoot ~ suit*. Danes typically replace both with a sound between /ʃ/ and /sj/. This distinction should be given a relatively low priority since most RP speakers nowadays pronounce words like *suit, superb, sue* without /j/, i.e. /suːt, suːˈpɜːb, suː/ (Windsor Lewis 1969: 85; Knowles 1987: 73; Ramsaran 1990: 184). Thus a lot of effort is wasted in trying to get learners to say /sj/ where they can simply use /s/. Even in words like *assume, consume*, where the majority of RP speakers still use /sj/ (84 per cent of 'the poll panel' in the *Longman Pronunciation Dictionary* (Wells 1990: 45) expressed a preference for /sj/ in *assume*), it is not a bad teaching strategy to point out to students that they can use /s/, since this to an English ear sounds better than the Danish realisation. Rather than working on making a /ʃ ~ sj/ distinction, which applies to a relatively small number of words, it would be more profitable to focus on the importance of making a /ʃ ~ s/ contrast by emphasising the importance of lip rounding in the articulation of /ʃ/ (see p. 435). This is particularly important (1) preceding close front vowels and (2) in final position, where a Danish version of /ʃ/ often sounds like /s/ to an English ear, so that the opposition between *she* and *see* and *swish* and *Swiss* is lost.

Similarly, too much emphasis has been placed on teaching students to make the opposition /tʃ ~ tj/ (*chew ~ tune*) and /dʒ ~ dj/ (*Jew ~ dew*). Although in traditional descriptions of RP these are said to be regularly distinguished (at least in stressed syllables), many younger educated English speakers these days pronounce both /tʃ/ and /tj/ as [tʃ] and both /dʒ/ and /dj/ as [dʒ]. Again, as in the case of /ʃ/, it would be more fruitful to work on obtaining an acceptable pronunciation of /tʃ/ and /dʒ/, for instance by emphasising the importance of lip rounding (see p. 435). The lack of lip rounding is particularly noticeable in word-final position, where the opposition between *catch* and *cats* and between *age* and *AIDS* may be lost.

NEGLECTED AREAS AND FALSE DESCRIPTIONS

Palatalisation

An example of a feature which has been neglected by teachers simply because it has not been described is the too clear palatalised quality of Danish realisations of English /tʃ, dʒ, ʃ, w, l, n/. This palatalisation effect can probably be attributed to a difference in articulatory setting in the two languages (Honikman 1964; Collins and Mees, this volume). In Danish, the front of the tongue is tenser than in English and raised towards the palate, giving a [j]-like colouring to a whole range of consonants, most noticeable with Danish /l, n/. Consequently, Danish renderings of English /tʃ, dʒ, ʃ/ result in a [j] off-glide, so that an English ear perceives them as [t], [d], [s] followed by [j]: *chew, Jew, shoe* *[tjuː, djuː, sjuː]. Danish attempts at English /l/ are affected similarly by palatalisation, resulting in an [l] which is markedly clearer than English clear [l]. Danish /n/ is subject to the same effect, particularly noticeable in connection with back vowels (e.g. *John*). Finally, Danish realisations of English /w/ sound more like a labial-palatal [ɥ] than the labial-velar sound characteristic of English.

For /tʃ, dʒ, ʃ/ the most effective remedy is to encourage the learner to pronounce these consonants with strongly rounded protruding lips, which provides the darker quality and more grave friction characteristic of the English consonants.[6]

The advice for /tʃ, dʒ, ʃ/ also holds for /w/, where strong lip rounding should be accompanied by an [u]-like vowel rather than the [y]-like realisation which is heard from Danes. The most difficult sounds to tackle are /l/ and /n/. The palatalised quality of Danish /l/ is obviously most problematic for Danish renderings of English *dark* [ɫ]. A possible approach is to start from Danish /ð/, as described on page 440. As far as /n/ is concerned we simply have not found a successful teaching strategy yet.

Glottal reinforcement and glottal replacement

A second neglected area is the improvement which is obtained from encouraging students to employ glottal reinforcement or glottal replacement. Jespersen (1950: 41) states that as 'the use of glottal stop is never indispensable in English it is probably not advisable to try to make the foreign learner acquire it, but he should know of its existence'. Davidsen-Nielsen (1983: 48) also recommends the learner to avoid the use of glottal stop. In our experience, however, it is easy to teach Danes to glottally reinforce syllable-final English /p, t, k, tʃ/ since they can draw on Danish *stød* (Fischer-Jørgensen 1989), which occurs with long Danish vowels (e.g. *ti* /tiː?/ 'ten', *by* /byː?/ 'city') and voiced consonants (e.g. *tand* /tan?/ 'tooth', *vild* /vil?/ 'wild'). Perhaps because the glottal stop has been associated with low-status dialects (Wells 1982: 261) teachers of English have traditionally been wary of it. Yet over the last decades the use of glottal reinforcement appears to be strongly on the increase in RP (Wells 1982: 261). Thus there is no longer any need to warn foreigners not to use it. On the contrary, it should be recommended to the Danish learner as a means of sounding authentically English (Mees and Collins 1987: 21). Glottal reinforcement comes naturally to a lot of Danes and the only thing one has to point out carefully to them is not to overuse the feature. As stated above, Danish *stød* occurs with long vowels and voiced consonants and consequently Danes sometimes wrongly extend the use of glottal stop to English voiced consonants in words like *tribe, food, age*, etc.

In addition, Danes should be advised to use glottal replacement for syllable-final /t/ preceding most consonants (e.g. *brightness, hot dog*) to avoid the typical Danish error of replacing /t/ by /d/. Ramsaran (1990: 187) observes that, in RP, 'the use of pre-consonantal glottal stop . . . as a full replacement for the voiceless alveolar plosive is increasingly common not only before obstruents but also before sonorant consonants'.

Final nasals and /l/

Yet another area which has not received enough attention from teachers is the length of final nasals and /l/. Hardly any of our students have ever been told that the Danish nasals cannot be transferred to English without modification, but once it is pointed out to them that final English nasals (and /l/) are *longer* than their Danish counter-parts, they can easily hear that this is the case and have no problem saying them correctly. Despite the fact that the phenomenon has been described (Davidsen-Nielsen *et al.*, 1982: 11), few teachers seem to deal with it.

/ð/

A final area which has been ignored by teachers is the pronunciation of English /ð/. Although the difference between the English and Danish consonants has been described in detail both in earlier books (e.g. Jespersen 1950: 71) and in more recent publications (e.g. Davidsen-Nielsen 1983: 53), few teachers have focused on this problem. Danish /ð/, which occurs in postvocalic position only (e.g. *bad* /bað/ 'bath'), differs from English /ð/ in having the tongue tip lowered, the blade/front being raised in the direction of the alveolar ridge and the anterior portion of the hard palate. The sound is typically realised as an approximant, except in Danish as spoken on the stage. The obvious advice to give students is to raise the tongue tip, as suggested by both Jespersen and Davidsen-Nielsen.

However, a point which is not made by either of these authors is that the Danish sound is also characterised by distinct velarisation, which is probably the reason why English speakers interpret it as /l/ (Windsor Lewis 1969: 11). The secondary articulation of velarisation has the effect of lowering and centralising preceding front vowels, particularly /iː/ and /ɪ/. On our tapes O'Connor warns IL about the 'baneful effect' her realisation of /ð/ has on the vowel, e.g. in *with*. He also points out that unlike most other pronunciation errors made by Danes, which they share with speakers of many other different nationalities, a Danish realisation of English /ð/ immediately identifies a speaker as a Dane.

Front vowels

In the course of the last decades the /æ/ vowels in English and Danish have moved in opposite directions; English /æ/ has become more open (Ramsaran 1990: 186), whereas both long and short Danish *a* have become considerably closer (Kristensen 1986: 134–5). The result is that the advice given by Davidsen-Nielsen (1983: 80–1) to set out from either long Danish /aː/ in *bade* 'to bathe', *gane* 'palate' or the short Danish vowel in *hat* 'hat', *kan* 'can' is now inapplicable. Danish learners should aim at a considerably more open quality. Certainly, the pronunciation of long Danish /aː/ is no lower than [ɛː] (see, for instance, Kristensen 1986: 23; Grønnum and Thorsen 1991: 138), and although the corresponding short vowel is somewhat more open, it is rarely as open as English /æ/.[7] And in many Danish accents (e.g. Copenhagen, Århus) the two vowels are considerably closer than the Standard Danish realisation (Andersen and Hjelmslev 1967: 334–5; Kristensen 1986: 77–8).

The advice to aim at a more open quality holds true of the whole set of English short, front vowels. Danish learners tend to pronounce English words like *sit, set, sat* with vowel qualities more like those of *seat, sit, set*. As in the case of Danish /a/, most Danish books on English have not taken account of the fact that Danish /ɛ/ has become closer over the last few decades – compare the placement of Danish /a/ and /ɛ/ in Andersen and Hjelmslev (1967: 330) with that of Grønnum and Thorsen (1991: 138) – and describe English /e/ as being closer than its Danish counterpart (e.g. Davidsen-Nielsen 1983: 80–1). It is important to make students aware that English /e/ and /æ/ are especially open before dark [ɫ], e.g. *fell, shall*, which in Danish speakers' renderings tend to sound like *fill* and *shell*. Davidsen-Nielsen (1983: 79) describes English /ɪ/ as having a noticeably more open allophone in word-final position than elsewhere, the second /ɪ/ in *pretty* being said to be more *open* than the first. In fact, final English /ɪ/ is generally nowadays much closer (Wells 1982: 257–8, 294, 299) although it is not quite as close as the sound used by Danish learners. Danes typically employ their short, close /i/, as in *fattig* /'fadi/ ['fæ̞di] 'poor', whereas the Danish /e/ vowel in *til* /tel/ [te̞l] 'to' is a much better substitution.

437

NEW TEACHING STRATEGIES

Plosives

The difficulty the Danish learner experiences with respect to the English plosives is not so much a result of problems in terms of the actual articulation but more the result of a lack of awareness that any problem exists.

Danish has an opposition between /p, t, k/ and /b, d, g/. However, this applies in initial position only. The two sets of consonants are distinguished by the feature of aspiration only, all Danish plosives being lenis and voiceless.

In other contexts, the opposition is neutralised, and the set /b, d, g/ is employed irrespective of what the spelling might suggest. In medial position, and in final position before another word, there is never aspiration, so that, for instance, *lappe* /'labə/ 'to patch' and *labbe* /'labə/ 'to lap up' are both realised as ['labə].

In final position before a pause, aspiration may or may not occur. Hence *lab* /lab/ 'paw' may be pronounced as either [lapʰ] or [lab] in the same speaker's rendering of the word. The same applies to *lap* /lab/ 'patch'.

As the distribution of Danish plosives is widely different from English, it is surprising that this fact is not even mentioned in Steller and Sørensen (1988: 33–4), and most advanced students of English (if our students are typical) seem to be quite unaware of it. Færch *et al.* (1984: 137) comment:

> in areas in which the sound systems of Danish and English partially overlap, such as medial plosives, errors persist. It is quite possible that the attention of learners has been consciously directed to new, 'difficult' sounds, whereas the fortis/lenis distinction in medial plosives is one to which they have not been sensitised to the same degree.

The main difficulty is raising the learner's awareness, since the learner mistakenly believes that there is a sound/spelling relationship for Danish plosives in *all* positions and, consequently, is under the false impression that the patterns of the English and Danish plosives are identical.

A possible explanation for the learner's misconception can perhaps be found in the way Danish spelling is taught in schools, where for the sake of clarity teachers add aspiration to words spelt with medial or final *p*, *t* or *k*, e.g.

I said ['lapʰə] *lappe* 'to patch ', not ['labə] *labbe* 'to lap up'.
I said [tykʰ] *tyk* 'fat', not [tyg] *tyg* 'chew'.[8]

How do we make learners aware that they have a problem at all? Providing them with detailed descriptions of the Danish and English plosives has not proved to be a successful method. The still sceptical student is stunned by the mass of detail. A practical approach is more rewarding.

Some textbooks have illustrated the problem by inventing sentences with predictable Danish errors of the following type:

1   with a cab (for *cap*) on his head
2   I heard (for *hurt*) my bag (for *back*) yesterday.

Generally this fails to convince the learner who has never been conscious of any communication problems of this kind. A better approach is to set out from perception. As with most other contrasts, we suggest starting with a listening test to make the student acknowledge that he/she has a problem. The learner has to identify medial or final plosives in isolated words and in sentences where either member of a minimal pair would fit in naturally.[9] For example:

Do you repair clocks/clogs?

Exercises of this type raise students' awareness and act as an incentive to practise the contrasts they should maintain. Improvement is most noticeable if one limits advice to the following simple instructions:

1   Consistently follow the spelling: *p* is always /p/, *t* is always /t/, etc.
2   Use aspiration with /p, t, k/ medially, and finally before another word. Also use glottal reinforcement with syllable-final /p, t, k/.
3   Remember the difference in the length of the preceding vowel.

Note that in final position before a pause, observing the third rule, i.e. that of vowel length variation, seems to help more towards acquiring an acceptable pronunciation than getting the feature of aspiration right.

Apart from the three rules given above applying to the whole set of plosives, there is an additional problem with /t/. Especially in the rendering of younger Danish speakers, /t/ is noticeably affricated, e.g. *tea* sounds like [tsiː]. Danes do not readily accept this criticism of their /t/ pronunciation. This is because very strong affrication is a stigmatised feature in Danish, being characteristic, for instance, of lower-class Copenhagen speech. In certain cases, /t/ is even realised as [s], so that *Tivoli* almost becomes ['siwli].

/z/

Danish has no /z/ phoneme, and the typical Danish substitution is /s/. Older English readers and older books on phonetics (e.g. Jespersen 1950) described lenis plosives as 'voiced'. Consequently, teachers took great pains to instruct their pupils to voice final /z/ – with devastating results. Windsor Lewis (1969: 11) observes:

in their over-anxiety to avoid the wrong phoneme many Scandinavians – and particularly teachers are at fault here – produce the
totally un-English allophone in this situation of a strongly voiced
sound. To an English speaker this may sound distractingly odd or he
may sometimes get the impression of hearing an extra syllable, e.g.
buzzer instead of *buzz.*

Alternatively, a [ð] sound is inserted, a fact stated emphatically by
Jespersen (1950: 71), who says that 'Danish people often have difficulties
with [z], particularly in the word *please*, which few Danes pronounce
correctly. *There is absolutely no [ð]-sound in the word.*' In actual fact, the typical
Danish mistake is to pronounce /z/ as [ðs] (see also Davidsen-Nielsen *et al.*
1982: 12) rather than [ðz]. It would appear that the learner distributes the
features 'voiced' and 'alveolar' of the English /z/ phoneme across two
phonemes from his/her own language, taking alveolar from Danish /s/
and taking voice from Danish /ð/, which is the only voiced fricative in
Danish (see Livbjerg 1985: 23–6 for a similar interpretation of learner
strategies). If our assumption is correct, it explains why Jespersen's advice
to 'begin by practising [pliːs] *and then voice the [s]*' (our emphasis) does not
work, because we are then back to where we started.

More recent Danish pronunciation books are aware that final lenis
obstruents are generally devoiced in English, hence this overvoicing
instruction has been abandoned. Nevertheless, many learners still have a
[ðs] problem, especially in words like *please, is, says, has, does, was, because,*
and it is not enough simply to ask them to omit [ð].

A successful way out of the substitution of [ðs] for /z/ is to ask the
student to start by exaggerating the length of the vowel, adding a very
unenergetic consonant, which is deliberately described as an [s]-sound to
avoid attempts at voicing leading to the insertion of [ð]. O'Connor taught
IL this method, asking her to add 'a very soft [s]', awakening the same
associations as intended by the term weak. Once this approach has
eradicated [ð], 'it is also useful to practise the distinction between /-z/,
/-ðz/ and /-s/ by means of words like *seize, seethes, cease*' (Davidsen-Nielsen
et al. 1982: 12).

Dark [ɫ]

As stated on page 435 above, Standard Danish /l/ is palatalised. Unlike RP
/l/, it has the same quality in all contexts. Thus one of the most difficult
sounds to teach a Danish learner is dark [ɫ]. The traditional approach –
recommending the learner to say a half-close, back vowel simultaneously
with /l/ (Davidsen-Nielsen 1983: 62; Gimson 1989: 206) – does not always
achieve the desired effect. Frequently, it results in a back vowel *followed* by
clear [l], e.g. feel [fiːol].

An alternative approach, which appears to be successful particularly with more advanced students, is to remind Danes that they have velarisation of a type similar to that found in English dark [ł] in Danish /ð/, as in *bad* 'bath'. In fact, this word is overwhelmingly interpreted by English speakers as *bell*. By starting from Danish /ð/, students can be made to feel how a velarised quality is achieved. Danish /ð/ has the tongue *tip* lowered, the blade being raised loosely in the direction of the alveolar ridge (see p. 436). If one points out that the tongue tip should be raised rather than lowered, an acceptable realisation of English velarised [ł] is often obtained.

American-type pronunciations

Some students have no probems with the articulation of dark [ł]. It is a well-known fact that some Danish learners – especially those with a good ear and well-developed powers of imitation – have become enamoured of some features which are characteristic of American English. Only with the greatest difficulty can they be persuaded to remove these realisations from a pronunciation which is otherwise based on an RP model. One feature is the use of dark [ł], which they employ in all positions of the word, another is postvocalic /r/.

When asked why, these students say that they find these features 'delightfully un-Danish', and some say they think they started noticing and mimicking them when watching American films or television programmes even before they started learning to speak English. Dark [ł] is not found in Danish (see p. 440), and Danish /r/ is only realised as a true consonant in the context before a vowel. In postvocalic environments it is either pronounced as an open back vowel [ɒ] (*Per* boy's name, *mor* 'mother', *stærk* 'strong') or it is elided (*far* 'father', *får* 'sheep'). Thus from a linguistic point of view there is no immediate reason why students should start pronouncing these sounds when speaking English.

We could, of course, argue that 'there is nothing reprehensible about sounding "mid-Atlantic"', but for *our* course participants 'keeping exclusively to one accent is an ideal goal' (Færch *et al.* 1984: 122). See also Færch *et al.* (1984: 120–2) for a discussion on accents and norms of pronunciation.

/ʌ/ ~ /ɑ/

The most significant vowel problem for Danish learners is the opposition between *luck* and *lock*. Both are replaced by the Danish sound in *godt* 'good', *kop* 'cup'. The vowel in such Danish words is realised with a wide range of sociolinguistically determined variants including allophones similar to both RP *luck* and RP *lock*. Each speaker of Danish obviously has his/her own *godt* variant, which is employed for both English vowel phonemes. Making a distinction between the English sounds seems as unnatural to the Danish speaker as using two different sociolects in Danish. The problem is further complicated by the fact that both English vowels can be represented by *o* in the spelling.

Various different approaches have been taken in often futile attempts to make Danes acquire the *luck* ~ *lock* contrast. Approaches which would seem logical unfortunately do not always work. Teachers and textbook authors have typically concentrated on the acquisition of English /ʌ/, recommending the Dane to adopt the *luck*-like allophones of the Danish *godt* vowel. However, this vowel appears to be difficult for most Danes to accept and use because of its upper-class 'affected' associations.

In actual fact, a *luck*-type vowel occurs in *Standard* Danish, in words like *tak* ('thank you'), without any form of social stigma attached to it. It is even possible to find minimal pairs that correspond with the English *luck* ~ *lock* distinction: *lak* ~ *lok* ('laquer' ~ 'lock of hair'), and Davidsen-Nielsen *et al.* (1982: 15–16) recommend Danish learners to use this distinction as an approach. In practice, however, this procedure is rarely successful, as most learners persist in associating the sound with the above 'affected' sociolect.

Contrary to the normal approach of regarding *luck* as the problem, our experience is that the most rewarding approach is to set out from English *lock*. Since Danish learners think they pronounce their *godt* vowel as a rounded open back vowel, it is RP *lock* they *think* they master. Most speakers of Standard Danish in reality produce a less retracted vowel which is more like *luck*. We therefore recommend concentrating on *lock*, emphasising its backness: 'retract the tongue so far that it almost makes you retch'. This drastic description has been chosen in favour of reminding the students of the similarity between RP *lock* and certain low-status variants of the Danish *godt* vowel, in order to avoid the same type of rejection of the sound as with the affected variant. Irrespective of what Danish learners think, rounding is less important than the back quality. O'Connor even explicitly recommended an unrounded sound in his instructions to IL when her attempts at English *lock* resulted in a sound similar to a typical German vowel in *Gott* ('God').

For the few learners who – after having accepted the necessity of operating with an /ʌ/ ~ /ɒ/ distinction in their English – can be persuaded to associate the *luck* sound with the unstigmatised vowel in *lak*, and can therefore use this vowel to acquire the precise RP /ʌ/ quality, a new difficulty arises, namely that of avoiding confusing it with 'the neighbouring vowel /æ/' (Davidsen-Nielsen 1983: 82) as in *lack* and *luck*, *match* and *much*.

However, if the *lack* ~ *luck* distinction is taken as the point of departure, isolated from the *luck* ~ *lock* contrast, as in Davidsen-Nielsen (1983: 82–3), students are simply sceptical and uncooperative. To quote them, they 'have never felt in danger of saying "I wish you lack" or "thank you very match"'.

CONCLUSION

This paper has tried to stress the fact that in order to achieve improvement in the pronunciation of learners, it is necessary to focus on the learner not only in terms of choosing priorities according to the level and purpose of his/her training (whether it be mere communication or a high degree of correctness) but especially in terms of learner mentality.

NOTES

1 We wish to thank Beverley Collins, Niels Davidsen-Nielsen, Kirsten Haastrup, Arnt Lykke Jakobsen and Jack Windsor Lewis for helpful comments on earlier versions of this paper.

2 For systematic treatments of the problems of Danish learners of English based on a contrastive approach, see Davidsen-Nielsen (1983), Livbjerg and Mees (1988) and Mees and Collins (1987).

3 In some cases, arguments could be put forward for allocating certain pronunciation problems to different categories from the ones selected, since there is a degree of overlap.

4 Strictly speaking, /ð/ does not carry phonemic status, although it is generally treated as such in Danish pronunciation books (e.g. Grønnum and Thorsen 1991).

5 In fact, this observation can be found as early as Jespersen (1897–9: sections 265 and 267).

6 It is worth mentioning, however, that O'Connor found the palato-alveolar consonants of both IL and her colleague *too* 'low-pitched' and warned them against excessive rounding. The pronunciation of these two speakers is typical of their age group, i.e. people who are over the age of forty today. On listening to the tapes we have become convinced that the error is more likely to be due to the retraction of the tongue recommended in Jespersen (1950: 76), the textbook of their day.

7 An additional difficulty for the learner is that the letter 'æ' in Danish represents a half-close vowel, [e], which is closer than the RP vowel in *bed*.

8 Mothers do the same when correcting their infants. The following dialogue between a mother and her two-year-old daughter was overheard by IL:

> Infant: ['sogə], attempting to say *suppe* 'soup' (Standard Danish ['sobə]) thus getting place of articulation wrong but medial neutralisation right.
> Mother: No, ['sobə], then, immediately correcting herself, ['sopʰə], and repeating with even stronger aspiration, ['sopʰə].

9 The tapes accompanying Andersen and Bauer (1975) and Livbjerg and Mees (1988) have exercises of this kind.

REFERENCES

Andersen, E. and Bauer, L. (1975) *Engelske Udtaleøvelser,* Copenhagen: Gyldendal.
Andersen, P. and Hjelmslev, L. (1967) *Fonetik,* 4th edn, Copenhagen: Rosenkilde & Bagger (first published 1954).

Davidsen-Nielsen, N. (1970) *Engelsk Fonetik*, Copenhagen: Gyldendal.
—— (1983) *Engelsk Udtale i Hovedtræk*, 2nd edn, Copenhagen: Gyldendal (first published 1975).
Davidsen-Nielsen, N., Færch, C. and Harder, P. (1982) *The Danish Learner*, Tunbridge Wells: Taylor.
Færch, C., Haastrup K. and Phillipson, R. (1984) *Learner Language and Language Learning*, Copenhagen: Gyldendal.
Fischer-Jørgensen, E. (1989) *A Phonetic Study of the Stød in Standard Danish*, Turku: Turku University, Dept of Phonetics.
Gimson, A. C. (1989) *An Introduction to the Pronunciation of English*, London: Edward Arnold; 4th edn, revised by S. Ramsaran (first published 1962).
Grønnum, N. and Thorsen, O. (1991) *Fonetik for Sprogstuderende*, 5th edn, Copenhagen: University of Copenhagen, Dept of Phonetics (first published 1977).
Honikman, B. (1964) 'Articulatory settings', in D. Abercrombie, D. G. Fry, P. A. D. MacCarthy, N. C. Scott and J. L. Trim (eds), *In Honour of Daniel Jones*, London: Longman, pp. 73–84.
Jacobsen, B. (1974) *Engelsk Fonetik for EA-Studiet*, Århus: Århus School of Business, Dept of English.
Jespersen, O. (1897–9) *Fonetik*, Copenhagen: Det Schubotheske Forlag.
—— (1950) *English Phonetics*, 5th edn, revised and translated by B. Jürgensen, Copenhagen: Gyldendal (first published 1912).
Jones, D. (1977) *An Outline of English Phonetics*, 9th edn, Cambridge: Cambridge University Press (first published 1918).
Knowles, G. (1987) *Patterns of Spoken English*, London and New York: Longman.
Kristensen, K. (1986) *Dansk for Svenskere*, Malmö: Gleerups.
Livbjerg, I. (1985) 'More tips of the slongue', *SPRINT* (Sproginstitutternes Tidsskrift), Copenhagen Business School: Faculty of Modern Languages, 23–8.
Livbjerg, I. and Mees, I. M. (1988) *Practical English Phonetics*, Copenhagen: Schønberg.
Mees, I. M. and Collins, B. (1987) *Sound English*, Copenhagen: Nyt Nordisk Forlag Arnold Busck.
O'Connor, J. D. (1967) *Better English Pronunciation*, Cambridge: Cambridge University Press.
Ramsaran, S. (ed.) (1990) *Studies in the Pronunciation of English: A Commemorative Volume in Honour of A. C. Gimson*, London and New York: Routledge.
Roach, P. (1983) *English Phonetics and Phonology*, Cambridge: Cambridge University Press.
Steller, P. and Sørensen, K. (1988) *Engelsk Grammatik*, 3rd edn, Copenhagen: Munksgaard (first published 1966).
Wells, J. C. (1982) *Accents of English*, Cambridge: Cambridge University Press.
—— (1990) *Longman Pronunciation Dictionary*, London: Longman.
Wells, J. C. and Colson, G. (1971) *Practical Phonetics*, Bath: Pitman.
Windsor Lewis, J. (1969) *A Guide to English Pronunciation*, Oslo: Universitetsforlaget.

37

Describing the pronunciation of loanwords from English

J. Posthumus
Anglistisch Instituut, University of Groningen

In the linguistic description of loanwords from English into another language the pronunciation aspect is definitely the most problematical. Whereas matters of spelling, morphology and also semantics can be confidently described in terms of the customary linguistic concepts, the fleeting and possibly variable sounds used in their pronunciation are not so easily placed in a categorial framework that can do justice to the facts. To the casual observer it may even seem as if speakers here move in a kind of phonetic no man's land between the English donor language and their own receiving language.

In this article I intend to chart this somewhat uncertain territory, and to develop a framework within which the phonetic data can be described and explained. In doing so I will draw upon my experience of the behaviour of English loanwords in Dutch. Though facts of detail will naturally differ for different receiving languages, I take the principles applied here to be generally valid.

ENGLISH PRONUNCIATION?

It is sometimes naively assumed that English loanwords should be pronounced exactly as in English, and that falling below the standard of an authentic English accent is to be considered a regrettable shortcoming. Accordingly, a well-reputed general Dutch dictionary to this day carries an appendix listing (in IPA transcription) the correct English pronunciation of all the English loanwords contained in its pages.[1] The list is even preceded by a brief guide explaining the value of the phonetic symbols, and informing speakers of Dutch about some of the finer points of English pronunciation, such as the obligatory aspiration of the fortis plosives.

The provision of instructions of this kind shows a complete ignorance of the basic realities of loanword pronunciation in native language settings. Here adaptation of the foreign sounds to the native sound system is normal practice. Actually, the introduction of a sample of authentic English pronunciation into the flow of Dutch speech produces a rather special effect. Such 'code-switching' is indeed only appropriate in special circumstances, as when a speaker, for instance, uses a longer English quotation or for some reason or other wants to stress the English provenance of a maybe as yet relatively unfamiliar term. In all other cases, however, a too perfect English accent is out of place, and may even carry the danger of causing the speaker not to be understood.

The fallacy of a supposedly normative English pronunciation still carries another danger. It may lead observers of loanword pronunciations to investigate and judge how far certain realisations of speech sounds can still be said to fall within the English phoneme areas. Given the fact that the phoneme areas of two languages will often overlap considerably, and that phonological adaptation of the foreign sounds is to be expected, this is looking at the facts through the wrong end of the telescope. What should be done instead is to judge whether the sounds used by the speaker of the receiving language fit within the phoneme areas of his–her own variety of native speech.

TRANSPHONEMISATION AND THE UNITS OF ADAPTATION

The pronunciation form of English loanwords in the receiving language normally establishes itself as the result of a process of 'transphonemisation' (Filipović 1960: 12). This means that every English phoneme is replaced by what is felt to be its native counterpart. Such substitutions are made on quite regular lines: the great majority of the counterparts are entirely self-evident, though in certain cases different choices may be open to the speaker.

A contrastive analysis of the two sound systems involved will of course throw some light on the substitutions that take place. A thorough and fairly lengthy contrastive analysis, indeed, often precedes the discussion of substitutions made.[2] Two cautionary remarks are in place here: first of all, a great deal of the differential detail that is thrown up turns out to be irrelevant to the transphonemisation process: second, the phonemic systems that are being compared may well have been constructed on such rigorously economic lines that certain quite normally functioning equivalences are missed. It is more fruitful, therefore, to take cognisance of the adaptation features with a mind free from preconceptions induced by a formal contrastive analysis. Contrastive analysis, in other words, had better be used in its weak function as an explanatory device after the event, rather than in its strong predictive function.

A better starting-point to discover the trajectories of the transphonemisation process is to observe what practical equations are actually made by the speakers of the receiving language. Plentiful information about this is available from the EFL classroom, where teachers of English are supervising the learning efforts of their pupils. Such information naturally tends to find its way into EFL textbooks (see e.g. the substitution tables in Gussenhoven and Broeders 1976: 88, 142–3, and 1981: 65, 111–12). While many of these features are branded there as undesirable behaviour, which has to be modified to reach the desired goal of a correct English accent, no such stigma attaches to them in loanword pronunciation. There, as pointed out above, substitution of native sounds is the normal thing.

A further important point is that a realistic table of substitution units for all the English phonemes should not restrict itself to what we might call the central, or primary, phonemes of the native sound system. If all the paths of transphonemisation are to be properly explained and evaluated, the inventory must indeed move beyond the confines of the primary system, and come to include any further marginal or secondary features that are conventionally used in the pronunciation of foreign words. In other words, it must give full recognition to all the relatively stable phonemic substitutional devices that can in some way be fitted into or connected with the native system.[3]

By means of the substitution units contained in such a comprehensive framework, it should be possible to describe all loanword pronunciations that in one way or another are adapted to the native system. The only pronunciations it cannot deal with are the exceptional authentic English pronunciations mentioned above (pp. 445–6), which, if they occur at all, can be described in terms of the English sound system. Variant adapted pronunciations will often differ in that one will contain a phoneme belonging to the secondary set which in the other has been replaced by a primary one. Such forms may well exist side by side, possibly as variants with higher and lower social prestige, and without the first being a transient form that in time will inexorably be replaced by the latter, further adapted form.

By incorporating both primary and secondary features as stable units in the substitution pattern, this approach essentially differs from that embodied in Filipović's (1958) 'Phonetic Compromise'. For, in the face of much evidence to the contrary, this latter concept, which is even claimed to be a universal in loanword adaptation, actually supposes all adaptation forms that occupy a place somewhere in between the foreign phoneme and the fully native one to be only short-lived.[4]

The points made above will now be illustrated from the transphonemisation tables that govern the pronunciation of English loanwords in Dutch.[5] The sounds of each language are indicated in the tables by means of an IPA notation customarily used in descriptions of that language. Sounds indicated by the same symbol may be taken to be generally identical. An overlap column has been added to show similarities that, owing to the different notational conventions, might otherwise remain obscured.

English into Dutch: the transphonemisation of the vowels

A conventional contrastive phonemic analysis reveals that the Dutch vowel system contains obvious parallels[6] for many English vowels. Problems of various kinds seem to arise in the case of nos 1, 4, 7, 9, 11, 15, 17, 18, 19 and 20. Yet all these English vowels have quite stable counterparts that turn out to be compatible with the Dutch system. Drawing upon the set of loan vowels that are conventionally used in the pronunciation of loanwords, the Dutch speaker can first of all find excellent parallels for vowels 7 and 19. The feature of vowel lengthening, used in Dutch as a conventional marker of foreignness, produces a good likeness also for English nos 1 and 9. In the case of the latter vowels further adaptation to short /i/ and /u/, which belong in the primary set of Dutch vowels, is possible. If this further adaptation takes place, nos 8 and 9 are conflated, something that invariably happens also in the case of nos 3 and 4. Dutch counterparts to the diphthongs nos 15 and 17 are found in other marginal elements used in a few interjections.[7] Lastly close approximations of the English centring diphthongs nos 18 and 20 exist in Dutch where short /i/ and /u/ are followed by /r/, in which environment the vowel is lengthened and an [ə]

Table 37.1 English and Dutch vowel correspondences

	E	D1	D2	Overlap	Comment
1	iː	(iː)	i		
2	ɪ	ɪ			
3	e	ɛ		++	
4	æ	ɛ		+	Distinction between 3 and 4 is lost
5	ɑː	aː		++	Before ⟨r⟩ also /ɑr/
6	ɒ	ɔ		+	
7	ɔː	(ɔː)			Before ⟨r⟩ also /ɔr/
8	ʊ	u		+	
9	uː	(uː)	u		Distinction between 8 and 9 may be lost
10	ʌ	ʉ		+	
11	ɜː	øːr		++	D allophone before /r/
12	ə	ə			
13	eɪ	eː		+++	In spite of the usual notation D. /eː/
14	əʊ	oː		++	and /oː/ are noticeably diphthongal
15	aɪ	ɑ+j		+++	
16	aʊ	ɔu		++	
17	ɔɪ	ɔ+j		+++	
18	ɪə	iː+r		++	Before /r/ D /i/ is long with [ə]-glide
19	ɛə	(ɛː)		+++	
20	ʊə	uː+r		++	Before /r/ D /u/ is long with [ə]-glide

Note: E = English phoneme; D1 = Dutch phoneme; in parentheses: secondary phoneme; D2 = further substitution by primary Dutch phoneme. In cases where the different vowel notation suggests a different sound value, the number of pluses indicates the degree of overlap.

glide is produced. A suitable allophone of Dutch /ø/ before /r/ also serves as a natural parallel for English no. 11.

In describing phonological substitution pictures, the possibility of spelling influence must not be overlooked. In the transphonemisation process spelling and phonology often go hand in hand, witness such English loanwords as *hit* or *sex*. In cases where English and the receiving language have different grapheme/phoneme relationships, however, the loanword may come to be pronounced in accordance with the spelling/ sound relationships of the receiving language. Spelling then plays a primary rather than a contributory role in determining the phonemic substitution. Thus the variant Dutch substitutes used by certain speakers for vowel no. 10 clearly correlate with the spelling ⟨u⟩ or ⟨o⟩. In variants where a postvocalic /r/ appears, as with vowels nos 5, 7 and 11, and with the centring diphthongs, spelling may be no more than a contributory factor, since the possibility must not be ruled out that the speaker has taken a rhotic accent of English for a model.

English into Dutch: the transphonemisation of the consonants

With the consonants the chosen equivalents are even less problematical than with the vowels. Here too, small contrastive differences in the realisation of the natural counterparts, such as English aspiration of fortis plosives, or a different formation of /r/ and /w/, are a matter of indifference in the substitution process. The only potential trouble spots are consonants nos 6, 9, 10, 13, 14, 16 and 17 in Table 37.2. For no. 6 the loan consonant /g/ is available, which on further adaptation is replaced by the spelling-induced velar fricative /ɣ/ of the primary system. Nos 13 and 14 are little trouble if the corresponding marginal Dutch fricatives, in economical inventories mostly notated as /s/+/j/, or /z/+/j/, are called into play.[8] Nos 16 and 17, the affricates, do not exist in Dutch, but careful speakers tend to put them together from their constituent elements. Through their relative unfamiliarity they are, however, subject to reduction and may then lose their first element. Spelling, of course, has taken over in certain words where the voiced affricate may appear as /j/. The English dental fricatives (nos 9 and 10) have no near equivalents in the extended system. In the very few loanwords in which it occurs, the fortis member no. 9 tends to appear as /t/, no doubt largely owing to spelling influence. The voiced member (no. 10) exclusively occurs in the definite article of a borrowed phrase like *to the point*, and is then pronounced /d/, which happens to be the phonological substitution used by all beginning Dutch learners of English.

Most of the positional variants shown in Table 37.2 are a matter of final devoicing. As Dutch, like German, has no voiced final obstruents, these come to be devoiced when they occur in loanwords. This feature of the

Table 37.2 English and Dutch consonant correspondences

	E	D1	D2	Pos. final	Comment
1	p	p			
2	t	t			
3	k	k			
4	b	b		p	Final devoicing normal
5	d	d		t	Final devoicing normal
6	g	(g)	ɣ	k	Final devoicing normal
7	f	f			
8	v	v		f	Final devoicing normal
9	θ	t			
10	ð	d			
11	s	s			
12	z	z		s	Final devoicing normal
13	ʃ	(ʃ)		s	Final /s/ considered slipshod
14	ʒ	(ʒ)			
15	h	h			
16	tʃ	t+ʃ	j	ts	Final /ts/ considered slipshod
17	dʒ	d+ʒ		ts	Final devoicing and cf 16
18	m	m			
19	n	n			
20	ɤ	ŋ			
21	l	l			
22	r	r			Dutch /r/ alveolar or uvular
23	j	j			
24	w	w			Dutch /w/ labiodental

Note: E = English phoneme; D1 = Dutch phoneme, in parentheses = secondary phoneme; D2 = further substitution by primary Dutch phoneme. Pos. = positional variant.

Dutch sound system is so deeply rooted that loanword pronunciations that do have voiced final obstruents must be classed as quotation forms. Positional variants also occur with the palatoalveolars: in final position /ʃ/ tends to become /s/. That pronunciation, though not infrequently heard, has lower social status and is therefore avoided by careful speakers.

It will have been seen that by means of these regular substitutions, which remain inside the extended Dutch phonemic system, a fairly close approximation to the English pronunciation forms is achieved. Dutch here has the advantage, of course, of having a sound system that, in both the number and the nature of its phonemes, differs not too drastically from that of English. For other languages with smaller phoneme systems, no doubt a greater number of the English phonemic contrasts will be lost. The guiding principle, however, should always be that loanword pronunciations are described in terms of the native phonemic system, which should be extended, wherever appropriate, with all relatively stable elements that can be called into play for the pronunciation of foreign words.

The system advocated here is also suitable for the recording of actual loanword pronunciations in dictionaries. What we have termed English quotation forms, forms that contain phonemes that cannot be accommodated in the (extended) native system, should in the first instance have no place there.[9] Commendably, only fully adapted pronunciation forms are given in Rey-Debove and Gagnon's *Dictionnaire des anglicismes* (1984). The German *Duden* dictionaries, however, for example, the *Duden Fremdwörterbuch* (1990) and the *Deutsches Universal Wörterbuch* (1989), use a curiously mixed system of native and unmistakably foreign sound symbols, which seems uninformed by a clear view of transphonemisation processes.

SUMMARY

The above can be summarised in the following guidelines for describing the pronunciation of English loanwords:

1 Separate off authentic English pronunciations; these rarely used forms can, if the need arises, be transcribed in terms of the English phonemic system.
2 The variety of adapted forms, which are the ones normally used in loanword pronunciation, are to be described in terms of the native phonemic system, which for this purpose should be augmented with all relevant marginal elements that can be seen as logical extensions of this native system.
3 The natural equivalents used by speakers of the receiving language in the transphonemisation process can most reliably be found by studying all relatively stable substitutions made by learners. Contrastive analysis is best used as an explanatory force after the event rather than as a predictive device.
4 Variant adapted forms can be looked for in places where the substitution, for lack of a direct natural equivalent, is not a straightforward matter. The variation shown often consists in a member of the secondary set of phonemes being replaced by one of the primary set.
5 The influence of spelling alongside the transphonemisation process should be duly recognised. It may play a contributory part in the phonemic substitutions, or sometimes also be the prime motivator.

NOTES

1 The reference is to Koenen, *Verklarend Handwoordenboek der Nederlandse Taal* (1897), now in its 29th edition (1992). The pronunciation list with its introductory comment first appeared in the 11th edition (1916).
2 This goes both for a relatively old study such as Stene (1940), and for quite recent contributions about phonological adaptation of anglicisms in Romanian and French, in Filipović (1991).

3   The educated speaker of Dutch has a well-established set of twelve such marginal phonemes at his/her disposal. The nine vowels and three consonants concerned can be seen as more or less natural extensions of the primary system, in that they either fill gaps in that system, or, where the vowels are concerned, are lengthened or nasalised versions of members of the primary set. (For details see Posthumus 1986: 35–6).

4   In his 1958 article Filipović, for instance, considered the French loans in English ending in -age, such as garage, camouflage, etc., to be on the way to exchanging their French-type pronunciation for the English-type ending prevalent in words like courage, wastage, etc. However, more than thirty years on, John Wells, in his Longman Pronouncing Dictionary (1990), still gives the French-type form as the first pronunciation. Nor is there any evidence to support the postulated universal occurrence of the 'phonetic compromise': on the contrary, many equations are unmistakable cases of direct equivalence without any occurrence of intermediate forms. After all, vowels in any two languages, even if not perfectly identical, will often show a considerable degree of overlap, and differential features such as the aspiration of fortis plosives and the approximant nature of English /r/ are simply ignored in the adaptation process.

5   What follows here is treated at greater length in Posthumus (1986: 34–51).

6   Such 'obvious parallels' must show a sufficient degree of phonetic similarity; they need not be phonetically identical.

7   Or less often, and more clumsily, in the combinations /aːj/ and /oːj/, which occur in many native Dutch words.

8   The velar fricative /ɣ/ and the two palato-alveolars /ʃ/ and /ʒ/ also occur in native Dutch words, the first as a positional allophone of /k/, the latter as coalescences of /s/ or /z/ + /j/, or as allophones of /s/, or /z/ before /j/.

9   By way of an extra service, the authentic English pronunciation could nevertheless be given for those words and phrases which may be expected to be frequently used as such quotation forms.

REFERENCES

Duden: Deutsches Universalwörterbuch, 2nd edn (1989) ed. G. Drosdowski, Mannheim, Vienna, Zürich: Dudenverlag.

Duden Fremdwörterbuch, 5th edn (1990) Mannheim, Vienna, Zürich: Bibliographisches Institut.

Filipović, R. (1958) 'The phonetic compromise', Studia Romanica et Anglica Zagrabiensia 5: 77–88.

—— (1960) The Phonemic Analysis of English Loan-words in Croatian, Zagreb: University of Zagreb Institute of Linguistics.

—— (ed.) (1991) The English Element in European Languages, Vol. 3, Zagreb: University of Zagreb Institute of Linguistics.

Gussenhoven, C. and Broeders, A. (1976) The Pronunciation of English: A Course for Dutch Learners, Groningen: Wolters–Noordhoff–Longman.

—— (1981) English Pronunciation for Student Teachers, Groningen: Wolters–Noordhoff–Longman.

Koenen, M. J. (1897) Verklarend Handwoordenboek der Nederlandse Taal, Groningen: Wolters.

Posthumus, J. (1986) A Description of a Corpus of Anglicisms, Groningen: Anglistisch Instituut RUG.

Rey-Debove, J. and Gagnon, G. (1984) *Dictionnaire des anglicismes*, Paris: Le Robert.
Stene, E. A. (1940) *English Loan-words in Modern Norwegian*, London: Oxford University Press.
Wells, J. C. (1990) *Longman Pronouncing Dictionary*, Harlow: Longman.

38

What do EFL teachers need to know about pronunciation?

David Taylor
University of Leeds

In two recent papers (Taylor 1990, 1991) I make the point that pronunciation teaching does not seem to have absorbed the implications of the fact
that 'a substantial and ever-increasing proportion of English transactions
take place between non-native speakers' (Taylor 1991). At the same time
the communicative approach and other developments in language-
teaching methodology and in education generally, such as needs analysis,
curriculum development, syllabus planning and design, which have had
considerable effects on the way we teach and the materials we use, seem to
have had little effect on the way we teach pronunciation, on the materials
we use for teaching it, or indeed, more fundamentally, on the aims of
pronunciation teaching. This latter point has also been taken up in an
important paper by Pennington and Richards (1986).

There has been a general failure, it seems, to clarify the aims and
objectives of English pronunciation teaching. Discussions of these rarely go
beyond a vaguely stated ambition to make learners *intelligible*. The meaning
of the term intelligible, with rare exceptions, is hardly explored, while the
question of whom the learners should be intelligible to is scarcely ever
raised. In as much as this issue is discussed, the assumption is that foreign
learners of English need to be intelligible to native speakers (Leather 1983:
198; Sridhar 1985: 101; Smith 1987: xi). Even Pennington and Richards
(1986), in a pioneering study which has done much to bring important
issues in pronunciation teaching back on to the agenda, make this
assumption. They refer several times to a 'target culture' (e.g. pp. 213, 215),
which they seem to assume is native speaking. There is thus little
consideration of the possibility that there may be more non-native speakers
of English than native speakers and that transactions and interactions in
English among non-native speakers (with no native speaker involved) may
well outnumber those that involve native speakers interacting with other
native speakers (Taylor 1991).

The other aspect of intelligibility, namely that it is a two-way process and
that learners not only need to make themselves intelligible to others

(whoever these others may be) but also to find others intelligible, is equally neglected. Pronunciation teaching has tended to concentrate on production, and to be seen as separate from listening comprehension, which in turn has tended to neglect the question of what varieties of English need to be understood, again making the assumption that it is the native speaker, although without making clear precisely which native speakers are to be understood. The concept of native speaker may itself be nebulous and ill-defined. What is certain, though, is that native speakers, however defined, pronounce English in a bafflingly wide variety of ways. What all this means is that the communicative needs of learners have not been taken into account as far as pronunciation teaching is concerned. Clearly, in these circumstances, when these important issues are neglected, it is very difficult to clarify the aims and to specify the objectives of pronunciation teaching within an English language teaching programme. As a result, in the absence of any clearly stated aims and objectives, it is virtually impossible, if we take the classic curriculum model, to give proper attention to the vital questions of teaching methodologies and teaching materials.

As has been argued recently (Richards 1984, 1990), much work in language teaching in general has tended to ignore these broader curriculum development issues, and it is therefore no surprise to find this happening to an even greater extent in the narrower and relatively neglected field of pronunciation teaching. It is no doubt this combination of factors which has led to the present situation, where pronunciation has not been given the attention it deserves and where the contribution that phonetics and phonology can make has consequently been overlooked, or, at best, misunderstood.

In addition, as I have argued elsewhere (Taylor 1990), past traditions of pronunciation teaching may have themselves contributed to this present situation, in that they have predominantly adopted a phonetic rather than a phonological approach. This has meant an overemphasis on form at the expense of function and has reinforced the lack of attention to the communicative needs of the learners. We have, in other words, tended to concentrate too much on achieving accurate pronunciation of sound segments and have not paid enough attention to the way these segments work together as a functional sound system (see also Pennington and Richards 1986). Although some have started to pay more attention to suprasegmental features such as stress, rhythm and intonation, embodying a more functional approach and taking into account discourse features (a good example is Brazil et al. 1980), this has so far had a limited impact and has not been enough to compensate for the predominantly phonetic and segmental approach. As Pennington and Richards (1986) lucidly and forcefully point out in an excellent discussion of just this issue, it remains true that pronunciation teaching has not been properly integrated into the wider context of language teaching.

The situation can be summarised by saying that the communicative needs of learners have not been taken into account, with the result that aims and objectives for pronunciation teaching have not been clearly worked out. Consequently methodology and materials have not been related to the needs of the learners, but have rather derived from a phonetics-dominated, largely segmental approach. What we need to do, therefore, is to go through the whole syllabus/curriculum-planning process with reference to the teaching of English pronunciation, to work out the needs of the learners, formulate appropriate aims and objectives, choose and devise appropriate methodologies and materials in the light of these aims and objectives, and finally work out the implications of this for the pre-service and in-service training of teachers.

It is essential to the nature of such a process that it is sensitive to the wider context in which it takes place and thus takes account of the political, cultural, social and educational factors operating in that milieu. In the absence of any particular context, therefore, it is impossible for us in the present paper to go through the process outlined above in any detail. We must confine ourselves to some broad strategic remarks relating to global factors affecting the teaching of pronunciation. We can at least define the broad general context and the factors at work in it and draw upon general principles which can guide the planning process in particular circumstances.

We must start, I think, with the present position of the English language and go back to the point made at the beginning. Figures given by Kachru (1985: 15) and Crystal (1988) suggest that English now has some 300–400 million non-native speakers in addition to its 340 million native speakers. If these figures are anything like correct, then, as suggested above, we must recognise that many transactions and interactions in English involve no native speaker at all. In the light of this, the assumption underlying most pronunciation teaching that non-native speakers are going to interact primarily with native speakers can no longer be valid. Thus non-native speakers are inevitably going to have to be intelligible to a wide range of other English speakers, both native and non-native. At the same time they will have to understand a wide range of Englishes, both native and non-native. This immediately becomes an important factor in determining the aims and objectives of pronunciation teaching as well as posing the question of standards, models and targets. (These terms are themselves problematic, as has been pointed out (Brown 1989; Taylor 1990).)

Given this situation, what is an appropriate model or target that can guide us in setting our aims and objectives? We may wonder whether it is still appropriate to choose a native-speaker model, probably spoken by relatively few (as is the case with RP) and by its nature fairly narrowly defined. And of course teaching a native-speaker model is no preparation for dealing with the wide range of English pronunciations that we may assume the learner is likely to encounter. I have attempted to resolve this problem of standards, models and targets by suggesting in a recent paper (Taylor 1991) that we teach to a transcription rather than a standard model of pronunciation.

A transcription system such as that used by John Wells in his recent pronouncing dictionary (Wells 1990) does not simply record one particular variety of English pronunciation but can in fact be used to cover virtually all native-speaker varieties of English (including American English). We could take advantage of this fact to help us solve the problem of standards and targets. We can think of a transcription as characterising a range of permitted variation. As such a transcription represents a wide range of possible pronunciations but within certain limits set by the phonological nature of the transcription system, we could take the transcription itself as the target. In other words, our target would be anything that could be transcribed in a standard transcription such as the Wells one. This would help us to tackle the problem of what standard to choose and go some way towards establishing a common goal for pronunciation teaching.

It would also help us to be clearer about what we mean by intelligibility. Our aim is to make our learners intelligible. As was pointed out above, it is impossible to know precisely to whom they should be intelligible and conversely whom they in turn should find intelligible. Having a common goal should go some way towards resolving these difficulties. If we are all teaching towards the same target, which allows wide variation within set limits, then it becomes easier to set aims and objectives for pronunciation teaching. We can take into account our own particular circumstances, but at the same time the common goal ensures that the implications of the fact that English is an international language are not ignored. (An interesting discussion of some of the issues involved in maintaining the international intelligibility of English is to be found in Abbott (1991), although he comes to a different conclusion regarding a desirable model.)

Transcription is of course limited in the extent to which it can represent prosodic features such as stress, rhythm, intonation and accent placement, and, as we have seen, these play an important part in what Pennington and Richards (1986: 208) describe as 'the interactional dynamics of the communication process'. We must, therefore, in adopting a transcription as the basis of our pronunciation teaching, make sure that we do not neglect prosodic features. Fortunately, there are relatively simple ways in which we can incorporate at least the essentials of these, with their crucial dynamic, interactional and functional dimensions, into our transcription and our pedagogical description of English pronunciation (Taylor 1993). The one exception is rhythm, whose description and representation both remain problematic.

If this argument is accepted, what are the consequences for the education and training of teachers of English? If they are to understand the common goal and the aims that follow from it, and are to be able in turn to set their own particular objectives that derive from the aims, then they need to have a good understanding of the principles of phonology and of phonological transcription to grasp the overall framework, as well as a sound understanding of phonetics in order to judge the degree of variation that can be tolerated within the overall framework set by the system and the phonological transcription. Teachers will need a clear understanding of the relationship between phonetics and phonology on the one hand and between transcription and pronunciation on the other. In particular, they will need to be clear about the abstract nature of phonological transcription. At the same time, given the importance of prosodic and discourse features, and in view of the fact that we are looking at pronunciation from a dynamic, interactional, functional perspective, it would seem essential to adopt what Pennington and Richards (1986: 209) call a 'top–down' approach, focusing on high level, long-term aims, giving an overall framework which will allow detailed phonetic or phonological objectives to take their place in the proper context of the relevant prosodic and discourse features.

From the point of view of preparing our teachers, then, we have on the one hand to provide them with more detailed phonetic and phonological knowledge at all levels and on the other to give them a broad perspective that takes into account all the relevant grammatical, semantic, discourse and pragmatic factors that enter into transactions and interactions in English. This is by no means an easy task and it is not at all obvious how we should go about it. What I propose to do in the remainder of this paper is to give in a programmatic way some suggestions as to how we might structure a teacher education programme and give some idea as to what such a programme might contain.

Adopting a top–down approach as advocated above implies a much more functional and phonological (in the widest sense) perspective for pronunciation teaching. It is perhaps fortunate that this comes at a time when phoneticians themselves are suggesting that they need to be more aware of the phonological implications of what they are doing, especially as regards transcription (Kohler 1990a, 1990b; Ladefoged 1990a, 1990b), and when there is a lively debate going on about the nature of the relationship between phonetics and phonology (Ohala 1990; Pierre-humbert 1990). We cannot therefore avoid these and other theoretical issues; but discussion of theory must take place in relation to practice. This is why it is important to integrate pronunciation into the general context of language teaching and to link it to statements of overall aims and objectives. In our preparation of teachers for pronunciation teaching, we must, as in other areas of teacher education, aim for the integration of theory and practice (Taylor 1985).

In the light of these considerations, let us sketch out a rough outline of what the pronunciation component of a teacher education course might look like. A needs analysis from the point of view of pronunciation and oral comprehension would lead to the formulation of appropriate aims and objectives for the particular group of learners. The trainee teachers could not at this point formulate the aims and objectives in any detail, as they would lack the phonetic and phonological knowledge to do so; but this exercise would have the great advantage of making them realise what they need to know in terms of phonetics and phonology. The consideration of practical ends would thus lead to the discussion of theoretical issues and help bring about the desired integration of theory and practice. Study of phonetics, phonology and transcription would then lead back to practical issues.

The exact details of such a programme will depend on individual circumstances, but already one can see what it might contain. The content would not perhaps be very different from that of a traditional phonetics course. What would be different would be the orientation and the approach. The starting-point would be the needs of the learners, and the end-point would be the needs of the teachers. All the phonetics and phonology come in in relation to these two sets of needs. The needs of the learners would determine what the teachers need to know. The teacher educators and the teachers themselves would have to ask themselves the question, 'What do teachers need to know in order to help the learners learn what they need to know?' Details of the content of the programme would be decided in the light of answers to questions like these, while the top-down approach would provide overall coherence and a means of relating the various phonetic and phonological phenomena to one another.

In all probability we would be dealing with such traditional questions as the distinction between phonetics and phonology, the organs of speech, the classification and description of vowels and consonants, word stress, sentence stress, weak forms, intonation, transcription, etc., but all these would come up within the framework set by the consideration of the needs of both teachers and learners. As well as relevance as determined by these criteria we would have to take into account feasibility and learnability. Some aspects of pronunciation do not seem to be easily teachable. This applies particularly to intonation, where much if not most of what learners acquire seems to be picked up naturally rather than learned as a result of any formal teaching (Taylor 1993). We should concentrate, then, on those aspects of pronunciation that can be presented clearly and understandably, in a way that makes sense to both teachers and learners and which gives some insight into the broad workings and functions of English pronunciation.

In our concern to develop a more phonological approach to the teaching of pronunciation, and to relate it properly to both the communicative context and the general language-teaching context we must be careful not to let the pendulum swing too much back the other way. To adopt a more phonological approach is not to neglect the phonetic aspects. Indeed a true phonological approach forces us to take proper account of phonetic factors and to recognise the interdependence of phonetics and phonology (Ohala 1990). In fact good phoneticians have always recognised this, and J. D. O'Connor's *Phonetics* (1973) is a fine example of a study of phonetics which owes its success precisely to the fact that it gives proper attention to phonological considerations. Nevertheless, it may be that, as far as teaching pronunciation is concerned, phoneticians may be forced to become a little more phonology-minded, while phonologists will need to think more about phonetic matters.

We need also to be on our guard against too phonological an approach, an example of which is to be found in Kreidler's recent book (1989), where an admirable attempt to develop a phonological approach to English pronunciation ultimately fails because a satisfactory balance between phonetics and phonology has not been struck (see also Taylor 1989). Cases like these strengthen the argument for teachers to have a sound under-standing of both phonetics and phonology.

We are saying, in effect, that teachers need to know more about phonetics and phonology, not less. Of course, this does not necessarily mean more of what has traditionally been provided on teacher education courses. The implications of the approach we have been outlining point towards some kind of applied phonology and applied phonetics on the analogy with applied linguistics which is distinguished from linguistics. But this parallel is probably misleading in that the term *applied linguistics* can be used to refer to notions and activities which sometimes have a close connection with linguistics proper but at other times seem to have little direct connection. Syllabus planning and design, for example, is often thought of as being part of applied linguistics and indeed applied linguistics is sometimes used to cover the whole field of language teaching.

To avoid these difficulties, I would prefer to talk about pedagogical phonology and pedagogical phonetics. There is a better parallel here, with pedagogical grammar, which is now a well-established term. Just as a pedagogical grammar can be regarded as a description of the grammar of a language made for teaching and learning purposes, to aid in the teaching and learning of that language, so pedagogical phonetics and phonology can be regarded as a description of the sound system and pronunciation of a language for the purposes of allowing teachers to teach it more effectively and learners to learn it more effectively. The point about pedagogical grammars is that they are not the same as linguistic grammars because they have different functions and uses. Similarly, pedagogical phonetics and phonology would acquire their distinctive character through their partic-ular purpose.

One of the main points at issue has already been mentioned, namely that of learnability and feasibility. As I argue in my article on intonation for teachers (Taylor 1993), where I have attempted to work out a description of intonation and accent for pedagogical purposes, there is little point in presenting an account of such complexity that teachers and learners find it difficult to grasp, with the result that they cannot make proper use of it. These are the dangers of too phonetic an approach. We must not allow teachers and learners to become discouragingly bogged down in excessive detail. We need a coherent framework which can help us to make sense of most of what we come across. We should be looking for broad general principles within which to work. We thus come back to the top–down approach suggested by Pennington and Richards (1986) which can help to provide such a framework, and, what is more, can give us criteria which will help us to judge at every stage what level of detail is appropriate. In this way we can devise a programme which will have a high pay-off for learners and teachers, in the sense of being accessible, easily perceived as relevant, and in the end, usable by them in their different ways.

As far as teacher education is concerned, an approach such as that outlined above, where consideration of the needs of the learners leads to the formulation of appropriate aims and objectives for pronunciation teaching, which in turn leads to reflection on what teachers need to know in order to achieve such aims and objectives, fits in well with current thinking about the preparation of teachers. Following Schön (1983, 1988), a reflective approach towards the preparation of language teachers has been developed (Richards 1990; Wallace 1990). One of the great advantages of pedagogical phonetics and phonology is that they are part of a reflective cycle and so contribute to the consciousness-raising which is such an important part of the reflective approach.

The renewed attention paid to transcription in the suggested approach will, for example, bring in, in a motivated way, not only the question of the relation between phonetics and phonology, but also increased awareness of crucial aspects of English pronunciation, which would have perhaps previously been dealt with in a rather decontextualised way but which here come in in a meaningful context where their relevance and importance can be clearly seen. Teachers are thus brought to reflect on their own needs in relation to the needs of their learners. This in turn can promote a spirit of active learning and of collaborative learning which is very much in tune with the general educational principles underlying language teaching today. Teachers can be brought to relate what they learn about pronunciation to their own classrooms. Possibilities of action research are opened up, particularly in the field of in-service teacher education. All this further reinforces the integration of pronunciation teaching into the main stream of language teaching and of language teacher education. 'Pronunciation comes in from the cold' might be one way of describing this process.

DAVID TAYLOR

Although this discussion has been rather programmatic in character, this is in keeping with the suggested top–down approach, where general principles and frameworks are considered first, leaving details to be filled in later at the appropriate stage and in a way relevant to the teaching and learning context. It is up to all of us now, in our own particular circumstances, to think through the whole process and to fill in the detail accordingly. I hope I have said enough to enable us to see the possibility of a new lease of life for phonetics and phonology, in the context of pronunciation teaching and language teaching in general, building on the tradition of O'Connor and his colleagues, who were always aware of the phonological aspect of phonetics and who never lost sight of the teaching and learning dimension of their work.

REFERENCES

Abbott, G. (1991) 'English across cultures: the Kachru catch', *English Today* 7, 4: 55–7.
Brazil, D., Coulthard, M. and Johns, C. (1980) *Discourse Intonation and Language Teaching*, London: Longman.
Brown, A. (1989) 'Models, standards, targets/goals and norms in pronunciation teaching', *World Englishes* 8: 193–200.
Crystal, D. (1988) *The English Language*, Harmondsworth: Penguin.
Kachru, B. B. (1985) 'Standards, codification and sociolinguistic realism: the English language in the outer circle', in R. Quirk and H. G. Widdowson (eds), *English in the World: Teaching and Learning the Language and Literatures*, Cambridge: Cambridge University Press, pp. 11–30.
Kohler, K (1990a) 'Illustrations of the IPA: German', *Journal of the International Phonetic Association* 20, 1: 48–50.
—— (1990b) 'Illustrations of the IPA: comment on German', *Journal of the International Phonetic Association* 20, 2: 44–6.
Kreidler, C. W. (1989) *The Pronunciation of English: A Course Book in Phonology*, Oxford: Basil Blackwell.
Ladefoged, P. (1990a) 'Some reflections on the IPA', *Journal of Phonetics* 18, 3: 335–46.
—— (1990b) 'Illustrations of the IPA: phonology and the IPA', *Journal of the International Phonetic Association* 20, 2: 47.
Leather, J. (1983) 'Second-language pronunciation learning and teaching', *Language Teaching* 16, 198–219.
O'Connor, J. D. (1973) *Phonetics*, Harmondsworth: Penguin.
Ohala, J. J. (1990) 'There is no interface between phonology and phonetics: a personal view', *Journal of Phonetics* 18, 2: 153–71.
Pennington, M. C. and Richards, J. C. (1986) 'Pronunciation revisited', *TESOL Quarterly* 20, 2: 207–25.
Pierrehumbert, J. (1990) 'Phonological and phonetic representation', *Journal of Phonetics* 18, 3: 375–94.
Richards, J. C. (1984) 'Language curriculum development', *RELC Journal* 15, 1: 5–29.
—— (1989) 'Beyond training: approaches to teacher education in language teaching', *Perspectives* (City Polytechnic of Hong Kong) 1, 1: 1–12.

—— (1990) *The Language Teaching Matrix*, Cambridge: Cambridge University Press.

Schön, D. (1983) *The Reflective Practitioner: How Professionals Think in Action*, New York: Basic Books.

—— (1988) *Educating the Reflective Practitioner: Towards a New Design for Teaching and Learning in the Professions*, San Francisco and London: Jossey-Bass.

Smith, L. E. (1987) Preface, in L. E. Smith (ed.) *Discourse across Cultures: Strategies in World Englishes*, New York and London: Prentice Hall, pp. xi–xii.

Sridhar, K. K. (1985) Review of L. Smith (ed.) *Readings in English as an International Language* (Pergamon, 1985) *RELC Journal* 16: 101–6.

Taylor, D. S. (1985) 'The place of methodology in the training of language teachers and the integration of theory and practice', *System* 13, 1: 37–41.

—— (1989) Review of Charles W. Kreidler, *The Pronunciation of English: A Course Book in Phonology*, *RELC Journal* 20, 2: 83–7.

—— (1990) 'The place of phonetics, phonology and transcription in English language teaching', in V. Bickley (ed.) *Language Use, Language Teaching and the Curriculum*, Hong Kong: Institute for Language in Education, pp. 384–92.

—— (1991) 'Who speaks English to whom? The question of teaching English pronunciation for global communication', *System* 19, 4: 425–35.

—— (1993) 'Intonation and accent in English: what teachers need to know', *International Review of Applied Linguistics* 21, 1: 2–21.

Wallace, M. J. (1990) *Training Foreign Language Teachers: A Reflective Approach*, Cambridge: Cambridge University Press.

Wells, J. C. (1990) *The Longman Pronunciation Dictionary*, London: Longman.

INDEX

ABBA 175
Abberton, E.R.M. 231, 234
Abbott, G. 457
Abe, I. 283
Abercrombie, D. xii, 135, 136, 137, 174, 231, 270, 274, 357, 364, 367
accent placement and intonational stereotypes 220–1
accommodative processes in dialect interviews 310
Adnyamathanha 14
Agar, M. 313–15, 317
Aitken, A.J. 367
Akamatsu, T. xv, 3, 5
algorithms and spelling aloud 151–3
Allan, K. 163, 165–6
allegro speech 3, 4, 5
alveolar articulations and Australian coronals 13–17, 22–4, 27, 32–3, 35
alveolar stops and nasals, assimilations of 49–67
alveopalatal articulations and Australian coronals 13, 15, 18, 26, 32
ambisyllabicity, phonetic interpretation of 358–60, 365; and non-segmental phonology 354–6
Amerman, L.E. 339
anacrusis 275
analytic/semantic listening 97, 98
Anderson, J.M. 354, 437, 443
apical contrasts and Australian coronals 13–17, 21–5, 27, 32, 34–5
Arandic languages 14
archiphonemes 3, 5, 6; and Australian coronals 33, 34
Armstrong, L.E. 180, 188, 291, 336, 337
Arnold, G.F. ix, xii, 145, 147–8, 155, 170, 188, 215–17, 219, 241, 255, 288, 290–1, 293–5

Aronsen, A.E. 237
articulatory settings 138; Danish 416–18 (Fig. 34.1 p. 417); General American 418–41; in Foreign language teaching 415–24 (Fig. 34.1 p. 417)
assimilation 3, 4, 5; of alveolar consonants and nasals 60–6; of velar consonants and palatal consonants 49–51, 57–60, 64–6
'attitudinal' meanings and modality features 200
Australian coronals 13–35; palatographic data on 17–31 (Figs 2.1.–2.12)
Australian English 155
automated telecommunications applications, voice types in 85–95
Avery, P. 11
Aydelott Uttman, J.G. 174

Baldwin, J. xix, 302, 308
Ball, V. 234
Bani, E. 16
Barnard, J.R.L. 163
Barney, H.L. 99
Barry, W.J. 236–7, 403
Bauer, L. xix, 321–2, 333, 443
Beach D.M. 121–4
Beckman, M. 222
Belfast, and social distribution of intonation patterns 180–6
Belfast and Derry, and rising tones 156–8, 171
Bell, A. 311
Bennet, J.A.W. 321
'berry name' task 245
Berry, M. 207
Better English Pronunciation xii

Bilton, L. 155
Bing, J.M. 263
Bird, S. 364
Birmingham and Manchester, and
    rising tones 162–3, 170
Boas, F. 336, 338
Bolinger, D.L. 159, 165, 171, 180, 187,
    199, 222, 256, 278, 283, 289
'boosted' accents, and declination
    244–6, 253
boundaries, of intonation units 270–7
    (Table 20.1 p. 275)
Boyanus, S.C. 336–7
Boyce, S.E. 12, 35
Brazil, D. 270–1, 291, 293, 455
Brazilian-Portugese, and English
    pronunciation 292
Bremner, C. 168
Britain, D. 156, 165, 166
Broadbent, D.E. 99
Broeders, A. 447
Brown, G. 180, 199, 271–3, 456
Bryan, M.A. 427
Burgess, O.N. 155
Busby P.A., 13
Bushman xvi
Butcher, A. xv, 17, 23

Cairo Arabic 140
Cameroon 13
Canadian English xx, xxi
Cantonese xvii, 197, 199, 202, 204; and
    English intonation 293
Capell, A. 15
Cardinal Vowel System 99, 115, 141
Carrol, P.J. 14
Catalan 11
Catford, J.C. 17, 40, 336, 418–19, 423
Cepstral techniques, and recording
    fundamental frequency 237
Chadwick, N. 14
Chambers, J.K. 385–8, 390, 392–3
Chapallaz ix
Charles-Luce, J. 11
checking and High Rise tone 164, 167
Ching, M. 166, 168
Chomsky, N. 187, 353
'chunking', and spelling aloud 148
Clark, J. 336, 339
Clavering, E. 160
Clements, G.N. 11, 354
Clézio, Yves le xxi, 427
clicks, place of articulation features

121–8, (Tables 8.1–8.2 p. 126)
Coleman, J. 351, 354
Collins, B. xxi, 416, 420–1, 423, 435–6,
    443
Colson, G. 433
Communicative Grammar of English, A 293
computer-incorporated recorded vocal
    responses xvi
concave family, the, and intonation
    patterns, and social class in Belfast
    182–4 (Fig. 13.2 p. 183)
'conceptual stylistic' hypothesis and
    rising tones 169–71
Concise Oxford Dictionary, The 320
'connected speech' 145
Connell, B. xv
consonant associated resonance 335–49
'consonant capture' 301–9
consonant clusters 308
consonant 'resonance' xx
consonants, clear and dark 130–42
    (Figs 9.1–9.2 p. 132), 342–3, 345–6,
    348
Coustenoble, H ix, x
contour interaction 243; and tone
    sequence models 242–4 (Fig. 17.1
    p. 243; Fig 17.2 p. 245), 252–3
Contreras, H. 256
convex family, the, and intonation
    patterns, and social class in Belfast
    184
Cooper, W.E. 241
coronals, Australian 13–35
Coupland, N. xix, 310, 312, 314, 316
Cowie, R. xvii, (and Douglas-Cowie) 185
Cruttenden, A. xvii, 112, 116, 155–7,
    160, 168, 180,187, 222, 255, 256, 263
Crystal, D. xvi, 163, 215, 217, 241, 244,
    263, 272, 275, 277, 292–3, 295, 456
Currie, K.L. 158, 199

Daniloff, R.G. 339
Danish, and EFL 432–44; and segmental
    errors in English pronunciation
    432–44
Davey, D. 156, 293, 295
Davidsen-Nielsen, N. 433–7, 440, 442–3
de Pijper, J.R. 180
declarative imperatives, and Hungarian
    stylised falling tone 280–1
declination xviii, and contour
    interaction 242–4; and emphasis
    241–54; and intonational typology

191–6; and modality features 200, 205; and prominence features 199
Delbridge, A. 163
deletion 302, 308
dental articulations (and Australian coronals) 13, 27, 32
Deutsches Universal Worterbuch 451
dialect and sociolinguistics 310–19
Dialects in Contact 311
Dictionnaire des Anglicismes 451
Dinnsen, D.A. 11
distance and the stylised fall 283–4
'distinctive feature' 6
Dixon, R.M.W. 13, 14, 15, 16, 32, 35
Djapu 15
Djingulu 14
Doddington, G. 81, 82
Doke, C.M. 121–2, 124, 336
double letters, and spelling aloud 145, 151, 152
double-laminal languages (and Australian coronals) 14, 15, 25, 27, 32
Douglas, W. 16
Douglas-Cowie, E. xvii
'drop', the, and Scouse 161
Duckworth, M. 234
Duden Fremdworterbuch 451
Dutch and English loanwords 445–53
Dyirbal 16

East Midlands English 379–84 (Table 30.1 p. 381)
Eastern Arrernte 25–7, 32
Eastern Kunwinjku 30
EFL, 147, 255–63, 288–95; and Danish 432–44; and English loanwords in Dutch 447–50 (Tables 37.1–37.2 pp. 448–50); and non-native speaker interaction 454–63; and pronunciation 454–63; and Shilluk 425–31
Eijkman, L.P.H. 415
Eilers, R.E. 117
electropalatography (EPG) 41–6 (Figs 3.1–3.3), 50–68 (Figs 4.1–4.8)
Elements xii
elisions 3, 4
Ellison collection 100
Elyan, O.H. 180
emphasis and declination in English intonation 241–54 (Figs 17.1–17.3; Tables 17.1–17.4)

English Allegro speech 3, 4
English intonation, teaching xix, 288–96
English Pronouncing Dictionary 410
English stylised fall 283
Entropic Signal Processing System software 102
'envelope features' and intonation typology 190–6 (Figs 14.1–14.10), 200, 205
Esling, J. xx, 395–6, 416, 418–19, 423
Eastern Torres Strait 36
Etuk, B. 47
Eulugbe 47
Evans, N. 14–16, 35

Faber, D. 263
Faerch, C. 438, 441
Fairbanks, G. 100, 102
fall, stylised and plain 284–6
falling tone, stylisation of in Hungarian intonation 278–87
Fant, G. 125
Filipovic, R. 446–7, 451–2
Finnish: and English intonation 293; and word stress 266
Firth, J.R. 17, 350, 353
Firthian phonology xx, 350–1, 353, 358
Fischer-Jorgensen, E. 418–21, 435
Fishman, J. 313
flaps, and taps 39–40, 46–7
Fletcher, C. xii
Fonagy, I. 171, 213, 227
Forensic Phonetics, International Association for 304
forensic phonetics xviii, xix, 302, 304, and speech fundamental frequency 230–40 (Figs 16.1–16.2 p. 232; Tables 16.1–16.2 pp. 235–6)
forensic speaker recognition xvi; field procedures in 68–84
Fourcin, A.J. 231
Fowler, C.A. 339, 353
Fox, T. xvii, 192, 206, 208, 215, 217
Francis, D. 166
Free vs Read speech, and fundamental frequency 236
French, P. xviii, 236, 302
'frequency compression', and fundamental frequency for telephone conversations 238
Fry, D. ix, 358

Fudge, E. 350
fudging in Midlands and Southern
dialects 385–94 (Map 31.1 p. 391)
Fujimara, O. 101, 359
Fujisaki, H. 207
functionalists 5
fundamental frequency, and
declination 246, 251, 254
fundamental frequency, over telephone
and face-to-face 230–40 (Figs
16.1–16.2 p. 232; Tables 16.1–16.2
pp. 235–6)

Gagnon, G. 451
Garding, E. 207
General American English (GA) xx, xxi;
and articulatory settings 415–24; and
pronunciation 155, 289
General Australian English 40, 247
German Federal Criminal Police Office
(BKA) 69, 72, 82
German xvii, 11
Gibbon, D. 272–3, 283
Giegerich, H. 207, 355
Giles 310, 313–14
Gimson, A.C. ix, x, xxii, 4, 5, 6, 49, 288,
290–1, 293–4, 305, 362, 402, 406–7,
409–11, 433, 440
Glasgow, and rising tones 158, 171
Glass, A. 16
glottal stops 306–7
Goddard, C. 16
Gold Rabiner algorithm, and
fundamental frequency 237
Goldsmith, J.A. 206, 352–3
Goodwin case, the 302
Goon Show 175
Gooniyandi 14–15
Graddol, D. 237
Grammar of Spoken English 293
Grant, W. 336
Green, I.P. 15
Gregg, R. 395–6
Gregory, O.D. 289
Grice, M. 213, 215, 222, 224–5, 403
Gronnum 433, 437, 443
Groundwork of English Intonation 292
Gupapuyngu 14–15
Gussenhoven, C. 215–18, 220, 222, 225,
228, 263, 278, 279, 283, 447
Guugu Yimidhirr 21, 24–5, 27–8, 32
Guy, G. 156, 163–5, 180
Guyanese Creole 339

Hackett, D. 16
Haldenby, C. 155
Halle, M. 121, 125, 207, 353
Halliday, M.A.K. xviii, 155–6, 189,
255–6, 263, 270–1, 273–4, 276,
290–1, 293, 310, 312, 314
Hamilton, P. 13, 35
Hannah, J. 315
Hardcastle, B. xvi
Harvey, M. 11
Haskins laboratory x
Haviland, J. 36
Heffner, R.M.S. 336
Helson, H. 99
Henderson, E.J.A. 336, 338
Hercus, L.A. 14, 15
hesitation noises (and the postura) 139
Hess, W. 231, 237
Hewitt, D.S. 367
Higginbottom, E. 355
Higgins, J. xix
Higgs, J. 418, 423
high fall, the 155
High Rise Tone xvii, 157, 168–71; and
New Zealand English 324; and North
America 165–8; and the Pacific rim
163–5; and social status 164
Hinch, H.H. 16
Hirson, A. xviii, 234
Hirst, D. 191
Hjelmslev, L. 437
Hockett, C.F. 96, 188
Hogg, R. 208
Hollien, H. 81, 236
Holmes, J. 324
Hombert, J.M. 191
homophones in English xx, 326–33
Honikman, B. 138–9, 415–16, 419, 422,
435
Hornby, A.S. 326
Horvath, B. 156
Hottentot xvi
House, A.S. 102, 115
House, J. xvii, 116, 212, 214, 220
Howard, D. xviii, 237
Hughes, E. 160
Huguenot substratum 304
Hull English 155
Hungarian xix
Hungarian intonation, stylisation of
falling tone in 278–87
Hurford, J. xvi, 116–17
Hyman, L.M. 12

Ibibio xv, 42–4, 46–7
idiomatic intonation 145–54
Indefrey, H. 231
Indian English 176–8
infant language, and syllable timing 268
infantile boasts, and the stylised
    Hungarian falling tone 282–3
International Association for Forensic
    Phonetics, Conference 1992, 238
Intonation of Colloquial English xii, 262
intonation patterns, and social class in
    Belfast 180–6, (Fig. 13.1 p. 181; Fig.
    13.2 p. 183)
intonation stereotypes 211–29;
    phonological analysis of 215–20; and
    telephone dialogues 212–15
intonation typology, principles of
    187–210
'intonation unit' 189
intonation units, boundaries of xviii,
    270–7 (Table 20.1 p. 275)
intonational patterns, and synthetic
    speech 241–2
intonational 'universals' 187
invariance, lack of 96

Jacobsen, B. 434
Jagst, L. 15
Jakobson, R. 121–2, 124–5
James, E. 166
Janubi 425
Japanese 197, 199–201, 205, 207; and
    English intonation 292; and Ibibio
    46
Jarman, E. 156–7, 180
Jassem, W. xviii, 272–3, 275, 277, 338
jaw movement 139
Jenner, B.R.A. 416, 421
Jernudd, B. 17, 23
Jesperson, O. 134, 434–6, 439–440, 443
Johnson, M. 213, 215, 222, 224–5
Jones, B. xii
Jones, D. ix, x, xvi, 3, 134–5, 137–8, 141,
    291, 336, 339, 354, 362, 402, 405–6,
    409–10, 432, 434
Joos, M.A. 99

Kachru, B.B. 176, 456
Kagaya, R. 121
Kahn, D. 355
Kayardild 14
Keating, P.A. 11, 35, 340, 348
Kelly, J. xx, 335, 339–42, 353

Kemp, A. 116
Kennedy, R. 16
Kenyon, J.S. 323, 410
Keyser, S.J. 353
Khartoum Arabic 425
Khoe languages of Botswana 123–4
Khoisan languages xvi, 121–8
Kingdom, R. 146, 188, 225, 241, 255–6,
    289, 292–5
Kiparsky, P. 11
Kitja 15
Kitzing, P. 234
Klatt, D.H. 352, 360
Klein, E. 364
Klokeid, T.J. 16
Knott, T.A. 323, 410
Knowles, G. 136–7, 141, 160–2, 171,
    415–16, 433, 434
Koenen, M.J. 451
Kohler, K. 4, 122, 458
Koster, J.P. 76
Kreidler, C.W. 418, 460
Kristensen, K. 437
Krio 177
Kunwinjku 14–16, 19–20, 23, 33
Kunzel, H. xvi

labialisation xvi
Labov, W. 164, 310–13, 321
Ladd, R. xix, 116, 158, 187, 191, 211–12,
    215, 218, 220–2, 224–5, 228, 242,
    256, 263, 278, 283, 286
Ladefoged, P. 17, 40, 96, 99, 121–4, 339,
    371, 458
Laferriere, M. 396
Lag, I.A. 351
Lakoff, R. 166
laminal articulations (and Australian
    coronals) 13–14, 28–9, 32–5
laryngography 61–6 (Figs 4.5–4.8),
    232–7
Lass, R. 355
last lexical item rule 256
Laughren, M. 16
Lavendera, B.R. 310
Laver, J. xii, xvi, 137, 415–16, 421, 422–3
Leather, J. 454
Leben, W. 279
Leech, G. 293
Lehiste, I. 169
Levinson, S. 212
Levitt, A.G. 174
lexical phonology 11

Liberman, M. 180, 211, 215, 218, 244–7, 251–3, 279, 283, 364
Lincolnshire English 155
Lindblom, B.E.F. 98, 100
Lindsay, G. 158, 222
Lindsey, G. 360
linear family, and intonational patterns and class distinction in Belfast 184
Linguistic Atlas of England, The 388, 392
Little Bo Peep 130–1, 133, 141–2
Livbjerg, I. xxi, 440, 443
Liverpool English, and the High Rise tone 160–1, 170–1
Lloyd James, A. 174
loanwords from English, pronunciation of 445–53 (Table 38.1 p. 448; Table 37.2 p. 450)
Local, J. xx, 236, 339–41, 351, 353, 357
Lodge, D. 166
Lombard, E. 238
London Bus numbers 146
Long Term Averaged Spectrum (LTAS) 69
Longman Pronunciation Dictionary, The 404, 434, 452
loosening of articulation xv
Lovins, J.B. 359
'Low Rise' 157
Lowe, B.M. 14–15
Lower Cross languages, of Nigeria 42
Luganda 337

Mackay, I.R.A. 418
Maddieson, I. 17, 116, 121–3, 127
Maidment, J. xx
Mandarin xvii, 196, 198–200, 202, 204–5
Maori English 324
Marrithiyel 15
Martinet, A. 3–4, 6
Mauny 15
McCawley, J.D. 207
McClure, D. xx
McConnell-Ginet 180
McCully, C.B. 208
McDonald, M. 15
McElholm, D.D. 146, 157
McEntee, J. 14
McGlone, R.E. 17
McGregor, R.L. 156, 163, 180
McGregor, W.B. 14–15
McKenzie, P. 14
Mees, I. xxi, 313, 416, 419–21, 423, 435–6, 443

Mende xvii, 190, 193, 195, 197, 199, 201, 204–5
Meyerhoff, M. 324
Microspeech Laboratory programme, the 234
Milroy, L. 313
Milton, R. 326
minimal pairs in English 326–34
Mitchell, A.G. 163
'Mittelding' realisations 12, 24, 34
mixing, in Midland and Southern dialects of English 385–94 (Map 31.1 p. 391)
'modality' features, and intonational typology 190, 200–5 (Figs 14.13–14.18 pp. 200–6)
Mollinjin, G.P. 15
morphological boundaries, and sonorant left capture 409
Morphy, F. 15
Moulton, W. 395, 397, 419
Murrinh-Patha 14–15, 19–21, 23–4

Nairn, M. xvi
natural syllabic structure, and consonant capture 304–5, 307–9
Nespor, M. 207
neutralisations 3, 5–7, 11–35
New York Times, The 168
New Zealand English, and the High Rise tone 165; and spelling pronunciation 320–5
Newcastle, and the High Rise tone 159–60, 170
Newman, J. 165
Ngaanyatjarra 21, 23, 25, 33
Ngangumarta 15, 19–21, 23–4, 29
Nolan, F. xviii, 244
non-segmental phonology 350–66 (Figs 28.1–28.6 pp. 352–63)
North America, and the High Rise tone 165–8
North Wind and the Sun, The xviii, 267
Northern English 50
Norwegian, and English intonation 292
nuclear tone analysis 155
'nuclear tone' xvii, 197–200, 206, 208, 215, 218
nucleus placement (in English and Spanish) 225–65 (Table 18.1 p. 257)
numerical expressions 146
nurse-backing 379–84

O'Connor, J.D. biography x–xi; *Phonetics* xii, xxi; publications of, xii–xiv, 12, 39, 47, 49, 117, 145, 147, 148, 155, 170, 178, 180, 188, 215–17, 219, 241, 255, 270, 274–5, 277, 288, 290–1, 293–5, 301–2, 308, 320, 326, 336, 350, 362–4, 385, 393, 415, 421–2, 432–3, 437, 440, 442–3, 460, 462
O'Dell, M.L. 11
O'Grady, G.N. 15
Ochiai, K. 101
OED 2 xxi
Ogden, R. 351
Ohala, J.J. 187, 458, 460
Ohman, S.E.G. 339, 353
Oller, D.K. 117
On Dialect 387
Ortiz-Lira, H. xviii
Orton, H. 380, 388
Osborne, C.R. 14
Outline of English Phonetics 134, 291
Oxford Advanced Learners Dictionary 146, 326

Pacific Rim, and the High Rise tone 156, 163–4, 170
palatal articulations, and Australian coronals 13
palatisation 140–1
Palmer, H.E. 188, 241, 291
Passy, P. 3
patterns of interference 255–65
pauses, tentative and final 273
Pellowe, J. 156, 159, 180
Peninsula Times Tribune, The 166, 168
Pennington, M.C. 454–5, 457–8, 461
Peterson, G.E. 99
phonemes 5
'phonetic compromise' 447
phonetic interpretation, temporal and parametric 352–4, 358–9
Phonetic Lexicon, A 101–2
Phonetics in Linguistics xii
Phonetics xii, 178, 326, 460
phonological oppositions 5
phonologies, Australian 35
phonology, non-segmental 350–66 (Figs 28.1–28.6 pp. 352–63)
Pierrehumbert, J.B. 188, 191, 207–8, 215–18, 220, 222–5, 241, 244, 245–7, 251–3, 458
Pike, K.L. 39, 155, 174, 207–8, 215, 218, 272–5, 277, 283, 335, 401

pitch levels 155
'pitch-accent' theory, and intonational stereotypes 211–29
Pointon, G. xviii, 266
Polish 11, 339; and word stress 266
Pollard, C. 351
polysyllabic structures, and non-segmental phonology 354
Port, R.F. 11
postalveolar articulations, and Australian coronals 13–17, 22–4, 34
Posthumus, J. xxi, 452
postura xvi; tense and lax 142
Powesland, P. 313
Preston, D.R. 318
Prince, A.S. 364
Prince, E.F. 259
Pring, J. ix
Proffit, W.R. 17
'prominence' features and intonational typology 190, 197–200 (Figs 14.11–14.12 p. 198), 205, 217
prosody 174–8

Quirk, R. x, xvii, 159
'Quantal theory' 115

Raban, J. 166
Rabiner, L.R. 237
Rahilly, J. xvii
Ramsaran, S. 4, 410, 434, 436–7
rapping, and syllabic timing 177
Received Pronunciation, (RP) 155, 159, 303, 306 307, 317, 324, 327, 330, 377, 381, 393, 401, 406, 408–9, 434, 440–2
'relevant feature' 5, 6
'Resonance system' 348
resonance, and consonants 335–49
Rey-Debove 451
rhythm, and boundaries of intonation units 270–7; and duration in Spanish 266–9; English xvii; in English disyllabic feet 356–8; and non-segmental phonology 350–66; and spelling aloud 151
rhythmical change, documentation of 174–9
rhythmical empathy 174–5
Rice, K. 11
'rich points' 310–18
Richards, J.C. 454–5, 457–8, 461
'rise–fall' 157
rises, in English 155–72

Roach, P. 174, 175
Roach, P. 433
Rockey, D. 101
Rumsey, A. 16
Russian 11, 140, 337

Sag, I. 180, 351
Sagey, E. 121–2, 124
Samuels, M.L. 158
Sands, B. 121
Schmerling, S.F. 263
Schon, D. 461
Schubiger, M. 188
Schwartz, L.S. 168
Scollins, R. 380–3
Scottish English xx, 104, 346, vowels of
    367–78 (Figs 29.1–29.7 pp. 372-5)
'segment timed' phonology xviii, 268
Selkirk, E. 351, 355, 364
semantic listening, and analytic
    listening 97–8
Sheldon, P.D.S 147
Shetland English 140
Shieber, S.M. 351, 356
Shilluk xxi; and English accent 425–31;
    and English consonants 428–30; and
    English vowels 430, 431; sound
    system of 427–8
Shirt, M. 75–6, 82
Sievers, E. 134, 136
Silver-Corvalan, C. 256
Silverman, K. 241
Slavonic, and Romance languages 305
Slowiaczek, L.M. 11
Smith, H.L. Jr 188
Smith, L.E. 454
Snyman, J.W. 121–2
social class, and intonation patterns in
    Belfast 180–6
sociolinguistics, and phonetics 310–11
Some Mothers Do 'Ave 'Em 175
Sonnenschein, A.E. 269
sonorant left capture, and new syllabic
    consonants 408–9
Sorensen, J.M. 241
Sorensen, K. 433, 438
Southern British 50
Southern Sudanese Arabic 425
Spanish, and English intonation 292
speaker recognition (SR) 68–84 (Table
    5.1 p. 69; Fig. 5.1 p. 71); commercial
    69, 72–3; forensic 69, 72–3,
    semi-automatic 79

speaker recognition, by expert 75–9;
    high-level information and low-level
    information 75; by non-experts 74–5;
    the Yorkshire Ripper case 77
spectography 98; and emphasis and
    declination 251; in speaker
    recognition 77–9
'spelling aloud' 145–54 (Figs 10.1–10.4
    pp. 149–50)
spelling pronunciation xix; and New
    Zealand English 320–5, and
    prescriptivism 320–1
Squares, G. 162
'Squish' 357
Sridhar, K.K. 454
Steele, J. 274
Steller, P. 433, 438
Stene, E.A. 451
'step', the, and Scouse 161
stereotyped intonation, phonology of
    215–20
Stevens, K.N. 115
stops, taps and flaps 39–40, 46–7
Story of Arthur the Rat, The 231, 234, 239
Strang, B. 159, 320, 323
Strange, W. 100
Street, C.S. 14, 15
Strehlow, T.G.H. 14
stress in Spanish and English 266–9
stress timing and syllabic timing in
    English 175–8
Strevens, P. 419
structure and timing, in non-segmental
    synthesis 351–4 (Fig 28.1 p. 352)
Studdert-Kennedy, M. 100
Studies in the Pronunciation of English xxi
stylised contours and intonational
    stereotypes 211
'stylised fall', the xix
Summers, W. 236, 238
Suner, M. 256
Survey of English Dialects, The 381–3, 385,
    387–9, 393
Svartvik, J. 293
Swedish, and English intonation 292–3
Sweet, H. 134, 294, 415, 419
Sydney Morning Herald, The 163, 168
syllabic consonant formation 403–4,
    and American English 410
syllabic consonants, new, in English
    401–12
syllabification 404–7; and
    non-segmental phonology 350–66

synthetic speech 241
synthetic voice 212
Systemic Grammar 207
'systemic hypothesis' and High Rise tones 169–71

tagmemics 207
Taljaard, P.C. 121
Talma-Schilthuis, J.G. 421
tap articulations xv
tap, articulatory characteristics of 39–48; and flaps 39–40, 46–7; and stops 40, 46–7
Taylor, D. xxii, 454, 455
Taylor, D.S. 15, 456–61
telephone numbers, and idiomatic expressions 147
Tench, P. xviii
Tex-Mex 177
Thomas, A.R. 316
Thorsen, N. 199, 243, 433, 437, 443
threshold word length, and spelling aloud 148, 151
Time Magazine 166, 168
Times Educational Supplement xii
Times, The 168
Titford, J. 380–3
Tiwi 14
Tok Pisin 177
tonic segment, the 270
Tooley, O. ix
Trager, G.L. 188
Traill, T. xvi, 17, 121
'transparency' 12
transphonemisation, and English loanwords in Dutch 446–51 (Tables 37.1–37.2 pp. 448–50)
Trim, J. ix, 308, 350, 362–3
Trubetzkoy, N.S. 402
Trudgill, P. 310–11, 315, 385–8, 390, 392–3, 416
Tucker, A. 427

UCL, ix, x
underspecification 11, 12
Ungarinjih 15
Unification Grammar 351
'universal grammar' 187
Upton, C. xx
Urban North British 156, 162–3, 170

Vaissiere, J. 187, 191
Van Buuren, L. xvi, 290, 416

Van Valin Jr, R.D. 117
Vancouver English, low vowels of 395–400 (Tables 32.1–32.3 pp. 397–8)
Varga, L. xviii
velarisation 140–1
Verbrugge, R. 99–100
Verklarend Handwoordenboek der Nederlandse Taal 451
Vierregge, W.H. 97–8
Vincent, N. 352
vocatives, and stylisation of Hungarian falling tone 278–9
Vogel, I. 207
voice typing, in telecommunications applications 85–95
Vonwiller, J. 164–5, 180
Vowel, Consonant and Syllable – a Phonological Definite 350
vowel merger, and British East Midlands accents 379–84 (Table 30.1 p. 381)
vowel quality, effect of context on transcription 96–118 (Tables 7.1–7.14 pp. 101–10)
vowels, and Scottish English 367–78; and Vancouver English 395–400

Wakelin, M. 314
Wall, A. 320–1, 323
Wallace, M.J. 461
Wallis, J. 136
Walpiri 15, 19–21, 23, 29, 33
Wangkumara 15
Ward, I.C. 180, 188, 291, 336
Warkentyne, H. xx, 395
Waves+ Software 102
Weinreich, U. 314
Wells, J.C. xxi, xxii, 305–6, 310, 317, 327, 355, 367, 379–80, 383, 395, 404, 406, 410–11, 418, 422, 427, 430, 433, 434, 436–7, 452, 457
Welmers, W.E. 193
Welsh 315–17
Wembawemba 14–15
Western Arrernte 14
Western Desert Language 15, 25, 30
Western Torres-Straight 15, 24–5, 30, 33–4
Whitley, E. 351
Wilkins, D. 15
Williams, C.J. 15
Windsor Lewis, J. 146, 178, 215, 217–18, 228, 289, 292–5, 305, 315, 404, 406

407, 434, 437, 439–40
Witten, I.H. 272
Wong, R. 416, 418–19, 423
Wordick, F.J.F 14, 15
Wurm, S.A. 15

Yallop, C. 14, 336, 339
Yanyuwa 25, 27
Yidiny 15

Yindjibarndi 14–15
Yorktalk 350–66
Youd, N. 212, 214, 220
Yule, G. 273
Yuwaalarraay 15

Zulu xvii, 191, 194–5, 197, 204–5
Zwaardemaker, H. 415